© IMAGES.COM/CORBIS

MICROECONOMICS
Principles & Applications, 6e

Robert E. **HALL**

Department of Economics, Stanford University

Marc **LIEBERMAN**

Department of Economics, New York University

SOUTH-WESTERN
CENGAGE Learning·

Australia · Brazil · Japan · Korea · Mexico · Singapore · Spain · United Kingdom · United States

SOUTH-WESTERN
CENGAGE Learning

**Microeconomics: Principles &
Applications, 6th Edition**
Robert E. Hall and Marc Lieberman

Vice President of Editorial, Business:
Jack W. Calhoun

Publisher: Joe Sabatino

Executive Editor: Michael Worls

Senior Developmental Editor: Susanna C.
Smart

Senior Marketing Manager: John Carey

Senior Marketing Communications
Manager: Sarah Greber

Senior Content Project Manager: Tim Bailey

Media Editor: Sharon Morgan

Manufacturing Planner: Kevin Kluck

Production Service: MPS Limited,
a Macmillan Company

Senior Art Director: Michelle Kunkler

Cover and Internal Designer: jen2design

Cover Image: © Images.com/Corbis

Rights Acquisitions Specialist, Text: Deanna
Ettinger

Rights Acquisitions Specialist, Text: Sam
Marshall

For product information and technology assistance, contact us at
Cengage Learning Customer & Sales Support, 1-800-354-9706

For permission to use material from this text or product,
submit all requests online at **www.cengage.com/permissions**
Further permissions questions can be emailed to
permissionrequest@cengage.com

Exam*View*® is a registered trademark of eInstruction Corp. Windows is a
registered trademark of the Microsoft Corporation used herein under license.

Library of Congress Control Number: 2011941987

ISBN-13: 978-1-111-82256-9

ISBN-10: 1-111-82256-5

South-Western
5191 Natorp Boulevard
Mason, OH 45040
USA

Cengage Learning products are represented in Canada by
Nelson Education, Ltd.

For your course and learning solutions, visit **www.cengage.com**

Purchase any of our products at your local college store or at our
preferred online store **www.cengagebrain.com**

Printed in the United States of America
2 3 4 5 6 7 16 15 14 13

BRIEF CONTENTS

CONTENTS

© IMAGES.COM/CORBIS

© IMAGES.COM/CORBIS

iv

Part III: Microeconomic Decision Makers

© IMAGES.COM/CORBIS

Microeconomics: Principles and Applications is about economic principles and how economists use them to understand the world. It was conceived, written, and for the sixth edition, substantially revised to help your students focus on those basic principles and applications.

We originally decided to write this book because we thought that existing texts tended to fall into one of three categories. In the first category are the encyclopedias—the heavy tomes with a section or a paragraph on every topic or subtopic you might possibly want to present to your students. These books are often useful as reference tools. But because they cover so many topics—many of them superficially—the central themes and ideas can be lost in the shuffle.

The second type of text we call the "scrapbook." In an effort to elevate student interest, these books insert multicolored boxes, news clippings, interviews, cartoons, and whatever else they can find to jolt the reader on each page. While these special features are often entertaining, there is a trade-off: These books sacrifice a logical, focused presentation of the material. Once again, the central themes and ideas are often lost.

Finally, a third type of text, perhaps in response to the first two, tries to do less in every area—a *lot* less. But instead of just omitting extraneous or inessential details, these texts often throw out key ideas, models, and concepts. Students who use these books may think that economics is overly simplified and unrealistic. After the course, they may be less prepared to go on in the field, or to think about the economy on their own.

A DISTINCTIVE APPROACH

Our approach is very different. We believe that the best way to teach principles is to present economics as a coherent, unified subject. This does not happen automatically. On the contrary, principles students often miss the unity of what we call "the economic way of thinking." The principles course then appears to be just "one thing after another," rather than the coherent presentation we aim for. For example, without proper guidance, students may view the analysis of goods markets, labor markets, and financial markets as entirely different phenomena, rather than as a repeated application of the same methodology with a new twist here and there.

CAREFUL FOCUS

Because we have avoided the encyclopedic approach, we have had to think hard about what topics are most important. As you will see:

We Avoid Nonessential Material

When we believed a topic was not essential to a basic understanding of economics, we left it out. However, we have striven to include core material to *support* an instructor who wants to present special topics in class. So, for example, we do not have separate chapters on environmental economics, agricultural economics, urban economics, health care economics, or comparative systems. But instructors should find in the text a good foundation for building any of these areas—and many others—into their course. And we have included examples from each of these areas as *applications* of core theory where appropriate throughout the text.

We Avoid Distracting Features

This text does not have interviews, news clippings, or boxed inserts with only distant connections to the core material. The features your students *will* find in our book are there to help them understand and apply economic theory itself, and to help them avoid common mistakes in applying the theory (the Dangerous Curves feature).

We Explain Difficult Concepts Patiently

By freeing ourselves from the obligation to introduce every possible topic in economics, we can explain the topics we *do* cover more thoroughly and patiently. We lead students, step-by-step, through each aspect of theory, through each graph, and through each numerical example. In developing this book, we asked other experienced teachers to tell us which aspects of economic theory were hardest for their students to learn, and we have paid special attention to these trouble spots.

We Use Concrete Examples

Students learn best when they see how economics can explain the world around them. Whenever possible, we develop the theory using real-world examples. You will find numerous references to real-world corporations and government policies throughout the text. We often use real-world data on our conceptual graphs. When we employ hypothetical examples because they illustrate the theory more clearly, we try to make them realistic. In addition, almost every chapter ends with a thorough, extended application (the "Using the Theory" section) focusing on an interesting real-world issue.

FEATURES THAT REINFORCE

To help students see economics as a coherent whole, and to reinforce its usefulness, we have included some important features in this book.

The Three-Step Process

Most economists, when approaching a problem, begin by thinking about buyers and sellers, and the markets in which they come together to trade. They move on to characterize a market equilibrium, and then explore how the equilibrium changes when conditions change. To understand what economics is about, students need to understand this process and see it in different contexts. To help them do so, we have identified and stressed a "three-step process" that economists use in analyzing problems. The three key steps are:

1. **Characterize the Market.** Decide which market or markets best suit the problem being analyzed, and identify the decision makers (buyers and sellers) who interact there.
2. **Find the Equilibrium.** Describe the conditions necessary for equilibrium in the market, and a method for determining that equilibrium.
3. **Determine What Happens When Things Change.** Explore how events or government policies change the market equilibrium.

The steps themselves are introduced toward the end of Chapter 3. Thereafter, the content of most chapters is organized around this three-step process. We believe this helps students learn how to think like economists, and in a very natural way. And they come to see economics as a unified whole, rather than as a series of disconnected ideas.

Dangerous Curves

Anyone who teaches economics for a while learns that, semester after semester, students tend to make the same familiar errors. In class, in office hours, and on exams, students seem pulled, as if by gravity, toward certain logical pitfalls. We've discovered in our own classrooms that merely explaining the theory properly isn't enough; the most common errors need to be *confronted*, and the student needs to be shown *specifically* why a particular logical path is incorrect. This was the genesis of our "Dangerous Curves" feature—boxes that anticipate the most common traps and warn students just when they are most likely to fall victim to them. We've been delighted to hear from instructors how effective this feature has been in overcoming the most common points of confusion for their students.

Using the Theory

This text is full of applications that are woven throughout the narrative. In addition, almost every chapter ends with an extended application ("Using the Theory") that pulls together several of the tools learned in that chapter. These are not news clippings or world events that relate only tangentially to the material. Rather, they are step-by-step presentations that are rich with real-world detail. The goal is to show students how the tools of economics can explain things about the world—things that would be difficult to explain without those tools.

Content Innovations

In addition to the special features just described, you will find some important differences from other texts in topical approach and arrangement. These, too, are designed to make the theory stand out more clearly, and to make learning easier. These are not pedagogical experiments, nor are they innovation for the sake of innovation. The differences you will find in this text are the product of years of classroom experience.

Scarcity, Choice, and Economic Systems (Chapter 2)

This early chapter, while covering standard material such as opportunity cost, also introduces some central concepts much earlier than other texts. Most importantly, it introduces the concept of *comparative advantage,* and the basic principle of *specialization and exchange.* We have placed them at the front of our book, because we believe they provide important building blocks for much that comes later. For example, comparative advantage and specialization *within* the firm help explain economies of scale (Chapter 7). International trade (Chapter 16) can be seen as a special application of these principles, extending them to trade between nations.

Working with Supply and Demand (Chapter 4)

Our Chapter 4—in addition to analyzing price ceilings and floors—introduces two concepts not often found in principles texts, but which have become increasingly relevant. The first is how supply and demand can be used for *stock variables,* and not just flow variables. In the chapter, we treat housing as a stock variable, and then apply the model to the recent housing boom and bust. We also believe that teaching the stock-flow distinction early—with the rather intuitive case of housing—makes it easier to think about stock variables later, when students learn about the stock market (in micro), and the money market (for those who go on to macro).

The second concept introduced in this chapter is *leverage.* Although it has been at the heart of recent economic turmoil, it has not been part of the traditional principles pedagogy. We've introduced leverage in a simple, intuitive way in the body of Chapter 4. We then delve a bit deeper in the short appendix to that chapter, which explains the concept of owners' equity (in a home), and presents a simple *leverage ratio* that students can work with. Teaching this concept early creates a fresh connection to current policy debates, and it lays the foundation for later applications in the text. Students will see how leverage contributed to the recent housing boom and bust (in Chapter 4) as well as the moral hazard problem in financial institutions (Chapter 15).

How Firms Make Decisions: Profit Maximization (Chapter 8)

Many texts introduce the theory of the firm using the perfectly competitive model first. While this has logical appeal to economists, we believe it is an unfortunate choice for students encountering this material for the first time. Leading with perfect competition forces students to simultaneously master the logic of profit maximization *and* the details of a rather counter-intuitive kind of market at the same time. Students quite naturally think of firms as facing *downward*-sloping demand curves—not horizontal ones. We have found that they have an easier time learning the theory of the firm with the more familiar, downward-sloping demand curve. Further, by treating the theory of the firm in a separate chapter, *before* perfect competition, we can separate concepts that apply in *all* market structures (the shapes of marginal and average cost curves, the MC and MR approach to profit maximization, the shutdown rule, etc.), from concepts that are unique to perfect competition (horizontal demand curve, marginal revenue the same as price, etc.). This avoids confusion later on.

Monopolistic Competition and Oligopoly (Chapter 11)

Two features of our treatment are worth noting. First, we emphasize advertising, a key feature of both of these types of markets. Students are very interested in advertising and how firms make decisions about it. Second, we have omitted older theories of oligopoly that raised more questions than they answered, such as the kinked demand curve model. Our treatment of oligopoly is strictly game theoretic, but we have taken great care to keep it simple and clear. Here, as always, we provide the important tools to *support* instructors who want to take game theory further, without forcing every instructor to do so by including too much.

Capital and Financial Markets (Chapter 13)

This chapter focuses on the common theme of these subjects: the present value of future income. Moreover, it provides simple, principles-level analyses of the stock and bond markets—something that students are hungry for but that many principles textbooks neglect.

Description versus Assessment (Chapters 14 and 15)

In treating product market structures, most texts switch back and forth between the *description and analysis* of different markets on the one hand and their *efficiency properties* on the other. Our book deals with description and analysis first, and only then discusses efficiency, in two comprehensive chapters. The first of these (Chapter 14) covers the concept and measurement of economic efficiency, using Pareto improvements as well as consumer and producer surplus. The second (Chapter 15) deals with market failures and government's role in economic efficiency. This arrangement of the material permits instructors to focus on *description and prediction* when first teaching about market structures—a full plate, in our experience. Moreover, two chapters devoted to efficiency allows a more comprehensive treatment of the topic than we have seen elsewhere. Finally, our approach—in which students learn about efficiency *after* they have mastered the four market structures—allows them to study efficiency with the perspective needed to really understand it.

Comparative Advantage and the Gains from International Trade (Chapter 16)

We've found that international trade is best understood through clear numerical examples, and we've developed them carefully in this chapter. We also try to bridge the gap between the economics and politics of international trade with a systematic discussion of winners and losers.

ORGANIZATIONAL FLEXIBILITY

We have arranged the contents of each chapter, and the table of contents as a whole, according to our recommended order of presentation. But we have also built in flexibility.

In Microeconomics

- Chapter 6 develops consumer theory with both marginal utility and (in an appendix) indifference curves, allowing you to present either method in class.
- If you wish to highlight international trade or present comparative advantage earlier in the course, you could assign Chapter 16 immediately following Chapter 3.
- If you wish to introduce consumer and producer surplus earlier in the course, all of Chapter 14 can be assigned after Chapter 10. And if you feel strongly that economic efficiency should be interwoven bit-by-bit with the chapters on market structure, Chapter 14 can be easily broken into parts. The relevant sections can then be assigned separately with Chapters 3, 5, 9, and 10.

Finally, we have included only those chapters that we thought were both essential and teachable in a yearlong course. But not everyone will agree about what is essential. While we—as authors—cringe at the thought of a chapter being omitted in the interest of time, we have allowed for that possibility. Nothing in Chapter 12 (Labor Markets), Chapter 13 (Capital and Financial Markets), Chapter 15 (Government's Role in Economic Efficiency), Chapter 16 (International Trade), is essential to any of the other chapters in the book. Skipping any of these should not cause continuity problems.

NEW TO THE SIXTH EDITION

Our previous (fifth) edition was our most significant revision yet. This will not surprise anyone who was teaching an economics principles course during or after September 2008, when the financial crisis hit its peak. One of us (Lieberman) was teaching macro principles at the time and had the daily task of integrating the flood of unprecedented events into the course. When the semester was over, the two of us thought long and hard about what worked, what didn't, and how the principles course—both micro and macro—should respond to the changes we had seen.

In planning this new edition, we were gratified that the major pedagogical changes we had made in the fifth edition still seemed, in retrospect, to be the right ones. So you will not find any radical changes in approach this

time. For faculty preparing lectures, this will be welcome news: Very few adjustments will be needed to present core concepts and models. For students, however, we think this revision will make a huge difference.

Our main goal in this edition was to provide students with a *smoother ride* through the text. Valuable suggestions from dozens of users—both instructors and students—were incorporated into every chapter. We paid particular attention to sections that were bogging students down, either deleting them or clarifying them. Many sections were rewritten from scratch to introduce a more careful, step-by-step approach. We removed some of the more complex Dangerous Curves boxes, trimmed down many others, and added about a dozen new ones. And, of course, we brought our examples and Using the Theory sections up to date, to engage with recent economic events.

Changes That May Be of Interest

Aside from the general updating and streamlining mentioned above, we want to call attention to a few changes that *might* affect lectures for some instructors.

Chapter 2 has a new section on markets, ownership, and the invisible hand, as well as a discussion of mixed economies. Chapter 3's Using the Theory section on oil markets is now a much simpler supply-and-demand analysis. Chapter 8 (Profit Maximization) has a new discussion of total revenue and elasticity. In Chapter 9 (Perfect Competition), we've deleted the vertical portion of the firm's supply curve (below the shutdown price), and offered an entirely new Using the Theory on the zero-profit result.

Chapter 11 (Imperfect Competition) has several changes. First, we've eliminated Nash equilibrium. We've found that—without a more advanced treatment (too advanced for the principles level), Nash equilibrium creates more confusion than understanding. But we've added a section on concentration ratios and the Herfindahl-Hirschman Index, and an appendix that presents a simple model of cartel pricing. Chapter 11 now covers antitrust policy related to mergers only, and we've moved our more general material on antitrust (including the Sherman and Clayton Acts) to Chapter 15.

Chapter 13 (Capital and Financial Markets) has a vastly simplified and shortened treatment of the bond market, involving fewer bolded terms and graphs. In Chapter 14 (Economic Efficiency), we moved (and expanded) the treatment of elasticity and deadweight losses from the Using the Theory section into the body of the chapter. The Using the Theory itself now covers only the land tax.

Chapter 15 has a few important changes. First, the discussion of the free-rider problem has been moved from externalities to public goods. Second, the discussion of the Coase theorem has been shortened and simplified. And the Using the Theory section on moral hazard and the financial crisis has been entirely rewritten from a different perspective. It also includes new material on the Dodd-Frank Act (as it relates to moral hazard).

Finally, for those who incorporate the end-of-chapter problems into their courses, we should point out that these, too, have undergone changes: Some deleted, and dozens substantially revised or entirely new.

For the Instructor

- The *Instructor's Manual* is revised by Dell Champlin, Oregon State University. The manual provides chapter outlines, teaching ideas, experiential exercises for many chapters, and solutions to all end-of-chapter problems.
- The *Instructor Companion Site* on the *Product Support Web Site*. This site at **http://login.cengage.com** features the essential resources for instructors, password-protected, in downloadable format: the *Instructor's Manual* in Word, the test banks in Word, and PowerPoint lecture and exhibit slides.
- The *Microeconomics Test Bank* is revised by Kenneth Slaysman of York College of Pennsylvania. It contains more than 2,500 multiple-choice questions. The test questions have been arranged according to chapter headings and subheadings, making it easy to find the material needed to construct examinations.
- *ExamView Computerized Testing Software.* ExamView is an easy-to-use test creation package compatible with both Microsoft Windows and Macintosh client software, and contains all of the questions in all of the printed test banks. You can select questions by previewing them on the screen, by number, or randomly. Questions, instructions, and answers can be edited, and new questions can easily be added.
- *PowerPoint Lecture and Exhibit Slides.* Available on the Web site and the IRCD, the PowerPoint presentations are revised by Andreea Chiritescu, Eastern Illinois University. These consist of speaking points in chapter outline format, accompanied by numerous key graphs and tables from the main text, many with animations to show movement of demand and supply curves.
- *CengageCompose.* With CengageCompose you can create your own print text to meet specific course learning objectives. Gather what you need from our vast library of market-leading course books and enrichment content, or add original material. Build your book the way you want it organized, personalized to your students. Publish your title with easy-to-use tools that guarantee you will get what you designed. For more information, contact your sales rep or go to **http://www.cengage.com/custom/**
- *WebTutor Toolbox.* WebTutor ToolBox provides instructors with links to content from the book companion Web site. It also provides rich communication tools to instructors and students, including a course calendar, chat, and e-mail. For more information about the WebTutor products, please contact your local Cengage sales representative.
- *CengageNOW* Ensure that your students have the understanding they need of procedures and concepts they need to know with CengageNOW. This integrated, online course management and learning system combines the best of current technology to save time in planning and managing your course and assignments. You can reinforce comprehension with customized student learning paths and efficiently test and automatically grade assignments with reports that correspond to AACSB standards. For your convenience, CengageNOW is also compatible with WebCT® and Blackboard®. For more information, visit **http://cengage.com/cengagenow.**

For the Student

- *Hall/Lieberman CourseMate.* Multiple resources for learning and reinforcing principles concepts are now available in one place!

  CourseMate is your one-stop shop for the learning tools and activities to help students succeed. Available for a minimal additional cost, CourseMate provides a wealth of resources that help them study and apply economic concepts. As students read and study the chapters, they can access video tutorials with *Ask the Instructor Videos*. They can review with *Flash Cards* and the *Graphing Workshop* as well as check their understanding of the chapter with *interactive quizzing*.

  CourseMate gives you BBC News videos, Econ-News articles, Economic Debates, Links to Economic Data, and more, organized by chapter to help your students get the most from *Microeconomics: Principles and Applications*, sixth edition, and from your lectures.

  Students can access CourseMate through CengageBrain at **www.cengagebrain.com**

- *Global Economic Watch.* A global economic crisis need not be a teaching crisis.

Students can now learn economic concepts through examples and applications using the most current information on the global economic situation. The Global Economic Resource Center includes:

- A 32-page eBook that gives a general overview of the events that led up to the current situation, written by Mike Brandl from the University of Texas, Austin
- A Blog and Community Site updated daily by an economic journalist and designed to allow you and your colleagues to share thoughts, ideas, and resources
- Thousands of articles from leading journals, news services, magazines, and newspapers revised four times a day and searchable by topic and key term
- Student and instructor resources such as PowerPoint® decks, podcasts, and videos
- Assessment materials allowing you to ensure student accountability

This resource can be bundled at no charge with this textbook. Visit www.cengage.com/thewatch for more information.

- *Tomlinson Economics Videos.* "Like Office Hours 24/7" Award winning teacher, actor, and professional communicator, Steven Tomlinson (PhD, economics, Stanford) walks students through all of the topics covered in principles of economics in an online video format. Segments are organized to follow the organization of the Hall/Lieberman text and most videos include class notes that students can download and quizzes to test their understanding. Find out more at www.cengage.com/economics/tomlinson.
- *Aplia.* Founded in 2000 by economist and Stanford professor Paul Romer, Aplia is dedicated to improving learning by increasing student effort and engagement. The most successful online product in economics by far, Aplia has been used by more than 1,000,000 students at more than 850 institutions. Visit www.aplia.com/cengage for more details. For help, answers, or a live demonstration, please contact Aplia at support@aplia.com.

ACKNOWLEDGMENTS

Our greatest debt is to the many reviewers who carefully read the book and provided numerous suggestions for improvements. While we could not incorporate all their ideas, we did carefully evaluate each one of them. We are especially grateful to the participants in our survey who helped us with the revision for this sixth edition. To all of these people, we are most grateful:

Sindy Abadie	Southwest Tennessee Community College
Eric Abrams	Hawaii Pacific University
Ljubisa Adamovich	Florida State University
Mehdi. Afiat	College of Southern Nevada
Brian A'Hearn	Franklin and Marshall College
Ali Akarca	University of Illinois, Chicago
Rashid Al-Hmoud	Texas Tech University
David Aschauer	Bates College
Richard Ballman	Augustana College
Gayle Bolash	Kent State University
James T. Bang	Virginia Military Institute
Chris Barnett	Gannon University
Parantap Basu	Fordham University
Tom Bernardin	Smith College
Tibor Besedes	Rutgers University
Gautam Bhattacharya	University of Kansas
Maharukh Bhiladwalla	New York University
Margot B. Biery	Tarrant County College
Edward Blackburne	Sam Houston State University
Sylvain Boko	Wake Forest University
Barry Bomboy	J. Sargeant Reynolds Community College
John L. Brassel	Southwest Tennessee Community College
Bruce Brown	Cal Poly Pomona and Santa Monica College
Mark Buenafe	Arizona State University
Steven Call	Metropolitan State College
Dell Champlin	Oregon State University
Kevin Carey	American University
Cheryl Carleton	Villanova University
Siddharth Chandra	University of Pittsburgh
Steven Cobb	Xavier University
Christina Coles	Johnson & Wales University
Maria Salome E. Davis	Indian River State College
Dennis Debrecht	Carroll College
Arthur M. Diamond, Jr.	University of Nebraska, Omaha
Selahattin Dibooglu	University of St. Louis, Missouri
James E. Dietz	California State University, Fullerton
Ferdinand DiFurio	Tennessee Tech University
Erol Dogan	New York University
Khosrow Doroodian	Ohio University

John Duffy	University of Pittsburgh	Farrokh Kahnamoui	Western Washington University
Debra S. Dwyer	SUNY, Stony Brook	Leland Kempe	California State University, Fresno
Stephen Erfle	Dickinson College	Jacqueline Khorassani	Marietta College
		Philip King	San Francisco State University
Barry Falk	Iowa State University	Scott Kjar	University of Minnesota Duluth
James Falter	Mount Mary College		
Sasan Fayazmanesh	California State University, Fresno	Frederic R. Kolb	University of Wisconsin, Eau Claire
William Field	DePauw University	Kate Krause	University of New Mexico
Lehman B. Fletcher	Iowa State University	Brent Kreider	Iowa State University
Richard Fowles	University of Utah	Eric R. Kruger	Thomas College
Mark Frascatore	Clarkson College	Viju Kulkarni	San Diego State University
Mark Funk	University of Arkansas at Little Rock		
		Matthew Lang	Xavier University
James R. Gale	Michigan Technological University	Nazma Latif-Zaman	Providence College
		Teresa Laughlin	Palomar College
Sarmila Ghosh	University of Scranton	Bruce Madariaga	Montgomery College
Satyajit Ghosh	University of Scranton	Judith Mann	University of California, San Diego
Michelle Gietz	Southwest Tennessee Community College		
		Thomas McCaleb	Florida State University
Scott Gilbert	Southern Illinois University, Carbondale	Mark McCleod	Virginia Tech University
		Michael McGuire	University of the Incarnate Word
Susan Glanz	St. John's University		
Michael J. Gootzeit	University of Memphis	Steve McQueen	Barstow Community College
John Gregor	Washington and Jefferson University	William R. Melick	Kenyon College
		Arsen Melkumian	West Virginia University
Jeff Gropp	DePauw University	Samuel Mikhail	Indian River State College
Arunee C. Grow	Mesa Community College	Frank Mixon	University of Southern Mississippi
Ali Gungoraydinoglu	The University of Mississippi		
		Shahruz Mohtadi	Suffolk University
Rik Hafer	Southern Illinois University	Gary Mongiovi	St. John's University
Robert Herman	Nassau Community College	Joseph R. Morris	Broward Community College-South Campus
Michael Heslop	Northern Virginia Community College		
		Paul G. Munyon	Grinnell College
Paul Hettler	California University of Pennsylvania		
		Rebecca Neumann	University of Wisconsin, Milwaukee
Roger Hewett	Drake University		
Andrew Hildreth	University of California, Berkeley	Chris Niggle	University of Redlands
Nathan Himelstein	Essex County College	Emmanuel Nnadozie	Truman State University
Stella Hofrenning	Augsburg College	Nick Noble	Miami University, Ohio
Shahruz Hohtadi	Suffolk University	Farrokh Nourzad	Marquette University
Daniel Horton	Cleveland State		
Jack W. Hou	California State University-Long Beach	Lee Ohanian	University of California, Los Angeles
Ann Horn-Jeddy	Medaille College		
Thomas Husted	American University	Andrew Paizis	New York University
		Jim Palmieri	Simpson College
Jeffrey Johnson	Sullivan University	Zaohong Pan	Western Connecticut State University
James Jozefowicz	Indiana University of Pennsylvania		
		Yvon Pho	American University
Jack Julian	Indiana University of Pennsylvania	Thomas Pogue	University of Iowa
		Gregg Pratt	Mesa Community College

Scott Redenius — Bryn Mawr College
Michael Reksulak — Georgia Southern University
Teresa Riley — Youngstown State University

William Rosen — Cornell University
Alannah Rosenberg — Saddleback College
Jeff Rubin — Rutgers University
Rose Rubin — University of Memphis

Thomas Sadler — Pace University
Jonathan Sandy — University of San Diego
Ramazan Sari — Texas Tech University
Mustafa Sawani — Truman State University
Edward Scahill — University of Scranton
Robert F. Schlack — Carthage College
Pamela M. Schmitt — U.S. Naval Academy
Mary Schranz — University of Wisconsin, Madison
Gerald Scott — Florida Atlantic University
Peter M. Shaw — Tidewater Community College
Alden Shiers — California Polytechnic State University

William Shughart — University of Mississippi
Kevin Siqueira — Clarkson University
William Doyle Smith — University of Texas, El Paso
Kevin Sontheimer — University of Pittsburgh
Mark Steckbeck — Campbell University
Richard Steinberg — Indiana University, Purdue University, Indianapolis

K. Strong — Baldwin-Wallace College
Martha Stuffler — Irvine Valley College
Mohammad Syed — Miles College

Manjuri Talukdar — Northern Illinois University
Kiril Tochkov — Binghamton University

John Vahaly — University of Louisville
Mikayel Vardanyan — Oregon State University

Thomas Watkins — Eastern Kentucky University
Hsinrong Wei — Baruch College, CUNY
Toni Weiss — Tulane University
Robert Whaples — Wake Forest University
Glen Whitman — California State University, Northridge

Michael F. Williams — University of St. Thomas
Melissa Wiseman — Houston Baptist University

Dirk Yandell — University of San Diego

Petr Zemcik — Southern Illinois University, Carbondale

Xiaodan Zhao — College of Saint Benedict and Saint John's University

We appreciate their input.

We also wish to acknowledge the talented and dedicated group of instructors who helped put together a supplementary package that is second to none. Dell Champlin, Oregon State University, revised the *Instructor's Manual,* and the test banks were carefully revised by Kenneth Slaysman of York College of Pennsylvania.

The beautiful book you are holding would not exist except for the hard work of a talented team of professionals. Book production was overseen by Tim Bailey, senior content project manager at Cengage Learning South-Western and undertaken by Lindsay Schmonsees, project manager at MPS Content Services. Tim and Lindsay showed remarkable patience, as well as an unflagging concern for quality throughout the process. We couldn't have asked for better production partners. Three former NYU students helped to locate and fix the few remaining errors: Madeline Merin, Joshua Savitt, and Matthew Weiner. The overall look of the book and cover was planned by Michelle Kunkler and executed by Jennifer Lambert. Deanna Ettinger managed the photo program, and Kevin Kluck made all the pieces come together in his role as manufacturing planner. We are especially grateful for the hard work of the dedicated and professional South-Western editorial, marketing, and sales teams. Mike Worls, executive editor, has once again shepherded this text through publication with remarkable skill and devotion. John Carey, senior marketing manager, has done a first-rate job getting the message out to instructors and sales reps. Susan Smart, who has been senior development editor on several editions, once again delved into every chapter and contributed to their improvement. She showed her usual patience, flexibility, and skill in managing both content and authors. Sharon Morgan, media editor, has put together a wonderful package of media tools, and the Cengage Learning South-Western sales representatives have been extremely persuasive advocates for the book. We sincerely appreciate all their efforts!

A Request

Although we have worked hard on the six editions of this book, we know there is always room for further improvement. For that, our fellow users are indispensable. We invite your comments and suggestions wholeheartedly. We especially welcome your suggestions for additional "Using the Theory" sections and Dangerous Curves. You may send your comments to either of us in care of South-Western.

Robert E. Hall

Marc Lieberman

ABOUT THE AUTHORS

Robert E. Hall

Robert E. Hall is the Robert and Carole McNeil Joint Professor of Economics at Stanford University and Senior Fellow at Stanford's Hoover Institution. His research focuses on the overall performance of the U.S. economy, including unemployment, capital formation, financial activity, and inflation. He has served as president, vice president, and Ely Lecturer of the American Economic Association and is a Distinguished Fellow of the association. Hall is an elected member of the National Academy of Sciences and Fellow of the American Academy of Arts and Sciences, the Society of Labor Economists, and the Econometric Society. He is director of the Research Program on Economic Fluctuations and Growth of the National Bureau of Economic Research. He was a member of the National Presidential Advisory Committee on Productivity. For further information about his academic activities, visit his Stanford Web site by googling "Robert E. Hall."

Marc Lieberman

Marc Lieberman is Clinical Professor of Economics at New York University. He received his PhD from Princeton University. Lieberman has taught graduate and undergraduate courses in microeconomics, macroeconomics, econometrics, labor economics, and international economics. He has taught Principles of Economics at Harvard, Vassar, the University of California at Santa Cruz, the University of Hawaii, and New York University. He has won NYU's Golden Dozen teaching award three times, and also the Economics Society Award for Excellence in Teaching. He was coeditor and contributor to *The Road to Capitalism: Economic Transformation in Eastern Europe and the Former Soviet Union*. Lieberman has consulted for Bank of America and for the Educational Testing Service. In his spare time, he is a professional screenwriter, and teaches screenwriting at NYU's School of Continuing and Professional Studies.

What Is Economics?

Economics. The word conjures up all sorts of images: manic stock traders on Wall Street, an economic summit meeting in a European capital, an earnest television news anchor announcing good or bad news about the economy. . . . You probably hear about economics several times each day. What exactly *is* economics?

First, economics is a *social science.* It seeks to explain something about *society,* just like other social sciences, such as psychology, sociology, and political science. But economists generally ask different questions about society than other social scientists do, such as:

- Why are some countries poor and others rich? How can we help the worst-off countries escape extreme poverty?

- When a nation is struck by a natural disaster—such as a hurricane or earthquake—how are people's jobs, incomes, and living standards affected?

- Why do Americans who graduate from college earn so much more than those who don't?

- What determines how much we pay for the things we buy every month? What happens when governments try to change these prices?

- Why do the prices of financial assets like stocks, bonds, and foreign currency fluctuate so widely? Can these price movements be predicted?

- What causes economies to occasionally go haywire, suffering months or years of falling production and sustained joblessness? How should governments respond?

In this book, you'll learn how economics can help us answer these and many other questions. You'll also see that the answers share a common starting point: an exploration of how individuals and societies make decisions when they are faced with scarcity.

In fact, a good definition of economics, which stresses its differences from other social sciences, is:

> *Economics is the study of choice under conditions of scarcity.*

Economics The study of choice under conditions of scarcity.

This definition may appear strange to you. Where are the familiar words we ordinarily associate with economics: "money," "stocks and bonds," "prices," "budgets," and so on? As you will soon see, economics deals with all of these things and more. But first, let's take a closer look at two important ideas in this definition: scarcity and choice.

1

SCARCITY AND INDIVIDUAL CHOICE

Think for a moment about your own life. Is there anything you don't have that you'd *like* to have? Anything you'd like *more* of? If your answer is "no," congratulations! You are well advanced on the path of Zen self-denial. The rest of us, however, feel the pinch of limits to our material standard of living. This simple truth is at the very core of economics. It can be restated this way: We all face the problem of **scarcity**.

Scarcity A situation in which the amount of something available is insufficient to satisfy the desire for it.

At first glance, it may seem that you suffer from an infinite variety of scarcities. There are so many things you might like to have right now—a larger room or apartment, a new car, more clothes . . . the list is endless. But a little reflection suggests that your limited ability to satisfy these desires is based on two more basic limitations: scarce *time* and scarce *spending power*.

> As individuals, we face a scarcity of time and spending power. Given more of either, we could each have more of the goods and services that we desire.

The scarcity of spending power is no doubt familiar to you. We've all wished for higher incomes so that we could afford to buy more of the things we want. But the scarcity of time is equally important. So many of the activities we enjoy—seeing movies, taking vacations, making phone calls—require time as well as money. Just as we have limited spending power, we also have a limited number of hours in each day to satisfy our desires.

Because of the scarcities of time and spending power, each of us is forced to make *choices*. We must allocate our scarce *time* to different activities: work, play, education, sleep, shopping, and more. We must allocate our scarce *spending power* among different goods and services: housing, food, furniture, travel, and many others. And each time we choose to buy something or do something, we also choose *not* to buy or do something else.

In fact, what we choose *not* to buy or do—"the road not taken" as the poet Robert Frost put it—leads to an interesting way of thinking about *cost*.

The Concept of Opportunity Cost

What does it cost you to go to the movies? If you answered 9 or 10 dollars because that is the price of a movie ticket, then you are leaving out a lot. Most of us are used to thinking of "cost" as the money we must pay for something. Certainly, the money we pay for goods or services is a *part* of its cost. But economics takes a broader view of costs. The true cost of any choice we make—buying a car, reading a book, or even taking a nap—is everything we must *give up* when we make that choice. This cost is called the *opportunity cost* of the choice because we give up the opportunity to enjoy other desirable things or experiences.

Opportunity cost What is given up when taking an action or making a choice.

> The **opportunity cost** of any choice is what we must forego when we make that choice.

Opportunity cost is the most accurate and complete concept of cost—the one we should use when making our own decisions or analyzing the decisions of others.

Suppose, for example, it's 8 P.M. on a weeknight, and you're spending a couple of hours reading this chapter. As authors, that thought makes us very happy.

We know there are many other things you could be doing: going to a movie, having dinner with friends, playing ping-pong, earning some extra money, watching TV. . . . But—assuming you're still reading and haven't run out the door because we've given you better ideas—let's relate this to opportunity cost.

What *is* the opportunity cost of reading this chapter? Is it *all* of those other possibilities we've listed? Not really, because in the time it takes to read this chapter, you'd probably be able to do only *one* of those other activities. You'd no doubt choose whichever one you regarded as best. So, by reading, you sacrifice only the *best* choice among the alternatives that you could be doing instead.

> *When the alternatives to a choice are mutually exclusive, only the next best choice—the one that would actually be chosen—is used to determine the opportunity cost of the choice.*

For many choices, the opportunity cost consists mostly of the money you actually pay out. If you spend $100 on a new pair of shoes, the most important thing you give up is $100, which is money you could spend on something else. But for other choices, money payments may be only a small part, or no part, of what is sacrificed. Doing a spring cleaning of your home, for example, will take you a lot of time, but very little money.

Economists often attach a monetary value to the time that we give up for a choice. This allows us to express a choice's opportunity cost in dollars—the number of dollars actually paid out plus the dollar value of the time given up. To see how this works, let's see how we might calculate the opportunity cost (in dollars) of an important choice you've already made: to attend college.

An Example: The Opportunity Cost of College

What is the opportunity cost of attending college for an academic year (9 months)? A good starting point is to look at the actual monetary costs—the annual out-of-pocket expenses borne by you or your family. Table 1 shows the College Board's estimates of these expenses for the average student (ignoring scholarships). For example, the third column of the table shows that the average in-state resident at a four-year state college pays $7,605 in tuition and fees, $1,137 for books and supplies, $8,535 for room and board, and $3,062 for transportation and other expenses, for a total of $20,339 per year.

TABLE 1

Average Out-of-Pocket Cost of a Year of College, 2010–2011

Type of Institution	Two-Year Public	Four-Year Public	Four-Year Private
Tuition and fees	$2,713	$7,605	$27,293
Books and supplies	$1,133	$1,137	$1,181
Room and board	$7,259	$8,535	$9,700
Transportation and other expenses	$3,532	$3,062	$2,302
Total out-of-pocket costs	$14,637	$20,339	$40,476

Source: *Trends in College Pricing*, 2010, The College Board, New York, NY.

Notes: Averages are enrollment-weighted by institution to reflect the average experience among students across the United States. Average tuition and fees at public institutions are for in-state residents only. Room and board charges are for students living on campus at four-year institutions and off-campus (but not with parents) at two-year institutions. Four-year private includes nonprofit only.

So, is that the average opportunity cost of a year of college at a public institution? Not really. Even if that is the amount you or your family actually pays out for college, this is not the dollar measure of the opportunity cost.

First, the $20,339 your family pays in this example most likely includes some expenses that are *not* part of the opportunity cost of college. These are payments you'd make whether or not you were in college. Let's suppose that if you *didn't* go to college, you would have lived in an apartment, and your expenses for rent and food would be equal to their college amounts: $8,535. Let's also suppose that you'd have transportation and other expenses equal to their college amounts: $3,062. Then these payments must be deducted from the opportunity cost of choosing college. Table 2 shows that when we deduct these payments, we're left with the additional dollars you pay out of pocket *because* you chose to attend college: $8,742. These dollars—spent on tuition and fees and books and supplies—are the only part of your money payments that are part of the opportunity cost. Money payments that are part of opportunity cost are called **explicit costs**. So your explicit costs of attending college are $8,742.

But college also has **implicit costs**—sacrifices for which no money changes hands. The biggest sacrifice in this category is *time*. But what is that time worth? That depends on what you *would* be doing if you weren't in school. For many students, the alternative would be working full-time at a job. If you are one of these students, attending college requires the sacrifice of the income you *could* have earned at a job—a sacrifice we call *foregone income*.

How much income is foregone when you go to college for a year? In 2010, the average yearly income of an 18- to 24-year-old high school graduate who worked full-time was about $24,000. If we assume that only nine months of work must be sacrificed to attend college (that is, you'd still work full-time in the summer), then foregone income is about 3/4 of $24,000, or $18,000. This is the implicit cost of a year of college.

Summing the explicit and implicit costs gives us a rough estimate of the opportunity cost of a year in college, as shown in Table 2. For a public institution, we have $8,742 in explicit costs and $18,000 in implicit costs, giving us an opportunity cost of $26,742 per year. Notice that this is even greater than the total charges estimated by the College Board we calculated earlier. When you consider this opportunity cost for four years, its magnitude might surprise you. Without financial aid in the form of tuition grants or other fee reductions, the average in-state resident will sacrifice about $107,000 over four years at a state college. At a private college, we'd find (using calculations similar to those in Table 2) a total opportunity cost of about $186,000.

Explicit cost The dollars sacrificed—and actually paid out—for a choice.

Implicit cost The value of something sacrificed when no direct payment is made.

TABLE 2

Sample Opportunity Cost Calculation for In-State Public University

Total out-of-pocket payments:		**$20,339**
minus { out-of-pocket expenses you'd have without college }		− $8,535 (room and board)
		− $3,062 (transportation and other)
= **Explicit cost of college**		= **$8,742**
plus implicit cost		+ $18,000 (9 months foregone income)
= **Opportunity cost of 1 year of college**		= **$26,742**

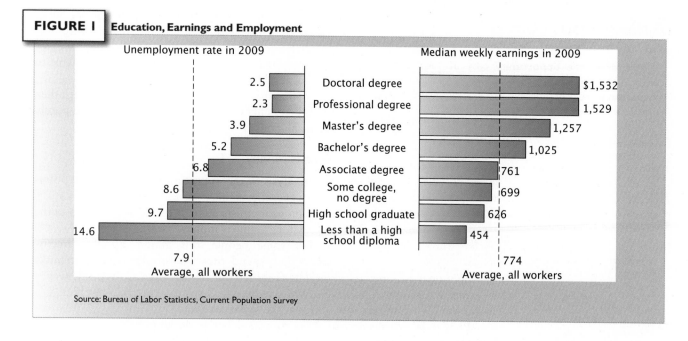

FIGURE 1 | **Education, Earnings and Employment**

Source: Bureau of Labor Statistics, Current Population Survey

Our analysis of the opportunity cost of college is an example of a general, and important, principle:

> *The opportunity cost of a choice includes both explicit costs and implicit costs.*

A Brief Digression: Is College the Right Choice?

Before you start questioning your choice to be in college, there are a few things to remember. First, for many students, scholarships reduce the costs of college to less than those in our example. Second, in addition to its high cost, college has substantial *benefits*, including financial ones.

Figure 1 shows two examples of these financial benefits for the year 2009. The right side of the figure shows that full-time workers with bachelor's degrees earned substantially higher incomes ($1,025 per week) than those with only a high-school diploma ($626 per week). Moreover, as seen in the left side, college graduates were more likely to find full-time jobs; the unemployment rate of those with bachelor's degrees (5.2%) was substantially lower than for high-school graduates (9.7%). These advantages in earnings and employment prospects are seen year after year, in good times and bad. In spite of its high cost, attending college appears to be one of the best *financial* investments you can make.[1]

Finally, remember that we've left out of our discussion many non-financial benefits of attending college. These may be harder to estimate in dollar terms, but they could be very important to you. Do you enjoy taking classes and learning new things more than you'd enjoy working at the job you would have gotten

[1] If you are studying microeconomics, you'll learn more about the value of college as an investment and how economists value future earnings in a later chapter.

⚠ DANGEROUS CURVES

If you think the opportunity cost of your time is zero . . . What if you can't work extra hours for additional pay, so you cannot *actually* turn time into money? Does this mean that the opportunity cost of your time is zero?

If you think the answer is yes, the authors of this textbook would like to hire you for help with some household chores for 25 cents per hour. Does this sound like a good deal to you? It would, if the opportunity cost of your time really had no value. If it doesn't sound like a good deal, then the time you'd be giving up must have some positive value to you. If pressed, you could state that value in money terms—and it would no doubt exceed 25 cents per hour.

© AXL/SHUTTERSTOCK.COM

instead? Do you have a more interesting social life in college than you'd otherwise have? In the future, will you get more satisfaction—above and beyond the extra earnings—from the jobs that will become available to you because of your college degree?

If you answered yes to any of these questions, then the full benefits of college are greater than the purely financial gains.

Time Is Money

Our analysis of the opportunity cost of college points out a general principle, one understood by economists and non-economists alike. It can be summed up in the expression, "Time is money."

For some people, this maxim applies directly: When they spend time on something, they *actually* give up money—money they *could* have earned during that time. Consider Jessica, a freelance writer with a backlog of projects on which she can earn $25 per hour. For each hour Jessica spends *not* working, she sacrifices $25.

What if Jessica decides to see a movie? What is the opportunity cost in dollar terms? Suppose the ticket costs $10, and the entire activity takes three hours—including time spent getting there and back. And suppose that working is Jessica's next best alternative to seeing the movie. The opportunity cost is the sum of the explicit cost ($10 for the ticket) and the implicit cost ($75 for three hours of forgone income), making the total opportunity cost $85.

The idea that a movie "costs" $85 might seem absurd to you. But if you think about it, $85 is a much better estimate than $10 of what the movie actually costs Jessica. To see the movie, Jessica does indeed sacrifice $85.

Our examples about the cost of college and the cost of a movie point out an important lesson about opportunity cost:

> *The explicit (direct money) cost of a choice may only be a part—and sometimes a small part—of the opportunity cost of a choice.*

SCARCITY AND SOCIAL CHOICE

Now let's think about scarcity and choice from *society's* point of view. What are the goals of our society? We want a high standard of living for our citizens, clean air, safe streets, good schools, and more. What is holding us back from accomplishing all of these goals in a way that would satisfy everyone? You already know the answer: scarcity. In society's case, the problem is a scarcity of **resources**—the things we use to make goods and services that help us achieve our goals.

Resources The labor, capital, land (including natural resources), and entrepreneurship that are used to produce goods and services.

The Four Resources

Resources are the most basic elements used to make goods and services. We can classify resources into four categories:

Labor The time human beings spend producing goods and services.

- **Labor**—the time human beings spend producing goods and services.
- **Capital**—any long-lasting tool that is itself produced and helps us make other goods and services.

Capital A long-lasting tool that is used to produce other goods.

More specifically, **physical capital** consists of things like machinery and equipment, factory buildings, computers, and even hand-tools like hammers and screwdrivers. These are all long-lasting *physical* tools that we produce to help us make other goods and services.

Physical capital The part of the capital stock consisting of physical goods, such as machinery, equipment, and factories.

Another type of capital is **human capital**—the skills and knowledge possessed by workers. These satisfy our definition of capital: They are *produced* (through education and training), they help us produce *other* things, and they last for many years, typically through an individual's working life.

Human capital The skills and training of the labor force.

Note the word *long-lasting* in the definition. If something is used up quickly in the production process—like the flour a baker uses to make bread—it is generally *not* considered capital. A good rule of thumb is that capital should last at least a year, although most types of capital last considerably longer.

The **capital stock** is the total amount of capital at a nation's disposal at any point in time. It consists of all the capital—physical and human—created in previous periods that is still productively useful.

Capital stock The total amount of capital in a nation that is productively useful at a particular point in time.

- **Land**—the physical space on which production takes place, as well as the useful materials—*natural resources*—found under it or on it, such as crude oil, iron, coal, or fertile soil.

Land The physical space on which production takes place, as well as the natural resources that come with it.

- **Entrepreneurship**—the ability (and the willingness to *use* it) to combine the *other* resources into a productive enterprise. An entrepreneur may be an *innovator* who comes up with an original idea for a business or a *risk taker* who provides her own funds or time to nurture a project with uncertain rewards.

Entrepreneurship The ability and willingness to combine the *other* resources—labor, capital, and land—into a productive enterprise.

Anything *produced* in the economy comes, ultimately, from some combination of these four resources.

Think about the last lecture you attended at your college. Some resources were used *directly*: Your instructor's labor and human capital (his or her knowledge of economics); physical capital (the classroom building, a blackboard or projector); and land (the property on which your classroom building sits). Somebody played the role of entrepreneur, bringing these resources together to create your college in the first place. (If you attend a public institution, the entrepreneurial role was played by your state government.)

Many other inputs—besides those special inputs we call resources—were also used to produce the lecture. But these other inputs were themselves produced from resources, as illustrated in Figure 2. For example, the electricity used to power the lights in your classroom is an input, not a resource. But electricity is itself produced from resources, including crude oil, coal, or natural gas (land and natural resources); coal miners or oil riggers (labor); and electricity-generating turbines and power cables (capital).

Input Anything (including a resource) used to produce a good or service.

Opportunity Cost and Society's Trade-offs

For an individual, opportunity cost arises from the scarcity of time and money. But for society as a whole, opportunity cost arises from the scarcity of *resources*. Our desire for goods is limitless, but we have limited resources to produce them. Therefore,

virtually all production carries an opportunity cost: To produce more of one thing, society must shift resources away from producing something else.

DANGEROUS CURVES ⚠

Resources versus inputs The term *resources* is often confused with another more general term—**inputs.** An input is *anything* used to make a good or service. Inputs include not only resources but also many other things made from them (cement, rolled steel, electricity), which are, in turn, used to make goods and services. *Resources,* by contrast, are the *special* inputs that fall into one of four categories: labor, land, capital, and entrepreneurship. They are the ultimate source of everything that is produced.

FIGURE 2   **Resources and Production**

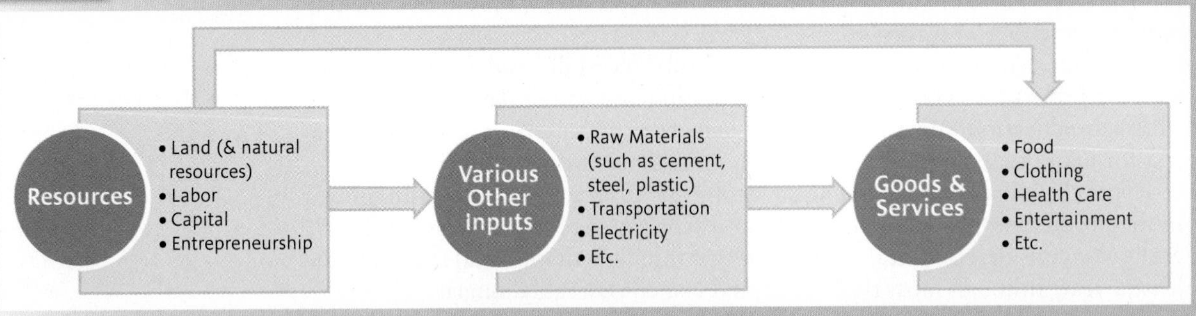

All goods and services come ultimately from the four resources. Resources are used directly by firms that produce goods and services. Resources are also used indirectly, to make the other inputs firms use to produce goods and services.

For example, we'd all like better health for our citizens. What would be needed to achieve this goal? Perhaps more frequent medical checkups for more people and greater access to top-flight medicine when necessary. These, in turn, would require more and better-trained doctors (labor and human capital), and more hospital buildings, laboratories, and high-tech medical equipment (physical capital). In order to produce more health care, we would have to pull resources— land, labor, capital, and entrepreneurship—out of producing other things that we also enjoy. We'd have more health care, but fewer movies, personal computers, cars, or other goods and services that would otherwise have been produced. The opportunity cost of improved health care, then, consists of those other goods and services we would have to do without.

THE WORLD OF ECONOMICS

The field of economics is surprisingly broad. It ranges from the mundane (why does a pound of steak cost more than a pound of chicken?) to the personal (how do couples decide how many children to have?) to the profound (could we ever have another Great Depression in the United States, with tens of millions plunged into sudden poverty?). With a field this broad, it is useful to have some way of classifying the different types of problems economists study and the different methods they use to analyze them.

Microeconomics and Macroeconomics

Microeconomics The study of the behavior of individual households, firms, and governments; the choices they make; and their interaction in specific markets.

The field of economics is divided into two major parts: microeconomics and macroeconomics. **Microeconomics** comes from the Greek word *mikros*, meaning "small." It takes a close-up view of the economy, as if looking through a microscope. Microeconomics is concerned with the behavior of *individual* actors on the economic scene—households, business firms, and governments. It looks at the choices they make and how they interact with each other when they come together to trade *specific* goods and services. What will happen to the cost of movie tickets over the next five years? How many management-trainee jobs will open up for college graduates? These are microeconomic questions because they analyze individual *parts* of an economy rather than the *whole*.

Macroeconomics—from the Greek *makros*, or "large"—takes an *overall* view of the economy. Instead of focusing on the production of carrots or computers, macroeconomics lumps all goods and services together and looks at the economy's *total output*. Instead of focusing on employment of management trainees or manufacturing workers, it considers *total employment* in the economy. Macroeconomics focuses on the big picture and ignores the fine details.

Macroeconomics The study of the behavior of the overall economy.

Positive and Normative Economics

The micro versus macro distinction is based on the level of detail we want to consider. Another useful distinction has to do with our *purpose* in analyzing a problem. **Positive economics** explains how the economy works, plain and simple. If someone says, "The decline in home prices during 2008 and 2009 was a major cause of the recent recession," he or she is making a positive economic statement. A statement need not be accurate or even sensible to be classified as positive. For example, "Government policy has no effect on our standard of living" is a statement that virtually every economist would regard as false. But it is still a positive economic statement. Whether true or not, it's about how the economy works and its accuracy can be tested by looking at the facts—and just the facts.

Positive economics The study of how the economy works.

Normative economics *prescribes solutions* to economic problems. It goes beyond just "the facts" and tells us what we should *do* about them. Normative economics requires us to make judgments about different outcomes and therefore depends on our values.

Normative economics The practice of recommending policies to solve economic problems.

If an economist says, "We should cut total government spending," he or she is engaging in normative economic analysis. Cutting government spending would benefit some citizens and harm others, so the statement rests on a value judgment. A normative statement—like "We should cut government spending"—cannot be proved or disproved by the facts alone.

Positive and normative economics are intimately related in practice. For one thing, we cannot properly argue about what we should or should not do unless we know certain facts about the world. Every normative analysis is therefore based on an underlying positive analysis. And a new understanding of positive economics often changes one's views on normative economics.

Why Economists Disagree about Policy

Suppose the country is suffering from a serious recession—a significant, nationwide decrease in production and employment. Two economists are interviewed on a cable news show.

Economist A says, "We should increase government spending on roads, bridges, and other infrastructure. This would directly create jobs and help end the recession." Economist B says, "No, we should cut taxes instead. This will put more money in the hands of households and businesses, leading them to spend more and create jobs that way." Why do they disagree?

The disagreement might be based on *positive* economics—different views about how the economy works. Economist A might think that government spending will create more jobs, dollar for dollar,

DANGEROUS CURVES ⚠️

Seemingly positive statements Be alert to statements that may *seem* purely positive, but contain hidden value judgments. Here's an example: "If we want to reduce greenhouse gas emissions, our society will have to use less gasoline." This may *sound* positive because it seems to refer only to a fact about the world. But it's also at least partly normative. Why? Cutting back on gasoline is just *one* policy among many that could reduce emissions. To say that we *must* choose this method makes a value judgment about its superiority to other methods. A purely positive statement on this topic would be, "Using less gasoline—with no other change in living habits— would reduce greenhouse gas emissions."

Similarly, be alert to statements that use vague terms that hide value judgments. An example: "All else equal, the less gasoline we use, the better our quality of life." Whether you agree or disagree, this is *not* a purely positive statement. People will disagree over the meaning of the phrase "quality of life" and what would make life better. This disagreement could not be resolved just by looking at the facts.

© AXL/SHUTTERSTOCK.COM

than will tax cuts. Economist B might believe the reverse. Positive differences like these can arise because our knowledge of how the economy works—while always improving—remains imperfect.

But the disagreement might also stem from a difference in values—specifically, what each economist believes about government's proper role in the economy. Those toward the left of the political spectrum tend to believe that government should play a larger economic role. They tend to view increases in government spending more favorably. Those toward the political right tend to believe that government's role should be smaller. They would prefer tax cuts that result in more private, rather than government, spending. This difference in values can explain why two economists—even if they have the same *positive* views about the outcome of a policy—might disagree about its wisdom.

> *Policy differences among economists arise from (1) positive disagreements (about the outcomes of different policies), and (2) differences in values (how those outcomes are evaluated).*

Policy disputes among economists are common. But on *some* policy issues, most economists agree. For example, in microeconomics there is wide agreement that certain types of goods and services should be provided by private business firms and that certain others are best provided by government.

In macroeconomics, almost all economists agree that some of the government policies during the Great Depression of the 1930s were mistakes that worsened and prolonged the economic downturn. When U.S. and global economies sank into a deep recession in 2008 and 2009, many feared a repeat of the Great Depression. Economists had some important disagreements about what the initial response of the U.S. and other governments should be. But they were virtually united in warning against repeating the mistakes of the 1930s.

Most governments heeded these warnings. Although the economic slump continued through 2010 and into 2011, another Great Depression was avoided. You will learn more about these areas of agreement among economists—as well as some important disagreements—in the chapters to come.

WHY STUDY ECONOMICS?

If you've read this far into the chapter, chances are you've already decided to allocate some of your scarce time to studying economics. We think you've made a wise choice. But it's worth taking a moment to consider what you might gain from this choice.

Why study economics?

To Understand the World Better

Applying the tools of economics can help you understand global and catastrophic events such as wars, famines, epidemics, and depressions. But it can also help you understand much of what happens to you locally and personally—the salary you will earn after you graduate or the rent you'll pay on your apartment. Economics has the power to help us understand these phenomena because they result, in large part, from the choices we make under conditions of scarcity.

Economics has its limitations, of course. But it is hard to find any aspect of life about which economics does not have *something* important to say. Economics cannot explain why so many Americans like to watch television, but it *can* explain how TV networks decide which programs to offer. Economics cannot protect you from a robbery, but it *can* explain why some people choose to become thieves and why no society has chosen to eradicate crime completely. Economics will not improve your love life, resolve unconscious conflicts from your childhood, or help you overcome a fear of flying, but it *can* tell us how many skilled therapists, ministers, and counselors are available to help us solve these problems.

To Achieve Social Change

If you are interested in making the world a better place, economics is indispensable. There is no shortage of serious social problems worthy of our attention—unemployment, hunger, poverty, disease, climate change, drug addiction, violent crime. Economics can help us understand the origins of these problems, explain why previous efforts to solve them haven't succeeded, and help us to design new, more effective solutions.

To Help Prepare for Other Careers

Economics has long been a popular college major for individuals intending to work in business. But it has also been popular among those planning careers in politics, international relations, law, medicine, engineering, psychology, and other professions. This is for good reason: Practitioners in each of these fields often find themselves confronting economic issues. For example, lawyers increasingly face judicial rulings based on the principles of economic efficiency. And doctors need to understand how new technologies or changes in health care policy can affect their practices.

To Become an Economist

Only a tiny minority of this book's readers will decide to become economists. This is welcome news to the authors, and after you have studied labor markets in your *microeconomics* course you will understand why. But if you do decide to become an economist—obtaining a master's degree or a PhD—you will find many possibilities for employment. The economists with whom you have most likely had personal contact are those who teach and conduct research at colleges and universities. But as many economists work outside of colleges and universities as work inside them. Economists are hired by banks to assess the risk of investing abroad; by manufacturing companies to help them determine new methods of producing, marketing, and pricing their products; by government agencies to help design policies to fight crime, disease, poverty, and pollution; by international organizations to help create and reform aid programs for less developed countries; by the media to help the public interpret global, national, and local events; and by nonprofit organizations to provide advice on controlling costs and raising funds more effectively.

THE METHODS OF ECONOMICS

One of the first things you will notice as you begin to study economics is the heavy reliance on *models*.

You have no doubt encountered many models in your life. As a child, you played with model trains, model planes, or model people (dolls). You may have also seen architects' cardboard models of buildings. These are all physical models, three-dimensional replicas that you can pick up and hold. Economic models, by contrast, are built with words, diagrams, and mathematical statements.

What, exactly, is a model?

A ***model*** *is an abstract representation of reality.*

Model An abstract representation of reality.

The two key words in this definition are *abstract* and *representation*. A model is not supposed to be exactly like reality. Rather, it *represents* reality by *abstracting* or *taking from* the real world. By including some—but not all—of the details of the real world, a model helps us understand the world more clearly.

The Art of Building Economic Models

When you build a model, how do you know which real-world details to include and which to leave out? There is no simple answer to this question. The right amount of detail depends on your purpose in building the model in the first place. There is, however, one guiding principle:

> *A model should be as simple as possible to accomplish its purpose.*

This means that a model should contain only the *necessary* details.

To understand this a little better, think about a map. A map is a model that represents a part of the earth's surface. But it leaves out many details of the real world. First, a map leaves out the third dimension—height—of the real world. Second, maps always ignore small details, such as trees and houses and potholes. But when you download a map, how much detail do you want it to have?

Suppose you're in Columbus, Ohio, and you want to drive from Port Columbus International Airport to the downtown convention center. You will need a zoomed-in, detailed street map, as on the left side of Figure 3. The zoomed-out highway map on the right doesn't show any streets, so it wouldn't do at all.

But if you instead wanted to find the best driving route from Columbus to Boston, you would want to zoom out to the highway map. The view with individual streets would have too much detail and be harder to use.

The same principle applies in building economic models. The level of detail that would be just right for one purpose will usually be too much or too little for another. When you feel yourself objecting to an economic model because something has been left out, keep in mind the purpose for which the model is built. In introductory economics, the purpose is entirely educational—to help you understand some simple yet powerful principles about how the economy operates. Keeping the models simple makes it easier to see these principles at work and remember them later.

FIGURE 3 Maps as Models

These maps are models. But each would be used for a different purpose.

Assumptions and Conclusions

Every economic model makes two types of assumptions: *simplifying* assumptions and *critical* assumptions.

A **simplifying assumption** is just what it sounds like—a way of making a model simpler without affecting any of its important conclusions. A road map, for example, makes the simplifying assumption, "There are no trees." Having trees on a map would only get in the way. Similarly, in an economic model, we might assume that there are only two goods that households can choose from or that there are only two nations in the world. We make such assumptions *not* because we think they are true, but because they make a model easier to follow and do not change any of the important insights we can get from it.

A **critical assumption**, by contrast, is an assumption that affects the conclusions of a model in important ways. When you use a road map, you make the critical assumption, "All of these roads are open." If that assumption is wrong, your conclusion—the best route to take—might be wrong as well.

In an economic model, there are always one or more critical assumptions. You don't have to look very hard to find them because economists like to make them explicit right from the outset. For example, when we study the behavior of business firms, our model will assume that firms try to earn the highest possible profit for their owners. By stating this critical assumption up front, we can see immediately where the model's conclusions spring from.

Simplifying assumption Any assumption that makes a model simpler without affecting any of its important conclusions.

Critical assumption Any assumption that affects the conclusions of a model in an important way.

Math, Jargon, and Other Concerns

Economists often express their ideas using mathematical concepts and a special vocabulary. Why? Because these tools enable economists to express themselves more precisely than with ordinary language. For example, when conflict raged across Libya in early 2011, someone who never studied economics might say, "Oil prices rose because there was a shortage of oil." That statement might not bother you right now. But in a few weeks, you'll be saying it something like this: "Oil prices rose because the supply curve for oil shifted leftward, while the demand curve continued to shift rightward."

Does the second statement sound strange to you? It should. First, it uses special terms—*demand curve* and *supply curve*—that you've yet to learn. Second, it uses a mathematical concept—*shifting curves*—with which you might not be familiar. But the first statement might mean a number of different things, some of which were *not* true at the time. The second statement—as you will see in Chapter 3—can mean only *one* thing. By being precise, we can steer clear of unnecessary confusion.

If you are worried about the special vocabulary of economics, you can relax. After all, you may never have heard the term "opportunity cost" before, but now you know what it means. New terms will be defined and carefully explained as you encounter them. Indeed, this textbook does not assume you have any special knowledge of economics. It is truly meant for a "first course" in the field.

But what about the math? Here, too, you can relax. While professional economists often use sophisticated mathematics to solve problems, only a little math is needed to understand basic economic *principles*. And virtually all of this math comes from high-school algebra and geometry.

Still, if you have forgotten some of your high-school math, a little brushing up might be in order. This is why we have included an appendix at the end of this chapter. It covers some of the most basic concepts—such as interpreting graphs, the equation for a straight line, and the concept of a slope—that you will need in this course. You may want to glance at this appendix now, just so you'll know what's there. Then, from time to time, you can go back to it when you need it.

HOW TO STUDY ECONOMICS

As you read this book or listen to your instructor, you may find yourself following along and thinking that everything makes perfect sense. Economics may even seem easy. Indeed, it *is* rather easy to *follow* economics, as it's based so heavily on simple logic. But *following* and *learning* are two different things. You will eventually discover (preferably *before* your first exam) that to learn economics, you must study it actively, not passively.

If you are reading these words while you are lying back on a comfortable couch, a phone in one hand and a remote in the other, you are going about it in the wrong way. Active studying means reading with a pencil in your hand and a blank sheet of paper in front of you. It means closing the book periodically and *reproducing* what you have learned. It means listing the steps in each logical argument, retracing the flow of cause and effect in each model, and drawing the graphs. It does require some work, but the payoff is a good understanding of economics and a better understanding of your own life and the world around you.

SUMMARY

Economics is the study of choice under conditions of scarcity. As individuals—and as a society—we have unlimited desires for goods and services. Unfortunately, our ability to satisfy those desires is limited, so we must usually sacrifice something for any choice we make.

The correct measure of the cost of a choice is not just the money price we pay, but the *opportunity cost*: what we must give up when we make a choice.

At the individual level, opportunity cost arises from the scarcity of time or money. For society as a whole, it arises from the scarcity of *resources*. The four types of resources are *land, labor, capital,* and *entrepreneurship*. All of the *inputs* we use to produce goods and services are either resources themselves or are made from resources. Therefore, to produce and enjoy more of one thing, society must shift resources away from producing something else. Every

society must choose which desires to satisfy and how to satisfy them. Economics provides the tools that explain those choices.

The field of economics is divided into two major areas. *Microeconomics* studies the behavior of individual households, firms, and governments as they interact in specific markets. *Macroeconomics*, by contrast, concerns itself with the behavior of the entire economy. It considers variables such as total output and total employment.

Economics makes heavy use of *models*—abstract representations of reality—to help us understand how the economy operates. All models are simplifications, but a good model will have just enough detail for the purpose at hand. The *simplifying* assumptions in a model just make it easier to use. The *critical* assumptions are the ones that affect the model's conclusions.

PROBLEM SET

Answers to even-numbered Problems can be found on the text Web site through www.cengagebrain.com

1. Discuss whether each statement is a purely positive statement, or whether it also contains normative elements and/or value judgments:
   a. An increase in the personal income tax will slow the growth rate of the economy.
   b. The goal of any country's economic policy should be to increase the well-being of its poorest, most vulnerable citizens.
   c. The best way to reduce the national poverty rate is to increase the federal minimum wage.

   d. The 1990s were a disastrous decade for the U.S. economy. Income inequality increased to its highest level since before World War II.

2. For each of the following, state whether economists would consider it a *resource*, and, if they would, identify which of the four types of resources the item is.
   a. A computer used by an FBI agent to track the whereabouts of suspected criminals.
   b. The office building in which the FBI agent works.

c. The time that an FBI agent spends on a case.
d. A farmer's tractor.
e. The farmer's knowledge of how to operate the tractor.
f. Crude oil.
g. A package of frozen vegetables.
h. A food scientist's knowledge of how to commercially freeze vegetables.
i. The ability to bring together resources to start a frozen-food company.
j. Plastic bags used by a frozen-food company to hold its product.

3. Suppose you are using the second map in Figure 3, which shows main highways only. You've reached a conclusion about the best way to drive from the Columbus city center to an area south of the city. State whether each of the following assumptions of the map would be a *simplifying* or *critical* assumption for your conclusion, and explain briefly. (Don't worry about whether the assumption is true or not.)
a. The thicker numbered lines are major highways without traffic lights.
b. The earth is two-dimensional.
c. When two highways cross, you can get from one to the other without going through city traffic.
d. Distances on the map are proportional to distances in the real world.

4. Suppose that you are considering what to do on an upcoming weekend. Here are your options, from least to most preferred: (1) study for upcoming midterms; (2) fly to Colorado for a quick ski trip; (3) go into seclusion in your dorm room and try to improve your score on a computer game. What is the opportunity cost of a decision to play the computer game all weekend? (Your answer will not be in dollars.)

5. Use the information in Table 1 (as well as the assumption about foregone income made in the chapter) to calculate the average opportunity cost of a year in college for a student at a four-year private institution under each of the following special assumptions:
a. The student receives free room and board at home at *no* opportunity cost to the parents.
b. The student receives an academic scholarship covering all tuition and fees (in the form of a grant, not a loan or a work-study aid).
c. The student works half-time while at school (assume for this problem that the leisure or study time sacrificed has no opportunity cost).

6. Use the information in Table 1 (as well as the assumption about foregone income made in the chapter) to compare the opportunity cost of attending a year of college for a student at a two-year public college, under each of the following special assumptions:
a. The student receives free room and board at home at *no* opportunity cost to the parents.
b. The student receives an academic scholarship covering all tuition and fees (in the form of a grant, not a loan or a work-study aid).
c. The student works half-time while at school (assume for this problem that the leisure or study time sacrificed has no opportunity cost).

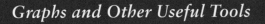
TABLES AND GRAPHS

A brief glance at this text will tell you that graphs are important in economics. Graphs provide a convenient way to display information and enable us to immediately *see* relationships between variables.

Suppose that you've just been hired at the advertising department of Len & Harry's—an up-and-coming manufacturer of high-end ice cream products located in Texas. You've been asked to compile a report on how advertising affects the company's sales. It turns out that the company's spending on advertising has changed repeatedly in the past, so you have lots of data on monthly advertising expenditure and monthly sales revenue, both measured in thousands of dollars.

Table A.1 shows a useful way of arranging this data. The company's advertising expenditures in different months are listed in the left-hand column, while the right-hand column lists total sales revenue ("sales" for short) during the same months. Notice that the data in this table is organized so that spending on advertising increases as we move down the first column. Often, just looking at a table like this can reveal useful patterns. In this example, it's clear that higher spending on advertising is associated with higher monthly sales. These two variables—advertising and sales—have a *positive relationship*. A rise in one is associated with a rise in the other. If higher advertising had been associated with

lower sales, the two variables would have a *negative* or *inverse relationship*: A rise in one would be associated with a fall in the other.

We can be even more specific about the positive relationship between advertising and sales: Logic tells us that the association is very likely *causal*. We'd expect that sales revenue *depends on* advertising outlays, so we call sales our *dependent variable* and advertising our *independent variable*. Changes in an independent variable cause changes in a dependent variable, but not the other way around.

To explore the relationship further, let's graph it. As a rule, the *independent* variable is measured on the *horizontal* axis and the *dependent* variable on the *vertical* axis. In economics, unfortunately, we do not always stick to this rule, but for now we will. In Figure A.1, monthly advertising expenditure—our independent variable—is measured on the horizontal axis. If we start at the *origin*—the corner where the two axes intersect—and move rightward along the horizontal axis, monthly advertising spending increases from $0 to $1,000 to $2,000 and so on. The vertical axis measures monthly sales—the dependent variable. Along this axis, as we move upward from the origin, sales rise.

The graph in Figure A.1 shows six labeled points, each representing a different pair of numbers from our table. For example, point *A*—which represents the numbers in the first row of the table—shows us that when

TABLE A.1

Advertising and Sales at Len & Harry's

Advertising Expenditures ($1,000 per Month)	Sales ($1,000 per Month)
2	24
3	27
6	36
7	39
11	51
12	54

FIGURE A.1   A Graph of Advertising and Sales

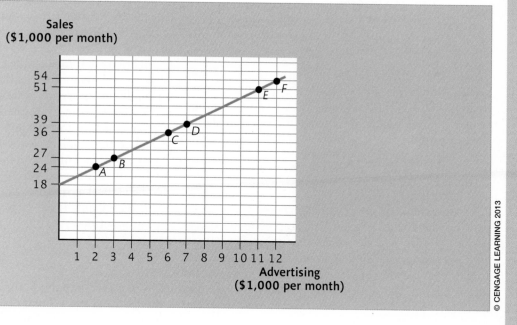

the firm spends $2,000 on advertising, sales are $24,000 per month. Point *B* represents the *second* row of the table, and so on. Notice that all of these points lie along a *straight line*.

Straight-Line Graphs

You'll encounter straight-line graphs often in economics, so it's important to understand one special property they possess: The "rate of change" of one variable compared with the other is always the same. For example, look at what happens as we move from point *A* to point *B*: Advertising rises by $1,000 (from $2,000 to $3,000), while sales rise by $3,000 (from $24,000 to $27,000). If you study the graph closely, you'll see that anywhere along this line, whenever advertising increases by $1,000, sales increase by $3,000. Or, if we define a "unit" as "one thousand dollars," we can say that every time advertising increases by one unit, sales rise by three units. So the "rate of change" is three units of sales for every one unit of advertising.

The rate of change of the *vertically* measured variable for a one-unit change in the *horizontally* measured variable is also called the *slope* of the line. The slope of the line in Figure A.1 is three, and it remains three no matter where along the line we measure it. For example, make sure you can see that from point *C* to point *D*, advertising rises by one unit and sales rise by three units.

What if we had wanted to determine the slope of this line, by comparing points *D* and *E* which have advertising rising by four units instead of just one? In that case, we'd have to calculate the rise in one variable *per unit* rise in the other. To do this, we divide the change in the vertically measured variable by the change in the horizontally measured variable.

$$\text{Slope of a straight line} = \frac{\text{Change in vertical variable}}{\text{Change in horizontal variable}}.$$

We can make this formula even simpler by using two shortcuts. First, we can call the variable on the vertical axis "*Y*" and the variable on the horizontal axis "*X*." In our case, *Y* is sales, while *X* is spending on advertising. Second, we use the Greek letter Δ ("delta") to denote the words "change in." Then, our formula becomes:

$$\text{Slope of a straight line} = \frac{\Delta Y}{\Delta X}.$$

Let's apply this formula to get the slope as we move from point *D* to point *E*, so that advertising (*X*) rises from 7 units to 11 units. This is an increase of 4, so $\Delta X = 4$. For this move, sales rise from 39 to 51, an increase of 12, so $\Delta Y = 12$. Applying our formula,

$$\text{Slope} = \frac{\Delta Y}{\Delta X} = \frac{12}{4} = 3.$$

This is the same value for the slope that we found earlier. Not surprising, since it's a straight line and a straight line has the same slope everywhere. The particular pair of points we choose for our calculation doesn't matter.

Curved Lines

Although many of the relationships you'll encounter in economics have straight-line graphs, many others do not. Figure A.2 shows *another* possible relationship between advertising and sales that we might have found from a different set of data. As you can see, the line is curved. But as advertising rises, the curve gets flatter and flatter. Here, as before, each time we spend another $1,000 on advertising, sales rise. But now, the rise in sales seems to get smaller and smaller. This means that the *slope* of the curve is *itself changing* as we move along this curve. In fact, the slope is getting smaller.

How can we measure the slope of a curve? First, note that since the slope is different at every point along the curve, we aren't really measuring the slope of "the curve" but the slope of the curve *at a specific point along it*. How can we do this? By drawing a *tangent line*—a straight line that touches the curve at just one point and that has the same slope as the curve at that point. For example, in the figure, a tangent line has been drawn for point B. To measure the slope of this tangent line, we can compare any two points on it, say, H and B, and calculate the slope as we would for any straight line. Moving from point H to point B, we are moving from 0 to 3 on the horizontal axis ($\Delta X = 3$) and from 21 to 27 on the vertical axis ($\Delta Y = 6$). Thus, the slope of the tangent line—which is the same as the slope of the curved line at point B—is

$$\frac{\Delta Y}{\Delta X} = \frac{6}{3} = 2$$

This says that, at point B, the rate of change is two units of sales for every one unit of advertising. Or, going back to dollars, the rate of change is $2,000 in sales for every $1,000 spent on advertising.

The curve in Figure A.2 slopes everywhere upward, reflecting a positive relationship between the variables. But a curved line can also slope downward

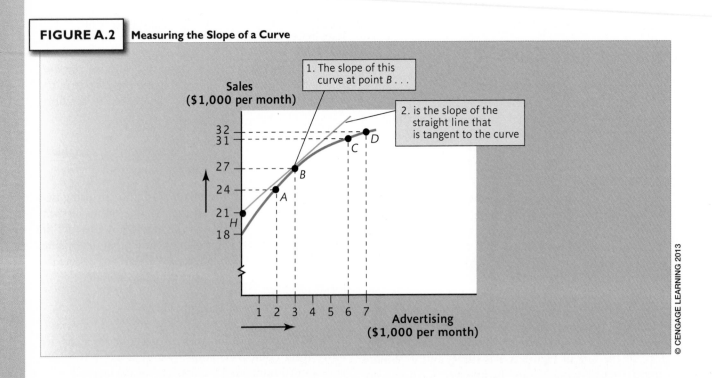

FIGURE A.2 **Measuring the Slope of a Curve**

1. The slope of this curve at point B . . .

2. is the slope of the straight line that is tangent to the curve

Sales ($1,000 per month)

Advertising ($1,000 per month)

to illustrate a negative relationship between variables, or it can slope first one direction and then the other. You'll see plenty of examples of each type of curve in later chapters, and you'll learn how to interpret each one as it's presented.

LINEAR EQUATIONS

Let's go back to the straight-line relationship between advertising and sales, as shown in Table A.1. What if you need to know how much in sales the firm could expect if it spent $5,000 on advertising next month? What if it spent $8,000 or $9,000? It would be nice to be able to answer questions like this without having to pull out tables and graphs to do it. As it turns out, anytime the relationship you are studying has a straight-line graph, it is easy to figure out an equation for the entire relationship—a *linear equation*. You then can use the equation to answer any such question that might be put to you.

All straight lines have the same general form. If Y stands for the variable on the vertical axis and X for the variable on the horizontal axis, every straight line has an equation of the form

$$Y = a + bX,$$

where a stands for some number and b for another number. The number a is called the vertical *intercept* because it marks the point where the graph of this equation hits (intercepts) the vertical axis; this occurs when X takes the value zero. (If you plug $X = 0$ into the equation, you will see that, indeed, $Y = a$.) The number b is the slope of the line, telling us how much Y will change every time X changes by one unit. To confirm this, note that when $X = 0$, the equation tells us that $Y = a$. When $X = 1$, it tells us that $Y = a + b$. So as X increases from 0 to 1, Y goes from a to $a + b$. The number b is therefore the change in Y corresponding to a one-unit change in X—exactly what the slope of the graph should tell us.

If b is a positive number, a one-unit increase in X causes Y to *increase* by b units, so the graph of our line would slope upward, as illustrated by the line in the upper left panel of Figure A.3. If b is a negative number, then a one-unit increase in X will cause Y to *decrease* by b units, so the graph would slope downward, as the line does in the lower left panel. Of course, b could equal zero. If it does, a one-unit increase in X causes no change

in Y, so the graph of the line is flat, like the line in the middle left panel.

The value of a has no effect on the slope of the graph. Instead, different values of a determine the graph's position. When a is a positive number, the graph will intercept the vertical Y-axis above the origin, as the line does in the upper right panel of Figure A.3. When a is negative, however, the graph will intercept the Y-axis *below* the origin, as the line in the lower right panel does. When a is zero, the graph intercepts the Y-axis right at the origin, as the line does in the middle right panel.

Let's see if we can figure out the equation for the relationship depicted in Figure A.1. There, X denotes advertising and Y denotes sales. Earlier, we calculated that the slope of this line, b, is 3. But what is a, the vertical intercept? In Figure A.1, you can see that when advertising outlays are zero, sales are $18,000. That tells us that $a = 18$. Putting these two observations together, we find that the equation for the line in Figure A.1 is

$$Y = 18 + 3X.$$

Now if you need to know how much in sales to expect from a particular expenditure on advertising (both in thousands of dollars), you would be able to come up with an answer: You'd simply multiply the amount spent on advertising by 3, add 18, and that would be your sales in thousands of dollars. To confirm this, plug in for X in this equation any amount of advertising in dollars from the left-hand column of Table A.1. You'll see that you get the corresponding amount of sales in the right-hand column.

HOW STRAIGHT LINES AND CURVES SHIFT

So far, we've focused on relationships where some variable Y depends on a single other variable X. But in many of our theories, we recognize that some variable of interest to us is actually affected by more than just one other variable. When Y is affected by both X and some third variable, changes in that third variable will usually cause a *shift* in the graph of the relationship between X and Y. This is because whenever we draw the graph between X and Y, we are holding fixed every other variable that might possibly affect Y.

FIGURE A.3 | Straight Lines with Different Slopes and Vertical Intercepts

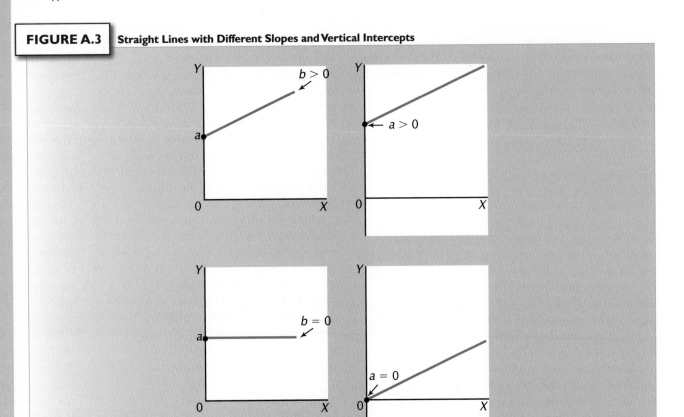

> *A graph between two variables X and Y is only a picture of their relationship when all other variables affecting Y are held constant.*

But suppose one of these other variables *does* change? What happens then?

Think back to the relationship between advertising and sales. Earlier, we supposed sales depended only on advertising. But suppose we make an important discovery: Ice cream sales are *also* affected by how hot the weather is. What's more, all of the data in Table A.1 on which we previously based our analysis turns out to have been from the month of June in different years, when

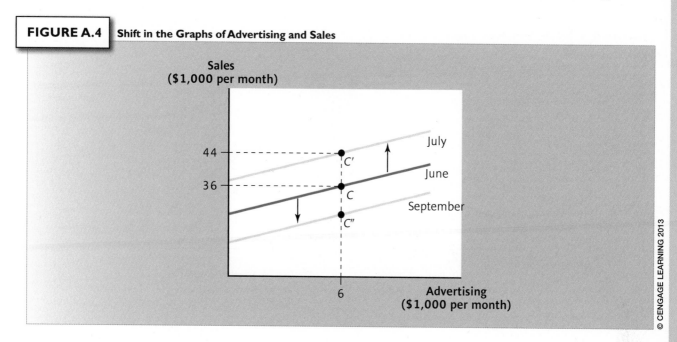

FIGURE A.4 **Shift in the Graphs of Advertising and Sales**

© CENGAGE LEARNING 2013

the average temperature in Texas is 80 degrees. What's going to happen in July, when the average temperature rises to 100 degrees?

In Figure A.4 we've redrawn the graph from Figure A.1, this time labeling the line "June." Often, a good way to determine how a graph will shift is to perform a simple experiment like this: Put your pencil tip anywhere on the graph labeled June—let's say at point C. Now ask the following question: If I hold advertising constant at $6,000, do I expect to sell more or less ice cream as temperature rises in July? If you expect to sell more, then the amount of sales corresponding to $6,000 of advertising will be *above* point C, at a point such as C′ (pronounced "C prime"), representing sales of $44,000. From this, we can tell that the graph will *shift upward* as temperature rises. In September, however, when temperatures fall, the amount of sales corresponding to $6,000 in advertising would be less than it is at point C. It would be shown by a point such as C″, (pronounced "C double-prime"). In that case, the graph would shift downward.

The same procedure works well whether the original graph slopes upward or downward and whether it is a straight line or a curved one. Figure A.5 sketches two examples. In panel (a), an increase in some third variable, Z, increases the value of Y for each value of X, so the graph of the relationship between X and Y shifts upward as Z increases. We often phrase it this way: "An

increase in Z causes an increase in Y, *at any value of X.*" In panel (b), we assume that an increase in Z *decreases* the value of Y, at any value of X, so the graph of the relationship between X and Y shifts *downward* as Z increases.

You'll notice that in Figures A.4 and A.5, the original line is darker, while the new line after the shift is drawn in a lighter shade. We'll often use this convention—a lighter shade for the new line—after a shift.

Shifts versus Movements Along a Line

If you look back at Figure A.1, you'll see that when advertising increases (say, from $2,000 to $3,000), we *move along* our line, from point A to point B. But you've just learned that when average temperature changes, the entire line *shifts*. This may seem strange to you. After all, in both cases, an independent variable changes (either advertising or temperature). Why should we move *along* the line in one case and *shift* it in the other?

The reason for the difference is that in one case (advertising), the independent variable is *in our graph*, measured along one of the axes. When an independent variable in the graph changes, we simply move along the line. In the other case (temperature), the independent variable does *not* appear in our graph. Instead, it's been in the background, being held constant.

FIGURE A.5   Shifts of Curved Lines

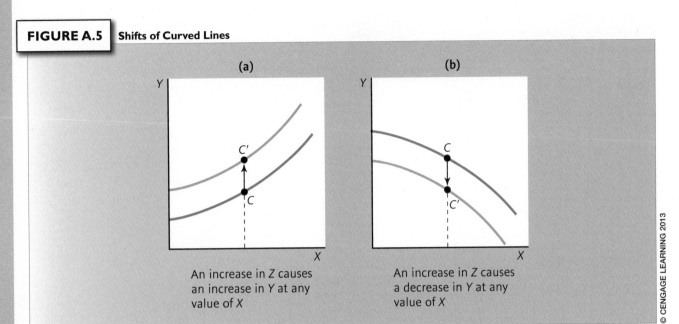

(a)

An increase in Z causes an increase in Y at any value of X

(b)

An increase in Z causes a decrease in Y at any value of X

Here's a very simple—but crucial—rule:

Suppose Y is the dependent variable, which is measured on one of the axes in a graph. If the independent variable measured on the other axis changes, we move along the line. But if any other independent variable changes, the entire line shifts.

Be sure you understand the phrase "any other independent variable." It refers to any variable that actually *affects* Y but is *not* measured on either axis in the graph.

This rule applies to straight lines as well as curved lines. And it applies even in more complicated situations, such as when *two different* lines are drawn in the same graph and a shift of one causes a movement along the other. (You'll encounter this situation in Chapter 3.) But for now, make sure you can see how we've been applying this rule in our example, where the three variables are total sales, advertising, and temperature.

SOLVING EQUATIONS

When we first derived the equation for the relationship between advertising and sales, we wanted to know what level of sales to expect from different amounts of advertising. But what if we're asked a slightly different question?

Suppose, this time, you are told that the sales committee has set an ambitious goal of $42,000 for next month's sales. The treasurer needs to know how much to budget for advertising, and you have to come up with the answer.

Since we know how advertising and sales are related, we ought to be able to answer this question. One way is just to look at the graph in Figure A.1. There, we could first locate sales of $42,000 on the vertical axis. Then, if we read over to the line and then down, we find the amount of advertising that would be necessary to generate that level of sales. Yet even with that carefully drawn diagram, it is not always easy to see just exactly how much advertising would be required. If we need to be precise, we'd better use the equation for the graph instead.

According to the equation, sales (Y) and advertising (X) are related as follows:

$$Y = 18 + 3X.$$

In the problem before us, we know the value we want for sales, and we need to solve for the corresponding amount of advertising. Substituting the sales target of $42 for Y, we need to find that value of X for which

$$42 = 18 + 3X.$$

In this case, X is the unknown value for which we want to solve.

Whenever we solve an equation for one unknown, say, *X*, we need to *isolate X* on one side of the equal sign and everything else on the other side of the equal sign. We do this by performing identical operations on both sides of the equal sign. Here, we can first subtract 18 from both sides, getting

$$24 = 3X.$$

We can then divide both sides by 3 and get

$$8 = X.$$

This is our answer. If we want to achieve sales of $42,000, we'll need to spend $8,000 on advertising.

Of course, not all relationships are linear, so this technique will not work in every situation. But no matter what the underlying relationship, the idea remains the same:

To solve for X in any equation, rearrange the equation, following the rules of algebra, so that X appears on one side of the equals sign and everything else in the equation appears on the other side.

Scarcity, Choice, and Economic Systems

In 2010, the U.S. Congress did something controversial: It voted to approve the Patient Protection and Affordable Care Act, which President Obama signed into law. The new law would eventually require most Americans to purchase health insurance or face a fine. It imposed new regulations on insurance companies and made many other changes in the way medical care would be provided and paid for. In the year leading up to the Act's passage, public opinion had been divided. The debate in Congress was intense. Even after the Act was passed, the controversy didn't die. Democrats in Congress were proud of the new law, while Republicans called it a disaster and vowed to repeal it or defeat it in the courts.

The debate over health care reform, like so many other public disagreements, was a debate about how society's resources should be used and about who should be making the decisions. How much of our resources should be used to produce medical services? How much should be devoted to national defense or education? Or to consumer goods that individuals choose for themselves? What are the consequences of these decisions, and how should they be made?

In this chapter, you'll learn a new framework for thinking about society's resources. Opportunity cost—which you learned about in the last chapter—plays a central role in this framework. So let's start with a simple model of opportunity cost for society's choices.

SOCIETY'S PRODUCTION CHOICES

Let's consider a specific choice that faces every society: how much of its resources to allocate toward national defense versus how much to use for civilian production. To make this choice more concrete, we'll make a simplifying assumption: In the economy we're studying, there is one kind of military good (tanks) and one kind of civilian good (wheat).

Table 1 lists some possible combinations of yearly tank production and yearly wheat production that this society could manage, given its available resources and the currently available production technology. For example, the first row of the table (choice A) tells us what would happen if all available resources were devoted to wheat production and no resources at all to producing tanks. The resulting quantity of wheat—1 million bushels per year—is the most this society could possibly produce. In the second row (choice B), society moves enough resources into tank production to make 1,000 tanks per year. This leaves fewer resources for wheat production, which now declines to 950,000 bushels per year.

© CENGAGE LEARNING 2013

Choice	Tank Production (number per year)	Wheat Production (bushels per year)
A	0	1,000,000
B	1,000	950,000
C	2,000	850,000
D	3,000	700,000
E	4,000	400,000
F	5,000	0

TABLE 1

Production of Tanks and Wheat

As we continue down the table, moving to choices C, D, and E, tank production increases by increments of 1,000. Finally, look at the last row (choice F). It shows us that when society throws all of its resources into tank production (with none for wheat), tank production is 5,000 and wheat production is zero.

The table gives us a quantitative measure of opportunity cost for this society. For example, suppose this society currently produces 1,000 tanks per year, along with 950,000 bushels of wheat (choice B). What would be the opportunity cost of producing another 1,000 tanks? Moving down to choice C, we see that producing another 1,000 tanks (for a total of 2,000) would require wheat production to drop from 950,000 to 850,000 bushels, a decrease of 100,000 bushels. Thus, the opportunity cost of 1,000 more tanks is 100,000 bushels of wheat. The opportunity cost of having more of one good is measured in the units of the other good that must be sacrificed.

The Production Possibilities Frontier

We can see opportunity cost even more clearly in Figure 1, where the data in Table 1 has been plotted on a graph. In the figure, tank production is measured along the horizontal axis, and wheat production along the vertical axis. Each of the six points labeled A through F corresponds to one of society's choices in the table. For example, point B represents 1,000 tanks and 950,000 bushels of wheat.

When we connect these points with a smooth line, we get a curve called society's **production possibilities frontier (PPF)**. Specifically, this PPF tells us the maximum quantity of wheat that can be produced for each quantity of tanks produced. Alternatively, it tells us the maximum number of tanks that can be produced for each different quantity of wheat.

Points outside the frontier are unattainable with the technology and resources at the economy's disposal. For example, locate the point (not marked in the figure) that would correspond to 4,000 tanks and 700,000 bushels of wheat, and label it "G." Point G would be unobtainable because if we were producing 4,000 tanks, we'd have enough resources left over to produce only 400,000 bushels of wheat, not 700,000. Producing at point G would require more land, labor, capital, and entrepreneurship than this economy has. Society's choices are limited to points on or inside the PPF.

Now recall our earlier example of moving from choice B to choice C in the table. When tank production increased from 1,000 to 2,000, wheat production decreased from 950,000 to 850,000. In the graph, this change would be represented by a movement along the PPF from point B to point C. We're moving rightward

Production possibilities frontier (PPF) A curve showing all combinations of two goods that can be produced with the resources and technology currently available.

| FIGURE I | The Production Possibilities Frontier |

At point A, all resources are used for wheat.

Moving from point A to point B requires shifting resources out of wheat and into tanks.

At point F, all resources are used for tanks.

Bushels of Wheat per Year

1,000,000
950,000
850,000
700,000
400,000

Number of Tanks per Year

1,000   2,000   3,000   4,000   5,000

© CENGAGE LEARNING 2013

(1,000 more tanks) and also downward (100,000 fewer bushels of wheat). Thus, the opportunity cost of 1,000 more tanks can be viewed as the vertical drop along the PPF as we move from point B to point C.

Increasing Opportunity Cost

Suppose we have arrived at point C, and society then decides to produce still more tanks. Once again, resources must be shifted into tank production to make an additional 1,000 of them, moving from point C to point D. This time, however, there is an even *greater opportunity cost*: Production of wheat falls from 850,000 to 700,000 bushels, a sacrifice of 150,000 bushels. The opportunity cost of 1,000 more tanks has risen. Graphically, the vertical drop along the curve is greater for the same move rightward.

Figure 2 shows that as we continue to increase tank production by increments of 1,000—moving from point C to point D to point E to point F—the opportunity cost of producing an additional 1,000 tanks keeps rising, until the last 1,000 tanks costs us 400,000 bushels of wheat. (You can also see this in the table, by running down the numbers in the right column. Each time tank production rises by 1,000, wheat production falls by more and more.)

The behavior of opportunity cost described here—the more tanks we produce, the greater the opportunity cost of producing still more—applies to a wide range of choices facing society. It can be generalized as the *law of increasing opportunity cost*.

According to the law of increasing opportunity cost, the more of something we produce, the greater the opportunity cost of producing even more of it.

FIGURE 2 | Increasing Opportunity Cost

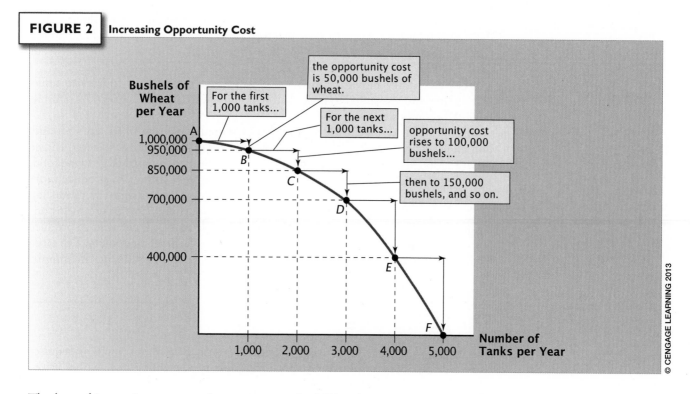

The law of increasing opportunity cost causes the PPF to have a concave (upside-down bowl) shape, becoming steeper as we move rightward and downward. That's because the slope of the PPF—the change in the quantity of wheat divided by the change in the quantity of tanks—can be interpreted as the change in wheat *per additional tank*. For example, moving from point *C* to point *D*, we give up 150,000 bushels of wheat to get 1,000 more tanks, or *150 bushels of wheat per tank*. Thus, the slope of the PPF between points *C* and *D* is approximately −150. (We say approximately because the PPF is curved, so its slope changes slightly as we move along the interval from *C* to *D*.) If we remove the minus sign from this slope and consider just its absolute value, it tells us the opportunity cost of *one more tank*.

Now—as we've seen—this opportunity cost increases as we move rightward. Therefore, the absolute value of the PPF's slope must rise as well. The PPF grows increasingly steeper, giving us the concave shape we see in Figure 1: 150 bushels of wheat.[1]

The Reason for Increasing Opportunity Cost

Why does opportunity cost increase as we move along a PPF? Because most resources—by their very nature—are better suited to some purposes than to others. If the economy were operating at point *A*, for example, we'd be using *all* of our resources for wheat, even those that are much better suited to making tanks. People who would be better at factory work than farming would nevertheless be pressed into working on farms. And we'd be growing wheat on all the land available, even land that would be fine for a tank factory but awful for growing crops.

---

[1] You might be wondering if the law of increasing opportunity cost applies in both directions. That is, does the opportunity cost of producing more wheat increase as we produce more of it? The answer is yes, as you'll be asked to show in an end-of-chapter problem.

Now, as we move rightward along the PPF, say from *A* to *B*, we would *first* shift those resources *best suited* to tank production—and least suited for wheat. So the first thousand tanks cause only a small drop in wheat production. This is why, at first, the PPF is very flat: a small vertical drop for the rightward movement.

As we continue moving rightward, however, we must shift resources to tanks that are less and less suited to tanks and more and more suited to wheat. As a result, the PPF becomes steeper.

The principle of increasing opportunity cost applies to most of society's production choices, not just that between wheat and tanks. If we look at society's choice between food and oil, we would find that some land is better suited to growing food, and other land is better suited to drilling for oil. As we continue to produce more oil, we would find ourselves drilling on land that is less and less suited to producing oil, but better and better for producing food. The opportunity cost of producing additional oil will therefore increase. The same principle applies if we want to produce more health care, more education, more automobiles, or more computers: The more of something we produce, the greater the opportunity cost of producing still more.

THE SEARCH FOR A FREE LUNCH

This chapter has argued that every decision to produce *more* of something requires us to pay an opportunity cost by producing less of something else. Nobel Prize–winning economist Milton Friedman summarized this idea in his famous remark, "There is no such thing as a free lunch." Friedman's point was that, even if a meal is provided free of charge to someone, society still uses up resources to provide it. Therefore, a "free lunch" is not *really* free: Society pays an opportunity cost by not producing other things with those resources. *Some* members of society will have less of something else.

The same logic applies to other supposedly "free" goods and services. From society's point of view, there is no such thing as a free sample at a supermarket or free medical care, even if people don't pay directly. Providing any of these things requires a sacrifice of *other* things, as illustrated by a movement along society's PPF.

But what if an economy is *not* living up to its productive potential, and is operating *inside* its PPF? For example, in Figure 3, suppose we are currently operating at point *W*, where we are producing 2,000 tanks and 400,000 bushels of wheat. Then we could move from point *W* to point *E* and produce 2,000 more tanks, with no sacrifice of wheat. Or, starting at point *W*, we could move to point *C* (more wheat with no sacrifice of tanks), or to a point like *D* (more of *both* wheat and tanks).

When we are operating inside the PPF, a "free lunch" may be possible, because we can have more of one thing (such as wheat or tanks) with no opportunity cost. However, in modern economies, these free lunches are not as easy to find or exploit as you may think. To see why, let's explore some reasons why an economy might be operating inside its PPF in the first place.

Productive Inefficiency

One reason we might be operating inside the PPF is that resources are not being used in the most productive way. Suppose, for example, that many people who could be outstanding wheat farmers are instead making tanks, and many who would be great at tank production are instead stuck on farms. Then switching people from one job

FIGURE 3 | Operating Inside the Production Possibilities Frontier

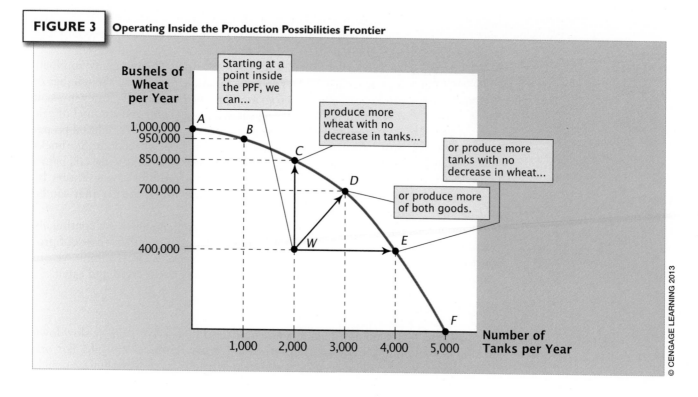

to the other could enable us to have more of *both* tanks *and* wheat. That is, because of the mismatch of workers and jobs, we would be *inside* the PPF at a point like *W*. Creating better job matches would then move us to a point *on* the PPF (such as point *E*).

Economists use the phrase *productive inefficiency* to describe this type of situation that puts us inside our PPF.

> *A firm, an industry, or an entire economy is **productively inefficient** if it could produce more of at least one good without producing less of any other good.*

Productively inefficient A situation in which more of at least one good can be produced without sacrificing the production of any other good.

The phrase *productive efficiency* means the absence of any productive *in*efficiency.

No firm, industry, or economy is ever 100 percent productively efficient. But in a well-functioning economy, cases of gross inefficiency are not as common as you might think. Business firms have strong incentives to identify and eliminate productive inefficiency, since any waste of resources increases their costs and decreases their profit. When one firm discovers a way to eliminate waste, others quickly follow.

For example, empty seats on an airline flight represent productive inefficiency. Since the plane is making the trip anyway, filling the empty seat would enable the airline to fly more people (produce more transportation services) without using any additional resources (other than the trivial resources of in-flight snacks). Therefore, more people could fly without sacrificing any other good or service. When American Airlines developed a computer model in the late 1980s to fill its empty seats by altering schedules and fares, the other airlines followed its example very rapidly. And when—in the late 1990s—Priceline.com enabled airlines to auction off empty seats on the Internet, several airlines jumped at the chance

and others quickly followed. As a result, a case of productive inefficiency in the airline industry—and therefore in the economy—was eliminated.

Starbucks provides another example. The company routinely uses efficiency experts to look for ways to increase the number of drinks served with a given amount of labor. In 2009, for example, it found that just by moving the whipped cream and caramel drizzle closer to where the drinks are handed to customers reduced preparation time from 45 seconds per drink to 37 seconds. Starbucks made these changes to save on labor costs and increase the company's profits. But from society's perspective, resource-saving efforts by Starbucks and other business firms free up labor time that can be used to produce other things.

Economists, logistics experts, business managers, and engineers are continually identifying and working to eliminate the most obvious and important cases of productive inefficiency. As a result, many of the "free lunches" we might think we can enjoy by eliminating productive inefficiency have already been served and eaten.

Recessions

Another reason an economy might operate inside its PPF is a *recession*—a slowdown in overall economic activity. During recessions, many resources are idle. For one thing, there is widespread *unemployment*—people who *want* to work but are unable to find jobs. In addition, factories shut down, so we are not using all of our available capital. An end to the recession would move the economy from a point *inside* its PPF to a point *on* its PPF—using idle resources to produce more goods and services without sacrificing anything.

This simple observation can help us understand an otherwise confusing episode in U.S. economic history. During the early 1940s, after the United States entered World War II and began using massive amounts of resources to produce military goods and services, the standard of living in the United States did *not* decline as we might have expected but actually improved slightly. Why?

When the United States entered the war in 1941, it was still suffering from the Great Depression—the most serious and long-lasting economic downturn in modern history, which began in 1929 and hit most of the developed world. As we joined the Allied war effort, the economy also recovered from the depression. (Indeed, for reasons you will learn when you study macroeconomics, U.S. participation in the war may have accelerated the depression's end.) So, in Figure 4, this moved our economy from a point like A, *inside* the PPF, to a point like B, *on* the frontier. Military production, such as tanks, increased, but so did the production of civilian goods, such as wheat. Although there were shortages of some consumer goods, the overall result was a rise in total production and an increase in the material well-being of the average U.S. citizen.

DANGEROUS CURVES

False benefits from employment Often, you'll hear an evaluation of some economic activity that includes "greater employment" as one of the benefits. For example, an article in the online magazine *Slate*, after discussing the costs of e-mail spam, pointed out that spam also has "a corresponding economic payoff. Anti-spam efforts keep well-paid software engineers employed."[2]

This kind of thinking is usually incorrect. True, when the economy is in recession, an increase in any kind of employment can be regarded as a benefit—especially to those who get the jobs. But this is a special, temporary situation. Once a recession ends, the software engineers—if not for the spam—would be employed elsewhere. At that point, employment in the spam-fighting industry—far from being a benefit—is actually part of the *opportunity cost* of spam: We sacrifice the goods and services these spam-fighting engineers would otherwise produce.

[2] Jeff Merron, "Workus Interruptus," *Slate*, Posted March 16, 2006, 12:06 PM ET.

Chapter 2: Scarcity, Choice, and Economic Systems 31

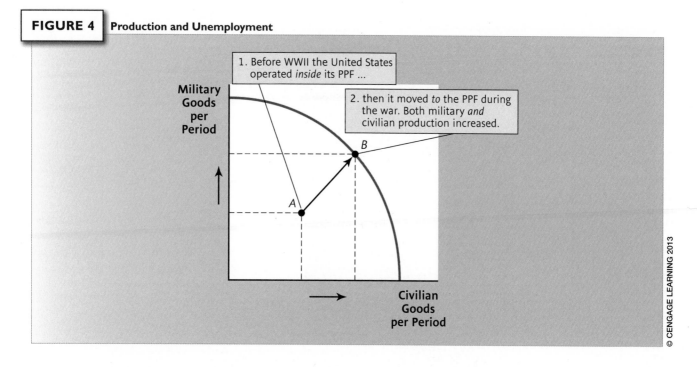

FIGURE 4 | **Production and Unemployment**

1. Before WWII the United States operated *inside* its PPF ...

2. then it moved *to* the PPF during the war. Both military *and* civilian production increased.

Military Goods per Period

B

A

Civilian Goods per Period

© CENGAGE LEARNING 2013

No government would ever *choose* war as a purely economic policy to end a downturn because other, economically superior policies could accomplish the same goal. But do these other methods of promoting recovery give us a free "lunch"? Yes... and no. When you study macroeconomics you'll learn that policies to cure or avoid recessions have risks and costs of their own. Indeed, when the Obama administration used some of these policies in 2009 and 2010 to help the economy recover from a deep recession, a heated debate broke out about whether the costs and risks were worth it.

Economic Growth

What if the PPF itself were to change? Couldn't we then produce more of everything? This is exactly what happens when an economy's productive capacity grows.

One way that productivity capacity grows is by an increase in available resources. Historically, the resource that has contributed most to rising living standards is capital. More physical capital (factory buildings, tractors, and medical equipment) or more human capital (skilled doctors, engineers, and construction workers) can enable us to produce more of *any* goods and services that use these tools.

The other major source of economic growth is *technological change*—the discovery of new ways to produce more from a given quantity of resources. The development of the Internet, for example, enabled people to find information in a few minutes that used to require hours of searching through printed documents. As a result, a variety of professionals—teachers, writers, government officials, attorneys, and physicians—can produce more of their services with the same amount of labor hours.

Figure 5 shows three examples of how economic growth can change the PPF. Panel (a) illustrates a change that initially affects only wheat production—say, the acquisition of more tractors (usable in wheat farming but not in tank-making) or the discovery of a new, higher-yielding technique for growing wheat. If we used *all* of our resources to produce wheat, we could now produce more of it than before. For

FIGURE 5   Economic Growth and the PPF

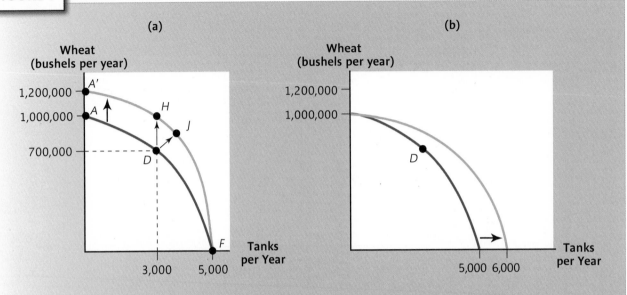

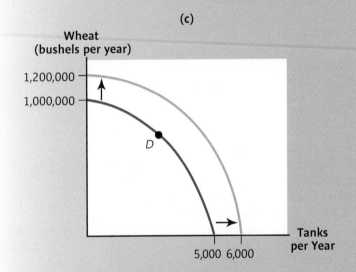

All three panels show economic growth from an increase in resources or a technological change. In panel (a), the additional resources or technological advance directly affect only wheat production. However, society can choose to have more wheat and more tanks if it desires, such as at point J. In panel (b), the additional resources or technological advance directly affect only tank production. But once again, society can choose to have more of both goods. In panel (c), the additional resources or technological advance directly affect production of both goods.

that reason, the vertical intercept of the PPF rises from point A to a point like A', where the economy could produce a maximum of 1,200,000 bushels per year. But the horizontal intercept of the PPF remains at point F, because the changes we're considering apply only to wheat. If we were to use all of our resources in tank production, we'd be able to produce the same number of tanks as before. So the final effect is to stretch the PPF upward along the vertical axis.

Suppose we were originally operating at point D on the old PPF. Then, with our new PPF, we could choose to produce more wheat and the same number of tanks (point H). Or we could produce more of *both* goods (point J). We could even choose to produce more tanks and the same amount of wheat as before. (See if you can identify this point on the new PPF.)

But wait . . . how can having more tractors or a new technique for growing wheat—changes that directly affect only the wheat industry—enable us to produce more tanks? The answer is: After the change in the PPF, society can choose to shift some resources out of wheat farming and have the same amount of wheat as before at point D, on the original PPF. The shifted resources can be used to increase tank production.

Panel (b) illustrates the opposite type of change in the PPF—from a technological change in producing tanks, or an increase in resources usable only in the tank industry. This time, the *horizontal* intercept of the PPF increases, while the vertical intercept remains unchanged. (Can you explain why?) As before, we could choose to produce more tanks, more wheat, or more of both. (See if you can identify points on the new PPF in panel [b] to illustrate all three cases.)

Finally, panel (c) illustrates the case where technological change occurs in both the wheat and the tank industries, or there is an increase in resources (such as workers or capital) that could be used in either. Now both the horizontal and the vertical intercepts of the PPF increase. But as before, society can choose to locate anywhere along the new PPF, producing more tanks, more wheat, or more of both.

Panels (a) and (b) can be generalized to an important principle about economic growth:

> *A technological change or an increase in resources, even when the direct impact is to increase production of just one type of good, allows us to choose greater production of all types of goods.*

This conclusion certainly *seems* like a free lunch. But is it?

Yes . . . and no. True, comparing the new PPF to the old, it looks like we can have more of something—in fact, more of everything—without any sacrifice. But Figure 4 tells only part of the story. It leaves out the sacrifice that creates the change in the PPF in the first place.

Consumption versus Growth

Suppose we want more capital, in order to shift the PPF outward as in the three panels of Figure 5. First, note that capital plays two roles in the economy. On the one hand, capital is a *resource* that we use to produce goods and services. On the other hand, capital is *itself* a good and is produced . . . using resources! A tractor, for example, is produced using land, labor, and *other* capital (a tractor factory and all of the manufacturing equipment inside the factory).

Each year, we must choose how much of our available resources to devote to producing capital, as opposed to other things. On the plus side, the more capital we produce this year, the more capital we'll have in the future to produce other things.

FIGURE 6 | How Current Production Affects Economic Growth

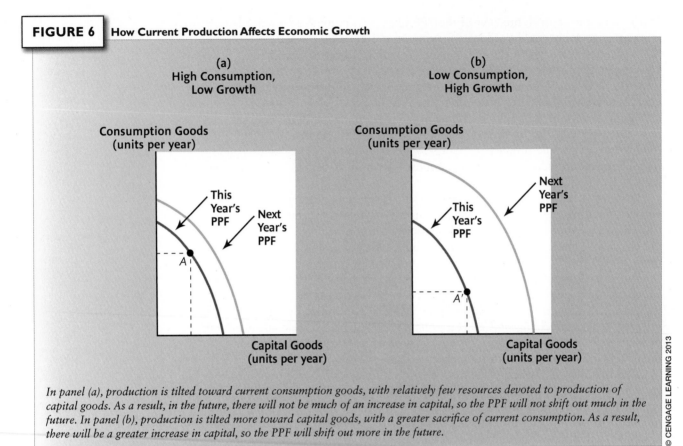

In panel (a), production is tilted toward current consumption goods, with relatively few resources devoted to production of capital goods. As a result, in the future, there will not be much of an increase in capital, so the PPF will not shift out much in the future. In panel (b), production is tilted more toward capital goods, with a greater sacrifice of current consumption. As a result, there will be a greater increase in capital, so the PPF will shift out more in the future.

(Remember: Capital, once produced, is a long-lasting tool.) But there's a trade-off: Any resources used to produce capital this year are *not* being used to produce *consumer goods*—food, health care, and other things that we can enjoy right now.

Figure 6 illustrates this trade-off. In each panel, the total quantity of capital goods is measured on the horizontal axis, and consumption goods on the vertical axis. In each panel, the darker curve is *this year's* PPF. In the left panel, point *A* shows one choice we could make this year: relatively high production of consumer goods and low production of capital goods. We'd have a relatively high standard of living this year (lots of consumer goods), but we'd be adding little to our total stock of capital during the year. As a result, *next year's* PPF—the lighter curve—will be shifted outward somewhat (because we'll have a bit more capital next year than we had this year), but not by much.

The right panel shows a different choice for the same economy. If we are situated at point *A'* on this year's PPF, we sacrifice more consumption goods now and produce more capital goods than at point *A* in the left panel. Living standards are lower this year. But next year, when we have considerably more capital, the PPF will have shifted outward even more. We can then choose a point on next year's PPF with greater production of consumer goods than we could have had if we had chosen point *A*. So, choosing point *A'* rather than *A* can lead to a greater rise in living standards next year, but requires greater sacrifice of consumer goods this year.

A similar trade-off exists when technological change drives growth. New technologies don't just "happen"—resources must be used *now* for research and development. These resources could have been used to produce other things that we'd enjoy today. For example, doctors who work at developing new drugs in pharmaceutical companies could instead be providing health care to patients right now. We could show this using the same PPFs as in Figure 6. But on the horizontal axis, instead of "capital goods," we'd have some measure of "research and development activities." And we'd come to the same conclusion about technological change that we came to earlier about having more capital:

In order to produce more goods and services in the future, we must shift resources toward R&D and capital production, and away from producing things we'd enjoy right now.

We must conclude that although economic growth—at first glance—*appears* to be a free lunch, someone ends up paying the check. In this case, the bill is paid by those who will have to make do with less in the present.

ECONOMIC SYSTEMS

As you read these words—perhaps sitting at home or in the library—you are experiencing a very private moment. It is just you and this book; the rest of the world might as well not exist. Or so it seems. . . .

Actually, even in this supposedly private moment, you are connected to others in ways you may not have thought about. In order for you to be reading this book, the authors had to write it. Someone had to edit it, to help make sure that all necessary material was covered and explained as clearly as possible. Someone else had to prepare the graphics.

And there's more. If you are reading a physical book (rather than reading online), people had to manufacture all kinds of goods: paper and ink, the computers used to keep track of inventory, and so on. And still others had to pack the book, ship it, unpack it, put it on a store shelf, and then sell it to you. It is no exaggeration to say that thousands of people were involved in making this book available to you.

Take a walk in your town or city, and you will see even more evidence of our economic interdependence: People are collecting garbage, helping schoolchildren cross the street, transporting furniture across town, constructing buildings, repairing roads, painting houses. Everyone is producing goods and services for *other people*.

Why is it that so much of what we consume is produced by other people? Why are we all so heavily dependent on each other for our material well-being? Why don't we all—like Robinson Crusoe on his island—produce our own food, clothing, housing, and anything else we desire? And how did it come about that *you*—who most likely did not produce any of these things yourself—are able to consume them?

These are all questions about our *economic system*—the way our economy is organized. Ordinarily, we take our economic system for granted, like the water that runs out of our faucets. But now it's time to begin looking at the plumbing—to learn how our economy serves so many millions of people, enabling them to survive and prosper.

Specialization and Exchange

If we were forced to, many of us could become economically *self-sufficient*. We could stake out a plot of land, grow our own food, make our own clothing, and build our own homes. But in no society is there such extreme self-sufficiency. On the contrary, every society has an economic system with two features: (1) **specialization,** in which each of us concentrates on a limited number of productive activities, and

Specialization A method of production in which each person concentrates on a limited number of activities.

(2) **exchange,** in which we obtain most of what we desire by trading with others rather than producing for ourselves.

> *Specialization and exchange enable us to enjoy greater production and higher living standards than would otherwise be possible. As a result, all economies exhibit high degrees of specialization and exchange.*

Where do the gains from specialization and exchange come from?

Development of Expertise. Each of us can learn only so much in a lifetime. By limiting ourselves to a narrow set of tasks—fixing plumbing, managing workers, writing music, or designing Web pages—we can hone our skills. We can become experts at one or two things, instead of remaining amateurs at a lot of things. An economy of experts will produce more than an economy of amateurs.

Minimizing Downtime. When people specialize, and thus spend their time doing one type of task, there is less unproductive "downtime" from switching activities. On a smaller scale, we see this in most households every night, when it's time to wash the dishes. "I'll wash, you dry" enables both members of a couple to keep doing their part nonstop, and the dishes get done faster.

Comparative Advantage. We would gain from developing expertise and minimizing downtime even if everyone, initially, had identical capabilities. But a third gain arises because of our *differences:* We are not all equally suited to different tasks. This idea applies not just to labor, but to the other resources as well. Not all plots of land are equally suited for all crops, nor are all types of capital equipment equally suited for all types of production. When we allocate our resources according to their *suitability* for different types of production, we get further gains from specialization. The principle behind this gain—*comparative advantage*—is such a central idea in economics that it gets its own section.

Comparative Advantage

Imagine a shipwreck in which there are only two survivors—let's call them Maryanne and Gilligan—who are washed ashore on opposite ends of a deserted island. Initially they are unaware of each other, so each is forced to become completely self-sufficient. And there are only two kinds of food on the island: fish and berries.

Table 2 shows how much time it takes for each castaway to pick a cup of berries or catch one fish. For simplicity, we'll assume that the time requirement remains constant, no matter how much time is devoted to these activities.

On one side of the island, Maryanne finds that it takes her 1 hour to catch a fish and 1 hour to pick a cup of berries, as shown in the first row of the table. On the other

TABLE 2

Labor Requirements for Fish and Berries

	Labor Required For:	
	1 Fish	1 Cup of Berries
Maryanne	1 hour	1 hour
Gilligan	3 hours	1½ hours

side of the island, Gilligan—who is less adept at both tasks—requires 3 hours to catch a fish and 1½ hours to pick a cup of berries, as listed in the second row of the table. Since both castaways would want some variety in their diets, we can assume that each would spend part of their time catching fish and part picking berries.

Suppose that, one day, Maryanne and Gilligan discover each other. After rejoicing at the prospect of human companionship, they decide to develop a system of production that will work to their mutual benefit. Let's rule out two of the gains from specialization that we discussed earlier (minimizing downtime and developing expertise). Will it still make sense for these two to specialize? The answer is yes, as you will see after a small detour.

Absolute Advantage: A Detour

When Gilligan and Maryanne sit down to figure out who should do what, they might fall victim to a common mistake: basing their decision on *absolute advantage*.

> *An individual has an **absolute advantage** in the production of some good when he or she can produce it using fewer resources than another individual can.*

Absolute advantage The ability to produce a good or service, using fewer resources than other producers use.

On the island, labor is the only resource. The castaways might (mistakenly) reason as follows: Maryanne can catch a fish more quickly than Gilligan (see Table 2), so she has an *absolute advantage* in fishing. Therefore, Maryanne should be the one to catch fish.

But wait! Maryanne can also pick berries more quickly than Gilligan, so she has an absolute advantage in that as well. If absolute advantage is the criterion for assigning work, then Maryanne should do *both* tasks. This, however, would leave Gilligan doing nothing, which is certainly *not* in the pair's best interests.

What can we conclude from this example? That absolute advantage is an unreliable guide for allocating tasks to different workers.

Comparative Advantage

The correct principle to guide the division of labor on the island is comparative advantage:

> *A person has a **comparative advantage** in producing some good if he or she can produce it with a smaller opportunity cost than some other person can.*

Comparative advantage The ability to produce a good or service at a lower opportunity cost than other producers.

Notice the important difference between absolute advantage and comparative advantage: You have an *absolute* advantage in producing a good if you can produce it using fewer *resources* than someone else can. But you have a *comparative* advantage if you can produce it with a smaller *opportunity cost*. As you'll see, these are not necessarily the same thing.

Who Has a Comparative Advantage in What?

Let's first see who has a comparative advantage in fishing. To do this, we need to calculate the opportunity cost—for each castaway—of catching one more fish.

For Maryanne, catching one more fish takes one more hour. That requires one hour less picking berries, and that, in turn, means sacrificing 1 cup of berries. We can summarize it this way:

Maryanne: 1 more fish ⇒ 1 more hour fishing
⇒ 1 less hour picking berries ⇒ 1 less cup berries

Even castaways do better when they specialize and exchange with each other, instead of trying to be self-sufficient.

© COURTESY OF NEAL PETERS COLLECTION

Therefore, for Maryanne: *the opportunity cost of one more fish is 1 cup of berries.* Because we've assumed that the time requirements for each activity don't change, this opportunity cost of 1 more fish remains constant, no matter how many fish Maryanne catches.

Doing the same analysis for Gilligan, who needs three hours to catch a fish, we find:

<u>Gilligan</u>: 1 more fish $\Rightarrow$ 3 more hours fishing
$\Rightarrow$ 3 fewer hours picking berries $\Rightarrow$ 2 fewer cups berries

So for Gilligan, the *opportunity cost of one more fish is 2 cups of berries.* Because Maryanne has the lower opportunity cost for one more fish (1 cup of berries rather than 2 cups), *Maryanne has the comparative advantage in fishing.*

Now let's see who has the comparative advantage in picking berries. We can summarize the steps as follows:

<u>Maryanne</u>: 1 more cup berries $\Rightarrow$ 1 more hour picking berries
$\Rightarrow$ 1 less hour fishing $\Rightarrow$ 1 less fish

<u>Gilligan</u>: 1 more cup berries $\Rightarrow$ 1½ more hours picking berries
$\Rightarrow$ 1½ fewer hours fishing $\Rightarrow$ ½ less fish

You can see that the opportunity cost of one more cup of berries is 1 fish for Maryanne, and ½ fish for Gilligan.[3] When it comes to berries, Gilligan has the lower opportunity cost. So Gilligan—who has an *absolute* advantage in nothing—has a *comparative* advantage in berry picking.

Gains from Comparative Advantage

What happens when each castaway produces more of their comparative advantage good? The results are shown in Table 3. In the first row, we have Maryanne catching one more fish each day (+1) at an opportunity cost of one cup of berries (−1). In the second row, we have Gilligan producing one fewer fish (−1), which enables him to produce two more cups of berries (+2).

Now look at the last row. It shows what has happened to the production of both goods on the island as a result of this little shift between the two. While fish production remains unchanged, berry production rises by one cup. If the castaways specialize and trade with each other, they can both come out ahead: consuming the same quantity of fish as before, but more berries.

As you can see in Table 3, when each castaway moves toward producing more of the good in which he or she has a *comparative advantage*, total production rises. Now, let's think about this. If they gain by making this small shift toward their comparative advantage goods, why not make the change again? And again after that? In fact, why not keep repeating it until the opportunities for increasing total island production are exhausted, which occurs when one or both of them is devoting all of their time to producing just their comparative advantage good, and none of the other? In the end, specializing according to comparative advantage and exchanging with each other gives the castaways a higher standard of living than they each could achieve on their own.

---

[3] Of course, no one would ever catch half a fish unless they were using a machete. The number just tells us the rate of trade-off of one good for the other.

© CENGAGE LEARNING 2013

TABLE 3

A Beneficial Change in Production

	Change in Fish Production	Change in Berry Production
Maryanne	+1	−1
Gilligan	−1	+2
Total Island	+0	+1

Beyond the Island

What is true for our shipwrecked island dwellers is also true for the entire economy:

> *Total production of every good or service will be greatest when individuals specialize according to their comparative advantage.*

When we turn from our fictional island to the real world, is production, in fact, consistent with the principle of comparative advantage? Indeed it is. A journalist may be able to paint her house more quickly than a house painter, giving her an *absolute* advantage in painting her home. Will she paint her own home? Except in unusual circumstances, no, because the journalist has a *comparative* advantage in writing news articles. Indeed, most journalists—like most college professors, attorneys, architects, and other professionals—hire house painters, leaving them more time to practice the professions in which they have a comparative advantage.

Even fictional superheroes seem to behave consistently with comparative advantage. Superman can no doubt cook a meal, fix a car, chop wood, and do virtually *anything* faster than anyone else on earth. Using our new vocabulary, we'd say that Superman has an absolute advantage in everything. But he has a clear *comparative* advantage in catching criminals and saving the universe from destruction, which is exactly what he spends his time doing.

International Comparative Advantage

You've seen that comparative advantage is one reason people *within* a country can benefit from specializing and trading with each other. The same is true for trading among *nations*. We say that

> *A nation has a comparative advantage in producing a good if it can produce it at a* lower opportunity cost *than some other nation.*

To illustrate this, let's consider a hypothetical world that has only two countries: the United States and China. Both are producing only two goods: soybeans and T-shirts. And—to keep our model simple—we'll assume that these goods are being produced with just one resource: labor.

Table 4 shows the amount of labor, in hours, required to produce one bushel of soybeans or one T-shirt in each country. We'll assume that hours per unit remain *constant*, no matter how much of a good is produced. For example, the entry "5 hours" tells us that it takes 5 hours of labor to produce one bushel of soybeans in China. This will be true no matter how many bushels China produces.

TABLE 4

Labor Requirements for
Soybeans and T-Shirts

	Labor Required For:	
	1 Bushel of Soybeans	1 T-Shirt
United States	½ hour	¼ hour
China	5 hours	1 hour

In the table, the United States has an *absolute advantage* in producing both goods. That is, it takes fewer resources (less labor time) to produce either soybeans or T-shirts in the United States than in China. But—as you are about to see—China has a *comparative* advantage in one of these goods.

Determining a Nation's Comparative Advantage

Just as we did for our mythical island, we can determine comparative advantage for a country by looking at opportunity cost.

Let's first look at the opportunity cost of producing, say, 10 more bushels of soybeans. (Using 10 bushels rather than just one bushel enables us to use round numbers in this example.) For the United States, these 10 bushels would require 5 hours. That means 5 fewer hours spent producing T-shirts. Since each T-shirt requires ¼ hour, 5 fewer hours means sacrificing 20 T-shirts. We can summarize it this way:

United States: 10 more bshls soybeans ⇒ 5 more hours producing soybeans
⇒ 5 fewer hours producing T-shirts
⇒ 20 fewer T-shirts

Therefore, for the U.S. the opportunity cost of 10 more bushels of soybeans is 20 T-shirts.

Doing the same analysis for China, where it takes 5 hours to produce each bushel of soybeans, we find:

China: 10 more bshls soybeans ⇒ 50 more hours producing soybeans
⇒ 50 fewer hours producing T-shirts
⇒ 50 fewer T-shirts

So for China, the opportunity cost of 10 bushels of soybeans is 50 T-shirts. Since the U.S. has the lower opportunity cost for soybeans (20 T-shirts rather than 50), the U.S. *has the comparative advantage in soybeans.*

Now let's see who has the comparative advantage in T-shirts. We can choose any number of T-shirts to start off our analysis, so let's (arbitrarily) consider the opportunity cost of producing 40 more T-shirts:

United States: 40 more T-shirts ⇒ 10 more hours producing T-shirts
⇒ 10 fewer hours producing soybeans
⇒ 20 fewer bshls soybeans

China: 40 more T-shirts ⇒ 40 more hours producing T-shirts
⇒ 40 fewer hours producing soybeans
⇒ 8 fewer bshls soybeans

	Soybeans (Bushels)	T-Shirts	
United States	+10	−20	**TABLE 5**
China	−8	+40	**A Beneficial Change in World Production**
Total World Production	**+2**	**+20**	© CENGAGE LEARNING 2013

The opportunity cost of 40 more T-shirts is 20 bushels of soybeans for the U.S., but only 8 bushels for China. So China, with the lower opportunity cost, has a *comparative* advantage in T-shirts.

Global Gains from Comparative Advantage

What happens when each nation produces more of its comparative advantage good? The results, for our example, are shown in Table 5. In the first row, we have the U.S. producing 10 more bushels of soybeans (+10) at an opportunity cost of 20 T-shirts (−20). In the second row, China produces 8 fewer bushels of soybeans (−8), and 40 more T-shirts (+40).

As you see in our example, world production of *both* goods increases: 2 more bushels of soybeans and 20 more T-shirts. With greater world production, each country can enjoy a higher standard of living. How will the potential gains in living standards be shared among the two countries? That depends on how many T-shirts trade for a bushel of soybeans in the international market where these goods are traded. You'll learn more about this—and other aspects of international trade—in a later chapter. But you can already see how this example illustrates a general point:

Total production of every good or service is greatest when nations shift production toward their comparative advantage goods and trade with each other.

Resource Allocation

Specialization and exchange permit a society to sustain higher levels of production than would otherwise be possible. But an economic system must do more than just increase production. It must also solve the thorny problem of *resource allocation*—deciding how society's scarce resources will be divided among competing claims and desires.

More specifically, resource allocation means coming up with answers to three important questions:

1. **Which goods and services should be produced with society's resources?**
   Should we produce more consumer goods for enjoyment now or more capital goods to increase future production? Should we produce more health care, and if so, what should we produce less of? In other words, where on the production possibilities frontier should the economy operate?

2. **How should they be produced?**
   Most goods and services can be produced in a variety of different ways, with each method using more of some resources and less of others. For example, there

are many ways to dig a ditch. We could use *no capital at all* and have dozens of workers digging with their bare hands. We could use *a small amount of capital* by giving each worker a shovel and thereby use less labor, since each worker would now be more productive. Or we could use *even more capital*—a power trencher—and dig the ditch with just one or two workers. Every economic system has some mechanism to select *how* goods and services will be produced from the many options available.

3. *Who* should get them?

This is where economics interacts most strongly with politics. There are so many ways to divide ourselves into groups: men and women, rich and poor, skilled and unskilled, workers and owners, families and single people, young and old . . . the list is almost endless. How should the products of our economy be distributed among these different groups and among individuals within each group? Determining *who* gets the economy's output is always the most controversial aspect of resource allocation. Over the last half-century, our society has become more sensitized to the way goods and services are distributed, and we increasingly ask whether that distribution is fair.

How do societies determine the answers to these questions about resources? Historically, three main methods have evolved: *tradition, command,* and *the market.* We can label an economic system based on which of the three methods is dominant. Let's consider each type of economic system in turn.

The Traditional Economy

> **Traditional economy** An economy in which resources are allocated according to long-lived practices from the past.

In a **traditional economy,** resources are allocated according to the long-lived practices of the past. Tradition was the dominant method of resource allocation for most of human history and remains strong in many tribal societies and small villages in parts of Africa, South America, Asia, and the Pacific. Typically, traditional methods of production are handed down by the village elders, and traditional principles of fairness govern the distribution of goods and services.

Economies in which resources are allocated mostly by tradition tend to be stable and predictable. But these economies have one serious drawback: They don't grow. With everyone locked into the traditional patterns of production, there is little room for innovation and technological change. Traditional economies are therefore likely to be stagnant economies.

The Command Economy

> **Command or centrally planned economy** An economic system in which resources are allocated according to explicit instructions from a central authority.

In a **command economy,** resources are allocated mostly by explicit instructions from some higher authority. Because the government must plan these instructions in advance, command economies are also called **centrally planned economies.**

But command economies are disappearing fast. Until about 25 years ago, examples would have included the former Soviet Union, Poland, Romania, Bulgaria, Albania, China, and many others. Beginning in the late 1980s, all of these nations began abandoning central planning because the system had so many problems.

To be fair, command economies did have some major achievements too. In their early years, production in China and the former Soviet Union grew rapidly, enabling these countries to provide everyone with a job and basic consumer goods like food, clothing, and shelter. But their governments often enforced commands through brute force, and millions who were suspected of opposing the government were imprisoned or killed. In their final decades, command economies were unable to keep up with the rising expectations of their populations. Living standards stagnated, and popular dissatisfaction—both political and economic—eventually led to the abandonment of strict central planning. The only command economies left today are North Korea and Cuba, although Cuba began taking major steps away from central planning in 2011.

The Market Economy

The third method of allocating resources—and the one with which you are no doubt most familiar—is "the market." In a **market economy,** instead of following long-held traditions or commands from above, people are largely free to do what they want with the resources at their disposal. In the end, resources are allocated as a result of individual decision making. *Which* goods and services are produced? The ones that producers *choose* to produce. *How* are they produced? However producers *choose* to produce them. *Who* gets these goods and services? Anyone who *chooses* to buy them.

Of course, in a market economy, freedom of choice is constrained by the resources one controls. And in this respect, we do not all start in the same place in the economic race. Some of us have inherited great financial wealth, intelligence, talent, or beauty; and some, such as the children of successful professionals, are born into a world of helpful personal contacts. Others, unfortunately, will inherit none of these advantages. In a market system, those who control more resources will have more choices available to them than those who control fewer resources. Nevertheless, given these different starting points, individual choice plays the major role in allocating resources in a market economy.

But wait . . . isn't there a problem here? People acting according to their own desires, without command or tradition to control them? This sounds like a recipe for chaos! How, in such a free-for-all, could resources possibly be *allocated*?

The answer is contained in two words: *markets* and *prices.*

Market economy An economic system in which resources are allocated through individual decision making.

UNDERSTANDING THE MARKET

The market economy gets its name from something that nearly always happens when people are free to do what they want with the resources they possess. Inevitably, people decide to specialize in the production of one or a few things—often organizing themselves into business firms—and then sellers and buyers *come together to trade.* A **market** is a collection of buyers and sellers who have the potential to trade with one another.

In some cases, the market is *global;* that is, the market consists of buyers and sellers who are spread across the globe. The market for oil is an example of a global market, since buyers in any country can buy from sellers in any country. In other cases, the market is local. Markets for restaurant meals, haircuts, and taxi service are examples of local markets.

Markets play a major role in allocating resources by forcing individual decision makers to consider very carefully their decisions about buying and selling. They do so because of an important feature of every market: the *price* at which a good is bought and sold.

Market A group of buyers and sellers with the potential to trade with each other.

The Importance of Prices

A **price** is *the amount of money a buyer must pay to a seller for a good or service.* Price is not always the same as *cost.* In economics, as you've learned in this chapter, cost means *opportunity cost*—the *total* sacrifice needed to buy the good. While the money price of a good is a *part* of its opportunity cost, it is not the only cost. For example, the price does not include the value of the time sacrificed to buy something. Buying a new jacket will require you to spend time traveling to and from the store, trying on different styles and sizes, and waiting in line at the cash register.

Price The amount of money that must be paid to a seller to obtain a good or service.

Still, in most cases, the price of a good is a significant part of its opportunity cost. For large purchases, such as a home or automobile, the price will be *most* of the opportunity cost. And this is why prices are so important to the overall working of the economy: They confront individual decision makers with the costs of their choices.

Consider the example of purchasing a car. Because you must pay the price, you know that buying a new car will require you to cut back on purchases of other things. In this way, the opportunity cost to *society* of making another car is converted to an opportunity cost *for you*. If you value a new car more highly than the other things you must sacrifice for it, you will buy it. If not, you won't buy it.

Why is it so important that people face the opportunity costs of their actions? The following thought experiment can answer this question.

A Thought Experiment: Free Cars

Imagine that the government passes a new law: When anyone buys a new car, the government will reimburse that person for it immediately. The consequences would be easy to predict.

First, on the day the law was passed, everyone would rush out to buy new cars. Why not, if cars are free? The entire stock of existing automobiles would be gone within days—maybe even hours. Many people who didn't value cars much at all, and who seldom used them, would find themselves owning several—one for each day of the week or to match the different colors in their wardrobe. Others who weren't able to act in time—including some who desperately needed a new car for their work or to run their households—would be unable to find one at all.

Over time, automobile companies would drastically increase production to meet the surge in demand for cars. So much of our available labor, capital, land, and entrepreneurial talent would be diverted to making cars that we'd have to sacrifice huge quantities of all other goods and services. Thus, we'd end up *paying* for those additional cars in the end, by having less education, less medical care, perhaps even less food—all to support the widespread, frivolous use of cars. Almost everyone would conclude that society had been made worse off with the new "free-car" policy. By eliminating a price for automobiles, we would sever the connection between society's opportunity cost of producing cars and individuals' decisions to buy them. And we would create quite a mess for ourselves.

> *When resources are allocated by the market, and people must pay for their purchases, they are forced to consider the opportunity cost to society of the goods that they consume. In this way, markets help to create a sensible allocation of resources.*

Markets, Ownership, and the Invisible Hand

The complete label for market economies is *market capitalism*. While the market describes how resources are allocated, capitalism refers to one way that resources are *owned*. Under **capitalism**, most resources are owned by private citizens, who are mostly free to sell or rent them to others as they wish. The alternative mode of ownership is **socialism**, a system in which most resources are owned by the state, as in the former Soviet Union.

The market and capitalism go hand in hand, and for good reason. If individuals are left free to make decisions about resources, we want them to make their decisions carefully, in a socially useful way, and not waste society's scarce resources or use them frivolously. Private ownership of resources provides incentives for people to make careful, socially beneficial decisions.

This insight was best expressed by Adam Smith (1723–1790), the Scottish social philosopher who is often regarded as the first economist. In *The Wealth of Nations*, published in 1776, Smith argued that private resource owners are guided as if by an *invisible hand* to benefit society as a whole. As Smith put it, a private resource owner in a market economy

> . . . neither intends to promote the public interest, nor knows how much he is promoting it . . . he intends only his own gain, and he is in this, as in many other cases, led by an invisible hand to promote an end which was no part of his intention. Nor is it always the worse for the society that it was no part of it. By pursuing his own interest he frequently promotes that of the society more effectually than when he really intends to promote it.[4]

The key to this insight is that trade in a market economy is *voluntary*. No trade can take place unless both sides believe they will benefit from it. So in order to enjoy gains from trading, you must find a way to use your resources that will make someone else better off if they trade with you. For example, if you own land or a factory, or you have a skill, you will earn income only if you make your resources available for production. And those who buy or rent your resources will earn the most income for themselves by using your resources in the most productive way possible. In this way, our self-serving desires push the economy to be *productively efficient* (to operate on, rather than inside, the PPF). Moreover, business owners will earn income only if they produce goods that people actually want to buy (like chocolate ice cream), rather than goods that no one wants (broccoli-flavored ice cream). By producing and selling the most desirable goods, resource owners, business owners, and consumers all gain. Even though our motives may be selfish, our decisions benefit others in the economy too.

The U.S. Market System in Perspective

The United States has always been considered a leading example of a market economy. Each day, millions of distinct items are produced and sold in markets. Our grocery stores are always stocked with broccoli and tomato soup, and the drugstore always has tissues and aspirin—all due to the choices of individual producers and consumers. The goods that are traded, the way they are traded, and the price at which they trade are determined by the traders themselves.

But even in the United States, there are numerous cases of resource allocation *outside* the market. Many economic decisions are made within families, where tradition often dominates. For example, even when children get an allowance or have other earnings, they don't have to pay for goods consumed within the home. Other decisions within the family are based on command ("No TV until you finish your homework!").

In the broader economy, we find many examples of resource allocation by command. Various levels of government collect, in total, about one-third of our incomes as taxes. We are *told* how much tax we must pay, and those who don't comply suffer serious penalties, including imprisonment. Government—rather than individual decision makers—spends the tax revenue. In this way, the government plays a major role in allocating resources—especially in determining which goods are produced and who gets them.

[4] Adam Smith, *The Wealth of Nations* (Modern Library Classics Edition, 2000), p. 423

Mixed Economy A market economy in which the government also plays an important role in allocating resources.

There are also other ways, aside from strict commands, that the government limits our market freedoms. Regulations designed to protect the environment, maintain safe workplaces, and ensure the safety of our food supply are just a few examples of government-imposed constraints on our individual choice. Thus, the U.S. economy—like every other market economy today—uses both command and the market to allocate resources. For this reason, modern market economies are sometimes called **mixed economies**.

Changing the Mix

Many of the most controversial political debates in the United States are about the right mix between command and the market for allocating resources—a normative issue about which people can disagree. For example, consider the 2010 health care legislation mentioned at the beginning of this chapter. Opponents argued that the new law tilted the mix too far toward command and away from the market. After all, the law *requires* people to purchase health insurance, and it imposes stricter limits on the behavior of private decision makers (e.g., health insurance companies). But supporters argued that making health care available to more Americans was an important social goal that could best be accomplished by increasing the government's role. They felt this tilt away from the market was appropriate and necessary.

In countries that formerly used central planning—such as Russia and China—government's role in allocating resources has shrunk dramatically. But in market economies such as the United States, government has become more involved in resource allocation over the years. This is especially true of many Western European countries, such as France, Germany, and Sweden. Compared to the United States, citizens in these countries pay a higher percentage of their income in taxes, businesses face more restrictions on their activities, and *social safety nets* (government-run programs to assist the poor and the unemployed) are more generous.

Still, in Europe—as in the United States—the market remains dominant. For each example of resource allocation by command or a serious restriction of some market freedom, we can find hundreds of examples where individuals make choices according to their own desires. The goods and services that we buy, the jobs at which we work, the homes in which we live—in almost all cases, these result from market choices.

A Look Ahead …

The market is simultaneously the most simple and the most complex way to allocate resources. For each buyer and seller, the market is simple. There are no traditions or commands to be memorized and obeyed. Instead, we enter the markets we *wish* to trade in, and we respond to prices there as we *wish* to, unconcerned about the overall process of resource allocation.

But from the economist's point of view, the market is quite complex. Resources are allocated indirectly, as a by-product of individual decision making, rather than through easily identified traditions or commands. As a result, it often takes some skillful economic detective work to determine just how individuals are behaving and how resources are being allocated as a consequence.

How can we make sense of all of this apparent chaos and complexity? That is what economics is all about. You will begin your detective work in Chapter 3, where you will learn about the most widely used model in economics: supply and demand.

USING THE THEORY

ARE WE SAVING LIVES EFFICIENTLY?

Earlier in this chapter, you learned that instances of gross productive inefficiency are not as easy to find in our economy as one might imagine. But many economists argue that our allocation of resources to lifesaving efforts is a glaring exception. In this section, we'll use some of the tools and concepts you've learned in this chapter to ask whether we are saving lives efficiently.

Lifesaving and the PPF

Let's view "saving lives" as the output—a service—produced by the "lifesaving industry." This industry consists of private firms (such as medical practices and hospitals), as well as government agencies (such as the Department of Health and Human Services or the Environmental Protection Agency). In a productively efficient economy, we must pay an opportunity cost whenever we choose to save additional lives. That's because saving more lives—by building another emergency surgery center, running an advertising campaign to encourage healthier living, or requiring the use of costly but safe materials instead of cheaper but toxic ones—requires resources. And these resources could be used to produce other goods and services instead.

Figure 7 illustrates this opportunity cost with a production-possibilities frontier. The number of lives saved per year is measured along the horizontal axis, and the quantity of all other goods

---

FIGURE 7 | **Efficiency and Inefficiency in Saving Lives**

This PPF shows society's choice between saving lives (measured along the horizontal axis) and all other production (on the vertical axis). Operating on the curve (at points like A, A', or A") would be productively efficient. But if the life-saving industry is not efficient, then society is operating inside the PPF (at a point like B). Eliminating the inefficiency would enable us to save more lives, or have more of other goods, or both.

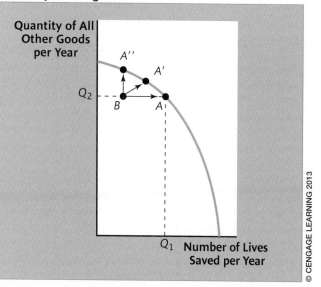

(lumped together into a single category) is measured on the vertical axis. A productively efficient economy would be *on* the frontier. Point A on the PPF is one such productively efficient point, where we would save Q_1 lives per year, and produce the quantity Q_2 of all other goods. Once we are on the frontier, we can only save more lives by pulling resources away from producing other goods and paying an opportunity cost in other goods forgone.

But what if there is productive *in*efficiency in the economy? And what if the source of the inefficiency is in lifesaving itself? More specifically, what if the "lifesaving industry" could save more lives using the current quantity of resources, simply by reallocating those resources among different types of lifesaving activities? In that case, we would be currently operating at a point like B, *inside* the PPF. By eliminating the inefficiency, we could move *to* the frontier. For example, we could save more lives with no sacrifice of other goods (a move from point B to point A) or have more of other goods while saving the same number of lives (a move to point A'') or have more of both (point A').

Lifesaving in the United States

Economists argue that the United States and many other countries do, in fact, suffer from productive inefficiency in saving lives. How have they come to such a conclusion?

The first step in the analysis is to remember that, in a market economy, resources sell at a price. We can use the dollar cost of a lifesaving method to measure the value of the resources used up by that method. Moreover, we can compare the "cost per year of life saved" of different methods.

For example, one study showed that in the United States, we spend roughly $382 million on heart transplants each year, and thereby add about 1,600 years to the lives of heart patients. Thus, the cost per year of life saved from heart transplants is $381,000,000/1,600 = $238,000 (rounded to the nearest thousand).

The upper part of Table 6 lists this cost per life-year saved for heart transplants and several other methods we currently use to save lives in the United States. Some of these methods reflect legal or regulatory decisions (such as the ban on chlorobenzilate pesticides), while others are common or often-used medical care practices (such as flu shots and heart transplants).

You can see that the cost per life-year saved ranges widely. It costs just a few hundred dollars to save a year of life by giving flu shots or having doctors warn patients to quit smoking. But it costs millions of dollars for each life-year saved with certain regulations, such as workplace arsenic exposure.

Our society has largely exhausted the potential to save lives from some of the examples listed in the upper part of the table. For example, most doctors *do* warn their smoking patients to quit. But some methods—though common—are not fully exploited. Millions of people do *not* currently get flu shots, for example. Moreover, some methods of saving lives that are *not* common practice (shown in the bottom half of the table) are relatively low-cost. Whenever we use up resources for less cost-effective methods before fully exploiting more cost-effective methods, we are being productively *in*efficient in life saving.

To see why, let's do some thought experiments. First, let's imagine that we shift resources from heart transplants to *intensive* antismoking efforts. Then for each year of life we decided not to save with heart transplants, we would free up $238,000 in medical resources. If we applied those resources toward intensive antismoking efforts, at a cost of $3,518 per year of life saved, we could then save $238,000/$3,518 = 67 life-years instead of just one. In other words, we could increase the number of

TABLE 6	
The Cost of Saving Lives	

Method	Cost per Life-Year Saved (2010 dollars)
Common Practice or Regulation	
Flu vaccinations	$210
Brief physician antismoking intervention (Single personal warning from Physician to stop smoking)	$215
Chlorination of drinking water	$4,700
Trihalomethane limits for drinking water	$16,600
Benzene emissions regulations	$155,000
Heart transplants	$238,000
Reflective devices on heavy trucks	$287,000
Applying chlorobenzilate pesticide ban to citrus fruit	$1,812,000
Limits on workplace arsenic exposure	$2,452,000
Proposed or Possible	
Increase random motor vehicle inspections	$2,300
Replace ambulances with helicopters for medical emergencies	$3,337
Intensive antismoking intervention (Physician identification of smokers; three physician counseling sessions; two sessions with smoking cessation specialists; provision of nicotine patch or gum)	$3,500
Install more automated external defibrillators in workplaces	$7,500
Build additional trauma centers	$36,000
Intensive blood pressure counseling (2 years of monitoring and counseling for normal-weight patients with high blood-pressure)	$65,000
Change in cigarette warning labels (2010 FDA proposal to add color-coded graphics)	$110,000
Meningococcal vaccine for adolescents	$134,000
Triple the wind resistance of new buildings	$3,900,000
Seat belts on school buses	$4,300,000

Note: Author calculations used to adjust results to 2010 dollars, and (for a few studies) from cost per life saved to cost per life-year saved.

Sources: Tammy O. Tengs et al. (1995) "Five hundred life-saving interventions and their cost effectiveness," *Risk Analysis* 15 (3); Malcolm Law and Jin Ling Tan (October 1995) "An analysis of the effectiveness of interventions intended to help people stop smoking," *Archives of Internal Medicine* 155 (18); Jerry Cromwell et al. (1997) "Cost-effectiveness of the clinical practice recommendations in the AHCPR guideline for smoking cessation," *Journal of the American Medical Association* 278 (21); P.A. Gearhart and A. R. Wuerz (October 1997) "Cost-effectiveness analysis of helicopter EMS for trauma patients," *Annals of Emergency Medicine* 30 (4); W. Kip Viscusi (February 2006) "Regulation of health, safety and environmental risks," *Harvard John M. Olin Discussion Paper Series*, Discussion Paper No. 544; Ellen J. McKenzie et al. (July 2010) "The value of trauma center care," *Journal of Trauma-Injury Infection & Critical Care* 69(1):1–10; S. K. Datta et al. (August 2010) "Economic analysis of a tailored behavioral intervention to improve blood pressure control for primary care patients," *American Heart Journal* 160 (2) (results for men and women have been averaged); Colin W. Shephard et al. (May 2005) "Cost-effectiveness of conjugate meningococcal vaccination strategies in the United States," *Pediatrics* 115 (5); "Proposed rules: Required warnings for cigarette packages and advertisements," *Federal Register*, Nov 12, 2010.

life-years saved without any increase in the total value of resources used, and without any sacrifice in other goods and services.

But why pick on heart transplants? We use hundreds of millions of dollars worth of resources limiting arsenic exposure in the workplace, costing us about $2.5 million per life-year saved. Suppose these resources were used instead to install automated external defibrillators in more workplaces, which cost $7,500 per life-year saved. Then, for each life-year lost to arsenic exposure, we'd save $2.5 million/$7,500 = 333 life-years through defibrillators.

How much does this productive inefficiency in life saving cost us? One study looked at 185 actual and potential life-saving methods, and found that merely shifting resources around so that the most cost-effective methods were fully exploited would more than double the number of life-years saved.[5] All without any sacrifice in other goods and services.

Of course, allocating lifesaving resources is much more complicated than our discussion so far has implied. For one thing, the benefits of lifesaving efforts are not fully captured by "life-years saved" (or even by an alternative measure, which accounts for improvement in *quality* of life). The cost per life-year saved from mandating seat belts on school buses is extremely high—more than $4 million. This is mostly because very few children die in school bus accidents—about 11 per year in the entire United States—and, according to the National Traffic Safety Board, few of these deaths would have been prevented with seat belts. But mandatory seat belts—rightly or wrongly—might decrease the anxiety of millions of parents as they send their children off to school. How should we value such a reduction in anxiety? Hard to say. But it may be reasonable to include it as a benefit—at least in some way—when deciding about resources.

[5] Tammy O. Tengs, "Dying Too Soon: How Cost-Effectiveness Analysis Can Save Lives," *National Center for Policy Analysis Report*, No. 204, May 1997.

SUMMARY

The *production possibilities frontier* (PPF) is a simple model to illustrate the opportunity cost of society's choices. When we are *productively efficient* (operating *on* the PPF), producing more of one thing requires producing less of something else. The *law of increasing opportunity cost* tells us that the more of something we produce, the greater the opportunity cost of producing still more. Even when we are operating inside the PPF—say because of productive inefficiency or a recession—it is not necessarily easy or costless to move to the PPF and avoid opportunity cost.

In a world of scarce resources, each society must have an *economic system*: its way of organizing economic activity. All economic systems feature *specialization,* in which each person and firm concentrates on a limited number of productive activities, and exchange, through which we obtain most of what we desire by trading with others. Specialization and exchange enable us to enjoy higher living standards than would be possible under self-sufficiency.

One way that specialization increases living standards is by allowing each of us to concentrate on tasks in which we have a *comparative advantage.* When individuals within a country produce more of their comparative advantage goods and exchange with others, living standards in that country are higher. Similarly, when individual nations specialize in their comparative advantage goods and trade with other nations, global living standards rise.

Every economic system determines how resources are allocated. Resources can be allocated by *tradition, command,* or *the market.* In a *market economy,* resources are allocated primarily through individual choice. Prices play an important role in markets by forcing decision makers to take account of society's opportunity cost when they make choices. Another feature of market economies—*capitalism* (private ownership of resources)—helps to direct resources in ways that create benefits for others.

PROBLEM SET

Answers to even-numbered Problems can be found on the text Web site through www.cengagebrain.com

1. Redraw Figure 1, but this time identify a different set of points along the frontier. Starting at point F (5,000 tanks, zero production of wheat), have each point you select show equal increments in the quantity of wheat produced. For example, a new point H should correspond to 200,000 bushels of wheat, point J to 400,000 bushels, point K to 600,000 bushels, and so on. Now observe what happens to the opportunity cost of "200,000 more bushels of wheat" as you move leftward and upward along this PPF. Does the law of increasing opportunity cost apply to the production of wheat? Explain briefly.

2. How would a technological innovation in lifesaving—say, the discovery of a cure for cancer—affect the PPF in Figure 7?

3. How would a technological innovation in the production of *other* goods—say, the invention of a new kind of robot that speeds up assembly-line manufacturing—affect the PPF in Figure 7?

4. Suppose the Internet enables more production of other goods *and* helps to save lives (for simplicity, assume proportional increases). Show how the PPF in Figure 7 would be affected.

5. Suppose that one day, Gilligan (the castaway) eats a magical island plant that turns him into an expert at everything. In particular, it now takes him just half an hour to pick a cup of berries, and 15 minutes to catch a fish.
   a. Redo Table 2 in the chapter.
   b. Who—Gilligan or Maryanne—has a comparative advantage in picking berries? In fishing?
   c. Suppose that Gilligan reallocates his time to produce *two more units* of his comparative advantage good and that Maryanne does the same. Construct a new version of Table 3 in the chapter, showing how production changes for each castaway and for the island as a whole.

6. Suppose that two different castaways, Mr. and Mrs. Howell, end up on a different island. Mr. Howell can pick 1 pineapple per hour, or 1 coconut. Mrs. Howell can pick 2 pineapples per hour, but it takes her 2 hours to pick a coconut.
   a. Construct a table like Table 2 showing Mr. and Mrs. Howell's labor requirements.
   b. Who—Mr. or Mrs. Howell—has a comparative advantage in picking pineapples? In picking coconuts? Which of the two should specialize in which tasks?
   c. [Harder] Assume that Mr. and Mrs. Howell had originally washed ashore on different parts of the island, and that they originally each spent 12 hours per day working, spending 6 hours picking pineapples and 6 hours picking coconuts. How will their total production change if they find each other and begin to specialize?

7. You and a friend have decided to work jointly on a course project. Frankly, your friend is a less-than-ideal partner. His skills as a researcher are such that he can review and outline only two articles a day. Moreover, his hunt-and-peck style limits him to only 10 pages of typing a day. On the other hand, in a day you can produce six outlines or type 20 pages.
   a. Who has an absolute advantage in outlining, you or your friend? What about typing?
   b. Who has a comparative advantage in outlining? In typing?
   c. According to the principle of comparative advantage, who should specialize in which task?

8. Suppose that an economy's PPF is a straight line, rather than a bowed out, concave curve. What would this say about the nature of opportunity cost as production is shifted from one good to the other?

More Challenging

9. Go back to Table 5 in the chapter, which is based on the hours requirements in Table 4. Suppose that when trade opens up between the U.S. and China, the U.S. increases its production of soybeans by 100 bushels (instead of 10 as in the table). China increases its production of T-shirts by 400 (instead of 40). Assume that when the two countries trade with each other, each bushel of soybeans is exchanged for 3 T-shirts. Finally, suppose that the U.S. trades (exports) 90 bushels of soybeans to China.
   a. How many T-shirts from China will the U.S. receive in exchange for its soybean exports to China?
   b. After trading with China, how many more bushels of soybeans will be available for Americans to consume (compared to the situation before trade)? How many more T-shirts?
   c. After trading with the U.S., how many more bushels of soybeans will be available for the Chinese to consume? How many more T-shirts?
   d. Based on this example, consider the following statement: "When two countries trade with each other, one country's gain will always be the other country's loss." Is this statement true or false? Explain briefly.

10. Evaluate the following statement: "If the dollar values in Table 6 are accurate, it follows that providing meningococcal vaccines to all adolescents would be cheaper than installing seat belts on all school buses." True or false? Explain.

© CHRIS HOWEY/SHUTTERSTOCK.COM

CHAPTER 3

Supply and Demand

F ather Guido Sarducci, a character on the early episodes of the TV show *Saturday Night Live*, once observed that the average person remembers only about five minutes worth of material from college. He therefore proposed the "Five Minute University," in which you'd learn only the five minutes of material you'd actually remember. The economics course would last only 10 seconds, just enough time for students to learn to memorize three words: "supply and demand."

Of course, there is much more to economics than these three words. But supply and demand does play a central role in economics. What, exactly, does this familiar phrase really mean?

First, supply and demand is an economic *model,* designed to explain *how prices are determined in certain types of markets.*

But it's an important model because prices themselves play such an important role in the economy. Once the price of something has been determined, only those willing to pay that price will get it. Thus, prices determine which households will get which goods and services and which firms will get which resources. If you want to know why the cell phone industry is expanding while the video rental industry is shrinking, or why homelessness is a more pervasive problem in the United States than hunger, you need to understand how prices are determined. In this chapter, you will learn how the model of supply and demand works and how to use it.

MARKETS

Put any compound in front of a chemist, ask him what it is and what it can be used for, and he will immediately think of the basic elements—carbon, hydrogen, oxygen, and so on. Ask an economist almost any question about the economy, and he will immediately think about *markets.*

When you hear the word "market," you probably think of a specific location where buying and selling take place: a supermarket, a flea market, and so on. In economics, "market" has a broader meaning:

> *A market is a group of buyers and sellers with the potential to trade with each other.*

The buyers and sellers in a market don't have to be in the same location, or even in the same country. For example, a seafood company in Vietnam might sell frozen shrimp to an import company in New York, without anyone from either company meeting face to face. Both the seller in Vietnam and the buyer in New York are part of the frozen-shrimp market. Economists think of the economy as a collection of markets. There is a market for oranges, another for automobiles, another for real estate, and still others for corporate stocks, plumbers' services, land, euros, and anything else that is bought and sold.

Characterizing a Market

The first step in analyzing a market is to figure out *which* market you are analyzing. This might seem easy. But we can choose to define a market in different ways, depending on our purpose.

Broad versus Narrow Definition

Suppose we want to study the personal computer industry in the United States. Should we define the market very broadly ("the market for computers"), or very narrowly ("the market for ultra-light laptops"), or something in between ("the market for laptops")? The right choice depends on the problem we're trying to analyze.

For example, if we're interested in why computers *in general* have come down in price over the past decade, we'd treat all types of computers as if they were the same good. Economists call this process **aggregation**—combining a group of distinct things into a single whole.

Aggregation The process of combining distinct things into a single whole.

But suppose we're asking a different question: Why do laptops always cost more than desktops with similar computing power? Then we'd aggregate all laptops together as one good, and all desktops as another, and look at each of these more narrowly defined markets.

We can also choose to define the *geography* of a market more broadly or more narrowly, depending on our purpose. We'd analyze the *national* market for gasoline if we're explaining general nationwide trends in gas prices. But we'd define it more locally to explain, say, why gas prices are rising more rapidly in Los Angeles than in other areas of the country.

> In economics, **markets** *can be defined broadly or narrowly, depending on our purpose.*

Markets A group of buyers and sellers with the potential to trade with each other.

How markets are defined is one of the most important differences between *macro*economics and *micro*economics. In macroeconomics, goods and services are aggregated to the highest levels. Macro models even lump all consumer goods—breakfast cereals, smart phones, denim jeans, and so forth—into the single category "consumption goods" and view them as if they are traded in a single, national "market for consumption goods." Defining markets this broadly allows macroeconomists to take an overall view of the economy without getting bogged down in the details.

In microeconomics, by contrast, markets are defined more narrowly. Instead of asking how much we'll spend on *consumer goods,* a microeconomist might ask how much we'll spend on *health care* or *video games.* Even in microeconomics, there is always some aggregation, but not as much as in macroeconomics.

Product and Resource Markets

Figure 1, often called the simple **circular flow** model of the economy, illustrates two different types of markets and how they relate to each other. The upper half illustrates **product markets,** where goods and services are bought and sold. The blue arrows show the flow of products from the business firms who supply them to the

Circular flow A simple model that shows how goods, resources, and dollar payments flow between households and firms.

Product markets Markets in which firms sell goods and services to households.

FIGURE 1   The Circular Flow Model

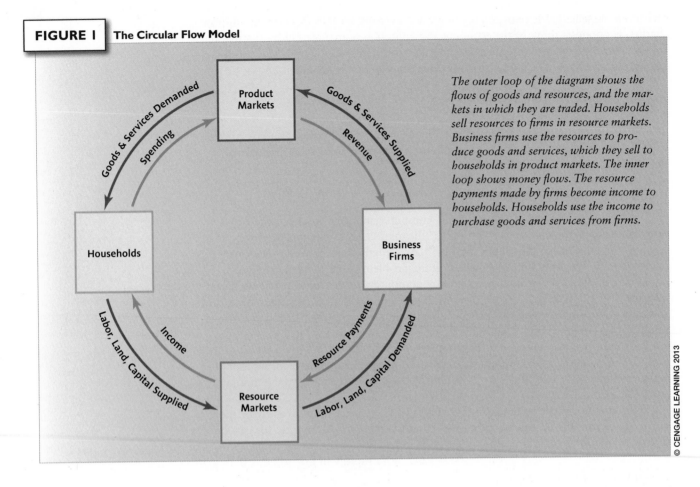

The outer loop of the diagram shows the flows of goods and resources, and the markets in which they are traded. Households sell resources to firms in resource markets. Business firms use the resources to produce goods and services, which they sell to households in product markets. The inner loop shows money flows. The resource payments made by firms become income to households. Households use the income to purchase goods and services from firms.

© CENGAGE LEARNING 2013

households who ultimately buy them. The green arrows show the associated flow of dollars from the households who spend the dollars, to the business firms who receive these dollars as revenue. (In the real world, businesses also sell products to the government and to other businesses, but this simple version leaves out these details.)

The lower half depicts a different set of markets: **resource markets,** where labor, land, and capital are bought and sold. Here, the roles of households and firms are reversed. The blue arrows show resources flowing from the households (who own and supply them) to the business firms (who demand them). The associated flow of dollars is indicated by the green arrows: Business firms pay for the resources they use, and households receive these payments as income.

In this chapter, we'll be using supply and demand to analyze product markets—particularly those where business firms supply goods and services that are bought by households. In later chapters, we'll look at resource markets, as well as some other types of markets that are not included in the circular flow depicted here. These include markets for existing homes, and markets for financial assets such as stocks and bonds.

Resource markets Markets in which households that own resources sell them to firms.

Competition in Markets

A final issue in defining a market is how prices are determined. In one type of market, individual buyers or sellers have some *control* over the price of the product. Microsoft—a major seller of operating systems and other software—operates in this kind of market. Microsoft can raise the price of its Windows operating system and sell fewer units, or lower its price and sell more. Markets like these—in which individual buyers or sellers can control or influence the price—are called *imperfectly competitive markets*.

In the other type of market, each buyer and seller is *confronted* with a market price that they can do little or nothing about. Consider the market for wheat. On any given day, there is a going price for wheat—say, $5.80 per bushel. If a farmer tries to charge more than that—say, $5.85 per bushel—he won't sell any wheat at all! His customers will instead go to one of his many competitors and buy the identical product from them for less. Each wheat farmer must take the price of wheat as a "given."

The same is true of a single wheat *buyer*: If he tries to negotiate a lower price from a seller, he'd be laughed off the farm. "Why should I sell my wheat to you for $5.75 per bushel, when there are others who will pay me $5.80?" Accordingly, each buyer must take the market price as a given.

The market for wheat is an example of a *perfectly competitive market*.

> *In **perfectly competitive markets** (or just **competitive markets**), each buyer and seller takes the market price as a given.*

Perfectly competitive market (informal definition) A market in which no buyer or seller has the power to influence the price.

But wait. If no individual buyer or seller can influence the price, then who decides what the price of wheat will be? The answer is: The "market" decides. If that sounds a bit mysterious or circular right now, don't worry. Explaining how prices are determined in competitive markets is exactly what supply and demand is all about.

> *The supply and demand model is designed to show how prices are determined in perfectly competitive markets.*

Applying Supply and Demand in the Real World

You'll learn more about what makes some markets perfectly competitive and others not when you are further into your study of *micro*economics. But here's a hint: In perfectly competitive markets, there are many buyers and sellers that are each very small relative to the total market, and the product is standardized, like wheat. In imperfectly competitive markets, by contrast, individual buyers or sellers can be a relatively large part of the market, or else the product of each seller is unique in some way.

But don't worry too much about perfect competition in this chapter, because the supply and demand model is often useful even when markets are *not* perfectly competitive. For example, in the market for hamburgers, there are high-priced restaurants and low-priced restaurants, so there is no single price for hamburgers in the market. Moreover, each restaurant (or restaurant chain) has some control over its own hamburger price. So the market for hamburgers is *not* strictly perfectly competitive.

But it is not too far from competitive. Most restaurants do regard the *range* of possible prices they can charge as given. The supply and demand model can help us see how this range of prices is determined, and what makes the average price of hamburgers rise or fall. In fact, if you ask an economist to explain or predict changes in the price of hamburgers, books, automobiles, or almost any other good or service, he or she will reach for the supply-and-demand model first. Supply and demand is the most versatile and widely used model in the economist's toolkit.

© JEFF GREENBERG/ALAMY

In the rest of this chapter, we will build the supply-and-demand model. As the name implies, the model has two major parts: *supply* and *demand*. Let's start by analyzing the demand side of the market.

DEMAND

It's tempting to think of the "demand" for a product as psychological—a pure "want" or "desire." But that kind of thinking can lead us astray. For example, you *want* all kinds of things: a bigger apartment, a better car, nicer clothes, more and better vacations. The list is endless. But you don't always *buy* them. Why not?

Because in addition to your wants—which you'd very much like to satisfy—you also face *constraints*. First, you have to *pay* for the products you want. Second, your spending power is limited, so every decision to buy one thing is also a decision *not* to buy something else (or a decision to save less, and have less buying power in the future). As a result, every purchase confronts you with an opportunity cost. Your "wants," together with the real-world constraints that you face, determine what you will choose to buy in any market. Hence, the following definition:

*The **quantity demanded** of a good or service is the number of units that all buyers in a market would choose to buy over a given time period, given the constraints that they face.*

Quantity demanded The quantity of a good that all buyers in a market would choose to buy during a period of time, given their constraints.

Since this definition plays a key role in any supply and demand analysis, it's worth taking a closer look at it.

Quantity Demanded Implies a **Choice.** Quantity demanded doesn't tell us the amount of a good that households feel they "need" or "desire" in order to be happy. Instead, it tells us how much households would choose to buy *when they take into account the opportunity cost* of their decisions. The opportunity cost arises from the constraints households face, such as having to pay a given price for the good, limits on spendable funds, and so on.

Quantity Demanded Is **Hypothetical.** Will households actually be *able* to purchase the amount they want to purchase? As you'll soon see, usually yes. But there are special situations—analyzed in microeconomics—in which households are frustrated in buying all that they would like to buy. Quantity demanded makes no assumptions about the availability of the good. Instead, it's the answer to a hypothetical question: How much would households buy, given the constraints that they face, if the units they wanted to buy were available?

Quantity Demanded Depends on **Price.** The price of the good is just one variable among many that influences quantity demanded. But because the price is a key variable that our model will ultimately determine, we try to keep that variable front-and-center in our thinking. This is why for the next few pages we'll assume that all other influences on demand are held constant, so we can explore the relationship between price and quantity demanded.

The Law of Demand

How does a change in price affect quantity demanded? You probably know the answer to this already: When something is more expensive, people tend to buy less of it. This common observation applies to air travel, magazines, guitars, and virtually everything else that people buy. For all of these goods and services, price and quantity are *negatively related*: That is, when price rises, quantity demanded falls; when price falls, quantity demanded rises. This negative relationship is observed so regularly in markets that economists call it the *law of demand*.

> The **law of demand** states that when the price of a good rises and everything else remains the same, the quantity of the good demanded will fall.

Law of demand As the price of a good increases, the quantity demanded decreases.

Read that definition again, and notice the very important words, "everything else remains the same." The law of demand tells us what would happen *if* all the other influences on buyers' choices remained unchanged, and only one influence—the price of the good—changed.

This is an example of a common practice in economics. In the real world, many variables change *simultaneously*. But to understand changes in the economy, we must first understand the effect of each variable *separately*. So we conduct a series of mental experiments in which we ask: "What would happen if this one influence—and only this one—were to change?" The law of demand is the result of one such mental experiment, in which we imagine that the price of the good changes, but all other influences on quantity demanded remain constant.

Mental experiments like this are used so often in economics that we sometimes use a shorthand Latin expression to remind us that we are holding all but one influence constant: ***ceteris paribus*** (formally pronounced KAY-ter-is PAR-ih-bus, although it's acceptable to pronounce the first word as SEH-ter-is). This is Latin for "all else the same," or "all else remaining unchanged." Even when it is not explicitly stated, the *ceteris paribus* assumption is virtually always implied. The exceptions are cases where we consider two or more influences on a variable that change simultaneously, as we will do toward the end of this chapter.

Ceteris paribus Latin for "all else remaining the same."

The Demand Schedule and the Demand Curve

To make our discussion more concrete, let's look at a specific market: the market for real maple syrup in the United States. In this market, we'll view the buyers as U.S. households, whereas the sellers (to be considered later) are maple syrup producers in the United States or Canada.

Table 1 shows a hypothetical **demand schedule** for maple syrup in this market. This is *a list of different quantities demanded at different prices, with all other*

Demand schedule A list showing the quantities of a good that consumers would choose to purchase at different prices, with all other variables held constant.

TABLE 1

Demand Schedule for Maple Syrup in the United States

Price (per bottle)	Quantity Demanded (bottles per month)
$1.00	75,000
$2.00	60,000
$3.00	50,000
$4.00	40,000
$5.00	35,000

FIGURE 2   The Demand Curve

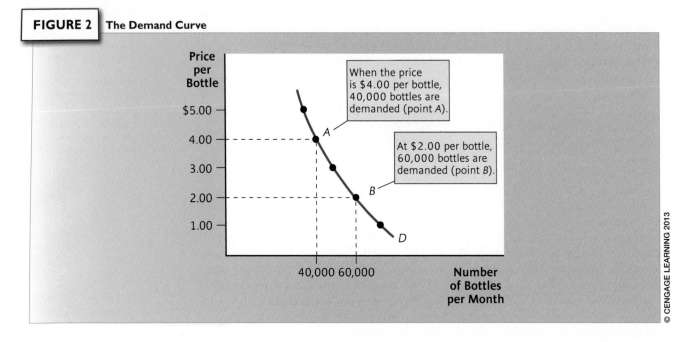

variables that affect the demand decision assumed constant. For example, the demand schedule tells us that when the price of maple syrup is $2.00 per bottle, the quantity demanded will be 60,000 bottles per month. Notice that the demand schedule obeys the law of demand: As the price of maple syrup increases, *ceteris paribus*, the quantity demanded falls.

Now look at Figure 2. It shows a diagram that will appear repeatedly in your study of economics. In the figure, each price-and-quantity combination in Table 1 is represented by a point. For example, point *A* represents the price $4.00 and quantity 40,000, while point *B* represents the pair $2.00 and 60,000. When we connect all of these points with a line, we obtain the famous *demand curve*, labeled with a *D* in the figure.

Demand curve A graph of a demand schedule; a curve showing the quantity of a good or service demanded at various prices, with all other variables held constant.

> The **demand curve** shows the relationship between the price of a good and the quantity demanded in the market, holding constant all other variables that influence demand. Each point on the curve shows the total quantity that buyers would choose to buy at a specific price.

Notice that the demand curve in Figure 2—like virtually all demand curves—*slopes downward*. This is just a graphical representation of the law of demand.

Shifts versus Movements Along the Demand Curve

Markets are affected by a variety of events. Some events will cause us to *move along* the demand curve; others will cause the entire demand curve to *shift*. It is crucial to distinguish between these two very different types of effects.

Let's go back to Figure 2. There, you can see that when the price of maple syrup rises from $2.00 to $4.00 per bottle, the number of bottles demanded falls from 60,000 to 40,000. This is a movement *along* the demand curve, from point *B* to point *A*. In general,

> a change in the price of a good causes a movement along the demand curve.

© CENGAGE LEARNING 2013

Price (per bottle)	Original Quantity Demanded (average income = $40,000)	New Quantity Demanded (average income = $50,000)
$1.00	75,000	95,000
$2.00	60,000	80,000
$3.00	50,000	70,000
$4.00	40,000	60,000
$5.00	35,000	55,000

TABLE 2

Increase in Demand for Maple Syrup in the United States

In Figure 2, a *fall* in price would cause us to move *rightward* along the demand curve (from point A to point B), and a *rise* in price would cause us to move *leftward* along the demand curve (from B to A).

Remember, though, that when we draw a demand curve, we assume all other variables that might influence demand are *held constant* at some particular value. For example, the demand curve in Figure 2 might have been drawn to give us quantity demanded at each price when average household income in the United States remains constant at, say, $40,000 per year.

But suppose average income increases to $50,000. With more income, we'd expect households to buy more of *most* things, including maple syrup. This is illustrated in Table 2. At the original income level, households would choose to buy 60,000 bottles of maple syrup at $2.00 per bottle. But after income rises, they would choose to buy more at that price—80,000 bottles, according to Table 2. A similar change would occur at any other price for maple syrup: After income rises, households would choose to buy more than before. In other words, the rise in income *changes the entire relationship between price and quantity demanded*. We now have a *new* demand curve.

Figure 3 plots the new demand curve from the quantities in the third column of Table 2. The new demand curve lies to the *right* of the old curve. For example, at a price of $2.00, quantity demanded increases from 60,000 bottles on the old curve

FIGURE 3 | A Shift of the Demand Curve

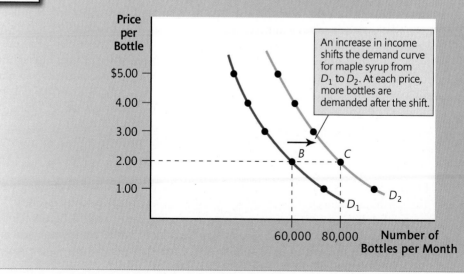

© CENGAGE LEARNING 2013

(point *B*) to 80,000 bottles on the *new* demand curve (point *C*). As you can see, the rise in household income has *shifted* the demand curve to the right.

More generally,

> *a change in any variable that affects demand—except for the good's price—causes the demand curve to shift.*

When buyers would choose to buy a greater quantity at any price, the demand curve shifts *rightward*. If they would decide to buy less at any price, the demand curve shifts *leftward*.

"Change in Quantity Demanded" versus "Change in Demand"

Language is important when discussing demand. The term *quantity demanded* means a *particular amount* that buyers would choose to buy at a specific price, represented by a single point on a demand curve. *Demand*, by contrast, means the *entire relationship* between price and quantity demanded, represented by the entire demand curve.

For this reason, when a change in the price of a good moves us *along* a demand curve, we call it a **change in quantity demanded.** For example, in Figure 2, the movement from point *A* to point *B* is an *increase* in quantity demanded. This is a change from one number (40,000 bottles) to another (60,000 bottles).

When something *other* than the price changes, causing the entire demand curve to shift, we call it a **change in demand.** In Figure 3, for example, the shift in the curve would be called an *increase in demand*.

Factors That Shift the Demand Curve

Let's take a closer look at what might cause a change in demand (a shift of the demand curve). Keep in mind that for now, we're exploring *one factor at a time*, always keeping *all other determinants of demand constant*.

Income. In Figure 3, an increase in **income** shifted the demand for maple syrup to the right. In fact, a rise in income increases demand for *most* goods. We call these **normal goods.** Housing, automobiles, health club memberships, and real maple syrup are all examples of normal goods.

But not all goods are normal. For some goods—called **inferior goods**—a rise in income would *decrease* demand—shifting the demand curve *leftward*. Regular-grade ground chuck is a good example. It's a cheap source of protein, but not as high in quality as sirloin. With higher income, households could more easily afford better types of meat—ground sirloin or steak, for example. As a result, higher incomes for buyers might cause the demand for ground chuck to *decrease*. For similar reasons, we might expect that Greyhound bus tickets (in contrast to airline tickets) and single-ply paper towels (in contrast to two-ply) are inferior goods.

> *A rise in income will* increase *the demand for a* normal *good, and* decrease *the demand for an* inferior *good.*

Wealth. Your **wealth** at any point in time is the total value of everything you *own* (cash, bank accounts, stocks, bonds, real estate or any other valuable property) minus the total dollar amount you *owe* (home mortgage, credit card debt, auto loan, student loan, and so on). Although income and wealth are different (see the nearby Dangerous Curves box), they have similar effects on demand. When people have more

---

Change in quantity demanded A movement along a demand curve in response to a change in price.

Change in demand A shift of a demand curve in response to a change in some variable other than price.

Income The amount that a person or firm earns over a particular period.

Normal good A good that people demand more of as their income rises.

Inferior good A good that people demand less of as their income rises.

Wealth The total value of everything a person or firm owns, at a point in time, minus the total amount owed.

wealth—because of an increase in the value of their stocks or bonds, for example—they have more funds with which to purchase goods and services. As you might expect,

> *an increase in wealth will* increase *demand (shift the curve rightward) for a normal good, and* decrease *demand (shift the curve leftward) for an inferior good.*

Prices of Related Goods. A **substitute** is a good that can be used in place of another good and that fulfills more or less the same purpose. For example, many people use real maple syrup to sweeten their pancakes, but they could use a number of other things instead: honey, sugar, jam, or *artificial* maple syrup. Each of these can be considered a substitute for real maple syrup.

When the price of a substitute rises, people will choose to buy *more* maple syrup. For example, when the price of jam rises, some jam users will switch to maple syrup, and the demand for maple syrup will increase. In general,

> *a rise in the price of a substitute increases the demand for a good, shifting the demand curve to the right.*

Of course, if the price of a substitute falls, we have the opposite result: Demand for the original good decreases, shifting its demand curve to the left.

A **complement** is the opposite of a substitute: It's used *together with* the good we are interested in. Pancake mix is a complement to maple syrup, since these two goods are used frequently in combination. If the price of pancake mix rises, some consumers will switch to other breakfasts—bacon and eggs, for—example—that *don't* include maple syrup. The demand for maple syrup will decrease.

> *A rise in the price of a complement decreases the demand for a good, shifting the demand curve to the left.*

To test yourself: How would a higher price for cashmere sweaters affect the demand for dry-cleaning services? How would it affect the demand for cotton or polyester sweaters?

Population. As the population increases in an area, the number of buyers will ordinarily increase as well, and the demand for a good will increase. The growth of the U.S. population over the last 50 years has been an important reason (but not the only reason) for rightward shifts in the demand curves for food, housing, automobiles, and many other goods and services.

Expected Price. If buyers expect the price of maple syrup to rise next month, they may choose to purchase more *now* to stock up before the price hike. If people expect the price to drop, they may postpone buying, hoping to take advantage of the lower price later.

> *In many markets, an expectation that price will rise in the future shifts the current demand curve rightward, while an expectation that price will fall shifts the current demand curve leftward.*

DANGEROUS CURVES ⚠️

Income versus wealth It's easy to confuse *income* with *wealth*, because both are measured in dollars and both are sources of funds that can be spent on goods and services. But they are not the same thing. Your income is how much you earn *per period of time* (such as $20 *per hour*; $3,500 *per month*; or $40,000 *per year*). Your wealth, by contrast, is the value of what you own minus the value of what you owe at a particular *moment in time*. (For example, if on December 31, 2012, the value of what you own is $12,000, and you owe $9,000, then you have $3,000 in wealth on that date.)

Someone can have a high income and low or even negative wealth (such as college students who get good jobs after graduation but still owe a lot on their student loans). And a person with great wealth could have little or no income (for example, if they make especially bad investment choices and earn little or no income from their wealth).

© AXL/SHUTTERSTOCK.COM

Substitute A good that can be used in place of some other good and that fulfills more or less the same purpose.

Complement A good that is used together with some other good.

Expected price changes for goods are especially important for goods that can be purchased and stored until needed later. Expected price changes are also important in the markets for financial assets such as stocks and bonds and in the market for housing, as you'll see in the next chapter.

Tastes. Not everyone likes maple syrup. And among those who do, some *really* like it, and some like it just a little. Buyers' basic attitudes toward a good are based on their *tastes* or *preferences*. Economists are sometimes interested in where these tastes come from or what makes them change. But for the most part, economics deals with the *consequences* of a change in tastes, whatever the reason for its occurrence.

When tastes change *toward* a good (people favor it more), demand increases, and the demand curve shifts to the right. When tastes change *away* from a good, demand decreases, and the demand curve shifts to the left. An example of this is the change in tastes away from cigarettes over the past several decades. The cause

FIGURE 4   **The Demand Curve—A Summary**

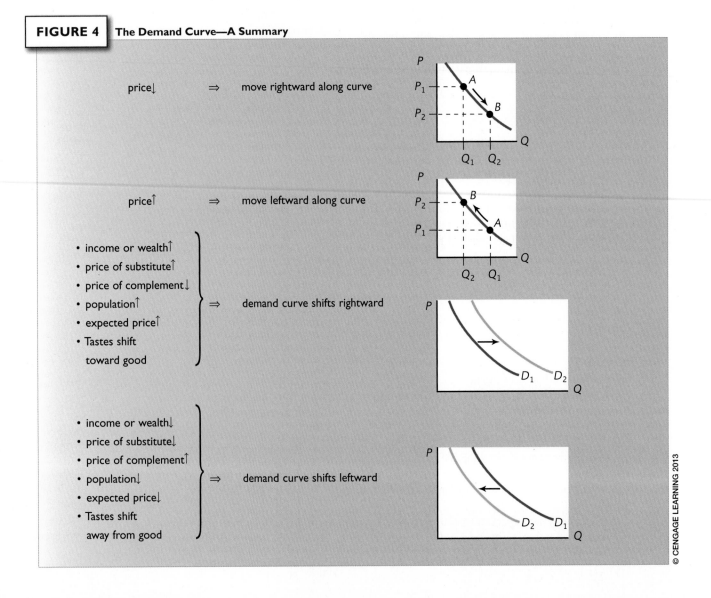

may have been an aging population, a greater concern about health among people of *all* ages, or successful antismoking advertising. But regardless of the cause, the effect has been to decrease the demand for cigarettes, shifting the demand curve to the left.

Other Shift Variables. Many other things, besides those we've discussed, can shift the demand curve. For example, if the government began to offer subsidies to households who buy maple syrup, demand would shift rightward. Also, if business firms (rather than just households) are among the buyers, then changes in the demand for their own products will influence their demand for maple syrup. We'll discuss additional shift variables in later chapters, as they become relevant.

Demand: A Summary

Figure 4 summarizes the key variables we've discussed that affect the demand side of the market and how their effects are represented with a demand curve. Notice the important distinction between events that move us *along* the curve (changes in price) and events that *shift* the curve.

SUPPLY

When most people hear the word *supply,* their first thought is that it's the amount of something "available," as if this amount were fixed in stone. For example, someone might say, "We can only drill so much oil from the ground," or "There are only so many apartments for rent in this town." And yet, the world's known oil reserves—as well as yearly production of oil—have increased dramatically over the last half century, as oil companies have found it worth their while to look harder for oil. Similarly, in many cities, low buildings have been replaced with high ones, and the number of apartments has increased. Supply, like demand, can change, and the amount of a good supplied in a market depends on the *choices* made by those who produce it.

What governs these choices? We assume that those who supply goods and services have a goal: to earn the highest profit possible. But suppliers also face constraints. First, in a competitive market, the price they can charge for their product is a *given*—the market price. Second, suppliers have to pay the *costs* of producing and selling their product. These costs will depend on the production process they use, the prices they must pay for their inputs, and more. Business firms' desire for profit, together with the real-world constraints that they face, determines how much they will choose to sell in any market. Hence, the following definition:

> ***Quantity supplied*** *is the number of units of a good that* all *sellers in the market would choose to sell over some time period, given the constraints that they face.*

Let's briefly go over the notion of quantity supplied to clarify what it means and doesn't mean.

Quantity supplied The specific amount of a good that all sellers in a market would choose to sell over some time period, given their constraints.

© AXL/SHUTTERSTOCK.COM

DANGEROUS CURVES

"Availability" and demand A common mistake is thinking that the amount of a good "available" should be a factor that influences demand. The reasoning might go like this: "If less maple syrup is available, people will have to buy less, so demand decreases." What's wrong with this? The most basic error involves forgetting that the demand curve comes from the answers to *hypothetical* questions, about how much people *would like* to buy at each price. A change in the amount available would not change how much people would *like* to buy at each price, and so it wouldn't affect the demand curve itself. As you'll see later in this chapter, changes in the amount of a good available *will* affect the price of the good and the amount ultimately bought. But this is represented by a movement along—not a shift of—the demand curve.

© JAMES MARSHALL/THE IMAGE WORKS

Quantity Supplied Implies a Choice. Quantity supplied doesn't tell us the amount of, say, maple syrup that sellers would like to sell *if* they could charge a thousand dollars for each bottle, and *if* they could produce it at zero cost. Instead, it's the quantity that firms *choose* to sell—the quantity that gives them the highest profit given the constraints they face.

Quantity Supplied Is Hypothetical. Will firms actually be *able* to sell the amount they want to sell at the going price? You'll soon see that they usually can. But the definition of quantity supplied makes no assumptions about firms' ability to sell the good. Quantity supplied answers the hypothetical question: How much *would* suppliers sell, given their constraints, if they were able to sell all that they wanted to?

Quantity Supplied Depends on Price.   The price of the good is just one variable among many that influences quantity supplied. But—as with demand—we want to keep that variable foremost in our thinking. This is why for the next couple of pages we'll assume that all other influences on supply are held constant, so we can explore the relationship between price and quantity supplied.

The Law of Supply

How does a change in price affect quantity supplied? When a seller can get a higher price for a good, producing and selling it become more profitable. Producers will devote more resources toward its production—perhaps even pulling resources from other goods they produce—so they can sell more of the good in question. For example, a rise in the price of laptop (but not desktop) computers will encourage computer makers to shift resources out of the production of other things (such as desktop computers) and toward the production of laptops.

In general, price and quantity supplied are *positively related:* When the price of a good rises, the quantity supplied will rise as well. This relationship between price and quantity supplied is called the law of supply, the counterpart to the law of demand we discussed earlier.

Law of supply As the price of a good increases, the quantity supplied increases.

> The **law of supply** states that when the price of a good rises, and everything else remains the same, the quantity of the good supplied will rise.

Once again, notice the very important words "everything else remains the same"— *ceteris paribus.* Although many variables influence the quantity of a good supplied, the law of supply tells us what would happen if all of them remained unchanged and only one—the price of the good—changed.

The Supply Schedule and the Supply Curve

Let's continue with our example of the market for maple syrup in the United States. Who are the suppliers in this market? Maple-syrup producers are located mostly in the forests of Vermont, upstate New York, and Canada. The market quantity supplied is the amount of syrup all of these producers together would offer for sale at each price for maple syrup in the United States.

Supply schedule A list showing the quantities of a good or service that firms would choose to produce and sell at different prices, with all other variables held constant.

Table 3 shows the **supply schedule** for maple syrup—a *list of different quantities supplied at different prices, with all other variables held constant.* As you can see, the supply schedule obeys the law of supply: As the price of maple syrup rises, the

TABLE 3

Supply Schedule for Maple Syrup in the United States

Price (per bottle)	Quantity Supplied (bottles per month)
$1.00	25,000
$2.00	40,000
$3.00	50,000
$4.00	60,000
$5.00	65,000

quantity supplied rises along with it. But how can this be? After all, maple trees must be about 40 years old before they can be tapped for syrup, so any rise in quantity supplied now or in the near future cannot come from an increase in planting. What, then, causes quantity supplied to rise as price rises?

Many things. With higher prices, firms will find it profitable to tap existing trees more intensively. Evaporating and bottling can be done more carefully, so that less maple syrup is spilled and more is available for shipping. Or syrup normally sold in other markets can be diverted and shipped to the U.S. market instead. For example, if the price of maple syrup rises in the United States (but not in Canada), producers would shift deliveries away from Canada so they could sell more in the United States, increasing supply to the U.S. market.

Now look at Figure 5, which shows a very important curve—the counterpart to the demand curve we drew earlier. In Figure 5, each point represents a price-quantity pair taken from Table 3. For example, point *F* in the figure corresponds to a price of $2.00 per bottle and a quantity of 40,000 bottles per month, while point *G* represents the price-quantity pair $4.00 and 60,000 bottles. Connecting all of these points with a solid line gives us the *supply curve* for maple syrup, labeled with an *S* in the figure.

FIGURE 5 **The Supply Curve**

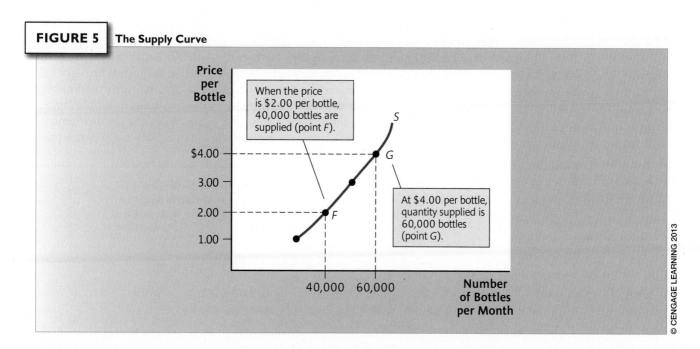

Supply curve A graph of a supply schedule, showing the quantity of a good or service supplied at various prices, with all other variables held constant.

> *The **supply curve** shows the relationship between the price of a good and the quantity supplied in the market, holding constant the values of all other variables that affect supply. Each point on the curve shows the quantity that sellers would choose to sell at a specific price.*

Notice that the supply curve in Figure 5—like all supply curves for goods and services—is *upward sloping*. This is the graphical representation of the law of supply.

Shifts versus Movements Along the Supply Curve

As with the demand curve, it's important to distinguish those events that will cause us to *move along* a given supply curve for the good, and those that will cause the entire supply curve to *shift*.

If you look once again at Figure 5, you'll see that if the price of maple syrup rises from $2.00 to $4.00 per bottle, the number of bottles supplied rises from 40,000 to 60,000. This is a movement *along* the supply curve, from point *F* to point *G*. In general,

> *a change in the price of a good causes a movement* along *the supply curve.*

In the figure, a *rise* in price would cause us to move *rightward* along the supply curve (from point *F* to point *G*) and a *fall* in price would move us *leftward* along the curve (from point *G* to point *F*).

But remember that when we draw a supply curve, we assume that all other variables that might influence supply are *held constant* at some particular values. For example, the supply curve in Figure 5 might tell us the quantity supplied at each price when the cost of an important input—transportation from the farm to the point of sale—remains constant.

But suppose the cost of transportation drops. Then, at any given price for maple syrup, firms would find it more profitable to produce and sell it. This is illustrated in Table 4. With the original transportation cost, and a selling price of $4.00 per bottle, firms would choose to sell 60,000 bottles. But after transportation cost falls, they would choose to produce and sell more—80,000 bottles in our example—assuming they could still charge $4.00 per bottle. A similar change would occur for any other price of maple syrup we might imagine: After transportation costs fall, firms would choose to sell more than before. In other words, *the entire relationship between price and quantity supplied has changed,* so we have a *new* supply curve.

Figure 6 plots the new supply curve from the quantities in the third column of Table 4. The new supply curve lies to the *right* of the old one. For example, at a price

TABLE 4

Increase in Supply of Maple Syrup in the United States

Price (per bottle)	Original Quantity Supplied	Quantity Supplied After Decrease in Transportation Cost
$1.00	25,000	45,000
$2.00	40,000	60,000
$3.00	50,000	70,000
$4.00	60,000	80,000
$5.00	65,000	90,000

| FIGURE 6 | A Shift of the Supply Curve |

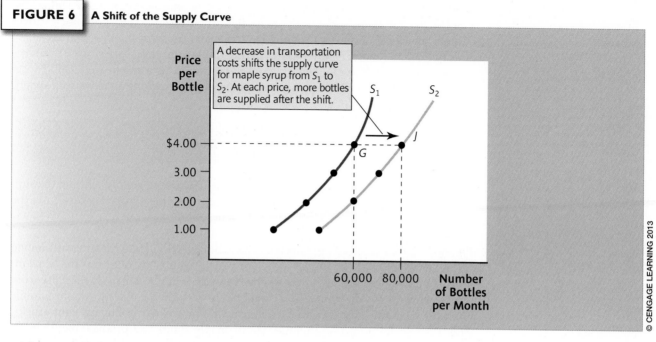

A decrease in transportation costs shifts the supply curve for maple syrup from S_1 to S_2. At each price, more bottles are supplied after the shift.

of $4.00, quantity supplied increases from 60,000 bottles on the old curve (point *G*) to 80,000 bottles on the *new* supply curve (point *J*). The drop in the transportation costs has *shifted* the supply curve to the right.

In general,

> *a change in any variable that affects supply—except for the good's price— causes the supply curve to shift.*

If sellers want to sell a greater quantity at any price, the supply curve shifts *right-ward*. If sellers would prefer to sell a smaller quantity at any price, the supply curve shifts *leftward*.

Change in Quantity Supplied versus Change in Supply

As we stressed in our discussion of the demand side of the market, be careful about language when thinking about supply. The term *quantity supplied* means a *particular amount* that sellers would choose to sell at a *particular* price, represented by a single point on the supply curve. The term *supply,* however, means the *entire relationship* between price and quantity supplied, as represented by the entire supply curve.

For this reason, when the price of the good changes, and we move *along* the supply curve, we have a **change in quantity supplied.** For example, in Figure 5, the movement from point *F* to point *G* is an *increase* in quantity supplied.

When something *other* than the price changes, causing the entire supply curve to shift, we call it a **change in supply.** The shift in Figure 6, for example, would be called an *increase in supply*.

Change in quantity supplied A movement along a supply curve in response to a change in price.

Change in supply A shift of a supply curve in response to a change in some variable other than price.

Factors That Shift the Supply Curve

Let's look at some of the *causes* of a change in supply (a shift of the supply curve). As always, we're considering *one* variable at a time, keeping all other determinants of supply constant.

Input Prices.   In Figure 6, we saw that a drop in transportation costs shifted the supply curve for maple syrup to the right. But producers of maple syrup use a variety of other inputs besides transportation: land, maple trees, sap pans, evaporators, labor, glass bottles, and more. A lower price for any of these means a lower cost of producing and selling maple syrup, making it more profitable. As a result, we would expect producers to shift resources into maple syrup production, causing an increase in supply.

In general,

> *a fall in the price of an input causes an increase in supply, shifting the supply curve to the right.*

Similarly, a rise in the price of an input causes a decrease in supply, shifting the supply curve to the left. If, for example, the wages of maple syrup workers rose, the supply curve in Figure 6 would shift to the left.

Price of Alternatives.   Many firms can switch their production rather easily among several different goods or services, each of which requires more or less the same inputs. For example, a dermatology practice can rather easily switch its specialty from acne treatments for the young to wrinkle treatments for the elderly. An automobile producer can—without too much adjustment—switch to producing light trucks. And a maple syrup producer could dry its maple syrup and produce maple *sugar* instead. Or it could even cut down its maple trees and sell maple wood as lumber. These other goods that firms *could* produce are called **alternate goods** and their prices influence the supply curve.

Alternate goods Other goods that firms in a market could produce instead of the good in question.

For example, if the price of maple *sugar* rose, then at any given price for maple *syrup,* producers would shift some production from syrup to sugar. This would be a decrease in the supply of maple syrup.

Another alternative for the firm is to sell the *same* good in a *different* market, which we'll call an **alternate market.** For example, since we are considering the market for maple syrup in the United States, the maple syrup market in Canada is a different market for producers. For any given price in the United States, a rise in the price of maple syrup in Canada will cause producers to shift some sales from the United States to Canada. In the U.S. market, this will cause the supply curve to shift leftward.

Alternate market A market other than the one being analyzed in which the same good could be sold.

> *When the price for an alternative rises—either an alternate good or the same good in an alternate market—the supply curve shifts leftward.*

Similarly, a decrease in the price of an alternate good (or a lower price in an alternate market) will shift the supply curve rightward.

Technology.   A *technological advance* in production occurs whenever a firm can produce a given level of output in a new and cheaper way than before.

Examples would include a new, more efficient tap that draws more maple syrup from each tree, or a new bottling method that reduces spillage. Advances like these would reduce the cost of producing maple syrup, making it more profitable, and producers would want to make and sell more of it at any price.

In general,

> *cost-saving technological advances increase the supply of a good, shifting the supply curve to the right.*

Number of Firms.   A change in the number of firms in a market will change the quantity that all sellers together would want to sell at any given price. For example, if—over time—more people decided to open up maple syrup farms because it was a profitable business, the supply of maple syrup would increase. And if maple syrup farms began closing down, their number would be reduced and supply would decrease.

> *An increase in the number of sellers—with no other change—shifts the supply curve rightward.*

Expected Price.   Imagine you're the president of Sticky's Maple Syrup, Inc., and you expect the market price of maple syrup—over which you, as an individual seller, have no influence—to rise next month. What would you do? You might want to postpone selling some of your maple syrup until later, when the price and your profit would be higher. Therefore, at any given price *now,* you might slow down production, or just slow down sales by warehousing more of what you produce. If other firms have similar expectations of a price hike, they'll do the same. Thus, an expectation of a *future* price hike will decrease supply *in the present.*

Suppose instead you expect the market price to *drop* next month. Then—at any given price—you'd want to sell more *now,* by stepping up production and even selling out of your inventories. So an expected future drop in the price would cause an increase in supply in the present.

Expected price is especially important when suppliers can hold inventories of goods for later sale, or when they can easily shift production from one time period to another.

> *In many markets, an expectation of a* future price rise *shifts the current supply curve* leftward. *Similarly, an expectation of a* future price drop *shifts the current supply curve* rightward.

Changes in Weather and Other Natural Events.   Weather conditions are an especially important determinant of the supply of agricultural goods.

> Favorable weather *increases crop yields, and causes a* rightward *shift of the supply curve for that crop.* Unfavorable weather *destroys crops and shrinks yields, and shifts the supply curve* leftward.

In addition to bad weather, natural disasters such as fires, hurricanes, and earthquakes can destroy or disrupt the productive capacity of *all* firms in a region. If many sellers of a particular good are located in the affected area, the supply curve for that good will shift leftward.

For example, companies in the industrial northeast of Japan are major global suppliers of many goods, including semiconductors, solar panels, automobiles and auto parts, steel, beer, paper, and more. When a powerful earthquake and tsunami struck Japan in 2011, it destroyed or disabled many factories and much of the transportation network in the area. Supply curves in global markets for those goods shifted leftward for weeks, and, in some cases, months, until production was restored.

Other Shift Variables.   Many other things besides those listed earlier can shift the supply curve. For example, a government tax imposed on maple syrup producers

would raise the cost of making and selling maple syrup. To suppliers, this would have the same effect as a higher price for transportation: It would shift the supply curve leftward. We'll discuss other shift variables for supply as they become relevant in this and later chapters.

Supply—A Summary

Figure 7 summarizes the various factors we've discussed that affect the supply side of the market, and how we illustrate them using a supply curve. As with demand, notice which events move us along the supply curve (changes in price) and which shift the curve. To test yourself, you might want to create a list of the shift variables in Figure 4 and Figure 7, in random order. Then explain, for each item, which curve shifts and in which direction.

FIGURE 7   **The Supply Curve—A Summary**

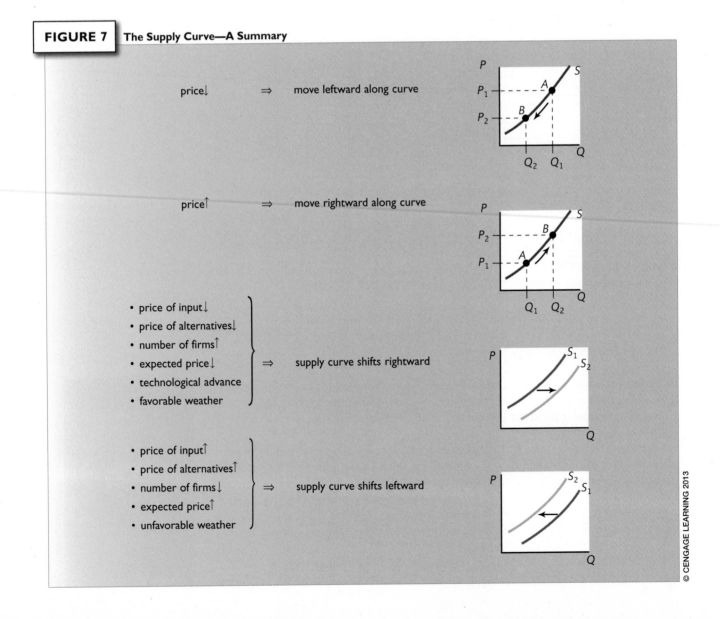

price↓   ⇒   move leftward along curve

price↑   ⇒   move rightward along curve

- price of input↓
- price of alternatives↓
- number of firms↑   ⇒   supply curve shifts rightward
- expected price↓
- technological advance
- favorable weather

- price of input↑
- price of alternatives↑
- number of firms↓   ⇒   supply curve shifts leftward
- expected price↑
- unfavorable weather

PUTTING SUPPLY AND DEMAND TOGETHER

Now that we've considered the demand and supply sides of the market separately, it's time to put the two sides together. As you are about to see, combining demand and supply will tell us how a market's price is determined.

Let's start by asking: What happens when buyers and sellers, each having the desire to trade, come together in a market? The two sides of the market certainly have different agendas. Buyers would like to pay the lowest possible price, while sellers would like to charge the highest possible price. Is there chaos when they meet, with each trade taking place at a wildly different price than the others? A casual look at the real world suggests not. In most markets, most of the time, there is order and stability in the encounters between buyers and sellers. In most cases, prices do not fluctuate wildly from moment to moment but seem to hover around a stable value. Even when this stability is short-lived—lasting only a day, an hour, or even a few minutes in some markets—for this brief time the market seems to be at rest. Whenever we study a market, therefore, we look for this state of rest—a price at which the market seems to settle, at least for a while.

Economists use the word *equilibrium* when referring to a state of rest. When a market is in equilibrium, both the price of the good and the quantity bought and sold each period have settled into a state of rest. More formally,

> the **equilibrium price** and **equilibrium quantity** are values for price and quantity in the market that, once achieved, will remain constant—unless and until the supply curve or the demand curve shifts.

Equilibrium price The market price that, once achieved, remains constant until either the demand curve or supply curve shifts.

Equilibrium quantity The market quantity bought and sold per period that, once achieved, remains constant until either the demand curve or supply curve shifts.

Finding the Equilibrium Price and Quantity

Look at Table 5, which combines the supply and demand schedules for maple syrup from Tables 1 and 3. We'll use Table 5 to find the equilibrium price in this market through the process of elimination.

Prices below the Equilibrium Price

Let's first ask what would happen if the price were less than $3.00 per bottle— say, $1.00. At this price, Table 5 tells us that buyers would want to buy 75,000 bottles each month, while sellers would offer to sell only 25,000. There would be an **excess demand** of 50,000 bottles. What would happen in this case? Buyers would

Excess demand At a given price, the amount by which quantity demanded exceeds quantity supplied.

TABLE 5

Finding the Market Equilibrium

Price (per bottle)	Original Demanded (bottles per month)	Quantity Supplied (bottles per month)	Excess Demand or Supply?	Consequence
$1.00	75,000	25,000	Excess Demand	Price will Rise
$2.00	60,000	40,000	Excess Demand	Price will Rise
$3.00	**50,000**	**50,000**	**Neither**	**No Change in price**
$4.00	40,000	60,000	Excess Supply	Price will Fall
$5.00	35,000	65,000	Excess Supply	Price will Fall

© CENGAGE LEARNING 2013

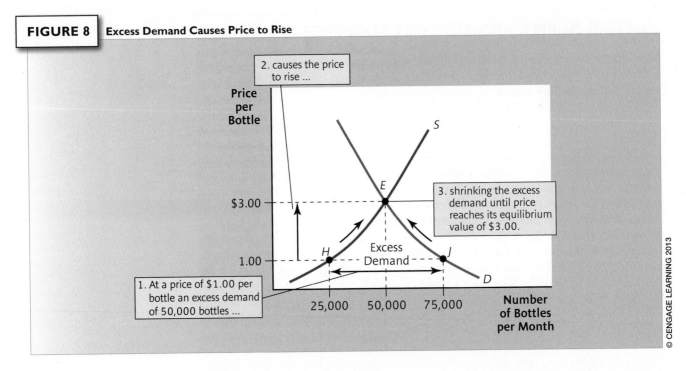

FIGURE 8   Excess Demand Causes Price to Rise

2. causes the price to rise ...

Price per Bottle

S

E

$3.00

3. shrinking the excess demand until price reaches its equilibrium value of $3.00.

H   Excess
1.00   Demand   J

D

25,000   50,000   75,000   Number of Bottles per Month

1. At a price of $1.00 per bottle an excess demand of 50,000 bottles ...

© CENGAGE LEARNING 2013

compete with each other to get more maple syrup than was available, and they would offer to pay a higher price rather than do without. The price would then rise. The same would occur if the price were $2.00 or any other price below $3.00.

We conclude that any price less than $3.00 cannot be an equilibrium price. If the price starts below $3.00, it would start rising—*not* because the supply curve or the demand curve had shifted, but from natural forces within the market itself. This directly contradicts our definition of equilibrium price.

Figure 8 illustrates the same process by putting the supply and demand curves together on the same graph. As you can see, at a price of $1.00, quantity supplied of 25,000 bottles is found at point *H* on the supply curve, while quantity demanded is at point *J* on the demand curve. The horizontal difference between the two curves at $1.00 is a graphical representation of the excess demand at that price. This excess demand would cause the price to rise.

How far will the price rise? Since excess demand is the only reason for the price to rise, it will stop rising when the excess demand is gone. And as you can see in Figure 8, the rise in price *shrinks* the excess demand in two ways. First, as price rises, buyers demand a smaller quantity—a leftward movement along the demand curve (from point *J* to point *E*). Second, sellers increase supply to a larger quantity—a rightward movement along the supply curve (from point *H* to point *E*). Finally, when the price reaches $3.00 per bottle, the excess demand is gone and the price stops rising.

This logic tells us that $3.00 is an *equilibrium* price in this market—a value that won't change as long as the supply and demand curves stay put.

Prices above the Equilibrium Price

We've shown that any price *below* $3.00 is not an equilibrium in our example. But could some price *above* $3.00—say, $5.00—be an equilibrium? Let's see.

Look again at Table 5. If the price were $5.00, quantity supplied would be 65,000 bottles per month, while quantity demanded would be only 35,000 bottles. There would be an **excess supply** of 30,000 bottles. Sellers would compete with each

Excess supply At a given price, the amount by which quantity supplied exceeds quantity demanded.

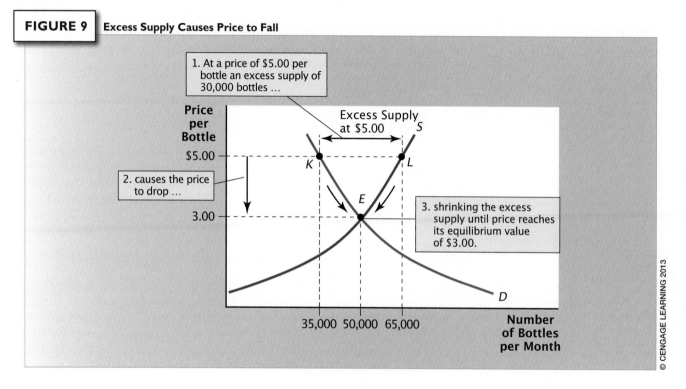

FIGURE 9 Excess Supply Causes Price to Fall

1. At a price of $5.00 per bottle an excess supply of 30,000 bottles ...

Price per Bottle

Excess Supply at $5.00

S

$5.00

K   L

2. causes the price to drop ...

E

3.00

3. shrinking the excess supply until price reaches its equilibrium value of $3.00.

D

35,000 50,000 65,000

Number of Bottles per Month

© CENGAGE LEARNING 2013

other to sell more maple syrup than buyers wanted to buy, and the price would fall. Thus, $5.00 cannot be the equilibrium price.

Figure 9 provides a graphical view of the market in this situation. With a price of $5.00, the excess supply is the horizontal distance between points K (on the demand curve) and L (on the supply curve). In the figure, the resulting drop in price would move us along both the supply curve (leftward) and the demand curve (rightward). As these movements continued, the excess supply of maple syrup would shrink until it disappeared, once again, at a price of $3.00 per bottle. Our conclusion: If the price happens to be above $3.00, it will fall to $3.00 and then stop changing.

You can see that $3.00 is the equilibrium price—and the *only* equilibrium price— in this market. Moreover, at this price, sellers would want to sell 50,000 bottles—the same quantity that households would want to buy. So, when price comes to rest at $3.00, quantity comes to rest at 50,000 per month—the *equilibrium quantity*.

Equilibrium on a Graph

No doubt, you have noticed that $3.00 happens to be the price at which the supply and demand curves cross. This leads us to an easy, graphical technique for locating our equilibrium:

> *To find the equilibrium in a competitive market, draw the supply and demand curves. Market equilibrium occurs where the two curves cross. At this crossing point, the equilibrium price is found on the vertical axis, and the equilibrium quantity on the horizontal axis.*

Notice that, in equilibrium, the market is operating on *both* the supply curve *and* the demand curve so that—at a price of $3.00—quantity demanded and quantity supplied are equal. There are no dissatisfied buyers unable to find goods they want to purchase, nor are there any frustrated sellers unable to sell goods they want to sell. Indeed, this is why $3.00 is the equilibrium price. It's the only price that creates consistency between what buyers choose to buy and sellers choose to sell.

But we don't expect a market to stay at any particular equilibrium forever, as you're about to see.

WHAT HAPPENS WHEN THINGS CHANGE?

Remember that in order to draw the supply and demand curves in the first place, we had to assume particular values for all the other variables—besides price—that affect demand and supply. If one of these variables changes, then either the supply curve or the demand curve will shift, and our equilibrium will change as well. Let's look at some examples.

Example: Income Rises, Causing an Increase in Demand

In Figure 10, point E shows an initial equilibrium in the U.S. market for maple syrup, with an equilibrium price of $3.00 per bottle and an equilibrium quantity of 50,000 bottles per month. Suppose that the incomes of buyers rise. We know that income is one of the shift variables in the demand curve (but not the supply curve). We also can reason that real maple syrup is a *normal good* (people want more as their income rises), so the demand curve will shift rightward. What happens then?

The old price—$3.00—is no longer the equilibrium price. How do we know? Because if the price *did* remain at $3.00 after the demand curve shifted, there would be an excess demand that would drive the price upward. The new equilibrium—at

| FIGURE 10 | A Shift in Demand and a New Equilibrium |

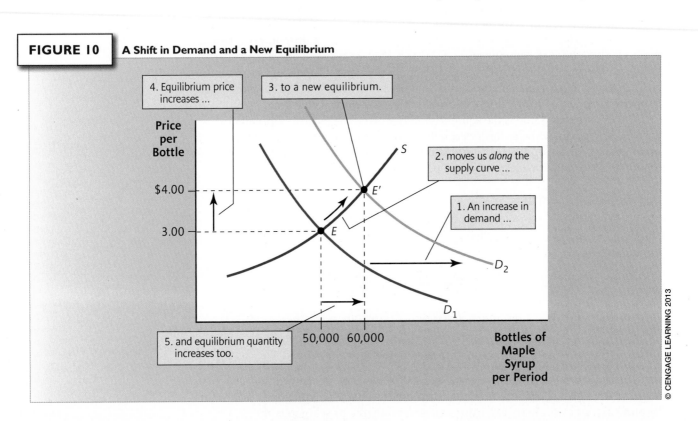

4. Equilibrium price increases ...

3. to a new equilibrium.

2. moves us *along* the supply curve ...

1. An increase in demand ...

5. and equilibrium quantity increases too.

© CENGAGE LEARNING 2013

point E'—is the new intersection point of the curves *after* the shift in the demand curve. Comparing the original equilibrium at point E with the new one at point E', we find that the shift in demand has caused the equilibrium price to rise (from $3.00 to $4.00) and the equilibrium quantity to rise as well (from 50,000 to 60,000 bottles per month).

Notice, too, that in moving from point E to point E', we move *along* the supply curve. That is, a shift of the demand curve has caused a movement along the supply curve. Why is this? The demand shift causes the *price* to rise, and a rise in price always causes a movement *along* the supply curve. But the supply curve itself does not shift because none of the variables that affect sellers—other than the price of the good—has changed.

In this example, income rose. But *any* event that shifted the demand curve rightward would have the same effect on price and quantity. For example, if tastes changed in favor of maple syrup, or a substitute good like jam rose in price, or a complementary good like pancake mix became cheaper, the demand curve for maple syrup would shift rightward, just as it did in Figure 10. So, we can summarize our findings as follows:

The Endless Loop of Erroneous Logic In trying to work out what happens after, say, a rise in income, you might find yourself caught in an endless loop. It goes something like this: "A rise in income causes an increase in demand. An increase in demand causes the price to rise. A higher price causes supply to increase. Greater supply causes the price to fall. A lower price increases demand ..." and so on, without end. The price keeps bobbing up and down, forever.

What's the mistake here? The first two statements ("a rise in income causes an increase in demand" and "an increase in demand causes price to rise") are entirely correct. But the next statement ("a higher price causes an increase in supply") is wrong, and so is everything that follows. A higher price does *not*, by itself, cause an "increase in supply" (a shift of the supply curve). It causes an increase in *quantity supplied* (a movement *along* the supply curve).

Here's the correct sequence of events: "A rise in income causes an increase in demand. An increase in demand causes price to rise. A higher price causes an increase in *quantity supplied,* moving us along the supply curve until we reach the new equilibrium, with a higher price and greater quantity."

> *A rightward shift in the demand curve causes a rightward movement* along *the supply curve. Equilibrium price and equilibrium quantity both rise.*

Example: Bad Weather, Supply Decreases

Unfavorable weather can affect supply for most agricultural goods, including maple syrup. An example occurred in 2007 and 2008, when abnormal weather patterns in Quebec and the northeastern U.S. slowed the flow of sap from maple trees. How did this affect the market for maple syrup?

As you've learned, weather can be a shift variable for the supply curve. Look at Figure 11. Initially, the supply curve for maple syrup is S_1, with the market in equilibrium at Point E. When bad weather hits, the supply curve shifts leftward— say, to S_2. The result: a rise in the equilibrium price of maple syrup (from $3.00 to $5.00 in the figure) and a fall in the equilibrium quantity (from 50,000 to 35,000 bottles).

Any event that shifts the supply curve leftward would have similar effects. For example, if the wages of maple syrup workers increase, or some maple syrup producers go out of business and sell their farms to housing developers, the supply curve for maple syrup would shift leftward, just as in Figure 11.

More generally,

> *A leftward shift of the supply curve causes a leftward movement* along *the demand curve. Equilibrium price rises, but equilibrium quantity falls.*

FIGURE 11   **A Shift of Supply and a New Equilibrium**

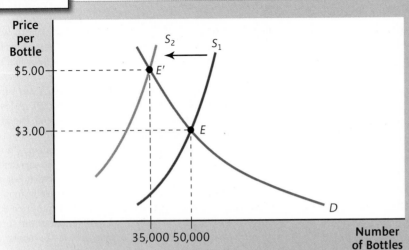

Unfavorable weather causes supply to decrease from S_1 to S_2. At the old equilibrium price of $3.00, there is now an excess demand. As a result, the price increases until excess demand is eliminated at point E′. In the new equilibrium, quantity demanded again equals quantity supplied. The price is higher, and fewer bottles are produced and sold.

Example: Higher Income and Bad Weather Together

So far, we've considered examples in which just one curve shifts due to a change in a single variable that influences *either* demand or supply. But what would happen if two changes affected the market simultaneously? Then both curves would shift.

Figure 12 shows what happens when we take the two factors we've just explored separately (a rise in income and bad weather) and combine them together. The rise in income causes the demand curve to shift rightward, from D_1 to D_2. The bad weather causes the supply curve to shift leftward, from S_1 to S_2. The result of all this is a change in equilibrium from point E to point $E′$, where the new demand curve D_2 intersects the new supply curve S_2.

Notice that the equilibrium price rises from $3.00 to $6.00 in our example. This should come as no surprise. A rightward shift in the demand curve, with no other change, causes price to rise. And a leftward shift in the supply curve, with no other change, causes price to rise. So when we combine the two shifts together, the price must rise. In fact, the increase in the price will be greater than would be caused by either shift alone.

But what about equilibrium quantity? Here, the two shifts work in *opposite* directions. The rightward shift in demand works to increase quantity, while the leftward shift in supply works to decrease quantity. We can't say what will happen to equilibrium quantity until we know which shift is greater and thus has the greater influence. Quantity could rise, fall, or remain unchanged.

In Figure 12, it just so happens that the supply curve shifts more than the demand curve, so equilibrium quantity falls. But you can easily prove to yourself that the other outcomes are possible. First, draw a graph where the demand curve shifts rightward by more than the supply curve shifts leftward. In your graph, you'll see that equilibrium quantity rises. Then,

⚠ **DANGEROUS CURVES**

Do Curves Shift Up and Down? Or Right and Left? When describing an increase in demand or supply, it's tempting to say "upward" instead of "rightward." Similarly, for a decrease, it's tempting to say "downward." But be careful! While this interchangeable language works for the demand curve, it does *not* work for the supply curve.

To prove this to yourself, look at Figure 6. There you can see that a rightward shift of the supply curve (an increase in supply) is also a *downward* shift. In later chapters, it will sometimes make sense to describe shifts as upward or downward. For now, it's best to avoid these terms and stick with *rightward* and *leftward*.

FIGURE 12   A Shift in Both Curves and a New Equilibrium

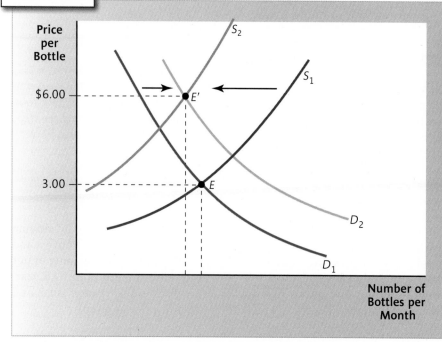

An increase in income shifts the demand curve rightward from D_1 to D_2. At the same time, bad weather shifts the supply curve leftward from S_1 to S_2. The equilibrium moves from point E to point E'. While the price must rise after these shifts, quantity could rise or fall or remain the same, depending on the relative sizes of the shifts. In the figure, quantity happens to fall.

draw one where both curves shift (in opposite directions) by equal amounts, and you'll see that equilibrium quantity remains unchanged.

We can also imagine other combinations of shifts. A rightward or leftward shift in either curve can be combined with a rightward or leftward shift in the other.

Table 6 lists all the possible combinations. It also shows what happens to equilibrium price and quantity in each case, and when the result is ambiguous (a question mark). For example, the top left entry tells us that when both the supply and demand curves shift rightward, the equilibrium *quantity* will always rise, but the equilibrium price could rise, fall, or remain unchanged, depending on the relative *size* of the shifts.

Do *not* try to memorize the entries in Table 6. Instead, remember the advice in Chapter 1: to study economics actively, rather than passively. This would be a good time to put down the book, pick up a pencil and paper, and see whether you can

TABLE 6

Effect of Simultaneous Shifts in Supply and Demand

	Increase in Demand (Rightward Shift)	No Change in Demand	Decrease in Demand (Leftward Shift)
• Increase in Supply (Rightward Shift)	$P?Q\uparrow$	$P\downarrow Q\uparrow$	$P\downarrow Q?$
• No change in Supply	$P\uparrow Q\uparrow$	No change in P or Q	$P\downarrow Q\downarrow$
• Decrease in Supply (Leftward Shift)	$P\uparrow Q?$	$P\uparrow Q\downarrow$	$P?Q\downarrow$

draw a graph to illustrate each of the nine possible results in the table. When you see a question mark for an ambiguous result, determine which shift would have to be greater for the variable to rise or to fall.

THE THREE-STEP PROCESS

In this chapter, we built a model—a supply and demand model—and then used it to analyze price changes in several markets. You may not have noticed it, but we took three distinct steps as the chapter proceeded. Economists take these same three steps to answer many questions about the economy, as you'll see throughout this book.

Let's review these steps:

Step 1—Characterize the Market: *Decide which market or markets best suit the problem being analyzed, and identify how trading occurs in that market.*

In economics, we make sense of the very complex, real-world economy by viewing it as a collection of *markets*. Each of these markets involves a group of buyers and sellers who have the potential to trade with each other. At the very beginning of our analysis, we must decide which market or markets to look at (such as the U.S. market for maple syrup), and specify how trading takes place in that market (such as a competitive market with buyers and sellers who take the price as given).

Step 2—Find the Equilibrium: *Describe the conditions necessary for equilibrium in the market, and a method for determining that equilibrium.*

Once we've defined a market, and put buyers and sellers together, we look for the point at which the market will come to rest—the equilibrium. In this chapter, we used supply and demand to find the equilibrium price and quantity in a competitive market, but this is just one example of how economists apply Step 2.

Step 3—What Happens When Things Change: *Explore how events or government policies change the market equilibrium.*

Once you've found the equilibrium, the next step is to ask how different events will *change* it. In this chapter, for example, we explored how rising income or bad weather (or both together) would affect the equilibrium price and quantity for maple syrup.

Economists follow this same three-step procedure to analyze important questions in both microeconomics and macroeconomics. In this book, we'll be taking these three steps again and again, and we'll often call them to your attention. In fact, we're about to use them again, in the Using the Theory section that follows.

THE PRICE OF OIL

Every day, the world produces about 90 million barrels of oil and uses up the same amount making and delivering almost all the products we consume. So when the price of oil changes, every part of the economy is affected. Rapid rises in oil prices have contributed to economic downturns in the U.S. and other countries. And because oil consumption contributes to greenhouse gas emissions, the quantity of oil produced and consumed has important implications for climate change. Not surprisingly, economists are often asked to explain the past behavior of oil's price and quantity and to predict how they might change in the future.

Figure 13 provides data on price and quantity in what is called the oil *spot market*—where actual barrels of crude oil are bought and sold. (There is also a *futures* market for oil, where people buy and sell contracts promising future delivery of oil. Futures contracts amount to "side bets" on the future price and normally have little direct impact on the current price in the spot market.)

The upper panel plots the average monthly spot price of oil (dollars per barrel) from January 2005 through mid-2011. We'll be analyzing three periods—labeled with arrows—during which the price of oil changed rapidly. The slopes of the arrows tell us the direction that oil prices changed during each period.

The lower panel shows world oil *production* (millions of barrels per day) over the same time frame, with the same three episodes labeled. But this time, the slopes of the arrows indicate the direction of change for production, rather than price.

Why did oil prices change so rapidly during these episodes? The three-step process—along with the supply and demand model you learned in this chapter—can help us answer. Let's go through each step carefully.

Characterize the Market

We'll view the market for oil as a *global* market. It costs just a couple of dollars to ship a barrel of oil halfway around the world, so oil sellers and oil buyers around the globe can easily trade with each other. And our goal is to explain why oil prices changed worldwide, rather than in any particular country or region.

We'll also view the market for oil as *competitive*, and use supply and demand in our analysis. Is this realistic? Yes… and no. Virtually all oil buyers, and many of the world's oil sellers, do take the market price as a given. When the price rises, these sellers want to produce and sell more, while the buyers want to purchase less.

But about a third of the world's oil is produced by the large, government-run companies that belong to OPEC (Organization of Petroleum Exporting Countries). OPEC producers often behave like private producers—viewing the price of oil as a given and changing their quantity supplied when the price changes. But sometimes, OPEC members act in concert to *influence* the market price by intentionally changing their total production. Because OPEC produces so much of the world's oil, an artificial change in OPEC's total production can shift the market supply curve significantly rightward or leftward, and thereby change the market price. (One of the OPEC countries—Saudi Arabia—is such a large producer that it can artificially shift the market supply curve all by itself.)

However, while OPEC can shift the supply curve, it cannot change one important fact about the oil market: The price rapidly adjusts to the *equilibrium* price, which is where the supply and demand curves intersect. So in the market for oil—as in the market for maple syrup—the model of supply and demand will help us explain why prices change.

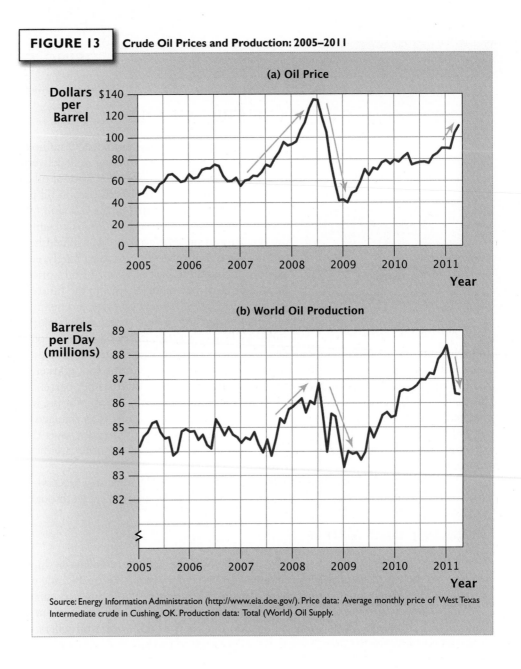

| FIGURE 13 | Crude Oil Prices and Production: 2005–2011 |

(a) Oil Price

Dollars per Barrel (vertical axis: $140, 120, 100, 80, 60, 40, 20, 0)

Year (horizontal axis: 2005, 2006, 2007, 2008, 2009, 2010, 2011)

(b) World Oil Production

Barrels per Day (millions) (vertical axis: 89, 88, 87, 86, 85, 84, 83, 82)

Year (horizontal axis: 2005, 2006, 2007, 2008, 2009, 2010, 2011)

Source: Energy Information Administration (http://www.eia.doe.gov/). Price data: Average monthly price of West Texas Intermediate crude in Cushing, OK. Production data: Total (World) Oil Supply.

Find the Equilibrium

Figure 14 shows market supply and demand curves for oil. The demand curve slopes downward, telling us that a rise in price, *ceteris paribus*, decreases the total quantity demanded in the market.[1] The supply curve slopes upward, telling us that a rise in price, *ceteris paribus*, increases the total quantity supplied to the market. The equilibrium price occurs where quantity supplied and demanded are equal. The curves in Figure 14

---

[1] Note that while ordinary households don't buy crude oil, they buy many goods and services—gasoline, motor oil, heating oil, electricity, plastic garbage bags, and more—that are made from oil. It is the manufacturers of these products—the actual buyers of oil—that want to purchase less oil when its price rises.

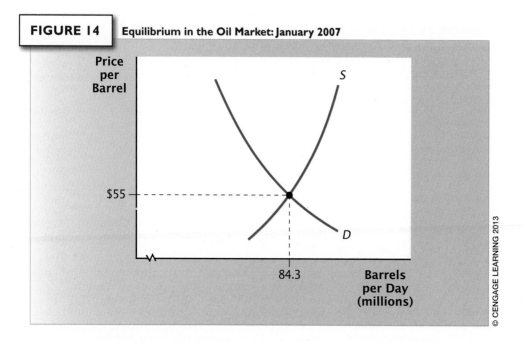

FIGURE 14   Equilibrium in the Oil Market: January 2007

have been drawn to illustrate the equilibrium in January 2007, when the price aver-aged $55 per barrel, and world production averaged 84.3 million barrels per day.

What Happens When Things Change?

When we looked at the market for maple syrup, you saw how an event (such as bad weather) changed the equilibrium price and quantity. Now let's do the same for oil, focusing on each of the three episodes marked in Figure 13.

January 2007 to July 2008: Oil Prices Spike Upward

From January 2007 to July 2008, oil prices rose from $55 to $133 per barrel. As a result, gasoline prices shot up around the globe (and rose from $2.27 to $4.11 per gallon in the United States). Some commentators on cable news shows and blogs argued that the price spike could *not* be explained by supply and demand, because total oil production was rising, not falling. Since more oil was being produced than ever before, they argued, supply and demand would predict a *lower* price, not the higher price we observed. The pundits suggested that some other explanation—such as a conspiracy among oil traders—must have been at fault.

While these commentators were right that oil production was rapidly rising (see the lower panel of Figure 13), their belief that the price should have been falling is *not* correct. As you've learned, price and quantity can rise together when the demand curve shifts rightward. And in 2007 and early 2008, all the evidence pointed to a significant, rapid rightward shift in demand. As Figure 15 shows, a rightward shift in demand—with no shift in supply—causes both price *and* quantity to rise.

But why did demand increase so rapidly?

Let's go back a bit. Even before 2007, the world's total production of goods and services—and the incomes of those who produced them—were growing at a rapid pace. And in 2007 and early 2008, growth accelerated. Not only were the advanced

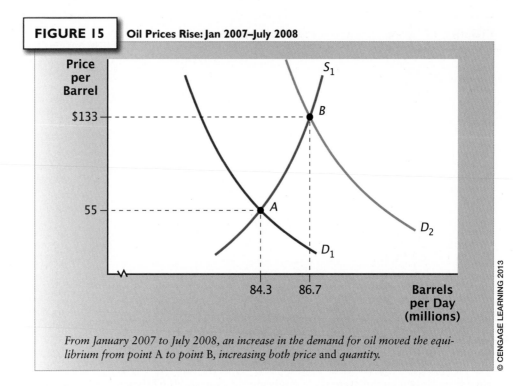

FIGURE 15   **Oil Prices Rise: Jan 2007–July 2008**

From January 2007 to July 2008, an increase in the demand for oil moved the equilibrium from point A to point B, increasing both price and quantity.

economies continuing to recover from earlier slowdowns, but several emerging economies grew especially fast. For example, incomes in China—which had been growing at 8 or 9 percent per year (already high)—grew by 12% in 2007. India's growth rate increased as well, from just under 6% to more than 9% per year. Moreover, these higher incomes enabled millions of people in emerging economies to afford cars for the first time, leading to a huge increase in demand for gasoline (and the crude oil from which gasoline is made). These changes caused the demand curve for oil to shift rightward.

If increases in supply had kept pace with the increases in demand, the price of oil would not have risen. (You can see this by drawing your own graph, in which both curves shift rightward by the same amount.) But during this period, no major new oil field was brought into production, and no new cost-saving technology was discovered. Nothing happened that might have shifted the supply curve significantly rightward. (Note that oil *production* rose, but this was a *movement along*—not a shift—of the supply curve.) So we had a rightward shift in demand, with no significant shift in supply, causing the price of oil to rise.

July 2008 to February 2009: Oil Prices Collapse

Look again at Figure 13, for the period from July 2008 to February 2009. In the upper panel, the price of oil plunged from $133 to $39 per barrel, while in the lower panel, oil production fell sharply, from 86.7 million to 83.8 million barrels per day. This change in price and quantity—the opposite of the one we just discussed—was caused by a *leftward* shift of demand, as shown in Figure 16.

Why did the demand curve shift leftward? In 2008, many of the world's economies suffered severe recessions. In the United States, total production fell by more than 4 percent, and millions of workers lost their jobs. In Europe and Japan, production fell even more sharply. Even in China and India, where production continued to increase,

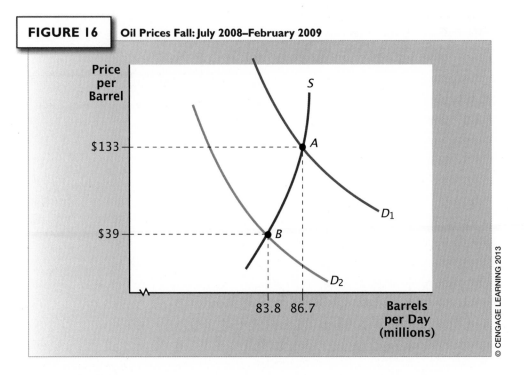

FIGURE 16   Oil Prices Fall: July 2008–February 2009

© CENGAGE LEARNING 2013

growth rates fell by one third or more. Worldwide demand for gasoline, jet fuel, and many other oil-based products plunged. As a result, the demand for oil itself decreased.

March and April 2011: Oil Prices Spike Again

Now take one more look at Figure 13. You can see in the figure that both price and quantity were steadily rising in the two years leading up to February 2011. In Europe, the U.S., and Japan, production was increasing. And in emerging economies like China and India, growth returned to its former rapid pace. These changes caused the demand curve to shift rightward during those two years, much as it had a few years earlier (depicted in Figure 15).

But in March and April, prices began shooting up suddenly. This time, both supply and demand played important roles.

Let's start with demand. With worldwide production and income continuing to rise, the demand curve continued shifting rightward. By some estimates, the demand curve for oil was increasing by about 500,000 barrels per day *every month*. So over this two-month period, the demand curve might have shifted rightward by $2 \times 500,000 = 1$ million barrels per day.

Second, the supply curve shifted sharply leftward, for two reasons. The first was internal conflict in Libya, which—in March and April—shut down most of that country's oil production. This alone removed about 1.3 million barrels per day from the market. Second, Saudi Arabia—which had often made up for past supply disruptions in the Middle East—did the opposite this time: It decreased production by about 200,000 barrels per day. In total, these two events caused the supply curve to shift leftward by about 1.5 million barrels per day.

The result is shown in Figure 17. Both the rightward shift in demand and the leftward shift in supply each contributed to the higher price of oil. But they had opposite effects on quantity. A rightward shift in demand tends to raise quantity, while a leftward shift in supply tends to lower it. Which effect dominated? If you

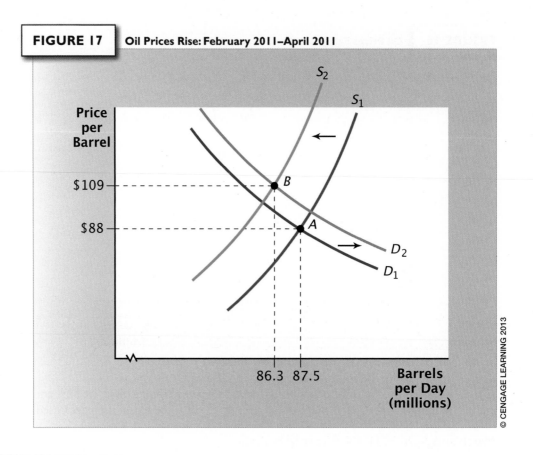

FIGURE 17 Oil Prices Rise: February 2011–April 2011

© CENGAGE LEARNING 2013

look back at Figure 13, you'll see that oil production fell during these two months. This tells us that the supply shift had the dominant effect on quantity, and that is what we've illustrated in Figure 17.

We'll be returning to oil prices later in this book. If you are studying micro-economics, you'll learn about some special features of oil and other commodities that explain why their prices can swing so widely and rapidly. If you are studying macroeconomics, you'll learn how sudden spikes in oil prices can cause (and have caused) recessions in the United States and other countries.

SUMMARY

In a market economy, prices are determined through the interaction of buyers and sellers in *markets. In perfectly competitive* markets, each buyer and seller regards the market price as given. If an individual buyer or seller has the power to influence the price of a product, the market is *imperfectly competitive.*

The model of *supply and demand* is designed to explain how prices are determined in perfectly competitive markets. The *quantity demanded* of any good is the total amount buyers would choose to purchase given the constraints that they face. The *law of demand* states that quantity demanded is negatively related to price; it tells us that the *demand curve* slopes downward. The demand curve is drawn for given levels of income, wealth, tastes, prices of substitute and complementary goods, population, and expected future price. If any of those factors changes, the demand curve will shift (a *change in demand*). A change in price, however, moves us *along* the demand curve (a *change in quantity demanded*).

The *quantity supplied* of a good is the total amount sellers would choose to produce and sell given the constraints that they face. According to the *law of supply,* supply curves slope upward. The supply curve will shift (a *change in supply*) if there is a change in the price of an input, the price of an alternate good, the price in an alternate market, the number of firms, expectations of future prices, or (for some goods) a change in weather. A change in the price of the good, by contrast, moves us *along* the supply curve (a *change in quantity supplied*).

Equilibrium price and quantity in a market are found where the supply and demand curves intersect. If either or both of these curves shift, price and quantity will change as the market moves to a new equilibrium.

Economists frequently use a three-step process to answer questions about the economy. The three steps—taken several times in this chapter—are to (1) characterize the market or markets involved in the question; (2) find the equilibrium in the market; and (3) ask what happens when something changes.

PROBLEM SET

Answers to even-numbered Problems can be found on the text Web site through www.cengagebrain.com

1. Consider the following statement: "In late 2008, as at other times in history, oil prices came down at the same time that the quantity of oil produced fell. There-fore, one way for us to bring down oil prices is to slow down oil production." True or false? Explain.

2. Discuss, and illustrate with a graph, how each of the following events, *ceteris paribus*, will affect the market for coffee:
    a. A blight on coffee plants kills off much of the Brazilian crop.
    b. The price of tea declines.
    c. Coffee workers organize themselves into a union and gain higher wages.
    d. Coffee is shown to cause cancer in laboratory rats.
    e. Coffee prices are expected to rise rapidly in the near future.

3. Consider the following passage from an article in the *New York Times* on March 9, 2011, "In the last few years, coffee yields have plummeted here [Colombia] and in many of Latin America's other premier coffee regions as a result of rising temperatures and more intense and unpredictable rains, phenomena that many scientists link partly to global warming... [while] global demand is soaring as the rising middle classes of emerging economies like Brazil, India and China develop the coffee habit." Illustrate the impact of these events in a supply and demand diagram of the global market for coffee. *Ceteris paribus*, can we determine the direction of change in equilibrium quantity? Of equilibrium price? Explain briefly.

4. In the late 1990s and through 2000, the British public became increasingly concerned about "Mad Cow Disease," which could be deadly to humans if they ate beef from these cattle. Fearing the disease, many consumers switched to other meats, like chicken, pork, or lamb. At the same time, the British government ordered the destruction of thousands of head of cattle. Illustrate the effects of these events on the equilibrium price and quantity in the market for British beef. Can we determine with certainty the direction of change for the quantity? For the price? Explain briefly.

5. The following table gives hypothetical data for the quantity of two-bedroom rental apartments demanded and supplied in Peoria, Illinois:

Monthly Rent	Quantity Demanded (thousands)	Quantity Supplied (thousands)
$ 800	30	10
$1,000	25	14
$1,200	22	17
$1,400	19	19
$1,600	17	21
$1,800	15	22

    a. Graph the demand and supply curves.
    b. Find the equilibrium price and quantity.
    c. Explain briefly why a rent of $1,000 cannot be the equilibrium in this market.
    d. Suppose a tornado destroys a significant number of apartment buildings in Peoria but doesn't affect people's desire to live there. Illustrate on your graph the effects on equilibrium price and quantity.

6. How would each of the following affect the market for denim jeans in the United States? Illustrate each answer with a supply-and-demand diagram.
    a. The price of denim cloth increases.
    b. An economic slowdown in the United States causes household incomes to decrease.

7. The following table gives hypothetical data for the quantity of gasoline demanded and supplied in Los Angeles per month.

Price per Gallon	Quantity Demanded (millions of gallons)	Quantity Supplied (millions of gallons)
$1.20	170	80
$1.30	156	105
$1.40	140	140
$1.50	123	175
$1.60	100	210
$1.70	95	238

a. Graph the demand and supply curves.
b. Find the equilibrium price and quantity.
c. Illustrate on your graph how a rise in the price of automobiles would affect the gasoline market.

8. The table at the end of this problem gives hypothetical data for the quantity of electric scooters demanded and supplied per month.
a. Graph the demand and supply curves.
b. Find the equilibrium price and quantity.
c. Illustrate on your graph how an increase in the wage rate paid to scooter assemblers would affect the market for electric scooters.
d. What would happen if there was an increase in the wage rate paid to scooter assemblers at the same time that tastes for electric scooters increased?

Price per Electric Scooter	Quantity Demanded	Quantity Supplied
$150	500	250
$175	475	350
$200	450	450
$225	425	550
$250	400	650
$275	375	750

9. Indicate which curve shifted—and in which direction—for each of the following. Assume that only one curve shifts.
a. The price of furniture rises as the quantity bought and sold falls.
b. Apartment vacancy rates increase while average monthly rent on apartments declines.
c. The price of personal computers continues to decline as sales skyrocket.

10. Consider the following forecast: "Next month, we predict that the demand for oranges will continue to increase, which will tend to raise the price of oranges. However, the higher price will increase supply, and a greater supply tends to lower prices. Accordingly, even though we predict that demand will increase next month, we cannot predict whether the price of oranges will rise or fall." There is a serious mistake of logic in this forecast. Can you find it? Explain.

11. A couple of months after Hurricane Katrina in 2005, an article in *The New York Times* contained the following passage: "Gasoline prices—the national average is now $2.15, according to the Energy Information Administration—have fallen because higher prices held down demand and Gulf Coast supplies have been slowly restored."[2] The statement about supply is entirely correct and explains why gas prices came down. But the statement about demand confuses two concepts you learned about in this chapter.
a. What two concepts does the statement about demand seem to confuse? Explain briefly.
b. On a supply-and-demand diagram, show what most likely caused gasoline prices to rise when Hurricane Katrina shut down gasoline refineries on the Gulf Coast.
c. On another supply-and-demand diagram, show what most likely happened in the market for gasoline as Gulf Coast refineries were repaired—and began operating again—after the hurricane.
d. What role did the *demand* side of the market play in explaining the rise and fall of gas prices?

12. Draw supply-and-demand diagrams for market *A* for each of the following. Then use your diagrams to illustrate the impact of the following events. In each case, determine what happens to price and quantity in each market.
a. *A* and *B* are substitutes, and the price of good *B* rises.
b. *A* and *B* satisfy the same kinds of desires, and there is a shift in tastes away from *A* and toward *B*.
c. *A* is a normal good, and incomes in the community increase.
d. There is a technological advance in the production of good *A*.
e. *B* is an input used to produce good *A*, and the price of *B* rises.

13. When we observe an increase in both price and quantity, we know that the demand curve must have shifted rightward. However, we cannot rule a shift in the supply curve as well. Prove this by drawing a supply-and-demand diagram for each of the following cases:
a. Demand curve shifts rightward, supply curve shifts leftward, equilibrium price and quantity both rise.
b. Demand and supply curves both shift rightward, equilibrium price and quantity both rise.
c. Evaluate the following statement: "During the oil price spike from 2007 to mid-2008, we know the supply curve could not have shifted leftward, because quantity supplied rose." True or False? Explain.

[2] "Economic Memo: Upbeat Signs Hold Cautions for the Future," *The New York Times*, November 30, 2005.

14. In early 2011, even though cotton prices were high, cotton farmers in China began to hoard (rather than sell) most of the crop they had harvested, filling spare rooms and even living areas of their homes with cotton. Given the cost and inconvenience of storing large amounts of cotton rather than selling it, what could explain this behavior? [Hint: Review the section of this chapter on factors that shift the supply curve.] Could this behavior explain why cotton prices were high during this period? Explain, using the concepts of supply and demand.

More Challenging

15. Suppose that demand is given by the equation $Q^D = 500 - 50P$, where Q^D is quantity demanded, and P is the price of the good. Supply is described by the equation $Q^S = 50 + 25P$, where Q^S is quantity supplied. What is the equilibrium price and quantity? (See Appendix.)

16. While crime rates fell across the country over the past few decades, they fell especially rapidly in Manhattan. At the same time, there were some neighborhoods in the New York metropolitan area in which the crime rate remained constant. Using supply-and-demand diagrams for rental housing, explain how a falling crime rate in Manhattan could make the residents in *other* neighborhoods *worse off*. (Hint: As people from around the country move to Manhattan, what happens to rents there? If people already living in Manhattan cannot afford to pay higher rent, what might they do?)

17. An analyst observes the following equilibrium price-quantity combinations in the market for restaurant meals in a city over a four-year period:

Year	P	Q (thousands of meals per month)
1	$12	20
2	$15	30
3	$17	40
4	$20	50

He concludes that the market defies the law of demand. Is he correct? Why or why not?

The unintended consequences of price ceilings—long lines, black markets, and, often, higher prices—explain why they are generally a poor way to bring down prices. Experience with price ceilings has generally confirmed this judgment. In the U.S., many states do have laws to limit price hikes during declared emergencies, thereby creating temporary price ceilings. But permanent or semipermanent price ceilings are exceedingly rare.

There is, however, one type of market in which several cities have imposed long-lasting price ceilings: the market for apartment rentals.

An Example: Rent Controls

Rent controls Government-imposed maximum rents on apartments and homes.

A price ceiling imposed in a rental housing market is called **rent control**. Most states have laws *prohibiting* rent control. But more than a dozen states do allow it. And in four of these states (New York, California, Maryland, and New Jersey), some form of rent control has existed in several cities and towns for decades.

In theory, rent control is designed to keep housing affordable, especially for those with low incomes. But for this purpose, it's a very blunt instrument because it doesn't target those with low incomes. Rather, *anyone* who was lucky enough to be living in one of the affected units when rent control was first imposed gets to pay less than market rent, as long as he or she continues to hold the lease on the unit. Many renters in cities such as New York and Santa Monica have higher incomes and living standards than do the owners from whom they rent.

Second, rent control causes the same sorts of problems as did our hypothetical price ceiling on maple syrup. It creates a persistent excess demand for rental units, so renters must spend more time and trouble finding an apartment. Typically, something akin to the black market develops: Real estate brokers quickly snap up the rent-controlled apartments (either because of their superior knowledge of the market, or their ability to negotiate exclusive contracts with the owners). Apartment seekers, who don't want to spend months searching on their own, will hire one of these brokers. Alternatively, one can sublet from a leaseholder, who will then charge market rent for the sublet and pocket the difference. Either way, many renters end up paying a higher cost for their apartments than the rent-controlled price.

Finally, rent controls cause a decrease in the quantity of apartments supplied (a movement along the supply curve). This is because lower rents reduce the incentives for owners to maintain existing apartments in rentable condition, and also reduce incentives to build new ones.

In our example of the market for maple syrup, the decrease in quantity supplied—combined with a black market—caused the average buyer to end up paying a higher price than before the ceiling was imposed (see point *T* in Figure 2). The same thing can happen in the apartment rental market. As supply decreases, the total money price of renting an apartment can rise above the original equilibrium price—if we include real estate commissions or the unofficial, higher rents paid by those who sublet.

Fighting the Market: Price Floors

Price floor A government-imposed minimum price in a market.

Sometimes, governments try to help sellers of a good by establishing a **price floor**—a minimum amount below which the price is not permitted to fall. The most common use of price floors around the world has been to raise prices (or prevent prices from falling) in agricultural markets. Price floors for agricultural goods are commonly called *price support programs*.

In the United States, price support programs began during the Great Depression, after farm prices fell by more than 50 percent between 1929 and 1932. The Agricultural Adjustment Act of 1933, and an amendment in 1935, gave the president the authority to intervene in markets for a variety of agricultural goods. Over the next 60 years, the United States Department of Agriculture (USDA) put in place programs to maintain high prices for cotton, wheat, rice, corn, tobacco, honey, milk, cheese, butter, and many other farm goods. Although some of these supports were removed in recent years, many remain. For example, government policy still maintains price floors for peanuts, sugar, and dairy products.

Let's consider dairy products, where the government has separate price floors for butter, cheese, and nonfat dry milk. These three price floors help to boost prices for *all* dairy products—even those without their own price floors. The price of fresh whole milk, for example, can only fall so far before the dairy industry would start producing less whole milk, and shifting production to butter, cheese, or nonfat dry milk, which have guaranteed minimum prices.

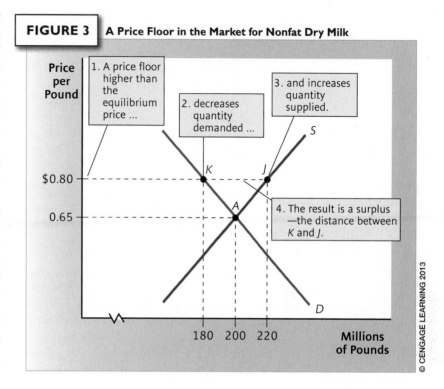

FIGURE 3   **A Price Floor in the Market for Nonfat Dry Milk**

But how does the government maintain its price floors for these three products? Let's narrow our focus to the market for nonfat dry milk—a market in which the USDA has been supporting prices for decades. In Figure 3—before any price floor is imposed—the market is in equilibrium at point A, with an equilibrium price of 65 cents per pound and an equilibrium quantity of 200 million pounds per month.

Now let's examine the impact of the price floor, which in recent years has been set at $0.80 per pound. At this price, producers want to sell 220 million pounds, while consumers want to purchase only 180 million pounds. There is an excess supply of 220 million − 180 million = 40 million pounds. Our short-side rule tells us that buyers determine the amount actually traded. They purchase 180 million of the 220 million pounds produced, and producers are unable to sell the remainder.

The excess supply of 40 million pounds would ordinarily push the market price down to its equilibrium value: $0.65. But now the price floor prevents this from happening. The result is a **surplus**—continuing extra production of nonfat dry milk that no one wants to buy at the going price.

Surplus An excess supply not eliminated by a fall in price, so that quantity supplied continues to exceed quantity demanded.

Maintaining a Price Floor

If the government merely *declared* a price floor of $0.80 per pound, many farmers who are unable to sell all of their product would be tempted to sell some illegally at a price below the floor. This would take sales away from other farmers trying to sell at the higher price, so they, too, would feel pressure to violate the floor. Soon, the price floor would collapse.

To prevent this, governments around the world have developed a variety of policies designed to prevent surplus goods from forcing down the price. One method, frequently used in the United States, is for the

DANGEROUS CURVES

Floor Above, Ceiling Below! It's tempting to think that a price floor should be set *under* the equilibrium price, or a price ceiling should be *above* the equilibrium price. After all, a floor is usually on the bottom of something, and a ceiling is on the top. Right? In this case, wrong! A price floor *below* the equilibrium price would have no impact, because the market price would *already* satisfy the requirement that it be higher than the floor. Similarly, a price ceiling set *above* the equilibrium price would have no impact (make sure you understand why). So remember: Always draw an effective price floor *above* the equilibrium price and an effective price ceiling *below* the equilibrium price.

government to promise to buy any unsold product at a guaranteed price. In the market for nonfat dry milk, for example, the government agrees to buy any unsold supplies from sellers at a price of $0.80 per pound. With this policy, no supplier would ever sell at any price *below* $0.80, since it could always sell to the government instead. With the price effectively stuck at $0.80, private buyers buy 180 million pounds—point *K* on the demand curve in Figure 3. But since quantity supplied is 220 million, at point *J*, the government must buy the excess supply of 40 million pounds per year. In other words, the government maintains the price floor by *buying up* the entire excess supply. This prevents the excess supply from doing what it would ordinarily do: drive the price down to its equilibrium value.

> *A price floor creates a surplus of a good. In order to maintain the price floor, the government must prevent the surplus from driving down the market price. In practice, the government often accomplishes this goal by purchasing the surplus itself.*

In 2009, for example, the USDA purchased more than 200 million pounds of non-fat dry milk, at a cost of almost $160 million.

Because purchasing surplus food is so expensive, price floors are usually accompanied by government efforts to *limit* any excess supplies. In the dairy market, for example, the U.S. government has developed a complicated management system to control the production and sale of milk to manufacturers and processors, which helps to limit the government's costs. In other agricultural markets, the government has ordered or paid farmers *not* to grow crops on portions of their land and has imposed strict limits on imports of food from abroad. As you can see, price floors often get the government deeply involved in production decisions, rather than leaving them to the market.

Price floors have certainly benefited farmers and helped them in times of need. But this market intervention has many critics—including most economists. They have argued that the government spends too much money buying surplus agricultural products, and the resulting higher prices distort the public's buying and eating habits—often to their nutritional detriment. For example, the General Accounting Office estimated that from 1986 to 2001, American consumers paid an extra $10.4 billion because of higher-than-equilibrium prices on dairy products. And this does not include the cost of the health effects—such as calcium and protein deficiencies among poor children—due to decreased milk consumption. The irony is that many of the farmers who benefit from price floors are wealthy individuals or large, powerful corporations that do not need the assistance. Economists argue that assistance to farmers would be more cost-effective if given directly to those truly in need, rather than supporting all farmers—rich and poor alike—with artificially high prices.

* * *

With price floors and price ceilings, the government tries to *prevent* the market price from reaching its equilibrium value. As you've seen, these efforts often backfire or have serious unintended consequences. But government can also intervene in a different way: It can try to influence the market outcome using *taxes* or *subsidies*—then stand out of the way and let the market help to achieve the desired outcome.

Manipulating the Market: Taxes

Taxes are imposed on markets to give the government revenue so it can provide public goods and services, to correct inequities in the distribution of income and wealth, or—our focus in this chapter—to change the price or quantity in a market.

A tax on a specific good or service is called an **excise tax**, which can be collected from either sellers or buyers. As you're about to see, the impact of a tax is the same, regardless of which side of the market (buyers or sellers) the tax is collected from.

An Excise Tax on Sellers

Let's explore the impact of an excise tax imposed on sellers with an example: Gasoline taxes. In the United States, the gasoline tax—collected from gasoline sellers—originated to fund the building and maintenance of the national highway system. But in recent years, many economists and others have wanted to increase this tax, for both geopolitical goals (to decrease U.S. imports of foreign oil) as well as environmental goals (to help fight pollution, traffic congestion, and climate change). Those who advocate a higher tax point out that gasoline taxes are much higher in Europe (approaching $5 per gallon in several European countries), while federal and state taxes on gasoline in the U.S. average only 48 cents per gallon.

In our example, we'll assume that initially there is no gas tax at all, and then we'll impose a tax of 60 cents per gallon on *sellers*. How would such a tax affect the market for gasoline?

Suppose that before the tax is imposed, the supply curve for gasoline is S_1 in Figure 4. (Ignore the curve above it for now.) Point A on this curve tells us that 400 million gallons will be supplied if the price is $3 per gallon. Let's state this another way: *In order for the gasoline industry to supply 400 million gallons they must get $3 per gallon.*

What happens when sellers must pay a tax of $0.60 on each gallon sold? What price must the industry charge now to supply the same 400 million gallons? The answer is $3.60, at point A'. Only by charging $0.60 more for each gallon could they continue to get the amount ($3) that makes it just worth their while to supply 400 million gallons. The same is true at any other quantity we might imagine: The price would have to be $0.60 more than before to get the industry to supply that same quantity. So imposing a $0.60 tax on gas suppliers shifts the entire supply curve *upward* by $0.60, to $S_{After Tax}$.

A tax collected from sellers shifts the supply curve upward by the amount of the tax.

Now look at Figure 5, which shows the market for gasoline. Before the tax is imposed, with supply curve S_1 and demand curve D, the equilibrium is at point A, with price at $3 and quantity at 400 million. After the $0.60 tax is imposed and the supply curve shifts up to $S_{After Tax}$, the new equilibrium price is $3.40, with 300 million gallons sold.

Who is paying this tax? Let's take a step back and think about it. The tax is *collected* from gas sellers. But who really *pays*—that is, who sacrifices funds they would otherwise have if not for the tax—is an entirely different question. The distribution of this sacrifice on each unit sold is called the **tax incidence**.

FIGURE 4 A Tax on Sellers Shifts the Supply Curve Upward

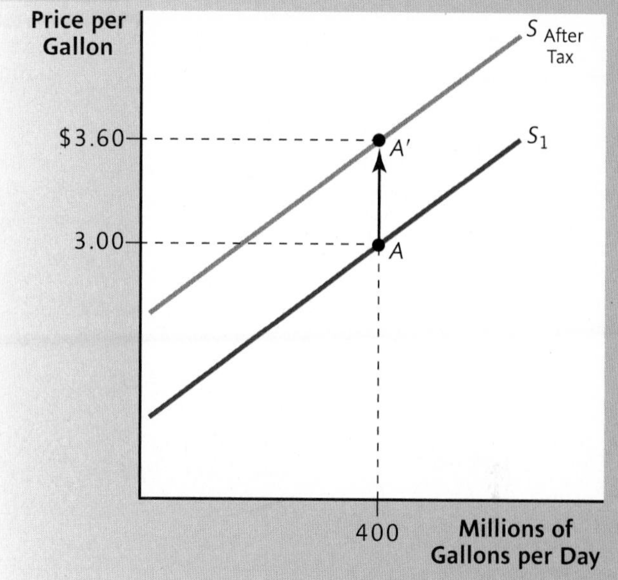

After a $0.60 per gallon tax is imposed on sellers, the price at which any given quantity would be supplied is $0.60 greater than before, so the supply curve shifts upward. For example, before the tax, 400 million gallons would be supplied at $3 per gallon (point A); after the tax, to get that same quantity supplied requires a price of $3.60 (point A').

Excise tax A tax on a specific good or service.

Tax incidence The division of a tax payment between buyers and sellers, determined by comparing the new (after tax) and old (pretax) market equilibriums.

FIGURE 5   The Effect of an Excise Tax Imposed on Sellers

After a $0.60 excise tax is imposed on sellers, the market equilibrium moves from point A to point B, with buyers paying sellers $3.40 per gallon. But sellers get only $3.40 − $0.60 = $2.80 after paying the tax. Thus, the tax causes buyers to pay $0.40 more per gallon, and sellers to get $0.20 less than before.

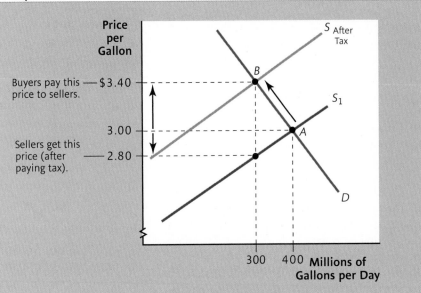

© CENGAGE LEARNING 2013

In our example, buyers paid $3.00 for each gallon before the tax, and $3.40 after. So buyers are really paying $0.40 of this tax each time they buy a gallon of gas in the form of a higher price.

What about sellers? Before the tax, they got $3.00 per gallon. After the tax, they collect $3.40 from drivers but $0.60 of that goes to the government. If we want to know how much sellers get after taxes, we have to go back to the old supply curve S_1, which lies below the new supply curve by exactly $0.60. In effect, the old supply curve deducts the tax and shows us what the sellers really receive. When the sellers charge $3.40, the original supply curve S_1 shows us that they receive only $2.80. This is $0.20 less than they received before, so sellers end up paying $0.20 of the tax.

Considering the impact on both buyers and sellers, we see that:

The incidence of a tax that is collected from sellers generally falls on both sides of the market. Buyers pay more, and sellers receive less, for each unit sold.

An Excise Tax on Buyers

Suppose that, instead of collecting the $0.60 tax from the sellers, the tax was collected directly from buyers. Before the tax is imposed, the demand curve for gasoline is D_1 in Figure 6. Point A on this curve tells us that 400 million gallons will be demanded by buyers each day if the price they have to pay is $3.00. Or, rephrased, *in order for buyers to demand 400 million gallons, each gallon must cost them $3.00.* If the cost per gallon is any more than that, buyers will not buy all 400 million gallons.

Now let's impose the $0.60 tax on buyers. (Imagine a government tax collector standing at the pump, requiring each buyer to hand over $0.60 for every gallon they buy.) What price would buyers now be willing to pay and still buy all 400 million gallons? The answer is $2.40, at point A'. We know this because only if they paid

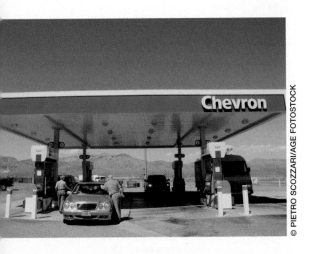

© PIETRO SCOZZARI/AGE FOTOSTOCK

$2.40 would gasoline continue to cost them the $3.00 per gallon which makes it just worth their while to demand all 400 million gallons. The same is true at any other quantity we might imagine: The price would have to be $0.60 less than before to induce buyers to demand that same quantity. So imposing a $0.60 tax on buyers shifts the entire demand curve *downward* by $0.60, to D_After Tax.

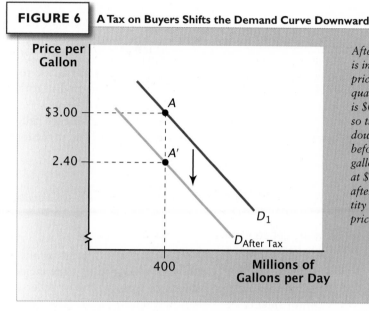

FIGURE 6   **A Tax on Buyers Shifts the Demand Curve Downward**

After a $0.60 per gallon tax is imposed on buyers, the price at which any given quantity would be demanded is $0.60 less than before, so the demand curve shifts downward. For example, before the tax, 400 million gallons would be demanded at $3 per gallon (point A); after the tax, that same quantity would be demanded at a price of $2.40 (point A').

© CENGAGE LEARNING 2013

A tax collected from buyers shifts the demand curve downward by the amount of the tax.

Figure 7 shows the impact on the market. Before the tax is imposed, with demand curve D_1 and supply curve S, the equilibrium is at point A, with price at $3.00 and quantity at 400 million. After the $0.60 tax is imposed, and the demand curve shifts down to $D_{After\ Tax}$, the new equilibrium price is $2.80, with 300 million gallons sold. With the tax imposed on buyers this time, the supply curve is not affected.

FIGURE 7   **The Effect of an Excise Tax Imposed on Buyers**

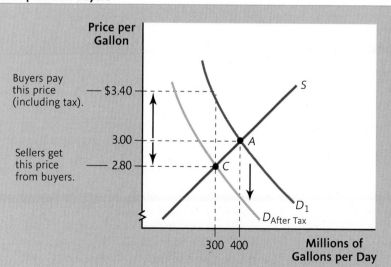

After a $0.60 excise tax is imposed on buyers, the market equilibrium moves from point A to point C, with buyers paying sellers $2.80 per gallon. But buyers pay a total of $2.80 + $0.60 = $3.40 per gallon when the tax is included. Thus, the tax causes buyers to pay $0.40 more, and sellers to get $0.20 less, just as when the tax is imposed on sellers.

© CENGAGE LEARNING 2013

What is the incidence of this tax? Let's see . . . Buyers paid $3.00 for each gallon of gas before the tax, and $2.80 after. But they also have to pay $0.60 to the government. If we want to know how much buyers pay *including* the tax, we have to go back to the old demand curve D_1, which lies above the new demand curve by exactly $0.60. As you can see, when buyers pay $2.80 to the gas station they pay a total of $3.40. This is $0.40 more than they paid in total before, so buyers end up paying $0.40 of the tax.

What about sellers? Sellers received $3.00 for each gallon before the tax and $2.80 after. So sellers are really paying $0.20 of this tax, in the form of a lower price.

> *The incidence of a tax that is collected from buyers falls on both sides of the market. Buyers pay more, and sellers receive less, for each unit sold.*

Tax Incidence versus Tax Collection

The numerical incidence of any tax will depend on the shapes of the supply and demand curves. But you may have noticed that the incidence in our example is the same whether the tax is collected from buyers or sellers. In both cases, buyers pay $0.40 of the tax per gallon and sellers pay $0.20. If you'll excuse the rhyme, this identical incidence is no coincidence.

> *The incidence of a tax (the distribution of the burden between buyers and sellers) is the same whether the tax is collected from buyers or sellers.*

Why? Because the two methods of collecting taxes are not really different in any important economic sense. Whether the tax collector takes the $0.60 from the gas station owner when the gas is sold, or takes $0.60 from the driver when the gas is sold, one fact remains: Buyers will pay $0.60 more than the sellers receive. The market finds a new equilibrium reflecting this. In our example, this new equilibrium occurs where each gallon costs drivers $3.40 in total, and the gas suppliers receive $2.80 of this, because that is the only incidence at which quantity demanded and supplied are equal.

Manipulating the Market: Subsidies

Subsidy A government payment to buyers or sellers on each unit purchased or sold.

A **subsidy** is the opposite of a tax. Instead of the government demanding a payment *from* the buyer or seller, the government makes a payment *to* the seller or buyer. And whereas a tax raises the price to the buyer and decreases purchases of the product, a subsidy does the reverse: It lowers prices to buyers and *encourages* people to buy it. In the United States, federal, state, and local governments subsidize a variety of goods and services, including medical care for the poor and elderly, energy-saving equipment, smoking-cessation programs, and college education.

A Subsidy to Buyers

Let's explore the impact of a subsidy given to buyers with an example: Tuition assistance to college students.

Every year in the United States, federal and state governments provide more than $100 billion in subsidies—scholarships and other assistance—to help students pay the cost of a college education. The reasons for these policies are clear: We want to

FIGURE 8 | **A Subsidy for Students Attending College**

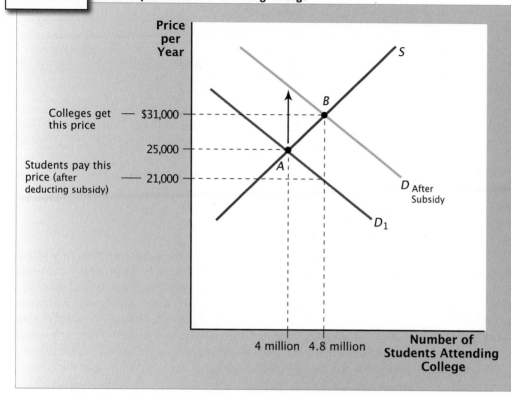

After a $10,000 subsidy is given to college students, the market equilibrium moves from point A to point B, with students paying colleges $31,000 per year. But students pay a total of $31,000 − $10,000 = $21,000 when their subsidy is deducted. Thus, the subsidy causes students to pay $4,000 less per year, and it causes colleges to get $6,000 more per year.

© CENGAGE LEARNING 2013

encourage more people to get college degrees. A college education gives substantial benefits to the degree-holders themselves, in the form of higher future incomes. And a more educated population creates benefits for society as a whole. There are also important equity considerations: Financial assistance increases the number of students from poor households, many of whom might otherwise have to forgo the benefits of college.

Figure 8 shows the market for attending college. Initially, without any government involvement, demand curve D_1 intersects supply curve S at point A. Four million students attend college each year, with each paying a total of $25,000 in tuition.

Now, let's introduce financial assistance: a subsidy of $10,000 per year for each student. And we'll assume here that the subsidy is paid out to buyers—college students—to help them pay tuition.

The subsidy shifts the demand curve *upward* by $10,000, to $D_{\text{After Subsidy}}$. Why? Before the subsidy, 4 million students would attend college when the price was $25,000. So *after* the subsidy, those same 4 million would attend at a price of $35,000 (indicated by the tip of the vertical arrow in Figure 8). After all, paying $35,000 with a $10,000 subsidy is the same as paying $25,000 with no subsidy. This reasoning applies to any other number of students we might imagine: After the subsidy, that same number of students would attend college if the price were $10,000 higher than before.

> *A subsidy paid to buyers shifts the demand curve upward by the amount of the subsidy.*

After the demand curve shifts upward, the market equilibrium moves from point *A* to point *B*. In the new equilibrium, 4.8 million students decide to attend college. But notice that the price is higher as well: Colleges are now charging $31,000 per year.

In general,

> *A subsidy paid to buyers benefits both sides of a market. Buyers pay less and sellers receive more for each unit sold.*

In the end, who benefits from the subsidy? Colleges benefit: They get more for each student who attends ($31,000 instead of $25,000). Students benefit as well: They pay $31,000 to the colleges, but the government pays $10,000 of that, so the cost to students has dropped to $21,000.

However, notice that the $10,000 subsidy has *not* reduced the cost of college by a full $10,000. In our example, only $4,000 of the subsidy ends up as a direct benefit to the student, while the other $6,000 goes to the college.

A Subsidy to Sellers

As you learned earlier, the burden (incidence) of a tax is the same, regardless of whether it is collected from sellers or buyers. What about a subsidy? Is the benefit to each side of the market the same, regardless of which side the payment is given to? Indeed it is.

We leave it to you to do the analysis, but here's a hint: If the subsidy in our example had been paid to colleges (the sellers) instead of students (the buyers), the supply curve would shift *downward* by the amount of the subsidy. If you draw the graph, using the same initial supply and demand curves as in Figure 8 and the same $10,000 subsidy, you'll see that students will pay $21,000 (and not receive anything from the government), while colleges will collect $31,000 when we include the subsidy they receive. What buyers end up paying, and what sellers end up receiving, is the same as in Figure 8.

In general,

> *The distribution of benefits from a subsidy is the same, regardless of whether the subsidy is paid to buyers or sellers.*

* * *

In this chapter, we've considered only one impact of taxes and subsidies: How they change the market price. But taxes and subsidies also change the market *quantity* and they affect taxpayers (through their impact on the government budget). If you are studying microeconomics, you'll learn how economists take account of all these effects in a later chapter. You'll also learn which types of taxes and subsidies can help the economy function more effectively.

SUPPLY AND DEMAND IN HOUSING MARKETS

So far in this text book, we've used supply and demand to analyze a variety of markets—for maple syrup, crude oil, higher education, and more. All of these markets have one thing in common: they are markets in which business firms sell currently produced goods or services.

But the supply-and-demand model is a versatile tool. With a bit of modification, we can use it to analyze almost any market in which something is traded at a price, including markets for labor, foreign currencies, stocks, bonds, and more. Our only requirement is that there are many buyers and sellers, and each regards the market price (or a narrow range of prices) as given. In the remainder of this chapter, we'll use supply and demand to understand a type of market that has been at the center of recent economic events: the market for residential housing.

What's Different about Housing Markets

Housing markets differ in an important way from others we've considered so far. When people buy maple syrup, they buy newly produced bottles, not previously owned ones. But when people shop for a home, they generally consider newly constructed homes and previously owned homes to be very close substitutes. After all, a house is a house. If properly maintained, it can last for decades or even centuries. Indeed, most of the homes that people own, and most that change hands each year, were originally built and sold long before.

This key difference—that housing markets are dominated by previously owned homes—means we'll need to think about supply and demand in a somewhat different way. To understand this new approach, we first need to take a short detour.

A Detour: Stock and Flow Variables

Many economic variables fall into one of two categories: *stocks* or *flows*.

> A **stock variable** *measures a quantity at a moment in time. A **flow variable** measures a process that takes place over a period of time.*

Stock variable A variable representing a quantity at a moment in time.

Flow variable A variable representing a process that takes place over some time period.

To understand the difference, think of a bathtub being filled with water. At any given moment, there are a certain number of gallons actually *in* the tub. This volume of water is a *stock variable:* a quantity that exists at that moment in time (such as 15 gallons). But each minute, a certain volume of water flows *into* the tub. This rate of flow is a *flow variable:* a process that takes place over a *period* of time (such as 2 gallons per minute).

In this book, you've encountered both types of variables. In Chapter 3, for example, the quantity of maple syrup demanded or supplied was a flow: a certain number of bottles bought or sold *per month*. Similarly, household income is a flow: so many dollars earned *per month* or *per year*. But household *wealth*—the total value of what someone owns minus the total owed—is a stock variable. Wealth is a certain number of dollars measured at a particular point in time.

Stocks versus Flows in the Housing Market

Now back to housing. Which of these two concepts—stock or flow—should we use in our supply-and-demand model for housing? Let's see.

If we use the now-familiar flow approach to supply and demand, then the "supply of housing" would be the number of homes everyone wants to sell per period, and the "demand for housing" would be the number that people want to buy per period. Both supply and demand would refer to a process (selling and buying) that takes place over a period of time.

If we use the stock approach, then the "supply of housing" would be the number of homes *available*—say, 100 million U.S. homes on January 1, 2013. This would be the total number of homes *in existence* at that time (often called the *housing stock*). The "demand for housing" would be the total number that people want to *own*. Both supply and demand would refer to quantities at a moment in time.

For some purposes, the two approaches would work equally well. But in many situations, the flow approach to the housing market creates confusion. For example, suppose that in a particular month, the number of homes people want to *sell* at any price decreases, because more homeowners want to continue living in their current homes rather than sell them. Using the flow approach, we'd have to say that the "supply of homes" is decreasing, because supply in the flow approach measures desired home *selling* during the month. But the total number of homes in *existence* and available for ownership would *not* be falling. In fact, if new homes are being built during the month (as usually happens), the number of homes available would actually be *rising*. Thus, the flow approach suggests something counter-intuitive: that "supply" is falling, even when the number of homes in existence is unchanged or rising.

To help us avoid this and other confusions, we'll use the stock approach to housing in this chapter. In the stock approach, the "supply of homes" is the number of homes available for ownership, and it rises if and only if the total number of homes in existence rises.

When we view demand and supply as stocks (rather than flows), equilibrium occurs when the total number of homes people *want to own* (demand) is equal to the total number *available* (supply). To see how this works, let's take a closer look at supply and demand as stock variables, and illustrate them graphically.

The Supply Curve for Housing

In Figure 9, panel (a) shows a supply curve for a local housing market in a small city. The average price of a home in this market is measured along the vertical axis, and the number of homes is on the horizontal axis. Remember that we are viewing housing supply as a stock variable. Accordingly,

Supply curve for housing A vertical line showing the total number of homes in a market that are available for ownership.

> *the **supply curve for housing** tells us the number of homes in a market that are available for ownership—the housing stock.*

It's a vertical line because, no matter what the price, the housing stock at any point in time is fixed, determined by the number of homes that were built in the past and

---

FIGURE 9 | **The Supply Curve in a Housing Market**

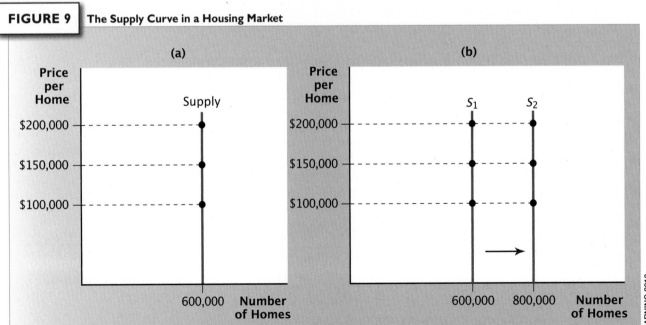

In panel (a), the supply curve tells us the number of homes (600,000) that exist at a particular time. It is a vertical line because the housing stock at any time does not depend on the price. Panel (b) shows the impact of building 200,000 new homes over the year. The housing stock rises to 800,000 so the supply curve shifts rightward, from S_1 to S_2.

still suitable for ownership. In the figure, we've assumed that the housing stock is currently 600,000, so the supply curve is a vertical line at 600,000.

Shifts versus Movements Along the Supply Curve

When the price of homes changes, we move *along* (up or down) the vertical supply curve for housing. Note that a change in the average price will not affect the current housing stock. A drop in the price from $200,000 to $100,000 will not cause existing houses to self-destruct, and a rise in the price from $100,000 to $200,000 will not cause more homes to suddenly appear.

Over time, however, the housing stock can change, causing the supply curve to *shift*. For example, if new homes are being built, the housing stock will rise over time. A year from now, more homes will be available for ownership than there are today. So the supply curve one year from now will lie further to the right than the current supply curve. Panel (b) of Figure 9 shows the rightward shift in the supply curve from its current position (S_1) to its position one year later (S_2) when 200,000 new homes are built over the year.

Could the supply curve ever shift *leftward*? Yes, if the housing stock *decreased*. This could occur if an earthquake or other natural disaster destroyed existing homes. After the disaster, fewer homes would be available at any price, so the supply curve would shift leftward.

The Demand Curve for Housing

As we did with supply, we will view the demand for homes as a stock variable. Specifically,

> the **demand curve for housing** tells us, at each price, the total number of homes that everyone in the market would like to own, given the constraints that they face.

Demand curve for housing A curve showing, at each price, the total number of homes that everyone in the market would like to own, given the constraints that they face.

Note the last phrase in that definition. As always, "demand" in a market takes into account the real-world constraints that people face. Home ownership is costly. So in deciding whether they want to own a home, people consider the cost, as well as their limited income and the alternatives to owning that are available to them.

Figure 10(a) shows the demand curve for housing in the small city that we've been considering. To keep things simple, we'll assume for now that households or families in this city can own just one home each. In that case, the demand curve tells us the number of families who want to be home owners at each price. (Later in the chapter, we'll discuss the role of owning multiple homes in the recent housing boom.)

As you can see in the figure, the demand curve slopes downward: As the average price of a home in this city falls, more people want to own them. To see why, let's take a closer look at the cost of home ownership.

Behind the Demand Curve: Ownership Costs

People deciding whether they want to own a home will compare the costs and benefits of owning a home with the costs and benefits of the next best alternative: renting. There are several advantages to owning rather than renting, including greater control over your living environment and the possibility that the home will increase in value. For many decades, owning a home was thought to be one of the most stable and profitable investments a family could make.

© AXL/SHUTTERSTOCK.COM

DANGEROUS CURVES

Misinterpreting the Supply and Demand Curves for Homes It's very easy to slip into thinking that the supply and demand curves for housing have the "flow" interpretation of the previous chapter, instead of the proper "stock" interpretation here. So remember: the supply curve does *not* represent the number of homes people want to sell each period. Rather, it represents the number of homes that *exist* at a point in time. Similarly, the demand curve does *not* tell us how many homes people would like to buy each period. Rather, it tells us how many homes people want to *own* at a point in time.

FIGURE 10   The Demand Curve in a Housing Market

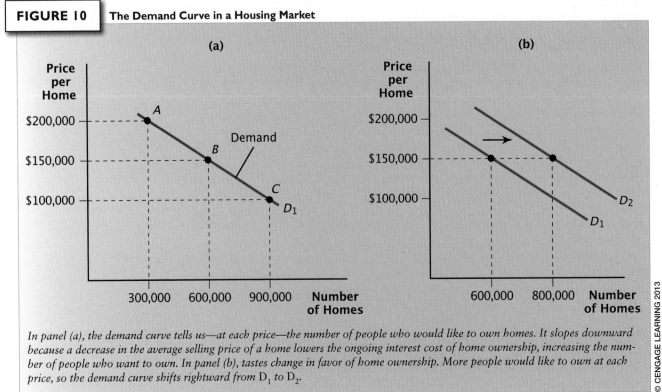

(a)

Price per Home

$200,000 — A

$150,000 — B   Demand

$100,000 — C   D₁

300,000   600,000   900,000   **Number of Homes**

(b)

Price per Home

$200,000 —

$150,000 —

$100,000 —   D₂   D₁

600,000   800,000   **Number of Homes**

© CENGAGE LEARNING 2013

In panel (a), the demand curve tells us—at each price—the number of people who would like to own homes. It slopes downward because a decrease in the average selling price of a home lowers the ongoing interest cost of home ownership, increasing the number of people who want to own. In panel (b), tastes change in favor of home ownership. More people would like to own at each price, so the demand curve shifts rightward from D₁ to D₂.

But owning a home also entails costs, including maintenance, property taxes, and—the largest component—interest. As you are about to see, the interest cost of owning a home depends on the current price of the house—the price that it *could* be sold for. This is true for prospective owners (those thinking of *becoming* home owners by buying a home) and also for those who already own a home, even if they bought it long ago.

Costs for Prospective Home Owners. Let's first consider those thinking of *becoming* owners by buying a home. Suppose that a buyer pays entirely with his or her own funds. Then those funds can no longer be invested elsewhere, so the buyer will be forgoing interest. The greater the price of the home, the more the buyer will have to pay, and the more interest the buyer will forgo each year.

Most prospective home owners, however, do *not* pay the entire purchase price themselves. Instead, they pay for a small part of the purchase with their own funds—called the *down payment*—and *borrow* the rest, getting a housing loan called a **mortgage**. The mortgage is paid back monthly over many years. For most of that time, the monthly payments will consist largely of interest charges. So, once again, the owner has an interest cost. For a given down payment, the greater the price of the home, the more the buyer will have to borrow, and the higher the monthly interest payments on the mortgage.

Summing up so far, we've seen that for *prospective* home owners, higher home prices lead to greater interest costs, and therefore a greater cost of owning. But what about ownership costs for those who *already* own their home?

Costs for Current Owners. You might think that, once someone has already purchased a home, the interest cost is based on the price paid earlier, at the time of purchase, and is not affected if the price of the home changes later. But in fact, any change in the home's price—even after it was purchased—will change the owner's costs.

Mortgage A loan given to a home-buyer for part of the purchase price of the home.

To see why, remember that anyone who already owns a home could always choose to sell it. The owner could then pay back any amount remaining on the mortgage and also get some cash back (since the selling price is usually greater than the amount owed on the mortgage). That cash could earn interest. Continued ownership, therefore, means *continued forgone interest*.

Of course, the higher the price at which a house *could* be sold, the more interest the owner sacrifices by *not* selling. So once again, higher home prices mean more forgone interest, and therefore higher ownership costs.

Let's summarize what we've found about ownership costs:

> *Both current and prospective homeowners face an interest cost of ownership. This cost rises when current home prices rise, and falls when current home prices fall.*

Now you can understand why the demand curve in Figure 10(a) slopes downward. When housing prices fall and nothing else changes, the ongoing interest cost of owning a home declines as well. With lower costs, more people than before will prefer to own homes, so the quantity of homes demanded increases.

Shifts versus Movements Along the Demand Curve

As with any demand curve, when we change the price and move along the curve, we hold constant all other influences on demand. For example, in Figure 10(a), if the price of a home falls from $150,000 to $100,000, *ceteris paribus*, we move along the demand curve from point B to point C. The number of families who want to own rises from 600,000 to 900,000.

But as we make this movement, we hold constant all other influences on demand, such as the cost of the main alternative (*renting* a home), interest rates in the economy, tastes for home ownership, expectations about future home prices, average income, population—anything that might affect the number of homes demanded *other* than the current price of a home. If any of these other factors change, the demand curve will shift.

Suppose, for example, that tastes in this city shift away from renting apartments toward owning homes. Then at each price, more people would want to be homeowners than before. This is illustrated in Figure 10(b), where the demand curve shifts rightward from D_1 to D_2.

Housing Market Equilibrium

Figure 11 combines the supply and demand curves from Figures 9(a) and 10(a). The equilibrium, as always, occurs where the two curves intersect, at point B, with the average price of a house in this city at $150,000. But because this is a new type of market, it's worth spending a little time understanding *why* equilibrium occurs at this price.

Suppose the price of homes in this area were $100,000, which is less than the equilibrium price. Point C on the demand curve tells us that 900,000 people want to own homes at this price. But the supply curve tells us that only 600,000 homes are available—that is, only 600,000 homes *can* be owned. So with a price of $100,000, there is an excess demand for homes. What will happen?

People who want homes, but don't yet have them, will try to buy them from the current owners, bidding up prices. Because the housing stock is constant (at least for now), the rise in price will *not* change the quantity of homes available. But it *will* move us along the demand curve (upward and leftward from point C), as higher home prices drive up ownership cost and reduce the number of people who want to

FIGURE 11   Equilibrium in a Housing Market

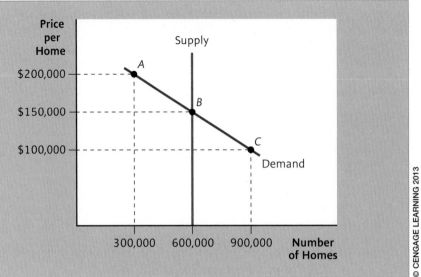

The equilibrium in this market is at point B, where the price of homes is $150,000. If the price were higher—say $200,000— the number of homes people want to own (300,000 at point A) would be less than the number in existence and currently owned (600,000). Owners would try to sell, and the price would fall until all 600,000 homes were demanded. If the price were lower than the equilibrium price—say $100,000—the number of homes people want to own (900,000 at point C) would be greater than the number in existence and currently owned (600,000). People would try to buy homes, and the price would rise until only 600,000 were demanded.

own. The price will continue rising until the number of people who *want* to own a home is equal to the number of homes that *can* be owned: the 600,000 that exist. This occurs when the price reaches $150,000, at point *B*.

What if the price started *higher* than $150,000—say, $200,000? Then only 300,000 people would want to own homes, at point *A*. But remember: 600,000 homes exist, and at any time, every one of them must be owned by *someone*. So at a price of $200,000, half of the current homeowners prefer *not* to own. They will try to sell, and home prices will fall. As home prices drop, and we move rightward along the demand curve, more people decide they want to own. The price continues dropping until it reaches $150,000, at point *B*, where people are content to own all 600,000 homes in existence.

> *The equilibrium price in a housing market is the price at which the quantity of homes demanded (the number that people want to own) and quantity supplied (the housing stock) are equal.*

What Happens When Things Change

So far, in Figure 11, we've identified the equilibrium at a particular point in time. We did so by assuming that the housing stock was fixed at 600,000, and all influences on demand other than the price of homes were held constant.

But *over time,* in most housing markets, both the supply and demand curves will shift rightward. The supply curve shifts rightward as the housing stock rises (new homes are built). And the demand curve shifts rightward for a variety of reasons, including population growth and rising incomes. As a result, the market equilibrium will move rightward over time as well. But what happens to home *prices* depends on the *relative* shifts in the supply and demand curves. Let's look at three possibilities.

Equal Changes in Supply and Demand: A Stable Housing Market

Figure 12 illustrates a stable housing market, in which increases in the housing stock just keep pace with increases in demand over time. Let's start with the initial situation, at point *B*, with a housing stock of 600,000 homes and a price of $150,000. Over the

© CENGAGE LEARNING 2013

FIGURE 12 | **A Stable Housing Market**

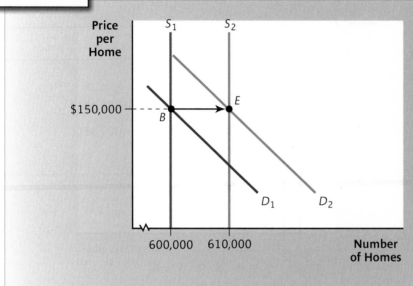

When the supply of homes increases at the same rate as demand for them, the equilibrium price remains unchanged. In the figure, the rightward shift in the supply curve (from S_1 to S_2) is equal to the rightward shift in the demand curve (from D_1 to D_2). Equilibrium moves from point B to point E, but the price remains at $150,000.

next year, population and income growth shifts the demand curve rightward to D_2. At each price, the demand for homes is 10,000 more than before. New construction increases the housing stock by 10,000 as well, shifting the supply curve to S_2. The equilibrium moves to point E, with a new, higher housing stock of 610,000, and an unchanged equilibrium price of $150,000.

> *When the housing stock grows at the same rate as housing demand, housing prices remain unchanged.*

We should note that Figure 12 is not entirely realistic. In most housing markets, construction costs for labor and raw materials tend to rise over time, as more homes are built. In order to cover these rising costs and continue increasing the housing stock, average home prices must rise, at least modestly. You'll learn more about these types of market adjustments when you study perfectly competitive markets in more detail, in microeconomics. In the figure, we've ignored rising construction costs.

But in some cases, we observe home prices rising *much* faster than can be explained by rising construction costs alone. When home prices rise especially rapidly, we know that increases in demand must be outpacing increases in supply. Let's consider two possible ways this could happen.

Restrictions on New Building: Rapidly Rising Prices

In some housing markets, local restrictions on new building can prevent the housing stock from keeping up with ongoing increases in demand. This is illustrated in Figure 13. As in our previous example, the initial market equilibrium is at point B, with price equal to $150,000. And once again, the demand curve shifts rightward over the year by 10,000 units, due to population and income growth. But now, we assume that restrictions allow construction of only 3,000 new homes, so the supply curve shifts by less than in the previous figure: to S_2'. After the demand shift, people want to own 610,000 homes (at point F) at a price of $150,000, but only 603,000 exist. The excess demand of 7,000 homes drives up home prices, and we move

curve for homes in Las Vegas shifted rapidly rightward, reaching D_{2006} in mid-2006. As housing prices rose, new construction picked up as well, increasing the housing stock and shifting the supply curve rightward, ultimately to S_{2006}. But, as discussed in this chapter, when demand increases rapidly, the housing stock often lags behind. That is what happened in Las Vegas. As shown in the figure, demand increased substantially more than supply, so home prices soared—rising to $324,000 in June 2006.

Unfortunately, what happened in Vegas didn't stay in Vegas. The same bubbles developed in many areas of the country—especially in towns and cities in California, Arizona, and Florida.

The Housing Bust: A Sudden Drop in Demand

Every bubble bursts at some point. If nothing else, there are natural limits to its growth. If home prices had continued to rise at such a rapid pace, eventually new buyers would not be able to make monthly mortgage payments, even with low interest rates. The speculation would ultimately slow, and then reverse direction when people realized that prices were no longer rising.

But a bubble can burst before it reaches a natural limit. And in U.S. housing markets, problems began to occur in mid-2006, largely due to two simultaneous events: (1) oil and gasoline prices spiked, so many new homeowners were having difficulty making their monthly mortgage payments; and (2) interest rates on a large group of adjustable rate mortgages reset to higher levels. Suddenly, people noticed a disturbing rise in defaults—especially on subprime mortgages with no down payments. Around the world, lenders to the U.S. mortgage market began to take a closer look at the housing market, and they did not like what they saw: more ARMs resetting to higher levels over the next several years, and more defaults down the road. Everyone suddenly took notice of how high home prices had risen, and how far they could fall.

For the first time, it seemed, investors began to ask questions about the statistical analysis used by financial institutions to measure the risk of ARMs and subprime mortgages, and the risks of their associated mortgage-backed securities. And it turned out that every financial institution had made the same assumption: That housing prices would continue rising or, at worst, fall only modestly. No one seemed to consider what would happen if home prices fell more dramatically.

Now, with the prospect of higher default rates, and the possibility of falling home prices, the former flood of funding for new mortgages turned into a drought. Interest rates on new mortgages—to the extent they were available at all—rose. The demand curve for housing shifted leftward. And the fears of mortgage lenders became self-fulfilling: Housing prices fell.

Moreover, once housing prices began to fall, speculative fever worked in reverse. By 2007, what had been a near-certain, highly leveraged gain for home buyers turned into the prospect of a highly leveraged loss. Anyone buying a home with a traditional down payment risked losing the entire investment in a few years or less. And many of those who already owned homes suddenly wished they didn't. The demand curve for housing shifted further leftward, and housing prices fell even more rapidly.

An Example: The Bust in Las Vegas

Figure 17 illustrates how these events affected the housing market in Las Vegas. Initially, at the peak of the bubble in mid-2006, with demand curve D_{2006} and supply curve S_{2006}, the market was at point B, with the average price of a home at $324,000.

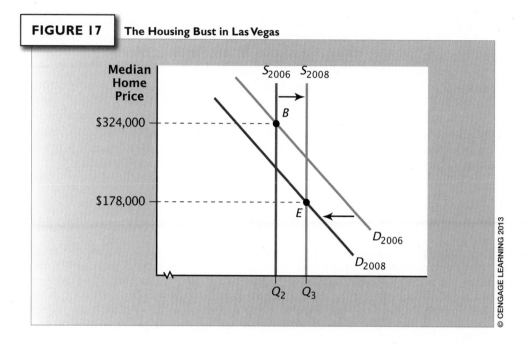

FIGURE 17   **The Housing Bust in Las Vegas**

But then the demand curve shifted leftward, and by late 2008, it reached a location like that of D_{2008}.

The supply curve, of course, did *not* shift leftward. Houses generally last a long time, and the homes built during the bubble had now become permanent additions to the housing stock. In fact, the supply curve continued to shift *rightward* for a few years, as construction projects initiated during the boom years were finished and added to the housing stock. Due to the leftward shift in demand and the rightward shift in supply, the average price of a Las Vegas home fell from $324,000 to $178,000.

The Long Housing Slump

From the end of 2008 through 2011, the U.S. economy suffered the aftermath of an unusually severe recession. High unemployment and declining incomes left millions of homeowners struggling to pay their monthly mortgage bills, leading to further defaults. Defaults rose even among those who *could* afford the monthly payments, but whose homes were now worth less than the amount they owed on their mortgages. In 2008, 2009, and 2010, financial institutions foreclosed on close to 3 million homes, and several million additional homes had received legal notices and remained in the foreclosure pipeline. Each foreclosure meant another homeowner who was no longer willing or able to own a home, shifting the demand curve for housing further to the left.

If you flip back to Figure 15, however, you'll see that U.S. home prices stabilized a bit in 2009 and early 2010. In part, this may reflect efforts by the Obama administration and Congress. The Making Home Affordable Program, begun in early 2009, provided incentives for banks and homeowners to renegotiate mortgage agreements and prevent foreclosures. Other programs offered additional tax benefits to new home buyers. These programs were meant to offer some financial relief to struggling families.

But they were also designed with another purpose in mind: to slow and perhaps reverse the decrease in demand for housing. If successful, these programs would cause housing prices to bottom out sooner, and at a higher price, than otherwise. If you are studying macroeconomics, you'll learn in a later chapter that rising home prices (or at least stable home prices) could have helped the economy recover from recession.

Unfortunately, the government's efforts were too small in scope and too slow in execution. As Figure 15 shows, they had a temporary effect at best. In 2010, home prices resumed their downward trajectory. And by mid-2011, the average U.S. home price (adjusted for inflation) had fallen to 40% of its peak five years earlier.

SUMMARY

The model of supply and demand is a powerful tool for understanding all sorts of economic events. For example, governments often intervene in markets through *price ceilings* or *price floors,* designed to prevent the market from reaching equilibrium. Economic analysis shows that these policies are often ineffective in achieving their goal of helping one side of the market, and they often create additional problems.

Governments also intervene to change the market equilibrium itself, using taxes and subsidies. Taxes raise the full price consumers pay and lower the net price that sellers receive, regardless of which side of the market (buyers or sellers) the tax is collected from. Subsidies have the opposite effect: lowering the net price that buyers pay and raising the full price that sellers receive, regardless of which side of the market (buyers or sellers) receive the subsidy.

Supply and demand can also be used to understand markets other than those for currently produced goods and services. One important example is the market for residential housing, which can be usefully analyzed as a *stock variable* (a quantity that exists at a particular point

in time), rather than a *flow variable* (a process that takes place over a period of time). In the housing market, the supply curve tells us the quantity of homes in existence, and the demand curve tells us the number of homes that the population would like to own. The demand curve slopes downward because housing entails an ongoing ownership cost, with interest cost (paid or foregone) one of its major components. The lower the price of a home, the lower the monthly ownership cost, and the more attractive owning is compared to renting.

In a stable housing market, the housing stock keeps pace with demand growth, so prices remain stable. But restrictions on new building, or a sudden acceleration of demand, can cause housing prices to soar. Because people usually buy homes with *mortgage loans,* housing is a highly *leveraged* financial investment: The value of the home is a multiple of the funds invested. As a result, the demand for housing is especially sensitive to changes in expected prices. This played a role in the most recent housing boom and the housing bust that followed.

PROBLEM SET

Answers to even-numbered Problems can be found on the text Web site through www.cengagebrain.com

1. Suppose the market for rice has the following supply and demand schedules:

P (per ton)	Q^D (tons)	Q^S (tons)
$10	100	0
$20	80	30
$30	60	40
$40	50	50
$50	40	60

To support rice producers, the government imposes a price floor of $50 per ton.
   a. What quantity will be traded in the market? Why?
   b. What steps might the government have to take to enforce the price floor?

2. In Figure 2, a price ceiling for maple syrup caused a shortage, which led to a black market price ($4) higher than the initial equilibrium price ($3). Suppose that the price ceiling remains in place for years. Over time, some maple syrup firms go out of business. With fewer firms, the supply curve in the figure shifts leftward by 10,000 bottles per month. After the shift in the supply curve:
   a. What is the shortage caused by the $2 price ceiling? (Provide a numerical answer.)
   b. If all of the maple syrup is once again purchased for sale on the black market, will the black market price be greater, less than, or the same as that in Figure 2? Explain briefly.

3. In the chapter, you learned that one way the government enforces agricultural price floors is to buy up the excess supply itself. If the government wanted to follow a similar kind of policy to enforce a price *ceiling* (such as rent control), and thereby prevent black-market-type activity, what would it have to do? Is this a sensible solution for enforcing rent control? Briefly, why or why not?

4. In Figure 5, explain why the incidence of a $0.60 tax imposed on sellers could not be split equally between buyers and sellers, given the specific supply and demand curves as drawn. [Hint: What price would gasoline sellers have to charge after the tax if there were an even split? What would happen in the market if sellers charged this price?]

5. Figure 8 shows the impact of a $10,000 subsidy on the market for college education when the subsidy is paid to college students. Starting with the same initial supply and demand curves, show what happens when the same $10,000 subsidy per student is paid to the *colleges* they attend. Suggestion: Trace the relevant curves from the figure on your own sheet of paper. [Hint: If a subsidy is paid directly to the colleges, which curve will shift? In what direction?]

6. State whether each of the following is a stock variable or a flow variable, and explain your answer briefly.
   a. Total farm acreage in the U.S.
   b. Total spending on food in China
   c. The total value of U.S. imports from Europe
   d. Worldwide iPhone sales
   e. The total number of parking spaces in Los Angeles
   f. The total value of human capital in India
   g. Investment in new human capital in India

7. In a study session, one of your fellow students says, "I think our econ text book has a mistake: It shows the supply curve for housing as a vertical line, which implies that a rise in price causes no change in quantity supplied. But everyone knows that if home prices rise, construction firms will build more homes and supply them to the market. So the supply curve should be drawn with an upward slope: higher price, greater quantity supplied." Explain briefly the mistake this student is making.

8. Suppose you buy a home for $200,000, using your own funds. The annual interest rate you could earn by investing your funds elsewhere is 5%. (Ignore any sales commissions or fees associated with buying or selling a home.)
   a. If the price at which you could sell the home remains at $200,000, what is your annual interest cost of home ownership?

   b. Suppose that, after a few years of owning, home prices rise dramatically, and you can now sell your home for $300,000. If you continue to own, what is your annual interest cost now?
   c. Suppose once again that, after a few years of owning, you can now sell your home for $300,000. But the interest rate you could earn by investing your funds elsewhere has risen to 7%. If you continue to own, what is your annual interest cost now?

9. Suppose you buy a home for $200,000, making a $40,000 down payment and taking out a mortgage for the rest. The annual interest rate on your mortgage is 5%, which is also the interest rate you can earn when you invest your funds elsewhere. (Ignore any possible tax benefits from your mortgage, as well as commissions or fees from buying or selling a home.)
   a. If the price at which you could sell the home remains at $200,000, what is your annual interest cost of home ownership? [Hint: Be sure to include both actual interest payments and foregone interest.]
   b. Suppose that, after a few years of owning, you still owe the same amount on your mortgage, but you could now sell your home for $300,000. If you continue to own, what is your annual interest cost now? [Hint: When calculating the foregone interest component, note that if you sell your home, you'll have to pay off the mortgage.]

10. Every year, the housing market in Monotone, Arizona, has the same experience: The demand curve for housing shifts rightward by 500 homes, 500 new homes are built, and the price of the average home doesn't change. Using supply and demand diagrams, illustrate how each of the following new events, *ceteris paribus*, would affect the price of homes in Monotone over the current year, and state whether the price rises or falls.
   a. Because of special tax breaks offered to Monotone home builders, 800 new housing units are built during the current year.
   b. Because of events in the overall economy, interest rates fall.
   c. The Monotone city council passes a new zoning law that prevents *any* new home construction in Monotone during the year.
   d. Because of the new zoning law, and the resulting change in home prices, people begin to think that homes in Monotone are a better investment than they had thought before.
   e. Five hundred new homes are built in Monotone during the year. But that same year, an earthquake destroys 2,000 preexisting homes. As a result of the earthquake, 3,000 homeowners decide they no longer want to live in or own homes in Monotone.

11. Every year in Houseville, California, builders construct 2,000 new homes—the most the city council will allow them to build. And every year, the demand curve for housing shifts rightward by 2,000 homes as well. Using supply and demand diagrams, illustrate how each of the following new events, *ceteris paribus,* would affect the price of homes in Houseville over the current year, and state whether home prices would rise or fall.
    a. Houseville has just won an award for the most livable city in the United States. The publicity causes the demand curve for housing to shift rightward by 5,000 this year.
    b. Houseville's city council relaxes its restrictions, allowing the housing stock to rise by 3,000 during the year.
    c. An earthquake destroys 1,000 homes in Houseville. There is no effect on the demand for housing, and the city council continues to allow only 2,000 new homes to be built during the year.
    d. The events in a., b., and c. all happen at the same time.

12. [Requires appendix.] Suppose you buy a home for $400,000 with a $100,000 down payment and finance the rest with a home mortgage.
    a. Immediately after purchasing your home, before any change in price, what is the value of your *equity* in the home?
    b. Immediately after purchasing your home, before any change in price, what is your simple leverage ratio on your investment in the home?
    c. Now suppose that over the next three years, the price of your home has increased to $500,000. Assuming you have not borrowed any additional funds using the home as collateral, but you still owe the entire mortgage amount, what is the new value of your equity in the home? Your new simple leverage ratio?
    d. Evaluate the following statement: "An increase in the value of a home, with no additional borrowing, increases the degree of leverage on the investment in the home." True or false? Explain.

13. [Requires appendix.] Suppose, as in the previous problem, you buy a home for $400,000 with a down payment of $100,000 and take out a mortgage for the remainder. Over the next three years, the price of the home rises to $500,000. However, during those three years, you also borrow $50,000 in *additional* funds using the home as collateral (called a "home equity loan"). Assume that, at the end of the three years, you still owe the $50,000, as well as your original mortgage.
    a. What is your equity in the home at the end of the three years?

    b. How many times are you leveraged on your investment in the home at the end of the three years?
    c. By what percentage could your home's price fall (after it reaches $500,000) before your equity in the home is wiped out?

14. [Requires appendix.] A homeowner is said to be "under water" if he or she owes more on the mortgage than the home is worth. Suppose someone bought a home for $300,000 with a $60,000 down payment, and took out a mortgage loan for the rest. A few years later, the value of the home has fallen by 15%, but the amount owed on the home has not changed.
    a. In this example, how much was borrowed to buy the home?
    b. What was the leverage ratio when the home was first purchased?
    c. After the home drops in value, is the homeowner under water?
    d. Answer the three questions above again, this time assuming that the down payment was only $30,000.
    e. Based on your answers above, when home prices are falling, what is the general relationship between the degree of leverage on a home and the likelihood that the owner will end up "under water" on the home?

More Challenging

15. [Requires appendix.] Suppose, as in a previous problem, you buy a home for $400,000 with a down payment of $100,000 and take out a mortgage for the remainder. Over the next three years, the price of the home rises to $500,000. However, during those three years, you borrow the *maximum* amount you can borrow without changing the value of your home equity. Assume that, at the end of the three years, you still owe all that you have borrowed, including your original mortgage.
    a. How much do you borrow (beyond the mortgage) over the three years?
    b. What is your simple leverage ratio at the end of the three years?
    c. By what percentage could your home's price fall (from $500,000) before your equity in the home is wiped out?

16. [Requires appendix.] Could any combination of home price, mortgage, or further borrowing on a home result in a simple leverage ratio of 1/2? If yes, provide an example. If no, briefly explain why.

This appendix discusses the concept of *leverage:* what it means, how it can be measured, and its implications for owning an asset. Our focus here is on the housing market. But leverage can be applied to many other markets, as you will see later in this text book.

Let's start by exploring how the housing market would operate *without* leverage. Imagine that you had to pay for a home in full, using only your own funds. In that case, if you have $100,000 available for buying a home, you could buy a home worth $100,000 and no more.

Suppose you bought a home for $100,000, and, over the year, housing prices rose 10%. The home would then be worth $110,000. If you then sold it (and if we ignore selling costs and maintenance), your $100,000 investment would have turned into $110,000—a capital gain of $10,000. This gives you a 10% rate of return on your financial investment of $100,000. We'll also note that, if the price of the home *fell* by 10%, down to $90,000, you would have a capital *loss* of $10,000—again, 10% of your financial investment. Notice that, when you use only your own funds, your rate of return on your investment (+10% or −10%) is the same as the rate of change for the home's price.

But as discussed in the chapter, most people do not buy a home using only their own funds. In the United States and many other countries, you will use your own funds for just *part* of the purchase—called the *down payment*—and borrow the remainder. This allows you to buy a home worth substantially more than you are investing yourself. Using borrowed money to buy a home is an example of a *leveraged* financial investment.

To see how this works in practice, let's once again assume you have $100,000 of your own funds available to invest in a home. But now, you'll use it as a down payment, equal to 20% of the home's purchase price. You'll buy a home for $500,000, and take out a mortgage loan for the amount not covered by your down payment: $400,000.

Panel (a) of Figure A.1 illustrates how this works: You use your own $100,000, plus $400,000 from the mortgage lender, to purchase a home worth $500,000. In return, you sign a mortgage contract, promising to pay back $400,000 in monthly payments over a few decades.

Now let's suppose, once again, that housing prices rise by 10% over the year. Because you own a $500,000 home, its price has risen to $550,000. Panel (b) shows what happens when you sell this home. You sell the house for $550,000, pay back what you owe the bank ($400,000),

and the mortgage contract is paid in full. You now have $150,000 left over. Remember: Your original investment was $100,000, and you now have $150,000, for a capital gain of $50,000. Thus, a 10% rise in housing prices has given you a 50% annual rate of return on your investment.

Of course, if the price *fell* by 10%, your home would be worth only $450,000. If you sold it at that price, and paid off the $400,000 loan, you'd be left with only $50,000 of the $100,000 you started with. In that case, you'd have *lost* 50% of your initial investment.

As you can see, when you borrow to buy a home, the potential capital gains and losses on your original investment are magnified. This magnification of gains and losses through borrowing is called leverage.

Measuring Leverage

For many purposes, it's useful to calculate the *degree* of leverage associated with an investment, such as a home purchase. There are various ways of measuring leverage, but all of them rely on the concept of *equity*:

> An owner's equity *in an asset is the difference between the asset's value and any unpaid debts on the asset (that is, debts for which the asset was used as collateral):*

Equity in Asset = Value of Asset − Debt Associated with Asset

Notice that an owner's equity depends on the asset's *value*. For assets owned by individuals or families, we use the *current market value* of the asset—the price at which it could be sold.[2] So, for example, a homeowner's equity is the price at which the home could be sold, minus any debts for which the home was used as collateral. The equity represents the part of the asset's value that truly belongs to its owner. It is what the owner would get if the asset were sold, after paying back the associated debt.

The concept of equity leads directly to one way of measuring leverage, which we'll call the *simple leverage ratio:*

> *The **simple leverage ratio** is the ratio of an asset's value to the owner's equity in the asset:*

[2] Owner's equity for a business firm is defined very much like equity for a household: The total value of its assets minus what it owes to others. But for firms, asset values are typically based on historical prices paid, rather than current market value.

FIGURE A.1   Leveraged Buying and Selling

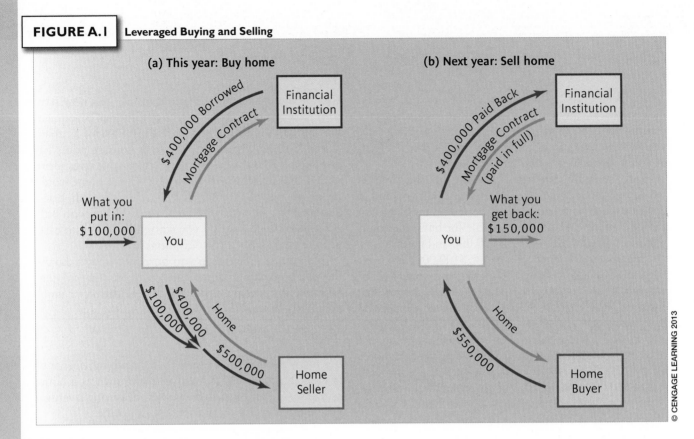

$$\text{Simple Leverage Ratio} = \frac{\text{Value of Asset}}{\text{Equity in Asset}}$$

Now, let's apply these concepts to home ownership. Suppose, as in our first example, you use only your own funds to buy a $100,000 home, and you never use the home as collateral for a loan. Using the definitions above, your equity in the home is $100,000 − $0 = $100,000. Your simple leverage ratio is $100,000/$100,000 = 1. A leverage ratio of 1 means no leverage at all: There is no borrowing to magnify capital gains and losses.

Now let's calculate the leverage ratio in our second example, in which you make a $100,000 down payment on a $500,000 home and borrow the remaining $400,000. Your equity in the home is $500,000 − $400,000 = $100,000. And your simple leverage ratio is $500,000/$100,000 = 5. In words, we'd say you are "leveraged five times."

Leverage and Rate of Return

The simple leverage ratio serves as a "rate-of-return multiplier." That is, we can multiply the rate of change in a home's price by the leverage ratio to get the rate of return on the (leveraged) investment. For example, we found earlier that, when you invest $100,000 to buy a $500,000 home and are leveraged 5 times, a 10% rise in housing

prices over the year gives you a 50% annual rate of return on your investment. Your rate of return is five times the percentage increase in the home's price.[3]

As you can see, when asset prices rise, leverage can increase your rate of return dramatically. But when asset prices fall, leverage increases the chance of wiping out your entire investment. With no leverage, your home's price would have to fall by 100% before your owner's equity would disappear. If you are leveraged 5 times, a drop of 20% eliminates your equity. And if you're leveraged 20 times, it takes only a 5% drop in prices to wipe out your entire investment.

One last word. In this appendix, we've been applying the concept of leverage, and the simple leverage ratio, to a single asset. But leverage can also refer to the *combined* assets of a household or business firm, or even to an entire sector of the economy. As you'll see in later chapters, high leverage played a crucial role in creating the financial crisis of 2008.

---

[3] More accurately, the leverage ratio is a multiplier for your *gross* rate of return, which ignores the annual cost of the borrowed funds. Your net rate of return (accounting for the cost of borrowing) will be lower. In our example, suppose that—based on the interest rate and tax benefits on your mortgage—your annual interest cost is 3% of the amount borrowed. Then borrowing costs for the year would be 0.03 × $400,000 = $12,000. Deducting this cost from your $50,000 capital gain leaves you with a $38,000 net gain for the year. So the *net* rate of return on your $100,000 investment would be $38,000/$100,000 = 38%.

CHAPTER 5

© FRANCES ROBERTS/ALAMY

Elasticity

Imagine that you are the mayor of a large U.S. city. Every day, the headlines blare about local problems—poverty, crime in the streets, the sorry state of public education, roads and bridges that are falling apart—and you, as mayor, are held accountable for all of them. Of course, you could help alleviate these problems, if only you had more money to spend on them. You've already raised taxes as much as you can, so where to get the money?

One day, an aide bounds into your office. "I've got the perfect solution," he says, beaming. "We raise mass transit fares." He shows you a sheet of paper on which he's done the calculation: Each year, city residents take 500 million trips on public transportation. If fares are raised by 50 cents, the transit system will take in an additional $250 million—enough to make a dent in some of the city's problems.

You stroke your chin and think about it. So many issues to balance: fairness, practicality, the political impact. But then another thought occurs to you: Your aide has made a serious mistake! Public transportation—like virtually everything else that people buy—obeys the law of demand. A rise in price—with no other change— will cause a decrease in quantity demanded. If you raise fares, each *trip* will bring in more revenue, but there will be *fewer trips* taken. Mass transit revenue might rise, or it might fall. How can you determine which will happen?

To answer that question, you need to know how *sensitive* mass transit ridership is to a change in price.

In this chapter, you will learn about *elasticities:* measures of the sensitivity of one variable to another. As you'll see, economists use a variety of different types of elasticities to make predictions and to recommend policy changes.

PRICE ELASTICITY OF DEMAND

One of the most important elasticities is the *price elasticity of demand,* which measures the sensitivity of quantity demanded to the price of the good itself. To make the measure meaningful, our elasticity calculation always compares the *percentage change* in quantity demanded with the *percentage change* in price. (See the nearby Dangerous Curves box to understand why using percentages is important.)

More specifically:

> The **price elasticity of demand** (E_D) *for a good is the percentage change in quantity demanded* ($\%\Delta Q^D$) *divided by the percentage change in price* ($\%\Delta P$):
>
> $$E_D = \frac{\%\Delta Q^D}{\%\Delta P}$$

Price elasticity of demand The sensitivity of quantity demanded to price; the percentage change in quantity demanded caused by a one percent change in price.

121

⚠ DANGEROUS CURVES

A tempting (but bad) measure of price sensitivity Why don't we measure price sensitivity more simply, dividing the change in quantity demanded by the change in price ($\Delta Q^D/\Delta P$), instead of using percentage changes?

Two reasons. First, the simpler measure would depend on how you choose to define quantity demanded. For example, suppose a $1 price hike caused music downloads to drop from 1,000,000 to 900,000 songs each day. Defining ΔQ^D as "songs per day," we'd get $\Delta Q^D/\Delta P = 100,000$ (ignoring the minus sign). But if we define Q^D as "songs per week," the same demand behavior would decrease quantity from 7,000,000 to 6,300,000, so we'd get $\Delta Q^D/\Delta P = 700,000$—a much larger number. Using percentage changes, by contrast, gives you the same percentage drop in quantity using either definition.

The simple measure also ignores the relative importance of changes in price and quantity, making it impossible to compare price sensitivities of different goods. For example, a $1 price hike is a relatively large increase for music downloads, but a relatively tiny increase for automobiles. Similarly, a decrease of "100,000 units" in quantity could be relatively large or small, depending on how many units were demanded before the price change. Percentage changes automatically account for the relative importance of a change.

For example, if the price of video games falls by 2%, and this causes the quantity demanded to rise by 6%, then $E_D = 6\%/2\% = 3.0$. We would say "the price elasticity of demand for video games is 3.0."

Of course, when price *falls* by 2%, that's a change of *negative* 2%, while quantity demanded changes by $+6\%$. So technically speaking, elasticity should be viewed as a negative number. In this book, we'll follow a common convention of dropping the minus sign. That way, when we compare elasticities and say that one is larger, we'll be comparing absolute values.

In our example, elasticity has the value 3.0. But what, exactly, does that number mean? Here is a straightforward way to interpret the number:

> *The price elasticity of demand* (E_D) *tells us the percentage change in quantity demanded for each 1 percent change in price.*

In our example, with $E_D = 3.0$, each 1% drop in price causes quantity demanded to rise by 3%.

Given this interpretation, it's clear that an elasticity value of 3.0 implies greater price sensitivity than an elasticity value of 2.0, or one of 0.7. More generally,

> *The greater the elasticity value, the more sensitive quantity demanded is to price.*

Calculating Price Elasticity of Demand

When we calculate price elasticity of demand, we imagine that *only price* is changing, while we hold constant all other influences on quantity demanded, such as buyers' incomes, the prices of other goods, and so on. Thus, we measure elasticity for a movement *along* an unchanging demand curve. In order to calculate an elasticity, we must first have some knowledge about the demand curve itself.

Figure 1, for example, shows a hypothetical demand curve in the market for avocados in a city. Suppose we want to measure elasticity along this demand curve between points *A* and *B*. As our first step, we'll calculate the percentage change in price.

Let's suppose we move from point *A* to point *B*. Price falls by $0.50. Since our starting price at point *A* was $1.50, this would be a 33% drop in price.

But wait . . . suppose we go in the reverse direction, from point *B* to *A*. Now our starting price would be $1.00, so the $0.50 price hike would be a 50% rise. As you can see, the percentage change in price (33% or 50%) depends on the direction we are moving. And the same will be true of quantity. If we calculate percentages in this way, our elasticity value will also depend on which direction we move.

This presents us with a problem. Ideally, we'd like our measure of price sensitivity to be the same, whether we go from *A* to *B* or from *B* to *A*, since each is simply the mirror image of the other. To accomplish this goal, elasticity calculations often use a special convention to get percentage changes: Instead of dividing the change in a variable by its *starting* value, we divide the change by the *average* of its starting and ending values. This is often called the "midpoint

FIGURE 1 | Using the Midpoint Formula for Elasticity

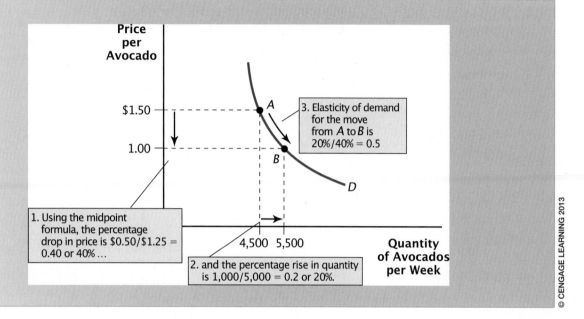

Price per Avocado

$1.50

1.00

A

B

D

3. Elasticity of demand for the move from A to B is 20%/40% = 0.5

1. Using the midpoint formula, the percentage drop in price is $0.50/$1.25 = 0.40 or 40% …

4,500 5,500

2. and the percentage rise in quantity is 1,000/5,000 = 0.2 or 20%.

Quantity of Avocados per Week

formula," because we are dividing the change by the midpoint between the old and new values.

> *When determining elasticities, we calculate the percentage change in a variable using the midpoint formula: the change in the variable divided by the average of the old and new values.*

For example, in Figure 1, between points A and B the average of the old and new price is ($1.50 + $1.00)/2 = $1.25. Using this average price as our base, the percentage change in price is $0.50/$1.25 = 0.40 or 40%. With the midpoint formula, the percentage change in price is the same whether we move from A to B, or from B to A.

More generally, when price changes from any value P_0 to any other value P_1, we define the percentage change in price ($\%\Delta P$) as

$$\%\Delta P = \frac{\Delta P}{P_{AV}}$$

where P_{AV} stands for the average of the old and new price. The percentage change in quantity demanded ($\%\Delta Q^D$) is calculated in a similar way:

$$\%\Delta Q^D = \frac{\Delta Q^D}{Q^D_{AV}}$$

Once again, we are using the average of the initial and the new quantity demanded as our base quantity.

The midpoint formula is an approximation to the actual percentage change in a variable, but it has the advantage of giving us consistent elasticity values when we reverse directions. We will use the midpoint formula only when *calculating elasticity values from data on prices and quantities*. For all other purposes, we'll calculate percentage changes in the normal way, using the starting value as the base.

FIGURE 2   Categories of Demand Behavior

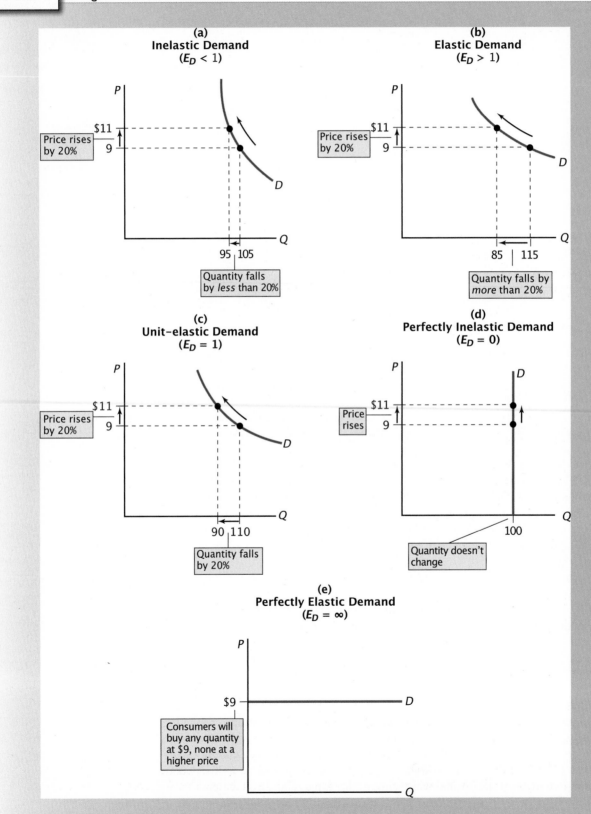

An Example

Let's calculate the price elasticity of demand for avocados along a part of the demand curve in Figure 1. As price falls from $1.50 to $1.00, quantity demanded rises from 4,500 to 5,500. Using the midpoint formula (and dropping negative signs):

$$\%\Delta Q^D = \frac{\Delta Q^D}{Q_{AV}} = \frac{5,500 - 4,500}{\left[\dfrac{(5,500 + 4,500)}{2}\right]} = \frac{1,000}{5,000} = 0.20 \text{ or } 20\%$$

$$\%\Delta P = \frac{\Delta P}{P_{AV}} = \frac{[\$1.00 - \$1.50]}{\left[\dfrac{(\$1.00 + \$1.50)}{2}\right]} = \frac{-\$0.50}{\$1.25} = -0.40 \text{ or } -40\%$$

Finally, we use these numbers (dropping the minus sign) to calculate the price elasticity of demand:

$$E_D = \frac{\%\Delta Q^D}{\%\Delta P} = \frac{20\%}{40\%} = 0.5$$

Or, in simple English, a 1% change in price causes a ½% change in quantity demanded.

Categorizing Demand

Economists have found it useful to divide demand behavior into categories, based on elasticity values.

These categories are illustrated in Figure 2. However, keep in mind that elasticity can change as we move along a demand curve. So the elasticities in Figure 2 apply to the specific price and quantity changes shown there.

Panel (a) illustrates the case of **inelastic demand**, defined as an elasticity value *less than one*. "Inelastic" means quantity demanded is relatively *in*sensitive to price changes. In the figure, a 20% price increase causes quantity demanded to fall by less than 20% (as you can verify). Whenever quantity changes by a smaller percentage than price, demand will be inelastic.

Inelastic demand A price elasticity of demand between 0 and 1.

Panel (b) shows **elastic demand**, which is an elasticity value *greater than one* (because quantity demanded changes by a larger percentage than the price). "Elastic" means quantity demanded is relatively sensitive to price changes. Here, the same 20% price increase causes quantity demanded to fall by more than 20%.

Elastic demand A price elasticity of demand greater than 1.

Panel (c) shows the special case of **unit-elastic demand**, which is an elasticity value *equal to one*. Unit-elasticity is an "in-between" case, where quantity demanded changes by the same percentage as the price (both 20% in the figure).

Unit elastic demand A price elasticity of demand equal to 1.

The last two panels illustrate elasticity values that apply in special situations. In panel (d), we have **perfectly inelastic demand**, defined as an elasticity value of *zero*. When demand is perfectly inelastic, the demand curve will be vertical, so a change in price causes no change at all in quantity demanded ($\%\Delta Q^D = 0$ for any $\%\Delta P$). Perfectly inelastic demand can occur along a segment of a demand curve (for price changes that people don't notice or choose to ignore), but it's mostly useful as a theoretical category—an extreme case of price insensitivity.

Perfectly inelastic demand A price elasticity of demand equal to 0.

Finally, panel (e) shows the opposite extreme case: **perfectly elastic demand**, defined as an elasticity value of *infinity*. Here, the demand curve is horizontal. As

Perfectly (infinitely) elastic demand A price elasticity of demand approaching infinity.

long as the price stays at one particular value (where the demand curve touches the vertical axis), *any* quantity might be demanded. But even the tiniest price rise would cause quantity demanded to fall to zero. $\%\Delta Q^D / \%\Delta P$ is infinite because no matter how small we make the percentage change in price (in the denominator), the percentage change in quantity (in the numerator) will always be infinitely larger.

Later (in Chapter 9), you'll see that perfectly elastic demand curves help us understand the behavior of individual firms in perfectly competitive markets. But for now, here's a hypothetical example. Imagine that the government were to lower the price of freshly printed 10 dollar bills just a tiny bit below $10. The quantity of 10 dollar bills demanded would be astronomically high. On the other hand, if the government charged even a tiny bit more than $10, almost no one would buy them. So the demand curve for new 10 dollar bills is essentially horizontal at a price of exactly $10.

Elasticity and Straight-Line Demand Curves

Figure 3 shows a linear (straight-line) demand curve for laptop computers. Each time the price drops by $500, the quantity of laptops demanded per week rises by 10,000. Because this behavior remains constant all along the curve, is the price elasticity of demand also constant?

Actually, no. Elasticity is the ratio of *percentage* changes; what remains constant along a linear demand curve is the ratio of *absolute* or *unit* changes.

In fact, we can show that as we move rightward along a downward-sloping linear demand curve, the elasticity always *decreases*. For example, let's calculate the elasticity between points *A* and *B*. Price falls from $2,000 to $1,500, a 28.6% drop using the midpoint formula. Quantity rises from 15,000 to 25,000, which is a 50% rise using the midpoint formula. Taking the ratio of these changes, we find

---

FIGURE 3   **How Elasticity Changes along a Straight-Line Demand Curve**

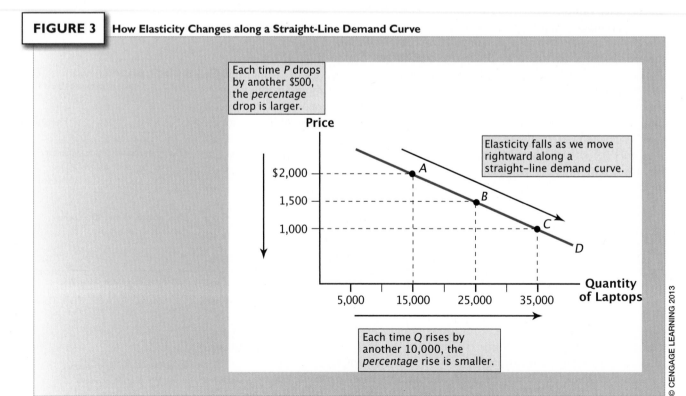

that the elasticity for a move from point *A* to *B* is 50% / 28.6% = 1.75.

Now let's calculate the elasticity between points *B* and *C*, where price falls from $1,500 to $1,000, and quantity rises from 25,000 to 35,000. For this change (as you can verify), price falls by 40% while quantity demanded rises by 33.3% (using the midpoint formula). So the elasticity for a move from point *B* to *C* is 33.3%/40% = 0.83.

Notice what's happened: as we've moved downward and rightward along this straight-line demand curve, elasticity has fallen from 1.75 to 0.83. Demand has become *less elastic*.

There is a good reason for this. As we travel down the demand curve, the average quantity we use as the base for figuring percentage changes keeps increasing. So a constant 10,000 increase in quantity becomes a smaller and smaller *percentage* increase. The opposite also happens with price: It keeps getting smaller, so the same $500 decrease in price becomes a growing *percentage* decrease. Thus, as we travel down a linear demand curve, with %ΔQ^D shrinking and %ΔP growing, the ratio %ΔQ^D/%ΔP decreases.

DANGEROUS CURVES

Mistakes in observing elasticities It's tempting to calculate an elasticity from simple observation: looking at what actually happened to buyers' purchases after some price changed. But this often leads to serious errors. Elasticity of demand tells us the effect of a price change on quantity demanded *if* all other influences on demand remain unchanged. That is, it measures price sensitivity *along* a single demand curve. But in the real world, these other influences may change in the months or years after a price change, causing the demand curve to shift. In that case, when you compare before and after, you are comparing points on two different demand curves. Some of the change in quantity demanded is caused by factors other than price.

Economists and statisticians have developed tools to isolate the effects of price changes when other things might be affecting demand at the same time. If you study economics further and take a course in econometrics, you'll learn some of these techniques.

> *Elasticity of demand varies along a downward-sloping straight-line demand curve. More specifically, demand becomes less elastic (E_D gets smaller) as we move downward and rightward.*

This is a special conclusion only for *linear* demand curves that slope *downward*. For *non*linear demand curves, moving down the curve can cause elasticity to rise, fall, or remain constant, depending on the shape of the curve. And as you've seen, if a linear demand curve is vertical or horizontal, elasticity will be constant (at zero or infinity, respectively).

Elasticity and Total Revenue

When the price of a good increases, the law of demand tells us that people will buy less of it. But this does not necessarily mean they will *spend* less on it. After the price rises, fewer units will be purchased in the market, but each unit will cost more. What happens to *total spending* on the good? Or, recognizing that total spending by all buyers equals the total revenue of all sellers, we can ask the same question this way: When price rises, what happens to the *total combined revenue* of all firms that sell in the market? Let's see. On the one hand, each unit sold can be sold for more, tending to increase revenue. On the other hand, fewer units will be sold, which works to decrease revenue. Which one will dominate?

The answer depends on the price elasticity of demand for the good. To see why, note that the total revenue of sellers in a market (*TR*) is the price per unit (*P*) times the quantity that people buy (*Q*):

$$TR = P \times Q.$$

When we raise price, *P* goes up, but *Q* goes down. What happens to the product depends on which one changes by a larger percentage.

FIGURE 4 **Elasticity and Total Revenue**

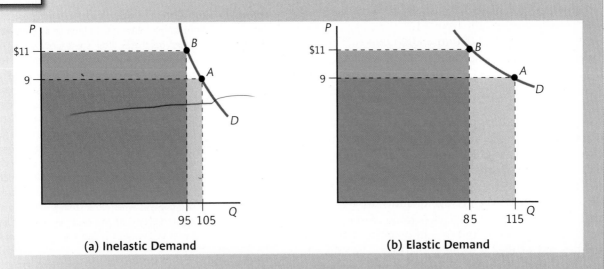

(a) Inelastic Demand   (b) Elastic Demand

In panel (a), demand is inelastic, so a rise in price causes total revenue to increase. Specifically, at a price of $9 (point A), total revenue is $9 × 105 = $945. When price rises to $11 (point B), total revenue increases to $11 × 95 = $1,045. In panel (b), demand is elastic, so a rise in price causes total revenue to decrease. Specifically, at a price of $9 (point A), total revenue is $9 × 115 = $1,035. When price rises to $11 (point B), total revenue falls to $11 × 85 = $935.

Suppose that demand is *inelastic* ($E_D < 1$). Then a 1% rise in price will cause quantity demanded to fall by *less* than 1%. So the greater amount sellers get on each unit outweighs the impact of the drop in quantity, and total revenue will *rise*.

The behavior of total revenue when demand is inelastic can be seen very clearly on a graph, once you learn how to interpret it. Look at the left panel of Figure 4, which duplicates the inelastic demand curve introduced earlier. On this demand curve, let's start at a price of $9, and look at the rectangle with a corner at point A. The height of the rectangle is the price of $9, and the width is the quantity of 105, so its *area* (height × width = $P \times Q$ = $9 × 105 = $945) is the total revenue of sellers when price is $9.

More generally,

> *At any point on a demand curve, sellers' total revenue is the area of a rectangle with height equal to price and width equal to quantity demanded.*

Now let's raise the price to $11. The total revenue is now the area of the rectangle with a corner at point B (with TR = $11 × 95 = $1,045). The rise in price has *increased* total revenue, because demand is inelastic.

Now suppose that demand is *elastic* ($E_D > 1$). Once again, a 1% rise in price causes quantity demanded to fall, but this time it falls by *more* than 1%. Sellers get more on each unit, but that is outweighed by the drop in the quantity they sell, and total revenue *falls*.

This is shown in the right panel of Figure 4, using the example of elastic demand from a few pages earlier. When the price is $9, TR is the area of the rectangle with a corner at point A, equal to $9 × 115 = $1,035. When the price rises to $11, TR becomes the area of the rectangle with corner at point B ($11 × 85 = $935). Because demand is elastic, the rise in price *decreases* total revenue.

TABLE 1

Demand Elasticity	Effect of Price *Increase*:	Effect of Price *Decrease*:
inelastic ($E_D < 1$)	total revenue ↑	total revenue ↓
unit elastic ($E_D = 1$)	no change in total revenue	no change in total revenue
elastic ($E_D > 1$)	total revenue ↓	total revenue ↑

© CENGAGE LEARNING 2013

TABLE 1

Effects of Price Changes on Revenue

We can conclude that:

An increase in price raises total revenue when demand is inelastic, and shrinks total revenue when demand is elastic.

What if the price fell instead of rose? Then, in Figure 4 we'd be making the reverse move: from point *B* to point *A* on each curve. And logic tells us that if demand is inelastic, total revenue must fall. If demand is elastic, the drop in price will cause total revenue to rise.

What happens if demand is unit elastic? You can probably guess. This would mean that a 1% change in price causes a 1% change in quantity, but in the opposite direction. The two effects on total revenue would cancel each other out, so total revenue would remain unchanged.

Table 1 summarizes these results about elasticity and total revenue. Don't try to memorize the table, but *do* use it to test yourself: Try to explain the logic for each entry.

Determinants of Elasticity

Table 2 lists the price elasticity of demand for a variety of goods and services. The numbers are not strictly comparable, because they were obtained using different statistical methods in different years. Still, they illustrate some interesting patterns that we can explore. Why, for example, is the demand for Tide Detergent, Pepsi, and Coke highly elastic, while the demand for gasoline and eggs is inelastic?

Availability of Substitutes

When close substitutes are available for a good, demand for it will be more elastic. If the price of ground beef rises, with all other prices held constant, consumers can easily switch to other forms of beef, or even chicken or pork. But when the price of gasoline rises, the substitutes that are available (mass transit, carpooling, biking, or even not going places) are not as close. Thus, it is not surprising that the demand for ground beef is more elastic than the demand for gasoline.

When close substitutes are available for a product, demand tends to be more elastic.

The availability of close substitutes often depends on how narrowly or broadly we define the market we are analyzing. Demand for Pepsi will be more elastic than demand for soft drinks, and the demand for soft drinks will be more elastic than the demand for all beverages. This is because when we determine the elasticity of demand in a market, we hold constant all prices outside of the market. So in determining the elasticity for Pepsi, we ask what happens when the price of Pepsi rises but the price of

TABLE 2

Some Short-Run Price Elasticities of Demand

Specific Brands		Narrow Categories		Broad Categories	
Tide Detergent	2.79	Transatlantic Air Travel	1.30	Recreation	0.90
Pepsi	2.08	Ground Beef	1.02	Clothing	0.72
Coke	1.71	Pork	0.78	Food	0.30
Kellogg's	2.93 to	Milk	0.54	Transportation	0.56
Corn Flakes	4.05	Cigarettes	0.25 to 0.70	Alcohol & Tobacco	0.26
		Electricity (New England)	0.19		
		Beer	0.26		
		Eggs	0.26		
		Gasoline	0.26		
		Health Insurance (individually purchased)	0.57		

Sources: "The price sensitivity of the demand for nongroup health insurance," Congressional Budget Office, August 2005; "Uncompensated own-price elasticity for broad consumption groups," U.S. Department of Agriculture, Economic Research Service, 2005; Bwo-Nung Huang, Chi-wei Yang, and Ming-jeng Hwang (2004) "New evidence on demand for cigarettes: A panel data approach," *The International Journal of Applied Economics* 1(1): 81–97; C. Akbay and E. Jones (2006) "Demand elasticities and price-cost margin ratios for grocery products in different socioeconomic groups," *Agricultural Economics—Czech* 52(5): 225–235; Mark A. Bernstein and James Griffin (2005) *Regional differences in the price-elasticity of demand for energy*, National Renewable Energy Laboratory/RAND Corporation; M. Espey (1996) "Explaining the variation in elasticity estimates of gasoline demand in the United States: A meta-analysis," *The Energy Journal* 17(3): 49–60; Sachin Gupta et al. (1996) "Do household scanner data provide representative inferences from brand choices? A comparison with store data," *Journal of Marketing Research* (Fall): 383ff; F. Gasmi, J. J. Laffont, and Q. Vuong (1992) "Econometric analysis of collusive behavior in a soft-drink market," *Journal of Economics and Management Strategy* (Summer): 277–311; J. M. Cigliano (1980) "Price and income elasticities for airline travel," *Business Economics* (September): 17–21; M. R. Baye, D. W. Jansen, and Jae-Woo Lee (1992) "Advertising effects in complete demand systems," *Applied Economics* (October): 1087–1096; Gary W. Brester and Michael K. Wohlgenant (1991) "Estimating interrelated demands for meats using new measures for ground and table cut beef," *American Journal of Agricultural Economics* (November): 1182–1194.

Coke remains constant. Since it is so easy to switch to Coke, demand is highly elastic. But in determining the elasticity for soft drinks, we ask what happens when the price of *all* soft drinks rise together, holding constant only the prices of things that are *not* soft drinks. Demand for soft drinks is therefore less elastic.

Some of the entries in Table 2 confirm this influence on elasticity. For example, the demand for transportation, a very broad category, is less elastic than the demand for transatlantic air travel. But other entries seem to contradict it. (Can you find one?) Remember, though, that there are other determinants of elasticity besides the narrowness or broadness of the market.

⚠ DANGEROUS CURVES

Even "necessities" obey the law of demand Don't make the common mistake of thinking that people *must* buy a constant quantity of goods they regard as necessities and cannot make do with any less. That would imply *perfectly inelastic* demand. Studies routinely show that demand for most goods regarded as necessities is inelastic, but not perfectly inelastic. People do find ways to cut back on these goods when their prices rise.

Necessities versus Luxuries

Goods that we think of as necessary for our survival or general well-being, and for which there are no close substitutes, are often referred to as "necessities." Most people would include the broad categories "food," "housing," and "medical care" in this category. When we regard something as a necessity, demand for it will tend to be less elastic. This is another reason why the elasticity of demand for gasoline is so small: Many people regard gasoline as a necessity.

By contrast, goods that we can more easily do without—such as entertainment or vacation travel—are often referred to as "luxuries." Demand for these goods will tend to be more elastic, since people will cut back their purchases more when price rises.

> *Goods we regard as necessities tend to have less elastic demand than goods we regard as luxuries.*

In Table 2, for example, among the broad categories, the demands for food and clothing are less elastic than the demand for recreation. Another example is health insurance. The table shows that demand for individually purchased health insurance is inelastic ($E_D = 0.57$). But among just those in fair or poor health, demand is even more inelastic ($E_D = 0.39$, not shown in the table). In this group, people are more likely to regard health insurance as a necessity.

Remember, though, that how broadly or narrowly we define the market makes an important difference. We may regard broadly defined "clothing" as a necessity. But "designer jeans" (not in the table) might be a luxury, with a highly elastic demand.

Importance in Buyers' Budgets

When a good takes up a large part of your budget initially, a rise in price has a large impact on how much you will have left to spend on other things. All else equal, this will tend to make demand more elastic. For example, a vacation trip to Paris would take a big bite out of most peoples' budgets. If the price of the vacation rises by, say, 20%, many people will start to consider other alternatives, since not doing so would mean a considerable sacrifice of other purchases.

Now consider the other extreme: ordinary table salt. A family with an income of $50,000 per year would spend less than 0.005% of its income on this good, so the price of salt could double or triple and have no significant impact on the ability to buy other goods. We would therefore expect the demand for table salt to be inelastic.

This insight helps us to explain some seemingly anomalous results in Table 2. Demand for food is more elastic than the demand for eggs. Based on the narrowness of definition, we would expect the reverse. But eggs make up a rather small fraction of the typical family's budget, and certainly smaller than food as a whole. This tends to reduce the elasticity of demand for eggs.

> *When spending on a good makes up a larger proportion of families' budgets, demand tends to be more elastic.*

Time Horizon

How much time we wait after a price change can have an important impact on the elasticity of demand. The elasticities of demand in Table 2 are all **short-run elasticities**: the quantity response is measured for just a short time (usually a year or less) after the price change.

A **long-run elasticity** measures the quantity response after more time has elapsed—typically a few years or more. For many goods, demand will be more

Short-run elasticity An elasticity measured just a short time after a price change.

Long-run elasticity An elasticity measured a year or more after a price change.

TABLE 3

Short-Run versus Long-Run Elasticities

Good	Area of Study	Short-Run Elasticity	Long-Run Elasticity
Gasoline	United States	0.26	0.58
	Britain	0.25	0.60
Electricity	U.S.–New England	0.19	0.33
	U.S.–Pacific Coast	0.19	0.25
Oil	United States	0.06	0.45
	France	0.07	0.57
	Japan	0.07	0.36
	Denmark	0.03	0.19
Mass Transit	Multi-Country	0.2 to 0.5	0.6 to 0.9

Sources: Molly Espey (1996) "Explaining the variation in elasticity estimates of gasoline demand in the United States: A meta-analysis," *The Energy Journal* 17(3): 49–60; Phil Goodwin, Joyce Dargay, and Mark Hanly (2004) "Elasticities of road traffic and fuel consumption with respect to price and income: A review," *Transport Reviews* 24(3) 275–292; ESRC Transport Studies Unit, University College London (www.transport.ucl.ac.uk); Mark A. Bernstein and James Griffin (2005) *Regional differences in the price-elasticity of demand for energy*, National Renewable Energy Laboratory/ RAND Corporation; John C.B. Cooper (March 2003) "Price elasticity of demand for crude oil: Estimates from 23 countries," *OPEC Review: Energy Economics & Related Issues* (27)1; Todd Litman (2004) "Transit price elasticities and cross-price elasticities," *Journal of Public Transportation* 7(2).

elastic in the long run than in the short run. Why? Because the longer we wait after a sustained price change, the more time consumers have to make adjustments in their lives that can affect their quantity demanded.

> *In markets where it takes a long time for buyers to fully adjust to a price change, demand will be more elastic in the long run than in the short run.*

Table 3 shows some examples of short-run and long-run elasticities related to energy and transportation. In each case, demand is more elastic in the long run than in the short run. For example, the *short-run* elasticity for gasoline in many countries is typically estimated around 0.26, while the long-run elasticity is two or three times higher. What accounts for the difference?

Table 4, provides some of the answers. It lists some of the ways people can adjust to a significant rise in the price of gasoline over the short run and the long

TABLE 4

Adjustments After a Rise in the Price of Gasoline

Short Run (less than a year)	Long Run (a year or more)
• Use public transit more often	• Buy a more fuel-efficient car
• Arrange a car pool	• Move closer to your job
• Check tire pressure more often	• Switch to a job closer to home
• Drive more slowly on the highway	• Move to a city where less driving is required
• Eliminate unnecessary trips	
• If there are two cars, use the more fuel-efficient one	

run. Remember that the adjustments in the long-run column are *additional* adjustments people can make if given enough time. While some of them may seem extreme, thousands of families made these changes during the latter half of the 1970s, after the OPEC nations reduced oil supplies and the price of gasoline roughly quadrupled.

Our analysis of short-run and long-run elasticities might have raised a question in your mind. Isn't price elasticity of demand measured *along* a demand curve? Indeed it is. But then how can we get two different elasticity measures from the same market? The answer is: There can be more than one demand curve associated with a market.

For some (but not all) goods, people need time to fully adjust to a price change. The relevant demand curve will then depend on the time horizon we are analyzing. *Short-run* demand curves show quantity demanded at different prices when people only have a short period of time (a few weeks or a few months) to adjust. A *long-run* demand curve shows quantity demanded after buyers have had much longer—say, a year or more—to adjust to a price change.

The two demand curves in Figure 5 illustrate how this works in the U.S. market for gasoline. We assume that initially we are at point *A*, with a price of $2 per gallon and quantity demanded of 400 million gallons per day. As long as the price—and every other influence on demand—remains the same, we would stay at point *A*.

© AXL/SHUTTERSTOCK.COM

DANGEROUS CURVES ⚠️

Slope and elasticity In Figure 5, when the price rises from $2 to $3, demand is more elastic along the flatter curve D_{LR} than along the steeper demand curve D_{SR}. So it's tempting to conclude that "flatter demand curves are more elastic than steeper curves." But be careful. As you learned earlier, except in special cases, elasticity changes as we move along a demand curve. Some segments of the flatter curve may be less elastic than some segments of the steeper curve. In general, elasticity applies to a given movement along a demand curve, not to the entire demand curve.

Still, when two different demand curves share a common point (such as point *A* in Figure 5), we can say the following: *For a given price change* and *starting at that shared point,* demand will be more elastic along the flatter curve. The reason: With the same starting point and the same price change, quantity will change by more (in both units and percentage) along the flatter curve. With %ΔP the same and %ΔQ^D greater, elasticity will be greater for the move along the flatter curve.

FIGURE 5 | **Short-Run versus Long-Run Price Elasticity of Demand**

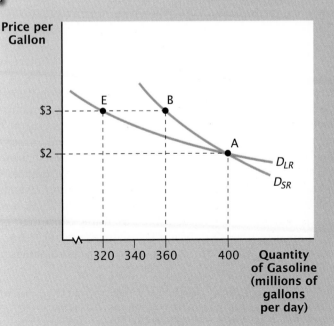

When the price of gasoline rises by $1, the decrease in quantity demanded (and the price elasticity of demand) depends on how long we wait before measuring buyers' response. If we waited just a few months after the price change, we'd move along demand curve D_{SR}, from point A to point B. If we waited a year or longer, we'd move from point A to point E along demand curve D_{LR}, with quantity demanded falling even more.

© CENGAGE LEARNING 2013

But now, suppose the price rises from $2 to $3 and stays there. To find the daily quantity demanded *a few months later,* we would move along a demand curve like D_{SR}. This demand curve has a very low elasticity of demand because there is not much time for gasoline buyers to adjust. For example, they might cut out some unnecessary trips, but they are unlikely to purchase a more fuel-efficient car in this time frame. Using demand curve D_{SR}, we end up at point *B*, with gasoline demand equal to 360 million gallons per day.

But if we measure the demand response a year or longer after the price change—enough time for a significant number of people to replace their cars or make other difficult adjustments—we would move along a demand curve like D_{LR}. The price increase—over the long run—would cause us to move from point *A* to point *E*, where quantity demanded has fallen to 320 million gallons per day.

An Example: Elasticity and Mass Transit

Earlier in this chapter, you were asked to imagine that you were a mayor trying to determine whether raising mass transit fares would increase or decrease city revenues. Now you know that the answer depends on the price elasticity of demand for mass transit.

As you can see in Table 3, the demand for mass transit services is *inelastic* in both the short run and the long run. This means that a rise in fares would likely raise mass transit revenue for a city. Let's illustrate with some sample calculations.

Suppose New York City raised subway and bus fares from $2.25 to $2.70, a 20% increase.[1] What would happen to revenue in the long run? From Table 3, the long-run elasticity is between 0.6 and 0.9, so let's choose an estimate that falls near the middle of that range: 0.7. Using this elasticity, each 1% increase in fares would cause a 0.7% decrease in ridership. So our 20% fare hike would decrease ridership by 20 × 0.7 = 14%. New Yorkers take about 2 billion trips each year, so a 14% decrease would bring trips down to 1.72 billion per year.

Now let's calculate revenue, before and after the price hike. At the original price of $2.25, total revenue is 2 billion trips × $2.25 per trip = $4.5 billion. After the price hike, total revenue would be 1.72 billion trips × $2.70 per trip = $4.64 billion. We conclude that raising the fare would increase mass transit revenue by about $0.14 billion, or $14 million per year in the long run.

Why, then, doesn't New York City raise the fare to $2.70? In fact, why doesn't it go further, to $3? Or $5? Or even $10?

For two reasons. First, elasticity estimates come from *past* data on the response to price changes. When we ask what would happen if we raise the price, we are extrapolating from these past responses. For small price changes, the extrapolation is likely to be fairly accurate. But large price changes move us into unknown territory, and elasticity may change. Demand could be *elastic* for a very large price hike, and then total revenue would fall. This puts a limit on fares, even if a city's goal is the maximum possible revenue.

A second (and more important) reason is that generating revenue is only *one* consideration in setting mass transit fares. City governments also want to provide affordable transportation to city residents, reduce traffic congestion on city streets, and limit pollution. A fare increase, even if it would raise total revenue, would work against these other goals. This is why most cities keep the price of mass transit below the revenue-maximizing price.

---

[1] Notice that we're calculating percentage changes the conventional way, rather than with the midpoint formula. In general, we use the midpoint formula only when calculating an elasticity value. Here we're using an elasticity that has already been determined for us.

PRICE ELASTICITY OF SUPPLY

The counterpart to the price elasticity of demand is the price elasticity of supply, which measures the sensitivity of quantity supplied to price. More specifically,

> *the **price elasticity of supply** is the percentage change in quantity supplied (%ΔQ^S) divided by the percentage change in price (%ΔP):*
>
> $$\frac{\%\Delta Q^S}{\%\Delta P}$$

price elasticity of supply The percentage change in quantity supplied caused by a 1 percent change in price.

Because price and quantity supplied move in the same direction, the result is a positive number.

The price elasticity of supply measures the sensitivity of quantity supplied to price changes as we move *along* the supply curve. A large value for the price elasticity of supply means that quantity supplied is very sensitive to price changes. For example, an elasticity value of 5 would imply that if price increased by 1%, quantity supplied would rise by 5%.

Determinants of Supply Elasticity

A major determinant of supply elasticity is the ease with which suppliers can find profitable activities that are *alternatives* to producing the good in question. In general, supply will tend to be more elastic when suppliers can switch to producing alternate goods more easily.

When can we expect suppliers to have easy alternatives? First, the nature of the good itself plays a role. All else equal, the supply of envelopes should be more elastic than the supply of microprocessor chips. This is because envelope producers can more easily modify their production lines to produce alternative paper products. Microprocessor suppliers, however, would be hard-pressed to produce anything other than computer chips.

The narrowness of the market definition matters too—especially *geographic* narrowness. For example, the market for oranges in Illinois should be more supply-elastic than the market for oranges in the United States. In the Illinois market, a decrease in price would imply we are holding constant the price of oranges in *all other states*. This gives suppliers an easy alternative: They could sell their oranges in other states! Similarly, the supply of oranges to Chicago would be even more elastic than the supply of oranges to Illinois.

Finally, the *time horizon* is important. The longer we wait after a price change, the greater the supply response to a price change. As we will see when we discuss the theory of the firm, there usually is *some* response to a price change right away: Existing firms will speed up or slow down production in their current facilities. But further responses come about as firms have time to change their plant and equipment, and new firms have time to enter or leave an industry.

Calculating a Supply Elasticity

Figure 6 illustrates how we can calculate the short-run and long-run elasticities of supply for U.S. corn farmers. Initially, the market is at point *A*, with a price of $4.50 per bushel and quantity supplied of 190 million bushels per week. When the price rises to $5.50 per bushel, and we measure the quantity supplied a short time (say a month or two) later, we move along supply curve S_{SR} and quantity supplied rises to 210 million bushels per week.

FIGURE 6   Short-Run versus Long-Run Price Elasticity of Supply

When the price of corn rises from $4.50 to $5.50 per bushel, the increase in quantity supplied (and the price elasticity of supply) depends on how long we wait before measuring the response. If we wait just a few months after the price change, we'd move along supply curve S_{SR}, from point A to point B. If we wait a year or longer, we'd move along supply curve S_{LR}, from point A to point C. The same rise in price causes a greater increase in quantity supplied after a year or longer, because farmers can make further adjustments in quantity supplied if given more time.

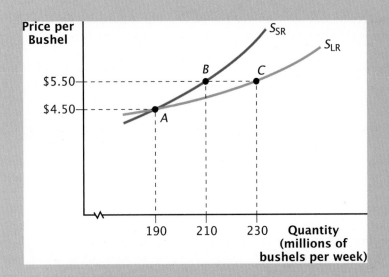

Using the midpoint rule, the percentage change in the price is $1/$5.00 = 20%, while the percentage change in quantity is 20/200 = 10%. Therefore, the short-run supply elasticity for corn is equal to $\%\Delta Q^S/\%\Delta P = 10\%/20\% = 0.50$.

What if we waited longer after the price hike (a year or longer) before measuring the quantity response? Then we would move along a more-elastic supply curve such as S_{LR}. Quantity is more sensitive to price in the long run, because farmers have the time to make further adjustments to increase production, such as shifting from other crops to corn.

> In general, long-run supply elasticities are greater than short-run supply elasticities.

OTHER ELASTICITIES

The concept of *elasticity* is a very general one. It can be used to measure the sensitivity of virtually *any* variable to any other variable. All types of elasticity measures, however, share one thing in common: They tell us the percentage change in one variable caused by a 1% change in the other. Let's look briefly at two additional elasticity measures, and what each of them tells us.

Income Elasticity of Demand

Income elasticity of demand The percentage change in quantity demanded caused by a 1 percent change in income.

You learned in Chapter 3 that household income is one of the variables that influences demand. The *income elasticity of demand* tells us how *sensitive* quantity demanded is to changes in buyers' incomes. The **income elasticity of demand** is the percentage change in quantity demanded ($\%\Delta Q^D$) divided by the percentage change in income, with all other influences on demand—including the price of the good—remaining constant:

$$\text{Income Elasticity} = \frac{\%\ \text{Change in Quantity Demanded}}{\%\ \text{Change in Income}}$$

Keep in mind that while a price elasticity measures the sensitivity of demand to price as we *move along the demand curve* from one point to another, an income elasticity tells us the relative *shift* in the demand curve—the percentage increase in quantity demanded *at a given price*.

With income elasticities (unlike price elasticities), the sign of the elasticity value matters. Income elasticity will be positive when a rise in price causes quantity demanded to rise. Such goods are called *normal* goods, as you learned in Chapter 3. But income elasticity can also be negative, when a rise in income *decreases* demand for a good (*inferior* goods).

Income elasticity is positive for normal goods, but negative for inferior goods.

An accurate knowledge of income elasticity can be crucial in predicting the growth in demand for a good as income grows over time. For example, economists know that different types of countries have different income elasticities of demand for oil. (In less-developed countries undergoing rapid industrialization, the income elasticity of demand for oil is typically twice as large as in developed countries). These income elasticities, along with forecasts of income growth in different developing and developed countries, are used to predict global demand for oil and forecast future oil prices.

Cross-Price Elasticity of Demand

A cross-price elasticity relates the percentage change in quantity demanded for one good to the percentage change in the price of another good. More formally, we define the **cross-price elasticity of demand** of good X with good Z as:

$$\frac{\%\ \text{Change in Quantity Demanded of }X}{\%\ \text{Change in Price of }Z}$$

Cross-price elasticity of demand The percentage change in the quantity demanded of one good caused by a 1 percent change in the price of another good.

In words, a cross-price elasticity of demand tells us the percentage change in quantity demanded of a good for each 1% increase in the price of some other good, while all other influences on demand remain unchanged.

With a cross-price elasticity (as with an income elasticity), the sign matters. A *positive* cross-price elasticity means that the two goods are *substitutes:* A rise in the price of one good increases demand for the other good. For example, Coke and Pepsi are clearly substitutes, and the cross-price elasticity of Pepsi with Coke has, in one study, been estimated at 0.8.[2] This means that a 1% rise in the price of Coke, holding constant the price of Pepsi, causes a 0.8% *rise* in the quantity of Pepsi demanded.

A *negative* cross-price elasticity means that the goods are *complements:* A rise in the price of one good *decreases* the demand for the other. Thus we'd expect higher gasoline prices to decrease the demand for large, fuel-inefficient cars. Indeed, when gasoline prices spiked in 2007 and 2008, the demand for SUVs and other gas-guzzling vehicles plunged.

[2] F. Gasmi, J. J. Laffont, and Q. Vuong, "Econometric Analysis of Collusive Behavior in a Soft Drink Market," *Journal of Economics and Management Strategy*, Summer, 1992, pp. 277–311.

USING THE THEORY

APPLICATIONS OF ELASTICITY

Elasticity is among the most widely used tools in microeconomics. You've already seen one example of how economists use elasticity: predicting mass transit revenues. In this section, we'll discuss three additional examples in which elasticity is key to analyzing events in markets.

The War on Drugs: Should We Fight Supply or Demand?

Every year, the U.S. government spends about $10 billion intervening in the market for illegal drugs like cocaine, heroin, and marijuana. Most of this money is spent on efforts to restrict the supply of drugs. But many economists argue that society would be better off if antidrug efforts were shifted from the supply side to the demand side of the market. Why? The answer hinges on the price elasticity of demand for illegal drugs.

Look at panel (a) of Figure 7, which shows the market for heroin if there were no government intervention. The equilibrium would be at point A, with price P_1 and quantity Q_1. Total revenue of sellers—and total spending by buyers—would be the area of the shaded rectangle, $P_1 \times Q_1$. Now let's explore two potential strategies for reducing heroin use.

FIGURE 7 | **The War on Drugs**

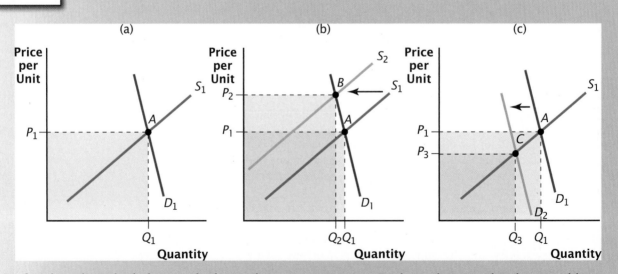

Panel (a) shows the market for heroin in the absence of government intervention. Total expenditures—and total receipts of drug dealers—are given by the area of the shaded rectangle. Panel (b) shows the effect of a government effort to restrict supply: Price rises, but total expenditure increases. Panel (c) shows a policy of reducing demand: Price falls, and so does total expenditure.

Decreasing Supply

Panel (b) shows the impact of a policy to restrict supply through any one of several methods, including vigilant customs inspections, arrest and stiff penalties for drug dealers, or efforts to reduce drug traffic from producing countries like Colombia, North Korea, and Thailand. The decrease in supply is represented by a leftward shift of the supply curve, establishing a new equilibrium at price P_2 and quantity Q_2. As you can see, supply restrictions, if they successfully reduce the equilibrium quantity of heroin, will also raise its equilibrium price.

But now let's consider the impact of this policy on the users' total *expenditure* on drugs. Although the research is difficult, a number of studies have concluded that the demand for addictive drugs such as heroin and cocaine is very price *inelastic*. This is not surprising, given their addictive properties. As you've learned, when demand is inelastic, a rise in price will *increase* the revenue of sellers, which is the same as the total expenditure of buyers. This means that a policy of restricting the supply of illegal drugs, if successful, will also increase the total expenditure of drug users on their habit. In panel (b), total expenditure rises from the area of the shorter rectangle to the area of the taller one.

The change in total expenditure has serious consequences for our society. Many drug users support their habit through crime. If the total expenditure needed to support a drug habit rises, they may commit more crimes—and more serious ones. And don't forget that the total expenditure of drug users is also the total *revenue* of the illegal drug industry. The large revenues—and the associated larger profits to be made—attract organized as well as unorganized crime and lead to frequent and very violent turf wars.

The same logic, based on the inelastic demand for illegal drugs, has led many economists to advocate the controlled legalization of most currently illegal drugs. Others advocate a shift of emphasis away from decreasing supply and toward decreasing demand, which we explore next.

Decreasing Demand

Policies that might decrease the demand for illegal drugs and shift the demand curve leftward include stiffer penalties on drug *users,* heavier advertising against drug use, and greater availability of treatment centers for addicts. In addition, more of the effort against drug sellers could be directed at retailers, rather than those higher up the chain of supply. It is the retailers who promote drugs to future users and thus increase demand.

Panel (c) illustrates the impact such policies might have on the market for heroin. As the demand curve shifts leftward, price *falls* from P_1 to P_3, and quantity demanded falls from Q_1 to Q_3. Now, we cannot say whether the drop in quantity will be greater in panel (b) or panel (c) (it depends on the relative sizes of the shifts). But we *can* be sure that a demand-focused policy will have a very different impact on equilibrium price, moving it down instead of up. Moreover, the demand shift will decrease total expenditure on drugs—to the *inner* shaded rectangle—since both price and quantity decrease. This can contribute to a lower crime rate by drug users and make the drug industry less attractive to potential dealers and producers.

Forecasting Price in an Oil Crisis

In Chapter 3, you saw how conflict in Libya and the resulting decrease in oil supply caused a price spike in early 2011. Table 5 shows other oil supply disruptions in recent history, and the percentage of the world's oil production directly affected.

TABLE 5

Oil Supply Disruptions

Event	Date	Percent of World Output Lost
OPEC Embargo	November 1973	7.5%
Iranian Revolution	November 1978	7%
Iran-Iraq War	October 1980	6%
Persian Gulf War I	August 1990	9%
Venezuelan Strikes and Persian Gulf War II	December 2002	4%
Libyan Conflict	March 2011	1.6%

Sources: James D. Hamilton, "Historical Oil Shocks" (manuscript, February 1, 2011) and U.S. Energy Information Administration (www.eia.gov)

In all of these cases, increased output by other producers (due to the rise in oil's price or a decision by OPEC) offset some of the lost production. But the question arises: What if a *major* supply disruption occurred, and *only* a price hike could restore the market to equilibrium? For example, the Persian Gulf—which has been a geopolitical hot spot for decades—produces more than a quarter of the world's oil. If an event disrupted supplies from this region, what would happen to the price of oil? Not surprisingly, elasticity plays a crucial role in answering this question.

To see why elasticity matters, Figure 8 shows two versions of the oil market. Panel (a) is a fictional version—what the market would look like if both supply and demand were very elastic in the short run. Panel (b) shows a more realistic picture of the oil market—very inelastic supply and demand in the short run. In both panels, our initial equilibrium is point *A*—with price equal to $100 per barrel, and quantity equal to 90 million barrels per day, their approximate values in mid-2011.

Now, let's suppose that 9 million barrels of Persian Gulf oil (about one-third of the region's production) were temporarily removed from the market. In both panels, the supply curves shift leftward, creating an excess demand of 9 million barrels at the original price. And in both panels, the price will rise. The price will continue rising—causing quantity supplied to increase and quantity demanded to decrease—until the excess demand has been eliminated. The excess demand we need to eliminate is 10% of the original market quantity (9 million out of 90 million barrels per day).

How much will the price have to rise? That depends on both the price elasticity of demand and the price elasticity of supply. Suppose, first, that supply and demand are both very elastic, as in panel (a). Then only a relatively small price increase is needed to increase quantity supplied and decrease quantity demanded by the needed amounts. In the figure, we assume that the price elasticities of demand and supply are both equal to 2.0. In that case, a price rise of just 2.5% (from $100 to $102.50) will do the trick. When the price rises by 2.5%, quantity supplied increases by 5% and quantity demanded falls by 5%, giving us a combined adjustment of 10 percentage points. This would shrink the excess demand by the needed 10% of the market, or 9 million barrels per day, and bring the market back to equilibrium.[3]

[3] Notice that we are using the standard definition of percentage changes—rather than the midpoint rule—to calculate the price hikes in this example. By common practice, the midpoint method is used only when calculating an elasticity value from data on price and quantity. Here we are *using* an elasticity value that has already been calculated for us.

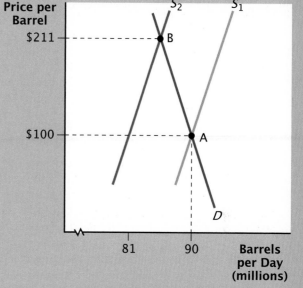

FIGURE 8   A Decrease in Oil Supply: Elastic versus Inelastic Demand

If either supply or demand is very elastic, only a relatively small price increase will be needed to restore equilibrium after a decrease in supply. Panel (a) illustrates the case in which both supply and demand are very elastic. The leftward shift in the supply curve causes equilibrium price to rise from $100 to $102.50. Panel (b) has the same leftward shift in the supply curve, but with much less elastic supply and demand. A much larger rise in price (from $100 to $211) is needed to restore equilibrium after the decrease in supply.

Now look at panel (b), which is drawn to illustrate the more realistic situation of very inelastic demand and supply. Specifically, we've used short-run elasticity estimates of 0.03 for supply and 0.06 for demand. Once again, the same 9 million barrel excess demand—about 10% of the original market—must be eliminated by an increase in price. But now, with supply and demand so inelastic, it will take a much larger price increase to do the job. Each 1% rise in price causes quantity supplied to rise by just .03%, and quantity demanded to fall by just 0.06%, reducing the excess demand by just 0.03 + 0.06 = 0.09 percentage points. To eliminate the entire excess demand requires the price to rise by about 111%—to $211 per barrel. (The 111% price increase raises quantity supplied by 111% × .03 = 3.33%, and shrinks quantity demanded by 111% × 0.06 = 6.66%, giving us the needed combined adjustment of 10 percentage points.) The new price—$211— would be an all-time high for oil's price, even after adjusting for general inflation.

A few provisos, though. First, with price increases this large, our results are only a very rough approximation. Demand might be more elastic for such large price changes, because oil and oil-related products will take a much larger bite out of the typical family's budget. Greater elasticity would cause the price to rise by less than it does in our example.

Second, if more cost-effective alternative energy sources become available, the short-run price elasticity of demand for oil will be greater in the future than it is today. (As you've learned, the availability of substitutes increases the price elasticity of demand.) With a larger elasticity, price would rise by less, so oil-consuming nations would be better cushioned from supply disruptions. Indeed, this is a major reason (aside from concerns about climate change) that governments in the U.S. and other countries are trying to speed the development of alternatives to oil.

Spikes in Food Prices

From mid-2010 to mid-2011, prices for wheat, corn, soybeans, sugar, and other food crops spiked around the world. Even before then, prices had been trending upward due to increases in demand. But the price increases that began in June 2010 were too rapid to be explained by rising demand alone. A much more important reason was decreases in supply caused by bad weather for crops in several parts of the world.

A decrease in supply in the market for crops works just like it does in the market for oil. In both cases, after the supply curve shifts leftward, the price will rise to eliminate the excess demand. And, as in the case of oil, supply and demand for food crops turns out to be very *inelastic*. Why?

Demand is inelastic for several reasons. First, food—especially staples like wheat or corn—are commonly regarded as necessities. Second, in large parts of the world only a small percentage of income is spent on these foods. As you've learned, when a good makes up a relatively small percentage of household budgets, demand is less elastic.

Supply is inelastic—at least in the short run—because farm output depends primarily on planting decisions made many months earlier, and then on weather conditions while crops are growing. If crop prices rise after planting, farmers can take *some* steps to increase output during the current season (e.g., harvesting more intensively, intensifying efforts to reduce spoilage in storage and transportation). But these steps can increase quantity supplied only a bit.

Figure 9 illustrates the impact of bad weather in the market for wheat. Initially, in June 2010, with supply curve S_{2010}, the price of wheat averaged $4.16 per bushel at point A. Then bad weather struck: a severe drought in Russia and Ukraine and too much rain in Northern Europe and Canada. By May 2011, the supply curve had shifted leftward, to S_{2011}, creating an excess demand for wheat at the initial price. With very inelastic supply and demand, the price increase had to be huge to close the gap. The result was a new equilibrium at point B, with the price rising to $8.16 per bushel.

Food prices have always fluctuated with changes in weather. But in recent years, bouts of bad weather have caused prices to spike by much more than in the past. One reason may be that bad-weather events themselves have become more severe due to climate change. But another explanation is that demand for food crops have very likely become more *inelastic* in recent years.

Why has the demand for food staples become more inelastic? Mostly because incomes have grown in formerly poor countries like China and India, so basic commodities like wheat, rice, corn, and soybeans now take a smaller fraction of the typical family's budget. As you've learned, all else equal, the smaller the fraction of the budget, the more inelastic is demand. But as you've also learned, as demand becomes more inelastic, any excess demand for food will cause prices to rise by even more.

This explanation—if true—has a dark implication. Not everyone is enjoying higher incomes. It is those left behind—and for whom basic staples remain a large part of their budget—that remain most sensitive to price changes. Therefore, as

FIGURE 9   Bad Weather and Food Prices with Inelastic Supply and Demand

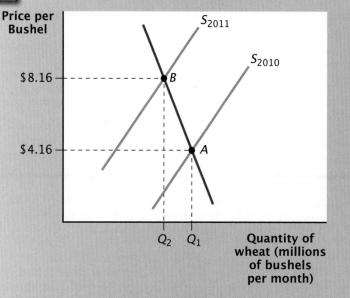

When the supply of wheat decreased from mid-2010 to mid-2011, creating an excess demand at the original price of $4.16 per bushel, the price spiked upward. A large price rise was needed to eliminate the excess demand because both the supply and the demand for wheat are so inelastic in the short run.

demand becomes more inelastic, not only does bad weather cause prices to rise more, but the poor must bear a greater share of the burden of adjustment than before. In essence, if farm output shrinks and those with higher incomes and bigger budgets cut back less, then those with the lowest incomes must cut back even more.

SUMMARY

A useful tool for analyzing markets is *elasticity*: a measure of the sensitivity of one economic variable to another. The *price elasticity of demand* is defined as the percentage change in quantity demanded divided by the percentage change in price that caused it, without the negative sign. In general, price elasticity of demand varies along a demand curve. In the special case of a straight-line demand curve, demand becomes more and more elastic as we move upward and leftward along the curve.

Along an elastic portion of any demand curve, a rise in price causes sellers' revenues (and consumers' expenditures) to fall. Along an *inelastic* portion of any demand curve, a rise in price causes sellers' revenues and consumers' expenditures to increase.

Generally speaking, demand for a good tends to be more elastic (1) the less we regard the good as a "necessity," (2) the easier it is to find substitutes for the good, (3) the greater the share of households' budgets that is spent on the good, and (4) the more time we allow for quantity demanded to respond to the price change.

In addition to price elasticity of demand, there are three other commonly used elasticities. The *price elasticity of supply* is the percentage change in quantity supplied divided by the percentage change in price. Price elasticity of supply is usually greater in the long run than in the short run, and greater when the market we are analyzing is more narrowly defined. The *income elasticity of demand* is the percentage change in quantity demanded divided by the percentage change in income that causes it. The *cross-price elasticity of demand* is the percentage change in the quantity demanded of one good divided by the percentage change in the price of some other good. For income and price elasticities, the sign can be either positive or negative.

Finally, the *price elasticity of supply* is the percentage change in quantity supplied divided by the percentage change in price.

PROBLEM SET

Answers to even-numbered Problems can be found on the text Web site through www.cengagebrain.com

1. Using Figure 5, calculate the price elasticity of demand when gasoline rises from $2 per gallon to $3 per gallon over:

   a. the short run.
   b. the long run.

2. Table 2 shows a short-run elasticity of demand for cigarettes. The same study suggested that the long-run elasticity of demand for cigarettes ranges from 1.0 to 2.5. Which is larger—short-run or long-run elasticity? Is this what we would expect? What adjustments might smokers be able to make in the long run that they cannot make in the short run that can explain the difference between short-run and long-run elasticities?

3. Some studies suggest that "tooth extraction" is an inferior good. Which measure of elasticity (price elasticity of demand, price elasticity of supply, income elasticity, or cross-price elasticity) would provide evidence to support this claim? What would we look for in this elasticity measure to determine if tooth extraction were inferior?

4. In Table 2, the price elasticity of demand for Kellogg's Corn Flakes includes a wide range of estimates. It turns out one end of the range is observed for low-income households, while the other is observed for high-income households. Identify which end of the range most likely corresponds to which type of household, and explain briefly. [Hint: It has to do with one of the determinants of elasticity.]

5. The demand for bottled water in a small town is as follows:

P (per bottle)	Q_D (bottles per week)
$1.00	500
$1.50	400
$2.00	300
$2.50	200
$3.00	100

   a. Is this a straight-line demand curve? How do you know?
   b. Calculate the price elasticity of demand for bottled water for a price rise from $1.00 to $1.50. Is demand elastic or inelastic for this price change?
   c. Calculate the price elasticity of demand for a price rise from $2.50 to $3.00. Is demand elastic or inelastic for this price change?
   d. According to the chapter, demand should become less elastic as we move downward and rightward along a straight-line demand curve. Use your answers in *b.* and *c.* to confirm this relationship.

   e. Create another column for total revenue on bottled water at each price.
   f. According to the chapter, a rise in price should *increase* total revenue on bottled water when demand is inelastic, and *decrease* total revenue when demand is elastic. Use your answers in *b.* and *c.* and the new total revenue column you created to confirm this.

6. In 2010, Apple wanted to lower the price of downloading TV shows from iTunes from $1.99 to $0.99. But Apple had to get permission from, and convince, the management of the networks with whom they share the revenue from each download. Apple argued that lowering the price would benefit both Apple and the networks. Managers at the networks disagreed, and wanted the price kept at $1.99.

   a. What did Apple believe about the price elasticity of demand for downloaded shows?
   b. What did the networks believe about the price elasticity of demand for downloaded shows?

7. In the chapter, we calculated the likely long-run change in revenue if New York City were to raise mass transit fares from $2.25 to $2.70. Use the same procedure to calculate the *short-run* impact of this fare hike. This time, use an elasticity of 0.35, which is in the middle of the short-run estimates in Table 3.

8. The Dangerous Curves box titled "Slope and Elasticity," states that when two demand curves share a point, then for a given price change and starting at that shared point demand will be more elastic along the flatter curve. Does this statement remain true if we replace the word "starting" with the word "ending"? Explain why or why not.

9. The demand for rosebushes in a market is as follows:

Price (per rosebush)	Quantity Demanded (rosebushes per week)
$10	230
$11	150
$12	90
$13	40

   a. Is this a straight-line demand curve? How do you know?
   b. Calculate the price elasticity of demand for roses for a price increase from $10 to $11. Is demand elastic or inelastic for this price change?
   c. Calculate the price elasticity of demand for roses for a price increase from $12 to $13. Is demand elastic or inelastic for this price change?

10. Refer to Table 2 in this chapter and answer the following questions:
    a. Which is more elastically demanded: cigarettes or pork? Does this make sense to you? Explain briefly.
    b. If the price of milk rises by 5%, what will happen to the quantity demanded? (Be specific.)

11. Once again, refer to Table 2 in this chapter and answer the following questions:
    a. Is the demand for recreation more or less elastic than the demand for clothing?
    b. If 10,000 2-liter bottles of Pepsi are currently being demanded in your community each month, and the price increases by 10%, what will happen to quantity demanded? Be specific.
    c. By how much would the price of ground beef have to increase (in percentage terms) in order to reduce quantity demanded by 5%?

12. Three Guys Named Al, a moving company, is contemplating a price hike. Currently, they charge $30 per hour, but Al thinks they could get $40. Al disagrees, saying it will hurt the business. Al, the brains of the outfit, has calculated the price elasticity of demand for their moving services in the range from $30 to $40 and found it to be 0.5.
    a. Based on total revenue alone, should they do as Al suggests and raise the price? Why or why not?
    b. Currently, Three Guys is the only moving company in town. Al reads in the paper that several new movers are planning to set up shop there within the next year. Twelve months from now, is the demand for Three Guys' services likely to be more elastic, less elastic, or the same? Why?

13. In Figure 6, calculate the *long-run* price elasticity of supply when price rises from $4.50 to $5.50.

14. Each of the following tells us something specific about the nature of spiral notebooks: either that the demand for them is elastic or inelastic; that they are normal or inferior; or that they are substitutes or complements for another good. In each case, state the relevant conclusion about spiral notebooks.
    a. The income elasticity of demand for spiral notebooks is −0.5
    b. The price elasticity of demand for spiral notebooks is 1.5
    c. The cross-price elasticity of demand for spiral notebooks with tablet computers is 0.8

More Challenging

15. In the Using the Theory section of this chapter, we determined how much oil prices might rise if 9 million barrels per day in Persian Gulf oil became unavailable. The analysis used short-run price elasticities (0.06 for demand, and 0.03 for supply). In the long run, both elasticities should be larger. Suppose the long-run price elasticities are 0.3 for supply, and 0.4 for demand, and that 9 million barrels of Persian Gulf oil became unavailable—this time permanently. Starting at a price of $100 per barrel, and giving producers and consumers a few years to adjust, what would be the new price of oil?

16. In mid-2011, the International Monetary Fund came out with some controversial estimates of price elasticities of demand for oil—much lower than estimates in previous research. Their estimate for the long-run price elasticity of demand was 0.072, and for income elasticity of demand they estimated 0.294. Assuming that the long-run price elasticity of supply is 0.3, and that world income grows by 40% over the next 10 years, use the IMF's estimates to forecast the percentage increase in oil's price over the next 10 years.

CHAPTER 6

Consumer Choice

You are constantly making economic decisions. Some of them are rather trivial. (Have coffee at Starbucks or more cheaply at home?) Others can have a profound impact on your life. (Live with your parents a while longer or get your own place?) The economic nature of all these decisions is rather obvious, since they all involve *spending*.

But in other cases, the economic nature of your decisions may be less obvious. Did you get up early today in order to get things done, or did you sleep in? At this very moment, what have you decided *not* to do in order to make time to read this chapter? These are economic choices, too, because they require you to allocate a scarce resource—your *time*—among different alternatives.

To understand the economic choices that individuals make, we must know what they are trying to achieve (their goals) and the limitations they face in achieving them (their constraints).

Of course, we are all different from one another . . . when it comes to *specific* goals and *specific* constraints. But at the highest level of generality, we are all very much alike. All of us, for example, would like to maximize our overall level of *satisfaction*. And all of us, as we attempt to satisfy our desires, come up against the same types of constraints: too little income or wealth to buy everything we might enjoy, and too little time to do everything we'd like to do.

We'll start our analysis of individual choice with constraints, and then move on to goals. In most of the chapter, we will focus on choices about *spending*: how people decide what to buy. This is why the theory of individual decision making is often called "consumer theory." Later, in the Using the Theory section, we'll broaden our analysis to include decisions involving scarce *time*.

THE BUDGET CONSTRAINT

In making decisions about spending, we must all face two facts of economic life: (1) We have to pay for the goods and services we buy, and (2) we have limited funds to spend. These two facts are summarized by our *budget constraint*:

> **Budget constraint** The different combinations of goods a consumer can afford with a limited budget, at given prices.

*A consumer's **budget constraint** identifies which combinations of goods and services the consumer can afford with a limited budget, at given prices.*

Consider Max, a devoted fan of both movies and the local music scene, who has a total entertainment budget of $100 each month. The price of a movie is $10, while hearing a rock concert at his favorite local club costs him $20. If Max were to spend all of his $100 budget on concerts at $20 each, he could see at most five each month. If he were to spend it all on movies at $10 each, he could see 10 of them.

But Max could also choose to spend *part* of his budget on concerts and *part* on movies. In this case, for each number of concerts, there is some *maximum* number of movies that he could see. For example, if he goes to one concert per month, it will cost him $20 of his $100 budget, leaving $80 available for movies. Thus, if Max were to choose one concert, the *maximum* number of films he could choose would be $80/$10 = 8.

The table in the bottom half of Figure 1 identifies Max's possible choices. Each row of the table specifies a number of concerts Max might attend, and it also tells us the maximum number of movies that he could see with the funds left over. Note that each combination in the table is affordable for Max, since each will cost him exactly $100. For example, combination *A* (the first row) represents no concerts and

FIGURE 1 | The Budget Constraint

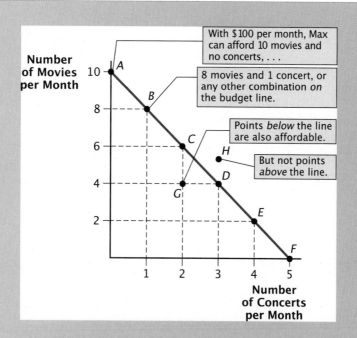

Max's Consumption Possibilities with Income of $100

	Concerts at $20 each		Movies at $10 each	
	Quantity	**Total Expenditure on Concerts**	**Quantity**	**Total Expenditure on Movies**
A	0	$ 0	10	$100
B	1	$ 20	8	$ 80
C	2	$ 40	6	$ 60
D	3	$ 60	4	$ 40
E	4	$ 80	2	$ 20
F	5	$100	0	$ 0

10 movies. Combination *F* (the last row) represents 5 concerts and no movies. In each of the combinations between *A* and *F*, Max attends both concerts and movies.

Figure 1 also shows these combinations on a graph. The number of movies is measured along the vertical axis and the number of concerts along the horizontal. Each of the points *A* through *F* corresponds to one of the rows in the table. If we connect all of these points with a straight line, we have a graphical representation of Max's budget constraint, which we call Max's **budget line.**

Note that any point below or to the left of the budget line is affordable. For example, two concerts and four movies—indicated by point *G*—would cost only $40 + $40 = $80. Max could certainly afford this combination. On the other hand, he *cannot* afford any combination *above* and to the right of this line. Point *H*, representing 3 concerts and 5 movies, would cost $60 + $50 = $110, which is beyond Max's budget. The budget line therefore serves as a *border* between those combinations that are affordable and those that are not.

Let's look at Max's budget line more closely. The *vertical intercept* is 10, the number of movies Max could see if he attended zero concerts. Starting at the vertical intercept (point *A*), notice that each time Max increases one unit along the horizontal axis (attends one more concert), he must decrease 2 units along the vertical (see three fewer movies). Thus, the slope of the budget line is equal to −2. The slope tells us Max's *opportunity cost* of one more concert. That is, the opportunity cost of one more concert is 2 movies forgone.

There is an important relationship between the opportunity cost and the *prices* of two goods. If we divide one money price by another money price, we get what is called a **relative price**, the price of one good *relative* to the other. Let's use the symbol P_c for the price of a concert and P_m for the price of a movie. Since $P_c = \$20$ and $P_m = \$10$, the *relative price of a concert* is the ratio $P_c/P_m = \$20/\$10 = 2$. Notice that this same number, 2, is the opportunity cost of another concert in terms of movies; and, except for the minus sign, it is also the slope of the budget line. That is, *the relative price of a concert, the opportunity cost of another concert, and the slope of the budget line* all have the same absolute value. This is one example of a general relationship:

> *If P_y is the price of the good on the vertical axis and P_x is the price of the good on the horizontal axis, then*
>
> P_x/P_y = *the relative price of good* X
>   = *the opportunity cost of one more unit of good* X
>   = *the absolute value of the slope of the consumer's budget line.*

Changes in the Budget Line

To draw the budget line in Figure 1, we have assumed given prices for movies and concerts and a given income that Max can spend on them. These "givens"—the prices of the goods and the consumer's income—are always *assumed constant* as we move along a budget line; if any one of them changes, the budget line will change as well. Let's see how.

Changes in Income

Suppose Max's available income increases from $100 to $200 per month. Then he can afford to see more movies, more concerts, or more of both, as shown by the change in his budget line in Figure 2(a). If Max were to devote *all* of his income to

---

Budget line The graphical representation of a budget constraint, showing the maximum affordable quantity of one good for given amounts of another good.

Relative price The price of one good relative to the price of another.

FIGURE 2   Changes in the Budget Line

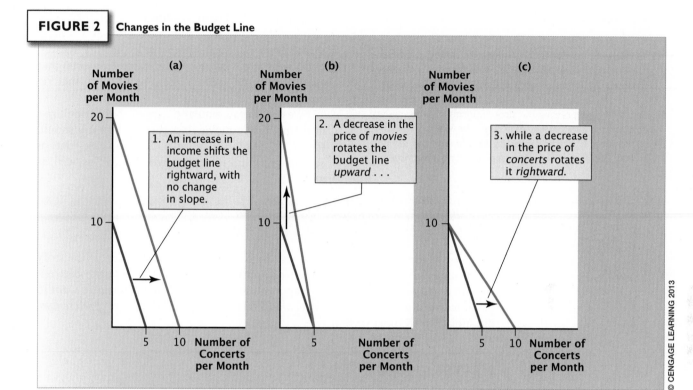

movies, he could now see 20 of them each month, instead of the 10 he was able to see before. Devoting his entire income to concerts would enable him to attend 10, rather than 5. Moreover, for any number of concerts, he will be able to see more movies than before. For example, choosing 2 concerts used to allow Max to see only 6 movies. Now, with a larger budget of $200, he can have 2 concerts and *16* movies.

Notice that the old and new budget lines in Figure 2(a) are parallel; that is, they have the same slope of −2. We have changed Max's income but *not* the prices. Since the ratio P_c/P_m has not changed, the spending tradeoff between movies and concerts and the slope of the budget line remain the same. Thus,

an increase in income will shift the budget line upward (and rightward). A decrease in income will shift the budget line downward (and leftward). These shifts are parallel: Changes in income do not affect the budget line's slope.

Changes in Price

Now let's go back to Max's original budget of $100 and explore what happens to the budget line when a price changes. Suppose the price of a movie falls from $10 to $5. The graph in Figure 2(b) shows Max's old and new budget lines. When the price of a movie falls, the budget line rotates outward; that is, the vertical intercept moves higher. The reason is this: When a movie costs $10, Max could spend his entire $100 on them and see 10; now that they cost $5, he can see a maximum of 20. The horizontal intercept—representing how many concerts Max could see with his entire budget—doesn't change at all, since there has been no change in the price of a concert. Notice that the new budget line is also *steeper* than the original one, with slope equal to $-P_c/P_m = -\$20/\$5 = -4$.

⚠ DANGEROUS CURVES

The budget line's slope It's tempting to think that the slope of the budget line should be $-P_y/P_x$, with the price of the vertical axis good y in the numerator. But notice that the slope is the other way around, $-P_x/P_y$, with P_x in the numerator. That's because we're expressing the slope in terms of prices (which are *not* on the axes), rather than quantities. We've given some intuition for this way of expressing the slope in our example with Max, but if you'd like a formal proof, see the footnote.[1]

© AXL/SHUTTERSTOCK.COM

Panel (c) of Figure 2 illustrates another price change. This time, it's a fall in the price of a *concert* from $20 to $10. Once again, the budget line rotates, but now it is the horizontal intercept (concerts) that changes and the vertical intercept (movies) that remains fixed.

We could draw similar diagrams illustrating a *rise* in the price of a movie or a concert, but you should try to do this on your own. In each case, one of the budget line's intercepts will change, as well as its slope:

> *When the price of a good changes, the budget line rotates: Both its slope and one of its intercepts will change.*

The budget constraint, as illustrated by the budget line, is one side of the story of consumer choice. It indicates the trade-off consumers *are able to* make between one good and another. But just as important is the trade-off that consumers *want to* make between one good and another, and this depends on consumers' *preferences*, the subject of the next section.

PREFERENCES

How can we possibly speak systematically about people's preferences? After all, people are different. They like different things. American teens delight in having Coke with dinner, while the very idea makes a French person shudder. What would satisfy a Buddhist monk would hardly satisfy the typical American.

And even among "typical Americans," there is little consensus about tastes. Some read Jane Austen, while others choose John Grisham. Some like to spend their vacations traveling, whereas others would prefer to stay home and sleep in every day. Even those who like Häagen-Dazs ice cream can't agree on which is the best flavor—the company notices consistent, regional differences in consumption. In Los Angeles, chocolate chip is the clear favorite, while on most of the East Coast, it's butter pecan—except in New York City, where coffee wins hands down.

In spite of such wide differences in preferences, we can find some important common denominators—things that seem to be true for a wide variety of people. In our theory of consumer choice, we will focus on these common denominators.

Rationality

One common denominator—and a critical assumption behind consumer theory—is that people *have* preferences. More specifically, we assume that you can look at two

---

[1] To prove that the slope of the budget line is $-P_x/P_y$, let Q_x and Q_y represent the quantities of good x and good y, respectively. Then the total amount a consumer spends on good y is P_yQ_y, and the total amount spent on good x is P_xQ_x. All along the budget line, the total amount spent on these two goods is equal to the total budget (B), so it must be that $P_xQ_x + P_yQ_y = B$. This is the equation for the budget line. Since the budget line graph has good y on the vertical axis, we can solve this equation for Q_y by rearranging terms: $Q_y = (B - P_xQ_x)/P_y$, which can be rewritten as $Q_y = (B/P_y) + (-P_x/P_y) Q_x$. This is the equation for a straight line. The first term in parentheses (B/P_y) is the vertical intercept, and the second term in parentheses ($-P_x/P_y$) is the slope. (See the mathematical appendix to Chapter 1 if you need to review slopes and intercepts.)

alternatives and state either that you prefer one to the other or that you are entirely indifferent between the two—you value them equally.

Another common denominator is that preferences are *logically consistent,* or *transitive.* If, for example, you prefer a sports car to a jeep, and a jeep to a motorcycle, then we assume that you will also prefer a sports car to a motorcycle. When a consumer can make choices, and is logically consistent, we say that she has **rational preferences.**

Notice that rationality is a matter of how you make your choices, and not what choices you make. You can be rational and like apples better than oranges, or oranges better than apples. You can be rational even if you like chocolate-covered anchovies! What matters is that you make logically consistent choices, and most of us usually do.

Rational preferences Preferences that satisfy two conditions: (1) Any two alternatives can be compared, and one is preferred or else the two are valued equally, and (2) the comparisons are logically consistent or transitive.

More Is Better

Another feature of preferences that virtually all of us share is this: We generally feel that *more is better.* Specifically, if we get more of some good or service, and nothing else is taken away from us, we will generally feel better off.

This condition seems to be satisfied for the vast majority of goods we all consume. Of course, there are exceptions. If you hate eggplant, then the more of it you have, the worse off you are. Similarly, a dieter who says, "Don't bring any ice cream into the house. I don't want to be tempted," also violates the assumption. The model of consumer choice in this chapter is designed for preferences that satisfy the "more is better" condition, and it would have to be modified to take account of exceptions like these.

So far, our characterization of consumer preferences has been rather minimal. We've assumed only that consumers are rational and that they prefer more rather than less of every good we're considering. But even this limited information allows us to say the following:

> *The consumer will always choose a point on the budget line, rather than a point below it.*

To see why this is so, look again at Figure 1. Max would never choose point *G,* representing 2 concerts and 6 movies, since there are affordable points—on the budget line—that we know make him better off. For example, compared to point *G,* point *C* has the same number of concerts, but more movies, while point *D* has the same number of movies, but more concerts. "More is better" tells us that Max will prefer *C* or *D* to *G,* so we know *G* won't be chosen. Indeed, if we look at any point below the budget line, we can always find at least one point on the budget line that is preferred, as long as more is better.

* * *

Knowing that Max will always choose a point *on* his budget line is a start. But how does he find the *best* point on the line—the one that gives him the highest level of satisfaction? This is where your *instructor's* preferences come in. There are two theories of consumer decision making, and they share much in common. First, both assume that preferences are rational. Second, both assume that the consumer would be better off with more of any good we're considering. This means the consumer will always choose a combination of goods *on,* rather than below, his budget line. Finally, both theories come to the same general conclusions about consumer behavior. However, to *arrive* at those conclusions, each theory takes a different road.

The next section presents the "Marginal Utility" approach to consumer decision making. If, however, your instructor prefers the "Indifference Curve" approach, you can skip the next section and go straight to the appendix. Then, come back to the section titled "Income and Substitution Effects," which is where our two roads converge once again.

One warning, though. Both approaches to consumer theory are *models*. They use graphs and calculations to explain how consumers make choices. While the models are logical, they may appear unrealistic to you. And in one sense, they *are* unrealistic: Few consumers in the real world are aware of the techniques we'll discuss, yet they make choices all the time.

Economists don't imagine that, when making choices, households or consumers actually *use* these techniques. Rather, the assumption is that people mostly behave *as if* they use them. Indeed, most of the time, in most markets, household behavior has proven to be consistent with the model of consumer choice. When our goal is to describe and predict how consumers are likely to behave in markets—rather than describe what actually goes on in their minds—our theories of consumer decision making can be very useful.

CONSUMER DECISIONS: THE MARGINAL UTILITY APPROACH

Utility A quantitative measure of pleasure or satisfaction obtained from consuming goods and services.

Marginal utility theory treats consumers as striving to maximize their **utility**—a *quantitative* measure of the consumer's well-being or satisfaction. Anything that makes the consumer better off is assumed to raise his utility. Anything that makes the consumer worse off will decrease his utility.

Utility and Marginal Utility

Figure 3 provides a graphical view of utility—in this case, the utility of a consumer named Lisa who likes ice cream cones. Look first at panel (a). On the horizontal axis, we'll measure the number of ice cream cones Lisa consumes each week. On the vertical axis, we'll measure the utility she derives from consuming each of them.

If Lisa values ice cream cones, her utility will increase as she acquires more of them, as it does in the figure. We'll suppose that when she has one cone, she enjoys total utility of 30 "utils," and when she has two cones, her total utility grows to 50 utils, and so on. Throughout the figure, the total utility Lisa derives from consuming ice cream cones keeps rising as she gets to consume more and more of them.

But notice something interesting—and important: Although Lisa's utility increases every time she consumes more ice cream, the *additional* utility she derives from each *successive* cone gets smaller and smaller as she gets more cones. We call the *change in utility* derived from consuming an *additional unit* of a good the *marginal utility*[2] of that additional unit.

Marginal utility The change in total utility an individual obtains from consuming an additional unit of a good or service.

> *Marginal utility is the change in utility an individual enjoys from consuming an additional unit of a good.*

[2] The term "marginal" is one that you'll encounter often in economics. The margin of a sheet of notebook paper is the area on the edge, just *beyond* the writing area. By analogy, a *marginal value* in economics measures what happens when we go a little bit *beyond* where we are now, by adding one more unit of something.

FIGURE 3   Total and Marginal Utility

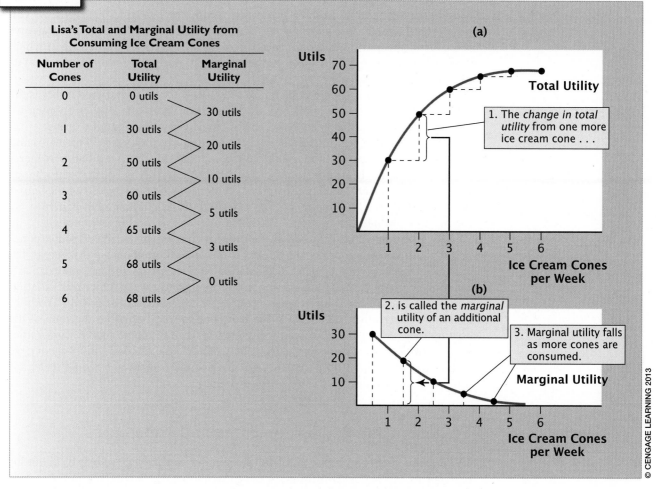

Lisa's Total and Marginal Utility from Consuming Ice Cream Cones

Number of Cones	Total Utility	Marginal Utility
0	0 utils	
		30 utils
1	30 utils	
		20 utils
2	50 utils	
		10 utils
3	60 utils	
		5 utils
4	65 utils	
		3 utils
5	68 utils	
		0 utils
6	68 utils	

(a)

Total Utility

1. The *change in total utility* from one more ice cream cone . . .

(b)

2. is called the *marginal utility* of an additional cone.

3. Marginal utility falls as more cones are consumed.

Marginal Utility

© CENGAGE LEARNING 2013

What we've observed about Lisa's utility can be restated this way: As she eats more and more ice cream cones in a given week, her *marginal utility* from another cone declines. We call this the **law of diminishing marginal utility**, which the great economist Alfred Marshall (1842–1924) defined this way:

> The marginal utility of a thing to anyone diminishes with every increase in the amount of it he already has.[3]

According to the law of diminishing marginal utility, when you consume your first unit of some good, like an ice cream cone, you derive some amount of utility. When you get your second cone that week, you enjoy greater satisfaction than when you only had one, but the extra satisfaction you derive from the second is likely to be smaller than the satisfaction you derived from the first. Adding the third cone to your weekly consumption will no doubt increase your utility further, but again the marginal utility you derive from that third cone is likely to be less than the marginal utility you derived from the second.

The table in Figure 3 will again help us see what's going on. The table in that figure summarizes the information in the total utility graph. The first two columns

Law of diminishing marginal utility As consumption of a good or service increases, marginal utility decreases.

[3] *Principles of Economics*, Book III, Ch. III, Appendix notes 1 & 2. Macmillan & Co., 1930.

show, respectively, the quantity of cones Lisa consumes each week and the total utility she receives each week from consuming them. The third column shows the *marginal* utility she receives from each successive cone she consumes per week. As you can see in the table, Lisa's total utility keeps increasing (marginal utility is always positive) as she consumes more cones (up to five per week), but the rate at which total utility increases gets smaller and smaller (her marginal utility diminishes) as her consumption increases.

Marginal utility is shown in panel (b) of Figure 3. Because marginal utility is the change in utility caused by a change in consumption from one level to another, we plot each marginal utility entry between the old and new consumption levels.

Notice the close relationship between the graph of total utility in panel (a) and the corresponding graph of marginal utility in panel (b). For every one-unit increment in Lisa's ice cream consumption, her marginal utility is equal to the change in her total utility. Diminishing marginal utility is seen in both panels of the figure: in panel (b), by the downward sloping marginal utility curve, and in panel (a), by the positive but *decreasing* slope (flattening out) of the total utility curve.

One last thing about Figure 3: By the time Lisa has consumed a total of five cones per week, the marginal utility she derives from an additional cone has fallen all the way to zero. At this point, she is fully satiated with ice cream and gets no extra satisfaction or utility from eating any more of it in a typical week. Once this satiation point is reached, even if ice cream were free, Lisa would turn it down ("Yechhh! Not more ice cream!!"). But remember from our earlier discussion that one of the assumptions we always make about preferences is that people prefer *more* rather than less of any good we're considering. So when we use marginal utility theory, we assume that marginal utility for every good is positive. For Lisa, it would mean she hasn't yet reached five ice cream cones per week.

Combining the Budget Constraint and Preferences

The marginal utility someone gets from consuming more of a good tells us about his *preferences*. His budget constraint, by contrast, tells us which combinations of goods he can *afford*. If we combine information about preferences (marginal utility values) with information about what is affordable (the budget constraint), we can develop a useful rule to guide us to an individual's utility-maximizing choice.

To develop this rule, let's go back to Max and his choice between movies and concerts. Table 1 shows some of Max's utility numbers for movies and concerts. Notice that, as was the case with Lisa and her ice cream cones, Max's *total* utility rises with each concert or movie he consumes. But his *marginal* utility falls as more of either good is added. For example, a second concert per month adds 800 utils to Max's total utility. But the third concert adds only 600.

Remember that we want to find Max's *best* (utility-maximizing) affordable combination of these two goods. That means we'll need to consider the combinations of the two goods that are on Max's budget line, as shown in Figure 4 (reproduced from Figure 1). Figure 4 also lists some of the utility information in Table 1, but rearranged to more easily see Max's available choices. There's a lot going on in that new table, so let's step through it carefully.

In column (1), the rows labeled A, B, C, and so forth correspond to possible combinations on Max's budget line. For example, the row labeled C corresponds to point C on the budget line: 2 concerts and 6 movies per month. (The unlabeled rows in between would require Max to see and pay for a half of a concert, which we assume he can't do.)

TABLE 1

Total and Marginal Utility of Concerts and Movies

Number of Concerts per Month	Total Utility	Marginal Utility	Number of Movies per Month	Total Utility	Marginal Utility
0	0		0	0	
		1,000			600
1	1,000		1	600	
		800			450
2	1,800		2	1,050	
		600			350
3	2,400		3	1,400	
		400			300
4	2,800		4	1,700	
		250			250
5	3,050		5	1,950	
		200			200
6	3,250		6	2,150	
					150
			7	2,300	
					100
			8	2,400	
					75
			9	2,475	
					60
			10	2,535	

© CENGAGE LEARNING 2013

Next, look at columns (2) and (5). Notice that the number of concerts runs from 0 to 5 as we travel down the rows. But the number of movies runs in the other direction, from 10 to 0. That's because—as we move along the budget line—attending more concerts means seeing fewer movies.

Now look at columns (3) and (6), which show the marginal utility from the "last" concert or movie. For example, in the row labeled C, the "last" concert Max sees is the second one, with marginal utility of 800 utils. In that same row, Max sees 6 movies, and the marginal utility from the last (sixth) movie is 200. These marginal utility numbers come from Table 1.

Now, look at column (4), which shows something new: the marginal utility *per dollar* spent on concerts. To get these numbers, we divide the marginal utility of the last concert (MU_c) by the price of a concert, giving us MU_c/P_c. This tells us the gain in utility Max gets *for each dollar he spends* on the last concert. For example, at point C, Max gains 800 utils from his second concert during the month, so his marginal utility *per dollar* spent on that concert is 800 utils/$20 = 40 utils per dollar. Marginal utility per dollar, like marginal utility itself, declines as Max attends more concerts. After all, marginal utility itself decreases, and the price of a concert isn't changing.

FIGURE 4   Consumer Decision Making

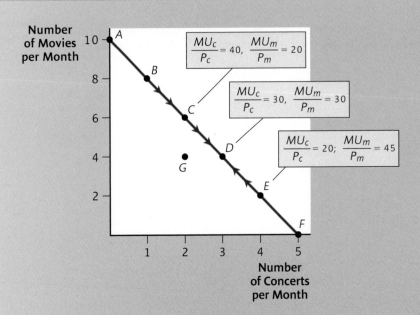

Budget = $100 per month

(1) Point on Budget Line	CONCERTS at $20 each			MOVIES at $10 each		
	(2) Number of Concerts per Month	(3) Marginal Utility from Last Concert (MU_c)	(4) Marginal Utility per Dollar Spent on Last Concert $\left(\dfrac{MU_c}{P_c}\right)$	(5) Number of Movies per Month	(6) Marginal Utility from Last Movie (MU_m)	(7) Marginal Utility per Dollar Spent on Last Movie $\left(\dfrac{MU_m}{P_m}\right)$
A	0			10	60	6
				9	75	7.5
B	1	1000	50	8	100	10
				7	150	15
C	2	800	40	6	200	20
				5	250	25
D	3	600	30	4	300	30
				3	350	35
E	4	400	20	2	450	45
				1	600	60
F	5	250	12.5	0		

The budget line shows the maximum number of movies Max could attend for each number of concerts he attends. He would never choose an interior point like G because there are affordable points—on the line—that make him better off. Max will choose the point on the budget line at which the marginal utilities per dollar spent on movies and concerts are equal. From the table, this occurs at point D.

The last column gives us similar information for movies: the marginal utility per dollar spent on the last movie (MU_m/P_m). As we travel *up* this column, Max attends more movies, and both marginal utility and marginal utility per dollar decline—once again, consistent with the law of diminishing marginal utility.

Now, Max's goal is to find the affordable combination of movies and concerts— the point on his budget line—that gives him the highest possible utility. As you are about to see, this will be the point at which *the marginal utility per dollar is the same for both goods*.

To see why, imagine that Max is searching along his budget line for the utility-maximizing point, and he's currently considering point *B*, which represents 1 concert and 8 movies. Is he maximizing his utility? Let's see. In row *B*, we see that Max's marginal utility *per dollar* spent on concerts is 50 utils, while his marginal utility per dollar spent on movies is only 10 utils. Since he gains more additional utility from each dollar spent on concerts than from each dollar spent on movies, he will have a net gain in utility if he shifts some of his dollars from movies to concerts. To do this, he must travel farther down his budget line.

Next suppose that, after shifting some of his spending from movies to concerts, Max arrives at point *C* on his budget line. What should he do then? At point *C*, Max's *MU* per dollar spent on concerts is 40 utils, while his *MU* per dollar spent on movies is 20 utils. Once again, he would gain utility by shifting dollars from movies to concerts, traveling down his budget line once again.

Now suppose that Max arrives at point *D*. At this point, the *MU* per dollar spent on both movies and concerts is the same: 30 utils. There is no further gain from shifting dollars from movies to concerts. At point *D*, Max has exploited all opportunities to make himself better off by moving down the budget line. He has maximized his utility.

But wait . . . what if Max had started at a point on his budget line *below* point *D*? Would he still end up at the same place? Yes, he would. Suppose Max finds himself at point *E*, with 4 concerts and 2 movies. Here, marginal utilities per dollar are 20 utils for concerts and 45 utils for movies. Now, Max could make himself better off by shifting spending away from concerts and toward movies. He will travel *up* the budget line, once again arriving at point *D*, where no further move will improve his well-being.

As you can see, it doesn't matter whether Max begins on his budget line. Wherever he starts, if he keeps shifting spending toward the good with greater marginal utility per dollar, he will always end up at point *D*. And because marginal utility per dollar is the same for both goods at point *D*, there is nothing further to gain by shifting spending in either direction.

What is true for Max and his choice between movies and concerts is true for *any* consumer and *any* two goods. We can generalize our result this way: For any two goods *x* and *y*, with prices P_x and P_y, whenever $MU_x/P_x > MU_y/P_y$, a consumer is made better off shifting spending toward *x* and away from *y*. When $MU_y/P_y > MU_x/P_x$, a consumer is made better off by shifting spending toward *y* and away from *x*. This leads us to an important conclusion:

> *A utility-maximizing consumer will choose the point on the budget line where marginal utility per dollar is the same for both goods ($MU_x/P_x = MU_y/P_y$). At that point, there is no further gain from reallocating spending in either direction.*

We can generalize this result to the more realistic situation of choosing combinations of more than two goods: different types of food, clothing, entertainment,

⚠️ DANGEROUS CURVES

Don't confuse MU with MU per dollar It's tempting to think that a consumer should shift spending to whichever good has greater marginal utility, rather than greater marginal utility *per dollar*. But a simple thought experiment can convince you why this is wrong. Imagine that you like to ski and you like going out for dinner. Currently, your marginal utility for one more skiing trip is 2,000 utils, and your marginal utility for an additional dinner is 1,000 utils. Should you shift your spending from dining out to skiing? It might seem so, since skiing has the higher marginal utility.

But what if skiing costs $200 per trip, while a dinner out costs only $20? Then, while it's true that another ski trip adds twice as much utility as another dinner out, it's also true that *skiing costs 10 times as much*. You would have to sacrifice 10 dinners out for 1 ski trip, and that would make you *worse off*.

Instead, you should shift your spending in the other direction: from skiing to dining out. Money spent on additional ski trips will give you 2,000 utils/$200 = 10 utils per dollar, while money spent on additional dinners will give you 1,000 utils/$20 = 50 utils per dollar. Dining out clearly gives you more bang for the buck than skiing, because its marginal utility *per dollar* is greater.

transportation, and so on. No matter how many goods there are to choose from, when the consumer is doing as well as possible, it must be true that $MU_x/P_x = MU_y/P_y$ for *any* pair of goods x and y. If this condition is *not* satisfied, the consumer will be better off consuming more of one and less of the other good in the pair.[4]

What Happens When Things Change?

If every one of our decisions had to be made only once, life would be much easier. But that's not how life is. Just when you think you've figured out what to do, things change. In a market economy, as you've learned, prices can change for any number of reasons. (See Chapter 3.) A consumer's income can change as well. These changes cause us to rethink our spending decisions: What maximized utility before the change is unlikely to maximize it afterward.

Changes in Income

Figure 5 illustrates how an increase in *income* might affect Max's choice between movies and concerts. As before, we assume that movies cost $10 each, that concerts cost $20 each, and that these prices do not change. Initially, Max has $100 in income to spend on the two goods, so his budget line is the line from point A to point F. As we've already seen, under these conditions, Max would choose point D (three concerts and four movies) to maximize utility.

Now suppose Max's monthly income (or at least the part he budgets for entertainment) increases to $200. Then his budget line will shift upward and outward in the figure. How will he respond? As always, he will search along his budget line until he finds the point where the marginal utility per dollar spent on both goods is the same. To help us find this point, Figure 5 includes some additional marginal utility values for combinations that weren't affordable before, but are affordable now. For example, the *sixth* concert—which Max couldn't afford in Figure 4—is now assumed to have a marginal utility of 200 utils.

With the preferences described by these marginal utility numbers, Max will search along his budget line for the best choice. This will lead him directly to point K, enjoying 6 concerts and 8 movies per month. For this choice, MU/P is 10 utils per dollar for both goods, so total utility can't be increased any further by shifting dollars from one good to the other.

Now let's take a step back from these calculations and look at the figure itself. We see that an increase in income has changed Max's best choice from point D on the old budget constraint to point K on the new one. In moving from D to K, Max chooses to buy more concerts (6 rather than 3) and more movies (8 rather than 4). As discussed in Chapter 3, if an increase in income (with prices held constant) increases the quantity

---

[4] There is one exception to this statement: Sometimes the optimal choice is to buy *none* of some good. For example, suppose that $MU_y/P_y > MU_x/P_x$, no matter how small a quantity of good x a person consumes. Then the consumer should always shift spending toward y and away from x until the quantity of good x is zero. Economists call this a "corner solution" because when there are only two goods being considered, the individual will locate at one of the end points of the budget line, in a corner of the diagram.

FIGURE 5   Effects of an Increase in Income

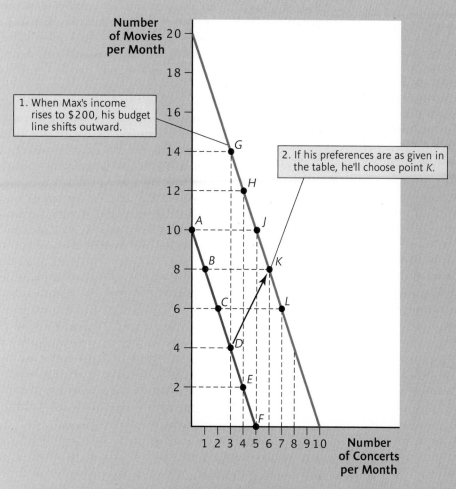

1. When Max's income rises to $200, his budget line shifts outward.

2. If his preferences are as given in the table, he'll choose point K.

Budget = $200 per month

(1) Point on New Budget Line	CONCERTS at $20 each			MOVIES at $10 each		
	(2) Number of Concerts per Month	(3) Marginal Utility from Last Concert (MU_c)	(4) Marginal Utility per Dollar Spent on Last Concert $\left(\dfrac{MU_c}{P_c}\right)$	(5) Number of Movies per Month	(6) Marginal Utility from Last Movie (MU_m)	(7) Marginal Utility per Dollar Spent on Last Movie $\left(\dfrac{MU_m}{P_m}\right)$
G	3	600	30	14	38	3.8
				13	40	4
H	4	400	20	12	45	4.5
				11	50	5
J	5	250	12.5	10	60	6
				9	75	7.5
K	6	200	10	8	100	10
				7	150	15
L	7	180	9	6	200	20

⚠ DANGEROUS CURVES

The special meaning of "inferior" in economics It's tempting to think that *inferior* goods are of lower quality than *normal* goods. But economists don't define normal or inferior based on the intrinsic properties of a good, but rather by the choices people make when their incomes increase. For example, Max may think that both movies and concerts are high-quality goods. When his income is low, he may see movies on most weekends because, being cheaper, they enable him to spread his budget further. But if his income increases, he might switch from movies to concerts on some nights and end up seeing fewer movies. In that case, his *behavior* tells us that movies are an inferior good for him.

© AXL/SHUTTERSTOCK.COM

of a good demanded, the good is *normal*. For Max, with the marginal utility values we've assumed in Figure 5, both concerts and movies would be normal goods.

But this is not the only possible result. If Max's preferences (and marginal utility values) had been different than those listed in Figure 5, he might have chosen more of one good and *less* of the other.

These possibilities are illustrated in Figure 6. Our previous result—based on the marginal utility numbers in Figure 5—had Max moving from point *D* on his initial budget line to point *K* on the new, higher one when his income rose. But with different preferences (different marginal utility values), his marginal utilities per dollar might have been equal at a point like *K'*, with 9 concerts and 2 movies. In this case, the increase in income would cause Max's consumption of concerts to increase (from 3 to 9), but his consumption of movies to *fall* (from 4 to 2). If so, movies would be an *inferior good* for Max—one for which demand decreases when income increases—while concerts would be a *normal* good.

Finally, let's consider another possible outcome for Max: point *K"*. At this point, he attends more movies and fewer concerts compared to point *D*. If point *K"* is where Max's marginal utilities per dollar are equal after the increase in income, then *concerts* would be the inferior good, and movies would be normal.[5]

A rise in income—with no change in prices—leads to a new quantity demanded for each good. Whether a particular good is normal (quantity demanded increases) or inferior (quantity demanded decreases) depends on the individual's preferences, as represented by the marginal utilities for each good, at each point along his budget line.

[5] If you are wondering how we would use marginal utility tables like those in Figures 4 and 5 when one of the goods is inferior, wait for the end of chapter problems. In Figures 4 and 5, we have made a special assumption: That the marginal utility values for one good do *not* depend on quantities of the *other* good. But this need not be the case, as you'll see in the problems.

| FIGURE 6 | Normal and Inferior Goods |

If income rises and concerts are inferior, Max moves to a point like *K"* (fewer concerts).

If income rises and movies are inferior, Max moves to a point like *K'* (fewer movies).

Number of Movies per Month

Number of Concerts per Month

© CENGAGE LEARNING 2013

Changes in Price

Let's explore what happens to Max when the *price of a concert decreases* from $20 to $10, while his income and the price of a movie remain unchanged. The drop in the price of concerts rotates Max's budget line rightward, pivoting around its vertical intercept, as illustrated in the upper panel of Figure 7. What will Max do after his budget line rotates in this way? As always, he will select the combination of movies and concerts on his budget line that makes him as well off as possible. This will be the combination at which the marginal utility per dollar spent on both goods is the same.

Once again, we've taken some of Max's marginal utility values from Figure 4 and added some additional numbers to construct the table in Figure 7. This table extends what we already knew about Max's preferences to cover the new, expanded possibilities.

With the preferences represented by these marginal utility numbers, Max will search along his budget line for the best choice. This will lead him directly to point *R*, where his quantities demanded are 5 concerts and 5 movies. Note that with each concert costing only $10 now, Max can afford this combination. Moreover, it satisfies our utility-maximizing rule: Marginal utility per dollar is 25 for both goods.

What if we dropped the price of concerts again—this time—to $5? Then Max's budget line rotates further rightward, and he will once again find the utility-maximizing point. In the figure, Max is shown choosing point *T*, attending 8 concerts and 6 movies. (The marginal utilities per dollar in the table cannot be used to find point *T*, because the table assumes the price of concerts is $10.)

The Consumer's Demand Curve

You've just seen that each time the price of concerts changes, so does the quantity of concerts Max will want to see. The lower panel of Figure 7 highlights this relationship by plotting the quantity of concerts demanded on the horizontal axis and the price of concerts on the vertical axis. For example, in both the upper and lower panels, point *D* tells us that when the price of concerts is $20, Max will see three of them. When we connect points like *D*, *R*, and *T* in the lower panel, we get Max's demand curve, which shows *the quantity of a good he demands at each different price*. Notice that Max's demand curve for concerts slopes downward—a fall in the price of concerts increases the quantity demanded—showing that Max's responses to price changes obey the law of demand.

But if Max's preferences—and his marginal utility values—had been different, could his response to a price change have *violated* the law of demand? The answer is yes . . . and no. Yes, it is theoretically possible. (As a challenge, try identifying points on the three budget lines that would give Max an *upward-sloping* demand curve.) But no, it does not seem to happen in practice.

To help you understand why and gain other insights, the next section takes a deeper look into the effects of a price change on quantity demanded.

INCOME AND SUBSTITUTION EFFECTS

Whether you've studied the marginal utility approach (the previous section) or the indifference curve approach (appendix), you've learned a logical process that leads directly to an individual's demand curve. But the demand curve actually summarizes the impact of two separate effects of a price change on quantity

FIGURE 7   Deriving the Demand Curve

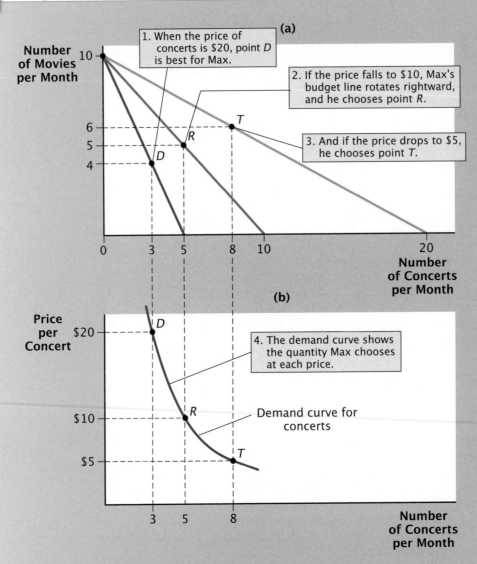

(a)

1. When the price of concerts is $20, point *D* is best for Max.

2. If the price falls to $10, Max's budget line rotates rightward, and he chooses point *R*.

3. And if the price drops to $5, he chooses point *T*.

Number of Movies per Month

Number of Concerts per Month

(b)

4. The demand curve shows the quantity Max chooses at each price.

Price per Concert

Demand curve for concerts

Number of Concerts per Month

Max's Choices with Budget of $100 per month

	CONCERTS at $10 each			MOVIES at $10 each		
(1) Point on New Budget Line	**(2)** Number of Concerts per Month	**(3)** Marginal Utility from Last Concert (MU_c)	**(4)** Marginal Utility per Dollar Spent on Last Concert $\left(\dfrac{MU_c}{P_c}\right)$	**(5)** Number of Movies per Month	**(6)** Marginal Utility from Last Movie (MU_m)	**(7)** Marginal Utility per Dollar Spent on Last Movie $\left(\dfrac{MU_m}{P_m}\right)$
	3	600	60	7	150	15
	4	400	40	6	200	20
R	**5**	**250**	**25**	**5**	**250**	**25**
	6	180	18	4	300	30
	7	100	10	3	350	35

demanded. As you are about to see, these two effects sometimes work together and sometimes oppose each other.

The Substitution Effect

Suppose the price of concerts falls and the price of movies remains the same. Concerts will become cheaper *relative to* movies. Or to put it another way, the relative price of concerts (*Pc/Pm*) will fall. Max can now get more entertainment from his budget by substituting concerts in place of movies, so he will demand more concerts.

This impact of a price decrease on quantity demanded is called a substitution effect: The consumer substitutes *toward* the good whose relative price has decreased.

> The **substitution effect** of a price change always moves quantity demanded in the opposite direction to the price change. When the price of a good decreases, the substitution effect works to increase quantity demanded; when price increases, the substitution effect works to decrease quantity demanded.

Substitution effect As the price of a good falls, the consumer substitutes that good in place of other goods whose prices have not changed.

The substitution effect is a powerful force in the marketplace. For example, while the price of cell phone calls began falling several years ago, the price of pay phone calls remained more or less the same. This fall in the relative price of cell phone calls caused consumers to substitute toward them and away from using regular pay phones. As a result, pay phones have almost disappeared in many areas of the country.

The substitution effect is also important from a theoretical perspective: It is the main factor responsible for the law of demand. Indeed, if the substitution effect were the *only* effect of a price change, the law of demand would be more than a law; it would be a logical necessity. But as we are about to see, a price change has another effect as well.

The Income Effect

In Figure 7 (or Appendix Figure A.5), when the price of concerts drops from $20 to $10, Max's budget line rotates rightward. Max now has a wider range of options than before: He can consume more concerts, more movies, or *more of both*. The price decline of *one* good increases his total purchasing power over *both* goods.

Income effect As the price of a good decreases, the consumer's purchasing power increases, causing a change in quantity demanded for the good.

A price cut gives the consumer a gift, which is rather like an increase in *income*. Indeed, in an important sense, it *is* an increase in *available* income: Point *D* (3 concerts and 4 movies) originally cost Max $100, but after the decrease in the price of concerts, the same combination would cost him just (3 × $10) + (4 × $10) = $70, leaving him with $30 in *available income* to spend on more movies or concerts or both. This leads to the second effect of a change in price:

> The **income effect** of a price change arises from a change in purchasing power over both goods. A drop in price increases total purchasing power, while a rise in price decreases total purchasing power.

© PHILIP JAMES CORWIN/CORBIS

Cheaper cell phone calls, and the substitution effect, have almost completely driven pay phones like this out of the market.

How will a change in purchasing power influence the quantity of a good demanded? That depends. Recall that an increase in income will increase the demand for normal goods and decrease the demand for inferior goods. The same is true for the *income effect* of a price cut: It can work to either *increase* or *decrease* the quantity of a good demanded, depending on whether the good is normal or inferior. For example, if concerts are a normal good for Max, then the income effect of a price cut will lead him to consume more of them; if concerts are inferior, the income effect will lead him to consume fewer.

Combining Substitution and Income Effects

Now let's look again at the impact of a price change, considering the substitution and income effects together. A change in the price of a good changes both the relative price of the good (the substitution effect) and the overall purchasing power of the consumer (the income effect). The ultimate impact of the price change on quantity demanded will depend on *both* of these effects. For normal goods, these two effects work together to push quantity demanded in the same direction. But for inferior goods, the two effects oppose each other. Let's see why.

Normal Goods. When the price of a normal good falls, the substitution effect *increases* quantity demanded. The price drop will also increase the consumer's purchasing power and—for a normal good—*increase* quantity demanded even further. The opposite occurs when price increases: The substitution effect decreases quantity demanded, and the decline in purchasing power further decreases it. Figure 8 summarizes how the substitution and income effects combine to make the price and quantity demanded of a normal good move in opposite directions:

> For normal goods, *the substitution and income effects work together, causing quantity demanded to move in the opposite direction of the price. Normal goods, therefore, must always obey the law of demand.*

Inferior Goods. Now let's see how a price change affects the demand for *inferior* goods. As an example, consider intercity bus service. For many consumers, this is an inferior good: with a higher income, these consumers would choose quicker and more comfortable alternatives (such as air or train travel), and therefore demand *less* bus service. Now, if the price of bus service falls, the substitution effect would work, as always, to *increase* quantity demanded. The price cut will also, as always, increase the consumer's purchasing power. But if bus service is inferior, the rise in purchasing power will *decrease* quantity demanded. Thus, we have two opposing effects: the substitution effect, which increases quantity demanded, and the income effect, which decreases quantity demanded. In theory, either of these effects could dominate the other, so the quantity demanded could move in either direction.

In practice, however, the substitution effect virtually always dominates for inferior goods.

Why? Largely, because we consume such a wide variety of goods and services that a price cut in any one of them changes our purchasing power by only a small amount. For example, suppose you have an income of $20,000 per year, and you spend $500 per year on bus tickets. If the price of bus travel falls by, say, 20 percent, this would save you $100—like a gift of $100 in income. But $100 is only ½ percent of your income. Thus, a 20 percent fall in the price of bus travel would cause only

| FIGURE 8 | Income and Substitution Effects |

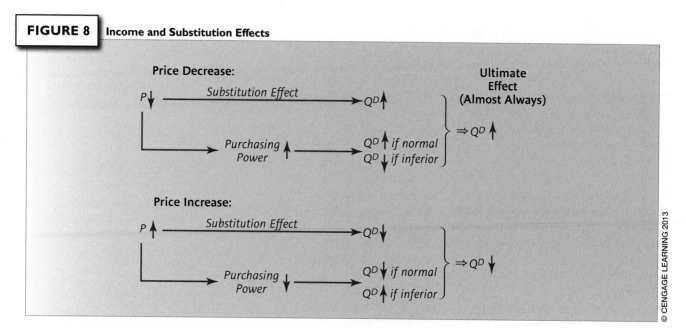

a ½ percent rise in your purchasing power. Even if bus travel is, for you, an inferior good, we would expect only a tiny decrease in your quantity demanded when your purchasing power changes by such a small amount. Thus, the income effect should be very small. On the other hand, the *substitution* effect should be rather large: With bus travel now 20 percent cheaper, you will likely substitute away from other purchases and buy more bus travel.

> *For inferior goods, the substitution and income effects of a price change work against each other. The substitution effect moves quantity demanded in the opposite direction of the price, while the income effect moves it in the same direction as the price. But since the substitution effect virtually always dominates, consumption of inferior goods—like normal goods—will virtually always obey the law of demand.*

CONSUMERS IN MARKETS

Since the market demand curve tells us the quantity of a good demanded by *all* consumers in a market, it makes sense that we can derive it by adding up the individual demand curves of every consumer in that market.

Figure 9 illustrates how this can be done in a small local market for bottled water, where, for simplicity, we assume that there are only three consumers—Jerry, George, and Elaine. The first three diagrams show their individual demand curves. If the market price were, say, $2 per bottle, Jerry would buy 4 bottles each week (point *c*), George would buy 6 (point *c'*), and Elaine would buy zero (point *c''*). Thus, the market quantity demanded at a price of $2 would be 4 + 6 + 0 = 10, which is point C on the market demand curve. To obtain the entire market demand curve, we repeat this procedure at each different price, adding up the quantities demanded by each individual to obtain the total quantity demanded in the market. (Verify on

FIGURE 9 | From Individual to Market Demand

The individual demand curves show how much bottled water will be demanded by Jerry, George, and Elaine at different prices. As the price falls, each demands more. The market demand curve in panel (b) is obtained by adding up the total quantity demanded by all market participants at different prices.

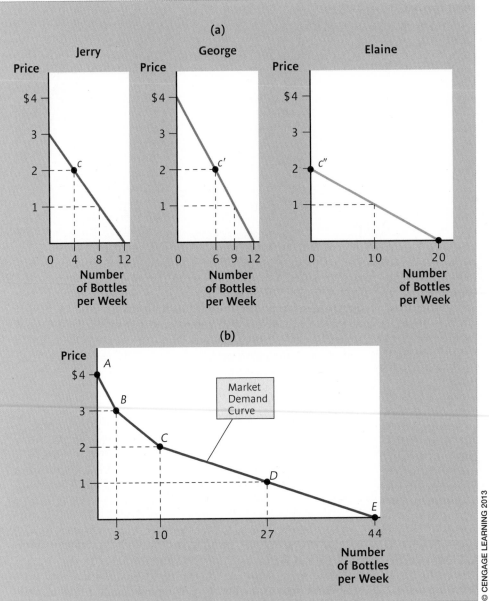

(a)

your own that points *A*, *B*, *D*, and *E* have been obtained in the same way.) In effect, we obtain the market demand curve by summing horizontally across each of the individual demand curves:

> *The market demand curve is found by horizontally summing the individual demand curves of every consumer in the market.*

Notice that as long as each individual's demand curve is downward sloping (and this will virtually always be the case), then the market demand curve will also be downward sloping. More directly, if a rise in price makes each consumer buy fewer units, then it will reduce the quantity bought by *all* consumers as well. Indeed, the market demand curve can still obey the law of demand even when *some* individuals in the market violate it. Thus, although we are already quite confident about the law of demand at the individual level, we can be even *more* confident at the market level. This is why we always draw market demand curves with a downward slope.

CONSUMER THEORY IN PERSPECTIVE

Our model of consumer theory—whether using marginal utility or indifference curves—has been kept simple. We've considered someone with a limited budget who must allocate his spending between two goods. But can the model explain and predict behavior in more complicated, real-world situations? In many cases, yes—with appropriate modification. In some cases, no. Let's first discuss how the model can be extended to analyze some more complex situations.

Extensions of the Model

One extension of the model—done in more advanced courses—is to incorporate choices among many goods, rather than just two. In that case, the calculations become more complicated, and we can no longer illustrate a consumer's choices on a two-dimensional graph. But the important conclusions we've reached (using either approach: marginal utility or indifference curves) remain the same.

Another extension is to recognize saving and borrowing. In our model, Max must spend his entire budget on movies and concerts, and he cannot spend more. But in the real world, people can spend more than their incomes by borrowing, or spend less than their incomes and save funds for future use. One way to incorporate these possibilities is to define one of the goods as "future consumption." In that case, saving means sacrificing consumption of all goods now in order to have more future consumption, and borrowing means the opposite.

More difficult extensions incorporate *uncertainty* and *imperfect information*. For example, we assumed that Max knows with certainty the outcomes of his choices: the number of movies and concerts he will get, and the satisfaction he will get from them. But in many situations, you make a choice and take your chances. When you buy a car, it might be a lemon; when you pay for some types of surgery, there is a risk that it may be unsuccessful. You can reduce the chance of a bad outcome by acquiring more information. But information is often costly to obtain. When uncertainty and/or imperfect information are important aspects of consumer decision making, additional tools are incorporated into the model. But the central idea—maximization of satisfaction based on rational preferences—remains in force.

Finally, you might think that consumer theory always regards people as relentlessly selfish, concerned only about their own consumption. In fact, when people trade in impersonal markets, this is mostly true: People *do* generally try to allocate their spending among different goods to achieve the greatest personal satisfaction. But in many areas of economic life, people act unselfishly. This, too, can be incorporated into the traditional model of consumer theory. One way is to treat the "satisfaction of others" (say, a family member or society at large) as another "good." Useful analyses of charitable giving, bequests, and voting behavior have been based on this type of modification of the model.

However, some real-world situations don't seem to fit the basic ideas of consumer theory at all. In recent decades, these situations have led to the creation of an entirely new branch of the field: *behavioral economics*.

Behavioral Economics

Behavioral economics
A subfield of economics focusing on decision-making patterns that deviate from those predicted by traditional consumer theory.

To understand what is different about behavioral economics, recall that traditional consumer theory assumes people make choices to maximize their satisfaction. These decisions are based on rational preferences: They compare alternative outcomes and choose the best among them in a logically consistent way. A subfield of economics called **behavioral economics** has shown that preferences are sometimes *irrational*. People sometimes make decisions—even highly consequential decisions—*against* their own interests, often in predictable ways. Businesses have long recognized and exploited these tendencies. Behavioral economists argue that government policy can exploit these same tendencies, mandating changes in how alternatives are presented to encourage people to choose more wisely.

In behavioral economics, the context in which choices are presented influences the actual decisions that people make. Here are a few of the decision-making concepts stressed by behavioral economics.

Salience. Consumers often make decisions based not just on the outcome, but on the *salience* of a particular outcome—the extent to which it "jumps out at them." For example, one study showed that people will consume 77% more M&Ms, on average, when the bowl contains 10 different colors as opposed to just seven different colors. Another study changed the price tags on certain grocery items to include sales tax, and then marked them as such. Sales on those items declined, even though there was no change in the buyer's required payment at checkout. In these cases, consumers seem to be responding to what jumps out at them—the M&M colors in the bowl or the number on the price tag—rather than basing their decisions on what they will have to pay (in money or extra pounds).

Salience also plays a role in major economic decisions, such as taking out mortgage loans, borrowing on credit cards, or buying insurance. Corporations exploit salience by arranging documents or bills to keep certain facts from standing out. For example, on a credit card bill, the minimum payment may be more prominent than the total balance due, encouraging the cardholder to run a balance. Relevant information—such as how much a cardholder has actually paid in fees and interest over the past year—is typically not displayed at all.

A city government in Sweden used some insights from behavioral economics to help fight obesity. The piano-key stairs play musical tones when climbed.

Preference for Defaults. If choices are based on rational preferences, the "default choice" should not matter. In our example, Max gets the most satisfaction from three concerts and four movies per month. Consumer theory suggests he will make that choice even if he is initially given some other combination, and must "opt out" of that combination to have his preferred choice.

But studies have repeatedly shown that people tend to stick to the default choice for some decisions. In employer-sponsored retirement plans, when the default is "no contribution" and employees can easily opt-in to contribute to a retirement fund, only a small percentage do. The share that chooses to contribute remains small even when the employer matches the contributions of the employees—a substantial gift. But when the default option is changed to "contribute," so that *not* contributing requires opting *out*, the contribution rate rises dramatically.

Why do people tend to stick with the default, even when opting in or opting out is quick and easy? Perhaps they become anxious when thinking about the future or when presented with complicated, consequential decisions. Regardless of the cause, marketers and business firms often exploit this tendency. For example, Web sites—when obligated to get users' permission to receive advertising e-mail—will often make "Yes, please send me e-mail from related businesses" the default choice.

Decision-Making Environment. Sometimes, the *environment* in which a decision is made can exert a strong and surprising influence. This violates traditional consumer theory, where preferences are assumed to be based on a comparison of alternatives, and not on how or where the alternatives are presented. In research on preventing obesity, for example, health economists found that students seated in large groups in the cafeteria will tend to eat more than those seated in small groups. Their decisions about how much to eat are influenced by the setting. In another study, irrelevant but appealing photographs on a loan application had a profound impact on the percentage of people applying for the loan. Retailers know that the environmental context matters, and try to influence purchasing decisions by controlling the music in the store, the scent in the air, or even the thickness of the carpet beneath customers' feet.

Self-Binding. In a famous story in Homer's *Odyssey*, Ulysses wants to hear the lovely, half-human female creatures called the Sirens sing as his ship passes near them. But their singing is so beautiful that, upon hearing it, sailors are always lured closer, ultimately smashing their ships or themselves on the rocks. So Ulysses instructs his shipmates to plug their own ears with wax and tie him to the ship's mast. They are told not to release him or obey him—no matter what he says—until they are well beyond the Sirens' voices and out of temptation.

From the perspective of rational preferences, Ulysses' strategy makes no sense. A decision maker should always prefer a wide array of choices to a narrow array. After all, if you know what you want, expanding your choices might not always make you better off, but it should *never* make you worse off.

Yet in daily life we often see decision makers act to limit their choices, just as Ulysses did. When a dieter says, "Don't bring any ice cream into the house; I don't want to be tempted," they are saying, "If you give me an additional choice to eat ice cream later, I will be worse off." They would prefer to bind themselves to a narrower set of choices, for their own long-run good. For similar reasons, people often publicly announce their New Year's resolutions, to make it harder for them to go back on their promises later. And some even buy software programs that block their own access to games, social networking sites, or other computer distractions for a set period of time, so they can get work done.

Jonathan Franzen, the award-winning and best-selling novelist, revealed that he applies this principle when writing:

> *Franzen works in a rented office that he has stripped of all distractions. He uses a heavy, obsolete Dell laptop from which he has scoured any trace of hearts and solitaire, down to the level of the operating system. Because Franzen believes you can't write serious fiction on a computer that's connected to the Internet, he not only removed the Dell's wireless card but also permanently blocked its Ethernet port. "What you have to do," he explains, "is you plug in an Ethernet cable with superglue, and then you saw off the little head of it."*

Lev Grossman, "Jonathan Franzen: Great American Novelist," *Time* Magazine, August 12, 2010.

Behavioral Economics and Policy

The insights of behavioral economics have begun to affect government policy. For example, in 2006, Congress changed the law governing pension plans, based on research by behavioral economists. For the first time, the government gave firms a financial incentive to make "automatic contribution" the default choice for their employees. In such plans, employees who do *not* want to contribute to their own retirement account must take action to opt out. Research has shown that at firms that have made this simple change, a significantly greater percentage of workers contribute to their retirement plan.

Another government policy based on self-binding has been instituted in some states with legal casino gambling. People with gambling problems can voluntarily put themselves on a list that bans them from any casino in the state for life. If caught violating the ban, the state will confiscate their winnings, and they will be subject to prosecution and even jail time. Thousands of former gamblers have put themselves on these lists.

In 2010, behavioral economics won a major policy victory when Congress created the new Consumer Financial Protection Bureau as part of a broad financial reform bill. The Bureau began operating in July 2011, and works to discourage some of the financial decisions that have gotten consumers into trouble. The insights of behavioral economics play an important role in its agenda.

For example, the bureau can require financial institutions to offer "vanilla" versions of mortgages, student loans, credit card agreements, and other financial products. These vanilla versions—treated as defaults—must be simply designed and easy to understand, without "teaser rates" or other enticements that might encourage people to borrow or invest irresponsibly. Consequential information must be prominently displayed in simple language, rather than buried in legal fine print. Consumers will remain free to choose more complex or innovative products—say, an adjustable rate mortgage with a low teaser rate and lots of fine print. But they will first have to opt out of the government-approved default versions. Because of the general preference for defaults, few people are expected to opt out. If so, fewer consumers will make decisions that will prove harmful to them in the long run.

Government policies like these, which arise from the insights of behavioral economics, are sometimes labeled "soft paternalism." The government is being paternalistic by using the law to encourage healthier or more responsible choices. But the paternalism is "soft": the government mandates *how* choices are presented, but ultimately leaves us free to choose. While there is some controversy over how far government should go in this direction, there is no doubt that behavioral economics has entered the mainstream of economic thought and has achieved considerable influence in government policy making.

Behavioral Economics and Traditional Theory

Traditional consumer theory assumes that consumers have rational preferences. Behavioral economics analyzes decisions that violate rational preferences. Which theory is better? The answer is: Neither. The best model to use depends on the issue we are analyzing.

In most markets, most of the time, consumer responses can be understood very well with the traditional model. For example, if we are trying to understand how a gasoline tax or a rise in mass transit fares would affect the demand for automobiles, virtually all economists would reach for the traditional model of consumer choice. We would assume that consumers have rational preferences, and act to achieve the highest level of satisfaction, because—for the most part—they would do so in choosing whether to buy a new car.

But to understand why consumers often buy particular models of cars that trap them into spending more on gasoline than they anticipated, traditional theory would leave us short. For this problem, the insights of behavioral economics would work best.

Thus, although behavioral economics is sometimes portrayed as an "alternative" or even a "replacement" for traditional economic theory, few if any economists see it that way. Instead, behavioral economics is more commonly viewed as an addition to the existing body of economic theory—an extra limb that extends the theory's reach.

USING THE THEORY

© JEFF GREENBERG/ALAMY

IMPROVING EDUCATION

So far in this chapter, we've considered the problem of a consumer trying to select the best combination of goods and services. But consumer theory can be extended to consider almost *any* decision among alternatives, including choices that cost us *time* rather than dollars. In this section, we apply the model of consumer choice to an important issue: improving the quality of education.[6]

Each year, various agencies within the U.S. Department of Education spend hundreds of millions of dollars on research to assess and implement new educational techniques. For example, suppose it is thought that computer-assisted instruction might help students learn better or more quickly. A typical research project to test this hypothesis would be a *controlled experiment* in which one group of students would be taught with the computer-assisted instruction and the other group would be taught without it. Then students in both groups would be tested. If the first group scores significantly higher, computer-assisted instruction will be deemed successful; if not, it will be deemed unsuccessful.

In 2011, the New York City public school system took this idea a step further, announcing that it planned to base 40% of each teacher's performance rating on how that teacher's students scored on standardized subject tests.

Many economists are suspicious of using student scores in a particular subject to evaluate teaching techniques or individual teachers. This approach treats students as passive responders to stimuli. Presented with a stimulus (a better teaching technique or a better teacher), students are assumed to give a simple response (scoring higher on the exam). Where in this model, economists ask, are students treated as *decision makers*, who must make *choices* about allocating their scarce time?

Let's apply our model of consumer choice to a student's time allocation problem. To keep things simple, we'll assume a bleak world in which there are only two activities: studying economics and studying French. Instead of costing money, each of these activities costs *time*, and there is only so much time available. And instead of buying quantities of two goods, students "buy" points on their exams with hours spent studying.

[6] This section is based on ideas originally published in Richard B. McKenzie and Gordon Tullock, *The New World of Economics,* 3d ed. (Burr Ridge, IL: Irwin, 1981).

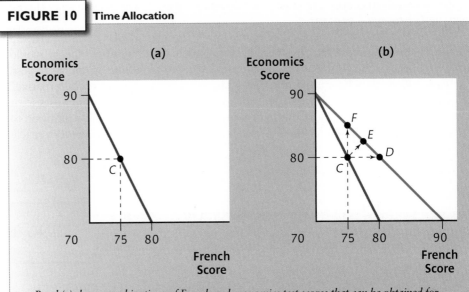

FIGURE 10   **Time Allocation**

Panel (a) shows combinations of French and economics test scores that can be obtained for a given amount of study time. The slope of −2 indicates that each additional point in French requires a sacrifice of 2 points in economics. The student chooses point C. Panel (b) shows that computer-assisted French instruction causes the budget line to rotate outward; French points are now less expensive. The student might move to point D, attaining a higher French score. Or she might choose F, using all of the time freed up in French to study economics. Or she might choose an intermediate point, such as E.

Panel (a) of Figure 10 shows how we can represent the time allocation problem graphically. The economics test score is measured on the vertical axis and the French score on the horizontal axis. The straight line in the figure is the student's budget line, showing the trade-off between economics and French scores. Our student can achieve any combination of scores on this budget line with her scarce time.

A few things are worth noting about the budget line in the figure. First, the more study time you devote to a subject, the better you will do on the test. But that means less study time for the other subject and a lower test score there. Thus, the opportunity cost of scoring better in French is scoring lower in economics, and vice versa. This is why the budget line has a negative slope: The higher the score in French, the lower the score in economics. As our student moves downward along the budget line, she is shifting hours away from studying economics and toward studying French.

Second, notice that the vertical and horizontal axes both start at 70 rather than 0. This is to keep our example from becoming too depressing. If our student devotes *all* her study time to economics and none to French, she would score 90 in economics but still be able to score 70 (rather than zero) in French, just by attending class and paying attention. If she devotes all her time to French, she would score 80 in French and 70 in economics. (*Warning*: Do not try to use this example to convince your economics instructor you deserve at least a 70 on your next exam.)

Finally, the budget line in our example is drawn as a straight line with a slope of −2. So each additional point in French requires our student to sacrifice two points in economics. This assumption helps make the analysis more concrete. But none of our conclusions would be different if the budget line had a different slope, or even if it were curved so that the trade-off would change as we moved along it. But let's take a moment to understand what our example implies.

As you've learned, the slope of any budget line is $-P_x/P_y$, where x is the good measured on the horizontal axis and y is the good measured on the vertical axis. We'll let P_F be the price of one point in French, and P_E be the price of one point in economics. Then, in our example, $-P_x/P_y$ translates into $-P_F/P_E$.

But what is the "price" of a test point in French or economics? Unlike the case of Max, who had to allocate his scarce funds between concerts and movies, our student must allocate her scarce *time* between the two "goods" she desires: test points in French and test points in economics. The *price* of a test point is therefore not a money price, but rather a *time price*: the number of study hours needed to achieve an additional point. For example, it might take an additional two hours of studying to achieve another point in French ($P_F = 2$) but just one hour to get another point in economics ($P_E = 1$). This would give us a budget line with a slope of $-P_F/P_E = -2/1 = -2$, which is the slope used in Figure 10(a).

Now let's turn our attention to student decision making. Our student values both her economics score and her French score. But among all those combinations of scores on her budget line, which is the best choice? That depends on the student's preferences, whether characterized by the marginal utility approach or the indifference curve approach. Suppose that initially, this student's best choice is at point C, where she scores 80 in economics and 75 in French.

Now, let's introduce a new computer-assisted technique in the French class, one that is, in fact, remarkably effective: It enables students to learn more French with the same study time or to study less and learn the same amount. This causes a *decrease* in the price of French points—it now takes less time to earn a point in French—so the budget line will rotate outward, as shown in panel (b) of Figure 10. On the new budget line, if our student devotes all of her time to French, she can score higher than before—90 instead of 80—so the horizontal intercept moves rightward. But since nothing has changed in her economics course, the vertical intercept remains unaffected. Notice, too, that the budget line's slope has changed to -1. Now, the opportunity cost of an additional point in French is one point in economics rather than two.

After the new technique is introduced in the French course, our *decision-making* student will locate at a point on her new budget line based once again on her preferences. Panel (b) illustrates some alternative possibilities. At point D, her performance in French would improve, but her economics performance would remain the same. This seems to be the kind of result education researchers have in mind when they design their experiments: If a successful technique is introduced in the French course, they expect to find the impact with a French test.

Point F illustrates a different choice: *Only* the economics performance improves, while the French score remains unchanged. Here, even though the technique in French is successful (it does, indeed, rotate the budget line outward), none of its success shows up in higher French scores.

But wait: How can a new technique in the French course improve performance in economics but not at all in French? The answer is found by breaking down the impact of the new technique into our familiar income and substitution effects. The new technique lowers the student's "time price" of getting additional points in French. The substitution effect (French points are relatively cheaper) will tend to improve her score in French, as she substitutes her time away from economics and toward French. But there is also an "*income*" effect: The "purchasing power" of her time has increased, since now she could use her fixed allotment of study time to "buy" higher scores in *both* courses. If performance in French is a normal good, this increase in "purchasing power" will work to increase her French score. But if French is an inferior good, it could work to *decrease* her French score. Point F could come about because French performance is *such* an inferior good that the negative income effect exactly cancels out the positive substitution effect. In this case, the education researchers will incorrectly judge the new technique a complete failure—it does not affect French scores at all.

Could this actually happen? Perhaps. It is easy to imagine a student deciding that 75 in French is good enough and using any study time freed up from better French instruction to improve her performance in some other course. More commonly, we expect a student to choose a point such as *E*, somewhere between points *D* and *F*, with performance improving in *both* courses. But even in this case, the higher French score measures just a *part* of the impact of the technique; the remaining effect is seen in a higher economics score.

Because students are free to allocate their study time as they choose, it is not surprising that many promising teaching techniques make little, if any, difference in student scores in a course. Much of the time freed up from an effective technique in one course might be spent on studying for other courses. And some of the freed-up time might be spent on sports, watching TV, earning money, sleeping, or other activities that go unmeasured. This suggests why educational research is conducted as it is: A more accurate assessment of teaching techniques or individual teachers would require a thorough accounting for all of a student's time, which is both expensive and difficult to achieve. Still, we should be cautious when interpreting results that, by design, ignore the choices students make in allocating their scarce time.

SUMMARY

The two components of consumer theory are the consumer's budget constraint and consumer preferences. The budget constraint tells us the combinations of goods a consumer can afford given the consumer's limited income and the prices charged for each good.

Graphically, the budget constraint is represented by the *budget line*. Only combinations on or below the budget line are affordable. An increase in income shifts the budget line outward. A change in the price of a good causes the budget line to rotate.

The consumer's goal is to achieve the highest level of satisfaction or *utility* affordable, given the consumer's budget constraint and unique preferences. Consumer theory assumes that preferences are *rational*, meaning a consumer can compare any two combinations of goods, and make logically consistent (transitive) choices among them. It also assumes that "more is better" for any good considered.

There are two alternative ways to represent consumer preferences, which lead to two different approaches to consumer decision making. The *marginal utility approach* is presented in the body of the chapter. In this approach, a utility-maximizing consumer chooses the combination of goods along her budget line at which the marginal utility per dollar spent is the same for all goods. When income or price changes, the consumer once again equates the marginal utility per dollar of both goods, resulting in a choice along the *new* budget line.

In the *indifference curve approach*, presented in the appendix, a consumer's preferences are represented by a collection of her *indifference curves*, called her *indifference map*. The highest level of utility or satisfaction is achieved at the point on the budget line that is also on the highest possible indifference curve. When income or price changes, the consumer moves to the point on the *new* budget line that is on the highest possible indifference curve.

Using either of the two approaches, we can trace the quantity of a good chosen at different prices for that good, and generate a downward sloping *demand* curve for that good. The downward slope reflects the interaction of the *substitution effect* and the *income effect*. For a normal good, both effects contribute to the downward slope of the demand curve. For an inferior good, the two effects oppose each other. But in virtually all cases, the substitution effect dominates the income effect, so—once again—the demand curve will slope downward.

Behavioral economics studies deviations from rational decision making. It focuses on how decisions are affected by the way in which alternatives are presented, and how consumers can be misled into making choices that do not maximize their utility. The insights of behavioral economics have begun to influence government policy in important ways.

PROBLEM SET

Answers to even-numbered Problems can be found on the text Web site through www.cengagebrain.com

1. Parvez, a pharmacology student, has allocated $120 per month to spend on paperback novels and hamburgers at his favorite burger joint. Novels cost $8 each; hamburgers cost $6 each. Draw his budget line.
   a. Draw and label a second budget line that shows what happens when the price of a hamburger rises to $10.
   b. Draw and label a third budget line that shows what happens when the price of a hamburger rises to $10 *and* Parvez's income rises to $240.

2. [Uses the Marginal Utility Approach] Now go back to the original assumptions of problem 1 (novels cost $8, hamburgers cost $6, and income is $120). Suppose that Parvez is spending $120 monthly on paperback novels and hamburgers. For novels, $MU/P = 5$; for hamburgers, $MU/P = 4$. Is he maximizing his utility? If not, should he consume (1) more novels and fewer hamburgers; or (2) more hamburgers and fewer novels? Explain briefly.

3. [Uses the Marginal Utility Approach] Anita consumes both pizza and Pepsi. The following tables show the amount of utility she obtains from different amounts of these two goods per week:

Pizza		Pepsi	
Quantity	Utility	Quantity	Utility
4 slices	115	5 cans	63
5 slices	135	6 cans	75
6 slices	154	7 cans	86
7 slices	171	8 cans	96

   Suppose Pepsi costs $1 per can, pizza costs $2 per slice, and Anita has $18 to spend on these two goods each week. What combination of pizza and Pepsi will maximize her utility?

4. Three people have the following individual demand schedules for Count Chocula cereal that show how many boxes each would purchase monthly at different prices:

Price	Person 1	Person 2	Person 3
$5.00	0	1	2
$4.50	0	2	3
$4.00	0	3	4
$3.50	1	3	5

   a. What is the market demand schedule for this cereal? (Assume that these three people are the only buyers.) Draw the market demand curve.
   b. Why might the three people have different demand schedules?

5. Suppose that 1,000 people in a market *each* have the same monthly demand curve for bottled water, given by the equation $Q^D = 100 - 25P$, where P is the price for a 12-ounce bottle in dollars.
   a. How many bottles would be demanded in the entire market if the price is $1?
   b. How many bottles would be demanded in the entire market if the price is $2?
   c. Provide an equation for the *market* demand curve, showing how the market quantity demanded by all 1,000 consumers depends on the price.

6. What would happen to the market demand curve for polyester suits, an inferior good, if consumers' incomes rose?

7. Larsen E. Pulp, head of Pulp Fiction Publishing Company, just got some bad news: The price of paper, the company's most important input, has increased.
   a. On a supply/demand diagram, show what will happen to the price of Pulp's output (novels).
   b. Explain the resulting substitution and income effects for a typical Pulp customer. For each effect, will the customer's quantity demanded increase or decrease? Be sure to state any assumptions you are making.

8. "If a good is inferior, a rise in its price will cause people to buy more of it, thus violating the law of demand." True or false? Explain.

9. Which of the following descriptions of consumer behavior violates the assumption of *rational preferences*? Explain briefly.
   a. Joseph is confused: He doesn't know whether he'd prefer to take a job now or go to college full-time.
   b. Brenda likes mustard on her pasta, in spite of the fact that pasta is not meant to be eaten with mustard.
   c. Brewster says, "I'd rather see an action movie than a romantic comedy, and I'd rather see a romantic comedy than a foreign film. But given the choice, I think I'd rather see a foreign film than an action movie."

10. [Uses the Indifference Curve Approach] Howard spends all of his income on magazines and novels. Illustrate each of the following situations on a graph, with the quantity of magazines on the vertical axis and the quantity of novels on the horizontal axis. Use two budget lines and two indifference curves on each graph.
   a. When the price of magazines rises, Howard buys fewer magazines and more novels.
   b. When Howard's income rises, he buys more magazines *and* more novels.
   c. When Howard's income rises, he buys more magazines but *fewer* novels.

11. [Uses the Marginal Utility Approach] In Figure 5, we assumed that after Max's income rose, his marginal utility values for any given number of movies or concerts remained the same as before. But now suppose that when Max's income rises, and he can consume more movies and concerts, *an additional movie has less value* to Max than before. In particular, assume that Max's marginal utility values are as in the table below. Fill in the blanks for the missing values, and find Max's utility-maximizing combination of concerts and movies. In Figure 5 in the chapter, locate the new combination as a point on the $200 budget line. (It will not be one of the labeled points.) With these new marginal utility values, is one of the two goods inferior? Explain.

Budget + $200 per month

Concerts at $20 each			Movies at $10 each		
(1) Number of Concerts per Month	(2) Marginal Utility from Last Concert (MU_C)	(3) Marginal Utility per Dollar Spent on Last Concert (MU_C/P_C)	(4) Number of Movies per Month	(5) Marginal Utility from Last Movie (MU_M)	(6) Marginal Utility per Dollar Spent on Last Movie (MU_M/P_M)
5	250		10	11	
			9	12	
6	180		8	12.5	
			7	13	
7	100		6	14	
			5	15	
8	50		4	16	
			3	18	
9	40		2	20	
			1	25	
10	30		0	—	—

12. [Uses the Marginal Utility Approach] In Figure 5, we assumed that after Max's income rose, his marginal utility values for any given number of movies or concerts remained the same as before. But now suppose that when Max's income rises, having the ability to enjoy more concerts or movies makes the *last movie* and the *last concert less valuable* to him, so all the marginal utility numbers shrink. In particular, assume that Max's marginal utility values are as in the following table. Fill in the blanks for the missing values, and find Max's utility-maximizing combination of concerts and movies. In Figure 5 in the chapter, locate the new combination as a point on the $200 budget line. (It will not be one of the labeled points.) With these new marginal utility values, is one of the two goods inferior? Explain.

Budget = $200 per month

Concerts at $20 each			Movies at $10 each		
(1) Number of Concerts per Month	(2) Marginal Utility from Last Concert (MU_C)	(3) Marginal Utility per Dollar Spent on Last Concert (MU_C/P_C)	(4) Number of Movies per Month	(5) Marginal Utility from Last Movie (MU_M)	(6) Marginal Utility per Dollar Spent on Last Movie (MU_M/P_M)
0	—		20	10	
			19	15	
1	36		18	18	
			17	20	
2	32		16	22	
			15	25	
3	28		14	30	
			13	35	
4	20		12	38	
			11	45	
5	15		0	—	

13. [Uses the Indifference Curve Approach]
   a. Draw a budget line for Cameron, who has a monthly income of $100. Assume that he buys steak and potatoes, and that steak costs $10 per pound and potatoes cost $2 per pound. Add an indifference curve for Cameron that is tangent to his budget line at the combination of 5 pounds of steak and 25 pounds of potatoes.
   b. Draw a new budget line for Cameron, if his monthly income falls to $80. Assume that potatoes are an inferior good to Cameron. Draw a new indifference curve tangent to his

new budget constraint that reflects this inferiority. What will happen to Cameron's potato consumption? What will happen to his steak consumption?

14. [Uses the Indifference Curve Approach]
    a. Draw a budget line for Rafaella, who has a weekly income of $30. Assume that she buys chicken and eggs, and that chicken costs $5 per pound while eggs cost $1 each. Add an indifference curve for Rafaella that is tangent to her budget line at the combination of 4 pounds of chicken and 10 eggs.
    b. Draw a new budget line for Rafaella, if the price of chicken falls to $3 per pound. Assume that Rafaella views chicken and eggs as substitutes. What will happen to her chicken consumption? What will happen to her egg consumption?

15. [Uses the Indifference Curve Approach]
    a. Draw a budget line for Lynne, who has a weekly income of $225. Assume that she buys food and clothes, and that food costs $15 per bag while clothes cost $25 per item. Add an indifference curve for Lynne that is tangent to her budget line at the combination of 3 items of clothing and 10 bags of food.
    b. Draw a new indifference curve diagram for Lynne, showing what will happen if her tastes change, so that she gets more satisfaction from an extra item of clothing, and less satisfaction from an extra bag of food.
    c. Draw a new indifference curve diagram for Lynne, showing what will happen if she decides to join a nudist colony.

More Challenging

16. The Smiths are a low-income family with $10,000 available annually to spend on food and shelter. Food costs $2 per unit, and shelter costs $1 per square foot per year. The Smiths are currently dividing the $10,000 equally between food and shelter. Use either the Marginal Utility Approach or Indifference Curve Approach.
    a. Draw their budget constraint on a diagram with food on the vertical axis and shelter on the horizontal axis. Label their current consumption choice. How much do they spend on food? On shelter?
    b. Suppose the price of shelter rises to $2 per square foot. Draw the new budget line. Can the Smiths continue to consume the same amounts of food and shelter as previously?

    c. In response to the increased price of shelter, the government makes available a special income supplement. The Smiths receive a cash grant of $5,000 that must be spent on food and shelter. Draw their new budget line and compare it to the line you derived in part a. *Could* the Smiths consume the same combination of food and shelter as in part a?
    d. With the cash grant and with shelter priced at $2 per square foot, *will* the family consume the same combination as in part a? Why or why not?

17. When an economy is experiencing inflation, the prices of most goods and services are rising but at different rates. Imagine a simpler inflationary situation in which *all* prices, and all wages and incomes, are rising at the same rate, say 5 percent per year. What would happen to consumer choices in such a situation? (Hint: Think about the budget line.)

18. [Uses the Indifference Curve Approach] With the quantity of popcorn on the vertical axis and the quantity of ice cream on the horizontal axis, draw indifference maps to illustrate each of the following situations. (Hint: Each will look different from the indifference maps in the appendix, because each violates one of the assumptions we made there.)
    a. Larry's marginal rate of substitution between ice cream and popcorn remains constant, no matter how much of each good he consumes.
    b. Heather loves ice cream but hates popcorn.

19. [Uses the Indifference Curve Approach] The appendix to this chapter states that when a consumer is buying the optimal combination of two goods x and y, then $MRS_{y,x} = P_x/P_y$. Draw a graph, with an indifference curve and a budget line, and with the quantity of y on the vertical axis, to illustrate the case where the consumer is buying a *non*-optimal combination on his budget line for which $MRS_{y,x} > P_x/P_y$.

of land and labor, the yield may continue to increase, but eventually the *size* of the increase—the marginal product of fertilizer—will begin to come down. This tendency is so pervasive and widespread that it has been deemed a law:

Law of diminishing (marginal) returns As more and more of any input is added to a fixed amount of other inputs, its marginal product will eventually decline.

> *The **law of diminishing (marginal) returns** states that as we continue to add more of any one input (holding the other inputs constant), its marginal product will eventually decline.*

The law of diminishing returns is a physical law, not an economic one. It is based on the nature of production—on the physical relationship between inputs and outputs with a given technology.

Figure 1 tells us that at Spotless diminishing returns set in after two workers have been hired. Beyond this point, the firm is crowding more and more workers into a car wash with just one automated line. Output continues to increase, since there is usually *something* an additional worker can do to move the cars through the line more quickly, but the increase is less dramatic each time.

THINKING ABOUT COSTS

The previous section dealt with *production*—the *physical* relationship between inputs and outputs. But a more critical concern for a firm is: What will it *cost* to produce any level of output? Everything you've learned about production will help you understand the behavior of costs.

Let's start by revisiting a familiar notion. In Chapter 1 you learned that economists always think of cost as *opportunity cost*—what we must give up in order to do something. This concept applies to the firm as well:

> *A firm's total cost of producing a given level of output is the opportunity cost of the owners—everything they must give up in order to produce that amount of output.*

Using the concept of opportunity cost can help us understand which costs matter—and which don't—when making business decisions.

The Irrelevance of Sunk Costs

Suppose that last year, Acme Pharmaceutical Company spent $10 million developing a new drug to treat acne that, if successful, would have generated millions of dollars in annual sales revenue. At first, the drug seemed to work as intended. But then, just before launching production, management discovered that the new drug didn't cure acne at all—but was remarkably effective in treating a rare underarm fungus. In this smaller, less lucrative market, annual sales revenue would be just $30,000. Now management must decide: Should they sell the drug as an antifungus remedy?

When confronted with a problem like this, some people will say: "Acme should *not* sell the drug. You don't sell something for $30,000 a year when it cost you $10 million to make it." Others will respond this way: "Of course Acme should sell the drug. If they don't, they'd be wasting that huge investment of $10 million." But to an economist, neither approach to answering this question is correct, because both use the $10 million development cost to reach a conclusion—and that cost is completely *irrelevant* to the decision.

The $10 million already spent on developing the drug is an example of a *sunk cost*. More generally,

> *a* **sunk cost** *is one that already has been paid, or must be paid, regardless of any future action being considered.*

In the case of Acme, the development cost has been paid already. The firm will not get this money back, whether it chooses to sell the drug in this new smaller market or not. Because the $10 million is not part of the opportunity cost of either choice—something that would have to be sacrificed *for* that choice—it should have no bearing on the decision. For Acme, as for any business,

> *Sunk costs should not be considered when making decisions.*

What *should* be considered are the costs that *do* depend on the decision about producing the drug, namely, the cost of actually manufacturing it and marketing it for the smaller market. If these costs are less than the $30,000 Acme could earn in annual revenue, Acme should produce the drug. Otherwise, it should not.

Look again at the definition of sunk cost, and you'll see that even a *future* payment can be sunk, if an *unavoidable commitment to pay it has already been made*. Suppose, for example, Acme Pharmaceuticals has signed a contract with a research scientist, legally binding the firm to pay her annual salary for three years even if she is laid off. Although some or all of the payments haven't yet been made, the future salary payments are sunk costs for Acme because they *must* be made no matter what Acme does. As sunk costs, they are irrelevant to Acme's decisions.

Our insight about the irrelevance of sunk costs applies beyond the business sector, to decisions in general. For example, suppose that after completing two years of medical school, you've decided that you've made a mistake: You'd rather be a lawyer. You might be tempted to stay in medical school because of the money and time you've already spent there. But you can't get your time back. And since you can't sell your two years of medical training to someone else, you can't get your money back either. Thus, the costs of your first two years in medical school have either *been* paid or the unavoidable *commitment* to pay them has already been made (say, because you've taken out a student loan that must be repaid in the future). They are sunk costs and should have no influence on your career decision. Only the costs that *depend* on your decision are relevant. If you choose to stay in medical school, you'll have to spend time, effort, and expense for your *remaining* years there. If you switch to law school, you'll spend the time, effort, and expense of three years *there*. These are the costs you should consider (and compare with the benefits) for each choice.

Explicit versus Implicit Costs

In Chapter 2, in discussing the opportunity cost of education, you learned that there are two types of costs: *explicit* (involving actual payments) and *implicit* (no money changes hands). The same distinction applies to costs for a business firm:

> *A firm's "cost" is its opportunity cost, which includes both implicit and explicit costs.*

Suppose you've opened a restaurant in a building that you already owned. You don't pay any rent, so there's no explicit rental cost. Is there a cost to using the building?

TABLE 2

A Firm's Costs

Explicit Costs	Implicit Costs
Rent paid out	Opportunity cost of:
Interest on loans	Owner's land and buildings (rent forgone)
Managers' salaries	Owner's money (investment income
Hourly workers' wages	forgone)
Cost of raw materials	Owner's time (labor income forgone)

© CENGAGE LEARNING 2013

To an accountant—who focuses on actual money payments—the answer is no. But to an economist—who thinks of opportunity cost—the answer is yes. By using your own building for your restaurant, you are sacrificing the opportunity to rent it to someone else. This *forgone rent* is an *implicit cost,* and it is as much a cost of production as the rent you would pay if you didn't own a building yourself. In both cases, something is given up to produce your output.

A similar logic applies to interest costs. Now suppose that instead of borrowing money to set up your restaurant, you used $100,000 of your own money. Therefore, you aren't paying any interest. But there is an opportunity cost: Your $100,000 *could* have been put in the bank or lent to someone else, where it would be earning interest for you. If the going interest rate is 5 percent, then each year that you run your restaurant, you are giving up $5,000 in interest you could have instead. This *forgone interest* is another implicit cost of your business.

Finally, suppose you decided to manage your restaurant yourself. Have you escaped the costs of hiring a manager? Not really, because you are still bearing an opportunity cost: You *could* do something else with your time. We measure the value of your time as the income you *could* earn by devoting your labor to your next-best income-earning activity. This *forgone labor income*—the wage or salary you could be earning elsewhere—is an implicit cost of your business, and therefore it is part of its opportunity cost.

Table 2 summarizes our discussion by listing some common categories of costs that business firms face, both explicit (on the left) and implicit (on the right). All of these are part of the firm's opportunity cost.

The Least-Cost Rule

Most firms can produce a given level of output in different ways. To produce a certain amount of corn, a farmer can use more harvesting machinery and save on labor costs, or use fewer machines and hire more labor. To get its packages to customers, FedEx can buy a greater number of smaller and cheaper jets, hiring more pilots and probably using more fuel. Or it can buy fewer larger and more expensive jets that require

⚠ DANGEROUS CURVES

Forgone interest can be tricky! Here are two common mistakes in calculating the implicit cost of funds you invest in your own business, such as the $100,000 in our restaurant example.

First, you might be tempted to count the entire $100,000 as a cost, rather than just the forgone interest on that sum. But a firm's costs are only the *ongoing, yearly costs* for the owner. (That's what we'll eventually compare to the ongoing, annual revenue.) The $100,000 initial investment is only paid out once, not every year. If you sell the business, you will presumably get that sum back. But as long as you continue to own the business, the interest that *could* be earned on that $100,000 ($5,000 per year in our example) is an ongoing, yearly cost.

A second mistake is not realizing that, if conditions change, some of the forgone interest on your initial investment can become a *sunk cost*. For example, suppose you invest $100,000 to open a restaurant, and then the restaurant industry falls out of favor. If you sell now, you will only get $40,000. Then the ongoing interest cost of owning the business has just dropped to $2,000 per year—the interest forgone on $40,000 at 5 percent. That's the only part you could recover if you sold the restaurant, rather than continuing to own it. The interest you could have earned on the other $60,000 you originally invested no longer matters. It's a sunk cost because, regardless of any decision you make now or in the future, you can *not* get that $60,000 back.

© AXL/SHUTTERSTOCK.COM

fewer pilots and possibly use less fuel. How does the firm choose? Since we assume that a firm strives to earn the maximum profit, it will choose the cheapest possible way to produce any given level of output. This leads to an important rule for calculating costs:

> The **least-cost rule** *states that a business firm will produce any given output level using the least-cost combination of inputs available to it.*

For any given output level, the least-cost input combination depends on the nature of the firm's technology, the prices the firm must pay for its inputs, and also the time horizon for the firm's planning. Recall that in the long run, all of the firm's inputs are variable, but in the short run, at least one of the firm's inputs is fixed. So in the short run, fewer choices are available to the firm. But even in the short run, as long as two or more inputs are variable, the firm will select the least-cost input combination for any output level it decides to produce. The appendix to this chapter presents, in more detail, how firms make that choice.

DANGEROUS CURVES

The least-cost rule When you read the *least-cost rule* of production, you might think that the firm's goal is to have the *lowest possible cost*. But that's not what the rule says. After all, the lowest possible cost could be achieved by not using any variable inputs and producing nothing!

The least-cost rule says something different: that any *given* level of output should be produced at the lowest possible cost for *that* output level.

Least-Cost Rule A firm produces any given output level using the lowest cost combination of inputs available.

COST IN THE SHORT RUN

Managers must answer questions about costs over different time horizons. One question might be, "How much will it cost to produce a given level of output *this year?*" Another might be, "How much will it cost us to produce a given level of output *three years from now and beyond?*" In this section, we'll explore managers' view of costs over a short-run time horizon—a time period during which *at least one* of the firm's inputs is fixed. That is, we'll be looking at costs with a *short-run* planning horizon.

Remember that no matter how much output is produced, the quantity of a fixed input *must* remain the same. Other inputs, by contrast, can be varied as output changes. Because the firm has these two different types of inputs in the short run, it will also face two different types of costs.

The costs of a firm's fixed inputs are called, not surprisingly, **fixed costs**. Like the fixed inputs themselves, fixed costs must remain the same no matter what the level of output. Typically, we treat rent and interest—whether explicit or implicit—as fixed costs, since producing more or less output in the short run will not cause these costs to change. Managers typically refer to fixed costs as their *overhead costs,* or simply, *overhead.*

Fixed costs Costs of fixed inputs, which remain constant as output changes.

The costs of obtaining the firm's variable inputs are its **variable costs**. These costs, like the usage of variable inputs themselves, will rise as output increases. Most businesses treat the wages of hourly employees and the costs of raw materials as variable costs, because quantities of labor and raw materials can usually be adjusted rather rapidly.

Variable costs Costs of variable inputs, which change with output.

Measuring Short-Run Costs

Let's return to our example, Spotless Car Wash. We'll assume that Spotless, like any firm, follows the least-cost rule. In the short run, Spotless cannot change the number of automated lines; its only variable input is labor. So the least-cost rule for Spotless

TABLE 3

Short-Run Costs for Spotless Car Wash

(1) Output (per Day)	(2) Capital	(3) Labor	(4) TFC	(5) TVC	(6) TC	(7) MC	(8) AFC	(9) AVC	(10) ATC
			Labor cost = $120 per worker per day				Capital cost = $150 per unit per day		
0	1	0	$150	$0	$150	—	—	—	—
						$ 4.00			
30	1	1	$150	$120	$270		$5.00	$4.00	$9.00
						$ 2.00			
90	1	2	$150	$240	$390		$1.67	$2.67	$4.33
						$ 3.00			
130	1	3	$150	$360	$510		$1.15	$2.77	$3.92
						$ 4.00			
160	1	4	$150	$480	$630		$0.94	$3.00	$3.94
						$ 5.00			
184	1	5	$150	$600	$750		$0.82	$3.26	$4.08
						$10.00			
196	1	6	$150	$720	$870		$0.77	$3.67	$4.44

is very simple: It will wash any given number of cars with the least amount of labor possible, using however many automated lines it happens to have already.

Look at Table 3, which rearranges the information from Table 1, given earlier in this chapter. As before, we assume that Spotless currently has one automated line. The first three columns of the table tell us the inputs Spotless will use for each output level.

In order to translate this information to *costs*, we need to know what Spotless must *pay* for its inputs. In Table 3, we suppose that the price of labor is $120 per worker per day, and each automated car-washing line costs $150 per day.[2]

How do Spotless's short-run costs change as its output changes? Get ready, because there are a surprising number of different ways to answer that question, as illustrated in the remaining columns of Table 3.

Total Costs

Columns 4, 5, and 6 in the table show three different types of total costs. In column 4, we have Spotless's **total fixed cost (TFC)**, the cost of all inputs that are fixed in the short run. Running down the column, you can see that this cost—because it is fixed—remains the same at $150 no matter how many cars are washed each day.

Column 5 shows **total variable cost (TVC)**, the cost of all variable inputs. For Spotless, labor is the only variable input. As output increases, more labor will be needed, so *TVC* will rise. For example, to wash 90 cars each day requires 2 workers,

Total fixed cost The cost of all inputs that are fixed in the short run.

Total variable cost The cost of all variable inputs used in producing a particular level of output.

[2] If Spotless rents its automated lines, $150 per day would be the explicit cost for renting an automated line. If it owns the lines, then $150 per day would be the interest forgone—an implicit cost. For example, if an automated line cost $912,500, and the interest rate is 6% per year, then each automated line causes Spotless's owners to sacrifice interest of 0.06 × $912,500 = $54,750 per year, which is $150 per day.

and each worker must be paid $120 per day, so *TVC* will be 2 × $120 = $240. But to wash 130 cars requires 3 workers, so *TVC* will rise to 3 × $120 = $360.

Finally, column 6 shows us that

> ***total cost* (TC)** *is the sum of all fixed and variable costs:*
>
> $$TC = TFC + TVC.$$

Total cost The costs of all inputs—fixed and variable—used to produce a given output level in the short run.

For example, at 90 units of output, *TFC* = $150 and *TVC* = $240, so *TC* = $150 + $240 = $390. Because total variable cost rises with output, total cost rises as well.

Now look at Figure 2, where we've graphed all three total cost curves for Spotless Car Wash. Both the *TC* and *TVC* curves slope upward, since these costs increase along with output. *TFC* is represented in two ways in the graph. One is the *TFC* curve, which is a horizontal line, since *TFC* has the same value at any level of output. The other is the *vertical distance* between the rising *TVC* and *TC* curves, since *TFC* is always the *difference* between *TVC* and *TC*. In the graph, this vertical distance must remain the same, at $150, no matter what the level of output.

Average Costs

While total costs are important, sometimes it is more useful to track a firm's costs *per unit* of output, which we call its *average cost*. There are three different types of average cost, each obtained from one of the total cost concepts just discussed.

> *The firm's **average fixed cost** (**AFC**) is its total fixed cost divided by the quantity (Q) of output:*
>
> $$AFC = \frac{TFC}{Q}.$$

Average fixed cost Total fixed cost divided by the quantity of output produced.

FIGURE 2 | **The Firm's Total Cost Curves**

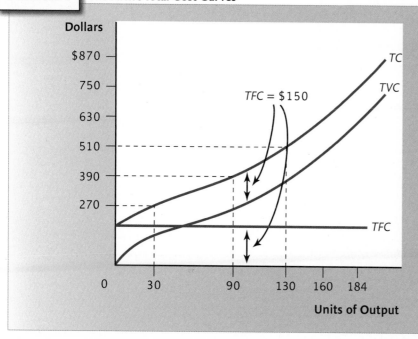

At any level of output, total cost (TC) is the sum of total fixed cost (TFC) and total variable cost (TVC).

No matter what kind of production or what kind of firm, *AFC* will always fall as output rises. Why? Because *TFC* remains constant, so a rise in *Q must* cause the ratio *TFC/Q* to fall.

Business managers often refer to this decline in *AFC* as "spreading their overhead" over more output. For example, a restaurant has overhead costs for its buildings, furniture, and cooking equipment. The more meals it serves, the lower will be its overhead cost per meal.

For Spotless Car Wash, look at column 8 of the table. When output is 30 units, *AFC* is $150/30 = $5.00. But at 90 units of output, *AFC* drops to $150/90 = $1.67. And *AFC* keeps declining as we continue down the column. The more output produced, the lower is the fixed cost per unit of output.

Next is average *variable* cost.

Average variable cost Total variable cost divided by the quantity of output produced.

> **Average variable cost (AVC)** *is the cost of the variable inputs per unit of output:*
>
> $$AVC = \frac{TVC}{Q}.$$

AVC is shown in column 9 of the table. For example, at 30 units of output, *TVC* = $120, so *AVC* = *TVC/Q* = $120/30 = $4.00.

What happens to *AVC* as output rises? If you run your finger down the *AVC* column in Table 3, you'll see a pattern: The *AVC* numbers first decrease and then increase. Economists believe that this pattern of decreasing and then increasing

---

FIGURE 3   **Average and Marginal Costs**

Average variable cost (AVC) and average total cost (ATC) are U-shaped, first decreasing and then increasing. Average fixed cost (AFC), the vertical distance between ATC and AVC, becomes smaller as output increases. The marginal cost (MC) curve is also U-shaped, reflecting first increasing and then diminishing marginal returns to labor. MC passes through the minimum points of both the AVC and ATC curves.

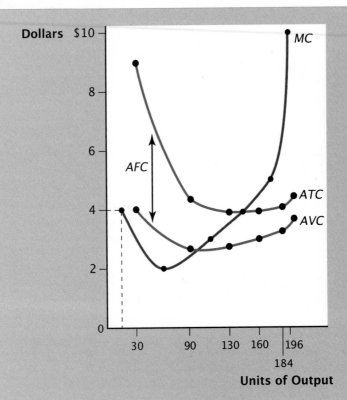

average variable cost is typical at many firms. When plotted in Figure 3, this pattern causes the *AVC* curve to have a U shape. We'll discuss the reason for this characteristic U shape a bit later.

The last average cost measure is average *total* cost.

> *Average total cost* (ATC) *is the total cost per unit of output:*
>
> $$ATC = \frac{TC}{Q}.$$

Values for *ATC* are listed in column 10 of Table 3. For example, at 90 units of output, *TC* = \$390, so *ATC* = *TC*/*Q* = \$390/90 = \$4.33. And a quick look at column 10 shows that as output rises, *ATC* first falls and then rises. So the *ATC* curve—like the *AVC* curve—is U-shaped. However—as you can see in Figure 3—it is not identical to the *AVC* curve. At each level of output, the vertical distance between the two curves is equal to average *fixed* cost (*AFC*). Since *AFC* declines as output increases, the *ATC* curve and the *AVC* curve must get closer and closer together as we move rightward.

Marginal Cost

The total and average costs we've considered so far tell us about the firm's cost at a particular *level* of output. For many purposes, however, we are more interested in how cost *changes* when output *changes*. This information is provided by another cost concept:

> *Marginal cost* (MC) *is the change in total cost* (ΔTC) *divided by the change in output* (ΔQ):
>
> $$MC = \frac{\Delta TC}{\Delta Q}.$$
>
> *It tells us how much cost rises per unit increase in output.*

For Spotless Car Wash, marginal cost is entered in column 7 of Table 3 and graphed in Figure 3. Since marginal cost tells us what happens to total cost when output *changes*, the entries in the table are placed *between* one output level and another. For example, when output rises from 0 to 30, total cost rises from \$150 to \$270. For this change in output, we have Δ*TC* = \$270 − \$150 = \$120, while Δ*Q* = 30, so *MC* = \$120/30 = \$4.00. This entry is listed *between* the output levels 0 and 30 in the table, and graphed *between* output levels in the figure.

Explaining the Shape of the Marginal Cost Curve

If you look carefully at the *MC* curve in Figure 3, you'll see that *MC* first declines and then rises. Why is this? Here, we can use what we learned earlier about marginal returns to labor. At low levels of employment and output, there are increasing marginal returns to labor: *MPL* = Δ*Q*/Δ*L* is rising. That is, each worker hired adds more to production than the worker before. But that means *fewer additional workers are needed to produce an additional unit of output*, so the *cost* of an additional unit of output (*MC*) must be falling. Thus, as long as *MPL* is rising, *MC* must be falling.

For Spotless, since *MPL* rises when employment increases from zero to one and again from one to two workers, *MC* must fall as the firm's output rises from zero to 30 units (produced by one worker) and then from 30 to 90 units (produced by two workers).

At higher levels of output, we have the opposite situation: Diminishing marginal returns set in and the marginal product of labor ($\Delta Q/\Delta L$) falls. Therefore, additional units of output require *more* and *more* additional labor. As a result, each additional unit of output costs more to produce. Thus, as long as *MPL* is falling, *MC* must be rising.

For Spotless, diminishing marginal returns to labor occur for all workers beyond the second, so *MC* rises for all increases in output beyond 90.

To sum up:

> *When the marginal product of labor (MPL) rises, marginal cost (MC) falls. When* MPL *falls,* MC *rises. Since* MPL *ordinarily rises and then falls,* MC *will do the opposite: It will fall and then rise. Thus, the* MC *curve is U-shaped.*

The Relationship between Average and Marginal Costs

Although marginal cost and average cost are not the same, there is an important relationship between them. Look again at Figure 3 and notice that all three curves—*MC*, *AVC*, and *ATC*—first fall and then rise, but not all at the same time. The *MC* curve bottoms out before either the *AVC* or *ATC* curve. Further, the *MC* curve intersects each of the average curves *at their lowest points*. These graphical features of Figure 3 are no accident; indeed, they follow from the laws of mathematics. To understand this, let's consider a related example with which you are probably more familiar.

An Example: Average and Marginal Test Scores

Suppose you take five tests in your economics course during the term, with the results listed in Table 4. To your immense pleasure, you score 100 on your first test. Your total score—the total number of points you have received thus far during the term—is 100. Your marginal score—the *change* in your total caused by the most

TABLE 4	Number of Tests Taken	Total Score	Marginal Score	Average Score
Average and Marginal Test Scores	0	0		—
			100	
	1	100		100
			50	
	2	150		75
			60	
	3	210		70
			70	
	4	280		70
			80	
	5	360		72

recent test—will also be 100, since your total rose from 0 to 100. Your average score so far is 100 as well.

Now suppose that, for the second test, you forget to study actively. Instead, you just read the text while simultaneously watching music videos and eavesdropping on your roommate's phone conversations. As a result, you get a 50, which is your marginal score. Since this score is lower than your previous average of 100, the second test will *pull your average down*. Indeed, whenever your score is lower than your previous average, it will pull down your average. In the table, we see that your average after the second test falls to 75.

Now you start to worry, so you turn off the TV while studying, and your performance improves a bit: You get a 60. Does the improvement in your score—from 50 to 60—increase your *average* score? No . . . your average will decrease once again, because your *marginal* score of 60 is *still* lower than your previous average of 75. As we know, when you score lower than your average, it pulls the average down, even if you're improving. In the table, we see that your average now falls to 70.

For your fourth exam, you study a bit harder and score a 70. This time, since your score is precisely *equal* to your previous average, the average remains unchanged at 70.

Finally, on your fifth and last test, your score improves once again, this time to 80. This time, you've scored *higher* than your previous average, pulling your average up from 70 to 72.

This example may be easy to understand because you are used to figuring out your average score in a course as you take additional exams. But the relationship between marginal and average spelled out here is universal: It is the same for grade point averages, batting averages—*and* costs.

Average and Marginal Cost

Now let's apply these insights to a firm's cost curves. Think of producing *one more unit* of output as similar to taking *one more test*. The cost of the unit is like the score on the test. If the cost is lower than the average cost so far, producing the next unit will *lower* the average cost (just like scoring lower than your previous average will lower your average score). On the other hand, if the cost for one more unit exceeds the previous average cost, producing that unit will *raise* average cost.

Let's start by applying this insight to the *AVC* curve in Figure 3. At first, marginal cost is not only falling; it is also less than *AVC*. So producing more output pulls the average down: *AVC* decreases. But then marginal cost starts rising. Eventually, *MC* rises above *AVC*, pulling the average up: *AVC* increases. Because *AVC* first decreases and then increases, the *AVC* curve is U-shaped.

> The U-shape of the *AVC* curve results from the U-shape of the *MC* curve, which in turn is based on increasing and then diminishing marginal returns to labor.

There is a similar relationship between *MC* and *ATC*, except for one additional complication. *ATC* is the sum of *AVC* and *AFC*. *AFC* *always* falls as output rises. So at low levels of output, when both *AVC* and *AFC* are falling, *ATC* decreases—even more rapidly than *AVC* does. When *AVC* starts to rise, the rising *AVC* and falling *AFC* compete with each other. But eventually, the rise in *AVC* wins out, and *ATC* begins to rise as well. This explains why the *ATC* curve is U-shaped.

> *The U shape of the* ATC *curve results from the behavior of both* AVC *and* AFC. *At low levels of output,* AVC *and* AFC *are both falling, so the* ATC *curve slopes downward. At higher levels of output, rising* AVC *overcomes falling* AFC, *and the* ATC *curve slopes upward.*

The relationships tell us something important about the crossing point between the *MC* curve and the average curves in Figure 3. Whenever the *MC* curve is below one of the average curves, the average curve slopes downward. Whenever the *MC* curve is above the average curve, the average curve slopes upward. Therefore, when *MC* goes from below the average to above the average—that is, where the *MC* curve *crosses* the average curve—the average must be at its very *minimum* (where it changes from a downward slope to an upward slope).

> *The* MC *curve crosses both the* AVC *curve and the* ATC *curve at their respective minimum points.*

If you look at Table 3, you'll see that when Spotless's output rises from 30 to 90, *MC* is below *AVC*, and *AVC* falls. When output rises from 90 to 130, *MC* is above *AVC*, and *AVC* rises. As a result, in Figure 3, the *MC* curve crosses the *AVC* curve where *AVC* bottoms out. The same relationship holds for the *MC* and *ATC* curves. But because of the competing affects of *AFC* and *AVC* on *ATC*, it takes longer for the *ATC* curve to hit bottom than the *AVC* curve. That's why minimum *ATC* occurs at a higher output than does minimum *AVC*.

Time to Take a Break. By now, your mind may be swimming with concepts and terms: total, average, and marginal cost curves; fixed and variable costs; explicit and implicit costs. . . . We are covering a lot of ground here and still have a bit more to cover: production and cost in the *long run*.

As difficult as it may seem to keep these concepts straight, they will become increasingly easy to handle as you use them in the chapters to come. But if this is your first trip through this chapter, now is a good time for a break. Then, when you're fresh, come back and review the material you've read so far. When the terms and concepts start to feel familiar, you are ready to move on to the long run.

PRODUCTION AND COST IN THE LONG RUN

Most of the business firms you have contact with—such as your supermarket, the stores where you buy clothes, your telephone company, and your Internet service provider—plan to be around for quite some time. They have a long-term planning horizon, as well as a short-term one. But so far, we've considered the behavior of costs only in the short run.

In the long run, costs behave differently, because the firm can adjust *all* of its inputs in any way it wants:

> *In the long run, there are no fixed inputs or fixed costs; all inputs and all costs are variable.*

How will the firm choose the inputs to use for any given output level? It will follow the *least-cost rule.*

Suppose Spotless wants to wash 196 cars per day. In the short run, of course, Spotless does not have to worry about what input mix to use: It is stuck with one automated line, and if it wants to wash 196 cars, it must hire six workers (see Table 3). Total cost in the short run will be 6 × $120 + $150 = $870.

In the long run, however, Spotless can vary the number of automated lines as well as the number of workers. Suppose, based on its production technology, Spotless can use four different input combinations to wash 196 cars per day. These are listed in Table 5. Combination *A* uses the least capital and the most labor—no automated lines at all and nine workers washing the cars by hand. Combination *D* uses the most capital and the least labor—three automated lines with only three workers. Since each automated line costs $150 per day and each worker costs $120 per day, it is easy to calculate the cost of each production method. Spotless will choose the one with the lowest cost: combination *C*, with two automated lines and four workers, for a total cost of $780 per day.

Retracing our steps, we have found that if Spotless wants to wash 196 cars per day, it will examine the different methods of doing so and select the one with the least cost. Once it has determined the cheapest production method, the other, more expensive methods can be ignored.

Table 6 shows the results of going through this procedure for several different levels of output. The second column, **long-run total cost** (*LRTC*), tells us the cost of producing each quantity of output *when the least-cost input mix is chosen.* For each output level, different production methods are examined, the cheapest one is chosen, and the others are ignored.

Notice that the *LRTC* of zero units of output is $0. This will always be true for any firm. In the long run, all inputs can be adjusted as the firm wishes, and the cheapest way to produce zero output is to use *no* inputs at all. (For comparison, what is the *short*-run total cost of producing zero units? Why can it never be $0?)

The third column in Table 6 gives the **long-run average total cost** (*LRATC*), the cost per unit of output in the long run:

$$LRATC = \frac{LRTC}{Q}.$$

Long-run average total cost is similar to average total cost, which was defined earlier. Both are obtained by dividing total cost by the level of output. There is one important difference, however: To calculate *ATC*, we used total cost (*TC*), which pertains to the short run, in the numerator. In calculating *LRATC*, we use *long-run* total cost (*LRTC*). Thus, *LRATC* tells us the cost per unit when the firm can vary *all* of its inputs and always chooses the cheapest input mix possible. *ATC*, however, tells us the cost per unit when the firm is stuck with some collection of fixed inputs and is able only to vary its remaining inputs, such as labor.

Long-run total cost The cost of producing each quantity of output when all inputs are variable and the least-cost input mix is chosen.

Long-run average total cost The cost per unit of producing each quantity of output in the long run, when all inputs are variable.

				TABLE 5
Method	Quantity of Capital	Quantity of Labor	Cost	**Four Ways to Wash 196 Cars per Day**
A	0	9	$1,080	
B	1	6	$ 870	
C	2	4	$ 780	
D	3	3	$ 810	

© CENGAGE LEARNING 2013

<table>
<tr><th>TABLE 6</th></tr>
</table>

**Long-Run Costs for
Spotless Car Wash**

Output	LRTC	LRATC
0	$ 0	—
30	$ 200	$6.67
90	$ 390	$4.33
130	$ 510	$3.92
160	$ 608	$3.80
184	$ 720	$3.91
196	$ 780	$3.98
250	$1,300	$5.20
300	$2,400	$8.00

The Relationship between Long-Run and Short-Run Costs

If you compare Table 6 (long run) with Table 3 (short run), you will see something important: For some output levels, *LRTC* is smaller than *TC*. For example, Spotless can wash 196 cars for an *LRTC* of $780. But earlier, we saw that in the short run, the *TC* of washing these same 196 cars was $870. There is a reason for this difference.

Look back at Table 5, which lists the four different ways of washing 196 cars per day. In the short run, the firm is stuck with just one automated line, so its only option is method *B*. In the long run, however, the firm can choose any of the four methods of production, including method *C*, which is cheapest. The freedom to choose among different production methods usually enables the firm to select a cheaper input mix in the long run than it can in the short run. Thus, in the long run, the firm may be able to save money.

But not always. At some output levels, the freedom to adjust all inputs doesn't save the firm a dime. In our example, the long-run cost of washing 130 cars is $510—the same as the short-run cost (compare Tables 6 and 3). For this output level, it just so happens that the least-cost output mix uses one automated line, which is what Spotless is stuck with in the short run. So if Spotless wants to wash 130 cars, it cannot do so any more cheaply in the long run than in the short run.

More generally,

> *the long-run total cost of producing a given level of output can be less than or equal to, but not greater than, the short-run total cost* (LRTC ≤ TC).

We can also state this relationship in terms of *average* costs. That is, we can divide both sides of the inequality by Q and obtain $LRTC/Q \le TC/Q$. Using our definitions, this translates to $LRATC \le ATC$.

> *The long-run average cost of producing a given level of output can be less than or equal to, but not greater than, the short-run average total cost* (LRATC ≤ ATC).

Average Cost and Plant Size

Often, economists refer to the collection of inputs that are fixed in the short run as the firm's **plant.** For example, the plant of a computer manufacturer, such as Dell, might include its factory buildings and the assembly lines inside them. The plant of the Hertz car-rental company would include all of its automobiles and rental offices.

Plant The collection of fixed inputs at a firm's disposal.

For Spotless Car Wash, we've assumed that the plant is simply the company's capital equipment—the automated lines for washing cars. If Spotless were to add to its capital, then each time it acquired another automated line, it would have a different, and larger, plant. Viewed in this way, we can distinguish between the long run and the short run as follows: *In the long run, the firm can change the size of its plant; in the short run, it is stuck with its current plant.*

Now think about the *ATC* curve, which tells us the firm's average total cost in the short run. This curve is always drawn for a specific plant. That is, the *ATC* curve tells us how average cost behaves in the short run, *when the firm uses a plant of a given size.* If the firm had a different-size plant, it would be moving along a different *ATC* curve. In fact, there is a different *ATC* curve for each different plant the firm could have. In the long run, then, the firm can choose to operate on *any* of these *ATC* curves. To produce any level of output, it will always choose that *ATC* curve—among all of the *ATC* curves available—with the lowest possible average total cost. This insight tells us something about the relationship between the firm's *ATC* curves and its *LRATC* curve.

Graphing the *LRATC* Curve

Look at Figure 4, which shows several different *ATC* curves for Spotless Car Wash. There is a lot going on in this figure, so let's take it one step at a time. First, find the curve labeled ATC_1. This is our familiar *ATC* curve—the same one shown in Figure 3—which we used to find Spotless's average total cost in the short run, when it was stuck with one automated line.

The other *ATC* curves refer to *different* plants that Spotless *might* have had instead. For example, the curve labeled ATC_0 shows how average total cost would behave if Spotless had a plant with *zero* automated lines washing all cars manually. ATC_2 shows average total cost with *two* automated lines, and so on. Since, in the long run, the firm can choose which size plant to operate, it can also choose on which of these *ATC* curves it wants to operate. And, as we know, in the long run, it will always choose the plant with the lowest possible average total cost for any output level it produces.

Let's take a specific example. Suppose that Spotless is planning to wash 130 cars per day. In the long run, what size plant should it choose? Scanning the different *ATC* curves in Figure 4, we see that the lowest possible per-unit cost—$3.92 per car—is at point *A* along ATC_1. The best plant for washing 130 cars per day, therefore, will have just one automated line. For this output level, Spotless would never choose a plant with zero lines, because it would then have to operate on ATC_0 at point *B*. Since point *B* is higher than point *A*, we know that point *B* represents a larger per-unit cost. Nor would the firm choose a plant with two lines—operating on ATC_2 at point *C*—for this would mean a still larger per-unit cost. Of all the possibilities for producing 130 units in the long run, Spotless would choose to operate at point *A* on ATC_1. So point *A* represents the *LRATC* of 130 units.

Now, suppose instead that Spotless wanted to produce 184 units of output in the long run. A plant with one automated line is no longer the best choice. Instead, the firm would choose a plant with *two* automated lines. How do we know? For an output of 184, the firm could choose point *D* on ATC_1, or point *E* on ATC_2. Since point *E* is lower, it is the better choice. At this point, average total cost would be $3.19, so this would be the *LRATC* of 184 units.

As you can see in the figure, with each firm producing 10,000 units (*less* than its MES), each is at point *A* on its *LRATC* curve. Cost per unit is $200—substantially above what cost per unit would be at the MES. There are unexploited economies of scale. We know that if this has been going on for a while, each firm must be charging *at least* $200; otherwise, it would not have been able to cover its costs and would have gone out of business.

Let's suppose (arbitrarily) that each of the six firms is charging a price of $220 per unit. (In coming chapters, you'll learn how the price is determined in different types of markets.) Since cost per unit is $200, each firm's total profit is $20 × 10,000 = $200,000 per month. All the firms are earning a profit, so you might think this situation could continue indefinitely.

But it likely won't. A market like this is ripe for mergers. Why? To keep our story as simple as possible, let's suppose for now that the total market demand remains at 60,000 units per month, no matter what happens to the price. Then it won't be long before one of the firms in this industry gets a brilliant idea: to lower its price below that of its competitors, so it can take some of the market away from them. The first firm to do so can even lower its price *below* $200 because, by doing so, it will increase the quantity it sells. As a result, it will slide down its *LRATC* curve and operate at a cost per unit under $200, and less than the cost per unit of its competitors.

Let's suppose that this first mover lowers the price to $190, which happens to be just enough to spur its sales to its MES of 20,000 units. For this firm, cost per unit falls to $80 (point *B*), so profit per unit rises to $190 − $80 = $110. With 20,000 units sold, the first mover's total profit rises to $110 × 20,000 = $2,200,000. Not a bad move!

Of course, this will not make the other firms in the industry happy. Because we assume that total sales are fixed at 60,000 units per month, the gain in sales by the first mover come at the expense of its competitors, who (we assume for now) have not yet lowered their own prices. As a result of the first mover *gaining* 10,000 units in sales, each of the remaining five firms has *lost* 2,000 in sales—declining to 8,000. These firms therefore move *leftward* and *upward* along *their LRATC* curves, to a point like C. Cost per unit for each of them is now $240.

These five slow-moving firms now have some unpleasant choices. If they *raise* their price above $240 to try to cover their costs on each unit, they will lose further sales, and slide further up their *LRATC* curve, with still higher cost. If they *lower* prices to get some of their sales back from the first mover, the result may be a price war, which could take the price down to $80, as the first mover tries to defend its market share so it can continue operating at its MES. (We'll have more to say about price wars and how they erupt in Chapter 11.)

But remember: It is impossible for *all* six firms to operate at their MES of 20,000 because we're assuming that the total demand for this product is fixed at 60,000. So if the price war leads all firms to charge a price of $80, with each firm having one-sixth of the market, then each firm, including the first mover, is once again producing 10,000 units, at a cost of $200 per unit. Only now, with a lower price, each will suffer a loss.

We could continue this story, with all six firms deciding to raise their prices back to $220, until a price war breaks out again. But you can see that this market, with six firms, is very unstable. There are too many firms to satisfy the market demand of 60,000 if all of them operate at their MES. Price wars are likely to break out periodically, with periodic losses by all firms. If they try to make an illegal agreement not to lower their prices, in most countries (including the United States) they risk jail terms and huge fines.

Is there any way out of this mess? The title of this section gives the answer. If three of the six firms each combine with one of the others, the result will be three larger firms splitting the market among them. Each could then fully exploit its economies of scale, raising its output to the MES of 20,000, without overshooting the market's total demand of 60,000. While these firms *may* still compete for market share, the fact that each is operating at its MES means that each continues to operate at the lowest possible cost per unit merely by *maintaining* its proportional market share.

Of course, our story made several simplifications. Firms in an industry aren't really identical. And we assumed that demand was fixed at 60,000 units. In reality, we know that market demand curves have some elasticity, and that changes in price lead to changes in total market demand. We could incorporate more realistic assumptions, but they would complicate the analysis without changing its central point: When there are too many firms for each to operate near its minimum efficient scale, mergers often follow.

Economies of scale play a large role in explaining mergers in industries with high-cost lumpy inputs, such as large expenses for physical infrastructure, R&D, design, or marketing. By merging with other firms, duplicate lumpy inputs can be eliminated, and the costs of those that remain can be spread over more units of output, substantially lowering the new, larger firm's cost per unit. The merger of United and Continental Airlines, for example, offered many opportunities to eliminate duplication of lumpy inputs. These include legal costs of contract negotiations with airports, labor unions, suppliers of food and fuel, and suppliers of aircraft. Other lumpy inputs include the costs of developing long-term strategies, marketing campaigns, and software. And further cost savings could come from a more efficient allocation of aircraft among different routes.

We'll have more to say about mergers and the behavior of large firms in future chapters. As you'll see, there are other motives for mergers that have nothing to do with economies of scale or costs. And even when a merger does bring down costs, it does not necessarily lead to lower prices for consumers. Indeed, economists become concerned when the number of firms in a market shrinks to just a few. This can mean less competition—and prices that are even higher than when the market had a greater number of higher cost firms.

SUMMARY

Business firms combine inputs to produce outputs. A firm's production *technology* determines the maximum output it can produce using different quantities of inputs. In the *short run,* at least one of the firm's inputs is fixed. In the *long run,* all inputs can be varied.

A firm's *cost of production* is the opportunity cost of its owners—everything they must give up in order to produce output. When firms can use different combinations of inputs, they follow the *least-cost rule,* producing any output level using the lowest-cost combination of inputs possible. Over the *short run,* a firm has at least one *fixed input* (an input whose usage cannot be changed), and has associated fixed costs. A firm's *variable inputs* (inputs whose usage can be changed) give rise to its *variable costs.*

Marginal cost is the change in total cost from producing one more unit of output. The *marginal cost curve* has a U shape, reflecting the underlying marginal product of labor. A variety of average cost curves can be defined. The *average variable cost curve* and the *average total cost curve* are each U-shaped, reflecting the relationship between average and marginal cost. The marginal cost curve must cross each of the average curves at their minimums.

In the long run, all inputs are variable, so all costs are variable costs. The firm's *long-run total cost curve* indicates the cost of producing each quantity of output with the least-cost input mix. The related *long-run average total cost (LRATC) curve* is formed by combining portions of different *ATC* curves, each portion representing a different plant size. The *LRATC* curve slopes downward when there are economies of scale, which continue until the firm reaches its *minimum efficient scale*.

The *LRATC* curve slopes upward when there are diseconomies of scale, and it is flat when there are constant returns to scale. Economies of scale can play a role in explaining mergers and acquisitions, especially when there are too many firms for each to operate at its minimum efficient scale.

PROBLEM SET

Answers to even-numbered Problems can be found on the text Web site through www.cengagebrain.com

1. The following table shows total output (in tax returns completed per day) of the accounting firm of Hoodwink and Finagle:

Number of Accountants	Number of Returns per Day
0	0
1	5
2	12
3	17
4	20
5	22

Assuming the quantity of capital (computers, adding machines, desks, etc.) remains constant at all output levels:
   a. Calculate the marginal product of each accountant.
   b. Over what range of employment do you see increasing returns to labor? Diminishing returns?
   c. Explain why *MPL* might behave this way in the context of an accounting firm.

2. In mid-2009, the Obama administration announced it would cancel orders for a new fleet of presidential helicopters. About $3 billion had already been spent on developing the helicopters, which had special protective and telecommunications features. But another $8 billion would have been needed to complete the project and deliver the fleet. The administration suggested it might look for a less expensive design and start from scratch. Some media commentators criticized the decision, arguing that cancelling the project would mean wasting the $3 billion already spent.
   a. Suppose that starting from scratch on a new proposal that would be just as good as the original would cost a total of $5 billion from beginning to end. Which would be the wiser choice— sticking with the original or starting from scratch? Why?
   b. Would your answer change if the new proposal would cost a total of $10 billion? Why or why not?

3. Down On Our Luck Studios has spent $100 million producing an awful film, *A Depressing Story About a Miserable Person*. If the studio releases the film, the most cost-effective marketing plan would cost an additional $5 million, bringing the total amount spent to $105 million. Box office sales under this plan are predicted to be $12 million, which would be split evenly between the theaters and the studio. Additional studio revenue from video and DVD sales would be about $2 million. Should the studio release the film? If no, briefly explain why not. If yes, explain how it could make sense to release a film that cost $105 million but earns only $12 million.

4. The following table gives the short-run and long-run total costs for various levels of output of Consolidated National Acme, Inc.:

Q	TC_1	TC_2
0	0	350
1	300	400
2	400	435
3	465	465
4	495	505
5	540	560
6	600	635
7	700	735

   a. Which column, TC_1 or TC_2, gives long-run total cost, and which gives short-run total cost? How do you know?
   b. For each level of output, find short-run *TFC*, *TVC*, *AFC*, *AVC*, and *MC*.
   c. At what output level would the firm's short-run and long-run input combinations be the same?
   d. Starting from producing two units, Consolidated's managers decide to double their production to four units. So they simply double all of their inputs in the long run. Comment on their managerial skills.
   e. Over what range of output do you see economies of scale? Diseconomies of scale? Constant returns to scale?

5. In a recent year, a long, hard winter gave rise to stronger-than-normal demand for heating oil. The following summer was characterized by strong demand for gasoline by vacationers. Show what these two events might have done to the short-run *MC*, *AVC*, and *ATC* curves

of American Airlines. (Hint: How would these events affect the price of oil and the price of jet fuel made from oil?)

6. Draw the long-run total cost and long-run average cost curves for a firm that experiences:
   a. Constant returns to scale over all output levels.
   b. Diseconomies of scale over low levels of output, constant returns to scale over intermediate levels of output, and economies of scale over high output levels. Does this pattern of costs make sense? Why or why not?

7. Ludmilla's House of Schnitzel is currently producing 10 schnitzels a day at point A on the following diagram. Ludmilla's business partner, Hans (an impatient sort), wants her to double production immediately.

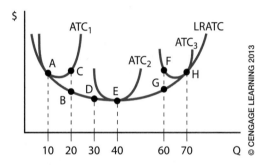

   a. What point will likely illustrate Ludmilla's cost situation for the near future? Why?
   b. If Ludmilla wants to keep producing 20 schnitzels, at what point does she want to be eventually? How can she get there?

   c. Eventually, Ludmilla and company do very well, expanding until they find themselves making 70 schnitzels a day. But after a few years, Ludmilla discovers that profit was greater when she produced 20 schnitzels per day. She wants to scale back production to 20 schnitzels per day, laying off workers, selling off equipment, renting less space, and producing fewer schnitzels. Hans wants to reduce output by just cutting back on flour and milk and laying off workers. Who's right? Discuss the situation with reference to the relevant points on the diagram.
   d. Does the figure tell us what output Ludmilla should aim for? Why or why not?

8. Clean 'n' Shine is a competitor to Spotless Car Wash. Like Spotless, it must pay $150 per day for each automated line it uses. But Clean 'n' Shine has been able to tap into a lower-cost pool of labor, paying its workers only $100 per day. Clean 'n' Shine's production technology is given in the following table. To determine its short-run cost structure, fill in the blanks in the table.
   a. Over what range of output does Clean 'n' Shine experience increasing marginal returns to labor? Over what range does it experience diminishing marginal returns to labor?
   b. As output increases, do average fixed costs behave as described in the text? Explain.
   c. As output increases, do marginal cost, average variable cost, and average total cost behave as described in the text? Explain.
   d. Looking at the numbers in the table, but without drawing any curves, is the relationship between MC and AVC as described in the text? What about the relationship between MC and ATC?

Short-Run Costs for Clean 'n' Shine Car Wash

(1) Output (per Day)	(2) Capital	(3) Labor	(4) TFC	(5) TVC	(6) TC	(7) MC	(8) AFC	(9) AVC	(10) ATC
0	1	0	$___	$___	$___		—	—	—
						$___			
30	1	1	$___	$___	$___		$___	$___	$___
						$___			
70	1	2	$___	$___	$___		$___	$___	$___
						$___			
120	1	3	$___	$___	$___		$___	$___	$___
						$___			
160	1	4	$___	$___	$___		$___	$___	$___
						$___			
190	1	5	$___	$___	$___		$___	$___	$___
						$___			
210	1	6	$___	$___	$___		$___	$___	$___

9. In Table 3, when output rises from 90 to 130 units, marginal cost is $3.00. For this change in output, marginal cost is greater than the previous *AVC* ($2.67) but less than the previous *ATC* ($4.33). According to the relationship between marginals and averages you learned in this chapter:
    a. What should happen to *AVC* due to this change in output? Does it happen?
    b. What should happen to *ATC* due to this change in output? Does it happen?

10. A soft drink manufacturer that uses just labor (variable) and capital (fixed) paid a consulting firm thousands of dollars to calculate short-run costs at various output levels. But after the cost table (see below) was handed over to the president of the soft drink company, he spilled Dr Pepper on it, making some of the entries illegible. The consulting firm, playing tough, is demanding another payment to provide a duplicate table.
    a. Should the soft-drink president pay up? Or can he fill in the rest of the entries on his own? Fill in as many entries as you can to determine your answer. (Hint: First, determine the price of labor.)
    b. Do *MC, AVC,* and *ATC* have the relationship to each other that you learned in this chapter? Explain.

Output per Day	Units of Capital	Number of Workers	*TFC*	*TVC*	*TC*	*MC*	*AFC*	*AVC*	*ATC*
0	10	0	$1,000	?	?		?	?	?
						?			
20,000	10	100	?	$9,000	?		?	?	?
						?			
40,000	10	?	?	?	?		?	?	$0.325
						?			
60,000	10	225	?	?	?		?	?	?
						?			
80,000	10	?	?	?	$30,000		?	?	?

11. "If a firm has diminishing returns to labor over some range of output, it cannot have economies of scale over that range." True or false? Explain briefly.

More Challenging

12. A study[3] of immunizing children in poor countries against diphtheria, pertussis, and tetanus estimated that, in the long run, a 10% increase in the number of children vaccinated increases the total cost of vaccinations by 8.4%. According to this study:
    a. Is immunization over this range characterized by economies of scale, constant returns to scale, or diseconomies of scale?
    b. [More difficult] We can define long-run marginal cost (*LRMC*) as the cost of increasing output by one unit when *all* inputs can be varied (as they can be in the long run). Based on the study, at current vaccine levels, would *LRMC* for vaccinations be greater than, less than, or equal to long-run average total cost (*LRATC*)? Why?
    c. If we want to know what it will cost to vaccinate *additional* children, and we use "cost per vaccine" as given by the current *LRATC*, do we overestimate, underestimate, or accurately estimate the cost per additional vaccine?

13. A firm has the strange *ATC* curve drawn in the following figure. Sketch in the marginal cost curve this firm must have. (Hint: Use what you know about the marginal-average relationship. Note that this *MC* curve does *not* have a standard shape.)

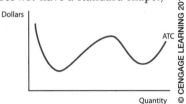

14. The following curve shows the *marginal* product of labor for a firm at different levels of employment.
    a. Show what the corresponding total product curve would look like.
    b. Do the total and marginal product curves for this firm ever exhibit diminishing marginal returns to labor? Increasing marginal returns to labor?

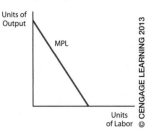

[3] David Bishal, Michael McQuestion, Rochika Chaudhry, and Alyssa Wigton, "The Costs of Scaling Up Vaccination in the World's Poorest Countries," *Health Affairs,* (Vol 25, No. 2) March/April 2006.

When a firm can vary more than one input, it can usually choose to produce any given output level in different ways. For example, in the long run, a car wash can vary both its labor and the number of automated car washing lines it uses. If it acquires more automated lines, it can wash the same number of cars with less labor. Even in the short run, a firm can often vary more than one input. A farmer might be able to achieve the same total yield using less fertilizer if he hires more labor to care for and harvest the crop.

When a firm can choose among different methods of production, it will choose to produce any given level of output in the cheapest way possible. This appendix presents a graphical technique to show how a firm with two variable inputs finds this least-cost production method. The technique can be used over any time horizon—short run or long run—as long as there are two inputs whose quantities can be varied within that horizon. Finally, at the end of this appendix, the technique will be generalized to the case of *more than two* variable inputs.

ISOQUANTS

Imagine that you own an artichoke farm, and you are free to vary two inputs: labor and land. Your output is measured in "boxes of artichokes per month." Your farm's production technology determines the maximum possible number of boxes you could produce in a given

month using different combinations of labor and land. Alternatively, it tells us all the different input mixes that could be used to produce any given quantity of output.

Table A.1 lists some of the information we could obtain based on the technology of production on your farm. Notice that, to produce each of the three output levels included in the table, there are many different combinations of inputs you could use. For example, the table tells us that your farm could produce 4,000 boxes of artichokes using 2 hectares of land and 18 workers, or 3 hectares and 11 workers, or 5 hectares and 5 workers, and so on.

(Note: If it seems to you that no artichoke farm would ever use some of these combinations—such as 14 hectares of land and 2 workers—you are right. But that is because of the relative *costs* of labor and land, which we haven't discussed yet. Table A.1 simply tells us what is *possible* for the firm, not what is economically sensible.)

The information in the table can also be illustrated with a graph. In Figure A.1, the quantity of land is plotted along the horizontal axis, and the number of workers on the vertical axis. Each combination of the two inputs is represented by a point. For example, the combination *3 hectares, 11 workers* is represented by the point labeled *B*, while the combination *5 hectares, 12 workers* is represented by point *F*.

Now let's focus on a single output level: 4,000 boxes per month. The middle columns of Table A.1 shows 5 of the different input combinations that can produce this output level, each represented by a point in

© CENGAGE LEARNING 2013

TABLE A.1

Production Technology for an Artichoke Farm

2,000 Boxes of Artichokes per Month		4,000 Boxes of Artichokes per Month		6,000 Boxes of Artichokes per Month	
Hectares of Land	Number of Workers	Hectares of Land	Number of Workers	Hectares of Land	Number of Workers
1	15	2	18	4	23
2	7	3	11	5	12
3	4	5	5	7	6
6	2	7	3	11	4
12	1	14	2	17	3

© IMAGES.COM/CORBIS

FIGURE A.1 An Isoquant Map

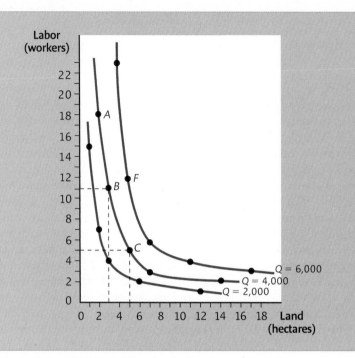

Each of the curves in the figure is an isoquant, showing all combinations of labor and land that can produce a given output level. The middle curve, for example, shows that 4,000 units of output can be produced with 11 workers and 3 hectares of land (point B), with 5 workers and 5 hectares of land (point C), as well as other combinations of labor and land. Each isoquant is drawn for a different level of output. The higher the isoquant line, the greater the level of output.

Figure A.1. When we connect all 5 points with a smooth line we get the curve labeled "$Q = 4,000$" in Figure A.1. This curve is called an **isoquant**[4] ("iso" means "same," and "quant" stands for "quantity of output").

> *Every point on an isoquant represents an input mix that produces the same quantity of output.*[5]

Figure A.1 also shows two additional isoquants. The higher one is drawn for the output level $Q = 6,000$, and the lower one for the output level $Q = 2,000$. When these curves are shown together on a graph, we have an **isoquant map** for the firm.

Things to Know About Isoquants

As we move along any isoquant, the quantity of output remains the same, but the combination of inputs changes. More specifically, as we move along an isoquant, we are *substituting one input for another.* For example, as we move from point B to point C along the isoquant labeled $Q = 4,000$,

the quantity of land rises from 3 to 5 hectares, while the number of workers falls from 11 to 5. You are substituting land for labor, while maintaining the same level of output. Since each of the two inputs contributes to production, every time you increase one input, you must decrease the other in order to maintain the same level of output.

> *An increase in one input requires a decrease in the other input to keep total production unchanged. This is why isoquants always slope downward.*

What happens as we move from isoquant to isoquant? Whenever we move to a higher *isoquant* (moving northeasterly in Figure A.1), the quantity of output increases. Moving directly northward means you are using more labor with the same amount of land, and moving directly eastward means you are using more land with the same amount of labor. When you move both north and east simultaneously (as in the move from point B to point F), you are using more of *both* inputs. For all of these movements, output increases. For the same reason, if we move southwestward, output decreases.

> *Higher isoquants represent greater levels of output than lower isoquants.*

[4] Bolded terms in this appendix are defined in the glossary.
[5] If you've read the appendix to Chapter 5, you will recognize that isoquants are similar to indifference curves. But while an indifference curve represents different combinations of two *goods* that give the same level of *consumer satisfaction*, an isoquant represents different combinations of two *inputs* that give the same level of *firm output*.

Finally, notice something else about Figure A.1: As we move rightward along any given isoquant, it becomes flatter. To understand why, we must take a closer look at an isoquant's slope.

The Marginal Rate of Technical Substitution

The (absolute value of the) slope of an isoquant is called the **marginal rate of technical substitution (MRTS).** As the name suggests, it measures the rate at which a firm can substitute one input for another while keeping output constant. In our example, if we use "L" for labor and "N" for land, the $MRTS_{L,N}$ tells us how many *fewer* workers you can employ each time you use *one more hectare of land*, and still maintain the same level of output.

For example, if you move from point A to point B along isoquant $Q = 4,000$, you use 1 more hectare and 7 fewer workers, so the $MRTS_{L,N} = 7/1 = 7$ for that move. Going from point B to point C, you use 2 more hectares of land, and 6 fewer workers, so the $MRTS_{L,N} = 6/2 = 3$.

Using this new term, the changing slope of an isoquant can be expressed this way:

> *as we move rightward along any given isoquant, the marginal rate of technical substituation decreases.*

But why does the $MRTS_{L,N}$ decrease? To answer this question, it helps to understand the relationship between the *MRTS* and the *marginal products* of land and labor. You've already learned that the marginal product of labor (*MPL*) is a firm's additional output when one more worker is hired and all other inputs remain constant. The marginal product of land (*MPN*, using "N" for land) is defined in a similar way: It's the additional output a firm can produce with one additional unit of land (one more hectare, in our example), holding all other inputs constant.

Suppose that, starting from a given input mix, you discover that your *MPN* is 21 boxes of artichokes, and your *MPL* is 7 boxes. Then conduct the following mental experiment: Add one hectare of land, with no change in labor, and your output *increases* by 21 boxes. Then give up 3 workers, with no change in land, and your output *decreases* by 3 × 7 = 21 boxes. In this case, adding 1 hectare of land, and hiring 3 fewer workers leaves your output unchanged. The slope of the isoquant for a move like this would be $\Delta L/\Delta N = -3/1 = -3$.

More generally, each time we change the amount of labor (*L*), the firm's output will change by $\Delta L \times MPL$. Each time we change the firm's land (*N*), the change in

output will be $\Delta N \times MPN$. If we want the net result to be zero change in output, we must have

$$\Delta L \times MPL + \Delta N \times MPN = 0 \text{ or}$$
$$\Delta L \times MPL = -\Delta N \times MPN.$$

Rearranging this equation gives us:

$$\Delta L/\Delta N = -MPN/MPL.$$

The left-hand side is the ratio of the change in labor to the change in land needed to keep output unchanged, that is, *the slope of the isoquant.* The right-hand side tells us that this slope is equal to the ratio of the marginal products of land and labor, except for the sign, which is negative. That is,

> *At each point along an isoquant with land measured horizontally, and labor measured vertically, the (absolute value of the) slope of the isoquant, which we call the $MRTS_{L,N}$, is the ratio of the marginal products, MPN/MPL.*

Now, what does this have to do with the shape of the isoquant? As we move rightward and downward along an isoquant, the firm is acquiring more and more land, and using less and less labor. The marginal product of land will decrease—since land is becoming more plentiful—and the marginal product of labor will increase—since labor is becoming more and more scarce. Taken together, these changes tell us that the ratio *MPN/MPL* must fall and so must the slope of the isoquant.

> *An isoquant becomes flatter as we move rightward because the MPN decreases, while the MPL increases, so the ratio—MPN/MPL—decreases.*

ISOCOST LINES

An isoquant map shows us the different input mixes capable of producing different amounts of output. But how should the firm *choose* among all of these input mixes? In order to answer that question, we must know something about input *prices*. After all, if you own an artichoke farm, you must *pay* for your land and labor.

To keep the math simple, let's use round numbers. We'll suppose that the price of labor—the wage—is $500 per month ($P_L = \$500$), and the price of land—what you must pay in rent to its owner, or your implicit cost if you own the land yourself—is $1,000 per hectare per month ($P_N = \$1,000$). An **isocost line** ("same cost" line) tells us all combinations of the two inputs that would require the same total outlay for the firm. It is very much like the *budget line* you learned about in Chapter 5, which showed all combinations of two *goods* that resulted in the same cost for the consumer. The difference is that an isocost line represents total cost to a *firm* rather than a consumer, and is based on paying for *inputs* rather than goods.

Figure A.2 shows three isocost lines for your artichoke farm. The middle line (labeled $TC = \$7,500$) tells us all combinations of land and labor that would cost $7,500 per month. For example, point G represents the combination *3 hectares, 9 workers,* for a total cost of $3 \times \$1,000 + 9 \times \$500 = \$7,500$.

Things to Know about Isocost Lines

Notice that all three isocost lines in Figure A.2 *slope downward.* Why is this? As you move rightward in the figure, you are using more land. If you continued to use an unchanged amount of labor, your cost would therefore increase. But an isocost line shows us input combinations with the *same* cost. Thus, to keep your cost unchanged as you use more land (move rightward), you must also employ *fewer* workers (move downward).

> *If you use more of one input, you must use less of the other input in order to keep your total cost unchanged. This is why isocost lines always slope downward.*

Notice, though, that the *slope* of the isocost line remains *constant* as we move along it. That is, isocost lines are *straight lines.* Why? Let's find an expression for the slope of the isocost line. Each time you change the number of workers by ΔL, your total cost will change by $P_L \times \Delta L$. Each time you change the amount of land you use by ΔN, your total cost will change by $P_N \times \Delta N$. In order for your total cost to remain the same as you change the amounts of both land and labor, the changes must satisfy the equation:

$$P_L \times \Delta L + P_N \times \Delta N = 0,$$

or

$$P_L \times \Delta L = -P_N \times \Delta N$$

which can be rearranged to

$$\Delta L/\Delta N = -P_N/P_L.$$

The term on the left is the change in labor divided by the change in land that leaves total cost unchanged—the slope of the isocost line. The term on the right is the (negative of the) ratio of the inputs' prices. In our example, with $P_N = \$1,000$ and $P_L = \$500$, the slope of the isocost line is $-\$1,000/\$500 = -2$.

Now you can see why the isocost line is a straight line: As long as the firm can continue to buy its inputs at unchanged prices, the ratio $-P_N/P_L$ will remain constant. Therefore, the slope of the isocost line will remain constant as well.

FIGURE A.2 | Isocost Lines

Each of the lines in the figure is an isocost line, showing all combinations of labor and land that have the same total cost. The middle line, for example, shows that total cost will be $7,500 if 9 workers and 3 hectares of land are used (point C). All other combinations of land and labor on the middle line have the same total cost of $7,500. Each isocost line is drawn for a different value of total cost. The higher the isocost line, the greater is total cost.

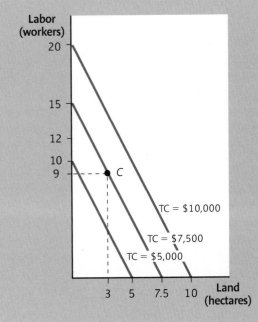

The slope of an isocost line with land (N) on the horizontal axis and labor (L) on the vertical axis is $-P_N/P_L$. This slope remains constant as we move along the line.

Finally, there is one more thing to note about isocost lines. As you move in a northeasterly direction in Figure A.2, to higher isocost lines, you are paying for greater amounts of land and labor, so your total cost must rise. For the same reason, as you move in a southwesterly direction, you are paying for smaller amounts of land and labor, so your total costs fall.

Higher isocost lines represent greater total costs for the firm than lower isocost lines.

In Figure A.2, the highest line represents all input combinations with a total cost of $10,000, and the lowest line represents all combinations with a total cost of $5,000.

THE LEAST-COST INPUT COMBINATION

Now we are ready to combine what we know about a firm's production—represented by its isoquants—with our knowledge of the firm's costs—represented by its isocost lines. Together, these will allow us to find the least-cost input combination for producing any level of output a firm might choose to produce.

Suppose you want to know what is the best way to produce 4,000 boxes of artichokes per month. Figure A.3 reproduces the isoquant labeled $Q = 4,000$ from Figure A.1, along with the three isocost lines from Figure A.2. You would like to find the input combination that is *capable* of producing 4,000 boxes (an input combination *on the isoquant* $Q = 4,000$), with the lowest possible cost (an input combination on the lowest possible isocost line). As you can see in the diagram, there is only one input combination that satisfies both requirements: point *C*. At this point, the firm uses 5 hectares of land, and 5 workers, for a total cost of $5 \times \$1,000 + 5 \times \$500 = \$7,500$. As you can see, while there are other input combinations that can also produce 4,000 boxes, such as point *J* or point *K*, each of these lie on a higher isocost line ($TC = \$10,000$) and will require a greater total outlay than the least-cost combination at point *C*.

The least-cost combination will always be found where the isocost line is *tangent* to the isoquant. This is where the two lines touch each other at a single point, and both lines *have the same slope*.

The least-cost input combination for producing any level of output is found at the point where an isocost line is tangent to the isoquant for that output level.

This result will prove very useful. We already know that the slope of the isoquant at any point is equal to $-MPN/MPL$. And we know that the slope of the isocost line is equal to $-P_N/P_L$. Putting the two together, we know that when you have found the least-cost input combination for any output level,

$$-MPN/MPL = -P_N/P_L$$

or

$$MPN/MPL = P_N/P_L.$$

The term on the left-hand side is just the $MRTS_{L,N}$—the marginal rate of technical substitution between labor and land. We conclude that:

When a firm is using the least-cost combination of two inputs (L and N) for a particular output level, the firm's MRTS between the two inputs (MPN/MPL) will equal the ratio of input prices (P_N/P_L).

In our example, $P_N/P_L = \$1,000/\$500 = 2$. This tells us that, at point C, the ratio $MPN/MPL = 2$ as well.

Finally, we can rearrange the equation $MPN/MPL = P_N/P_L$ to get:

$$MPN/P_N = MPL/P_L.$$

This form of the equation gives us another insight. It says that when you have found the least-cost input mix for any output level, the marginal product of land divided by the price of land will be equal to the marginal product of labor divided by the price of labor.

How can we interpret the marginal product of an input divided by its price? It gives us the additional output from spending one more *dollar* on the input. For example, if the (monthly) price of a hectare of land is $1,000, and using one more hectare increases your output by 21 boxes ($MPN = 21$), then an additional *dollar* spent on land will give you 1/1,000 of a hectare, which, in turn, will increase your output by $(1/1,000) \times 21 = 21/1,000$ or .021 boxes. So, $MPN/P_N = 21/1,000$ is the additional output from one more dollar spent on land. As a kind of shorthand, we'll call MPN/P_N the "marginal product per dollar" of land.

FIGURE A.3 | The Least-Cost Input Combination for a Given Output Level

To produce any given level of output at the least possible cost, the firm should use the input combination where the isoquant for that output level is tangent to an isocost line. In the figure, the input combinations at points J, C, and K can all be used to produce 4,000 units of output. But the combination at point C (5 workers and 5 hectares of land), where the isoquant is tangent to the isocost line, is the least expensive input combination for that output level.

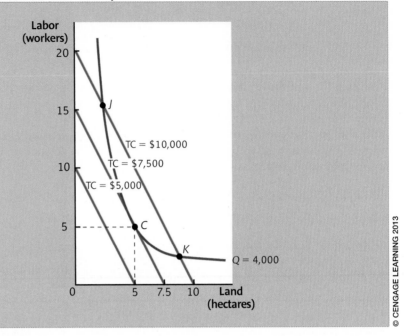

Using this language, we can state our result this way:

> When a firm is using the least-cost combination of land and labor for any output level, the marginal product per dollar of land (MPN/P_N) must equal the marginal product per dollar of labor (MPL/P_L).

In the next section, where this result is stated more generally, you will learn the intuition behind it.

Generalizing to the Case of More than Two Inputs

When a firm can vary three or more inputs, we cannot illustrate isoquants and isocost lines on a two-dimensional graph. Nevertheless, the conclusions we reached for the two-input case can be generalized to any number of inputs.

Suppose a firm has several variable inputs, which we can label $A, B, C, \ldots$, with marginal products MPA, MPB, MPC, … and input prices P_A, P_B, P_C, …. Then for any level of output, the least-cost combination of all of these inputs will always satisfy:

$$MPA/P_A = MPB/P_B = MPC/P_C = \ldots$$

That is,

> When a firm with many variable inputs has found its least-cost input mix, the marginal product per dollar of any input will be equal to the marginal product per dollar of any other input.

How do we know this must always be true? First, remember that MPA/P_A tells us the additional output the firm will produce *per additional dollar spent on input A*. Next, suppose we have two inputs, A and B, for which MPA/P_A is *not* equal to MPB/P_B. Then we can show that the firm can always shift its spending from one input to another, lowering its cost while leaving its output unchanged.

Let's take a specific example. Suppose that $MPA/P_A = 2$, and $MPB/P_B = 3$. Then the firm can easily save money by shifting dollars away from input A toward input B. Each dollar shifted away from A causes output to decrease by 2 units, while each dollar shifted toward input B causes output to rise by 3 units. Thus, the firm could shift dollars away from input A, and use only *some* of those dollars to increase the amount of input B, and still keep its production unchanged.

The same holds for any other two inputs we might compare: Whenever the marginal product per dollar is different for any two inputs, the firm can always shift its spending from the input with the lower marginal product per dollar to the input with the higher marginal product per dollar, achieving lower total cost with no change in output.

8

How Firms Make Decisions: Profit Maximization

© FRANCES ROBERTS/ALAMY

In March 2011, Apple began selling a new and improved version of its original iPad. Among the changes on the new iPad 2 were a second (front-facing) camera, more memory and a faster processor. It was also lighter and thinner than its predecessor.

But well before the launch date, Apple had several important decisions to make. From which companies should it buy the components? Where should the new product be assembled? How much should Apple spend on advertising? And finally: What price should it charge for the product, and what rate of production should it plan for?

These last decisions—what price to charge and how much to produce—are the focus of this chapter. In the end, Apple decided to charge $499 for the basic model, and sold about 22 million iPad 2s over the next 6 months. But why didn't Apple charge a lower price that would allow it to sell even more units? Or a higher price that would give it more profit on each unit sold?

Although this chapter concentrates on firms' decisions about price and output level, the tools you will learn apply to many other firm decisions. How much should Master-Card spend on advertising? How late should Starbucks keep its coffee shops open? How many copies should the *Wall Street Journal* give away free to potential subscribers? Should movie theaters offer Wednesday afternoon showings that only a few people attend? This chapter will help you understand how firms answer these sorts of questions.

THE GOAL OF PROFIT MAXIMIZATION

To analyze decision making at the firm, let's start with a very basic question: What is the firm trying to maximize?

Economists have given this question a lot of thought. Some firms—especially large ones—are complex institutions in which many different groups of people work together. A firm's owners will usually want the firm to earn as much profit as possible. But the workers and managers who actually run the firm may have other agendas. They may try to divert the firm away from profit maximization in order to benefit themselves. We'll explore these situations later in the book (Chapter 15). But in this chapter, we assume that workers and managers are faithful servants of the firm's owners. That is,

We will view the firm as a single economic decision maker whose goal is to maximize its owners' profit.

This assumption explains what firms actually do with reasonable—and sometimes remarkable—accuracy. Part of the reason the assumption seems to describe firm behavior so well is that when managers deviate from it too much and for too long, they are typically replaced. Another reason is that so many managers—especially of the largest business firms—have taken several economics courses as part of their management education. In fact, the economic theory of profit maximization has so permeated the language and culture of modern business that it's sometimes hard to distinguish where economic theory ends and business practice begins.

UNDERSTANDING PROFIT

Profit is defined as the firm's *sales revenue* minus its *costs of production*. There is widespread agreement over how to measure the firm's revenue—the flow of money into the firm. But there are two different conceptions of the firm's costs, and each of them leads to a different definition of profit.

Two Definitions of Profit

One definition of profit is used by accountants. With a few exceptions, accountants consider only *explicit* costs, where money is actually paid out.[1] If we deduct only the costs recognized by accountants, we get one definition of profit:

Accounting profit Total revenue minus accounting costs.

$$\text{Accounting profit} = \text{Total revenue} - \text{Accounting costs.}$$

But economics, as you have learned, has a much broader view of cost—*opportunity cost*. For the firm's owners, opportunity cost is the total value of *everything* sacrificed to produce output. This includes not only the explicit costs recognized by accountants—such as wages and salaries and outlays on raw materials—but also *implicit costs*, when something is given up but no money changes hands. For example, if an owner contributes his own time or money to the firm, there will be forgone wages or forgone investment income—both implicit costs for the firm.

This broader conception of costs leads to a second definition of profit:

Economic profit Total revenue minus all costs of production, explicit and implicit.

$$\text{Economic profit} = \text{Total revenue} - \textit{All} \text{ costs of production}$$
$$= \text{Total revenue} - (\text{Explicit costs} + \text{Implicit costs})$$

The difference between economic profit and accounting profit is an important one; when they are confused, some serious (and costly) mistakes can result. An example might help make the difference clear.

Suppose you own a firm that produces T-shirts, and you want to calculate your profit over the year. Your bookkeeper provides you with the following information:

Total Revenue from Selling T-shirts		$300,000
Cost of raw materials	$ 80,000	
Wages and salaries	150,000	
Electricity and phone	20,000	
Advertising cost	40,000	
Total Explicit Cost		290,000
Accounting Profit		$ 10,000

© CENGAGE LEARNING 2013

[1] One exception is *depreciation*, a charge for the gradual wearing out of the firm's plant and equipment. Accountants include this as a cost, even though no money is actually paid out.

From the looks of things, your firm is earning a profit, so you might feel pretty good. Indeed, if you look only at money coming in and money going out, you have indeed earned a profit: $10,000 for the year . . . an accounting profit.

But suppose that in order to start your business you invested $100,000 of your own money—money that *could* be earning $6,000 in interest if you sold the business, got your $100,000 back, and put it in the bank. Also, you are using two extra rooms in your own house as a factory—rooms that *could* be rented out for $4,000 per year. Finally, you are managing the business full-time, without receiving a separate salary, and you could instead be working at a job earning $40,000 per year. All of these costs—the interest, rent, and salary you *could* have earned—are implicit costs that have not been taken into account by your bookkeeper. They are part of the opportunity cost of your firm because they are sacrifices you made to operate your business.

Now let's look at this business from the economist's perspective and calculate your *economic* profit.

Total Revenue from Selling T-shirts		$300,000
Cost of raw materials	$ 80,000	
Wages and salaries	150,000	
Electricity and phone	20,000	
Advertising cost	40,000	
Total Explicit Costs	$290,000	
Investment income forgone	$ 6,000	
Rent forgone	4,000	
Salary forgone	40,000	
Total Implicit Costs	$ 50,000	
Total Costs		$340,000
Economic Profit		−$ 40,000

From an economic point of view, your business is not profitable at all, but is actually losing $40,000 per year! But wait—how can we say that your firm is suffering a loss when it takes in more money than it pays out? Because, as we've seen, your *opportunity cost*—the value of what you are giving up to produce your output—includes more than just money costs. When *all* costs are considered—implicit as well as explicit—your total revenue is not sufficient to cover what you have sacrificed to run your business. You would do better by shifting your time, your money, and your spare room to some alternative use.

Which of the two definitions of profit is the correct one? Either one of them, depending on the reason for measuring it. For tax purposes, the government is interested in profits as measured by accountants. The government cares only about the money you've earned, not what you *could* have earned had you done something else with your money or your time.

However, for our purposes—understanding the behavior of firms—economic profit is clearly better. Should your T-shirt factory stay in business? Should it expand or contract in the long run? Will other firms be attracted to the T-shirt industry? It is economic profit that will help us answer these questions, because it is economic profit that you and other owners care about.

The proper measure of profit for understanding and predicting the behavior of firms is economic profit. Unlike accounting profit, economic profit recognizes all the opportunity costs of production—both explicit costs and implicit costs.

Why Are There Profits?

When you look at the income received by households in the economy, you see a variety of resource payments. Those who provide firms with land receive *rent*—the payment for land. Those who provide labor receive a wage or salary. And those who lend firms money so they can purchase capital equipment receive interest. The firm's profit goes to its owners. But what do the owners of the firm provide that earns them this payment?

Economists view profit as a payment for entrepreneurship, which is just as necessary for production as are land, labor, or machinery. Entrepreneurs' two contributions to production are *risk taking* and *innovation*.

Consider a successful restaurant. The land, labor, and capital it uses to make and serve meals did not simply come together on their own. Someone had to recognize that a particular restaurant could be successful in a particular location and figure out how to set it up—*innovation*. And someone had to provide the *funds* to get the restaurant up and running, even though it might fail and the investment might be lost—*risk taking*. In the case of a single restaurant and many other small businesses, a sole individual might play both entrepreneurial roles—innovator and risk taker.

For larger business ventures, these two roles are often played by different sets of people. Google was started by two Stanford students (Larry Page and Sergey Brin) who came up with the idea for a new Internet search algorithm, and then spent considerable effort designing the service and planning their future company. They were entrepreneurs who contributed mostly *innovation*. But *other* entrepreneurs—the individuals and venture capital partners that provided funds to launch the new company—played the role of *risk takers*. Had Google not been successful, these investors would have lost part or all of the money they had put into the new firm. In hindsight, the fact that Google was such a good investment seems inevitable, as successful investments often do. But in the early days, Google—like any startup—was a risky venture.

Society benefits from entrepreneurial activity. Without it, the businesses we often take for granted—restaurants, movie studios, farms, Web sites, computer manufacturers, and more—would not exist. But in general, people will make the effort to innovate and take on financial risks only if there is a potential for reward. Entrepreneurs—as owners of the businesses that they help create—are rewarded by earning profit if their businesses are successful. At Google, for example, both the innovators (Page and Brin) and the risk takers (the investors) shared ownership of the new firm, and earned profits as Google became successful. Over the years, as Google sought new funds to expand the company, new investors risked their funds. They, too, became owners, and they were rewarded with a share of the firm's growing profits.

THE FIRM'S CONSTRAINTS

If the firm were free to earn whatever level of profit it wanted, it would earn virtually infinite profit. This would make the owners very happy. Unfortunately for owners, though, the firm is not free to do this; it faces *constraints* on both its revenue and its costs.

The Demand Curve Facing the Firm

The constraint on the firm's revenue arises from a familiar concept: the demand curve. This curve always tells us the quantity of a good buyers wish to buy at different prices. But which buyers? And from which firms are they buying? Depending on how we answer these questions, we might be talking about different types of demand curves.

Market demand curves—like the ones you studied in Chapters 3 and 4—tell us the quantity demanded by *all* consumers from *all* firms in a market. In this chapter, we look at another kind of demand curve:

> The **demand curve facing the firm** *tells us, for different prices, the quantity of output that customers will choose to purchase from that firm.*

Demand curve facing the firm A curve that indicates, for different prices, the quantity of output that customers will purchase from a particular firm.

Notice that this new demand curve—the demand curve facing the firm—refers to only *one* firm, and to *all buyers* who are potential customers of that firm.

What does the demand curve facing the firm look like? That depends. Recall from Chapter 3 that firms can sell their products in two different types of markets: perfectly competitive markets (where they take the *market price as a given*) and *imperfectly* competitive markets (where the *firm must decide what price to charge*). We'll postpone our analysis of perfectly competitive markets until the next chapter. In this chapter, we'll deal with firms in imperfectly competitive markets that must decide what price to charge. If a manager thinks, "I'd like to sell more of my product, but then I'd have to lower my price, so I wonder if it's worth it," the manager is operating in an imperfectly competitive market.

Let's consider the demand curve faced by Ned, the owner and manager of Ned's Beds, a manufacturer of bed frames. Figure 1 lists the different prices that Ned could charge for each bed frame and the number of them (per day) he can sell at each price. The figure also shows a graph of the demand curve facing Ned's firm. For each price (on the vertical axis), it shows us the quantity of output the firm can sell (on the horizontal axis). Notice that, like the other types of demand curves we have studied, the demand curve facing the firm slopes downward. In order to sell more bed frames, Ned must lower his price.

The definition of the demand curve facing the firm suggests that once it selects a price, the firm has also determined how much output it will sell. But, as you saw a few chapters ago, we can also flip the demand relationship around: Once the firm has selected an output level, it has also determined the maximum price it can charge. This leads to an alternative definition:

> The demand curve facing the firm shows us the maximum price the firm can charge to sell any given amount of output.

Looking at Figure 1 from this perspective, we see that the horizontal axis shows alternative levels of output, and the vertical axis shows the price Ned will charge if he sells each quantity of output.

Because of the demand curve that Ned faces, he can choose *either* the price he charges *or* the quantity of beds he will sell. Once he chooses one of these, the other is determined for him by the demand curve. Economists typically focus on the choice of output level, with the price implied as a consequence. We will follow that convention in this textbook.

© MASTERFILE (ROYALTY-FREE DIV.)

Like many other firms, a furniture manufacturer must determine either its price for its products, or its level of output; once it chooses price, its level of output is determined, and vice versa.

FIGURE 1 | The Demand Curve Facing the Firm

(1) Price	(2) Output	(3) Total Revenue	(4) Total Cost	(5) Profit
>$650	0	0	$ 300	−$ 300
$650	1	$ 650	$ 700	−$ 50
$600	2	$1,200	$ 900	$ 300
$550	3	$1,650	$1,000	$ 650
$500	4	$2,000	$1,150	$ 850
$450	5	$2,250	$1,350	$ 900
$400	6	$2,400	$1,600	$ 800
$350	7	$2,450	$1,900	$ 550
$300	8	$2,400	$2,250	$ 150
$250	9	$2,250	$2,650	−$ 400
$200	10	$2,000	$3,100	−$1,100

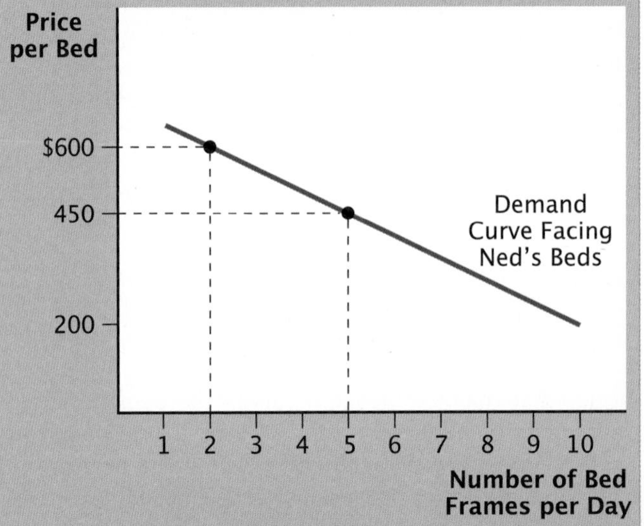

The table presents information about Ned's Beds. Data from the first two columns are plotted in the figure to show the demand curve facing the firm. At any point along that demand curve, the product of price and quantity equals total revenue, which is given in the third column of the table.

© CENGAGE LEARNING 2013

Demand and Total Revenue

Total revenue The total inflow of receipts from selling a given amount of output.

A firm's **total revenue** is the total inflow of receipts from selling output. Each time the firm chooses a level of output, it also determines its total revenue. Why? Because once we know the level of output, we also know the highest price the firm can charge. Total revenue, which is the number of units of output times the price per unit, follows automatically.

The third column in Figure 1 lists the total revenue of Ned's Beds. Each entry is calculated by multiplying the quantity of output (column 2) by the price per unit (column 1). For example, if Ned's firm produces 2 bed frames per day, he can charge $600 for each of them, so total revenue will be 2 × $600 = $1,200. If Ned increases output to 3 units, he must lower the price to $550, earning a total revenue of 3 × $550 = $1,650. Because the firm's demand curve slopes downward, Ned must lower his price to sell more beds. With more units of output, but each one selling at a lower price, total revenue could rise or fall. Scanning the total revenue column, we see that for this firm, total revenue first rises and then begins to fall.

Total Revenue and Elasticity

There is a connection between the behavior of total revenue and the price elasticity of demand you learned about in Chapter 5. In that chapter, we looked at elasticity as we moved along a *market* demand curve. But the same concept can be applied to the demand curve facing a *single firm*.

When the firm lowers its price, it will sell more output. If demand for the firm's output is elastic ($E_D > 1$), then lowering the price by a given percentage will cause quantity sold to rise by *more* than that percentage. In that case, the firm's total revenue will rise. In Table 1, total revenue rises for all changes in output between 0 and 7 units. This tells us that demand must be elastic along the demand curve between 0 and 7 units.

TABLE 1

More Data for Ned's Beds

Output	Total Revenue	Marginal Revenue	Total Cost	Marginal Cost	Profit
0	0		$ 300		−$ 300
		$650		$400	
1	$ 650		$ 700		−$ 50
		$550		$200	
2	$1,200		$ 900		$ 300
		$450		$100	
3	$1,650		$1,000		$ 650
		$350		$150	
4	$2,000		$1,150		$ 850
		$250		$200	
5	$2,250		$1,350		$ 900
		$150		$250	
6	$2,400		$1,600		$ 800
		$ 50		$300	
7	$2,450		$1,900		$ 550
		−$ 50		$350	
8	$2,400		$2,250		$ 150
		−$150		$400	
9	$2,250		$2,650		−$ 400
		−$250		$450	
10	$2,000		$3,100		−$1,100

On the other hand, if demand is inelastic ($E_D < 1$), lowering the price by a given percentage causes quantity sold to rise by a *smaller* percentage. The firm's total revenue will fall. In Table 1, total revenue falls for all changes in output between 7 and 10 units, so demand is inelastic over that interval.

The Cost Constraint

Every firm struggles to reduce costs, but there is a limit to how low costs can go. These limits impose a second constraint on the firm. Where do the limits come from? They come from concepts that you learned about in Chapter 6. Let's review them briefly.

First, the firm has a given production technology, which determines the different combinations of inputs the firm can use to produce its output.

Second, the firm must pay *prices* for each of the inputs that it uses, and we assume there is nothing the firm can do about those prices. Together, the firm's technology and the prices of the inputs determine the cheapest way to produce any given level of output. And once the firm finds this least-cost method, it has driven the cost of producing that output level as low as it can go.

The fourth column of Figure 1 lists Ned's total cost—the lowest possible cost of producing each quantity of output. *More output always means greater costs*, so the numbers in this column are always increasing. For example, at an output of zero, total cost is $300. This tells us we are looking at costs in the short run, over which some of the firm's costs are *fixed*. (What would be the cost of producing 0 units if this were the long run?) If output increases from 0 to 1 bed frame, total cost rises from $300 to $700. This increase in total costs—$400—is caused by an increase in *variable* costs, such as labor and raw materials.

THE PROFIT-MAXIMIZING OUTPUT LEVEL

In this section, we ask a very simple question: How does a firm find the level of output that will earn it the greatest possible profit? We'll look at this question from several angles, each one giving us further insight into the behavior of the firm.

The Total Revenue and Total Cost Approach

At any given output level, the data in Figure 1 tell us (1) how much revenue the firm will earn and (2) its total cost of production. We can then easily see how much profit the firm earns at each output level, which is the difference between total revenue (*TR*) and total cost (*TC*).

> *In the total revenue and total cost approach, we see the firm's profit as the difference between* TC *and* TR *at each output level. The firm chooses the output level where profit is greatest.*

Let's see how this works for Ned's Beds. Column 5 of Figure 1 lists total profit at each output level. If the firm were to produce no bed frames at all, total revenue (*TR*) would be 0, while total cost (*TC*) would be $300. Total profit would be $TR - TC = 0 - \$300 = -\$300$. We would say that the firm earns a profit of negative $300 or a **loss** of $300 per day. Producing one bed frame would raise total revenue to $650 and total cost to $700, for a loss of $50. Not until the firm produces 2 bed frames does total revenue rise above total cost and the firm begin to make a profit. At 2 bed frames per day, *TR* is $1,200 and *TC* is $900, so the firm earns a profit of $300. Remember that as long as we have been careful to include *all* costs in *TC*—implicit as well as explicit—the profits and losses we are calculating are *economic* profits and losses.

In the total revenue and total cost approach, locating the profit-maximizing output level is straightforward: We just scan the numbers in the profit column until we find the largest value, $900, and the output level at which it is achieved, 5 units per day. We conclude that the profit-maximizing output for Ned's Beds is 5 units per day.

Loss The difference between total cost (*TC*) and total revenue (*TR*), when *TC* > *TR*.

The Marginal Revenue and Marginal Cost Approach

There is another way to find the profit-maximizing level of output. This approach, which uses *marginal* concepts, gives us some powerful insights into the firm's

⚠ DANGEROUS CURVES

Maximize profit, not revenue You may be tempted to forget about profit and think that the firm should produce where its total revenue is maximized. As you can see in Figure 1 (column 3), total revenue is greatest when the firm produces 7 units per day, but at this output level, profit is not as high as it could be. The firm does better by producing only 5 units. True, revenue is lower at 5 units, but so are costs. It is the *difference* between revenue and cost that matters, not revenue alone.

© AXL/SHUTTERSTOCK.COM

decision-making process. It is also closer to the trial-and-error procedure at some firms, in which small experimental changes are made to determine the impact on profit.

Recall that *marginal* cost is the *change* in total cost per unit increase in output. Now, let's consider a similar concept for revenue.

> **Marginal revenue (MR)** *is the change in the firm's total revenue (ΔTR) divided by the change in its output (ΔQ):*
>
> $$MR = \frac{\Delta TR}{\Delta Q}$$
>
> MR *tells us how much revenue rises per unit increase in output.*

Marginal revenue The change in total revenue from producing one more unit of output.

Table 1 reproduces the *TR* and *TC* columns from Figure 1, but adds columns for marginal revenue and marginal cost. (In the table, output is always changing by one unit, so we can use Δ*TR* alone as our measure of marginal revenue.) For example, when output changes from 2 to 3 units, total revenue rises from $1,200 to $1,650. For this output change, *MR* = $450. As usual, marginals are placed *between* different output levels because they tell us what happens as output *changes* from one level to another.

Understanding Marginal Revenue

There are two important things to notice about marginal revenue. First, if an increase in output causes total revenue to rise, *MR* must be positive. In the table, total revenue rises for all increases in output from 0 to 7 units and, as you can see, *MR* is positive for all those changes. On the other hand, when an increase in output causes total revenue to fall, *MR* is negative, which occurs for all increases in output beyond 7 units.

The second thing to notice about *MR* is a bit more complicated: Each time output increases, *MR* is *smaller* than the price the firm charges at the new output level. For example, when output increases from 2 to 3 units, the firm's total revenue rises by $450—even though it sells the third unit for a price of $550. This may seem strange to you. After all, if the firm increases output from 2 to 3 units, and it gets $550 for the third unit of output, why doesn't its total revenue rise by $550?

The answer is found in the firm's downward-sloping demand curve, which tells us that to sell more output, the firm must cut its price. Look back at Figure 1 of this chapter. When output increases from 2 to 3 units, the firm must lower its price from $600 to $550. Moreover, the new price of $550 will apply to *all three* units the firm sells.[2] This means it *gains* some revenue—$550—by selling that third unit. But it also *loses* some revenue—$100—by having to lower the price by $50 on each of the two units of output it could have otherwise sold at $600. Marginal revenue will always equal the *difference* between this gain and loss in revenue—in this case, $550 − $100 = $450.

> *When a firm faces a downward-sloping demand curve, each increase in output causes a revenue gain, from selling additional output at the new price, and a revenue loss, from having to lower the price on all previous units of output. Marginal revenue is therefore less than the price of the last unit of output.*

[2] Some firms can charge two or more different prices for the same product. We'll explore some examples in Chapter 10.

Using MR and MC to Maximize Profits

Now we'll see how marginal revenue, together with marginal cost, can be used to find the profit-maximizing output level. The logic behind the MC and MR approach is this:

> *An increase in output will always raise profit as long as marginal revenue is greater than marginal cost* (MR > MC).

Notice the word *always*. Let's see why this rather sweeping statement must be true. Table 1 tells us that when output rises from 2 to 3 units, *MR* is $450, while *MC* is $100. This change in output causes both total revenue and total cost to rise, but it causes revenue to rise by *more* than cost ($450 > $100). As a result, profit must increase. Indeed, looking at the profit column, we see that increasing output from 2 to 3 units *does* cause profit to increase, from $300 to $650.

The converse of this statement is also true:

> *An increase in output will always lower profit whenever marginal revenue is less than marginal cost* (MR < MC).

For example, when output rises from 5 to 6 units, *MR* is $150, while *MC* is $250. For this change in output, both total revenue and total cost rise, but cost rises *more,* so profit must go down. In Table 1, you can see that this change in output does indeed cause profit to decline, from $900 to $800.

These insights about *MR* and *MC* lead us to the following simple guideline the firm should use to find its profit-maximizing level of output:

> *To find the profit-maximizing output level, the firm should increase output whenever* MR > MC, *but* not *increase output when* MR < MC.

Let's apply this rule to Ned's Beds. In Table 1 we see that when moving from 0 to 1 unit of output, *MR* is $650, while *MC* is only $400. Since *MR* is larger than *MC*, making this move will increase profit. Thus, if Ned is producing 0 beds, he should always increase to 1 bed. Should he stop there? Let's see. If he moves from 1 to 2 beds, *MR* is $550, while *MC* is only $200. Once again, *MR* > *MC*, so Ned should increase output to 2 beds. You can verify from the table that if Ned finds himself producing 0, 1, 2, 3, or 4 beds, *MR* > *MC* for an increase of 1 unit, so he will always make greater profit by increasing production.

Until, that is, output reaches 5 beds. At this point, the picture changes: From 5 to 6 beds, *MR* is $150, while *MC* is $250. For this move, *MR* < *MC*, so profits would decrease. Thus, if Ned is producing 5 beds, he should *not* increase to 6. The same is true at every other output level beyond 5 units: Ned should *not* raise his output beyond 5 beds, since *MR* < *MC* for each increase. We conclude that Ned maximizes his profit by producing 5 beds per day—the same answer we got using the *TR* and *TC* approach earlier.

One final note: It sometimes happens that—for some increase in output—*MR* is precisely equal to *MC*, although this does not occur in Table 1. What should the firm do if *MR* and *MC* have the same value as output rises? In that case, both cost *and* revenue would rise by equal amounts, so increasing output would cause *no change* in profit. The firm should not care whether it makes this change in output or not. There can be more than one profit-maximizing output level when *MR* = *MC* for a change in output, as you'll see in some of the end-of-chapter problems.

Profit Maximization Using Graphs

Both approaches to maximizing profit (using totals or using marginals) can be seen even more clearly when we use graphs. In Figure 2(a) and (b), the data from Table 1 have been plotted—the *TC* and *TR* curves in the upper panel, and the *MC* and *MR* curves in the lower one.

Before we actually *use* the graphs, notice how they illustrate the relationship between total revenue and marginal revenue that you learned about earlier, and saw in Table 1. For all output levels between 0 and 7 units, the total revenue curve slopes upward—telling us that an increase in output raises total revenue. Over this range of output, marginal revenue is positive (the *MR* curve is above the horizontal axis). But beyond 7 units, total revenue slopes downward—increases in output beyond 7 units cause total revenue to fall. Marginal revenue is negative over this range of output (the *MR* curve drops below the horizontal axis).

The *TR* and *TC* Approach Using Graphs

Now let's see how we can use the *TC* and *TR* curves to guide the firm to its profit-maximizing output level. We know that the firm earns a profit at any output level where *TR* > *TC*—where the *TR* curve lies *above* the *TC* curve. In Figure 2(a), you can see that all output levels from 2 through 8 units are profitable for the firm. The *amount* of profit is simply the *vertical distance* between the *TR* and *TC* curves, whenever the *TR* curve lies above the *TC* curve. Since the firm cannot sell part of a bed frame, it must choose whole numbers for its output, so the profit-maximizing output level is simply the whole-number quantity at which this vertical distance is greatest—5 units of output. Of course, the *TR* and *TC* curves in Figure 2 were plotted from the data in Table 1, so we should not be surprised to find the same profit-maximizing output level—5 units—that we found before when using the table.

We can sum up our graphical rule for using the *TR* and *TC* curves this way:

> *To maximize profit, the firm should produce the quantity of output where the vertical distance between the* TR *and* TC *curve is greatest and the* TR *curve lies above the* TC *curve.*

The *MR* and *MC* Approach Using Graphs

Figure 2 also illustrates the *MR* and *MC* approach to maximizing profits. As usual, the marginal data in panel (b) are plotted *between* output levels, since they tell us what happens as output changes from one level to another.

In the diagram, as long as output is less than 5 units, the *MR* curve lies above the *MC* curve (*MR* > *MC*), so the firm should produce more. For example, if we consider the move from 4 to 5 units, we compare the *MR* and *MC* curves at the midpoint between 4 and 5. Here, the *MR* curve lies above the *MC* curve, so increasing output from 4 to 5 will increase profit.

But now suppose the firm is producing 5 units and considering a move to 6. At the midpoint between 5 and 6 units, the *MR* curve has already crossed the *MC* curve, and now it lies *below* the *MC* curve. For this

DANGEROUS CURVES ⚠️

Misusing the gap between *MR* and *MC* A common error is to think a firm should produce the level of output at which the difference between *MR* and *MC* is as large as possible, like 2 or 3 units of output in Figure 2. But if the firm produces 2 or 3 units, it would leave some profitable increases in output unexploited—increases where *MR* > *MC*. As long as *MR* is even a tiny bit larger than *MC*, it pays to increase output, since doing so will add more to revenue than to cost. The firm should be satisfied only when the difference between *MR* and *MC* is as *small* as possible, not as *large* as possible.

FIGURE 2 | **Profit Maximization**

Panel (a) shows the firm's
total revenue (TR) and total
cost (TC) curves. Profit is
the vertical distance between
the two curves at any level of
output. Profit is maximized
when that vertical distance
is greatest—at 5 units of
output.

Panel (b) shows the firm's
marginal revenue (MR) and
marginal cost (MC) curves.
Profit is maximized at the
level of output closest to
where the MR and MC
curves cross—at 5 units of
output.

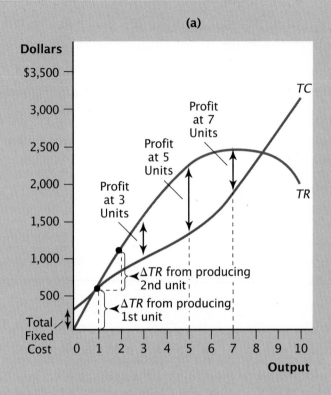

(a)

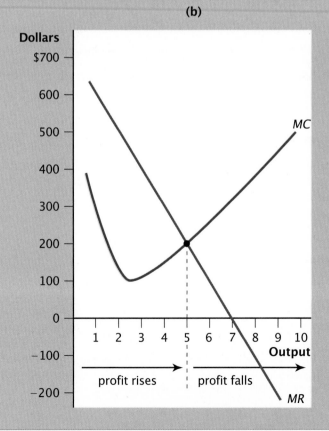

(b)

move, $MR < MC$, so raising output would *decrease* the firm's profit. The same is true for every increase in output beyond 5 units: The *MR* curve always lies below the *MC* curve, so the firm will decrease its profits by increasing output. Once again, we find that the profit-maximizing output level for the firm is 5 units.

Notice that the profit-maximizing output level—5 units—is the level closest to where the *MC* and *MR* curves cross. This is no accident. For each change in output that *increases* profit, the *MR* curve will lie above the *MC* curve. The first time that an output change *decreases* profit, the *MR* curve will cross the *MC* curve and dip below it. Thus, the *MC* and *MR* curves will always cross closest to the profit-maximizing output level.

With this graphical insight, we can summarize the *MC* and *MR* approach this way:

> *To maximize profit, the firm should produce the quantity of output closest to the point where* MC = MR—*that is, the quantity of output at which the* MC *and* MR *curves intersect.*

This rule is very useful, since it allows us to look at a diagram of *MC* and *MR* curves and *immediately* identify the profit-maximizing output level. In this text, you will often see this rule. When you read, "The profit-maximizing output level is where *MC* equals *MR*," translate to "The profit-maximizing output level is closest to the point where the *MC* curve crosses the *MR* curve."

A Proviso. There is, however, one important exception to this rule. Sometimes the *MC* and *MR* curves cross at two different points. In this case, the profit-maximizing output level is the one at which the *MC* curve crosses the *MR* curve *from below.*

Figure 3 shows why. At point *A*, the *MC* curve crosses the *MR* curve from *above.* Our rule tells us that the output level at this point, Q_1, is *not* profit maximizing. Why not? Because at output levels lower than Q_1, $MC > MR$, so profit *falls* as output increases toward Q_1. Also, profit *rises* as output increases *beyond* Q_1, since $MR > MC$ for these moves. Since it never pays to increase *to* Q_1, and profit rises when increasing *from* Q_1, we know that Q_1 cannot possibly maximize the firm's profit.

 FIGURE 3   **Two Points of Intersection**

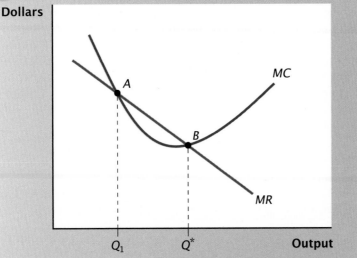

Sometimes the MR *and* MC *curves intersect twice. The profit-maximizing level of output is always found where* MC *crosses* MR *from below.*

But now look at point *B,* where the *MC* curve crosses the *MR* curve from below. You can see that when we are at an output level lower than *Q**, it always pays to increase output, since *MR* > *MC* for these moves. You can also see that, once we have arrived at *Q**, further increases will reduce profit, since *MC* > *MR*. *Q** is thus the profit-maximizing output level for this firm—the output level at which the *MC* curve crosses the *MR* curve *from below.*

What about Average Costs?

You may have noticed that this chapter has discussed *most* of the cost concepts introduced in Chapter 7. But it has not yet referred to *average* cost. There is a good reason for this. We have been concerned about how much the firm should produce if it wishes to earn the greatest possible level of profit. To achieve this goal, the firm should produce more output whenever doing so *increases* profit, and it needs to know only *marginal* cost and *marginal* revenue for this purpose. The different types of average cost (*ATC, AVC,* and *AFC*) are simply irrelevant. Indeed, a common error—sometimes made even by business managers—is to use *average* cost in place of *marginal* cost in making decisions.

For example, suppose a yacht maker wants to know how much his total cost will rise in the short run if he produces another unit of output. It is tempting—*but wrong*—for the yacht maker to reason this way: "My cost per unit (*ATC*) is currently $50,000 per yacht. Therefore, if I increase production by 1 unit, my total cost will rise by $50,000; if I increase production by 2 units, my total cost will rise by $100,000, and so on."

There are two problems with this approach. First, *ATC* includes many costs that are *fixed* in the short run—including the cost of all fixed inputs, such as the factory and equipment and the design staff. These costs will *not* increase when additional yachts are produced, and they are therefore irrelevant to the firm's decision making in the short run.

Second, *ATC changes* as output increases. The cost per yacht may rise above $50,000 or fall below $50,000, depending on whether the *ATC* curve is upward or downward sloping at the current production level. Note that the first problem—including fixed costs—could be solved by using *AVC* instead of *ATC*. The second problem—changes in average cost—remains even when *AVC* is used.

The correct approach, as we've seen in this chapter, is to use the *marginal cost* of a yacht and to consider increases in output one unit at a time. The firm should produce the output level where its *MC* curve crosses its *MR* curve from below. Average cost doesn't help at all; it only confuses the issue.

Does this mean that all of your efforts to master *ATC* and *AVC*—their definitions, their relationship to each other, and their relationship to *MC*—were a waste of time? Far from it. As you'll see, average cost will prove *very* useful in the chapters to come. You'll learn that whereas marginal values tell the firm *what* to do, averages can tell the firm *how well* it is doing. But average cost should *not* be used in place of marginal cost as a basis for decisions.

The Marginal Approach to Profit

The *MC* and *MR* approach for finding the profit-maximizing output level is actually a very specific application of a more general principle:

Marginal approach to profit A firm maximizes its profit by taking any action that adds more to its revenue than to its cost.

> *The **marginal approach to profit** states that a firm should take any action that adds more to its revenue than to its costs.*

In this chapter, the action being considered is whether to increase output by 1 unit. We've learned that the firm should take this action whenever $MR > MC$.

But the same logic can be applied to *any other decision* facing the firm. Should a restaurant owner take out an ad in the local newspaper? Should a convenience store that currently closes at midnight stay open 24 hours instead? Should a private kindergarten hire another teacher? Should an inventor pay to produce an infomercial for her new gizmo? Should a bank install another ATM? The answer to all of these questions is yes—*if* the action would add more to revenue than to costs. In future chapters, we'll be using the marginal approach to profit to analyze some other types of firm decisions.

DEALING WITH LOSSES

So far, we have dealt only with the pleasant case of profitable firms and how they select their profit-maximizing output level. But what about a firm that cannot earn a positive profit at *any* output level? What should it do? The answer depends on what time horizon we are looking at.

The Short Run and the Shutdown Rule

In the short run, the firm cannot escape paying for its fixed inputs. There is not enough time to sell a factory or get out of lease and rental agreements. But the firm can *still* make decisions about production. And one of its options is to *shut down*—to stop producing output, at least temporarily.

At first glance, you might think that a loss-making firm should always shut down its operation in the short run. After all, why keep producing if you are not making any profit? In fact, it makes sense for some unprofitable firms to continue operating.

Imagine a firm with the TC and TR curves shown in the upper panel of Figure 4 (ignore the TVC curve for now). No matter what output level the firm produces, the TC curve lies above the TR curve, so it will suffer a loss—a negative profit. For this firm, the goal is still profit maximization. But now, the highest profit will be the one with the *least negative value*. In other words, profit maximization becomes *loss minimization*.

If the firm keeps producing, then the smallest possible loss is at output level Q^*, where the distance between the TC and TR curves is smallest. Q^* is also the output level we would find by using our marginal approach to profit. (If increasing output adds more to revenue than to costs, then increasing output will make any loss *smaller*.) This is why, in the lower panel of Figure 4, the MC and MR curves must intersect at (or very close to) Q^*.

The question is: Should this firm produce at Q^* and suffer a loss? The answer is . . . maybe. It depends on which choice—either producing at Q^* or shutting down and not producing anything—leaves the firm with the *smaller* loss.

One way to figure out what the firm should do is to think about its fixed costs. In the short run, a firm must continue to pay its total fixed cost (TFC) no matter what level of output it produces—even if it produces nothing at all. If the firm shuts down, it will therefore have a loss equal to its TFC, since it will not earn any revenue. But if, by producing some output, the firm can cut its loss to something *less* than TFC, then it should stay open and keep producing.

But we can also look at the firm's decision from the viewpoint of total variable cost (TVC). Business managers often call TVC the firm's *operating cost*, since the firm only pays these variable costs when it continues to operate. If a

6. At its best possible output level, a firm has total revenue of $3,500 per day and total cost of $7,000 per day. What should this firm do in the short run if:
   a. the firm has total *fixed* costs of $3,000 per day?
   b. the firm has total *variable* costs of $3,000 per day?

7. Suppose you own a restaurant that serves only dinner. You are trying to decide whether or not to rent out your dining room and kitchen during mornings to another firm, The Breakfast Club, Inc., that will serve only breakfast. Your restaurant currently has the following monthly costs:

Rent on building:	$ 2,000
Electricity:	$ 1,000
Wages and salaries:	$15,000
Advertising:	$ 2,000
Purchases of food and supplies:	$ 8,000
Your forgone labor income:	$ 4,000
Your forgone interest:	$ 1,000

   a. Which of your current costs are implicit, and which are explicit?
   b. Suppose The Breakfast Club, Inc., offers to pay $800 per month to use the building. They promise to use only their own food, and also to leave the place spotless when they leave each day. If you believe them, should you rent out your restaurant to them? Or does it depend? Explain.

8. Suppose that, due to a dramatic rise in real estate taxes, total fixed cost at Neds Beds rises from $300 to $1,300 per day. Use the data of Table 1 to answer the following:
   a. What does the tax hike do to Ned's *MC* and *MR* curves?
   b. In the short run, how many beds should Ned produce after the rise in taxes?

9. A firm's *marginal profit* can be defined as the change in its profit when output increases by one unit.
   a. Compute the marginal profit for each change in output at Ned's Beds in Table 1.
   b. State a complete rule for finding the profit-maximizing output level in terms of marginal profit.

10. In the chapter, you learned about the relationship between price elasticity of demand and total revenue, and also between total revenue and marginal revenue.
    a. Using the information in Figure 1, calculate the price elasticities of demand for Ned's Beds when price changes from $450 to $400, from $400 to $350, and from $350 to $300.
    b. Now shift your attention from Figure 1 to *Table* 1 in the chapter. Is the behavior of total revenue in the table consistent with each of the elasticities that you found in part a.? Explain briefly.

c. Is the behavior of *marginal* revenue in the table consistent with each of the elasticities that you found in part a.? Explain briefly.

11. Kyle, Stan, and Eric have created a new app that enables someone to point a smartphone at a person's face while he or she is talking and tell you the probability that he or she is lying. They originally spent $80,000 to develop and patent the app. They could sell the patent to a large firm for $1,000,000 and get out of the business, but it would take them a year to arrange the sale. Currently, they are selling the app themselves, charging the profit-maximizing price of $10 per download and selling 1,000 downloads per year. The only actual *payment* they make to run the business is a flat $200 per month ($2,400 per year) to an Internet service provider. The interest rate in the economy—which they could earn on alternative investments—is 5% per year.
    a. What is the annual *accounting* profit of their business?
    b. What is the annual *economic* profit of their business?
    c. Based on the information given in the problem, what is the marginal cost of selling another download?
    d. Based on the answers above, should Kyle, Stan, and Eric continue to run the business in the short run (the next few months)?
    e. Based on the answers above, and assuming economic and accounting profit remain unchanged in the long run, should Kyle, Stan, and Eric continue to run the business in the long run (the next few years)?
    f. One day Kyle thinks he's discovered that demand for their apps is elastic over the entire price range from $15 to $5 per download. If Kyle is correct, should they keep the price at $10? Lower it? Raise it? Explain your answer briefly.

12. A bakery currently charges $1.50, the profit-maximizing price, for each gourmet cookie, and it sells 5,000 cookies per month. The bakery's rent and utility costs are a flat fee of $4,000 per month, and it has just signed a lease obligating it to make the payments for one year. To make each cookie costs $1 in labor and raw materials, regardless of how many cookies are made. The bakery has no costs other than those listed
    a. What is the monthly economic profit earned by the bakery?
    b. Over the short run (for the next few months), should the bakery keep operating or shut down? Why?
    c. Assuming that the bakery's current "plant" is also its *least-cost* plant, should the bakery plan to exit or stay in business *a year from now*?

More Challenging

13. Suppose Ned's Beds does *not* have to lower the price in order to sell more beds. Specifically, suppose Ned can sell all the beds he wants at a price of $275 per bed.

    a. What will Ned's *MR* curve look like? (Hint: How much will his revenue rise for each additional bed he sells?)

    b. In Table 1, how would you change the numbers in the marginal revenue column to reflect the constant price for beds?

    c. Using the marginal cost and *new* marginal revenue numbers in Table 1, find the number of beds Ned should sell.

14. Howell Industries specializes in precision plastics. Their latest invention promises to revolutionize the electronics industry, and they have already made and sold 75 of the miracle devices. They have estimated average costs as given in the following table:

Unit	ATC
74	$10,000
75	$12,000
76	$14,000

Backus Electronics has just offered Howell $150,000 if it will produce the 76th unit. Should Howell accept the offer and manufacture the additional device?

© JENNIFER MACKENZIE/ALAMY

CHAPTER 9

Perfect Competition

When we observe buyers and sellers in action, we see that different goods and services are sold in vastly different ways. Consider advertising. Every day, we are inundated with sales pitches for a long list of products: toothpaste, perfume, automobiles, cat food, ahtletic shoes, banking services, and more. But not everyone advertises what they have for sale. Farmers don't advertise when they want to sell their wheat or corn. Nor do shareholders or bondholders advertise when they want to sell stocks or bonds. Why, in a world full of advertising, don't the sellers of wheat, shares of stock, corn, crude oil, copper, or foreign currency advertise what they are selling?

Or consider profits. Anyone starting a business hopes to make as much profit as possible. Yet some companies—Microsoft, Google, and PepsiCo, for example—earn sizable profits for their owners year after year, while at other companies, such as American Airlines, Ford, and most small businesses, economic profit may fluctuate from year to year, but on average it is very low.

When economists turn their attention to these observed differences in trading, they think immediately about *market structure,* the subject of this and the next two chapters. We've used this term informally before, but now it's time for a formal definition:

> By **market structure,** *we mean all the characteristics of a market that influence the behavior of buyers and sellers when they come together to trade.*

Market structure The characteristics of a market that influence how trading takes place.

In microeconomics, we can divide markets for goods and services into four basic kinds of market structure: *perfect competition, monopoly, monopolistic competition,* or *oligopoly.* The subject of this chapter is perfect competition. In the next two chapters, we'll look carefully at the other market structures.

WHAT IS PERFECT COMPETITION?

The phrase "perfect competition" should sound familiar, because you encountered it earlier, in Chapter 3. There you learned (briefly) that the famous supply and demand model explains how prices are determined in *perfectly competitive markets.* Now we're going to take a much deeper and more comprehensive look at perfectly competitive markets. By the end of this chapter, you will understand very clearly how perfect competition and the supply and demand model are related.

Let's start with the word *competition* itself. When you hear that word, you may think of an intense, personal rivalry, like that between two boxers competing in a ring or two students competing for the best grade in a small class. But there are other, less personal forms of competition. If you took the SAT exam to get into college, you were competing with thousands of other test takers in rooms just like yours, all across the country. But the competition was *impersonal:* You were trying to do the best that you could do, trying to outperform others in general, but not competing with any one individual in the room. In economics, the term "competition" is used in the latter sense. It describes a situation of diffuse, impersonal competition in a highly populated environment.

The Four Requirements of Perfect Competition

Perfect competition is a market structure with four important characteristics:
1. *There are large numbers of buyers and sellers, and each buys or sells only a tiny fraction of the total quantity in the market.*
2. *Sellers offer a standardized product.*
3. *Sellers can easily enter into or exit from the market.*
4. *Buyers and sellers are well-informed.*

Perfect competition A market structure in which there are many buyers and sellers, the product is standardized, sellers can easily enter or exit the market, and buyers and sellers are well-informed.

These four conditions probably raise more questions than they answer, so let's see what each one really means.

A Large Number of Buyers and Sellers

In perfect competition, there must be many buyers and sellers. How many? It would be nice if we could specify a number—like 1,000—for this requirement. Unfortunately, we cannot, since what constitutes a large number of buyers and sellers can be different under different conditions. What is important is this:

In a perfectly competitive market, the number of buyers and sellers is so large that no individual decision maker can significantly affect the price of the product by changing the quantity it buys or sells.

Think of the world market for wheat. On the selling side, there are hundreds of thousands of individual wheat farmers—more than 250,000 in the United States alone. Each of these farmers produces only a tiny fraction of the total market quantity. If any one of them were to double, triple, or even quadruple production, the impact on total market quantity and market price would be negligible. The same is true on the buying side: There are so many small buyers that no one of them can affect the market price by increasing or decreasing its quantity demanded. Most agricultural markets have a large-enough number of buyers and sellers to meet this requirement, as do markets for many commodities, such as gold or silver.

Now think about the market for branded athletic shoes. Four large firms—Nike, Adidas (including Reebok), New Balance, and Puma—account for about 70 percent of worldwide sales in this market. If any one of these producers decided to change its output by even 10 percent, the impact on total quantity supplied—and market price—would be *very* noticeable. The market for athletic shoes fails the large-number-of-small-firms requirement, so it is not an example of perfect competition.

A Standardized Product Offered by Sellers

In a perfectly competitive market, buyers do not perceive differences between the products of one seller and another. For example, buyers of wheat will ordinarily have no preference for one farmer's wheat over another's, so wheat would surely pass the standardized product test. The same is true of many other agricultural products—for example, corn syrup and soybeans. It is also true of commodities like specific grades of crude oil, gold and silver, and financial instruments such as the stocks and bonds of a particular firm. (One share of eBay stock is indistinguishable from another.)

When differences among firms' products matter to buyers, the market is not perfectly competitive. For example, most consumers perceive differences among the various brands of coffee on the supermarket shelf and may have strong preferences for one particular brand. Coffee, therefore, fails the standardized product test of perfect competition. Other goods and services that would fail this test include automobiles, colleges, and magazines.

Easy Entry into and Exit from the Market

Entry into a market is rarely free; a new seller must always incur *some* costs to set up shop, begin production, and establish contacts with customers. But a perfectly competitive market has no *significant* barriers or special costs to discourage new entrants: Any firm wishing to enter can do business on the same terms as firms that are already there. For example, anyone who wants to start a wheat farm can do so, facing the same costs for land, farm equipment, seeds, fertilizer, and hired labor as existing farms. The same is true of anyone wishing to open up a dry-cleaning shop, restaurant, or dog-walking service. Each of these examples would pass the easy-entry test of perfect competition.

In many markets, however, there are significant barriers to entry. For example, local zoning laws may place strict limits on how many businesses—movie theaters, supermarkets, hotels—can operate in a local area. The brand loyalty enjoyed by existing producers of breakfast cereals, instant coffee, and soft drinks would require a new entrant to wrest customers away from existing firms—a very costly undertaking. We will discuss these and other barriers to entry in more detail in later chapters.

Perfect competition also requires easy *exit*: A firm suffering a long-run loss must be able to sell off its plant and equipment and leave the industry without obstacles. Some markets satisfy this requirement, and some do not. Plant-closing laws or union agreements can require lengthy advance notice and high severance pay when workers are laid off. Or capital equipment may be so highly specialized—perhaps designed to produce just one type of automobile—that it cannot be sold off if the firm decides to exit the market. These and other barriers to exit do not conform to the assumptions of perfect competition.

Well-Informed Buyers and Sellers

In perfect competition, both buyers and sellers have all information relevant to their decision to buy or sell. For example, they know about the quality of the product and the prices being charged by competitors. In most agricultural and commodities markets—wheat, copper, crude oil, or platinum—traders are well-informed in this way. In most other types of markets, buyers and sellers are *reasonably* well-informed. For example, if you buy a shirt at the Gap, you have a very good idea what you are getting, and you can easily find out the prices being charged for similar items in other stores.

But in some markets, this assumption may not be realistic. When individuals sell used cars to other individuals (via Internet sites like autotrader.com or Craigslist), the seller knows if he is unloading a lemon. But a buyer usually doesn't—unless he or she goes through considerable time and expense to have a mechanic examine the car. In the market for home insurance against fire and theft, *you* may know whether you smoke in bed or leave your door unlocked when not at home. But—unless you have a record of past insurance claims—the insurance company has no easy way of finding this out. Markets for used cars and home insurance thus violate the easily obtained information requirements of perfect competition. We'll explore the consequences of these and other information problems in Chapter 15.

Is Perfect Competition Realistic?

The four assumptions a market must satisfy to be perfectly competitive (or just "competitive," for short) are rather restrictive. Do any markets satisfy all these requirements? How broadly can we apply the model of perfect competition when we think about the real world?

In some cases, the model fits remarkably well. We have seen that the market for wheat, for example, passes all four tests for a competitive market: many buyers and sellers, standardized output, easy entry and exit, and well-informed buyers. Indeed, most agricultural markets satisfy the strict requirements of perfect competition quite closely, as do many financial markets and some markets for consumer goods and services.

But in the vast majority of markets, one or more of the assumptions of perfect competition will, in a strict sense, be violated. This might suggest that the model can be applied only in a few limited cases. Yet when economists look at real-world markets, they use the perfect competition model more than any other market model. Why is this?

First, the model of perfect competition is powerful. Using simple techniques, it leads to important predictions about a market's response to changes in consumer tastes, technology, and government policies. While other types of market structure models also yield valuable predictions, they are often more cumbersome and their predictions less definitive.

Second, many markets, while not strictly perfectly competitive, come *reasonably* close. The more closely a real-world market fits the model, the more accurate our predictions will be when we use it.

THE PERFECTLY COMPETITIVE FIRM

A market is a collection of individual decision makers. The decisions made by individuals, collectively, affect the market. And the market, in turn, influences the choices made by individuals. This is why, in learning about perfect competition, we'll be going back and forth between the competitive firm and the market in which it operates.

In Figure 1(a), we start with the market—specifically, the competitive market in which gold is produced and sold. The intersection of the market supply and demand curves determines the market price of gold which, in the figure, is $800 per ounce. This is all familiar territory, which you learned in Chapter 3. But now, let's turn our attention to one of the many sellers in this market: Small Time Gold Mines, a small mining company.

The Competitive Firm's Demand Curve

Panel (b) of Figure 1 shows the demand curve facing Small Time Gold Mines. Notice the special shape of this curve: It is horizontal, or perfectly price elastic. This tells us that no matter how much gold Small Time produces, it will always sell it at the same price—$800 per ounce. More generally:

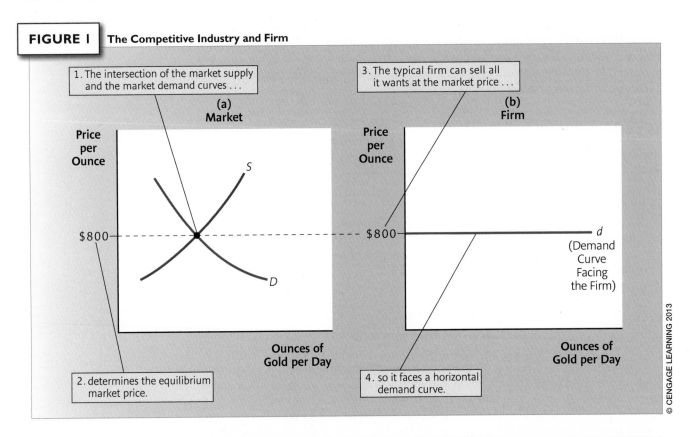

FIGURE 1   The Competitive Industry and Firm

1. The intersection of the market supply and the market demand curves . . .

(a) Market

3. The typical firm can sell all it wants at the market price . . .

(b) Firm

2. determines the equilibrium market price.

4. so it faces a horizontal demand curve.

A perfectly competitive firm faces a demand curve that is horizontal (perfectly elastic) at the market price.

⚠ DANGEROUS CURVES

Two demand curves in perfect competition In the model of perfect competition, there are *two different* demand curves, as shown in Figure 1. One is the familiar *market demand curve* (labeled with an uppercase *D*). The other is the *demand curve facing the individual firm* (labeled with a lowercase *d*). If you forget the distinction, you'll get confused. For example, you might start thinking that perfectly competitive markets are for special products with perfectly elastic demand. True, the demand curve facing the individual firm is perfectly elastic, but this has nothing to do with buyers' elasticity of demand for the product itself. The elasticity of demand for the *product* is given by the (downward sloping) *market* demand curve.

Why should this be?

First, in perfect competition, output is standardized—buyers do not distinguish the gold of one mine from that of another. If Small Time were to charge a price even a tiny bit higher than other producers, it would lose all of its customers; they would simply buy from Small Time's competitors. The horizontal demand curve captures this effect. It tells us that if Small Time raises its price above $800, it will not just sell *less* output, it will sell *no* output.

Second, Small Time is only a tiny producer relative to the entire gold market. No matter how much it produces and sells, it cannot make a noticeable difference in market quantity supplied, and so it cannot affect the market price. Once again, the horizontal demand curve describes this effect very well: The firm can increase its production without having to lower its price.

All of this means that Small Time has no control over the price of its output—it simply accepts the market price as given.

Price taker A firm that treats the price of its product as given and beyond its control.

*In perfect competition, the firm is a **price taker**: It treats the price of its output as given.*

The horizontal demand curve facing the firm and the corresponding price-taking behavior of firms are hallmarks of perfect competition. When a manager thinks, "If we produce more output, we will have to lower our price in order to sell it" then the firm faces a *downward sloping* demand curve and it is *not* a competitive firm. The manager of a competitive firm will instead think, "We can sell all the output we want at the going price, so how much should we produce?"

Notice that, since a competitive firm takes the market price as given, its only decision is *how much output to produce and sell.* And that decision will determine the firm's cost of production, as well as its total revenue. Let's see how this works in practice with Small Time Gold Mines.

Cost and Revenue Data for a Competitive Firm

Table 1 shows cost and revenue data for Small Time. In the first two columns are different quantities of gold that Small Time could produce each day and the selling price per ounce. Because Small Time is a competitive firm (a price taker), the price remains constant at $800 per ounce, no matter *how* much gold it produces.

TABLE 1

Cost and Revenue Data for Small Time Gold Mines

(1) Output (Ounces of Gold per Day)	(2) Price (per Ounce)	(3) Total Revenue	(4) Marginal Revenue	(5) Total Cost	(6) Marginal Cost	(7) Profit
0	$800	$ 0		$1,100		−$1,100
			$800		$ 900	
1	$800	$ 800		$2,000		−$1,200
			$800		$ 400	
2	$800	$1,600		$2,400		−$ 800
			$800		$ 100	
3	$800	$2,400		$2,500		−$ 100
			$800		$ 200	
4	$800	$3,200		$2,700		$ 500
			$800		$ 300	
5	$800	$4,000		$3,000		$1,000
			$800		$ 500	
6	$800	$4,800		$3,500		$1,300
			$800		$ 700	
7	**$800**	**$5,600**		**$4,200**		**$1,400**
			$800		$ 900	
8	$800	$6,400		$5,100		$1,300
			$800		$1,100	
9	$800	$7,200		$6,200		$1,000
			$800		$1,300	
10	$800	$8,000		$7,500		$ 500

© CENGAGE LEARNING 2013

Run your finger down the total revenue and marginal revenue columns. Since price is always $800, each time the firm produces another ounce of gold, total revenue rises by $800. This is why marginal revenue—the additional revenue from selling one more ounce of gold—remains constant at $800.

Figure 2 plots Small Time's total revenue and marginal revenue. Notice that the total revenue (*TR*) curve in the upper panel is a *straight line* that slopes upward; each time output increases by one unit, *TR* rises by the same $800. That is, the slope of the *TR* curve is equal to the price of output.

FIGURE 2   Profit Maximization in Perfect Competition

Panel (a) shows a competitive firm's total revenue (TR) and total cost (TC) curves. TR is a straight line with slope equal to the market price. Profit is maximized at 7 ounces per day, where the vertical distance between TR and TC is greatest. Panel (b) shows that profit is maximized where the marginal cost (MC) curve intersects the marginal revenue (MR) curve, which is also the firm's demand curve.

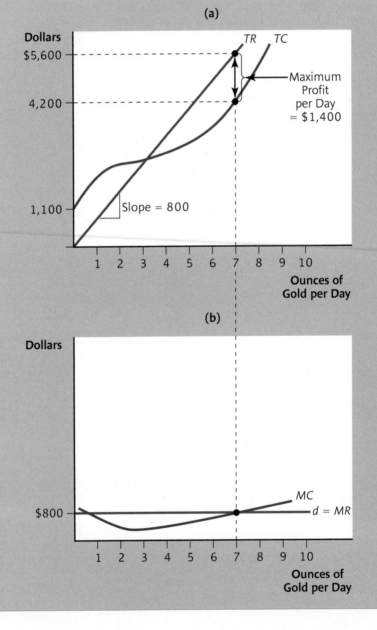

The marginal revenue (*MR*) curve in the lower panel is a *horizontal* line at the market price. In fact, the *MR* curve is the same horizontal line as the demand curve facing the firm. Why? Remember that marginal revenue is the additional revenue the firm earns from selling an additional unit of output. For a price-taking competitive firm, that additional revenue will always be the unchanging price it gets for each unit—in this case, $800.

> *For a competitive firm, marginal revenue is the same as the market price. For this reason, the marginal revenue curve and the demand curve facing the firm are the same: a horizontal line at the market price.*

In panel (b), we have labeled the horizontal line "*d* = *MR*," since this line is both the firm's demand curve (*d*) *and* its marginal revenue curve (*MR*).

Columns 5 and 6 of Table 1 show total cost and marginal cost for Small Time. There is nothing special about cost data for a competitive firm. In Figure 2, you can see that marginal cost (*MC*)—as usual—first falls and then rises. (You may want to look at Chapter 7 to review why this cost behavior is so common.)

Finding the Profit-Maximizing Output Level

A competitive firm—like any other firm—wants to earn the highest possible profit, and to do so, it should use the principles you learned in Chapter 7. Although the diagrams look a bit different for competitive firms, the ideas behind them are the same. We can use either Table 1 or Figure 2 to find the profit-maximizing output level. And we can use the techniques you have already learned: the total revenue and total cost approach, or the marginal revenue and marginal cost approach.

The Total Revenue and Total Cost Approach

The *TR* and *TC* approach is the most direct way of viewing the firm's search for the profit-maximizing output level. Quite simply, at each output level, subtract total cost from total revenue to get total profit:

$$\text{Total Profit} = TR - TC$$

Then we just scan the different output levels to see which one gives the highest number for profit.

In Table 1, total profit is shown in the last column. A simple scan of that column tells us that $1,400 is the highest daily profit that Small Time Gold Mines can earn. To earn this profit, the first column tells us that Small Time must produce 7 ounces per day, its profit-maximizing output level.

The same approach to maximizing profit can be seen graphically, in the upper panel of Figure 2. There, total profit at any output level is the distance between the *TR* and *TC* curves. As you can see, this distance is greatest when the firm produces 7 units, verifying what we found in the table.

This approach is simple and straightforward, but it hides the interesting part of the story: the way that *changes* in output cause total revenue and total cost to change. The other approach to finding the profit-maximizing output level focuses on these changes.

The Marginal Revenue and Marginal Cost Approach

In the *MR* and *MC* approach, the firm should continue to increase output as long as marginal revenue is greater than marginal cost. You can verify, using Table 1, that if the firm is initially producing 1, 2, 3, 4, 5, or 6 units, it will find that $MR > MC$ when it raises output by one unit, so producing more will raise profit. Once the firm is producing 7 units, however, $MR < MC$, so further increases in output will reduce profit.

Alternatively, using the graph in panel (b) of Figure 2, we look for the output level at which $MR = MC$. As the graph shows, there are two output levels at which the MR and MC curves intersect. However, we can rule out the first crossing point because there, the MC curve crosses the MR curve from above. Remember that the profit-maximizing output is found where the MC curve crosses the MR curve from *below*, at 7 units of output.

You can see that finding the profit-maximizing output level for a competitive firm requires no new concepts or techniques; you have already learned everything you need to know in Chapter 8. In fact, the only difference is one of appearance. Ned's Beds—our firm in Chapter 8—did *not* operate under perfect competition. As a result, both its demand curve and its marginal revenue curve sloped *downward*. Small Time, however, operates under perfect competition, so its demand and MR curves are the same horizontal line.

Measuring Total Profit

You have already seen one way to measure a firm's total profit on a graph: the vertical distance between the TR and TC curves. In this section, you will learn another graphical way to measure profit.

To do this, we start with the firm's *profit per unit,* which is the revenue it gets on each unit minus the cost per unit. Revenue per unit is just the price (P) of the firm's output, and cost per unit is our familiar average total cost, so we can write:

$$\text{Profit per unit} = P - ATC.$$

In Figure 3(a), Small Time's ATC curve has been plotted (calculated from the data in Table 1). When the firm is producing at the profit-maximizing output level, 7 units, its ATC is $TC/Q = \$4,200/7 = \$600$. Since the price of output is \$800, profit *per unit* = $P - ATC = \$800 - \$600 = \$200$. Graphically, this is the vertical distance between the firm's demand curve and its ATC curve at the profit-maximizing output level.

Once we know Small Time's profit per unit, it is easy to calculate its *total* profit: Just multiply profit per unit by the number of units sold. Small Time is earning \$200 profit on each ounce of gold, and it sells 7 ounces in all, so total profit is $\$200 \times 7 = \$1,400$.

Now look at the blue-shaded rectangle in Figure 3(a). The height of this rectangle is profit per unit, and the width is the number of units produced. The *area* of the rectangle—height $\times$ width—equals Small Time's profit:

> *A firm earns a profit whenever* P > ATC. *Its total profit at the best output level equals the area of a rectangle with height equal to the distance between* P *and* ATC, *and width equal to the quantity of output.*

In the figure, Small Time is fortunate: At a price of \$800, there are several output levels at which it can earn a profit. Its problem is to select the one that makes its profit as large as possible. (We should all wish for such problems.)

But what if the price had been lower than \$800—so low, in fact, that Small Time could not make a profit at *any* output level? Then the best it can do is to choose the smallest possible loss. Just as we did in the case of profit, we can measure the firm's total loss using the ATC curve.

FIGURE 3   Measuring Profit or Loss

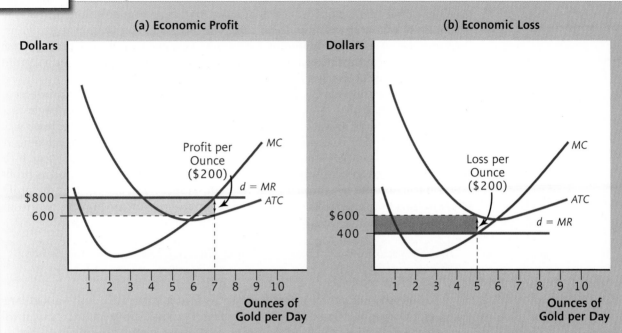

The competitive firm in panel (a) produces where marginal cost equals marginal revenue, or 7 units of output per day. Profit per unit at that output level is equal to revenue per unit ($800) minus cost per unit ($600), or $200 per unit. Total profit (indicated by the blue-shaded rectangle) is equal to profit per unit times the number of units sold, $200 × 7 = $1,400. In panel (b), we assume that the market price is lower, at $400 per ounce. The best the firm can do is to produce 5 ounces per day and suffer a loss shown by the red area. It loses $200 per ounce on each of those 5 ounces produced, so the total loss is $1,000—the area of the red-shaded rectangle.

Panel (b) of Figure 3 reproduces Small Time's ATC and MC curves from panel (a). This time, however, we have assumed a lower price for gold—$400—so the firm's d = MR curve is the horizontal line at $400. Since this line lies everywhere below the ATC curve, profit per unit (P − ATC) is always negative: Small Time cannot make a positive profit at *any* output level.

With a price of $400, the MC curve crosses the MR curve from below at 5 units of output. Unless Small Time decides to shut down (we'll discuss shutting down for competitive firms later), it should produce 5 units. At that level of output, ATC is $600, and profit per unit is P − ATC = $400 − $600 = −$200, a *loss* of $200 per unit. The total loss is loss per unit (negative profit per unit) times the number of units produced, or −$200 × 5 = −$1,000. This is the area of the red-shaded rectangle in Figure 3(b), with height of $200 and width of 5 units:

A firm suffers a loss whenever P < ATC *at the best level of output. Its total loss equals the area of a rectangle with height equal to the distance between* P *and* ATC, *and width equal to the quantity of output.*

DANGEROUS CURVES

Misusing profit per unit It is tempting—but *wrong*—to think that the firm should produce where profit *per unit* (P − ATC) is greatest. The firm's goal is to maximize *total* profit, not profit per unit. Using Table 1 or Figure 3(a), you can verify that while Small Time's profit *per unit* is greatest at 6 units of output, its *total* profit is greatest at 7 units.

The Firm's Short-Run Supply Curve

A competitive firm is a price taker: It takes the market price as given and then decides how much output it will produce at that price. If the market price changes for any reason, the price taken as given by the firm will change as well. The firm will then have to find a new profit-maximizing output level. Let's see how the firm's profit-maximizing output changes as the market price rises or falls.

Figure 4(a) shows *ATC*, *AVC*, and *MC* curves for a competitive producer of wheat. The figure also shows five hypothetical demand curves the firm might face, each corresponding to a different market price for wheat. If the market price were $7 per bushel, the firm would face demand curve d_1, and its profit-maximizing output level—where *MC* and *MR* intersect—would be 7,000 bushels per year. If the price dropped to $5 per bushel, the firm would face demand curve d_2, and its profit-maximizing output level would drop to 5,000 bushels. You can see that the profit-maximizing output level is always found by traveling from the price, across to the firm's *MC* curve, and then down to the horizontal axis. In other words,

> *as the price of output changes, the firm will slide along its* MC *curve in deciding how much to produce.*

But there is one problem with this: If the firm is suffering a loss—a loss large enough to justify shutting down—then it will *not* produce along its *MC* curve; it will produce zero units instead. Thus, in order to know for certain how much output the firm will produce, we must bring in the shutdown rule.

FIGURE 4 | **Short-Run Supply under Perfect Competition**

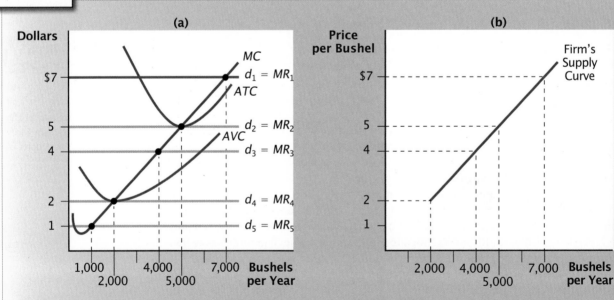

Panel (a) shows a typical competitive firm facing various market prices. For prices between $2 and $7 per bushel, the profit-maximizing quantity is found by sliding along the MC *curve. Below $2 per bushel, the firm is better off shutting down, because P < AVC. Panel (b) shows the firm's supply curve, which is the same as its* MC *curve for all prices above the shutdown price of $2 per bushel.*

The Shutdown Price

In Chapter 8, you learned that a firm should shut down in the short run if, at its best positive output level, it finds that $TR < TVC$. (In words, if the firm cannot even cover its operating costs, it should not continue to operate.) If $TR > TVC$, the firm should continue to operate.

But when we use a graph such as Figure 4(a), which has different prices *per unit* on the vertical axis and has curves showing cost *per unit*, it will be helpful to express this shutdown rule in "per unit" terms. Let's start with the rule from Chapter 8:

$$\text{Shut down if } TR < TVC$$

Next, with lowercase q representing the individual firm's output level, we divide both sides of the inequality by q:

$$\text{Shut down if } (TR/q) < (TVC/q)$$

Finally, we recognize that TR/q is just revenue per unit, or the price (P), and TVC/q is the firm's average variable cost (AVC), giving us

$$\text{Shut down if } P < AVC$$

Now let's apply the shutdown rule to the firms in Figure 4(a). Suppose the price drops down to $4 per bushel. At this price, the best output level is 4,000 bushels, and the firm suffers a loss, since $P < ATC$. Should the firm shut-down? Let's see. At 4,000 bushels, it is also true that $P > AVC$, since the demand curve lies above the AVC curve at this output level. Thus, at a price of $4, the firm will stay open and produce 4,000 units of output.

Now, suppose the price drops all the way down to $1 per bushel. At this price, $MR = MC$ at 1,000 bushels. But notice that here $P < AVC$. Therefore, at a price of $1, this firm will shut down and produce *zero* units of output.

Finally, let's consider a price of $2. At this price, $MR = MC$ at 2,000 bushels, and here we have $P = AVC$. At $2, therefore, the firm will be indifferent between staying open and shutting down. We call this price the firm's **shutdown price**, since it will shut down at any price lower and stay open at any price higher.

> **Shutdown price** The price at which a firm is indifferent between producing and shutting down.

Note that the shutdown price is found at the *minimum* of the AVC curve. Why? As the price decreases, the best output level is found by sliding along the MC curve, until we reach the AVC curve. At that point, the firm will shut down. But—as you learned in Chapter 7—the point at which the MC curve reaches (crosses) the AVC curve is the *minimum* point of the AVC curve.

Now let's recapitulate what we've found about the firm's output decision. For all prices above the minimum point on the AVC curve, the firm will stay open and will produce the level of output at which $MR = MC$. For these prices, the firm slides along its MC curve in deciding how much output to produce. But for any price below the minimum AVC, the firm will shut down and produce zero units. We can summarize all of this information with the **firm's supply curve**, which tells us how much output the firm will produce at each price:

> **Firm's supply curve** A curve that shows the quantity of output a competitive firm will produce at different prices.

> *A competitive firm's supply curve is its* MC *curve for all prices above minimum* AVC. *For all prices below minimum* AVC, *the firm will shut down.*

In panel (b) of Figure 4, we have drawn the supply curve for our hypothetical wheat farmer. As price declines from $7 to $2, output is determined by the firm's MC curve. For all prices *below* $2—the shutdown price—the firm will not produce any output.

market arrives at its short-run equilibrium. On the right side, we add up the quantities supplied by all firms to obtain the market supply curve. On the left side, we add up the quantities demanded by all consumers to obtain the market demand curve.

At this stage, the market supply and demand curves show if/then relationships: *If* the price were such and such, *then* firms would supply this much and consumers would buy that much. But once we bring the two curves together and find their intersection point, we know the *equilibrium* price at which trading will actually take place. Finally, when we confront each firm and each consumer with the equilibrium price, we find the actual quantity each consumer will buy and the actual quantity each firm will produce.

Figure 7 gets more specific, illustrating two possible short-run equilibriums in the wheat market, depending on the position of the market demand curve. In panel (a), if the market demand curve were D_1, the short-run equilibrium price would be $7. Each firm would face the horizontal demand curve d_1 [panel (b)] and decide to produce 7,000 bushels. With 100 such firms, the equilibrium market quantity would be 700,000 bushels. Notice that, at a price of $7, each firm is enjoying an economic profit, since $P > ATC$.

If the market demand curve were D_2 instead, the equilibrium price would be $4. Each firm would face demand curve d_2 and produce 4,000 bushels. With 100 firms, the equilibrium market quantity would be 400,000. Here, each firm is suffering an economic loss, since $P < ATC$. These two examples show us that

> in short-run equilibrium, competitive firms can earn an economic profit or suffer an economic loss.

FIGURE 7   **Short-Run Equilibrium in Perfect Competition**

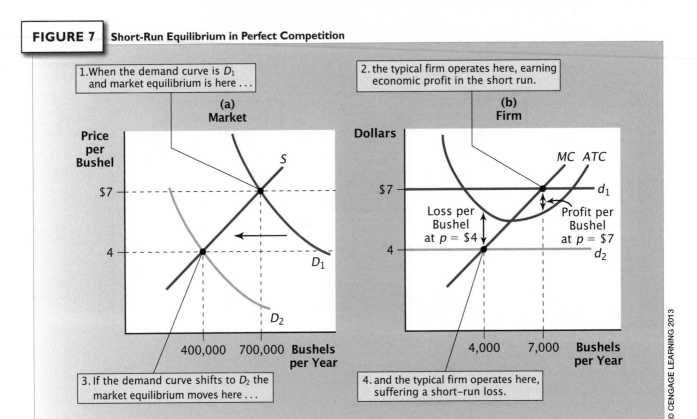

1. When the demand curve is D_1 and market equilibrium is here ...

2. the typical firm operates here, earning economic profit in the short run.

(a)
Market

(b)
Firm

3. If the demand curve shifts to D_2 the market equilibrium moves here ...

4. and the typical firm operates here, suffering a short–run loss.

Equilibrium in Perspective

We are about to leave the short run and turn our attention to what happens in a competitive market over the long run. But before we do, let's look once more at how a short-run equilibrium is established. One part of this process—combining supply and demand curves to find the market equilibrium—has been familiar to you all along. But now you can see how much information is contained within each of these curves. And you can appreciate what an impressive job the market does—coordinating millions of decisions made by people who may never even meet each other.

Think about it: So many individual consumers and firms, each with its own agenda, trading in the market. Not one of them has any power to decide or even influence the market price. Rather, the price is determined by *all* of them, adjusting until *total* quantity supplied is equal to *total* quantity demanded. Then, facing this equilibrium price, each consumer buys the quantity he or she wants, each firm produces the output level that it wants, and we can be confident that all of them will be able to realize their plans. Each buyer can find willing sellers, and each seller can find willing buyers.

> *In perfect competition, the market sums up the buying and selling preferences of individual consumers and producers, and determines the market price. Each buyer and seller then takes the market price as given, and each is able to buy or sell the desired quantity.*

This process is, from a certain perspective, a thing of beauty, and it happens each day in markets all across the world—markets for wheat, corn, barley, soybeans, apples, oranges, gold, silver, copper, and more. And something quite similar happens in other markets that do not strictly satisfy our requirements for perfect competition—markets for television sets, books, air conditioners, fast-food meals, bottled water, blue jeans. . . . The list is virtually endless.

COMPETITIVE MARKETS IN THE LONG RUN

The long run is a time horizon sufficiently long for firms to vary *all* of their inputs. This includes inputs that were treated as fixed in the short run, such as plant and equipment. Logically, then, the long run must be enough time for *new* firms to acquire those inputs and enter the market as *new* suppliers. And it is also long enough for existing firms to sell all such inputs and exit the market.

> *In the long run, new firms can enter a competitive market, and existing firms can exit the market.*

But what makes firms want to enter or exit a market? The driving force behind entry is economic profit, and the force behind exit is economic loss.

Profit and Loss and the Long Run

Recall that economic profit is the amount by which total revenue exceeds *all* costs of doing business. The costs we deduct include implicit costs like forgone investment income or forgone wages for

Long-run exit from a market can occur in different ways. An example is when a firm (such as this retailer) goes entirely out of business.

an owner who devotes money or time to the business. Thus, when a firm earns positive economic profit, we know the owners are earning *more* than they could by devoting their money and time to some other activity.

A temporary episode of positive economic profit will not have much impact on a competitive industry, other than the temporary pleasure it gives the owners of competitive firms. But when positive profit reflects basic conditions in the industry and is expected to continue, major changes are in the works. Outsiders, hungry for profit themselves, will want to enter the market and—since *there are no barriers to entry*—they can do so.

On the other hand, if firms already in the industry are suffering economic losses, they are not earning enough revenue to cover all their costs. There must be other opportunities that would more adequately compensate the owners for their money or time. If this situation is expected to continue over the firm's long-run planning horizon—a period long enough to vary *all* inputs—there is only one thing for the firm to do: exit the industry by selling off its plant and equipment, thereby reducing its loss to zero.

> *In a competitive market, economic profit and loss are the forces driving long-run change. The expectation of continued economic profit causes outsiders to enter the market; the expectation of continued economic losses causes firms in the market to exit.*

In the real world of business, entry and exit occur in a variety of different ways. Sometimes it involves the formation of an entirely new firm, such as JetBlue, an airline formed in 2000. Entry can also occur when an existing firm adds a new product line, as Apple did when it entered the wireless phone market in 2007. Or, in a local market, entry can occur when an existing firm creates a new branch, such as when Walmart or Starbucks builds a new store. In all of these cases, the number of sellers in the market increases.

Exit, too, can occur in different ways. Sometimes, it involves a firm going entirely out of business as did Borders bookstores in 2011. But exit can also occur when a firm switches out of a particular product line, even as it continues to produce other things. In 2009, for example, Condé Nast stopped publishing *Portfolio*, thus exiting the market for business-oriented magazines. But it continued to publish other monthlies—such as *Vogue, Allure,* and *Wired*—for other magazine markets.

Long-Run Equilibrium

Entry and exit—however they occur—are powerful forces in real-world competitive markets. They determine how these markets change over the long run, how much output will be available to consumers, and the prices they must pay. To explore these issues, let's see how entry and exit move a market to its long-run equilibrium from different starting points.

From Short-Run Profit to Long-Run Equilibrium

Suppose that the market for wheat is initially in a short-run equilibrium like point *A* in panel (a) of Figure 8, with market supply curve S_1. The initial equilibrium price is $9 per bushel. In panel (b), we see that a typical competitive firm—producing 9,000 bushels— is earning economic profit, since $P > ATC$ at that output level. As long as we remain in the short run, with no new firms entering the market, this situation will not change.

But as we enter the long run, much will change. First, economic profit will attract new entrants, increasing the number of firms in the market. Now remember (from Chapter 3) when we draw a market supply curve like S_1, we draw it for some *given* number of firms, and we hold that number constant. But in the long run, as the number of firms increases, the market supply curve will *shift rightward;* a greater

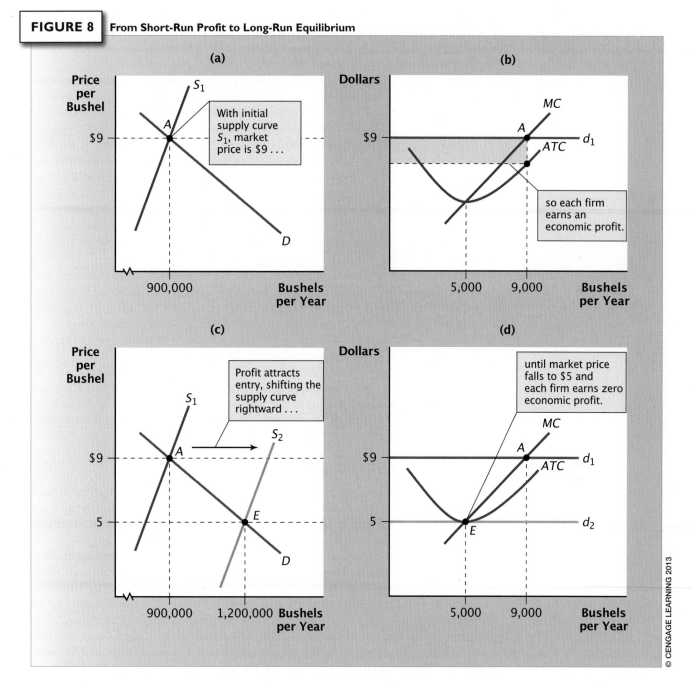

FIGURE 8 | **From Short-Run Profit to Long-Run Equilibrium**

(a)

Price per Bushel

$9 ----- A

With initial supply curve S_1, market price is $9 ...

S_1

D

900,000 · Bushels per Year

(b)

Dollars

$9 — A

MC

d_1

ATC

so each firm earns an economic profit.

5,000 · 9,000 · Bushels per Year

(c)

Price per Bushel

Profit attracts entry, shifting the supply curve rightward ...

S_1

S_2

$9 ----- A

5 ----- E

D

900,000 · 1,200,000 · Bushels per Year

(d)

Dollars

until market price falls to $5 and each firm earns zero economic profit.

MC

$9 — A

ATC

d_1

5 — E · d_2

5,000 · 9,000 · Bushels per Year

© CENGAGE LEARNING 2013

quantity will be supplied at any given price. As the market supply curve shifts rightward, several things happen:

1. The market price begins to fall—from $9 to $8 to $7 and so on.
2. As market price falls, the horizontal demand curve facing each firm shifts downward.
3. Each firm—striving as always to maximize profit—will slide down its marginal cost curve, decreasing output.[1]

[1] There is one other possible consequence that we ignore here: Entry into the industry, which changes the demand for the industry's inputs, may also change input prices. If this occurs, firms' cost curves can shift as well. We'll explore this possibility later in this chapter.

This process of adjustment, in the market and the firm, continues until the *reason for entry*—positive profit—no longer exists. That is, it will continue until the market supply curve shifts rightward enough, and the price falls enough, so that *each existing firm is earning zero economic profit*.

Panels (c) and (d) in Figure 8 show the final, long-run equilibrium. First, look at panel (c), which shows long-run market equilibrium at point E. The market supply curve has shifted to S_2, and the price has fallen to $5 per bushel. Next, look at panel (d), which tells us why the market supply curve stops shifting when it reaches S_2. With that supply curve, each firm is producing at the lowest point of its ATC curve, with $P = ATC = \$5$, and each is earning zero economic profit. With no economic profit, there is no further reason for entry, and no further shift in the market supply curve.

> *In a competitive market, positive economic profit continues to attract new entrants until economic profit is reduced to zero.*

Now you can see the role played by one of our assumptions about competitive markets: *easy entry*. With no significant barriers to entry, we can be confident that economic profit at the typical firm will attract new firms to the industry, driving down the market price until the economic profit disappears. If a permanent barrier—legal or otherwise—prevented new firms from coming into the market, this mechanism would not work, so long-run economic profit would be possible.

Before proceeding further, take a close look at Figure 8. As the market moves to its long-run equilibrium [point E in panels (c) and (d)], output at each firm *decreases* from 9,000 to 5,000 bushels. But in the market as a whole, output *increases* from 900,000 to 1,200,000 bushels. How can this be? (See if you can answer this question yourself. Hint: entry!)

From Short-Run Loss to Long-Run Equilibrium

We have just seen how, beginning from a position of short-run profit at the typical firm, a competitive market will adjust until the profit is eliminated. But what if we begin from a position of loss? As you might guess, the same type of adjustments will occur, only in the opposite direction.

This is a good opportunity for you to test your own skill and understanding. Study Figure 8 carefully. Then see if you can draw a similar diagram that illustrates the adjustment from short-run *loss* to long-run equilibrium. Use the same demand curve as in Figure 8, but draw in a new, appropriate market supply curve to create an initial equilibrium price of $3. Then let the market work. Show what happens in the market, and at each firm, as economic loss causes some firms to exit. If you do this correctly, you'll end up once again at a market price of $5, with each firm earning zero economic profit. Your graph will illustrate the following conclusion:

> *In a competitive market, economic losses continue to cause exit until the losses are reduced to zero.*

Notice the role played by our assumption of *easy exit* in competitive markets. When there are no significant barriers to exit, we can be confident that economic loss will eventually drive firms from the industry, raising the market price until the typical firm breaks even again. Significant barriers to exit (such as a local law forbidding a plant from closing down) would prevent this mechanism from working, and economic losses could persist even in the long run.

The Notion of Zero Profit in Perfect Competition

From the preceding discussion, you may wonder why anyone in his or her right mind would ever want to set up shop in a competitive industry or stay there for any length of time. In the long run, after all, they can expect zero economic profit. Indeed, if you want to become a millionaire, you would be well advised *not* to buy a wheat farm. But most wheat farmers—like most other sellers in competitive markets—do not curse their fate. On the contrary, they are likely to be reasonably content with the performance of their businesses. How can this be?

Remember that zero *economic* profit is not the same as zero *accounting* profit. When a firm is making zero *economic* profit, it is still making some accounting profit. In fact, the accounting profit is just enough to cover all of the owner's implicit costs, including compensation for any forgone investment income or forgone salary. Suppose, for example, that a farmer paid $100,000 for land and works 40 hours per week. Suppose, too, that the $100,000 *could* be invested in some other way and earn $6,000 per year, and the farmer *could* work equally pleasantly elsewhere and earn $50,000 per year. Then the farm's implicit costs will be $56,000, and zero economic profit means that the farm is earning $56,000 in *accounting profit* each year. This won't make a farmer ecstatic, but it will make it worthwhile to keep working the farm. After all, if the farmer quits and takes up the next best alternative, he or she will do no better.

To emphasize that zero economic profit is not an unpleasant outcome, economists often replace it with the term **normal profit**, which is a synonym for "zero economic profit," or "just enough accounting profit to cover implicit costs." Using this language, we can summarize long-run conditions at the typical firm this way:

Normal profit Another name for zero economic profit.

> In the long run, the competitive firm will earn normal profit—that is, zero economic profit.

Perfect Competition and Plant Size

There is one more characteristic of competitive markets in the long run that we have not yet discussed: plant size. It turns out that the same forces—entry and exit—that cause all firms to earn zero economic profit *also* determine the size of each firm's plant.

> In long-run equilibrium, a competitive firm will operate with the plant and output level that bring it to the bottom of its LRATC curve.

To see why, let's consider what would happen if this condition were violated. Figure 9(a) illustrates a firm in a perfectly competitive market. The firm faces a market price of P_1 and produces quantity q_1, where $MC_1 = MR_1$. With its current plant, the firm has average costs given by ATC_1. Note that the firm is earning zero profit, since average cost is equal to P_1 at the best output level.

But panel (a) does *not* show a true long-run equilibrium. How do we know this? First, in the long run, the typical firm will want to expand. Why? Because by increasing its plant size, it could slide down its $LRATC$ curve and produce more output at

FIGURE 9 Perfect Competition and Plant Size

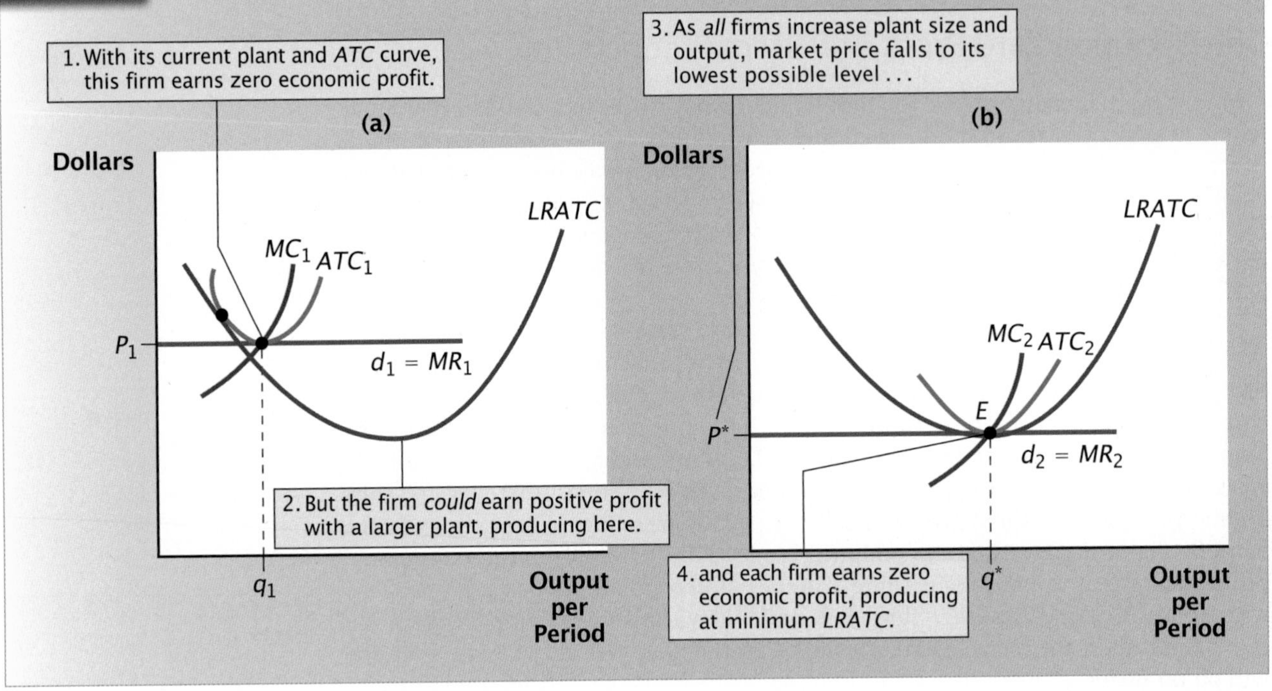

1. With its current plant and *ATC* curve, this firm earns zero economic profit.

3. As *all* firms increase plant size and output, market price falls to its lowest possible level . . .

(a)

Dollars

LRATC

MC_1 ATC_1

P_1

$d_1 = MR_1$

2. But the firm *could* earn positive profit with a larger plant, producing here.

q_1

Output per Period

(b)

Dollars

LRATC

MC_2 ATC_2

P^*

E

$d_2 = MR_2$

4. and each firm earns zero economic profit, producing at minimum *LRATC*.

q^*

Output per Period

a lower cost per unit. Since it is a perfectly competitive firm—a small participant in the market—it can expand in this way *without* worrying about affecting the market price. As a result, the firm, after expanding, could operate on a new, lower *ATC* curve, so that *ATC* is less than *P*. That is, by expanding, the firm could potentially earn an economic profit.

Second, this same opportunity to earn positive economic profit will attract new entrants that will establish larger plants from the outset.

Expansion by existing firms and entry by new ones increase market output and bring down the market price. (This would be illustrated by a rightward shift of the market supply curve, which is not shown in the figure.) The process will stop—and a long-run equilibrium will be established—only when there is no potential to earn positive economic profit with *any* plant size. As you can see in panel (b), this condition is satisfied only when each firm is operating at the minimum point on its *LRATC* curve, using the plant represented by ATC_2, and producing output of q^*. Entry and expansion must continue in this market until the price falls to P^* because only then will each firm—doing the best that it can do—earn zero economic profit. (*Question:* In the long run, what would happen to a firm if it refused to increase its plant size?)

A Summary of the Competitive Firm in the Long Run

Panel (b) of Figure 9 summarizes everything you have learned about the competitive firm in long-run equilibrium. The typical firm, taking the market price P^* as given, produces the profit-maximizing output level q^*, where $MR = MC$. Since this is the long run, each firm will be earning zero economic profit, so we also know that

$P^* = ATC$. But since $P^* = MC$ and $P^* = ATC$, it must also be true that $MC = ATC$. As you learned in Chapter 7, MC and ATC are equal only at the minimum point of the ATC curve. Thus, we know that each firm must be operating at the lowest possible point on the ATC curve for the plant it is operating. Finally, each firm selects the plant that makes its $LRATC$ as low as possible, so each operates at the minimum point on its $LRATC$ curve.

As you can see, there is a lot going on in Figure 9(b). But we can put it all together with a very simple statement:

> *In long-run equilibrium, the competitive firm operates where:*
> MC = *minimum* ATC = *minimum* LRATC = P.

In Figure 9(b), this equality is satisfied when the firm produces at point *E*, where its demand, marginal cost, ATC, and $LRATC$ curves all intersect. This is a figure well worth remembering, since it summarizes so much information about competitive markets in a single picture. (Here is a useful self-test: Close the book, put away your notes, and draw a set of diagrams in which one curve at a time does *not* pass through the common intersection point of the other three. Then explain which principle of firm or market behavior is violated by your diagram. Do this separately for all four curves.)

Figure 9(b) also explains one of the important ways in which perfect competition benefits consumers: In the long run, each firm is driven to the plant size and output level at which its cost per unit is as low as possible. This lowest possible cost per unit is also the price per unit that consumers will pay. If price were any lower than P^*, it would not be worthwhile for firms to continue producing the good in the long run. Thus, given the $LRATC$ curve faced by each firm in this industry—a curve that is determined by the technology of production and the prices of its inputs—P^* is the lowest possible price that will ensure the continued availability of the good. In perfect competition, consumers are getting the best deal they could possibly get.

WHAT HAPPENS WHEN THINGS CHANGE?

So far, you've learned how competitive firms make decisions, how these decisions lead to a short-run equilibrium in the market, and how the market moves from short- to long-run equilibrium through entry and exit. Now, it's time to ask: *What happens when things change?*

A Change in Demand

In Figure 10, panel (a) shows a competitive market that is initially in long-run equilibrium at point *A*, where the market demand curve D_1 and supply curve S_1 intersect. Panel (b) shows conditions at the firm, which faces demand curve d_1 and produces the profit-maximizing quantity q_1.

But now suppose that the market demand curve shifts rightward to D_2 and remains there. (This shift could be caused by any one of several factors. If you can't list some of them, turn back to Chapter 3.) Panels (c) and (d) show what happens. In the *short run*, the shift in demand moves the market equilibrium to point *B*, with market output Q_{SR} and price P_{SR}. At the same time, the demand curve facing each

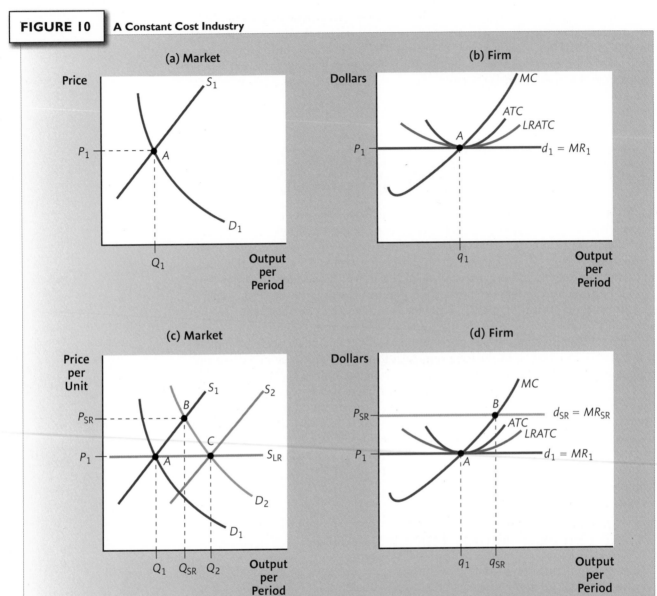

| FIGURE 10 | A Constant Cost Industry |

At point A in panel (a), the market is in long-run equilibrium. The typical firm in panel (b) operates at the minimum of its ATC and LRATC curves, and earns zero economic profit. The lower panels show what happens if demand increases. In the short run, the market reaches a new equilibrium at point B in panel (c), and the typical firm in panel (d) earns economic profit at the higher price P_{SR}. In the long run, profit attracts entry, increasing market supply and lowering price. Entry continues until economic profit at the typical firm in panel (d) is reduced to zero, which requires the price to drop to P_1, its original level. In panel (d), the typical firm returns to point A, and in panel (c), the new long-run market equilibrium is point C. The increase in demand raises output, but leaves price unchanged, as shown by the horizontal long-run supply curve connecting points A and C.

firm shifts upward, and each firm raises output to the new profit-maximizing level q_{SR}. At this output level, $P > ATC$, so each firm is earning economic profit. Thus, the short-run impact of an increase in demand is (1) a rise in market price, (2) a rise in market quantity, and (3) economic profits.

When we turn to the long run, we know that economic profit will attract the entry of new firms. And, as you learned a few pages ago, an increase in the number of firms shifts the market supply curve rightward, which drives down the price until the economic profit is eliminated. But how far must the price fall in order to bring this about? That is, how far can we expect the market supply curve to shift? That depends on whether or not the expansion of the industry causes each firm's cost curves to shift.

A Constant Cost Industry

Let's assume, for now, that a change in industry output (such as when new firms enter) has no impact on the cost curves of the individual firm. This is called a **constant cost industry**. Then in panel (c), entry will continue—and the supply curve will continue shifting rightward—until the price returns to P_1, its original level. (At any higher price, each firm would still be earning economic profit, and new firms would still be entering.) Our new long-run equilibrium occurs at point C, with the supply curve S_2, price P_1, and market quantity Q_2. Panel (d) shows what happens at the typical firm: The price moves back to P_1, so the demand curve facing the firm shifts back to d_1, and the typical firm returns to its original level of output q_1.

There is a lot going on in Figure 10. But we can make the story simpler if we *skip over* the short-run equilibrium at point *B,* and just ask: What happens in the *long run* after the demand curve shifts rightward? The answer is: The market equilibrium will move from point A to point C. A line drawn through these two points tells us, in the long run, the market price we can expect for any quantity the market provides. In Figure 10, this is the horizontal line, which is called the *long-run supply curve* (S_{LR}).

> The **long-run supply curve** *shows the relationship between market price and market quantity produced after all long-run adjustments have taken place.*

Notice that, because we are dealing with a constant cost industry, the long-run supply curve is horizontal.

> *In a constant cost industry, in which industry output has no effect on individual firms' cost curves, the long-run supply curve is horizontal. In the long-run, the industry will supply any amount of output demanded at an unchanged price.*

An Increasing Cost Industry

Our trip through Figure 10 illustrated the impact of an increase in demand for a constant cost industry, in which a rise in industry output has no impact on the cost curves of individual firms. But a constant cost industry is just one possible case.

In an **increasing cost industry**, the entry of new firms that use the same inputs as existing firms drives up input prices. This, in turn, causes each firm's *LRATC* curve to shift upward.

For example, corn farming uses a great deal of land in the Midwestern United States. Over the past decade, the demand for U.S. corn has increased dramatically, for two main reasons. First, increases in global incomes—especially in emerging market economies such as China and India—have raised the demand for corn (both for eating and for feeding poultry and livestock). Second, the United States has required gasoline refiners to blend increasing amounts of ethanol (made from corn) into gasoline. (In 2011, more than half of all U.S. corn produced was used to make ethanol.) As the demand for U.S. corn has increased, U.S. corn farms have expanded,

Constant cost industry An industry in which the long-run supply curve is horizontal because each firm's cost curves are unaffected by changes in industry output.

Long-run supply curve A curve indicating price and quantity combinations in an industry after all long-run adjustments have taken place.

Increasing cost industry An industry in which the long-run supply curve slopes upward because each firm's *LRATC* curve shifts upward as industry output increases.

⚠ DANGEROUS CURVES

Do demand shifts cause supply shifts? In Chapter 3, you learned that a change in price causes a movement *along the supply curve*. But in Figures 10 and 11, after the demand curve shifts rightward from D_1 to D_2, the price rises, and then . . . the *supply curve shifts!* So, now you may be wondering: When the demand curve shifts, does the resulting rise in price cause a movement *along* the supply curve, or a *shift* of the supply curve?

The complete answer is: both. But to avoid confusion, it's important to distinguish what happens in the short run and the long run. In Figures 10 and 11, you can see that the shift in demand first raises the price, moving us *along* the supply curve S_1 from point A to point B in the short run. This is just as you learned in Chapter 3, which only dealt with the short run. (In that chapter, we assumed the number of firms was constant.)

But now, we're extending our analysis further, into the long run. The rise in price causes new firms to enter by creating profit for firms already in the industry. An *increase in the number of firms* is a shift variable for the supply curve. This is why, in the long run, the supply curve shifts from S_1 to S_2.

and new farms have entered the industry. These new and expanding farms have bid up the price of farmland suitable for growing corn.

Because *every* farm in the industry—the existing ones as well as new entrants—must pay more for farmland, their *LRATC* curves have shifted upward (greater cost per unit at each output level).

Let's see how this changes the graphical analysis of an increase in demand. Panel (a) in Figure 11 shows a competitive market in an initial long-run equilibrium at point A. Panel (b) shows the situation of a single competitive firm (corn farm) in this market, facing demand curve d_1 and producing output level q_1. To keep the diagram simple, we've left out the *MC* and *ATC* curves for the firm and show the only cost curve that will matter to our analysis: the *LRATC* curve. Initially, the firm operates at the minimum point of $LRATC_1$.

Now suppose the demand curve shifts rightward to D_2 [panel (a)]. As a result, the short-run market equilibrium moves to point B, and price rises to P_{SR}. Because the typical firm enjoys economic profit (not shown), entry will occur in the long run, and the

FIGURE 11   An Increasing Cost Industry

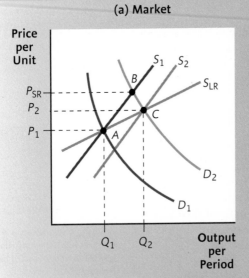

(a) Market

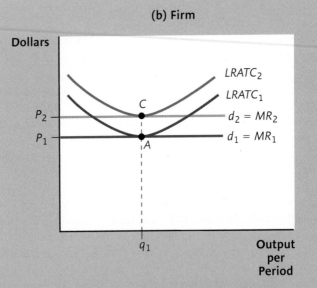

(b) Firm

Point A in both panels shows the initial long-run market equilibrium, with the typical firm earning zero economic profit. After demand increases, the market reaches a new short-run equilibrium at point B in panel (a). At the higher price, the typical firm earns economic profit (not shown). In the long run, profit attracts entry, supply increases and price begins to fall. But in an increasing cost industry, the rise in industry output also causes costs to rise, shifting up the LRATC curve. In the final, long-run market equilibrium (point C in both panels), price at P₂ is higher than originally, and the typical firm once again earns zero economic profit. The increase in demand raises both output and price, as shown [in panel (a)] by the upward-sloping long-run supply curve.

market supply curve shifts rightward. As usual, the supply curve will continue shifting rightward until economic profit is eliminated.

But this time, the entry of new firms and the rise in industry output causes the typical firm's *LRATC* curve to shift *upward* to $LRATC_2$. With higher long-run average cost, zero profit will occur at a price *higher* than the original price P_1. In Figure 11, the supply curve stops shifting when the price reaches P_2, with the new market equilibrium at point *C*. As panel (b) shows, once the price reaches P_2, the typical firm—facing the horizontal demand curve d_2—operates at the minimum point on $LRATC_2$, earning zero economic profit.

Let's now concentrate on just the long-run impact of the change in demand, which moves the equilibrium from point *A* to point *C*. Connecting these two equilibrium points gives us the long-run supply curve for this industry. As you can see, the curve slopes *upward*, telling us that the industry will supply greater output, but only with a higher price.

> *In an* increasing cost industry, *a rise in industry output shifts up each firm's* LRATC *curve, so that zero economic profit occurs at a higher price. The long-run supply curve slopes upward.*

The long-run supply curve tells us that an increasing cost industry will deliver more output, but only at a higher price. It also tells us that, if industry output decreases, the price will drop. This is because a decrease in output would cause each firm's *LRATC* curve to shift *downward* so that zero profit would be established at a *lower* price than initially.

A Decreasing Cost Industry

In a **decreasing cost industry,** a rise in industry output causes input prices to *fall*, and the *LRATC* curve to shift downward at each firm. This might occur for a number of reasons. As an industry expands, there might be more workers in the area with the needed skills, making it easier and less expensive for each firm to find and recruit qualified employees. Or transportation costs might decrease.

For example, suppose that a modest size city has just a few sushi restaurants. Periodically, a partially loaded truck makes a special trip from a distant larger city to deliver raw fish, nori seaweed, wasabi, and other special ingredients to these few restaurants. Transportation costs—part of the price of the ingredients—will be rather high.

Now suppose that demand for sushi meals increases. Profits at the existing restaurants attract entry. With more restaurants ordering ingredients, the same delivery truck makes the same trip, but now it is fully loaded and the transportation costs are shared among more restaurants. As a result, transportation costs at *each* restaurant decrease—and each restaurant's *LRATC* curve shifts down. Competition among the restaurants then ensures that prices will drop to match the lower *LRATC*. As a result, the long-run effect of an increase in demand is a *lower* price for eating sushi at a restaurant—a downward sloping long-run supply curve.

Decreasing cost industry An industry in which the long-run supply curve slopes downward because each firm's *LRATC* curve shifts downward as industry output increases.

DANGEROUS CURVES

Similar-sounding terms, but different concepts You've learned a number of different terms having to do with rising costs. A direct comparison can help to prevent confusing them.

Diseconomies of scale (from Chapter 7) refers to a rise in long-run average cost due to an increase in a firm's *own* output. This is illustrated by a movement *along* the upward sloping portion of the firm's *LRATC* curve.

Increasing-cost industry (from this chapter) refers to an upward *shift* of the entire *LRATC* curve, due to higher input prices caused by entry.

Increasing marginal cost refers to the upward-sloping portion of the firm's marginal cost curve. It is a short-run concept, associated with diminishing marginal returns (see Chapter 7).

Each of these terms has its opposite, having to do with *falling* costs: economies of scale, decreasing cost industry, and decreasing marginal cost. You might want to test yourself by explaining how these three terms differ from one another.

FIGURE 12	**A Decreasing Cost Industry**

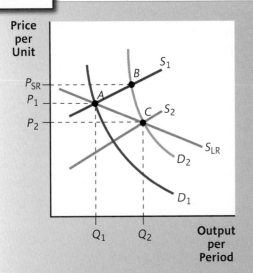
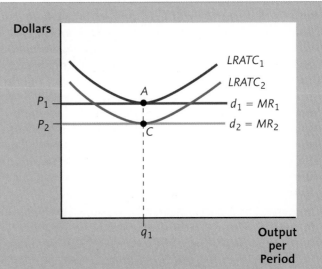

Point A in both panels shows the initial long-run market equilibrium, with the typical firm earning zero economic profit. After demand increases, the market reaches a new short-run equilibrium at point B in panel (a). At the higher price, the typical firm earns economic profit (not shown). In the long run, profit attracts entry, supply increases, and price begins to fall. But in a decreasing cost industry, the rise in industry output causes costs to fall, shifting down the LRATC curve. In the final, long-run market equilibrium (point C in both panels), price at P₂ is lower than originally, and the typical firm once again earns zero economic profit. The increase in demand raises output but lowers price, as shown [in panel (a)] by the downward-sloping long-run supply curve.

Figure 12 illustrates how a decreasing cost industry behaves after an increase in demand. In panel (a), after the demand curve shifts rightward, the market equilibrium moves from *A* to *B* in the short run. The typical firm earns economic profit (not shown). In the long run, profit causes entry. But now, as the industry expands, the *LRATC* curve at each firm shifts *downward*. With lower cost per unit, zero economic profit occurs at a long-run equilibrium price *lower than the original price*. In the figure, the market reaches its new long-run equilibrium at point *C*, at the new, lower price P_2.

When we draw a line through the initial equilibrium at point *A* and the new long-run equilibrium at point *C*, we get the long-run supply curve for this industry. As you can see, the curve slopes downward: In a decreasing cost industry, as industry output rises, the *price drops*.

> In a decreasing cost industry, *a rise in industry output shifts down each firm's* LRATC *curve, so that zero economic profit occurs at a lower price. The long-run supply curve slopes downward.*

The long-run supply curve tells us that in a decreasing cost industry, the more output produced, the lower the price. On the other hand, if industry output were to fall, the price would rise. This is because a decrease in output would cause each firm's *LRATC* curve to shift *upward*, so that zero profit would be established at a *higher* price than initially.

Market Signals and the Economy

The previous discussion of changes in demand included a lot of details, so let's take a moment to go over it in broad outline. You've seen that an *increase* in demand always leads to an *increase* in market output in the short run, as existing firms raise their output levels, and an even *greater* increase in output in the long run, as new firms enter the market.

We could have also analyzed what happens when demand *decreases,* but you'll be asked to do this on your own in the end-of-chapter problem set. If you do it correctly, you'll find that the leftward shift of the demand curve will cause a drop in output in the short run and an even greater drop in the long run. The effect on price will depend on the nature of the industry (i.e., whether it is a constant, increasing, or decreasing cost industry).

But now let's step back from these details and see what they really tell us about the economy. We can start with a simple fact: In the real world, the demand curves for different goods and services are constantly shifting. For example, over the last couple of decades, Americans have developed an increased taste for bottled water. The average American gulped down 8 gallons of the stuff in 1990, and more than three times that much—28 gallons—in 2010. As a consequence, the *production* of bottled water has increased dramatically. This seems like magic: Consumers want more bottled water and, presto, the economy provides it! Our model of perfect competition shows us the workings behind this apparent magic, the logical sequence of events leading from our desire to consume more bottled water and its appearance on store shelves.

The secret—the trick up the magician's sleeve—is this: As demand increases or decreases in a market, *prices change.* And price changes act as *signals* for firms to enter or exit an industry. How do these signals work? As you've seen, when demand increases, the price tends to initially *overshoot* its long-run equilibrium value during the adjustment process, creating sizable temporary profits for existing firms. Similarly, when demand decreases, the price falls *below* its long-run equilibrium value, creating sizable losses for existing firms. These exaggerated, temporary movements in price, and the profits and losses they cause, are almost irresistible forces, pulling new firms into the market or driving existing firms out. In this way, the economy is driven to produce whatever collection of goods consumers prefer.

Figure 13 illustrates the process. In the upper panel, as Americans shifted their tastes toward bottled water, the market demand curve for this good shifted rightward from D_1 to D_2. Initially, the price rose *above* its new long-run equilibrium value, to P_2, leading to high profits at existing bottled water firms such as Poland Spring and Arrowhead. High profits, in the long run, attracted entry—especially the entry of new brands from established firms not previously selling bottled water, such as Pepsi's Aquafina and Coke's Dasani. Entry shifted the supply curve rightward, to S_2, bringing the price back down somewhat to P_3. (We are viewing bottled water as an increasing cost industry.) As a result, production expanded to match the increase in demand by consumers. More of our land, labor, capital, and entrepreneurial skills are now used to produce bottled water. Where did these resources come from?

In large part, they were freed up from those industries that experienced a *decline* in demand. In these industries, lower prices have caused exit, freeing up land, labor, capital, and entrepreneurship to be used in other, expanding industries, such as the bottled water industry. The lower panel of Figure 13 shows a production possibilities frontier (PPF) for bottled water and other goods. As production of bottled water increases from Q_1 to Q_2 to Q_3, the production of other things decreases. (If we wanted

FIGURE 13   How a Change in Demand Reallocates Resources

In the upper panel, an increased desire for bottled water shifts the market demand curve rightward, from D_1 to D_2. Price and quantity rise in the short run, and we move from A to B along short-run supply curve S_1. The lower panel shows the corresponding short-run movement from A to B along the economy's PPF: Greater production of bottled water, less production of other things.

In the long run, the higher price creates economic profit, attracting new firms, and shifting the supply curve rightward (upper panel). Price falls and quantity rises further. In the figure, we assume bottled water is an increasing cost industry, so entry brings the price down to P_3, at point C, which is higher than the original price. In the lower panel, the further long-run increase in bottled water production moves us along the PPF, from B to C.

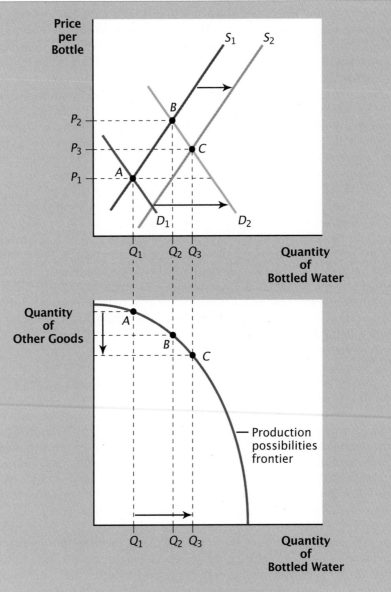

to illustrate economic growth at the same time, the entire PPF would shift outward. In that case, increased production of bottled water would mean that production of other things would *increase* by less than otherwise.)

This leads us to an important observation:

Market signals Price changes that cause changes in production to match changes in consumer demand.

> *In a market economy, price changes act as **market signals**, ensuring that the pattern of production matches the pattern of consumer demands. When demand increases, a rise in price signals firms to enter the market, increasing industry output. When demand decreases, a fall in price signals firms to exit the market, decreasing industry output.*

Importantly, in a market economy, no single person or government agency directs this process. There is no central command post where information about consumer demand is assembled, and no one tells firms how to respond. Instead, existing firms and new entrants, in their *own* search for higher profits, respond to market signals and help move the overall market in the direction it needs to go. This is what Adam Smith meant when he suggested that individual decision makers act—as if guided by an *invisible hand*—for the overall benefit of society, even though, as individuals, they are merely trying to satisfy their own desires.

A Change in Technology

You've just learned how production in perfectly competitive markets responds to changes in consumer demand. Demand for a good increases, and production rises. Demand decreases; production falls.

But the service of competitive markets extends to other types of changes as well. In this section, we'll explore how competitive markets ensure that the benefits of technological advances are enjoyed by consumers.

One industry that has experienced especially rapid technological changes is the solar power industry, which makes the solar panels that convert the sun's energy into electricity. A common measure of the price of a solar panel is "price per installed watt," which is the consumer's cost (including installation) for each watt of electricity-generating capacity. Rapid advances in technology have lowered the cost of producing and installing solar panels, resulting in lower prices for consumers—from $9.50 per installed watt in 2003 down to $7 per installed watt in 2010.

Figure 14 illustrates the market for solar panels as it undergoes technological change. In panel (a), the market begins at point A, where the price per installed watt is $9.50. In panel (b), the typical solar panel firm (which we'll assume both produces and installs the systems) produces quantity q_1 and—with long-run average cost curve $LRATC_1$—earns zero economic profit.

Now let's see what happens when a new technology lowers the cost of producing solar panels. Suppose first that only one firm uses the new technology. This firm will enjoy a downward shift in its $LRATC$ curve from $LRATC_1$ to $LRATC_2$. Because this firm is so small relative to the market, it can produce all it wants and continue to sell at $9.50. Although we have not drawn in the new MC curve, you can see that the firm has several output levels from which to choose where price exceeds cost per unit and it can earn economic profit.

But not for long. Eventually (in the long run), economic profit at this firm will cause two things to happen. First, all other firms in the market will have a powerful incentive to adopt the new technology so they can lower their costs too. Under perfect competition, they can do so; there are no barriers that prevent any firm from using the same technology as any other. As these other firms adopt the new technology, their $LRATC$ curves, too, will drop down to $LRATC_2$.

Second, outsiders will have an incentive to enter this industry and use the new technology, shifting the market supply curve rightward (from S_1 to S_2) and driving down the market price. The process will stop only when the market price has reached the level at which firms using the new technology earn zero economic profit. In Figure 14, this occurs at a price of $7 per installed watt.

From this example, we can draw two conclusions about technological change under perfect competition. First, what will happen to a solar panel maker that is reluctant to use the new technology? As other firms make the change, and the market

FIGURE 14 — Technological Change in Perfect Competition

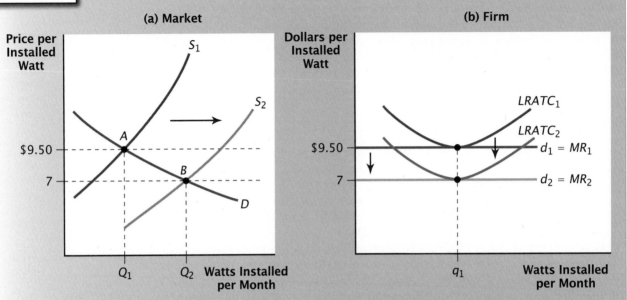

Technological change may reduce LRATC. In panel (b), the first solar panel firms to adopt new, cost-saving technologies earn economic profit in the short run, because they can initially sell at the old market price of $9.50 per installed watt. That profit leads its competitors to adopt the same technology and attracts new entrants. As market supply increases, price falls until it reaches $7 per installed watt, and each firm is once again earning zero economic profit.

price falls from $9.50 to $7, the reluctant firm will suffer an economic loss, because its average cost will remain at $9.50. Thus, a firm that refuses to adopt the new technology will be forced to exit the industry. In the end, all firms that remain in the market must use the new technology.

Second, who benefits from the new technology in the long run? Not the solar panel makers who adopt it. Some of them—the earliest adopters—may enjoy short-run profit before the price adjusts completely. But in the long run, all firms will be right back where they started, earning zero economic profit. The gainers are consumers of solar panels, because they benefit from the lower price.

More generally, we can summarize the impact of technological change as follows:

> *Under perfect competition, a technological advance leads to a rightward shift of the market supply curve, decreasing market price. In the short run, early adopters may enjoy economic profit, but in the long run, all adopters will earn zero economic profit. Firms that refuse to use the new technology will not survive.*

Technological advances in many competitive industries—farming, mining, lumber, communication, entertainment, and others—have indeed spread quickly, shifting market supply curves rapidly and steadily rightward over the past 100 years. Competitive firms in these industries have had to continually adapt to new technologies in order to survive, leading to huge rewards for consumers.

USING THE THEORY

REAL ESTATE AGENTS AND THE ZERO-PROFIT RESULT

In the body of the chapter, you learned that firms in perfectly competitive markets earn zero economic profit in the long run, due to easy entry and exit. In all of the examples we explored, entry and exit eliminate economic profit and loss by changing the market *price* of output.

But what about markets in which, for one reason or another, entry and exit do *not* affect the market price? Will the zero-profit result still hold? Yes—but with a twist. In these markets, instead of prices, *costs* adjust to eliminate economic profit and loss. Let's see how this works in the market for real estate agents' services.

First, some background. Most homeowners who want to sell a home sign a contract with a real estate agent, who is given the exclusive right to sell it for a period of time. The home seller pays the agent a commission, typically equal to 6 percent of the home's selling price. Half of this goes to the buyer's agent, leaving the seller's agent with a commission of 3 percent. So on a $100,000 home, the agent will earn a $3,000 commission, and on a one-million dollar home, the agent will earn $30,000.

We can view a real estate agent as a business firm that uses inputs (such as office space, transportation, a computer, and the agent's time), to produce an output: completed home sales. We'll assume for simplicity that all of these inputs can be changed on short notice, so we won't need to distinguish between short-run and long-run costs.

Panel (a) of Figure 15 shows the situation facing a typical agent in a city where, for simplicity, we assume every home initially sells for $200,000. (Ignore the higher demand curve for now.) The price of the agent's output is the commission (in dollars) on each sale. Our representative agent earns a commission of 3 percent per home, or $6,000 per home, no matter how many of them he or she sells. So the initial demand curve facing the agent, labeled $d_1 = MR_1$, is horizontal (infinitely elastic) at $6,000.

Because the demand curve is horizontal, our agent can sell as many homes as he or she wants without having to lower the price (commission) per sale. Why, then, doesn't an agent keep increasing the number of homes sold without limit, and earn an almost unlimited income?

Because of *costs*. To sell more homes requires greater amounts of inputs—especially the agent's time—so costs rise with output. Specifically, an agent who sells more homes must spend more time networking and canvassing neighborhoods to find clients, and more time on selling activities (showing homes to finicky buyers, negotiating with buyers' agents, and so forth). Each additional sale becomes more costly than the sale before, because the opportunity cost of the agent's time increases with each additional hour spent on these activities. This is why the *MC* curve slopes upward.

The profit-maximizing agent in the figure continues to increase the number of homes sold until the *MC* of one more sale equals the *MR* of $6,000, which occurs at point *A* (10 home sales per year). At that point, the agent's revenue is $6,000 × 10 = $60,000 per year in commissions. Note that at point *A* the agent's *ATC* (cost per sale) equals the commission per sale, so the agent is earning zero economic profit. Point *A* represents the typical agent when the market is in long-run equilibrium. Because

FIGURE 15 | **After Commissions Rise, Long-Run Profit Returns to Zero**

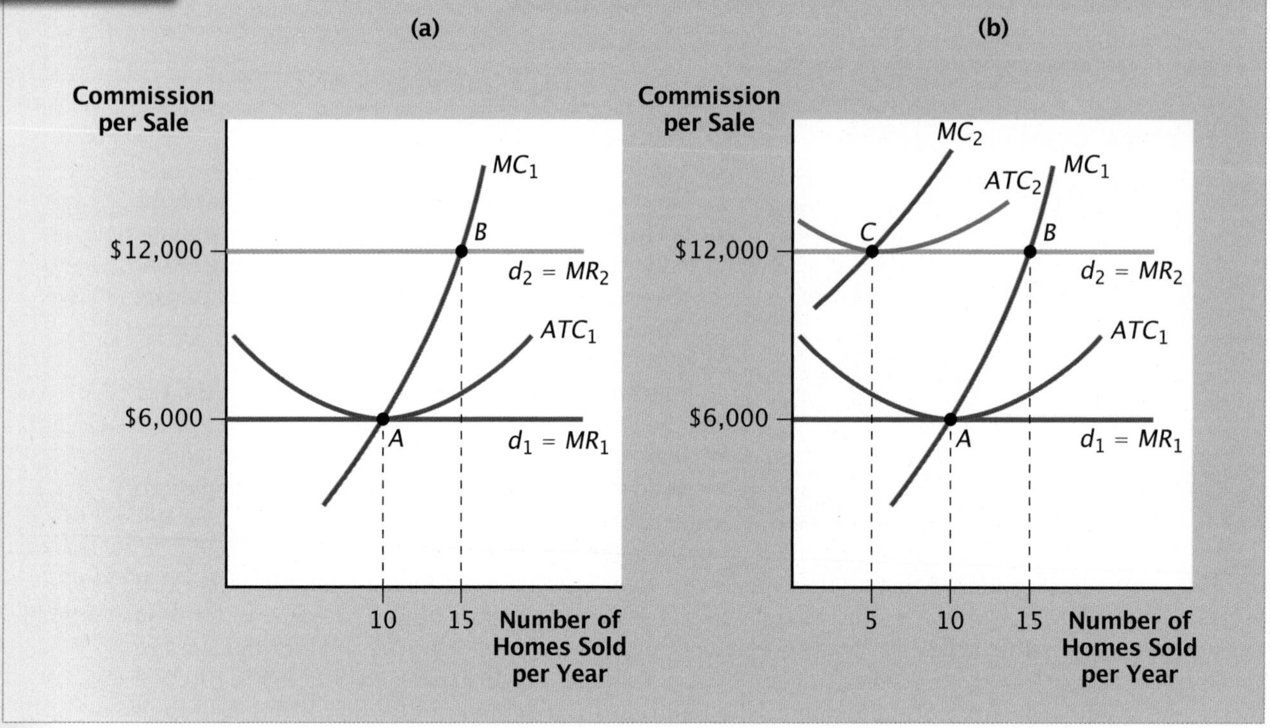

(a)

(b)

economic profit is zero, agents neither enter nor exit the market, so the number of agents remains constant.

Now, suppose the price of homes in the city doubles to $400,000 and stays there, but there is no change in the number of homes sold each year. The fixed 3 percent commission rate now translates to a higher *dollar* commission of $12,000. In panel (a), the demand curve facing the typical agent shifts upward, to $d_2 = MR_2$. The typical agent moves temporarily to point B, increasing sales to 15, which is where MC equals the now-higher MR of $12,000. The broker earns economic profit in the short run, because at 15 homes, the revenue per sale ($12,000) would be greater than the cost per sale (found on the ATC curve at 15). What about the long run? In a normal market, economic profit would attract entry, lowering the commission per sale until economic profit was back at zero. But real estate agents do not operate in a normal market, because their commission rate will remain at 3 percent. So with home prices at $400,000, the commission stays at $12,000. Does this mean that agents can continue to earn economic profit as long as home prices remain high?

The answer is no, because two things will happen in the market as the commission rises. First, with each current agent trying to sign more clients, and the total number of clients fixed (by assumption), each agent will have to work harder and longer to find new clients. Second, new agents will enter the market, attracted by the potential for economic profit. (In most states, you can become a licensed real estate agent after taking a short class and passing a test, at a cost of a few hundred dollars.) The entry of new agents will add further to the time and effort each agent will spend to find each client. Remember that an agent's time is an important component of costs. So after the commission rises to $12,000, and each agent must spend more time looking for clients, both the *ATC* curve (cost per sale) and the *MC* curve (cost per *additional* sale) will shift upward.

Panel (b) shows the new equilibrium in this market, after the *ATC* and *MC* curves have shifted upward, and each agent—doing the best he or she can do—is once again earning zero economic profit. This occurs at point *C*, where the typical agent still earns the higher commission of $12,000 on each sale, but now sells only 5 homes per year. We know that the cost curves must rise by just enough to create zero economic profit. If they rise by less, entry would still be occurring and the cost curves would still be rising, so we would not yet have reached our final equilibrium. (In the figure, the total revenue from commissions remains unchanged, because half as many homes are sold for twice the commission. Although a rise in home prices often seems to leave agents with the same total revenue—as discussed below—this need not be the case.)

Zero economic profit for real estate agents surprises some people, especially after home prices rise. At such times, people assume that real estate agents are "making a killing" (in our language, earning "great economic profit"). To be sure, there are always some star agents who attract a steady stream of new clients and do very well. They do even better when home prices are high. And for a short time (before entry occurs), even the *typical* agent may earn some economic profit.

But because new agents can enter the market quickly, adjustment to zero-profit equilibrium occurs quickly as well. So the typical agent will not benefit much, or benefit for very long, after home prices rise. And the theory is supported by research[2] showing that in areas with higher home prices, more agents compete for each client, so that each agent—with higher costs—sells fewer homes. For example, in 1990, the average home price in Boston was twice that in Minneapolis. But the typical Boston real estate agent sold half as many homes per year (3.3) as his counterpart in Minneapolis (6.6), resulting in the same total commission earnings per year.

A similar result occurs when home prices rise over time within a local market. From 1980 to 1990, those cities in which home prices rose most rapidly also experienced the most rapid entry of new agents. And the number of homes sold by a typical agent tended to fall by the same proportion as home prices (and commissions) rose.

Indirect evidence suggests that the same forces have continued to rule the market more recently. Figure 16 shows yearly membership in the National

[2] Chang-Tai Hsieh and Enrico Moretti, "Can Free Entry be Inefficient? Fixed Commissions and Social Waste in the Real Estate Industry," *Journal of Political Economy*, Vol 111, October 2003. See also Steven J. Dubner and Steven D. Levitt, "Endangered Species" posted on Freakonomics blog, March 5, 2006.

FIGURE 16   **Membership in National Association of Realtors**

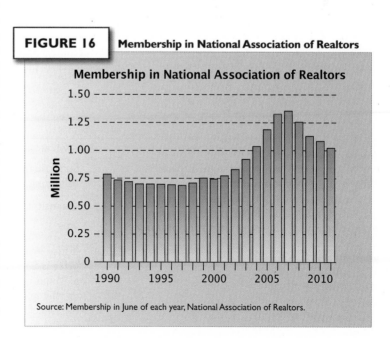

Source: Membership in June of each year, National Association of Realtors.

Association of Realtors. From 1998 to 2007—as home prices rose rapidly during the housing boom—the number of real estate agents grew rapidly as well, suggesting increased competition for clients and fewer home sales for each agent. Even as the average commission skyrocketed during the housing boom, the median income of real estate agents (not shown) changed very little.

Finally, notice what happened as housing prices and commissions began falling in 2008. Many agents exited, just as the theory predicts, reducing competition for clients among those that remained. You'll be asked to analyze the case of falling commissions and exit from the market in an end-of-chapter question.

SUMMARY

Perfect competition is a market structure in which (1) there are large numbers of relatively small buyers and sellers; (2) sellers offer a standardized product; (3) sellers can easily enter or exit from the market; and (4) buyers and sellers are well-informed. While few real markets satisfy these conditions precisely, the model is still useful in a wide variety of cases.

Each perfectly competitive firm faces a horizontal demand curve; it can sell as much as it wishes at the market price. The firm chooses its profit-maximizing output level by increasing output until marginal cost is equal to the market price. Its *short-run supply curve* is that part of its MC curve that lies above the average variable cost curve. Total profit is profit per unit $(P - ATC)$ times the profit-maximizing quantity.

In the short run, market price is determined where the market supply curve—the horizontal sum of all firms' supply curves—crosses the market demand curve. In short-run equilibrium, existing firms can earn a profit (in which case new firms will enter) or suffer a loss (in which case existing firms will exit). Entry or exit will continue until, in the long run, each firm is earning zero economic profit.

At each competitive firm in long-run equilibrium, price = marginal cost = minimum average total cost = minimum long-run average total cost.

When demand curves shift, prices change more in the short run than in the long run. The temporary, exaggerated price movements act as *market signals*, ensuring that output expands and contracts in each industry to match the pattern of consumer preferences.

In the long run, an increase in demand can result in a higher, lower, or unchanged market price, depending on whether the good is produced, respectively, in an *increasing cost industry, decreasing cost industry,* or *constant cost industry*. The long-run supply curve slopes upward in an increasing cost industry and slopes downward for a decreasing cost industry. In a constant cost industry, the long-run supply curve will be horizontal.

A technological advance in a perfectly competitive market causes the equilibrium price to fall and equilibrium quantity to rise. Each competitive firm must use the new technology in order to survive, but consumers reap all the benefits by paying a lower price.

PROBLEM SET

Answers to even-numbered Problems can be found on the text Web site through www.cengagebrain.com

1. Assume that the market for cardboard is perfectly competitive (if not very exciting). In each of the following scenarios, should a typical firm continue to produce or should it shut down in the short run? Draw a diagram that illustrates the firm's situation in each case.
   a. Minimum ATC = $2.00
      Minimum AVC = $1.50
      Market price = $1.75
   b. MR = $1.00
      Minimum AVC = $1.50
      Minimum ATC = $2.00

2. Suppose that a perfectly competitive firm has the following total variable costs (*TVC*):

Quantity:	0	1	2	3	4	5	6
TVC:	$0	$6	$11	$15	$18	$22	$28

It also has total fixed costs (*TFC*) of $6. If the market price is $5 per unit:
   a. Find the firm's profit-maximizing quantity using the marginal revenue and marginal cost approach.
   b. Check your results by re-solving the problem using the total revenue and total cost approach. Is the firm earning a positive profit, suffering a loss, or breaking even?

3. "A *profit-maximizing* competitive firm will produce the quantity of output at which price *exceeds* cost per unit by the greatest possible amount." True or false? Explain briefly. [Hint: See Figure 3(a).]

4. The following table gives quantity supplied and quantity demanded at various prices in the perfectly competitive meat-packing market:

Price (per lb.)	Q_S (in millions of lbs.)	Q_D (in millions of lbs.)
$1.00	10	100
$1.25	15	90
$1.50	25	75
$1.75	40	63
$2.00	55	55
$2.25	65	40

Assume that each firm in the meat-packing industry faces the following cost structure:

Pounds	TC
60,000	$110,000
61,000	$111,000
62,000	$112,000
63,000	$115,000

a. What is the profit-maximizing output level for the typical firm? (Hint: Calculate *MC* for each change in output, then find the equilibrium price, and calculate *MR* for each change in output.)
b. Is this market in long-run equilibrium? Why or why not? (Hint: Calculate *ATC*.)
c. What do you expect to happen to the number of meat-packing firms over the long run? Why?

5. Assume that the kitty litter industry is perfectly competitive and is presently in long-run equilibrium:
a. Draw diagrams for both the market and a typical firm, showing equilibrium price and quantity for the market, and *MC, ATC, AVC, MR,* and the demand curve for the firm.
b. Your friend has always had a passion to get into the kitty litter business. If the market is in long-run equilibrium, will it be profitable for him to jump in headfirst (so to speak)? Why or why not?
c. Suppose people begin to prefer dogs as pets, and cat ownership declines. Show on your diagrams from part (a) what happens in the industry and the firm in the long run, assuming that this is a constant cost industry.

6. In a perfectly competitive, increasing cost industry, is the long-run supply curve always flatter than the short-run market supply curve? Explain.

7. A student says, "My economics professor must be confused. First he tells us that in perfect competition, the demand curve is completely flat—horizontal. But then he draws a supply and demand diagram that has a downward-sloping demand curve. What's up with that?" Resolve this student's problem in a single sentence.

8. Assume that the firm shown in the following table produces output using one fixed input and one variable input.

Output	Price	Total Revenue	Marginal Revenue	Total Cost	Marginal Cost	Profit
0	$50	$0		$5		
					$35	
1	$50					
					$15	
2	$50					
					$35	
3	$50					
					$55	
4	$50					
					$65	

a. Complete this table and use it to find this firm's short-run profit-maximizing quantity of output. How much profit will this firm earn?
b. Redo the table and find the profit-maximizing quantity of output, if the price of the firm's fixed input rose from $5 to $10. How much profit will this firm earn now?
c. Now redo the original table and find the profit-maximizing quantity of output, if the price of the firm's variable input rose so that *MC* increased by $20 at each level of output. How much profit will this firm earn in this case?

9. Assume that the firm shown in the following table produces output using one fixed input and one variable input.
a. Complete this table and use it to find this firm's short-run profit-maximizing quantity of output. How much profit will this firm earn?

b. Redo the table and find the profit-maximizing quantity of output, if the price of the firm's fixed input fell by half. How much profit will this firm earn now?

c. Now redo the original table and find the profit-maximizing quantity of output, assuming the price of the variable input drops, and each *MC* value is 50% lower than before. How much profit will the firm earn in this case?

Output	Price	Total Revenue	Marginal Revenue	Total Cost	Marginal Cost	Profit
0	$3500	$0		$1000		
					$ 4000	
1	$3500					
					$ 3000	
2	$3500					
					$ 2000	
3	$3500					
					$ 1000	
4	$3500					
					$ 3000	
5	$3500					
					$ 4000	
6	$3500					
					$ 9000	
7	$3500					
					$36,000	
8	$3500					

10. Figure 11 shows the short-run and long-run adjustment process for an increasing cost industry responding to an increase in demand. Draw a similar two-panel diagram, illustrating the response of an increasing cost industry to a *decrease* in demand. Draw in the long-run supply curve. In the long run, will the price be higher or lower, compared to the initial price?

11. Figure 12 shows the short-run and long-run adjustment process for a decreasing cost industry responding to an increase in demand. Draw a similar two-panel diagram, illustrating the response of a decreasing cost industry to a *decrease* in demand. Draw in the long-run supply curve. In the long run,

will the price be higher or lower, compared to the initial price?

12. Draw a diagram similar to Figure 15, panel (b), but this time illustrate what happens to a typical real estate agent after a *fall* in home prices that causes the average commission to decrease from $6,000 to $3,000. Assume that the typical agent is initially selling 10 homes per year, and that the total number of homes sold in the market does not change. (Hint: If you do this correctly, your diagram should show each agent selling more homes than before.)

More Challenging

13. Draw a diagram for a perfectly competitive firm in long-run equilibrium. Include only the demand curve facing the firm and its *LRATC* curve. Then show the impact of an excise tax (some number of dollars per unit) imposed by the government *on this firm only* but not on any other firm in the market. Can we say what this firm will do in the long run?

14. In Chapter 4, you learned that when an excise tax is imposed on buyers or sellers in a competitive market, the equilibrium price rises, and the tax payment is shared between buyers and sellers. To obtain that result, we used the (short-run) market supply curve. Now let's extend the analysis to the long run. Draw a two panel diagram: one panel for the market (demand and short-run supply curves only), the other panel for the typical firm (demand and *LRATC* curves only). Suppose an excise tax (some number of dollars per unit) is imposed on *all* sellers (firms) in this market.
   a. Show what will happen in the *market* in the short run.
   b. Show what will happen in *both* diagrams (market and typical firm) in the long run, assuming that this is a *constant cost industry*. [Hint: After the tax is imposed, will the typical firm earn a profit or suffer a loss? Will entry or exit occur?]
   c. In the long run, do both buyers and sellers share in the payment of the excise tax? Explain briefly.

15. In recent years, Web sites such as zillow.com have made it easier for home sellers to figure out what price to charge for their home—one of the tasks that real estate agents perform for sellers. And a variety of other Web sites enable home buyers and sellers to find each other without using an agent at all. Suppose these new technologies catch on with half of the home sellers in an area, while the other half

continues to prefer selling with an agent. Assume that home prices and the commission rate stay unchanged.

Before accounting for entry or exit of agents:
a. Describe what would happen to a typical agent's *ATC* and *MC* curves.
b. What would happen to the number of homes sold by a typical agent?
c. What would happen to the economic profit of a typical agent?

Now take account of entry or exit of agents in response to the new technologies available for home selling. Compared to the results you found above, how will entry or exit affect:
d. A typical agent's *ATC* and *MC* curves?
e. The economic profit of the typical agent?
f. The number of homes sold by a typical agent?

© DAVID YOUNG-WOLFF/ALAMY

CHAPTER 10

Monopoly

"Monopoly" is as close as economics comes to a dirty word. It is often associated with thoughts of extraordinary power, unfairly high prices, and exploitation. Even in the board game *Monopoly*, when you take over a neighborhood by buying up adjacent properties, you exploit other players by charging them higher rent.

The negative reputation of monopoly is in many ways deserved. A monopoly, as the only firm in its market, has the power to act in ways that a perfectly competitive firm cannot. Adam Smith's "invisible hand"—which channels the behavior of perfectly competitive firms into a socially beneficial outcome—doesn't poke, prod, or even lay a finger on a monopoly firm. Left unchecked, it will *not* create the best of all possible worlds for consumers. Indeed, when a monopoly "takes over" a previously competitive industry, great harm can be done to consumers and society in general. Monopolies, therefore, present a problem that nations around the world address with the very *visible* hand of government policy.

At the same time, a mythology has developed around monopolies. The media often portray their power as absolute and unlimited, and their behavior as capricious and unpredictable. As you are about to see, this characterization goes too far. A monopoly's power may be formidable, but it's far from unlimited. And monopoly behavior—far from capricious—is remarkably predictable.

This chapter will help you understand what monopolies are, how they arise, how they behave, and how they respond to changing market conditions. Our focus here will be on *understanding* monopolies and *predicting* their behavior. A fuller assessment of monopolies and policies for dealing with them will be provided in Chapters 14 and 15.

WHAT IS A MONOPOLY?

In most of your purchases—a meal at a restaurant, a car, a college education—more than one seller is competing for your dollars, and you can choose which one to buy from. But in some markets, you have no choice at all. If you want to mail a letter for normal delivery, you must use the U.S. Postal Service. In most U.S. towns (at least for now), if you want cable television service, you must use the one cable television company in your neighborhood. Many cities have only a single local newspaper. And if you live in a very small town, you may have just one doctor, one gas station, or one movie theater to select from. These are all examples of *monopolies:*

Monopoly The only seller in a market, or a market with just one seller.

> *A monopoly refers to (1) a market in which only one firm sells a product with no close substitutes; or (2) the single firm that sells in that market.*

Notice the phrase "no close substitutes." This suggests that deciding whether a market or firm is a monopoly depends on the how easy it is for consumers to substitute the products of other sellers. This can be a matter of judgment.

Sometimes, the judgment is easy. At one extreme, think about the only doctor, attorney, or food market in a small, isolated town. Everyone would view these as monopolies, because no other firm in town offers a similar product or service. At the other extreme, think about Gap, Inc., the only seller of Gap jeans. Almost everyone would agree that Gap is not a monopoly, because other brands of jeans sold by other firms are very close substitutes.

But what about the sole cable company in a neighborhood? This is an "in-between" case. There are *reasonably* close substitutes for cable—including satellite TV and downloading shows from Netflix or iTunes. But for most consumers, these other services differ in major ways (convenience, experience, and the library of shows offered), so the substitutes are not *that* close to cable. So . . . is the cable company a monopoly? Economists typically answer yes. And we'll follow that convention in this chapter. But keep in mind that when we categorize "in between" cases as monopolies, we are making an important judgment: That the available substitutes are not very close.

How Monopolies Arise

The mere existence of a monopoly means that *something* is causing other firms to stay out of the market rather than enter and compete with the one firm already there. Broadly speaking, there must be some *barrier to entry*. The question, "Why is the market a monopoly?" then becomes, "What *barrier* prevents other firms from entering the market?" There are several possible answers.

Economies of Scale

One barrier to entry—and thus one explanation for a monopoly—is economies of scale. Recall from Chapter 7 that economies of scale in production causes a firm's long-run average cost curve to slope downward. That is, the more output the firm produces, the lower will be its cost per unit. If economies of scale persists through a large-enough range of output, then a single firm can produce for the entire market at lower cost than could two or more firms.

Figure 1 shows an example: the *LRATC* curve for a dry cleaner in a small town. We'll suppose the entire market for dry-cleaning services in this town never exceeds 300 pieces of clothing per day. In the figure, the *LRATC* curve slopes downward, exhibiting economies of scale. Why might this be? A dry-cleaning service uses a number of lumpy inputs: a parcel of land for the shop, a store clerk, a small dry-cleaning machine if the clothes are cleaned on-site, or daily transportation to an off-site cleaning plant. In the figure, we assume that cleaning more clothes—by spreading these costs among more units—causes cost per unit to decline all the way to 300 units and beyond. As a result, one dry cleaner could achieve a lower cost per unit than could two or more dry cleaners. For example, the *LRATC* curve tells us that one firm could clean 300 pieces of clothing at a cost of $5 per piece (point *A*). But if two dry cleaners were to split this same output level (150 pieces of clothing each), each would have a higher cost per unit of $12 at point *B*. For three dry cleaners, cost per article cleaned would be $15 at point *C*, and so on. The first dry cleaner to locate in the town will have a cost advantage over any potential new entrants. This cost advantage will tend to keep newcomers out of the market.

FIGURE 1   A Natural Monopoly

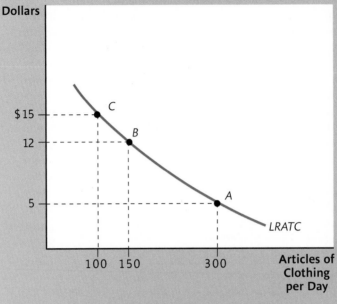

In the figure, the typical firm has an LRATC curve as shown, with economies of scale through an output level of 300, which is assumed to be the maximum market quantity. A single firm could serve the market at a cost of $5 per unit, operating at point A. Two firms splitting this market would each produce 150 units, with each operating at point B on its LRATC curve. Cost per unit would be $12, higher than with just one firm. Cost per unit would be even higher with three firms (each operating at point C). Since a single firm could produce at lower cost than two or more firms, this market tends naturally toward monopoly.

Natural monopoly A monopoly that arises when, due to economies of scale, a single firm can produce for the entire market at lower cost per unit than could two or more firms.

A monopoly that arises because of economies of scale is called a **natural monopoly.** Local monopolies are often natural monopolies. In a very small town, there might be one gas station, one food market, one doctor, and so on. In all these cases, because there are sizable lumpy inputs and the market is small, the first firm to enter the market will likely be the last.

Legal Barriers

Many monopolies arise because of legal barriers. Of course, since laws are created by human beings, this immediately raises the question: Why would anyone want to create barriers that lead to monopoly? As you'll see, the answer varies depending on the type of barrier being erected. Here, we'll consider two of the most important legal barriers that give rise to monopolies: protection of intellectual property and government franchise.

Protection of Intellectual Property

The words you are reading right now are an example of *intellectual property,* which includes literary, artistic, and musical works, as well as scientific inventions. The market for a specific intellectual property is a monopoly: One firm or individual owns the property and is the sole seller of the rights to use it. There is both good and bad in this. As you will learn in this chapter, prices tend to be higher under monopoly than under perfect competition, and monopolies often earn economic profit as a consequence. A higher price is good for the monopoly and bad for everyone else.

On the other hand, the promise of monopoly profit is what encourages the creation of original products and ideas in the first place. And this benefits the rest of us. Google's search engine, Apple's iPhone and iPad, Visex's cornea-shaping laser, and every film you've seen or novel you've read—all were launched by companies that took on considerable cost and risk for the prospect of future profit.

In dealing with intellectual property, government ideally strikes a compromise: It allows the creators of intellectual property to enjoy a monopoly and earn economic profit, *but only for a limited period of time*. Once the time is up, other sellers are allowed to enter the market, and it is hoped that competition among them will, in the end, bring down the price.

The two most important kinds of legal protection for intellectual property are *patents* and *copyrights*. New scientific discoveries and the products that result from them are protected by a **patent** obtained from the government. The patent prevents anyone else from selling the same discovery or product for about 20 years. If someone uses the discovery without obtaining (and paying for) permission from the patent owner, they can be sued. Every year, more than 2,000 patent infringement cases are brought before U.S. courts and thousands more in courts in other countries. Table 1 lists the largest awards granted by U.S. Courts (not including cases settled out of court before final verdict).

Patent A temporary grant of monopoly rights over a new product or scientific discovery.

Literary, musical, and artistic works are protected by a **copyright**, which grants exclusive rights over the material for at least 70 years and often longer. For example, the copyright on this book is owned by South-Western/Cengage Learning. No other company or individual can print copies and sell them to the public, and no one can quote from the book at length without obtaining the company's permission.

Copyright A grant of exclusive rights to sell a literary, musical, or artistic work.

Copyrights and patents are often sold to another person or firm, but this does not change the monopoly status of the market, since there is still just one seller. For example, the song "Happy Birthday" was originally written about a century ago, but first received copyright protection in 1935. Since then, the copyright has changed hands numerous times and is currently owned by Warner Music Group.

TABLE 1

Largest Patent Infringement Awards

Year	Patent Holder	Patent Infringer	Award (in millions)
1990	Polaroid	Eastman Kodak	$909.5
1994	Alpex Computer	Nintendo	$253.6
1996	Haworth	Steelcase	$211.5
1997	Proctor & Gamble	Paragon Trade Brands	$178.4
1998	Exxon, et al.	Mobil Oil and others	$171.0
2004	Eolas Technologies, et al.	Microsoft	$565.9
2007	Lucent Technologies	Microsoft	$769.0
2009	i4i	Microsoft	$290.0
2009	Rambus	Hynix	$397.0
2009	Uniloc	Microsoft	$338.0

Sources: "Industries Brace for Tough Battle over Patent Law," *Wall Street Journal*, p. 1, June 6, 2007; "Microsoft Told to Pay $338 Million over Piracy Patent," *Bloomberg.com*, April 8, 2009; "Microsoft Loses $200 Million Jury Verdict in i4i Patent Trial," *Bloomberg.com*, May 21, 2009; "Hynix Revises Down 2008 Earnings on Provisions for Rambus," *Bloomberg.com*, March 11, 2009. Some of the more recent awards are still being contested.

Of course you are free to sing this song at a private birthday party. But anyone who wants to use the song for profit—for example, by featuring it in a radio or television program—must pay a minimal royalty to Warner Music Group (at least until 2030, when the copyright expires).[1]

Government Franchise

Government franchise
A government-granted right to be the sole seller of a product or service.

Some firms have their monopoly status guaranteed through **government franchise**, a grant of exclusive rights over a product. Here, the barrier to entry is quite simple: Any other firm that enters the market will be prosecuted!

Governments often grant franchises when they think the market is a *natural monopoly*. In this case, a single large firm enjoying economies of scale would have a lower cost per unit than multiple smaller firms. Government tries to serve the public interest by *ensuring* that there are no competitors that would cause cost per unit to rise. In exchange for its monopoly status, the seller must submit to either government ownership and control or government regulation over its prices and profits. (We'll have more to say about the regulation of monopoly in Chapter 15.)

This is the logic behind the monopoly status of the U.S. Postal Service. Two postal companies would need many more carriers to deliver the same total number of letters each day, raising costs and, ultimately, the price of mailing a letter. The federal government has chosen to own and control this natural monopoly, rather than merely regulate. Federal law prohibits any other firm from offering normal letter delivery service.

Local governments, too, create monopolies by granting exclusive franchises in a variety of industries believed to be natural monopolies. These include utility companies that provide electricity, gas, and water, as well as garbage collection services.

Since ordinary letter delivery is a natural monopoly, the U.S. Postal Service has been granted an exclusive government franchise to deliver the mail.

Network Externalities

Imagine that you have created a new, superior operating system for personal computers. Compared to Microsoft Windows, your operating system is less vulnerable to viruses, works 10 percent faster, and uses 10 percent less memory. It even allows the user to turn off the caps-lock key, which most people use only by mistake.

Now all you need is a few million dollars to launch your new product. You manage to get appointments with several venture capital firms, specialists in funding new projects. But every time you make your pitch, and the venture capital people realize what you're proposing, you get the same reaction: hysterical laughter. "But really," you say. "It works better than Windows. I can prove it." "We believe you," they always respond. And they do. And then . . . they start laughing again.

Why? Because you're trying to enter a market with significant *network externalities*.

[1] The copyright on Happy Birthday has a long and complex history, and it may not even be valid. Although Warner Music Group collects about $2 million per year in royalties on the song, the charge for any one user is so low that no one has mounted a court challenge. For more information, see Robert Brauneis, "Copyright and the World's Most Popular Song," *GWU Legal Studies Research Paper No. 1111624* (2008).

> ***Network externalities*** *are the added benefits for all users of a good or service that arise because other people are using it too.*

Network externalities Additional benefits enjoyed by all users of a good or service because others use it as well.

When network externalities are present, joining a large network is more beneficial than joining a small network, even if the product in the larger network is somewhat inferior to the product in the smaller one. So once a network reaches a certain size, additional consumers will want to join just because so many others already have. And if joining the network requires you to buy a product produced by only one firm, that firm can rapidly become the leading supplier in the market.[2]

All of this applies to the market for computer operating systems. When you buy a Windows computer, you benefit from the existence of so many other Windows users in a variety of ways. First, you have access to a large number of other computers—owned by friends and coworkers—that you can easily operate. Second, you have access to more software programs (because software developers know they can reach a bigger market when they write programs for Windows). Finally, there are more people around who can help you when you have a problem, saving you the time and trouble of calling a help desk.

In addition to the advantages of *joining* a larger network, there is also an advantage in not leaving it once you've joined: avoiding *switching costs*. It takes time to learn to operate and get used to a new operating system. Although the time you've spent mastering Windows is a sunk cost, the time you'd have to spend mastering a new system can be avoided by staying in the network you're in.

Windows, the first operating system to be used by tens of millions of people, has clearly benefited from network externalities, as well as switching costs. To be sure, two competing operating systems—Apple's OS X and Linux—have managed to establish their own smaller networks that compete with Windows. And all three of these operating systems are threatened by cloud-based computing, which can be accessed with a variety of mobile operating systems. Still, as far as personal computer operating systems, Windows' large network has allowed it to retain its worldwide dominance for years.

Network externalities will not necessarily protect a monopoly from competitors forever. Consider MySpace, which was once the world's most popular social communication Web site, with a huge network of users. Until, that is, Facebook came onto the scene. Facebook first began growing its network among college students, who valued its exclusivity. When the company opened its service to the general public in 2006, its network was large enough to appeal to most MySpace users. By 2008, Facebook surpassed MySpace in total membership, and MySpace soon withered. (This is an example of network externalities in reverse: As more people drop out of a network such as MySpace, the network becomes less valuable to those who remain.)

But breaking through the barrier of network externalities, as Facebook did with MySpace, is more difficult than it might seem. Just ask Google, which tried several times in recent years to break Facebook's dominant position. In spite of Google's substantial customer base and vast resources, none of its Facebook-like services convinced Facebook users to switch. In 2011, Google tried again with Google+, which many observers judged superior in quality to Facebook. If—by the time you

---

[2] The term *externality* will be defined formally in Chapter 15. But if you're curious, an externality is a by-product of a transaction that affects someone other than the buyer or seller (someone external to the transaction). In the case of network externalities, by paying to join the network (e.g., buying a Windows computer), you make the network larger, benefiting others (everyone else with a Windows computer) who weren't involved in your transaction.

are reading this—Google+ has caught on, it will be Google's first success against Facebook in a string of failures.

MONOPOLY BEHAVIOR

The goal of a monopoly, like that of any firm, is to earn the highest profit possible. And, like other firms, a monopolist faces constraints.

Reread that last sentence because it is important. It is tempting to think that a monopolist—because it faces no direct competitors in its market—is free of constraints or that its constraints are noneconomic ones. For example, many people think that the only force preventing a monopolist from charging outrageously high prices is public outrage. In this view, a monopoly cable company would charge $500, $1,000, or even $10,000 per month if only it could "get away with it."

But with a little reflection, it is easy to see that a monopolist faces purely *economic* constraints that limit its behavior—constraints that are in some ways similar to those faced by other, nonmonopoly firms.

First, there is a constraint on the monopoly's *costs:* For any level of output the monopolist might produce, it must pay some total cost to produce it. This cost constraint is determined by the monopolist's production technology and by the prices it must pay for its inputs. In other words, a monopolist's cost constraints are the same as for any other type of firm, such as the perfectly competitive firm we studied in the previous chapter.

The monopolist also faces constraints on the price it can charge. This can be a bit confusing because a monopolist, unlike a competitive firm, is *not* a price taker: It does *not* take the market price as a given. But it does face a given demand curve for its product. Indeed, since a monopoly is the only firm in its market, its demand curve is the *market* demand curve. Thus, the monopoly faces a trade-off: The more it charges for its product, the fewer units it will be able to sell.

Single Price versus Price Discrimination

As you'll see later in this chapter, some firms—including some monopolies—can charge different prices to different consumers, based on differences in the prices they are willing to pay. This kind of pricing is called *price discrimination*. Other firms— we'll call them *single-price firms*—must charge the same price for every unit they sell, regardless of any differences in willingness to pay among their customers. For the next several pages, we'll assume we are dealing with a **single-price monopoly**. (In general, when economists use the term "monopoly" without a modifier, it means "single-price monopoly.") We'll deal with price discrimination later in the chapter.

Single-price monopoly
A monopoly firm that is limited to charging the same price for each unit of output sold.

Monopoly Price or Output Decision

Notice that the title of this section reads "price *or* output decision," not "price *and* output decision." The reason is that a monopoly does not make two separate decisions about price and quantity, but rather *one* decision. Once the firm determines its output level, it has also determined its price (the maximum price it can charge and still sell that output level). Similarly, once the firm determines its price, it has also determined its output level.

How does a monopoly determine its profit-maximizing output level (and therefore its profit-maximizing price)? The same way as any other firm: It considers how a change in output would affect revenue on the one hand and cost on the other. We'll start by exploring the relationship between output and revenue.

Output and Revenue

Table 2 shows some data for Patty's Pool, a firm that owns and operates the only swimming pool in a small town—a local monopoly. Patty earns revenue by charging an admission fee for using her pool.

The first two columns show various output levels (swimmers per day) and the highest price (admission fee) Patty could charge for each output level. These two columns tell us that Patty faces a downward-sloping demand curve: The lower the fee, the greater the number of people who will pay to swim each day. This demand curve is graphed in Figure 2 (as the upper curve).

The demand curve should look familiar to you. In Chapter 8, Ned's Beds had to lower its price in order to sell more bed frames. The firm faced a downward-sloping demand curve much like the one shown here. (Ned was not necessarily the only seller in his market, but as you'll see in the next chapter, monopolies are not the only firms that face downward-sloping demand curves.)

The third column of the table shows Patty's total revenue per day (quantity times price) at each output level. For example, at an output level of 3, her daily revenue will be 3 × $10 = $30. And the last column shows Patty's marginal revenue (MR), which is the increase in her revenue for a one-unit rise in output. For example, when

TABLE 2
Demand and Revenue
at Patty's Pool

Q (swimmers per day)	P (admission fee)	TR	MR
0	$13	$ 0	
			$12
1	$12	$12	
			$10
2	$11	$22	
			$ 8
3	$10	$30	
			$ 6
4	$ 9	$36	
			$ 4
5	$ 8	$40	
			$ 2
6	$ 7	$42	
			$ 0
7	$ 6	$42	
			−$ 2
8	$ 5	$40	
			−$ 4
9	$ 4	$36	

FIGURE 2   Demand and Marginal Revenue for Patty's Pool

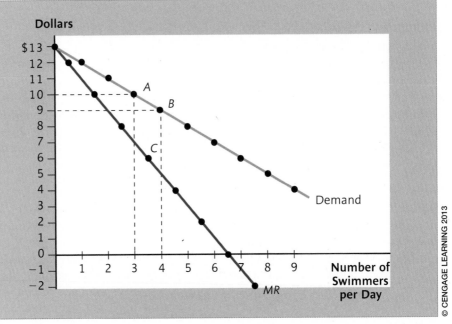

When a firm faces a downward-sloping demand curve, marginal revenue (MR) is less than price, and the MR curve lies below the demand curve. For example, moving from point A to point B, output rises from 3 to 4 units, while price falls from $10 to $9. For this move, total revenue rises from $30 to $36, so marginal revenue (plotted at point C) is only $6—less than the new price of $9.

Patty's output rises from 3 to 4, her total revenue rises from $30 to $36, so her marginal revenue for this change is $36 − $30 = $6.

The marginal revenue column is graphed in Figure 2, *below* the demand curve. Why below? Mathematically, this is because when the firm's demand curve slopes downward, marginal revenue is less than the price for all increases in output (except the increase from zero to one unit). To see this, look at what happens when we move from point *A* to point *B* along the demand curve, and output rises from 3 to 4 units. The new price is $9, but the marginal revenue from producing the fourth unit is $6 (at point *C*), which is less than the new price.

> *When any firm, including a monopoly, faces a downward-sloping demand curve, marginal revenue is less than the price of output. Therefore, the marginal revenue curve will lie below the demand curve.*

Why must marginal revenue be less than the price? Because when a firm faces a downward-sloping demand curve, it must lower the price in order to sell a greater quantity. The new, lower price applies to *all* units it sells, including those it was *previously* selling at some higher price.

For example, suppose Patty initially has 3 swimmers per day at $10 each. If she wants 4 swimmers, Table 1 tells us that she must lower her price to $9. Patty would *gain* $9 in revenue by admitting one more swimmer at that price. But she would also *lose* some revenue, because each of the first three swimmers that she *used* to charge $10 will now be charged $9—a *loss* of $3 in revenue. If we add the $9 gained on the fourth swimmer and subtract the $3 lost from lowering the price to the other three, the net impact on revenue is an increase of $6—less than the $9 price she is now charging.

Notice, too, that for increases in output beyond 7, marginal revenue turns negative. For these changes in output, Patty loses more in revenue from dropping the price on previous units than she gains by selling one new unit. No firm would ever want to operate where marginal revenue is negative, because it could then increase its revenue *and* have lower costs by *decreasing* output.

The Profit-Maximizing Output Level

Once we have a monopoly's marginal revenue curve, the profit-maximizing output level can be found by applying our (now familiar) rule from Chapter 8, which tells us how *any* firm can find its profit-maximizing output level:

> *To maximize profit, a monopoly—like any firm—should produce the quantity where* MC = MR *and the* MC *curve crosses the* MR *curve from below.*

Let's apply this rule to a different firm, Zillion-Channel Cable, a monopoly that sells cable television service to the residents of a small city. We'll assume that Zillion-Channel is free from government regulation and is free to set the profit-maximizing price.

In Figure 3, we've plotted the firm's demand curve, showing the number of cable subscribers at each monthly price. As with Patty's Pool, Zillion-Channel's marginal revenue curve lies below its demand curve. The figure also shows Zillion-Channel's marginal cost curve.

The greatest profit possible occurs at an output level of 50 thousand, where the *MC* curve crosses the *MR* curve from below. In order to sell this level of output, the firm will charge a price of $100, located at point *E* on its demand curve. You can see that for a monopoly, *price and output are not independent decisions, but different ways of expressing the same decision.* Once Zillion-Channel determines its profit-maximizing output level (50 thousand units), it has also determined its profit-maximizing price ($100), and vice versa.

FIGURE 3 | Monopoly Price and Output Determination

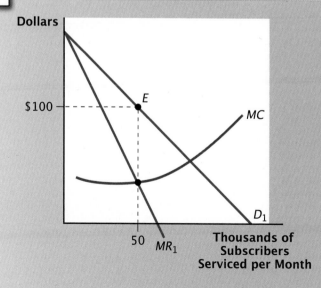

Like any firm, the monopolist maximizes profit by producing where MC equals MR. Here, that quantity is 50 thousand units. The price charged ($100) is read off the demand curve. It is the highest price at which the monopolist can sell the profit-maximizing level of output.

Monopoly and Market Power

Market power The ability of a seller to raise price without losing all demand for the product being sold.

A monopoly is an example of a firm with **market power**—the ability to raise price without causing quantity demanded to go to zero. Any firm facing a downward-sloping demand curve has market power: As it raises its price, quantity demanded falls, but some customers who value the firm's product will continue to buy it at the higher price. Only perfectly competitive firms, which face horizontal demand curves, have no market power at all. For a competitive firm, raising price even a tiny bit above the market price reduces quantity demanded to zero. This is why in Chapter 9 we referred to a competitive firm as a *price taker*: It must accept the market price as a given, so there is no decision about price.

Price setter A firm (with market power) that selects its price, rather than accepting the market price as a given.

By contrast, when a firm has market power, it is a **price setter**—it makes a choice about what price to charge. The choice is limited by constraints (such as the demand curve itself), but it is still a choice. Monopolies are one example of price-setting firms, but they are not the only example. In the next chapter, you'll learn about other market structures besides monopoly in which firms have market power and are therefore price setters.

Profit and Loss

In Figure 3, we've illustrated Zillion-Channel's price and output level, but we cannot yet see whether the firm is making an economic profit or loss. This will require one more addition to the diagram—the average cost curve. Remember that

$$\text{Profit per unit} = P - ATC.$$

At any output level, the price is read off the demand curve. Profit per unit, then, is just the vertical distance between the firm's demand curve and its *ATC* curve.

Figure 4 is just like Figure 3 but adds Zillion-Channel's *ATC* curve. As you can see, at the profit-maximizing output level of 50 thousand, price is $100 and average total cost is $70, so profit per unit is $30.

FIGURE 4 | A Monopoly Earning Profit

The monopoly in this figure is earning a profit. At the profit maximizing output level (50 thousand), profit per unit is equal to the difference between price ($100) and ATC ($70). Total profit is equal to profit per unit multiplied by the number of units, or $30 × 50,000 = $1,500,000, represented by the blue shaded rectangle.

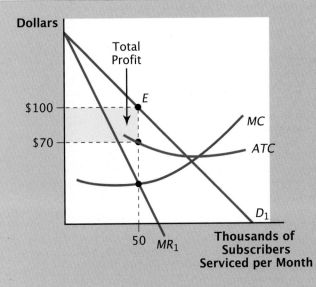

Now look at the blue rectangle in the figure. The height of this rectangle is profit per unit ($30), and the width is the number of units produced (50 thousand). The *area* of the rectangle—height × width—equals Zillion-Channel's total profit, or $30 × 50,000 = $1,500,000.

> *A monopoly earns a profit whenever* P > ATC. *Its total profit at the best output level equals the area of a rectangle with height equal to the distance between* P *and* ATC *and width equal to the level of output.*

This should sound familiar: It is exactly how we represented the profit of a perfectly competitive firm (compare with Figure 3(a) in Chapter 9). The diagram looked different under perfect competition because the firm's demand curve was horizontal, whereas for a monopoly it is downward sloping.

Figure 5 illustrates the case of a monopoly suffering a loss. Here, average costs are higher than in Figure 4, and the *ATC* curve lies everywhere above the demand curve. As a result, the firm will suffer a loss at any level of output. At the best output level (where *MC* = *MR*), the loss will be smallest. In the figure, this occurs at 50 thousand units, with *ATC* = $125 and price = $100, so the loss per unit is $25. The total loss ($1,250,000) is the area of the pink rectangle, whose height is the loss per unit ($25) and width is the best output level (50,000).

As you can see, being a monopolist is no guarantee of profit. If costs are too high, or demand is insufficient, a monopolist may break even or suffer a loss.

DANGEROUS CURVES ⚠️

A monopoly supply curve? A question may have occurred to you: Where is the monopoly's *supply curve*? The answer is that *there is no supply curve for a monopoly.* A firm's supply curve tells us how much output a firm will want to produce and sell when it is *presented* with different prices. This makes sense for a perfectly competitive firm that takes the market price as given and responds by deciding how much output to produce. A monopoly, by contrast, is *not* a price taker; it *chooses* its price. Since the monopolist is free to choose any price it wants—and it will always choose the *profit-maximizing* price and no other—the notion of a supply curve does not apply to a monopoly.

FIGURE 5 | **A Monopoly Suffering a Loss**

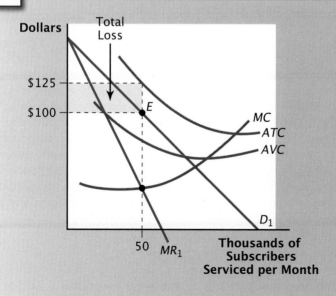

The monopoly in this figure is suffering a loss. At the profit maximizing output level (50 thousand), the loss per unit is equal to the difference between price ($100) and ATC ($125). The total loss is equal to loss per unit multiplied by the number of units, or $25 × 50,000 = $1,250,000, represented by the pink shaded rectangle.

> *A monopoly suffers a loss whenever* P < ATC. *Its total loss at the best output level equals the area of a rectangle with height equal to the distance between* ATC *and* P *and width equal to the level of output.*

EQUILIBRIUM IN MONOPOLY MARKETS

A monopoly market is in equilibrium when the only firm in the market, the monopoly firm, is maximizing its profit. After all, once the firm is producing the profit-maximizing quantity—and charging the highest price that will enable it to sell that quantity—it has no incentive to change either price or quantity, unless something in the market changes (which we'll explore later).

But for monopoly, as for perfect competition, we have different expectations about equilibrium in the short run and equilibrium in the long run.

Short-Run Equilibrium

In the short run, a monopoly may earn an economic profit or suffer an economic loss. (It may, of course, break even as well; see if you can draw this case on your own.) A monopoly that is earning an economic profit will, of course, continue to operate in the short run, charging the price and producing the output level at which *MR = MC*, as in Figure 4.

But what if a monopoly suffers a loss in the short run? Then it will have to make the same decision as any other firm: to shut down or not to shut down. The rule you learned in Chapter 8—that a firm should shut down if *TR < TVC* at the output level where marginal revenue and marginal cost are equal—applies to any firm, including a monopoly. And (as you learned in Chapter 9), the statement "*TR < TVC*" is equivalent to the statement "*P < AVC*." Therefore,

> *any firm—including a monopoly—should shut down if* P < AVC *at the output level where* MR = MC.

In Figure 5, Zillion-Channel is suffering a loss. But since *P* = $100 and *AVC* is less than $100 at an output of 50 thousand, we have *P > AVC*: The firm should keep operating. On your own, draw in an alternative *AVC* curve in Figure 5 that would cause Zillion-Channel to shut down. (Hint: It will be higher than the existing *AVC* curve.)

The shutdown rule should accurately predict the behavior of most privately owned and operated monopolies. But if a monopoly operates under a government franchise or regulation and produces a vital service such as transportation, mail delivery, or mass transit, the government may not allow it to shut down. If, for example, the monopoly suddenly finds that *P < AVC* at every output level (perhaps because the cost of a variable input suddenly rises or because the demand curve suddenly shifts leftward), the government might order the firm to continue operating, and use tax revenue to cover the loss.

Long-Run Equilibrium

One of the most important insights of the previous chapter was that perfectly competitive firms will *not* earn a profit in long-run equilibrium. Profit attracts new firms into the market, and market production increases. This, in turn, causes the market price to fall, eliminating any temporary profit earned by a competitive firm.

But there is no such process at work in a monopoly market, where barriers *prevent* the entry of other firms into the market. Outsiders will *want* to enter an industry when a monopoly is earning positive economic profit, but they will be *unable to do so*. Thus, the market provides no mechanism to eliminate monopoly profit.

> *Unlike perfectly competitive firms, monopolies may earn economic profit in the long run.*

What about economic loss? If a monopoly is franchised or regulated by the government, and it faces the prospect of long-run loss, the government may decide to subsidize it in order to keep it running. But if the monopoly is privately owned and controlled, it will not tolerate long-run losses. A monopoly suffering an economic loss that it expects to continue indefinitely should always exit the industry, just like any other firm.

> *A privately owned, unregulated monopoly suffering an economic loss in the long run will exit the industry, just as would any other business firm. In the long run, therefore, we should not find such monopolies suffering economic losses.*

Comparing Monopoly to Perfect Competition

We have already seen one important difference between monopoly and perfectly competitive markets: In perfect competition, economic profit is relentlessly reduced to zero by the entry of other firms; in monopoly, economic profit can continue indefinitely.

But monopoly also differs from perfect competition in another way:

> *All else equal, a monopoly market will have a higher price and lower output than a perfectly competitive market.*

To see why this is so, let's explore what would happen if a single firm took over a perfectly competitive market, changing the market to a monopoly. Panel (a) of Figure 6 illustrates a competitive market consisting of 100 identical firms. The market is in long-run equilibrium at point *E,* with a market price of $10 and market output of 100,000 units. In panel (b), the typical firm faces a horizontal demand curve at $10, produces output of 1,000 units, and earns zero economic profit.

Now, imagine that a single company buys all 100 firms, to form a monopoly. The new monopoly market is illustrated in panel (c). Under monopoly, the horizontal demand curve facing each firm becomes irrelevant. Now, the demand curve facing the monopoly is the downward-sloping *market* demand curve *D*—the same as the market demand curve in panel (a). Since the demand curve slopes downward, marginal revenue will be less than price, and the *MR* curve will lie everywhere below the demand curve. To maximize profit, the monopoly will want to find the output level at which $MC = MR$. But what is the new monopoly's *MC* curve?

We'll assume that the monopoly doesn't change the way output is produced. (This is part of the "all else equal" assumption in the highlighted statement above.) That is, each previously competitive firm will continue to produce its output with the same technology as before, only now it operates as one of 100 different plants that

FIGURE 6 — Comparing Monopoly and Perfect Competition

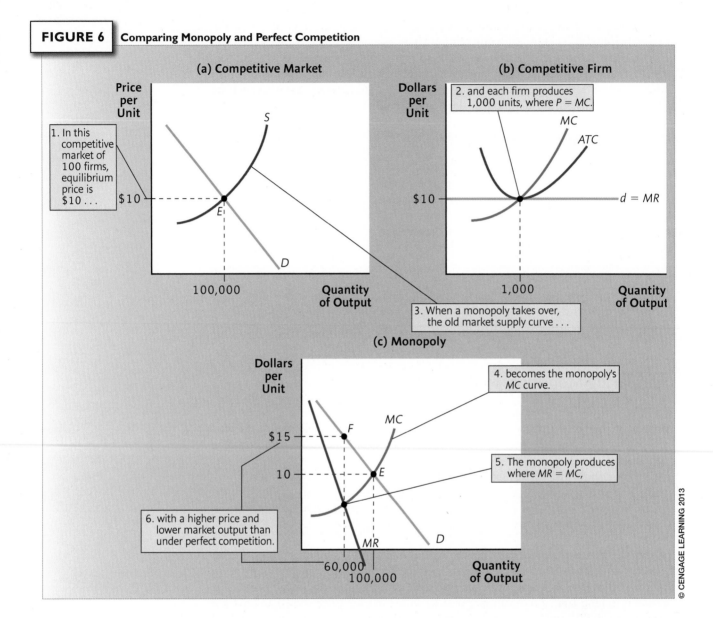

(a) Competitive Market

Price per Unit

1. In this competitive market of 100 firms, equilibrium price is $10 . . .

$10

S

E

D

100,000 — Quantity of Output

(b) Competitive Firm

Dollars per Unit

2. and each firm produces 1,000 units, where P = MC.

MC

ATC

$10

d = MR

1,000 — Quantity of Output

3. When a monopoly takes over, the old market supply curve . . .

(c) Monopoly

Dollars per Unit

4. becomes the monopoly's MC curve.

MC

$15 — F

10 — E

5. The monopoly produces where MR = MC,

6. with a higher price and lower market output than under perfect competition.

MR

D

60,000
100,000 — Quantity of Output

© CENGAGE LEARNING 2013

the monopoly controls. With this assumption, *the monopoly's marginal cost curve will be the same as the market supply curve in panel (a).* Why? First, remember that in a perfectly competitive industry the market supply curve is obtained by adding up each individual firm's supply curve, that is, each individual firm's marginal cost curve. Therefore, the market supply curve tells us the marginal cost—at each firm— of producing another unit of output for the market. When the monopoly takes over each of these individual firms, the market supply curve tells us how much it will cost the monopoly to produce another unit of output at each of its plants.

For example, point *E* on the market supply curve tells us that, when total supply is 100,000, each plant will be producing 1,000 units. Increasing output by one more unit will cost the monopoly $10 because that is the marginal cost at any of its plants. The same is true at every other point along the old competitive market supply curve: It will always tell us the new monopoly's cost of producing one more unit at any of the plants it now owns. In other words, the upward-sloping curve in panel (c), which is the market supply curve when the market is competitive, becomes the marginal cost curve for a single firm when the market is monopolized.

Now we have all the information we need to find the monopoly's choice of price and quantity. In panel (c), the monopoly's *MC* curve crosses the *MR* curve from below at 60,000 units of output. This will be the monopoly's profit-maximizing output level. To sell this much output, the monopoly will charge $15 per unit—point *F* on its demand curve.

Notice what has happened in our example: After the monopoly takes over, the price rises from $10 to $15, and market quantity drops from 100,000 to 60,000. The monopoly, compared to a competitive market, *charges more and produces less.*

Why does this happen? When the market was perfectly competitive, each firm could sell all the output it wanted at the given market price of $10, and each firm knew it could earn an additional $10 in revenue for each additional unit it sold. The best option for the firm was to increase output until marginal cost rose to $10.

But the new monopoly does *not* treat price, or marginal revenue, as given values. Instead, it knows that raising its own output *lowers* the market price. So if the monopoly goes all the way to the competitive output level (100,000 units in the figure), it will be producing units for which *MR* < *MC* (all units beyond 60,000). This will reduce its profit. To maximize profit, the monopoly has to stop short of the competitive output—producing 60,000 rather than 100,000. Of course, since the monopoly sells a lower market quantity, it will charge a higher market price.

Now let's see who gains and who loses from the takeover. By raising price and restricting output, the new monopoly earns economic profit. We know this because if the firm were to charge $10—the old competitive price—each of its plants would break even, giving it zero economic profit. But we've just seen that $10 is *not* the profit-maximizing price—$15 is. So, the firm must make higher profit at $15 than at $10, ensuring it will earn more than zero economic profit.

Consumers, however, lose in two ways: They pay more for the output they buy, and, due to higher prices, they buy less output. The changeover from perfect competition to monopoly thus benefits the owners of the monopoly and harms consumers of the product.

An Important Proviso

Keep in mind, though, an important proviso concerning this result: Comparing monopoly and perfect competition, we see that price is higher and output is lower under monopoly *if all else is equal.* In particular, we have assumed that after the market is monopolized, the technology of production remains unchanged at each of the monopoly's "plants" (i.e., at each of the previously competitive firms).

But a monopoly may be able to *change* the technology of production, so that all else would *not* remain equal. For example, a monopoly may have each of its new plants *specialize* in some part of the production process, or it may be able to achieve efficiencies in product planning, employee supervision, bookkeeping, or customer relations. These cost savings might shift down the monopoly's marginal cost curve. If you draw a new, lower *MC* curve in panel (c), you'll see that this works to *decrease* the monopoly's price and *increase* its output level—exactly the reverse of the effects discussed earlier. If the cost savings are great enough, and the *MC* curve drops low enough, a profit-maximizing monopoly could even charge a lower price and produce more output than would a competitive market. (See if you can draw a diagram to demonstrate this case.)

The general conclusion is this:

> *The monopolization of a competitive industry leads to two opposing effects. First, for any given technology of production, monopolization leads to higher prices and lower output. Second, changes in the technology of production made possible under monopoly may lead to lower prices and higher output. The ultimate effect on price and quantity depends on which effect is stronger.*

Government and Monopoly Profit

Monopolies, as you learned earlier, often exist with government permission. When we bring the government into our analysis, the monopoly's total profit may be less than that predicted by the analysis we've done so far. Government involvement reduces monopoly profit in two ways.

Government Regulation

As discussed earlier, in many cases of natural monopoly, a firm is granted a government franchise to be the sole seller in a market. This has been true of monopolies that provide water service, electricity, and natural gas. In exchange for its franchise, the monopoly must accept government regulation, often including the requirement that it submit its prices to a public commission for approval. The government will often want to keep prices high enough to keep the monopoly in business, but no higher. Since the monopoly will stay in business unless it suffers a long-run loss, the ideal pricing strategy for the regulatory commission would be to keep the monopoly's economic profit at zero.

Remember, though, that economic profit includes the opportunity cost of the funds invested by the monopoly's owners. If the public commission succeeds, the monopoly's *accounting* profit will be just enough to match what the owners could earn by investing their funds elsewhere—that is, the monopoly will earn zero economic profit. Government regulation of monopoly will be discussed further in Chapter 15.

Rent-Seeking Activity

Another factor that reduces a monopoly's profit comes from the interplay between politics and economics. As we've seen, many monopolies achieve and maintain their monopoly status due to legal barriers to entry. And many of these monopolies are completely unregulated. For example, a movie theater or miniature golf course may enjoy a monopoly in an area because zoning regulations prevent entry by competitors. Or, especially in less developed countries, a single firm may be granted the exclusive right to sell or produce a particular good even though it is not a natural monopoly. In all of these cases, the monopoly is left free to set its price as it wishes.

But legal barriers to entry—for example, zoning laws—are often controversial. After all, as you've learned, a monopoly may charge a higher price and produce less output than would a competitive market. Thus, government will be tempted to pull the plug on a monopoly's exclusive status and allow competitors into the market. The monopoly, in turn, will often take action to *preserve* legal barriers to entry. Economists call such actions *rent-seeking activity*.

Rent-seeking activity Any costly action a firm undertakes to establish or maintain its monopoly status.

> *Any costly action a firm undertakes to establish or maintain its monopoly status is called **rent-seeking activity**.*

In economics, the term *economic rent* refers to any earnings beyond the minimum needed in order for a good or service to be produced. For example, the minimum price to get *land* "produced" is zero, since it's a gift of nature. This is why all the earnings of landowners are called "rent." A monopoly's economic profit is another example of rent, since it represents earnings above the minimum needed to keep the monopoly in business.

In countries with the most corrupt bureaucracies, rent-seeking activity typically takes the form of outright bribes to government officials. But rent seeking occurs in virtually all countries. It includes the time and money spent lobbying legislators and the public for favorable policies. The costs of such activities can reduce a monopoly's profit below what the simple monopoly model would suggest.

WHAT HAPPENS WHEN THINGS CHANGE?

Once a monopoly is maximizing profit, it has no incentive to change its price or its level of output . . . unless something that affects these decisions changes. In this section, we'll consider two such events: a change in demand for the monopolist's product, and a change in its costs.

A Change in Demand

Back in Chapter 9 we saw that in a perfectly competitive market, an increase in demand caused an increase in market quantity. Does the same general conclusion hold for a monopolist? Let's see.

Panel (a) of Figure 7 shows Zillion-Channel Cable earning a positive profit in the short run. As before, it is producing 50 thousand units per month, charging $100 per unit, and earning a monthly profit of $1,500,000 (not shown in this figure). The fact that Zillion-Channel is a monopolist, however, does not mean that it is immune to shifts in demand.

What might cause a monopolist to experience a shift in demand? The list of possible causes is the same as for perfect competition. If you need a reminder of these causes, look back at Figure 4 in Chapter 3. For example, an increase in consumer tastes for the monopolist's good will shift its demand curve rightward, and a decrease in consumer incomes can shift it leftward.

Suppose that the demand for local cable service increases because a sitcom shown on one of Zillion-Channel's premium services attracts an enthusiastic following (an increase in tastes for cable services). In panel (b) of Figure 7, this is shown as a rightward shift of the demand curve from D_1 to D_2.

Notice that the marginal revenue curve shifts as well, from MR_1 to MR_2. Why is this? As you can see in the figure, a rightward shift in demand is also an *upward* shift in demand. At each quantity, the firm can charge a greater price than before. With a higher price, the rise in revenue (MR) for each increase in quantity will be greater as well. So the MR curve shifts upward (rightward), just like the demand curve. (If you want to demonstrate this with numbers, use Table 2. Cross out the price associated with each quantity and write in a price that's $2 greater instead. Then, recalculate the TR and MR columns. You'll see that marginal revenue for each increase in quantity is greater than before.)

With an unchanged cost structure, the new short-run equilibrium will occur where MR_2 intersects the unchanged MC curve. As you can see, the result is an increase in quantity to 75 thousand, and an increase in price to $125 per month. In this sense, monopoly markets behave very much like competitive markets.

FIGURE 7 | A Change in Demand

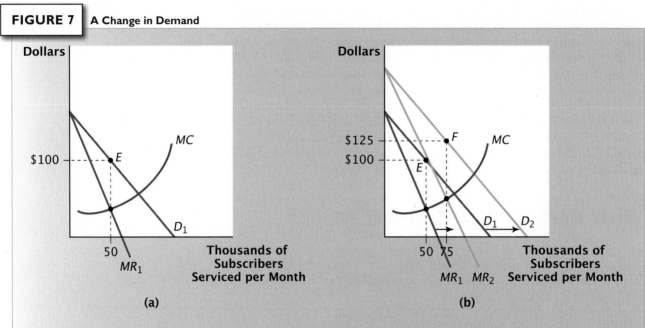

Panel (a) shows Zillion-Channel in equilibrium. It is providing 50 thousand units of cable TV service at a price of $100 per month. Panel (b) shows the same firm following an increase in demand from D_1 to D_2. With the increased demand, MR is higher at each level of output. In the new equilibrium, Zillion-Channel is charging a higher price ($125), providing more TV service (75 thousand units), and earning a larger profit.

What about the monopolist's profit, though? With both price and quantity now higher, total revenue has clearly increased. But total cost is higher as well. (Total cost always rises with greater output.) So it seems as if profit could either rise or fall.

It turns out, however, that profit *must* be higher in the new equilibrium at point F. We know that because Zillion-Channel has the option of continuing to sell its original quantity, 50 thousand, at a price higher than before. If, as we assume, it started out earning a profit at that output level, then the higher price would certainly give it an even *higher* profit. But the logic of $MR = MC$ tells us that the greatest profit of all occurs at 75 thousand units. So profit is certainly greater after the increase in demand.

We can conclude that:

> *A monopolist will generally react to an increase in demand by producing more output, charging a higher price, and earning a larger profit. It will react to a decrease in demand by reducing output, lowering price, and suffering a reduction in profit.*

A Cost-Saving Technological Advance

In Chapter 9, you learned that in a perfectly competitive market, all cost savings from a technological advance are passed along to consumers in the form of lower prices. Is the same true of monopoly? Let's see.

FIGURE 8 | A Cost-Saving Technological Change

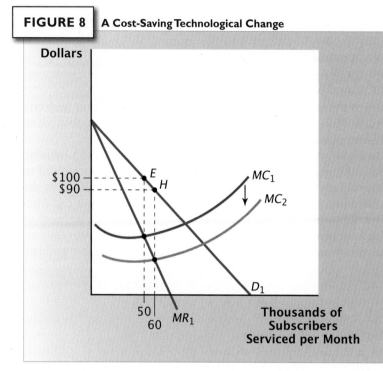

A cost-saving technological advance shifts the monopolist's marginal cost curve down, from MC$_1$ to MC$_2$. Consumers gain because the price falls, but the drop in price is less than the drop in marginal cost. The monopoly gains because its profit is greater.

Suppose a new type of cable box becomes available that breaks down less often, requiring fewer service calls. When Zillion-Channel Cable begins using this equipment, it finds that it gets fewer service calls, so its labor costs decrease by $20 per customer.

Figure 8 shows the result. Before the new equipment is used, Zillion-Channel is charging $100 and producing output of 50 thousand, where its *MR* and *MC* curves cross. The technological advance, when it's distributed to all of Zillion's customers, will lower not only the monthly cost per *current* customer (shifting down the *ATC* curve, which isn't shown, by $20), but also the monthly cost of servicing each *additional* subscriber. That is, Zillion's *marginal cost* curve will shift down by $20, from MC$_1$ to MC$_2$ (which *is* shown).

Zillion-Channel will now want to add subscribers. This is because, after the downward shift in the *MC* curve, *MR* exceeds *MC* at the original output of 50 thousand. An opportunity to raise profit by increasing output has been created. In the figure, the new intersection point between *MC* and *MR* occurs at an output level of 60 thousand, so that's Zillion-Channel's new profit-maximizing output level. The demand curve tells us that when output is 60 thousand, Zillion-Channel will charge a price of $90.

Furthermore, we know that Zillion-Channel's profits have increased. How? If Zillion-Channel had left its output unchanged, the downward shift in its *ATC* curve (not shown) would have raised its profit. Increasing output from 50 thousand to 60 thousand increased profit further (because *MR* > *MC* for that move). Thus, profit must be greater than before.

Let's summarize what's happened: Zillion-Channel's cost per subscriber decreased by $20, but its price decreased by only $10 (from $100 to $90), and its profit increased. It appears that while consumers do get some benefit from the technological change, they don't get all the benefit. Zillion-Channel keeps a chunk of the benefits for itself.

We can summarize our results this way:

> *In general, a monopoly will pass to consumers only part of the benefits from a cost-saving technological change. After the change in technology, the monopoly's profits will be higher.*

This stands in sharp contrast to the impact of technological change in perfectly competitive markets, where—as stated earlier—all of the cost saving is passed along to consumers in the long run.

But there's a silver lining for consumers. Suppose that Zillion-Channel's monthly costs *increased* by \$20 per subscriber, say, because of a rise in the wage rate needed to maintain its workforce. Figure 8 could be used to analyze this case as well. This time, the MC curve would shift *upward* by \$20, so we'd view MC_2 as the initial curve and MC_1 as the new one. And while the price of cable service would rise, it would rise by *less* than the \$20 increase in cost per unit (in our example, price would rise by only \$10). Zillion-Channel would bear part of the burden of the increase in costs, and its profits would fall.

> *In general, a monopoly will pass only part of a cost increase on to consumers in the form of a higher price. After the cost increase, the monopoly's profits will be lower.*

PRICE DISCRIMINATION

So far, we've analyzed the decisions of a single-price monopoly—one that charges the same price on every unit that it sells. But not all monopolies operate this way. For example, local utilities typically charge different rates per kilowatt-hour, depending on whether the energy is used in a home or business. Telephone companies charge different rates for calls made by people on different calling plans. Nor is this multiprice policy limited to monopolies: Movie theaters charge lower prices to senior citizens, airlines charge lower prices to those who book their flights in advance, and supermarkets and food companies charge lower prices to customers who clip coupons from their local newspaper.

In some cases, the different prices are due to differences in the firm's costs of production. For example, it may be more expensive to deliver a product a great distance from the factory, so a firm may charge a higher price to customers in outlying areas. But in other cases, the different prices arise not from cost differences but from the firm's recognition that *some customers are willing to pay more than others:*

Price discrimination Charging different prices to different customers for reasons other than differences in cost.

> **Price discrimination** *occurs when a firm charges different prices to different customers for reasons other than differences in costs.*

The term *discrimination* in this context requires some getting used to. In everyday language, *discrimination* carries a negative connotation: We think immediately of discrimination against someone because of his or her race, sex, or age. But a price-discriminating monopoly does not discriminate based on prejudice, stereotypes, or ill will toward any person or group; rather, it divides its customers into different categories based on their *willingness to pay* for the good—nothing more and nothing less. By doing so, a monopoly can squeeze even more profit out of the market. Why, then, doesn't *every* firm practice price discrimination?

Requirements for Price Discrimination

Although every firm would *like* to practice price discrimination, not all of them can. To successfully price discriminate, three conditions must be satisfied:

Market Power. To price discriminate, a firm must have *market power.* That is, the firm must face a downward-sloping demand curve so that it behaves as a price setter. To see why, think about a perfectly competitive firm that faces a horizontal demand curve and has no market power. If such a firm tried to charge some customers a higher price than others, the high-price customers would simply buy from other firms that are selling the same product at the market price. By contrast, all monopolies face a downward-sloping demand curve, so they meet the market power requirements.

Identifying Willingness to Pay. In order to determine which prices to charge to which customers, a firm must be able to identify how much different customers or groups of customers are willing to pay. But this is often difficult. Suppose your barber or hairstylist wanted to price discriminate. How would he determine how much you are willing to pay for a haircut? He could *ask* you, but . . . let's be real: You wouldn't tell him the truth, since you know he would only use the information to charge you more than you've been paying. Price-discriminating firms—in most cases—must be a bit sneaky, relying on more indirect methods to gauge their customers' willingness to pay.

For example, airlines know that business travelers, who must get to their destination quickly, are willing to pay a higher price for air travel than are tourists or vacationers, who can more easily travel by train, bus, or car. Of course, if airlines merely *announced* a higher price for business travel, then no one would admit to being a business traveler when buying a ticket. So the airlines must find some way to identify business travelers without actually asking. Their method is crude but reasonably effective: Business travelers typically plan their trips at the last minute and don't stay over Saturday night, while tourists and vacationers generally plan long in advance and do stay over Saturday. Thus, the airlines give a discount to any customer who books a flight several weeks in advance and stays over, and they charge a higher price to those who book at the last minute and don't stay over.[3]

Prevention of Resale. To price discriminate, a firm must be able to prevent low-price customers from reselling its product to high-price customers. This can be a vexing problem for many would-be discriminators. For example, when airlines began price discriminating, a resale market developed: Business travelers could buy tickets at the last minute from intermediaries, who had booked in advance at the lower price and then advertised their tickets for sale. To counter this, the airlines imposed the additional requirement of a Saturday stayover for the lower price. By adding this restriction, the airlines were able to substantially reduce the reselling of low-price tickets to business travelers.

It is often easy to prevent resale of a *service* because of its personal nature. A hairstylist can charge different prices to different customers without fearing that one customer

---

[3] It is sometimes argued that airlines' pricing behavior is based entirely on a cost difference to the airline. For example, it is probably more costly for an airline to keep seats available until the last minute because there is a risk that they will go unsold. The higher price for last-minute bookings would then compensate the airline for the unsold seats. (See, for example, the article by John R. Lott, Jr., and Russell D. Roberts in *Economic Inquiry*, January 1991.) But we know that cost differences are not the only reason for the price differential, or else the airlines would not have added the Saturday stayover requirement, which has nothing to do with their costs.

will sell her haircut to another. The same is true of the services provided by physicians, attorneys, and music teachers. Resale of *goods,* however, is much harder to prevent, since goods can be easily transferred from person to person without losing their usefulness.

Effects of Price Discrimination

Price discrimination always benefits the owners of a firm: When the firm can charge different prices to different consumers, it can use this ability to increase its profit. But the effects on consumers can vary. To understand how price discrimination affects the firm and the consumers of its product, consider Larisa, a monopolist who produces and sells Elvis dolls at flea markets. To keep our analysis as simple as possible, we'll assume that Larisa has no fixed costs, and that each doll costs $10 to make no matter how many she produces. Thus, Larisa's cost per doll (*ATC*) is $10 at every output level. Furthermore, because each additional doll costs $10 to make, her marginal cost (*MC*) is also $10 at any output level. This is why, in Figure 9(a), both the *MC* and *ATC* curves are represented by the same horizontal line at $10.

Let's first suppose that Larisa is a single-price monopolist, charging a pre-announced price on every doll she sells. The figure shows the demand and marginal revenue curves she would face on a typical day. Using the *MR* = *MC* rule, Larisa would earn maximum profit by selling 30 dolls per day, and charging $25 per doll. Her profit per unit would be $25 − $10 = $15, which is the vertical distance between the *ATC* curve and the demand curve at 30 units. Her total profit would be $15 × 30 dolls = $450 per day, which is equal to the area of the shaded rectangle.

Price Discrimination That Harms Consumers

Now suppose that Larisa discovers that on a typical day, some of her dolls are sold to particularly eager customers who show up first thing in the morning to buy them. Larisa figures she has found a way to identify those willing to pay more, so she charges the early-morning buyers $35 each and continues charging $25 to everyone else. The result, seen in panel (b), is that the first 10 dolls are now sold to those willing to pay $35 or more for them, and the remaining 20 dolls continue to sell for $25.

What will happen to Larisa's profit? Because she's selling the same total number of dolls each day, her costs are unchanged. In effect, she has merely raised the price of the first 10 dolls by $10 each (from $25 to $35), increasing her revenue by $10 × 10 dolls = $100. Thus, Larisa's profit must rise by $100. This *increase* in profit is represented by the darker shaded rectangle in Figure 9(b). (Make sure you see why.) Larisa's total profit is now equal to the areas of *both* shaded rectangles together—the lightly shaded one (her original profit of $450) and the darker one (her additional profit of $100). Thus, her total profit has risen to $550.

What about her customers? Those who pay a higher price than they otherwise would are harmed by her price discrimination (compared to the single-price outcome). Her other customers, who continue to pay $25, are unaffected. Thus, the increase in Larisa's profit is equal to the additional payments by the customers who pay more.

More generally,

> *Price discrimination can raise the price for some consumers above the price they would pay under a single-price policy. The additional profit for the firm comes at the expense of the consumers who pay more.*

FIGURE 9 | Two Kinds of Price Discrimination

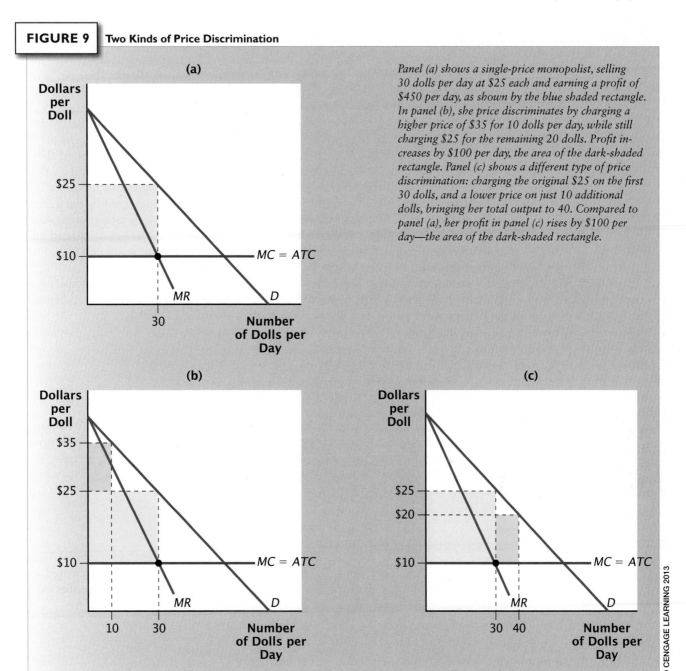

(a)

Panel (a) shows a single-price monopolist, selling 30 dolls per day at $25 each and earning a profit of $450 per day, as shown by the blue shaded rectangle. In panel (b), she price discriminates by charging a higher price of $35 for 10 dolls per day, while still charging $25 for the remaining 20 dolls. Profit increases by $100 per day, the area of the dark-shaded rectangle. Panel (c) shows a different type of price discrimination: charging the original $25 on the first 30 dolls, and a lower price on just 10 additional dolls, bringing her total output to 40. Compared to panel (a), her profit in panel (c) rises by $100 per day—the area of the dark-shaded rectangle.

(b)

(c)

© CENGAGE LEARNING 2013

Price Discrimination That Benefits Consumers

Let's go back to the initial, single-price policy and suppose that Larisa had discovered a different way to price discriminate. Observing that those who come late in the day are rushed and tend not to buy any dolls at $25, she decides to lower the price to $20 during her last hour of business. Sure enough, she sells an additional 10 dolls that way. The result is shown in panel (c), where Larisa charges $25 for the first 30 dolls, and $20 for an additional 10 beyond those. Her total output is now 40 dolls per day.

But wait: By pushing her output all the way to 40 dolls per day, isn't Larisa violating the *MC* = *MR* rule and decreasing her profit? Not really. The *MR* curve in the figure was drawn under the assumption that Larisa would have to lower her price on *all* dolls in order to sell more of them. But this is no longer the case. With price discrimination, the *MR* curve no longer tells us what will happen to Larisa's revenue when she increases her output.

In fact, we know that each doll she sells for $20 will now add a full $20 to her revenue. At the same time, each one adds only $10 to her cost. So she earns profit of $20 − $10 = $10 on each additional doll. She should sell as many of these additional dolls at $20 as people will buy. According to the demand curve, that is 10 dolls beyond the previous 30. Selling these 10 additional dolls increases her total profit by $10 × 10 = $100. This *increase* in profit is represented by the darker shaded rectangle in Figure 9(c). (Make sure you see why.) Larisa's total profit is once again equal to the areas of *both* shaded rectangles together—the lightly shaded one (her original profit of $450) and the darker one (her additional profit of $100). Her total profit has risen to $550.

In this case, Larisa's customers are better off, too. The first 30 customers are unaffected—they continue to pay $25. But with price discrimination, an additional 10 people are able to buy dolls at a price they are willing to pay.

More generally,

> *Price discrimination can lower the price for some consumers below the price they would pay under a single-price policy. Those consumers benefit, while the firm earns higher profit.*

Of course, it is possible for a firm to combine *both* types of price discrimination. That is, it could raise the price above what it would charge as a single-price monopoly for some consumers, and lower it for others. This would increase the firm's profit, while benefiting some consumers and harming others. In theory, a firm can go even further, as the next section discusses.

Perfect Price Discrimination

Suppose a firm could somehow find out the maximum price customers would be willing to pay for *each* unit of output it sells. Then it could increase its profits even further by practicing *perfect price discrimination:*

Perfect price discrimination Charging each customer the most he or she would be willing to pay for each unit purchased.

> Under **perfect price discrimination**, *a firm charges each customer the most the customer would be willing to pay for each unit he or she buys.*

Perfect price discrimination is very difficult to practice in the real world, since it would require the firm to read its customers' minds. However, many real-world situations come rather close to perfect price discrimination. Used-car dealers routinely post a sticker price far higher than the price they think they can actually get. They then size up each customer to determine the discount needed to complete the sale. The dealer may look at the customer's clothes and the car the customer is currently driving, inquire about the customer's job, and observe how sophisticated the customer is about cars. The aim is to determine the maximum price he or she would be willing to pay. A similar sizing up takes place in flea markets, yard sales, and many other situations in which the final price is *negotiated* rather than fixed in advance.

Suppose that Larisa becomes especially good at sizing up her customers. She learns how to distinguish true Elvis fanatics (a white, sequined jumpsuit is a dead giveaway) from people who merely want the doll as a gag gift. Moreover, by observing the way people handle the doll and listening to their conversations with their companions, Larisa can discern the exact maximum price each customer would pay. In effect, she knows exactly where on the demand curve each customer would be located. With her new skills, she can increase her profit by becoming a *perfect price discriminator:* For each unit along the horizontal axis, she will charge the price indicated by the vertical height of the demand curve.

How many dolls should Larisa sell now? To answer this question, we need to find the new output level at which $MR = MC$. But once again, the MR curve in the figure is no longer valid: It was based on the assumption that Larisa had to lower the price on *all* units each time she wanted to sell another one. Now, as a perfect price discriminator, she needs to lower the price only on the *additional* unit she sells, and her revenue will rise by the price of that additional unit. For example, if she is currently selling 30 dolls and wants to sell 31, she would lower the price just on the additional doll by a tiny bit—say, to $24.50—and in that case, her revenue would rise by $24.50.

> For a perfect price discriminator, marginal revenue is equal to the price of the additional unit sold. Thus, the firm's MR curve is the same as its demand curve.

Now it is easy to see what Larisa should do: Since our requirement for profit maximization is that $MC = MR$, and for a perfect price discriminator, MR is the same as price (P), Larisa should keep increasing output as long as MC is less than the price for the next unit. In Figure 10(b), she should increase output until she reaches point J, where the MC curve intersects the demand curve—at 60 units of output. At that point, the only way to increase sales would be to lower the price on an additional doll below $10, but since the marginal cost of a doll is always $10, we would have $P < MC$, and Larisa's profit would decline.

What is Larisa's profit-maximizing price? Think for a moment. Then see Footnote 4 for the answer.

What about Larisa's total profit? On each unit of output, she charges a price given by the demand curve and bears a cost of $10. Adding up the profit on *all* units gives us the area under the demand curve and above $10, or the area of triangle HBJ (shaded).

Now we can determine who gains and who loses when Larisa transforms herself from a single-price monopolist to a perfect price discriminator. Larisa clearly gains: Her profit increases, from the rectangle in Figure 10(a) to the larger, shaded triangle in Figure 10(b). Consumers of the product are the clear losers: Since they all pay the most they would willingly pay, no one gets to buy a doll at a price he or she would regard as a "good deal."

> A perfect price discriminator increases profit at the expense of consumers, charging each customer the most he or she would willingly pay for the product.

[4] Sorry, that's a trick question: There *is* no profit-maximizing price. As a perfect price discriminator, Larisa earns the highest profit by charging *different* prices to different customers.

SUMMARY

A *monopoly firm* is the only seller of a good or service in a market, where the market is defined broadly enough to include any close substitutes. Monopoly arises because of some *barrier to entry*: economies of scale, legal barriers, or *network externalities*. As the only seller, the monopoly faces the market demand curve and must decide what price (or prices) to charge in order to maximize profit.

A single-price monopolist will produce the quantity at which $MR = MC$ and set the price that will enable it to sell that quantity. Monopoly profit ($P - ATC$ multiplied by the quantity produced) can persist in the long run because of barriers to entry. However, government regulation and the costs of rent-seeking activity can reduce monopoly profit.

All else equal, a monopoly charges a higher price and produces less output than a perfectly competitive market. When demand for a monopoly's product increases, it will raise prices and increase production. When a monopoly's marginal costs decrease, it will pass only part of the cost savings on to consumers.

Some firms, including some monopolies, can practice *price discrimination* by charging different prices to different customers. Doing so requires the ability to identify customers who are willing to pay more and to prevent low-price customers from reselling to high-price customers. Price discrimination always benefits the monopolist (otherwise, it would charge a single price), but it can either benefit or harm consumers, depending on whether they face higher or lower prices after the discrimination. With *perfect price discrimination*, every consumer is charged the highest price they are willing to pay.

When a price discriminating firm faces more than one market, it maximizes its profits by equating the marginal revenue in each market to its marginal cost of production. This leads to a higher price in markets where buyers are less price-sensitive, and lower prices in markets where buyers are more price-sensitive.

PROBLEM SET

Answers to even-numbered Problems can be found on the text Web site through www.cengagebrain.com

1. In a certain large city, hot dog vendors are *perfectly competitive*, and face a market price of $1 per hot dog. Each hot dog vendor has the following total cost schedule:

Number of Hot Dogs per Day	Total Cost
0	$ 63
25	73
50	78
75	88
100	103
125	125
150	153
175	188
200	233

a. Add a *marginal cost* column to the right of the total cost column. (Hint: Don't forget to divide by the *change* in quantity when calculating MC.)
b. What is the profit-maximizing quantity of hot dogs for the typical vendor, and what profit (loss) will he earn (suffer)? Give your answer to the nearest 25 hot dogs.

One day, Zeke, a typical vendor, figures out that if he were the only seller in town, he would no longer have to sell his hot dogs at the market price of $1. Instead, he'd face the following demand schedule:

Price per Hot Dog	Number of Hot Dogs per Day
> $6.00	0
6.00	25
5.00	50
4.00	75
3.25	100
2.75	125
2.25	150
1.75	175
1.25	200

c. Add *total revenue* and *marginal revenue* columns to the table above. (Hint: Once again, don't forget to divide by the *change* in quantity when calculating MR.)
d. As a monopolist with the cost schedule given in the first table, how many hot dogs would Zeke choose to sell each day? What price would he charge?
e. A lobbyist has approached Zeke, proposing to form a new organization called "Citizens to Eliminate Chaos in Hot Dog Sales." The organization will lobby the city council to grant Zeke the only hot dog license in town, and it is guaranteed to succeed. The only problem is, the lobbyist is asking for a payment that amounts to $200 per business day as long as Zeke stays in business.

On purely economic grounds, should Zeke go for it? (Hint: If you're stumped, re-read the section on rent-seeking activity.)

2. Draw demand, *MR,* and *ATC* curves that show a monopoly that is just breaking even.

3. Below is demand and cost information for Warmfuzzy Press, which holds the copyright on the new best-seller, *Burping Your Inner Child.*

Q (No. of Copies)	P (per Book)	ATC (per Book)
100,000	$100	$20
200,000	$ 80	$15
300,000	$ 60	$16⅔
400,000	$ 40	$22½
500,000	$ 20	$31

   a. Determine what quantity of the book Warmfuzzy should print, and what price it should charge in order to maximize profit.
   b. What is Warmfuzzy's maximum profit?
   c. Prior to publication, the book's author renegotiates his contract with Warmfuzzy. He will receive a great big hug from the CEO, along with a one-time bonus of $1,000,000, payable when the book is published. This payment was not part of Warmfuzzy's original cost calculations. How many copies should Warmfuzzy publish now? Explain your reasoning.

4. Regarding Figure 11(b) in the chapter, one of your fellow students says, "I think the airline is making a mistake by charging students $70. It should drop the price further, so it could sell even *more* tickets than the 60 tickets in the figure. After all, as long as it charges even a little bit more than $40, its price will still be above its marginal cost, so it will still make a profit on each ticket." What is wrong with your fellow student's argument?

5. A doctor in a rural area faces the following demand schedule:

Price per Office Visit	Number of Office Visits per Day
$200	2
$175	3
$150	5
$125	8
$100	12
$ 75	18
$ 50	23
$ 25	25

The doctor's marginal cost of seeing patients is a constant $50 per patient.

   a. If the doctor must charge all patients the same price, what price will she charge, and how many patients will she see each day?
   b. If the doctor can perfectly price discriminate, how many patients will she see each day?

6. You are thinking about tutoring students in economics, and your research has convinced you that you face the following demand curve for your services:

Price per Hour of Tutoring	Number of Students Tutored per Week
> $50	0
$40	1
$35	2
$27	3
$26	4
$20	5
$15	6
< $15	6

Each student who hires you gets one hour of tutoring per week. You have decided that your time and effort are worth a constant $25 per hour (up to 6 hours per week), and that you will not tutor anyone for less than that.

   a. Suppose you are wary that your students might talk to each other about the price you charge, so you decide to charge them all the same price. Determine (1) how many students you will tutor; (2) what price you will charge; and (3) your weekly revenue from tutoring.
   b. Now suppose you discover that your students don't know each other, and you decide to perfectly price discriminate. Once again, determine (1) how many students you will tutor; (2) what price you will charge; and (3) your weekly revenue from tutoring.

Now suppose that your city requires all tutors to get a license, at a cost of $1,300 per year ($25 per week).

   c. Does it make sense for you to buy this license and be a tutor if you must charge each student the same price? Explain.
   d. Does it make sense for you to buy the license and be a tutor if you can perfectly price discriminate? Explain.

7. Draw demand, *MR, MC, AVC,* and *ATC* curves that show a monopolist operating at a loss that would cause it to *stay open* in the short run, but *exit* the industry in the long run. Then, show how a technological advance that lowers *only* the monopolist's *fixed costs* could cause a change in its long-run exit decision.

8. Answer the following:
   a. Complete the following table and use it to find this monopolist's short-run profit-maximizing level of output. How much profit will this firm earn?
   b. Redo the table to show what will happen to the short-run profit-maximizing level of output if the monopolist's marginal costs rise by $1 at each level of output. How much profit will the firm earn now?
   c. Redo the original table to show what will happen to the short-run profit-maximizing level of output if the monopolist's marginal cost at each level of output is $0.40 less than before. How much profit would the firm earn in this case?

Output	Price	Total Revenue	Marginal Revenue	Total Cost	Marginal Cost	Profit
0	$5.60			$ 0.50		
1	$5.50			$ 3.50		
2	$5.40			$ 5.45		
3	$5.30			$ 6.45		
4	$5.20			$ 6.90		
5	$5.10			$ 8.90		
6	$5.05			$13.40		
7	$4.90			$20.40		

9. In the short run, a monopoly uses both fixed and variable inputs to produce its output. Draw a diagram illustrating a monopoly breaking even. Then alter your graph to show why, if the price of using a fixed input rises, there will be no change in the monopoly's short-run equilibrium price or quantity. (Hint: Which curves shift if the price of a fixed input rises?)

10. Suppose that Patty's Pool has the demand data given in Table 2 in the chapter. Further, suppose that Patty has just two types of costs: (1) rent of $25 per day and (2) towel service costs equal to 50 cents per swimmer. Over the short run, rent is a fixed cost (Patty has a lease she can't get out of), but towel service is a variable cost (it varies with the number of swimmers). Patty's marginal cost is therefore constant at 50 cents.
    a. Under these cost conditions, what are Patty's short-run profit-maximizing output and price? What is her profit or loss per day?
    b. Now suppose that, in addition to the costs just described, the town imposes a "swimming excise tax" on Patty's Pool equal to $2 per swimmer. What are Patty's new short-run profit-maximizing output and price? What is her new profit per day? (Hint: First decide whether or not the excise tax affects Patty's marginal cost.)

c. In addition to the costs just described (including the swimming excise tax of $2 per swimmer), suppose the town imposes a "fixed swimming tax" requiring Patty to pay $2 per day for operating her pool, regardless of the number of swimmers. What are Patty's new short-run profit-maximizing output and price? What is her new profit per day? (Hint: First decide whether or not this new fixed swimming tax affects Patty's marginal cost.)
   d. Now suppose that costs are as in (c), except that the fixed swimming tax is $5 per day instead of $2 per day. What are Patty's new short-run profit-maximizing output and price? What is her new profit per day?
   e. With the $5 per day fixed swimming tax, what should Patty do in the short run? If Patty's long-run costs are the same as her short-run costs, what should she do in the long run? (Hint: Think about shutdown for short run; exit for long run.)
   f. Based on your answers to b, c, d, and e, assess the following statement: "When an excise (variable) tax is imposed on a monopoly, it will pass part, but not all, of the tax on to consumers in the form of a higher price. But a fixed tax has no effect on monopoly behavior over any time horizon." Are both of these sentences true? Explain briefly.

More Challenging

11. In Figure 13, the equation for each country's demand curve is $Q^D = 160 - 40\,P$, where Q^D represents millions of doses. Use this demand equation to answer the following questions:
    a. Suppose the price negotiated for Europe is $1 per dose (rather than $0.75 as in the chapter), and there is no parallel trade. How many doses would Europe buy, and what would be its contribution to R&D expenditures and profit? What would be the total contribution from the U.S. and Europe?
    b. Suppose that parallel trade occurs, and the price in both countries ends up converging to $1.00 per dose. How much would Pfycor collect in total to cover its R&D expenses and profit? How does this amount compare to what it collected without parallel trade, in part (a)?
    c. Suppose as in part (b) that parallel trade occurs. But this time, because they know parallel trade will occur, the pharmaceutical companies bargain harder, and end up with a negotiated price of $1.50 per dose in Europe. Once again, the price converges to the negotiated price in both countries. How much would Pfycor collect in total to cover its R&D expenses and profit? How does this amount compare to the total collected in part (a), without parallel trade and the lower

negotiated price? How does this amount compare to the total collected in the chapter, when Pfycor charged the monopoly price in both countries?

12. Suppose that Patty's Pool has the demand data given in Table 2. Further, suppose that Patty has just two types of costs: (1) rent of $24 per day and (2) towel and other service costs equal to $5 per swimmer. Over the short run, rent is a fixed cost, but towel and other service costs are variable costs. Patty's marginal cost is therefore constant at $5.

   a. Under these cost conditions, and assuming first that Patty is a *single-price monopolist*, what are Patty's short-run profit-maximizing output and price? What is her profit or loss per day? (Hint: Be sure to check the shutdown rule if you determine that she is suffering a loss.) In the long run, if Patty's rent remains the same as in the short run, should she stay in this business?

   b. Now suppose that Patty figures out a way to price discriminate by dividing her swimmers into two groups: those willing to pay the price in part *a* and those who would not be willing to pay that price but *would* swim if the price were $5. What is Patty's short-run profit-maximizing output now? What is her profit or loss per day? In the long run, if Patty's rent remains the same as in the short run, should she stay in this business?

(Hint: Be sure to recalculate the *TR* and *MR* numbers to answer this question. Also, if Patty is indifferent between two output levels, choose the higher one.)

   c. Let's say that Patty figures out a way to price discriminate by charging *three* different prices: a high price of $10 to those willing to pay that much to swim; a medium price equal to the price you found in part *a*; and a lower price of $5 to those who would not pay the price in part *a*, but would pay $5. What is Patty's short-run profit-maximizing output now? What is her profit or loss per day? In the long run, if Patty's rent remains the same as in the short run, should she stay in this business?

   d. Now suppose that Patty figures out a way to *perfectly* price discriminate, still facing the same demand curve given in Table 2 and Figure 2. What is Patty's short-run profit-maximizing output now? What is her profit or loss per day? In the long run, if Patty's rent remains the same as in the short run, should she stay in this business?

13. Suppose a single-price monopoly's demand curve is given by $P = 20 - 4Q$, where P is price and Q is quantity demanded. Marginal revenue is $MR = 20 - 8Q$. Marginal cost is $MC = Q^2$. How much should this firm produce in order to maximize profit?

CHAPTER 11

Monopolistic Competition and Oligopoly

On any given day, you are exposed to hundreds of advertisements. On the way to campus, you might see billboards suggesting that you stay at the Holiday Inn, eat at Burger King, or buy the latest, lightest, thinnest electronic device. While watching a single television show, you might encounter commercials for all three overnight delivery services (FedEx, UPS and the U.S. Postal Service). And as you search for information on the Internet, ads for vitamins, banking services, and vacation packages flash before your eyes. In all of these cases, firms are trying to convince you that their product is better or cheaper than those of its competitors.

Yet so far in this book, not much has been said about this kind of competitive advertising. That's because in the market structures we've studied so far, there is no reason for it. A perfectly competitive firm would not advertise quality or price, because each firm produces the same product as every other, and each sells at the same market price. Monopolies sometimes advertise, to make their product more appealing to consumers and shift the market demand curve rightward. But the most frequent and intense advertising about prices and product quality comes from two *other* market structures that you will learn about in this chapter. These two market structures fall into the general category of *imperfect competition*.

THE CONCEPT OF IMPERFECT COMPETITION

When thinking of market structure, perfect competition and monopoly can be viewed as the two extremes. In perfect competition, there are so many firms producing the same product that each takes the market price as given. In monopoly, there is only one firm in the market, producing a product without close substitutes. It can set its price without worrying about other firms that are selling a similar product.

Most markets, however, lie somewhere *between* these two extremes. In these markets, there is more than one firm, but each firm has some market power—some ability to set price.

Consider, for example, the market for wireless phone service in the United States. It is certainly not a monopoly, because there is more than one firm. But neither does it resemble perfect competition. For one thing, just three large firms (Verizon Wireless, AT&T, and Sprint) provide service to more than 80 percent of those with cell phones. Further, their service differs in important ways that matter to consumers: coverage, reliability, customer service, available phone models, and more. Thus, in terms of the number of firms and differences in the product, the market for wireless phone service falls somewhere between the extremes of monopoly and perfect competition.

Or consider restaurants. Even a modest-size city such as Cincinnati has thousands of different restaurants. This is certainly a large number of competitors. But they are not *perfect* competitors, because each one sells a product that is different in important ways—the type of food served, the recipes used, the atmosphere, the location, and even the friendliness of the staff. The markets for wireless phone service and restaurant meals in most cities are examples of **imperfect competition**. Imperfectly competitive markets have more than one firm (so they are not monopolies), but they violate one or more of the requirements of perfect competition.

In this chapter, we study two types of imperfectly competitive markets: *monopolistic competition* and *oligopoly*.[1]

Imperfect competition A market structure in which there is more than one firm but one or more of the requirements of perfect competition is violated.

MONOPOLISTIC COMPETITION

Suppose you live in a midsize or large city, and you're having a night out with friends when you notice the gas tank is empty. You pass several stations, looking for one with a decent convenience store, because one of your friends needs to get some hair gel. After filling up the tank, a lively discussion ensues because everyone wants to go to a different pizza place. Finally, after some cajoling and compromising, you head across town to your group's choice. Over dinner, you all decide to see a movie. But that leads to another discussion: which multiplex to go to. One has the advantage of being closest, but the popcorn is stale. A second has great popcorn but it's impossible to park. And a third has great parking and great popcorn, but it's a 20-minute drive.

Although most people would have no reason to notice, all of your purchases that night would have something in common. The gas station, the pizza place, and the movie theaters all sell their products under a market structure called **monopolistic competition**.

As the name suggests, monopolistic competition is a hybrid of perfect competition and monopoly, sharing some of the features of each. Specifically,

Monopolistic competition A market structure in which there are many firms selling products that are differentiated, and in which there is easy entry and exit.

> *a monopolistically competitive market has three fundamental characteristics:*
>
> 1. *differentiated products;*
> 2. *many buyers and sellers;*
> 3. *easy entry and exit.*

If you compare this list of characteristics with the list for perfect competition (in Chapter 9), you'll notice that the last two items are shared by both market structures. But the first item is new. Let's examine each of these characteristics in turn.

Differentiated Products

In perfect competition, sellers offer a standardized product. In *monopolistic competition,* by contrast, each seller produces a somewhat different product from the others. Two coffeehouses, two photocopy shops, or two supermarkets might be close substitutes for one another, but they are not the same. For this reason, a monopolistic competitor can raise its price (up to a point) and lose only *some* of its customers.

---

[1] Imperfect competition is sometimes defined as *any* market structure other than perfect competition, which would include monopoly as well.

The others will stay with the firm because they like its product, even when it charges somewhat more than its competitors.

Thus, a monopolistic competitor faces a *downward-sloping demand curve,* so it has market power. In this sense, it is more like a monopolist than a perfect competitor:

> *Because it produces a differentiated product, a monopolistic competitor faces a downward-sloping demand curve: It can sell more by charging less, or raise its price without losing all of its customers.*

What makes a product differentiated? Sometimes it is the *quality* of the product. By many objective standards, a Mercedes is a better car than a Hyundai and the Hilton has better hotel rooms than Motel 6. Another type of differentiation arises from differences in *location.* Even if two supermakets were otherwise identical, you will prefer the one closer to your home or office.

Product differences can also be entirely subjective. Objectively speaking, Colgate toothpaste may be neither better nor worse than Crest. But each has its own flavor and texture, and each appeals to different people. Even when two products *are* identical, if people *think* they are different, then as far as the market is concerned, they are different. For example, all bottles of bleach have identical ingredients—5.25 percent sodium hypochlorite and 94.75 percent water. But if *some* buyers think that Clorox bleach is different and would pay a bit more for it, then Clorox bleach is a differentiated product.

Because a monopolistic competitor faces a downward-sloping demand curve, the firm *chooses* its price. Like a monopoly, it is a *price setter.*

Many Buyers and Sellers

In *perfect* competition, the existence of many buyers and sellers helps ensure that no individual buyer or seller can influence the market price. In monopolistic competition, the "many buyers and sellers" assumption plays a different role: It rules out *strategic interaction* among firms in the market. That is, when a firm under monopolistic competition makes a decision (about price, advertising, product guarantees, etc.), it does not take into account how its decision will affect other firms and how they might respond. There are simply too many other firms, each supplying such a small part of the market, for any one of them to have much impact on the others.

Restaurants in most cities satisfy this requirement. With so many other restaurants, if one decides to offer an early-bird special or advertise in the local paper or put flyers under windshields, it usually doesn't worry how the other restaurants in the city will react.[2]

Easy Entry and Exit

In monopolistic competition, easy entry and exit play the same role as in perfect competition: ensuring that firms earn zero economic profit in the long run. Remember that "easy entry" does *not* mean that entry is effortless or inexpensive. Rather, it means that you can open up, say, a pizza place if you're willing to bear the same costs that existing pizza places must bear. There are no significant *barriers* to entry that keep out newcomers—no law, for example, that new pizza places must pay higher annual license fees than established ones.

[2] Monopolistic competitors do imitate the successful practices of others in the market, as you'll see in a few pages. But a monopolistic competitor does not take into account the *potential* for imitation when making a decision. In the second half of this chapter, when we study oligopoly, we'll examine what happens when firms *do* take into account the potential reactions of their rivals.

In monopolistic competition, however, our assumption about easy entry extends to business practices as well: Any firm can copy the successful practices of other firms. If one movie theater finds that offering lower prices for Wednesday-afternoon showings generates economic profit, any other movie theater can do the same. If Best Buy's multi-year replacement plan for electronic goods brings it profit, then other electronic goods retailers can choose to offer the same plan. Although it may take time, success will eventually lead to imitation. You'll see later how this extended view of entry—specific to monopolistic competition—plays a role in ensuring zero economic profit in the long run.

Monopolistic Competition in the Short Run

The individual monopolistic competitor behaves very much like a monopoly. Its goal is to maximize profit by producing where $MR = MC$. In the short run, the result may be economic profit, economic loss, or zero economic profit.

The key difference is this: While a monopoly is the *only* seller in its market, a monopolistic competitor is one of many sellers. When a *monopoly* raises its price, its customers must pay up or buy less of the product. When a *monopolistic competitor* raises its price, its customers have one additional option: They can buy a close substitute from some other firm. Thus, all else equal, the demand curve facing a firm will be more elastic under monopolistic competition than under monopoly.

Figure 1 illustrates the situation of a monopolistic competitor, Kafka Exterminators. The figure shows the demand curve, d_1, that the firm faces, as well as the marginal revenue, marginal cost, and average total cost curves. As a monopolistic competitor, Kafka Exterminators competes with many other extermination services in its local area. Thus, if it raises its price, it will lose some of its customers to the competition. If Kafka had a *monopoly* on the local extermination business, we would expect less price elasticity than in the figure, because customers would have to buy from Kafka or get rid of their bugs on their own.

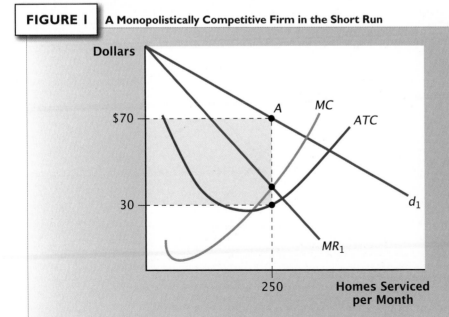

FIGURE 1   **A Monopolistically Competitive Firm in the Short Run**

Like any other firm, a monopolistic competitor maximizes profit by producing the level of output where its MR and MC curves intersect. Kafka exterminators maximizes profit by servicing 250 homes per month. The profit-maximizing price ($70) is found on the demand curve at an output level of 250 (point A). Profit per unit of $40 is the difference between the price ($70) and average total cost ($30) at output of 250. Total profit is profit per unit times output ($40 × 250 = $10,000), equal to the area of the shaded rectangle.

Like any other firm, Kafka Exterminators will produce where $MR = MC$. As you can see in Figure 1, when Kafka faces demand curve d_1 and the associated marginal revenue curve MR_1, its profit-maximizing output level is 250 homes serviced per month, and its profit-maximizing price is $70 per home. In the short run, the firm may earn an economic profit or an economic loss, or it may break even. In the figure, Kafka is earning an economic profit: Profit per unit is $P - ATC = \$70 - \$30 = \$40$, and total monthly profit—the area of the blue rectangle—is $\$40 \times 250 = \$10,000$.

Monopolistic Competition in the Long Run

If Kafka Exterminators were a monopoly, Figure 1 might be the end of our story. The firm could continue to earn economic profit forever, since barriers to entry would keep out any potential competitors.

But under monopolistic competition—in which there are no barriers to entry and exit—the firm will not enjoy its profit for long. New sellers will enter the market, attracted by the profits that can be earned there. Kafka will lose some of its customers to the new entrants. At any given price, Kafka will find itself servicing fewer homes than before, so the demand curve it faces will shift leftward. Entry will continue to occur, and the demand curve will continue to shift leftward, until Kafka and other firms are earning zero economic profit.

This process of adjustment is shown in Figure 2. The demand curve shifts leftward (from d_1 to d_2). The marginal revenue curve shifts left as well (from MR_1 to MR_2). Kafka's new profit-maximizing output level, 100, is found at the intersection point between its marginal cost curve and its *new* marginal revenue curve MR_2. Kafka's new price—found on its demand curve d_2 at 100 units—is $40. Finally, since ATC is also $40 at that output level, Kafka is earning zero economic profit—the

---

FIGURE 2   A Monopolistically Competitive Firm in the Long Run

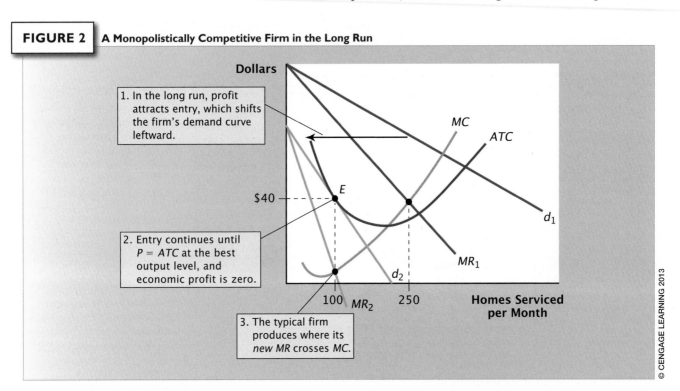

1. In the long run, profit attracts entry, which shifts the firm's demand curve leftward.

2. Entry continues until $P = ATC$ at the best output level, and economic profit is zero.

3. The typical firm produces where its *new MR* crosses *MC*.

© CENGAGE LEARNING 2013

best it can do in the long run.[3] In long-run equilibrium, the profit-maximizing price, $40, will always equal the average total cost of production.

We can also reverse these steps. If the typical firm is suffering an economic loss (draw this diagram on your own), *exit* will occur. With fewer competitors, those firms that remain in the market will gain customers, so their demand curves will shift *rightward*. Exit will cease only when the typical firm is earning zero economic profit, where the demand curve just touches the *ATC* curve at a point like *E* in Figure 2. Thus, the typical firm will earn zero economic profit in the long run, whether we start from a position of economic profit or economic loss:

> *Under monopolistic competition, firms can earn positive, negative, or zero economic profit in the short run. But in the long run, free entry and exit ensure that each firm earns zero economic profit, just as under perfect competition.*

Is this prediction of our model realistic? Indeed it is: In the real world, monopolistic competitors often earn economic profit or loss in the short run. But, given enough time, profits attract new entrants while losses result in an "industry shakeout" as firms exit. In the long run, restaurants, retail stores, hair salons, and other monopolistically competitive firms earn zero economic profit for their owners. That is, there is just enough accounting profit to cover the implicit costs of doing business—just enough to keep the owners from shifting their time and money to some alternative enterprise.

Excess Capacity Under Monopolistic Competition

Figure 3 reproduces the long-run equilibrium result in Figure 2, after entry has eliminated Kafka's economic profit at point *E*. At that point, the *ATC* curve has the same slope as the demand curve, a *negative* slope. Thus, in the long run, a monopolistic competitor always produces on the *downward-sloping* portion of its *ATC* curve and therefore *never produces at minimum average cost*. Indeed, its long-run output level is always *too small* to minimize cost per unit. The firm operates with *excess capacity*. (The output level at which cost per unit is minimized is often called "capacity output.")

In Figure 3, Kafka Exterminators *would* reach minimum cost per unit by servicing about 200 homes per month (the firm's capacity output), but in the long run, it will service only 100 homes per month.

[3] In the figure, we've assumed that as long-run adjustment takes place, the *ATC* and *MC* curves remain as drawn. That is, we assume that Kafka's optimal plant size and the prices it pays for its inputs remain unchanged in the long run. If these assumptions don't hold, the *ATC* and *MC* curves will shift during long-run adjustment, but our conclusion remains the same: Entry will occur until the demand curve shifts leftward by just enough to touch the *new ATC* curve, so that $P = ATC$ at the new profit-maximizing output level.

DANGEROUS CURVES

Contradictory curves A common error when drawing a monopolistic competitor in long-run equilibrium is to have the demand curve *cross* the *ATC* curve, rather than be *tangent* to the *ATC* curve as in Figure 2. An example of this mistake is drawn here, with a (supposed) long-run equilibrium output of Q_1. It is true that at Q_1, $P = ATC$, so economic profit would indeed be zero. But Q_1 is not the profit-maximizing output level. Why? Notice that there are *other* output levels (e.g., Q_2) where the demand curve lies *above* the *ATC* curve. Because $P > ATC$ at those output levels, the firm could earn an economic profit by producing them. Because Q_1 is *not* the profit-maximizing output level (since other output levels have positive profit), then Q_1 cannot be the output level at which the *MR* and *MC* curves intersect. One or more of these curves must be drawn incorrectly.

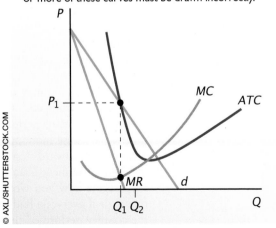

| FIGURE 3 | Excess Capacity in Monopolistic Competition |

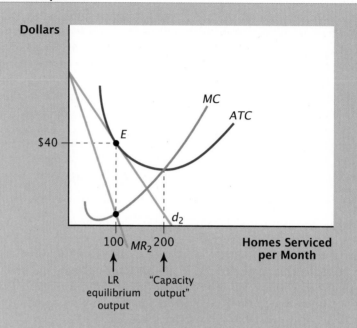

In long-run equilibrium, a monopolistic competitor earns zero profit and operates on the downward-sloping portion of its ATC curve (100 units, at point E). As a result, it does not use enough of its capacity to minimize its average total cost. "Capacity output" (where ATC is minimized) is 200 units. But for any rise in output beyond 100, MR < MC, so profit would decrease (the firm would go from zero to negative profit).

> *In the long run, a monopolistic competitor will operate with excess capacity—that is, it will not sell enough output to achieve minimum cost per unit.*

To see why a monopolistic competitor *cannot* minimize average cost in the long run, imagine that Kafka Exterminators started to increase the number of homes it serviced beyond 100, moving closer to 200. Each additional home serviced would cause cost to rise more than revenue would rise ($MC > MR$). Moreover, the firm would suffer a loss, since $P < ATC$ at all output levels greater than 100. Kafka would quickly return to its profit-maximizing output of 100 homes, where at least it breaks even.

Excess Capacity and Prices

Excess capacity suggests that monopolistic competition is costly to consumers, and indeed it is. Recall that under perfect competition, $P = $ minimum ATC in long-run equilibrium. (Look back at Figure 9 in Chapter 9.) But under monopolistic competition, $P > $ minimum ATC in the long run. Thus, if the ATC curves were the same, price would always be greater under monopolistic competition.

This reasoning may tempt you to leap to a conclusion: Consumers are better off under perfect competition. But don't leap so fast. Remember that in order to get the beneficial results of perfect competition, all firms must produce identical output. It is precisely because monopolistic competitors produce *differentiated* output—and therefore have downward-sloping demand curves—that $P > $ minimum ATC in the long run.

And consumers usually *benefit* from product differentiation. (If you don't think so, imagine how you would feel if every restaurant in your town served an identical menu, or if everyone had to wear the same type of clothing, or if every rock group in the country performed the same tunes in exactly the same way.) Seen in this light, we can regard the higher prices under monopolistic competition as the price we pay for product variety. Some may argue that there is too much variety in a market economy—how many different brands of toothpaste do we really need?—but few would want to transform all monopolistically competitive industries into perfectly competitive ones.

Nonprice Competition

As you've seen, a monopolistic competitor tries to earn the highest possible profit by moving *along* its demand curve until it finds the profit-maximizing output level. But a monopolistic competitor may also try to *shift* its demand curve rightward by making its own product more appealing and attracting customers from competitors.

> Any action a firm takes to shift the demand curve for its output to the right is called **nonprice competition**.

Nonprice competition Any action a firm takes to shift its demand curve rightward.

Better service, product guarantees, free home delivery, more attractive packaging, better locations, as well as advertising to inform customers about these things, are all examples of nonprice competition.

This type of competition is another reason why monopolistic competitors earn zero economic profit in the long run. If an innovative firm discovers a way to shift its demand curve rightward—say, by offering better service or more clever advertising—then in the *short run*, it may be able to earn a profit.

But not for long. Remember that in monopolistic competition, the "free entry" assumption includes the ability of new entrants, as well as existing firms, to replicate the successful business practices of others. If product guarantees are enabling some firms to earn economic profit, then *all* firms will offer product guarantees. If advertising is doing the trick, then *all* firms will start ad campaigns. In the long run, imitation by others will reverse any advantage that the initiators hoped to achieve, and will begin shifting their demand curves back again. At the same time, the costs of the nonprice competition shifts up each firm's *ATC* curve. After all, firms have to *pay* for advertising, product guarantees, or better staff training.

As you can see, even if nonprice competition leads to profits for the early adopters in the short run, we can identify *two* forces that shrink profit back to zero in the long run: (1) imitation by others reverses the initial rightward shift in demand; and (2) the costs of nonprice competition shift the *ATC* curve upward. In the end, each firm will once again earn zero economic profit, with its demand curve tangent to the new, higher *ATC* curve.

> In monopolistic competition, nonprice competition can temporarily increase demand for a firm's product and create economic profit in the short run. But in the long run, entry and emulation by other firms, as well as the cost of nonprice competition itself, ensure zero economic profit in the long run.

We will take a closer look at one form of nonprice competition, advertising, in the Using the Theory section at the end of the chapter. But first, in the next section, we'll take a look at a completely different type of imperfectly competitive market.

OLIGOPOLY

A monopolistic competitor enjoys a certain amount of independence. There are so many *other* firms selling in the market—each one such a small fish in such a large pond—that each of them can make decisions without worrying about how the others will react. For example, if a single pharmacy in a large city cuts its prices or begins advertising, it can safely assume that any other pharmacy that could benefit from price cutting or advertising has already done so, or will shortly do so, *regardless of its own actions*. Thus, there is no reason for the first pharmacy to take the reactions of other pharmacies into account when making its own decisions.

But in some markets, most of the output is sold by just a few firms. These markets are not monopolies (there is more than one seller), but they are not monopolistically competitive either. There are so few firms that the actions taken by any one will *very much* affect the others and will likely generate a direct response. Before the management team makes a decision, it must reason as follows: "If we take action *A,* our competitors will do *B,* and then we would do *C,* and they would respond with *D...,*" and so on. This kind of strategic interaction among firms is the hallmark of the market structure we call *oligopoly:*

Oligopoly A market dominated by a small number of strategically interacting firms.

> An **oligopoly** is a market dominated by a small number of strategically interacting firms.

The words "dominated by" are important in this definition. A market can have very many firms and still be considered an oligopoly market, as long as the top few firms sell a large share of the output in that market. For example, there are over 100 companies that offer wireless phone service in the United States. But the big three (AT&T, Verizon, and Sprint) dominate the market because they serve 80 percent of the customers.

Measuring Market Concentration

As you'll see later in this chapter, strategically interacting firms often try to raise their profits by colluding with each other to raise prices, to the detriment of consumers. Strategic interaction—and the likelihood of collusion—is greater when a market is highly *concentrated* (i.e., a large share of market production is concentrated among the top few firms). Therefore, it's useful to have some measure of market concentration.

The first step in obtaining such a measure is to define the relevant market itself. The approach taken by economists and government officials is to define a market just broadly enough so that it includes all "reasonably close" substitutes. Thus, we refer to the market for "breakfast cereals" rather than the market for food (which would be too broad) or the market for cornflakes (too narrow).

Once the market is defined, economists measure market concentration in two ways: *Concentration ratios* and the *Herfindahl-Hirschman Index.* Let's discuss each of these in turn and see how they apply to some real-world markets.

Concentration Ratios

Concentration ratio The percentage of total output or sales by a given number of the largest firms in the market.

The simplest measure of market concentration is a **concentration ratio,** defined as the percentage of total output or sales attributable to the top 4, 8, or any other number of the largest firms in the market. Table 1 shows 4-firm and 8-firm concentration ratios for several U.S. industries in 2007, the latest data available from the U.S. Census Bureau. For example, the 4-firm concentration ratio for breakfast cereals, 85.0, tells us that the top four U.S. firms produced 85% of total U.S. production. With so few firms accounting for such a large share of the market, it is safe to assume they interact strategically.

TABLE 1

Concentration Ratios and
HHI Values in Selected
Industries, 2007

Market	Total Number of Firms in Market	4-Firm Concentration Ratio	8-Firm Concentration Ratio	Herfindahl- Hirschman Index (HHI)
Beer	373	89.6	91.7	>2,000
Computers	413	89.5	94.9	>2,000
Breakfast Cereals	35	85.0	94.2	2,909
Tires	90	77.6	92.9	1,893
Automobiles	174	71.3	90.2	1,549
Soft Drinks	259	61.1	76.5	1,132
Ice Cream and Similar Frozen Deserts	347	57.6	71.3	1,174
Mattresses	452	57.0	67.7	916
Household & Institutional Furniture	15,898	16.7	23.0	94
Hospitals	6,505	7.4	10.9	–

Source: U.S. Census Bureau, Concentration Ratios—Share of Value Added, 2007.

By contrast, household furniture is characterized by very little market concentration; the top 8 firms account for less than a quarter of total output. Here, strategic interaction is likely to be very weak or nonexistent, and oligopoly analysis would contribute little to our understanding of firm and market behavior. For household furniture, the nonstrategic model of monopolistic competition would be a better fit.

The Herfindahl-Hirschman Index

Another measure of market concentration—which gives more weight to the presence of the largest firms—is the **Herfindahl-Hirschman Index** (HHI). To calculate the index, we first convert the percentage market share of each firm in the industry into a whole number, then square it, then sum the squared numbers. For example, if there is just one firm (a monopoly), its market share is 100%, so the HHI = 100^2 = 10,000. This is the largest value the HHI can have. If there are 100 firms, each with a 1% share, the HHI = $1^2 + 1^2 + 1^2 + \cdots$ = 100. With an even greater number of equal-sized firms, the HHI would be even smaller. In general, the fewer the number of firms in the market, the larger the HHI.

But the HHI is most useful when the firms are not of equal size. In that case, the larger firms will have more weight in the HHI value. For example, suppose a market has just four firms. Then the 4-firm concentration ratio will be 100%, regardless of how market share is distributed among these firms. If all four have equal market shares of 25%, the HHI will be $25^2 + 25^2 + 25^2 + 25^2$ = 2,500. But if some of the firms are larger than the others, the HHI will rise. For example, suppose two of these firms each have a 40% share, while the other two each have 10%. Then the HHI will be $40^2 + 40^2 + 10^2 + 10^2$ = 3,400. We'd naturally view the market as more concentrated in this second case, and this is reflected in its larger HHI value.

The HHI is used by two government agencies—the Federal Trade Commission and the Department of Justice—in deciding whether to approve or block mergers

Herfindahl-Hirschman Index (HHI): A measure of market concentration obtained by summing the squares of each firm's market share.

between firms. These agencies have even announced how they use the HHI, so firms can anticipate the government's response to proposed mergers.

The most recent guidelines—released in August 2010—state that mergers will generally not invite government scrutiny or opposition if they either (1) increase the HHI by less than 100; or (2) keep the HHI under 1,500. (An HHI under 1,500 is considered an "unconcentrated" market.) All other mergers can invite government investigation. And government opposition can be presumed for any merger that raises the HHI by more than 200 to a value of 2,500 or greater (the HHI threshold for a "highly concentrated" market).

True to its word, in September 2011, the U.S. Justice Department announced that it would go to court to block AT&T's planned acquisition of T-mobile. An end-of-chapter problem will help you see how the HHI figured into their decision.

Some Provisos on the Measures

"Official" concentration ratios and HHI values—such as those in Table 1—are based on data collected by the U.S. Census Bureau. In some cases, these measures distort the true degree of market concentration. For example, in the Census Bureau data, the market share of each firm is its percentage of *U.S. production* only. This does not matter much for breakfast cereals or ice cream, where almost all of the output is produced domestically. But it *does* matter in markets—such as computers—in which U.S.-made products compete with those made abroad. If foreign production were included, market shares for each firm producing in the U.S. would be smaller.

Another problem is that the census data is nationwide, while the relevant markets are sometimes local. For example, Table 1 shows that the largest eight U.S. hospitals account for only 10.9 percent of nationwide hospital services, suggesting very little market concentration. But residents in much of the country have access to only a few hospitals at best; in their *local* markets, these top few hospitals might have a combined 100 percent of the market. In general, local markets for hospital services and many other services are more concentrated than they appear in the official measures. Because of these problems, government agencies—when evaluating potential mergers—do not limit themselves to measures derived from Census Bureau data. They try to incorporate other factors, such as foreign production that competes with U.S. production, the local nature of many markets, and more.

How Oligopolies Arise

If a market has just a few sellers, we should naturally ask: Why aren't there more? After all, in some oligopoly markets, firms earn economic profit year after year. Why doesn't such profit attract entry, as it does in perfect competition and monopolistic competition? What *barriers to entry* keep out new competitors, leaving just a few firms with the market all to themselves?

Economies of Scale

One familiar barrier to entry is economies of scale. In Chapter 7, you learned that when a firm has economies of scale over a wide range of output, a large firm will have lower cost per unit than would a small firm. This can create a natural monopoly if a firm's minimum efficient scale (MES) occurs when it produces for the entire market. Or it can create a **natural oligopoly** if the MES occurs when a firm produces for

Natural oligopoly A market that tends naturally toward oligopoly because the minimum efficient scale of the typical firm is a large fraction of the market.

a large fraction of the market. Since small firms can't compete, only a few large firms survive, and the market becomes an oligopoly. Airlines, college textbook publishers, and passenger jet manufacturers are all examples of oligopolies in which economies of scale play a large role.

Reputation as a Barrier

A new entrant may suffer just from being new. Established oligopolists are likely to have favorable reputations. In many oligopolies—like the markets for soft drinks and breakfast cereals—heavy advertising expenditure has also helped to build and maintain brand loyalty. A new entrant might be able to catch up to those already in the industry, but only after a substantial period of high advertising costs, low revenue, and economic loss. This puts potential new firms at a disadvantage compared to those already in the industry, and it may discourage entry.

Strategic Barriers

Oligopoly firms often pursue strategies designed to keep out potential competitors. They can maintain excess production capacity as a signal to a potential entrant that, with little advance notice, they could easily saturate the market and leave the new entrant with little or no revenue. They can make special deals with distributors to receive the best shelf space in retail stores or make long-term arrangements with customers to ensure that their products are not displaced quickly by those of a new entrant.

Legal Barriers

Patents and copyrights, which can be responsible for monopoly, can also create oligopolies. For example, as of 2011, only two medications have shown (limited) promise in treating advanced melanoma (skin cancer), and both are protected by patents. Until their patents expire, or several new drugs are developed, the market for melanoma drugs will continue to be an oligopoly, in which two large pharmaceutical companies are the only sellers.

Other legal barriers arise when oligopoly firms lobby the government to preserve their market domination. One of the easiest targets is foreign competition. U.S. steel companies are relentless in their efforts to limit the amount of foreign—especially Japanese—steel sold in the U.S. market. In the past, they have succeeded in getting special taxes on imported steel and financial penalties imposed upon successful foreign steel companies. Other U.S. industries, including automobiles, textiles, and lumber, have had similar successes.

In local markets, zoning regulations may prohibit the building of a new supermarket, movie theater, or auto repair shop, thereby preserving the oligopoly status of the few firms already established there. Lobbying by established firms is often the source of these restrictive practices.

Oligopoly versus Other Market Structures

Of the market structures you have studied in this book, oligopoly presents the greatest challenge to economists. To see why, look at Figure 4. It shows some demand curve facing Apple iTunes for a subset of its music downloads: the most popular new releases. Let's first consider the curve labeled D_1. It shows (hypothetically) the number of songs Apple would sell at each price—*if* its chief competitor, Amazon, continued to charge $0.89 for the same songs. For example, with a price of $0.99 per song, Apple would sell 4 million songs per week (point A). With a higher price of

oil by setting the amount that each of its members can produce. In the mid-1970s, OPEC quadrupled its price per barrel in just two years, leading to a huge increase in profits for the cartel's members. In the late 1990s, OPEC exerted its muscle once again, doubling the price of oil over a period of 18 months.

If explicit collusion to raise prices is such a good thing for oligopolists, why don't they all do it? A major reason is that price-fixing agreements by private firms are illegal in the United States, Canada, the European Union, and many other developed countries, except in special circumstances where governments allow them. (OPEC has *not* been granted such permission by oil-importing country governments. But OPEC is a price-fixing agreement among oil-exporting country *governments*, rather than private firms, so it has not been prosecuted.)

Interestingly, authorities in both the United States and Europe now use a strategy based on the prisoner's dilemma game to uncover price-fixing agreements: The first manager to confess is given automatic amnesty, while those who don't confess (or confess too late) are treated harshly. The U.S. Department of Justice has reported that since this policy went into effect in 1993, the number of corporate confessions and applications for amnesty has increased dramatically. Table 2 lists some of the largest fines imposed by the U.S. and other governments in recent years, after price-fixing arrangements were exposed and prosecuted.

The chances of getting caught, and the severe penalties at stake, often lead oligopolists to other forms of collusion that are harder to detect and prosecute.

Tacit Collusion

Tacit collusion Any form of oligopolistic cooperation that does not involve an explicit agreement.

Any time firms cooperate *without* an explicit agreement, they are engaging in **tacit collusion**. In our gas station example, one of the gas stations would try to signal to the other that if one charges the high price, the other will too. If this works, both Gus

TABLE 2				
Some Recent U.S. Price-Fixing Cases	**Date of Fine**	**Company**	**Product**	**Fine**
	Various dates in 2008 and 2009	• Japan Airlines • British Airways • Korean Airlines • Qantas Airlines • 12 other airlines	Air freight	$1.6 billion combined
	October 2008	• Sasol • Exxon Mobil • Total SA • Six other firms	Paraffin Wax	$470 million combined
	October 2008	• Dole Food • Fresh Del Monte Produce	Bananas	$82 million combined
	November 2008	• Asahi Glass • Nippon Sheet Glass • Saint-Gobain	Car Windows	$1.7 billion combined
	November 2008–March 2009	• Sharp Corp • LG Display Co. • Chungwa Picture Tubes • Hitachi	LCD displays	$621 million combined

and Filip will earn higher profit than they could without cooperating, even though there is no explicit agreement. Tacit collusion is much harder to prosecute than explicit collusion, because there is no hard evidence of the agreement.

Tacit collusion depends crucially on adopting strategies that send the right signals and discouraging other firms from breaking the agreement. One type of strategy, called **tit-for-tat**, involves doing to the other player what he has just done to you. In our gas station duopoly, for example, Gus will pick the high price whenever Filip has set the high price in the previous play, and Gus will pick the low price if that is what Filip did in the previous play. With enough plays of the game, Filip may eventually catch on that he can get Gus to set the desired high price by setting the high price himself and that he should not exploit the situation by setting the low price, because that will cause Gus to set the low price next time. The result of every play will then be the cooperative outcome: The players move to the lower right-hand corner of Figure 6, with each firm earning the higher $50,000 in profit.

Tit-for-tat A game-theoretic strategy of doing to another player this period what he has done to you in the previous period.

Tit-for-tat strategies are prominent in the airline industry. When one major airline announces special discounted fares, its rivals almost always announce identical fares the next day. The response from the rivals not only helps them remain competitive, but also provides a signal to the price-cutting airline that it will not get away with being the only discounter. This is often sufficient to get the initial discounter to reverse course.

Another form of tacit collusion is **price leadership**, in which one firm, the *price leader,* sets its price, and other sellers copy that price. The leader may be the dominant firm in the industry (the one with the greatest market share, for example), or the position of leader may rotate from firm to firm. In recent decades, American Airlines has behaved as a price leader in many air-travel markets. American's price increases have often been matched within days by Delta, United, and other major airlines.

Price leadership A form of tacit collusion in which one firm sets a price that other firms copy.

With price leadership, there is no formal agreement. Rather, the choice of the leader, the criteria it uses to set its price, and the willingness of other firms to follow come about because the firms realize—without formal discussion—that the system benefits all of them.

The Limits to Collusion

It is tempting to think that collusion—whether explicit or tacit—gives oligopolies absolute power over their markets, leaving them free to jack up prices and exploit the public without limit. But oligopoly power, even when firms get away with collusion, has its limits.

First, even colluding firms are constrained by the market demand curve: A rise in price will always reduce the quantity demanded from all firms together. There is one price—the cartel monopoly price—that maximizes the total profits of all firms in the market, and it will never serve the group's interest to charge any price higher than this.

Second, oligopolies are often weakened—and sometimes destroyed—by new technologies. This is especially true of local oligopolies. A small town, for example, might be able to support only a few stores selling luggage, office equipment, or mattresses. But the Internet has enabled residents in small towns everywhere to choose among dozens or more online sellers of the same merchandise.

Third, collusion is limited by powerful incentives to cheat on any agreement. In Figure 6, for example, suppose Gus and Filip collude to end up in the lower right-hand corner ($50,000 in profit for each). Will they stay there? Perhaps not, because each player has an incentive to cheat by switching back to the low price. The other player may punish the cheater by lowering his own price, and cooperation may be restored. But periodic cheating often plagues oligopolies.

Even the explicit collusion practiced by the OPEC cartel periodically falls apart, because so many members cheat. One member may think that it can secretly sell a bit more than its allotted quantity of oil and earn more revenue. (While the *market* demand for oil is inelastic, the demand for any *one* member's oil is highly elastic.) But when *several* OPEC members use this reasoning and cheat, market quantity rises significantly and the market price falls. At that point, no one wants to stick to a profit-sacrificing agreement that no one else seems to be following, and cooperation breaks down. (Cheating in cartels is discussed further in the appendix.)

Finally, there is government. In this chapter, we've discussed two ways that government limits oligopoly power: (1) prosecuting managers who participate in price-fixing agreements, and (2) blocking mergers that would result in highly concentrated markets where collusion of all types is more likely. We'll discuss the legal basis for these policies, as well as other government actions to preserve competition in markets, in Chapter 15.

THE FOUR MARKET STRUCTURES: A POSTSCRIPT

You have now been introduced to the four different market structures: perfect competition, monopoly, monopolistic competition, and oligopoly. Each has different characteristics, and each leads to different predictions about pricing, profit, nonprice competition, and firms' responses to changes in their environments.

Table 3 summarizes some of the assumptions and predictions associated with each of the four market structures. While the table is a useful review of the *models* we have

TABLE 3

A Summary of Market Structures

	Perfect Competition	Monopolistic Competition	Oligopoly	Monopoly
ASSUMPTIONS:				
Number of firms	Many	Many	Few	One
Output of different firms	Standardized	Differentiated	Standardized or differentiated	—
View of pricing	Price taker	Price setter	Price setter	Price setter
Barriers to entry or exit?	No	No	Yes	Yes
Strategic interdependence?	No	No	Yes	No
PREDICTIONS:				
Price and output decisions	$MC = MR$	$MC = MR$	Through strategic interdependence	$MC = MR$
Short-run profit	Positive, zero, or negative	Positive, zero, or negative	Positive, zero, or negative	Positive, zero, or negative
Long-run profit	Zero	Zero	Positive or zero	Positive or zero
Advertising?	Never	Almost always	Maybe, if differentiated product	Sometimes

studied, it is not a how-to guide for classifying real-world markets: We cannot simply look at the array of markets we see around us and say, "This one is perfectly competitive," "That one is an oligopoly," and so on. Why not? Because the model we should choose to analyze any market depends on the question we are trying to answer.

Suppose we're interested in explaining why a particular barbecue restaurant with no nearby competitors earns economic profit year after year, or why it spends so much of its profit on rent-seeking activity (lobbying the local zoning board). Then, we would most likely use the monopoly model. Alternatively, if we want to explain why *most* barbecue restaurants do *not* earn much economic profit, or why they advertise so heavily, or why there is so much excess capacity (empty tables) in the industry, we would use the model of monopolistic competition. To explain a price war among the only two restaurants in a neighborhood, or to explore the possibility of explicit or tacit collusion in pricing or advertising, we would use the oligopoly model. And if we're interested in barbecue restaurants as an example of *restaurants in general,* and we want to explain why restaurant prices are rising, we might use the perfectly competitive model (supply and demand curves for restaurant meals).

The Nobel prize–winning economist Milton Friedman (1912–2006), explaining a point originally made by another great economist, Alfred Marshall (1842–1924), put it this way:

> Everything depends on the problem; there is no inconsistency in regarding the same firm as if it were a perfect competitor for one problem, and a monopolist for another.[7]

In other words, rather than viewing a given market as always conforming to this or that market structure model, we treat a market *as if* it can fit *each* of our models. And we choose whichever model best helps us understand the behavior we are analyzing at the time.

[7] Milton Friedman, "The Methodology of Positive Economics," in *Essays in Positive Economics*, University of Chicago Press, 1953.

USING THE THEORY

ADVERTISING IN MONOPOLISTIC COMPETITION AND OLIGOPOLY

We began this chapter by noting that firms in perfectly competitive markets never advertise because they produce a standardized product. Differentiated products are a defining characteristic of monopolistic competition and are often a characteristic of oligopoly (think of breakfast cereals, wireless services, and airlines). When a firm produces a differentiated product, it can gain customers by convincing them that its product is different and better in some way than that of its competitors. Advertising, whether it merely informs customers about the product ("The new Toyota Corolla gets 45 miles per gallon on the highway") or attempts to influence them more subtly and psychologically ("Our exotic perfume will fill your life with mystery and intrigue"), is one way to sharply differentiate a product in the minds of consumers. Since other firms will take advantage of the opportunity to advertise, any firm that *doesn't* advertise will be at a disadvantage. In this section, we use the tools we've learned in this chapter to look at some aspects of advertising under monopolistic competition and oligopoly.

How Advertising Affects Price in Monopolistic Competition

A monopolistic competitor advertises for two reasons: to shift its demand curve rightward (greater quantity demanded at each price) and to make demand for its output *less* elastic (so it can raise price and suffer a smaller decrease in quantity demanded). Advertising costs money, so in addition to its impact on the demand curve, it will also affect the firm's ATC curve. What is the ultimate impact of advertising on the typical firm?

Figure 9(a) shows demand and ATC curves for a company, Narcissus Fragrance, that manufactures and sells perfume. Initially, there is no advertising at all in the industry. Narcissus is in long-run equilibrium at point A, in panel (a), where its demand curve ($d_{no\ ads}$) and ATC curve ($ATC_{no\ ads}$) touch, so economic profit is zero. The firm charges $60 per bottle and sells at the profit-maximizing output level of 1,000 bottles per month. This is the output level where its marginal revenue and marginal cost curves (not shown) intersect.

Now suppose that we introduce advertising into this market. Initially, the first few firms that discover advertising may have a temporary advantage over firms that don't advertise. But remember that in monopolistic competition, any successful form of nonprice competition will be replicated by *all* firms (otherwise they would be at a competitive disadvantage). So let's skip over the temporary situation, in which only some firms advertise, and examine our new long-run equilibrium when *all* firms advertise. In the long run, how will advertising change the situation of a typical monopolistic competitor in this market?

One change is that, with each firm paying additional costs for advertising, cost per unit will be greater at every output level. So the typical firm's ATC curve will shift upward. In panel (a), we show that Narcissus's ATC curve shifts upward to ATC_{ads}. Notice, however, that the upward shift is smaller at higher output levels, as the cost of any given ad campaign is spread over a larger number of units.

In addition to the shift in ATC, we can expect that with all firms advertising, the demand for the product *in general* will increase. (More people are aware of the product, or have had their appetites stimulated.) And this, in turn, means that *each* firm should be able to sell more units at any given price than before: The demand curve facing each firm shifts rightward.

Where will each firm end up? We know that, in the long run, the combination of a rightward shift in demand and an upward shift in ATC must eventually lead to a new equilibrium in which economic profit is zero. To see why, remember that if advertising creates economic profit in the short run, entry will occur, and every firm's demand curve will then shift leftward. If advertising creates economic loss in the short run, exit will occur, and the remaining firms' demand curves will shift rightward. In the end, long-run equilibrium (a situation of neither entry nor exit) requires that the typical firm earn zero economic profit. And in monopolistic competition, as you've learned, this can only occur when the demand curve touches but does not cross the ATC curve, with $P = ATC$ at the profit-maximizing output level.

In panel (a), the new long-run equilibrium for our typical firm, Narcissus, occurs at point B. Narcissus sells 1,750 bottles of perfume and charges consumers a higher price ($100) than before. But because it has to pay for advertising, it is breaking even, just as it was in the initial long-run equilibrium without advertising.

| FIGURE 9 | Advertising in Monopolistic Competition |

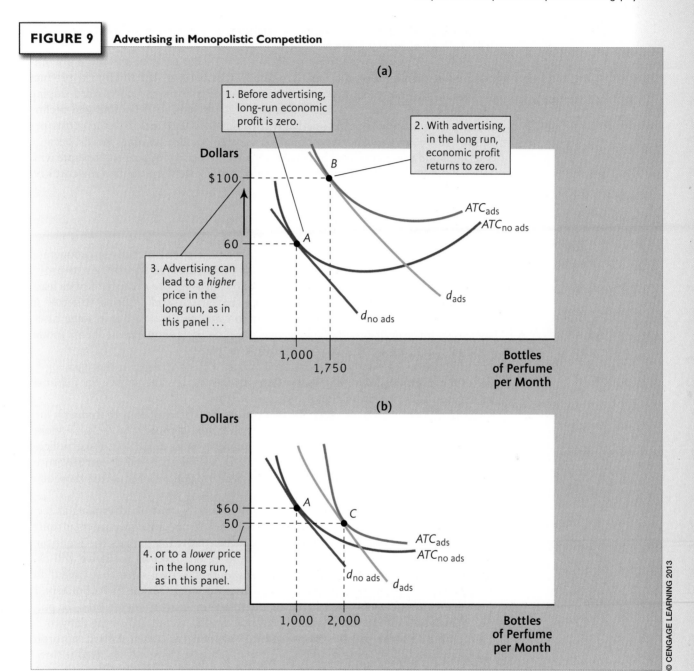

(a)

1. Before advertising, long-run economic profit is zero.

2. With advertising, in the long run, economic profit returns to zero.

3. Advertising can lead to a *higher* price in the long run, as in this panel …

Dollars

$100

60

ATC_{ads}
$ATC_{no\ ads}$
d_{ads}
$d_{no\ ads}$

1,000
1,750

Bottles of Perfume per Month

(b)

4. or to a *lower* price in the long run, as in this panel.

Dollars

$60
50

ATC_{ads}
$ATC_{no\ ads}$
$d_{no\ ads}$ d_{ads}

1,000   2,000

Bottles of Perfume per Month

In panel (a), the impact of advertising is to *raise* prices for consumers. When consumers buy perfume, they are now paying for the advertising as well as all the inputs they paid for before. But you may be surprised that advertising can also have the opposite result: It can actually *lower* prices for consumers.

Panel (b) illustrates this case. As before, we begin in a long-run equilibrium with no advertising in the market, and Narcissus operating at point *A*. When we introduce advertising to all firms, each firm (including Narcissus) sees its *ATC* curve shift upward, to ATC_{ads}. But this time, when long-run equilibrium is restored with zero economic profit (point C), Narcissus is charging only $50—less than the initial $60. Advertising has brought down the price of perfume.

How can this be? By advertising, each firm is able to produce and sell more output. This remains true even when *all* firms advertise because demand for the product in general has increased. Since the firm was originally on the downward-sloping portion of its *ATC* curve, we know that its *non*advertising costs per unit will decline as output expands. If this decline is great enough—as in panel (b)—then costs per unit will drop, even when the cost of advertising is included. In other words, because you and I and everyone else is buying more perfume, each producer can operate with lower costs per unit. In the long run, entry will force each firm to pass the cost savings on to us.

Advertising and Collusion in Oligopoly

In this chapter, you've learned that oligopolists have a strong incentive to cooperate. But cooperation—when it takes the form of tacit collusion—is difficult to prove. When one firm raises its prices and others follow, that *may* be because of price leadership, or it may be that costs in the industry have risen, and *all* firms—affected in the same way—have decided independently to raise their prices. But in some cases, such as strategic decisions about advertising, we can use a simple game theory model to show that collusion is almost certainly taking place.

Let's take the airline industry as an example. Polls have shown that passengers are very concerned about airline safety. Any airline that could convince the public of its superior safety record would profit considerably.

And there are so many different ways to interpret safety data that almost any airline could come up with a measure by which it would appear the "safest." Moreover, any airline that actually took steps to improve safety could tout those policies in its ads, taking business from other airlines. Yet airlines have never run advertisements with information about their safety or security policies or attacked those of a competitor. Let's see why.

Figure 10 shows some hypothetical payoffs from this sort of advertising as seen by two firms, United Airlines and American Airlines, competing on a particular route. Focus first on the top, green-shaded entries, which show the payoffs for American. If neither firm ran safety ads, American would earn a level of profit we will call *medium*, as a benchmark. If American ran ads touting its own safety, but United did not, American's profit would certainly increase—to "high" in the payoff matrix. If both firms ran safety ads—especially negative ads that attacked their rival—the public's demand for airline tickets would certainly decline. Reminded of the dangers of flying, more consumers would choose to travel by train, bus, or car. American's profit in this case would be lower than if *neither* firm ran ads, so we have labeled it "low" in the payoff matrix. Finally, the worst possible result for American—"very low" in the figure—occurs when United touts its own safety record, but American does not.

Now consider American's possible strategies. If United decides to run the ads (the top row), American's best action is to run them as well. If United does not run the ads (bottom row), American's best action is still to run the ads. Thus, American has a dominant strategy: Regardless of what United does, it should run the safety ads.

As you can verify, United, whose payoffs are in the lower, red-shaded entries, faces an entirely symmetrical situation. It, too, has the same dominant strategy: Run the ads. Thus, when each airline acts independently, the outcome of this game is shown in the upper left-hand corner, where each airline runs ads and earns a low profit.

FIGURE 10 · An Advertising Game

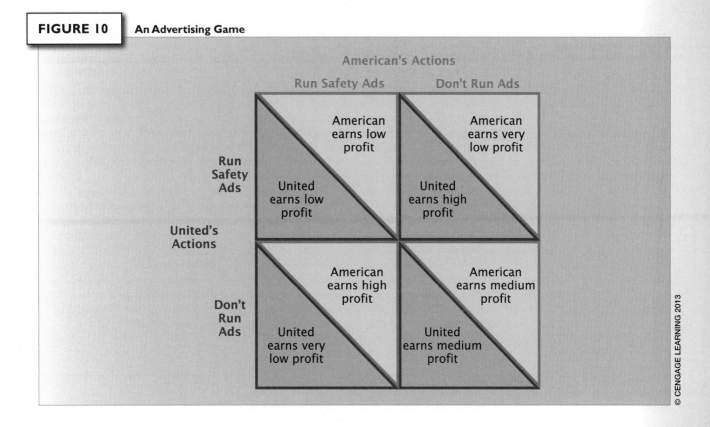

American's Actions

	Run Safety Ads	Don't Run Ads
Run Safety Ads	American earns low profit / United earns low profit	American earns very low profit / United earns high profit
Don't Run Ads	American earns high profit / United earns very low profit	American earns medium profit / United earns medium profit

United's Actions

© CENGAGE LEARNING 2013

So why don't we observe that outcome?

The answer is that the airlines are playing against each other repeatedly and reach the kind of cooperative equilibrium we discussed earlier. Each airline can punish its rival next time if it fails to cooperate this time. In the cooperative outcome, each airline plays the strategy that it will *not* run the ads as long as its rival does not. The game's outcome moves to the lower right-hand corner. Here, neither firm runs ads, and each earns medium rather than low profit. This is the result we see in the airline industry.

Until the 1980s, a similar collusive understanding seemed to characterize the automobile industry. As long as the "Big Three" dominated auto sales in the United States, the word *safety* was never heard in their advertising. There seemed to be an understanding that all three would earn greater profits if consumers were *not* reminded of the dangers of driving.

Things changed in the 1980s, however, as foreign firms' share of the U.S. market rose dramatically. One of the new players, Volvo, decided that its safety features were so far superior to its competitors that it no longer paid to play by the rules. Volvo began running television advertisements that not only stressed its own safety features but implied that competing products were dangerous. (On a rainy night, a worried father stops his son at the door, hands him some keys, and says, "Here, son, take the Volvo.") Once Volvo began running ads like these, the other automakers had no choice but to reciprocate. Now, automobile ads routinely mention safety features like antilock brakes and air bags. The tacit collusion of prior years has broken down.

SUMMARY

Monopolistic competition is a market structure in which there are many small buyers and sellers, easy entry and exit, and firms sell differentiated products. As in monopoly, each firm faces a downward-sloping demand curve, chooses the profit-maximizing quantity where $MR = MC$, and charges the maximum price it can for that quantity. As in perfect competition, short-run profit attracts new entrants. As firms enter the industry, the demand curves facing existing firms shift leftward. Eventually, each firm earns zero economic profit and produces at greater than minimum average cost.

An *oligopoly* is a market structure dominated by a small number of strategically interacting firms. Strategic interaction becomes more likely when there is a high degree of *market concentration*, which can be measured with a *concentration ratio* or the *Herfindahl-Hirschman Index*. New entry is deterred by economies of scale, reputational barriers, strategic barriers, and legal barriers. Because each firm, when making decisions, must anticipate its rivals' reactions, oligopoly behavior can be hard to

predict. However, one approach, *game theory*, has offered rich insights.

In game theory, a *payoff matrix* indicates the payoff to each firm for each combination of strategies adopted by that firm and its rivals. A *dominant strategy* is a strategy that is best for a particular firm regardless of what its rival does. If there is no cooperation among firms, any firm that has a dominant strategy will play it, and that helps predict the outcome of the game.

Sometimes oligopolists can cooperate to increase profits. *Explicit collusion* is an actual agreement, such as to raise prices in a *price-fixing agreement*. The most extreme form of price fixing is a cartel, in which firms agree to maximize their combined profits by acting as a monopoly. Because explicit collusion is illegal in the United States and many other countries, oligopoly firms often engage in *tacit collusion*, using tactics such as *tit-for-tat* or *price leadership* to reach a cooperative outcome. Collusion is often countered by cheating, by technological change, and by the government policies.

PROBLEM SET

Answers to even-numbered Problems can be found on the text Web site through www.cengagebrain.com

1. Draw the relevant curves to show a monopolistic competitor suffering a *loss* in the short run. What will this firm do in the long run if the situation does not improve? (Assume its *ATC* and *MC* curves don't change in the long run.) How would this action affect *other* firms in this market?

2. The owner of an optometry practice, in a city with more than a hundred other such practices, has the following demand and cost schedules for eye exams:

Price per Eye Exam	Eye Exams per Week	Total Cost per Week	Total Revenue per Week	Marginal Revenue	Marginal Cost
$100	100	$10,500			
$ 80	140	$10,800			
$ 60	200	$11,300			
$ 40	310	$12,290			
$ 20	550	$14,762			

   a. Fill in the columns for total revenue, marginal revenue, and marginal cost. (Remember to put *MR* and *MC between* output levels.)
   b. Briefly explain why an optometry practice (like this one) might face a downward-sloping demand curve, even if it is one out of more than a hundred. (Hint: What might make this market

monopolistically competitive rather than perfectly competitive?)

   c. Use the data you filled in for the marginal revenue and marginal cost columns to find the profit-maximizing price and the profit-maximizing number of eye exams per week for this practice.

3. Suppose that the cost data in problem 2 are for the short run, and that the owner of the practice suddenly realizes that she forgot to include her only fixed cost: her license fee of $2,600 per year (which is $50 per week). Should the practice shut down in the short run? Why or why not?

4. Tino owns a taco stand in Houston, Texas, where there are dozens of other taco stands. He faces the following demand and cost schedules for his taco plates (two tacos and a side of refried beans):

Price per Taco Plate	Taco Plates per Week	Total Cost per Week	Total Revenue per Week	Marginal Revenue	Marginal Cost
$5	50	$ 30			
$4	80	$ 50			
$3	150	$ 176			
$2	800	$1,476			
$1	1,100	$2,136			

a. Fill in the columns for total revenue, marginal revenue, and marginal cost and use the table to find the profit-maximizing price and the profit-maximizing number of taco plates per week for Tino's Taco Stand. (Remember to put *MR* and *MC between* output levels.)

b. Redo the table to show what will happen in the short run if Tino spends $100 on an advertising campaign that increases the quantity demanded at each output level by 20 percent. What will happen to his profit-maximizing price and profit-maximizing number of taco plates per week? Do you expect this outcome to persist? Explain.

5. Assume that the plastics business is monopolistically competitive.
a. Draw a graph showing the long-run equilibrium situation for a typical firm in the industry. Clearly label the demand, *MR, MC,* and *ATC* curves.
b. One of the major inputs into plastics is oil. Draw a new graph illustrating the short-run position of a plastics company after an increase in oil prices. Again, show all relevant curves.
c. If oil prices remain at the new, higher level, what will happen to get firms in the plastics industry back to a long-run equilibrium? (Assume the firm's *ATC* and *MC* curves don't change in the long run.)

6. Draw a diagram, including demand, marginal revenue, marginal cost, and any other curves necessary, to illustrate each of the following two situations for a monopolistic competitor:
a. The firm is suffering a loss, and it should shut down in the short run.
b. The firm is suffering a loss, but it should stay open in the short run.

7. Suppose there are five firms in a market, with the following market shares:
Firm A: 30%
Firm B: 25%
Firm C: 20%
Firm D: 15%
Firm E: 10%
a. What is the 4-firm concentration ratio?
b. What is the 8-firm concentration ratio?
c. What is the HHI?

8. Starting with the data in problem 7, suppose that Firm A manages to take 5 percentage points of market share away from Firm C.
a. What is the 4-firm concentration ratio now?
b. What is the 8-firm concentration ratio now?
c. What is the HHI now?
d. Comparing your answers with those in problem 7, which measures have changed, and which have remained the same?

9. Suppose there are only four ice cream manufacturers in a market, with the following market shares:
Delicious Brand: 35%
Better Ice Cream: 30%
To Die For: 25%
Sven and Mary's   10%

Sven and Mary want to give up making ice cream and retire. According to the U.S. government's 2010 guidelines, which (if any) of the other three companies would be permitted to purchase Sven and Mary's company without inviting government opposition?

10. In September 2011, the U.S. government announced that it would go to court to block AT&T's planned acquisition of T-Mobile. At the time, the market shares of the four largest wireless carriers (which together had about 90% of the market) were roughly as follows:
Verizon   33%
AT&T   31%
Sprint   16%
T-Mobile   10%

a. Ignoring the other small wireless firms not shown, what was the value of the HHI *before* the planned acquisition?
b. What would be the value of the HHI be if the proposed acquisition were completed?
c. Was the U.S. government's opposition to the merger consistent with its 2010 guidelines? Explain briefly.

11. In a small Nevada town, Ptomaine Flats, there are only two restaurants, the Road Kill Café and, for Italian fare, Sal Monella's. Each restaurant has to decide whether to clean up its act or continue to ignore health code violations.

Each restaurant currently makes $7,000 a year in profit. If they both tidy up a bit, they will attract more patrons but must bear the (substantial) cost of the cleanup; so they will both be left with a profit of $5,000. However, if one cleans up and the other doesn't, the influx of diners to the cleaner joint will more than cover the costs of the scrubbing; the more hygienic place ends up with $12,000, and the grubbier establishment incurs a loss of $3,000.
a. Write out the payoff matrix for this game, clearly labeling strategies and payoffs to each player.
b. What is each player's dominant strategy?
c. What will be the outcome of the game? Explain your answer.
d. Suppose the two restaurants believe they will face the same decision repeatedly. How might the outcome differ? Why?

e. Assume that if one cleans up and one stays dirty, the cleaner restaurant makes only $6,000 in profit. All other payoffs are the same as before. What will the outcome of the game be now without cooperation? With cooperation?

12. Assume that Nike and Adidas are the only sellers of athletic footwear in the United States. They are deciding how much to charge for similar shoes. The two choices are "High" (H) and "Outrageously High" (OH). Nike's payoffs are in the lower left of each cell in the payoff matrix below:

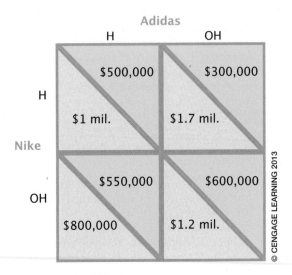

a. Do both companies have dominant strategies? If so, what are they?
b. What will be the outcome of the game?

13. [Requires Appendix] In Figure A.2, suppose that Bole is already cheating by selling 80 million pounds of bananas, while Bel Monte is sticking to its agreed allotment of 60 million, and earning profit of $15 million.
    a. If Bel Monte decides to cheat too and sell 80 million, what will be the new market price? [Hint: Use the fact that the demand curve is linear.]
    b. What will be Bel Monte's profit now?
    c. What will be Bole's profit now?

14. [Requires Appendix] In Figure A.2, suppose that both Bole and Bel Monte are each selling 80 million—in violation of the agreement. If one stays at 80 million, does the other have an incentive to increase sales by another 20 million? Explain briefly.

More Challenging

15. Suppose that the government has decided to tax all the firms in a monopolistically competitive industry by levying a fixed tax on each firm; that is, the amount of the tax is the same regardless of how much output the firm produces. In the short run, how would the tax affect the price, output level, and profit of a typical firm in that industry? What would be the effect in the long run?

16. Below, you will find the payoff matrix for a two-player game, where each player has three possible strategies: A, B, and C. The payoff for player 1 is listed in the lower left portion of each cell. Assume there is no cooperation among players.
    a. Does either player have a dominant strategy? If so, which player or players, and what is the dominant strategy?
    b. Can we predict the outcome of this game from the payoff matrix using the methods you've learned in the chapter? Why or why not?
    c. Suppose that strategy C is no longer available to either player. Does either player have a dominant strategy now? Can you now predict the outcome of the game? Explain.

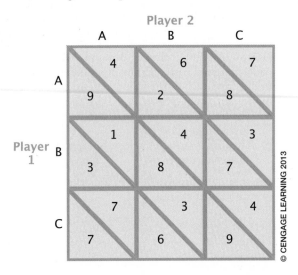

17. State whether each of the following is mathematically possible or impossible:
    a. A market has a 4-firm concentration ratio of 50%, and an HHI of 600.
    b. A market has a 4-firm concentration ratio of 50%, and an HHI of 3,000.
    c. A market has a 4-firm concentration ratio of 100%, and an HHI of 5,000.

This appendix discusses how a cartel might work among banana importers in a country that cannot grow its own bananas. To keep things simple, we'll assume that the cost for any banana importer (which includes purchasing the bananas themselves and transporting them) is a constant $0.15 per pound, no matter how many pounds are imported and sold. If importers were perfectly competitive firms (not shown in the figure), we know that easy entry and exit would ensure a long-run price of $0.15 per pound ($P = ATC$), with each firm earning zero economic profit.

But we'll instead suppose there are only *two* importers—we'll call them Bole and Bel Monte—and some barrier to entry keeps out other firms. Rather than charge the competitive price of $0.15 per pound, Bole and Bel Monte form a cartel, acting as a single profit-maximizing firm. Figure A.1 illustrates the market demand curve, which is also the demand curve facing the cartel. It also shows the cartel's marginal cost (the cost of importing an additional pound) and average total

cost (cost per imported pound), both represented by the horizontal line at $0.15. The profit-maximizing output level for the cartel is 120 million pounds of bananas per month, where the *MR* and *MC* curves intersect. At this output level, the cartel can charge $0.45 per pound. Total cartel profit—represented by the area of the shaded rectangle—is $0.30 (profit per pound) times 120 million pounds, or a total of $36 million per month. This is the highest combined profit that the two firms could earn.

Notice that the banana cartel—by restricting its output to 120 million pounds—causes the market price to rise above the competitive price of $0.15. This is why the formation of a cartel is often called a *price-fixing* agreement. To maintain total output at the profit-maximizing level, each member is allotted a fixed quantity, so that the allotments of all members sum to the desired market quantity. For example, Bole and Bel Monte might agree that each will sell exactly 60 million pounds. As long as each sticks to the agreement, market output will be

---

FIGURE A.1 | **The Profit Maximizing Price and Output Level for a Cartel**

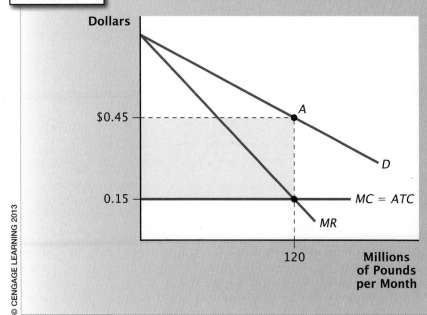

Facing the market demand curve D, a cartel's profit is maximized by the output level 120 million pounds (where MR = MC), charging $0.45 per pound. Total cartel profit is the area of the blue-shaded rectangle. The profit is divided among the members by allotting a quantity of output for each firm, such that the sum of each firm's quantity is the profit-maximizing total output (120 million pounds).

120 million, the price will remain at $0.45, and each firm will earn half of the total profit, or $18 million. Alternatively, if Bole is the larger firm, the cartel could allot, say, 80 million pounds to Bole and the remaining 40 million to Bel Monte, resulting in the same total profit, but different amounts for each.

The Incentive to Cheat

As discussed in the chapter, cartels often break down because of the incentive to cheat. For example, let's suppose the banana cartel is initially earning total profit of $36 million, as in Figure A.1, and splitting the output and profit equally. So Bole and Bel Monte are each selling 60 million pounds of bananas, and each is earning $18 million in profit.

Figure A.2 shows how one of the firms can come out ahead by cheating. In the figure, Bole sells 80 million pounds—which is 20 million beyond its allotment. Assuming that the other firm, Bel Monte, continues to abide by the agreement and sell 60 million pounds, total output now rises to 60 million + 80 million = 140 million. The increase in total output moves us from point A to point B on the market demand curve, causing the price to fall to

$0.40. Profit per pound falls to $0.40 − $0.15 = $0.25, and total profit for the cartel (the shaded rectangle) falls to $0.25 × 140 million = $35 million (compared to $36 million before). But notice that Bole—the cheater—is now earning profit of $0.25 per pound on 80 million pounds, so its total profit is $0.25 × 80 million = $20 million (compared to $18 million before). Bole's profit rises. Bel Monte's profit, by contrast, falls, because it is now earning $0.25 per pound on 60 million pounds, for a profit of $15 million (compared to $18 million before the cheating).

If accused of cheating by Bel Monte, Bole might respond with a lie: "Who me? I'm not cheating. Maybe the market price fell because the market demand curve shifted to the left. I'm still selling my 60 million pounds, and you should keep doing the same . . ." Unless Bel Monte has a way to monitor Bole's output and discover when Bole cheats, Bole has an incentive to keep cheating. In fact, cheating might be the *dominant strategy* for *both* Bole and Bel Monte—the best move for each, regardless of what the other does. (An end-of-chapter question will walk you through an example.) This is one of the reasons that price-fixing agreements often collapse.

FIGURE A.2 | **Cheating Reduces the Cartel's Total Profit**

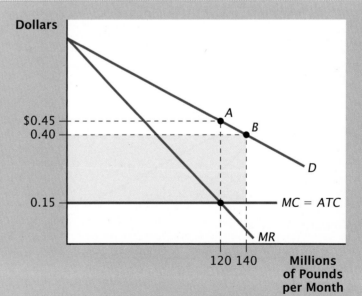

The cartel members initially sell 60 million pounds each (a total of 120 million pounds) and charge $0.45 per pound at point A. If one cartel member cheats by producing an extra 20 million pounds, total output rises to 140 million, and the market price falls to $0.40 (point B). Total cartel profit falls as well, to the area of the new shaded rectangle.

However (from separate calculations described in this appendix), the cheater's profit rises, while the non-cheater's profit falls.

CHAPTER 12

Labor Markets

© DREAMWORKS/THE KOBAL COLLECTION/ PICTURE DESK

When we went to do the deals for Shrek 2, *they were made in one day. It was that fast and that easy. It was also probably the biggest payday in movie history. They were each paid $10 million for what is in effect 18 hours of work.*

Jeffrey Katzenberg, cofounder of DreamWorks SKG, referring to payments made to Eddie Murphy, Mike Myers, and Cameron Diaz for voiceovers.[1]

Imagine, for a pleasant moment, that you are someone like Eddie Murphy, Mike Myers, or Cameron Diaz, doing voiceovers for a major studio production. Your work day might begin in a limousine, escorting you to the site of the day's recording. From the moment you arrive, you are doted on by assistants whose sole job is to keep you happy. You spend a few hours reading from a script. If you make a mistake, everyone laughs good-naturedly, and you get another chance to get it right—as many chances as you need. And after doing this each day for a few weeks, you pick up a check for $10 million.

Now, let's switch gears. Imagine that you are the typical short-order cook at a restaurant. You spend the day sweating over a hot grill, cooking several hundred meals, dealing with the tempers of waiters and waitresses who want you to do it faster, and who glare at you if you forget that a customer wanted French fries instead of home fries. For this work, you would earn about $9.50 per hour, giving you an income just under $20,000 for the year.

Granted, this is an extreme comparison. But we observe sizeable differences in job earnings throughout the spectrum of the labor market. For example, in 2011 the median American worker with a full-time job earned about $18 per hour. But among college graduates, the median was around $29. Workers at the top 5-percentile earned more than $50 per hour, and those at the top 1-percentile earned more than $100 per hour.

In addition to their labor earnings, some people earn income from other resources that they own, such as capital or land. But most of the inequality in incomes in the United States arises from differences in labor earnings. And inequality from earnings in the labor market has been growing steadily for the past three decades, largely because pay among those at the very top has grown much more rapidly than the pay of those lower down.

To understand where these pay differences come from—at the extremes and in the middle—you need to understand *labor markets,* the subject of this chapter.

[1] "Question and Answer: Movie Mogul Jeffrey Katzenberg," *Reel West* (Vol. 17, No. 4) July–August 2002.

These are the markets where people supply their labor to employers: business firms, government agencies, and others.

LABOR MARKETS IN PERSPECTIVE

Before we focus on labor markets specifically, let's begin with some perspective. Most of the markets we've analyzed so far (maple syrup, crude oil, pharmaceuticals, and more) were **product markets,** in which firms sell goods and services to households or other firms. Of course, products aren't made out of thin air, but rather from the economy's resources, such as labor, capital, and land. The use of these resources must be purchased from those who own them. Because resources are sometimes called factors of production, the markets in which they are traded are called **factor markets.** Labor markets, for example, are a type of factor market.

In this and the next chapter, we switch our focus from product markets to factor markets. Figure 1 illustrates how factor markets fit into the economy. It shows another version of the circular flow model from Chapter 3. In this version, we've left out the money flows in order to highlight the flows of products and resources. As you can see, in product markets households typically demand the products and firms supply them. In factor markets, these roles are reversed: Firms demand resources such as labor, land, or capital, and they are supplied by the households who own these resources.

The figure also illustrates how behavior in product and factor markets is connected. When households demand more of a good, firms respond by producing more,

Product markets Markets in which firms sell goods and services to households.

Factor markets Markets in which resources—labor, capital, land and natural resources, and entrepreneurship—are sold to firms.

FIGURE 1 | **Product Markets and Factor Markets**

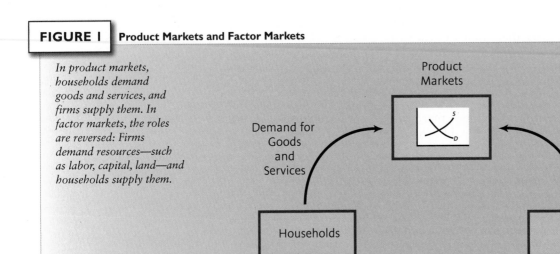

In product markets, households demand goods and services, and firms supply them. In factor markets, the roles are reversed: Firms demand resources—such as labor, capital, land—and households supply them.

Demand for Goods and Services

Product Markets

Supply of Goods and Services

Households

Firms

Supply of Resources

Demand for Resources

Factor Markets

© CENGAGE LEARNING 2013

which makes them demand greater quantities of resources. For example, if households want to buy more cars and Ford Motor Company produces more of them, the company will need to hire more labor, use more machinery, and so on. It will also use more inputs from other firms—glass, steel, tires—and these firms, in turn, will demand more resources. Thus, the demand for resources in the economy arises *from* the demand for goods and services.

> *The demand for a resource—such as labor—is a **derived demand**. That is, it arises from, and will vary with, the demand for the firm's output.*

Derived demand The demand for a resource that arises from, and varies with, the demand for the product it helps to produce.

Defining a Labor Market

When you begin working or searching for a job after college, you will become a seller in a labor market. But which labor market? As we've suggested several times in this book, how broadly or narrowly we define a market depends on the specific questions we wish to answer.

For example, suppose we want to understand why college graduates, on average, earn more than those with only high school diplomas. For this purpose, we would look at two broadly defined labor markets: one for all college graduates in the country, another for those with only high school diplomas. If we want to know how salaries in some professions (say, physicians) are determined, we'd look at the market for all physicians in the country. Or if we want to know why physicians in Boston earn unusually high wages, we'd narrow our definition even further, to the market for physicians in Boston.

The Wage Rate

Much of our focus in this chapter will be on *price* in a labor market: the *wage rate*. It is common to think of a wage rate as an hourly rate, in part because many jobs pay by the hour. But we can calculate an hourly wage rate for *anyone* who works, including a manager paid a salary, a sales representative paid by commission, or a movie star with a contract. The hourly wage rate is simply their total earnings over a week, month, or year divided by the number of hours worked during that period.

For example, if someone earns $80,000 in commissions during the year and works 2,000 hours that year, the hourly wage rate would be $80,000/2,000 = $40.

Competitive Labor Markets

In the first part of this chapter, we'll be looking at *perfectly competitive* labor markets. Competition in labor markets is analogous to competition in product markets. More specifically, a **perfectly competitive labor market** has the following four characteristics:

Perfectly competitive labor market A market with many well-informed buyers and sellers of standardized labor, with no barriers to entry and exit.

1. *Many buyers and sellers:* So many firms demand labor, and so many households supply it, that no decisions by a single firm or worker has a noticeable effect on the labor demanded or supplied in the market.
2. *Standardized labor quality:* To employers, any worker who meets the basic skill requirements for the job is considered just as productive as any other worker.

3. *Easy entry and exit:* No artificial barriers prevent workers from entering or leaving a labor market or from acquiring the basic skills needed to work there.
4. *Well-informed buyers and sellers:* Firms and households have all the information they need to make decisions about demanding or supplying labor.

Because labor quality is standardized, and each firm is such a small employer in the market, its employment decisions do not noticeably affect the market wage. Just as we call a firm in a competitive product market a "price taker," we can call a firm in a competitive *labor* market a "wage taker." The firm takes the wage rate as given.

How is the wage rate determined in a competitive labor market? The same way that a price is determined in *any* competitive market: by the forces of supply and demand.

LABOR DEMAND

When we refer to *labor demand* in a market, we mean the demand by *all* firms for the type of labor being traded in that market. For example, in the market for registered nurses in the United States, all employers of registered nurses—hospitals, medical practices, home health care providers, government agencies, and more—would demand this labor. In a more narrowly defined market—say, the market for *hospital nurses* in *Chicago*—we would view only hospitals located in Chicago as demanding labor.

The Labor Demand Curve

Labor demand curve Curve indicating the total number of workers all firms in a labor market want to employ at each wage rate.

Let's look at the market for all nurses in the United States. Figure 2 shows a hypothetical **labor demand curve** (L^D) for this broadly defined labor market. It tells us the number of nurses that *all* U.S. employers would want to hire at each wage rate.

FIGURE 2   **The Labor Demand Curve**

The labor demand curve slopes downward because, all else equal, firms want to employ fewer workers from a labor market when the wage rate is higher. For the hypothetical labor demand curve shown here, firms will want to hire 1 million nurses when the wage rate is $25 per hour, but only 0.5 million nurses at a wage rate of $35.

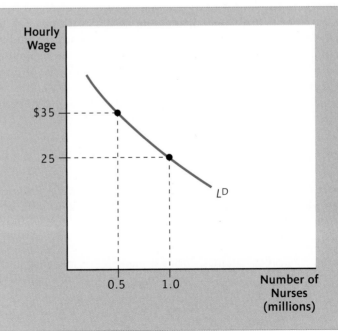

Notice that the labor demand curve slopes *downward:* A rise in the wage rate (from $25 to $35)—holding all other influences on demand constant—causes the quantity of labor demanded to fall (from 1.0 million to 0.5 million). This suggests that individual *firms* in this labor market want to employ fewer workers at higher wage rates. Why?

In the appendix, we show how to find a firm's specific quantity of labor demanded at a particular wage rate. Here, we focus on how a *change* in the wage rate affects the quantity of labor demanded.

The Output Effect

Over most time horizons, labor is considered a variable input, used to calculate the firm's marginal cost. So when the wage rate rises, a firm's *marginal cost curve* shifts upward. (It costs more to produce each *additional* unit of output when the wage is high than when the wage is low.) The upward shift in the marginal cost curve decreases the firm's profit-maximizing output level, as illustrated in Figure 3. Finally, remember that the demand for resources is a derived demand: As the firm's rate of *production* falls, so will the quantity of labor it wants to employ. This is the **output effect** of a wage change.

Output effect A change in the wage rate alters the profit-maximizing output level, and therefore changes the quantity of labor demanded.

For example, suppose the going wage rate for registered nurses rises from $25 to $35 per hour, and nothing else changes. Then a home health care firm—facing an increase in marginal cost at each output level—would want to serve fewer clients, and would employ fewer nurses. The same would happen at other firms that employ nurses: higher wages would lead to higher marginal costs, lower output, and a decrease in the quantity of nurses demanded.

The Input-Substitution Effect

A higher wage rate in a labor market has a second effect: It raises the price of that labor *relative to the price of other inputs*. The other inputs—now relatively cheaper—may

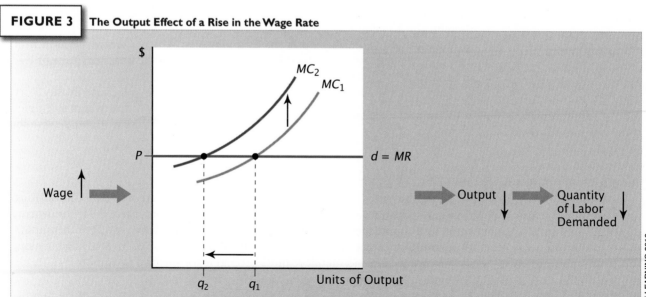

FIGURE 3   The Output Effect of a Rise in the Wage Rate

All else equal, a rise in the wage rate shifts up a firm's marginal cost curve, and therefore lowers its profit-maximizing output level (from q_1 to q_2). Because it is producing less output, the firm will want to employ fewer workers.

© CENGAGE LEARNING 2013

include capital or even other types of labor. As firms switch to using more of the other inputs whose prices have *not* risen, they demand less of the labor whose price *has* risen. This is the **input-substitution effect** of a wage change.

Input-substitution effect
A change in the wage rate alters the price of labor relative to the costs of other inputs, and therefore changes the quantity of labor demanded.

For example, a health care firm may use several types of labor to provide patient care, including nurses, nurse's aides, physician assistants, and more. All else equal, a rise in the wage rate of registered nurses would raise their price *relative* to the price of these other workers. To produce any *given* quantity of health care services, the firm's least-cost method may change: fewer nurses, more of the other types of labor.

In sum:

> *A market labor demand curve slopes downward because a rise in the wage rate has two effects: (1) It increases firms' marginal costs, causing them to decrease production and employ fewer workers (the output effect); and (2) it increases the relative cost of labor from that market, causing firms to substitute other inputs, such as capital or other types of labor (the input-substitution effect).*

Shifts in the Labor Demand Curve

You've seen that a change in the market wage rate moves us along a labor demand curve. But when the demand for labor is affected by something *other* than a change in the wage rate, the curve will shift. Let's discuss two important causes of such shifts.

Changes in Demand for the Product

Demand in a *product* market can increase for any number of reasons—increasing population, rising incomes, changes in tastes, and more (see Chapter 3). When demand increases in the product market, the labor demand curve will shift.

Let's take an example. Suppose that home health care firms (which employ a significant fraction of the nation's nurses) sell in a competitive *product* market. If demand for home health care increases, then its price will rise. This, in turn, will raise the profit-maximizing output level (number of patients served) at each firm, increasing the number of nurses they want to employ. (In the long run, it might lead to entry of new firms, increasing the demand for labor further.)

Notice that we have not referred to any change in the wage rate in this story. When the demand for the product—health care—rises, each firm wants to employ more nurses *at any given wage rate for nurses*. So the entire labor demand curve for nurses shifts rightward, as in Figure 4.[2]

Changes Involving Other Inputs

As we've discussed, firms use *other* inputs besides the labor we are considering. Changes in the price or availability of these other inputs can affect the labor demand curve. The effect depends on the relationship between the labor and the other input.

Complementary input An input that is used *by* a particular type of labor, making it more productive.

A **complementary input** is one that is used *by* the labor we're analyzing, making it more productive and therefore more profitable for the firm to employ.

---

[2] Even if home health care is *not* sold in a perfectly competitive market, an increase in demand for the product will still shift the labor demand curve rightward. As you've learned (see Chapters 10 and 11), when demand increases for the product of a monopoly or monopolistic competitor, its marginal revenue curve shifts upward (and rightward), and its profit-maximizing output level rises. Once again, because firms are producing more, they will want to use more labor at any given wage rate.

FIGURE 4 | A Rightward Shift in the Labor Demand Curve

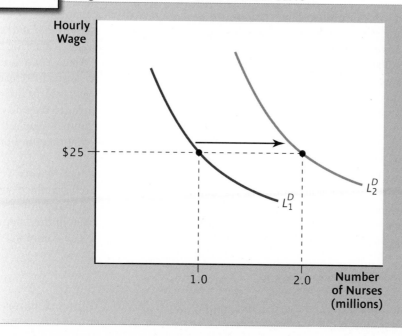

When firms in a labor market want to employ more labor at any given wage rate, the demand curve shifts rightward. Here, the number of nurses firms want to employ at a wage of $25 per hour rises from 1 million to 2 million. The rightward shift could be caused by an increased demand for a product that nurses help produce (such as home health care services), a new or cheaper complementary input, or a rise in the price of a substitutable input.

When a technological advance creates an entirely new complementary input, or when an existing one becomes cheaper, the demand curve for labor that uses the input will shift rightward.

For example, sophisticated diagnostic equipment used by nurses is complementary with their labor, because it enables them to care for more patients each day. When a drop in price causes firms to acquire more equipment, or when a new technology is put to use at the firm, nurses will be more productive and firms will want to hire more of them at each wage. The demand curve for nurses will shift rightward.

A **substitutable input** is one that can be used *instead* of a particular type of labor. We discussed an example of this type of input (other health care workers) earlier, as part of the input-substitution effect of a wage change for nurses. That effect moved us *along* a labor demand curve. But changes that originate with the substitutable inputs themselves can also cause the demand curve to *shift*.

Substitutable input An input that can be used *instead of* a particular type of labor.

When a technological change creates an entirely new substitutable input, or when an existing one becomes cheaper, the demand curve for the type of labor it replaces will shift leftward.

If, for example, the wage rate for physician assistants decreases, the least-cost combination of inputs for any level of production would change: more physician assistants, fewer nurses. This would shift the demand curve for nurses leftward.

LABOR SUPPLY

So far, we've considered the demand side of the labor market: firms that hire workers. Now we turn our attention to the *supply* side of the labor market: households that supply their labor to firms.

Variable Hours versus Fixed Hours

Some people have considerable freedom to vary how many hours they work. For example, many self-employed professionals—doctors, lawyers, freelance writers, and others—can adjust their work hours as they please, simply by increasing or decreasing the number of clients they serve. Even employees can sometimes vary their weekly hours by changing from full-time to part-time work or vice versa, or by accepting or refusing overtime. In cases like these—in which work hours can be varied—economists analyze the labor supply decision using a model of individual choice very similar to the one you learned for consumer theory in Chapter 6. However, instead of a limited budget that must be allocated to two different *goods,* the individual has a limited number of *hours* to allocate to two *activities*: working (earning income) and leisure.

In most labor markets, however, there is relatively little freedom to vary your weekly hours. Instead, your employer will expect you to work a predetermined shift: typically eight hours a day, five days a week. Your choice is not how many *hours* you want to work, but rather *whether to work at all* in that labor market. In this chapter, we'll focus on *fixed-hours* labor markets like these because they are so common.

The Labor Supply Curve

Labor supply curve A curve indicating the number of people who want jobs in a labor market at each wage rate.

Figure 5 shows a hypothetical **labor supply curve** (L^S) for registered nurses in the United States. It tells us the *number of people* who will want to work as nurses (supply their labor) at each hypothetical wage rate.

As you can see, the labor supply curve slopes upward: All else equal, a rise in the wage rate (from $25 to $35 in the figure) causes the quantity of labor supplied to rise (from 1.0 million to 1.2 million). Where would those 200,000 additional nurses come from? We'll suppose that the labor supply curve in the figure is drawn for a short-run time horizon: It traces out changes in quantity supplied that would

---

FIGURE 5 | **The Labor Supply Curve**

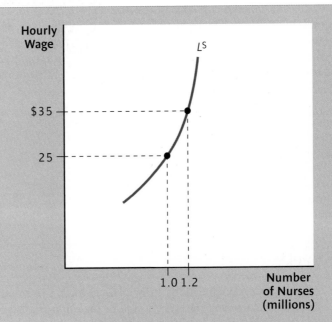

The labor supply curve in a market slopes upward because, all else equal (including the number of people qualified for that job), more people will want to work in that market when the wage rate rises. For the labor supply curve shown here, 1 million qualified nurses want to work in the nursing market if the wage rate is $25 per hour, while 1.2 million want to work as nurses if the wage rate is $35.

occur a few months after a change in the wage rate. This is not enough time for new workers—attracted by the higher wage—to enroll in nursing school and qualify to supply labor in this market. So the additional nurses would have to be those who already *are* qualified, but—before the wage increased—chose not to work as nurses. They might be retired, or temporarily not working, or working at some entirely different type of job. At a higher wage rate, some of them will decide it is worthwhile to re-enter this labor market and work as nurses.

> *The (short-run) supply of labor curve slopes upward. A rise in the wage rate causes some additional people—already qualified but previously not working in that labor market—to want to work there.*

Shifts in the Labor Supply Curve

A change in the wage rate moves us *along* a labor supply curve. But *other* changes that affect labor supply decisions will shift the entire curve. Here we'll discuss two of them.

Changes in the Number of Qualified People

When we draw a short-run supply curve in a labor market, we hold constant the number of people *qualified* to work in that market. But if the number of qualified people rises, the labor supply curve will shift rightward.

In the market for nurses, for example, the qualifications include having a degree from an accredited nursing program. As we move *along* the supply curve, we assume the total number of people with nursing degrees remains constant. As the wage rate changes, they can either choose to work as nurses or not. But over time, if more people acquire nursing degrees, more will want to work as nurses at any *given* wage. This is represented by a rightward shift in the labor supply curve for nurses, as illustrated in Figure 6.

FIGURE 6 | **A Rightward Shift in the Labor Supply Curve**

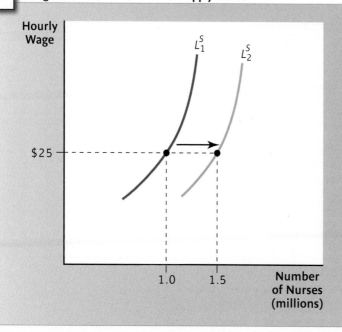

When more people want to work in a labor market at any given wage rate, the supply curve shifts rightward. Here, the number of people who want to work as nurses at a wage of $25 per hour rises from 1 million to 1.5 million. The rightward shift could be caused by an increase in the number of qualified nurses over time, a decrease in the pay or attractiveness of jobs in alternative labor markets, or a change in tastes in favor of nursing work.

Changes in *Other* Labor Markets

As long as some individuals can choose to supply their labor in more than one market, a change in the attractiveness of *other* jobs can shift the labor supply curve in the market we're analyzing. For example, suppose some of those with nursing degrees can instead teach science in a private high school, tutor other nursing students, or even open up a restaurant. If pay falls at these other jobs, or the jobs become less attractive for other reasons, then nursing becomes relatively *more* attractive at any given wage rate for nurses. The labor supply curve for nurses shifts rightward.

Changes in Tastes

Some people like working with numbers and hate working with people; others prefer the reverse. Some like danger and excitement, whereas others like safety and routine. A change in tastes in favor of particular kinds of work or working conditions will shift labor supply curves rightward in those labor markets. When a type of work falls into disfavor, the labor supply curve shifts leftward.

Tastes can also change for working *in general*. In the United States, women's labor force participation rate rose dramatically during the 1960s through the 1990s. The growth was especially rapid among married women: In 1960, less than one-third of married women were in the labor force; by 2000, almost two-thirds were. This change in the desire to work shifted labor supply curves rightward in many labor markets simultaneously.

LABOR MARKET EQUILIBRIUM

Figure 7 shows demand and supply curves in the market for nurses. By now you can certainly guess that the market equilibrium occurs at point *A*, with a wage rate of $25 per hour, and employment of 1 million nurses. But on your own, it's worthwhile to review the logic of equilibrium in this new context. Make sure you can see that

---

FIGURE 7 | **Equilibrium in a Labor Market**

The equilibrium wage rate and employment level in a labor market are found where the labor supply and labor demand curves intersect. Here, the equilibrium wage rate for nurses is $25 per hour, and equilibrium employment is 1 million. If the wage rate were greater than $25, the quantity of nurses supplied would exceed the quantity demanded, and the wage rate would fall. If the wage rate were less than $25, the quantity demanded would exceed the quantity supplied, and the wage rate would rise.

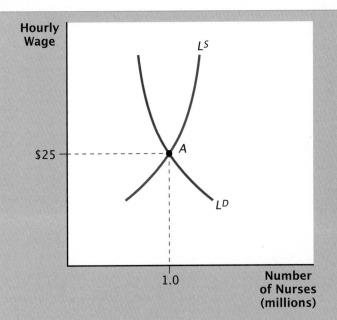

at any wage rate above $25, an excess *supply* of nurses would ultimately drive the market wage downward, as nurses competed to get available jobs. Similarly, at any wage rate lower than $25, an excess *demand* for labor would drive the wage rate upward, as firms competed to hire scarce nurses.

What Happens When Things Change

Events that shift a labor-demand or labor-supply curve will change both the equilibrium wage rate and employment level. Here we'll explore two examples.

An Increase in Labor Demand

Figure 8 shows what happens when the demand curve for nurses shifts rightward, with no shift in supply. The demand shift might be caused, for example, by an increase in demand in the *product market* for health care services. Indeed, in recent years, the demand for health care services has increased dramatically, due to an aging population, the availability of new treatments, and rising incomes.

In the figure, the demand curve shifts from L_1^D to L_2^D. At the old wage rate of $25, there is now an excess demand for nurses, causing the wage rate to rise. As the wage rate increases, the quantity of nurses demanded falls, moving us leftward along L_2^D. At the same time, the rising wage rate attracts qualified nurses back into the labor market, moving us *rightward* along the short-run labor supply curve L^S. In the figure, once the wage rate reaches $35, the quantity of nurses demanded and supplied are equal at the new, higher employment level of 1.2 million.

> *An increase in labor demand raises both the equilibrium wage rate and the equilibrium level of employment.*

Note that now that the wage is higher, more people might decide to become nurses. As we move into the long run, this increase in the number of qualified people would

© CENGAGE LEARNING 2013

FIGURE 8   **An Increase in Labor Demand**

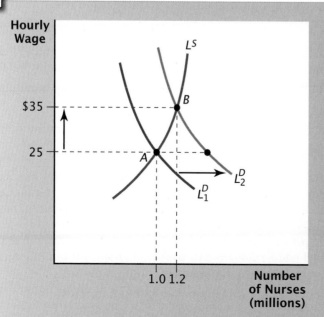

Initially, the market for nurses is in equilibrium at point A, with an hourly wage of $25 and 1 million people working as nurses. When labor demand increases (the labor demand curve shifts rightward), the equilibrium moves to point B. The wage rate rises to $35, and employment rises to 1.2 million.

FIGURE 9   An Increase in Labor Supply

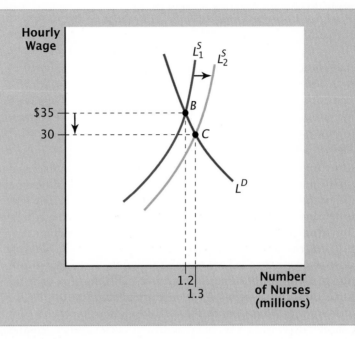

Initially, the market for nurses is in equilibrium at point B, with an hourly wage of $35 and 1.2 million people working as nurses. When labor supply increases (a rightward shift of the labor supply curve), the equilibrium moves to point C. The hourly wage falls to $30, and employment rises to 1.3 million.

© CENGAGE LEARNING 2013

start to shift the supply curve rightward as well. So let's now explore the impact of an increase in labor supply.

An Increase in Labor Supply

In Figure 9, we begin with the equilibrium reached in Figure 8, with a wage rate of $35 and employment of 1.2 million nurses (point *B*). Then we suppose that the number of people qualified as nurses increases. This might be a delayed reaction to the wage increase we explored in Figure 8 (nurses' wages, at $35, are higher than before). Or it could be that new scholarships or low-interest loans have become available, lowering the cost of attending nursing school. Regardless of the cause, as more nursing students complete their training, the number of qualified nurses will increase, and the labor supply curve shifts rightward. The equilibrium wage rate declines from $35 to $30, while equilibrium employment rises from 1.2 million to 1.3 million (point *C*).

WHY DO WAGES DIFFER?

Table 1 shows hourly earnings in 2010 for full-time workers in selected occupations. Each row of the table lists not only the median wage rate (in bold), but also the wage rate at the 10th and 90th percentiles for the occupation. For example, the second row shows that the bottom 10 percent of full-time physicians in general practice earned $23.56 per hour or less, while the top 10 percent earned $125.00 or more. And the bolded middle column tells us that in 2010, half of physicians earned less than $75.00 per hour while the other half earned more.

Note the inequality in wage rates among *different* occupations. These sharp differences occur even for jobs in the same industry, in which the work is often similar.

TABLE 1

Hourly Earnings of Full-time Workers in Selected Occupations, 2010

Occupation	10th Percentile	Median (50th Percentile)	90th Percentile
Airline pilots, co-pilots, and flight engineers	$38.31	$125.17	$ 171.41
Physicians, general practice	$23.56	$ 75.00	$ 125.00
College teachers, business	$26.71	$ 66.38	$ 80.80
Pharmacists	$48.50	$ 55.24	$ 60.50
Marketing managers	$28.26	$ 46.34	$ 76.92
College teachers, political science	$33.15	$ 40.35	$ 55.60
Registered nurses	$22.52	$ 30.46	$ 44.35
Electricians	$14.00	$ 22.50	$ 38.41
Truck drivers, heavy and tractor-trailer	$12.40	$ 18.13	$ 25.69
Preschool teachers	$ 9.75	$ 14.00	$ 35.33
Cabinetmakers	$11.30	$ 15.50	$ 23.00
Bank tellers	$10.00	$ 12.00	$ 16.04
Cooks, short order	$ 7.75	$ 9.50	$ 13.25
Cashiers	$ 7.75	$ 10.00	$ 14.55

Source: Selected data from *National Compensation Survey: Occupational Wages in the United States, 2010* (released May, 2011), Table 16, Bureau of Labor Statistics. The BLS data are based on a sample survey of about 22,000 business establishments and government agencies.

Compare, for example, the median hourly wage rate of a business professor ($66.38) and a political science professor ($40.35), or that of a physician ($75.00) and a registered nurse ($30.46).

But you can also see sharp differences in earnings *within* many occupations. For many of these jobs, the wage rate at the 90th percentile is many times greater than at the 10th.

This wage inequality—among and within occupations in the U.S. labor market—is *persistent*. The highest-paid and lowest-paid occupations have been so for decades. And year after year, the highest-paid workers within an occupation earn substantially more than the lowest.

Moreover, Table 1 understates differences in pay. It does not include bonuses, fringe benefits, or other additional labor earnings that are substantially greater for the highest-paying occupations and the highest-paid workers within each job. It also leaves out those at the very top—such as chief executive officers of top corporations, sports celebrities, and movie stars. For example, Eddie Murphy's wage rate on most films is between $10,000 and $20,000 per hour. (He earned a higher rate for *Shrek 2,* as you can calculate from information given earlier in this chapter.) And the top 25 hedge fund managers averaged more than $200,000 per *hour* (that is not a typo) in 2010.[3]

How can one hour of human labor have such different values in the market?

[3] Various sources and author's calculations, assuming a workweek of 80 hours. Assuming a more normal workweek of 40 hours, the wage rate would be $400,000 per hour.

An Imaginary World

To understand why wages differ in the real world, let's start by imagining an *unreal* world with three features:

1. All labor markets are perfectly competitive.
2. Except for differences in wages, all jobs are equally attractive to all workers.
3. In the long run, all workers can costlessly acquire the qualifications for any job. In such a world, we would expect every worker to earn an *identical* wage in the long run. Let's see why.

Figure 10 shows two different labor markets that initially have different wage rates. Panel (a) shows a local market for preschool teachers, with an initial equilibrium at point *A* and a wage of $14 per hour. Panel (b) shows the market for pharmacists, who, at point *B*, earn $55 per hour. In the figure, the labor supply curves are for a short-run period, during which the number qualified for each job is held constant. In our imaginary world, could this diagram describe the *long-run* equilibrium in these markets?

Absolutely not. Imagine that you are a preschool teacher. By our second assumption (all jobs are equally attractive), you would find being a pharmacist just as attractive as teaching school. But because pharmacists earn more, you would prefer to be one. By our third assumption, you can costlessly *qualify* to be a pharmacist. And by our first assumption (perfect competition), there are no barriers to prevent

---

FIGURE 10   Disappearing Wage Differentials

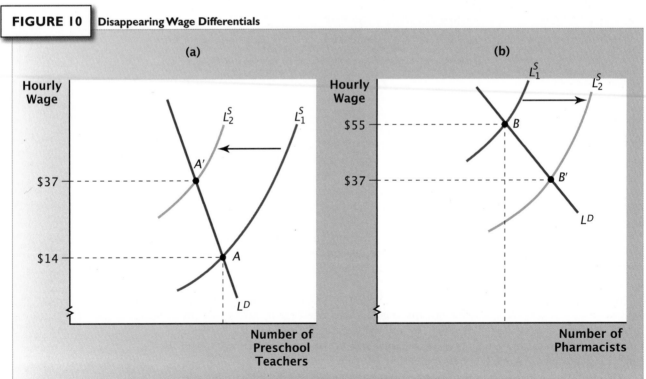

Initially, the supply and demand for preschool teachers in panel (a) determine an equilibrium wage of $14 per hour—at point A. In panel (b), the equilibrium wage for pharmacists is initially $55 per hour. If these markets are competitive, if the two jobs are equally attractive, and if all workers can costlessly acquire the qualifications to do either job, this wage differential cannot persist. Some preschool teachers will give up that occupation, reducing supply in panel (a), and become pharmacists, increasing supply in panel (b). This migration will continue until the wage in both markets is equal—at $37 in the figure.

you from becoming one. Thus, you—and many of your fellow preschool teachers—will begin to obtain the qualifications to be pharmacists, and eventually seek work in that market. In panel (a) the labor supply curve will shift leftward (exit from the market for preschool teachers), and in panel (b) the labor supply curve will shift rightward (entry into the market for pharmacists). As these shifts occur, the market wage rate of preschool teachers will rise and that of pharmacists will fall.

When will the entry and exit stop? When there is no longer any reason for a preschool teacher to want to be a pharmacist—that is, when both labor markets are paying the same wage rate ($37 in our example). In the long run, the market for preschool teachers reaches equilibrium at point A' and the market for pharmacists at point B'.

Our conclusion about preschool teachers and pharmacists would apply to *any* pair of labor markets we might choose. In our imaginary world, bank tellers and physicians, kitchen workers and nurses—all would earn the same wage. In this world, labor is like water in a swimming pool: It flows freely from end to end, ensuring that the level is the same everywhere. In our imaginary world, workers flow into labor markets with higher wages, evening out the wages in different jobs . . . *if* our three critical assumptions are satisfied.

But take any one of these assumptions away, and the equal-wage result disappears. This tells us where to look for the sources of wage inequality in the real world: a *violation* of one or more of our three assumptions.

Compensating Differentials

In our imaginary world, all jobs were equally attractive to all workers. But in the real world, jobs differ in hundreds of ways that matter to workers. When one job is more or less attractive than another for reasons other than a difference in pay, we can expect their wage rates to differ by a *compensating wage differential*:

> A **compensating wage differential** is the difference in wage rates that makes two jobs equally attractive to workers.

To see how compensating wage differentials come about, let's consider some of the important ways in which jobs can differ.

Nonmonetary Job Characteristics

Suppose you are an office worker in a skyscraper, and you could earn $1 more per hour than you currently earn by washing the building's windows . . . from the *outside*. Would you "flow" to the windowwasher labor market, like water in a pool? Probably not. The harder work and greater risk of death just wouldn't be worth the $1-per-hour difference.

Danger is an example of a **nonwage job characteristic**. It is an aspect of a job (good or bad) other than the wage rate that people care about. When you think about a career, whether you are aware of it or not, you are evaluating hundreds of nonwage job characteristics: the risk of death or injury, the amount of physical exertion required, the degree of intellectual stimulation, the potential for advancement, the cost of living and other conditions, where the job is located . . . the list goes on and on.

Compensating wage differential A difference in wages that makes two jobs equally attractive to a worker.

Nonwage job characteristic Any aspect of a job—other than the wage—that matters to a potential or current employee.

© PHOTOHOUSE/SHUTTERSTOCK.COM

Differences in nonwage job characteristics alone can stop the flow of workers from one labor market to another before the wages are equalized. If this were the only one of our special features that were violated, we would expect the compensating differential to be just enough to make the two jobs equally attractive.

To take an extreme example, suppose people had identical tastes for work, and that *everyone* would prefer to teach preschoolers rather than work in a pharmacy. Further, suppose these preferences were so strong that it would take a wage differential of $41 per hour to make the two jobs equally attractive. Then the long-run equilibrium would remain at the initial points *A* and *B*, with pharmacists earning a compensating wage differential of $55 − $14 = $41 per hour to make up for the less desirable features of their job. Even with the higher wage rate for pharmacists, preschool teachers would not want to switch jobs.

> *The nonmonetary characteristics of different jobs give rise to compensating wage differentials. Jobs considered intrinsically less attractive will tend to pay higher wages, other things being equal.*

Of course, different people have different tastes for working and living conditions. When labor markets are perfectly competitive, the entry and exit of workers automatically determines the compensating wage differential in each labor market.

What about *unusually attractive* jobs? Compared to the average job, these will generally pay *negative* compensating differentials. For example, many new college graduates are attracted to careers in the arts or the media. Since entry-level jobs in these industries are so desirable to so many people, they tend, on average, to pay lower wages than similar jobs in other industries.

Human Capital Requirements

In our imaginary world, everyone could costlessly acquire the qualifications to do any job. In the real world, many jobs require costly investments in human capital. All else equal, jobs that require more costly investments must pay more in the long run, or people wouldn't want to do them. (Although human capital may be a sunk cost for those who already have it, it is *not* sunk for those thinking about entering a profession to replace those retiring from it.)

> *Differences in human capital requirements give rise to compensating differentials. Jobs that require more costly training will tend to pay higher wages.*

For example, a pharmacist must have a PharmD degree, which requires at least six years of schooling after high school, including prerequisite science courses. In most states, substantially less schooling is required to qualify as a preschool teacher. If these two jobs paid the same wage, and everyone felt the jobs were otherwise equally attractive, no one would want to become a pharmacist. The number qualified to be pharmacists would decrease (through retirement), and the labor supply curve would shift leftward. This would cause the market wage for pharmacists to rise—until the difference in wages compensated pharmacists for the additional costs of qualifying.

Compensating wage differentials explain some of the wage differences we observe between jobs. The relatively high earnings of doctors, attorneys, research scientists, and college professors reflect—at least in part—compensating differentials for the especially high costs of qualifying for their professions.

The idea of compensating wage differentials dates back to Adam Smith, who first observed that unpleasant jobs seem to pay more than other jobs that require similar skills and qualifications. It is a powerful concept, and it can explain many of the differences we observe in wages . . . but not all of them.

Differences in Ability

In our discussion of compensating wage differentials and human capital requirements, we assumed that anyone willing to pay for human capital can acquire it. We've also been assuming that labor is standardized (one of the assumptions of a competitive labor market). So once someone *becomes* qualified, they can do the job just as well as anyone else.

But in the real world, abilities differ. And these differences in ability can create wage differences in two ways.

Differences in Ability to *Become* Qualified

Not everyone has the intelligence needed to be an astrophysicist, the steady hand to be a neurosurgeon, the quick-thinking ability to be a commodities trader, the well-organized mind to be a business manager, or the talent to be an artist or a ballet dancer. If you don't have the intrinsic talent or ability required in one of these jobs, you will not qualify even if you were to invest in the training.

Going back to Figure 10, suppose a wage differential of $10 per hour would compensate for the higher human capital investment required of the job in the right panel, and that initially we are at points *A* and *B* (with a differential much greater than $10). But now suppose that those working for lower wages in the left panel cannot switch to the high wage job on the right because—regardless of training or effort—they cannot master the skills required for that job. Then the "flow of labor" from one market to the other, which would ordinarily reduce the differential to $10, will not occur. The result is a persistent wage differential that *exceeds* any compensating wage differential.

This leads to an important conclusion:

> *All else equal, jobs that require skills that relatively few people have the ability to acquire will pay persistently higher wage rates—in excess of compensating wage differentials.*

Notice the word *relatively* in the highlighted statement. A wage rate is determined by both supply and demand. In order for your rare ability to acquire some skill to result in a higher wage, there must also be sufficient *demand* for the skill.

To take an extreme example, imagine that only 20 people on earth had the intrinsic ability, with proper training, to whistle out of their ears. But suppose that there is virtually no demand for employees or performers who develop that skill. Then, while the absolute number of people who had it would be very few, the *relative* number who had it (relative to the demand) would be very many. So the ability, while rare, would not give anyone who exploits it a higher wage.

On the other hand, hundreds of thousands of people have the intrinsic ability to complete law school, medical school, or business school. But because the demand for these professionals is high *relative* to the number who are able to qualify, their wage remains persistently *greater* than that needed to compensate for the cost of the training.

Differences in Ability *among* Those Qualified

Even among those qualified and working at a particular job, some are more able than others. This violates the "standardized labor" assumption of a perfectly competitive labor market. And it helps to explain much of the difference in pay we see *within* occupations in Table 1.

For example, the top 10 percent of marketing managers earn substantially more than the median, and almost three times as much as the bottom 10 percent. Some of this difference may be due to differences in nonwage job characteristics (marketing managers work under a variety of different conditions). But much of it is based on differences in ability. If Alicia can design a better marketing campaign than Emily, and if every employer knows this, then hiring Alicia will earn a firm more revenue than hiring Emily. Thus, in an otherwise competitive market, firms will be willing to pay a greater wage to Alicia than to Emily.

> *All else equal, those with greater ability to perform a job better—based on talent, experience, motivation, or perseverance—will be more valuable to their employers, and will generally be able to command a higher wage rate.*

Differences in ability also help explain why workers' pay tends to rise with age and experience on the job. Experience adds to a worker's human capital and can also reduce risk to employers. Hiring a new, untested worker—even one who seems to have great talent—is always a bit risky, because the worker's basic ability hasn't yet been proven. By contrast, hiring or continuing to employ someone with a history of advancement and accomplishments reduces this risk.

For these reasons, firms will typically pay more for a worker with a proven track record. Not surprisingly, when wage rates within an occupation are broken down by age (not shown in Table 1), workers who are older—and have been in their occupation longer—dominate the higher percentiles, while younger and newer entrants are more prevalent in the lower percentiles.

The Economics of Superstars

In 2000, at the age of 26, Alex Rodriguez signed a contract to play baseball for the Texas Rangers at an average salary of $25 million per year. (He later joined the New York Yankees, for an average annual salary of $27.5 million.) No one would argue that this unusually high pay is a compensating wage differential for the "unpleasantness" of playing professional baseball, or that—at age 26—Rodriguez had spent more years honing his skills than the average attorney, doctor, or engineer. Rather, let's state the obvious: Rodriguez is an *outstanding* baseball player, better than 99.999 percent of the population could ever hope to be. This is largely due to Rodriguez's exceptional gifts: both physical (agility, coordination, strength) and emotional (the temperament and character needed to hone and exploit those gifts).

Alex Rodriguez is an example of a *superstar*—an individual widely viewed as among the top few in his or her profession. In recent years, superstars have included actors such as Will Smith, Julia Roberts, and Angelina Jolie; talk show hosts Jay Leno and David Letterman; news anchors Brian Williams and Katie Couric; and novelists Stephen King and J. K. Rowling.

Exceptional ability may explain *why* someone is a superstar. But when we try to explain the extremely high wage rates of these superstars based solely on ability, we confront a puzzle. Clearly, Alex Rodriguez has more athletic ability and more skill in honing it, than almost anyone in the population, including other major-league baseball players. But can this explain a salary that is *25 times* that of the median major-league player? By any measure, is Rodriguez *25 times better* than these other players?

Many would agree that Eddie Murphy's voice work for *Shrek 2* was better than, say, the typical voiceovers on the Saturday morning cartoon shows. But Murphy's hourly pay—at about \$550,000 per hour—was about 3,000 times that of the typical cartoon voice actor. Is he *that much better?*

The very top athletes, writers, rock stars, comedians, talk show hosts, and movie directors all earn wage premiums that seem vastly out of proportion to their additional abilities. Why? The explanation in all these cases *is* based on ability—and also the exaggerated rewards that certain markets bestow on those deemed the best or one of the best in their field.[4]

An example can help us understand how this works. Say you like to read one mystery novel a month for entertainment. If you can choose between the best novel published that month or one that is almost—but not quite—as good, you will naturally choose the one you think is best. Only people who read *two* mystery novels each month would choose the best *and* the second best; only those who read three will choose the top three. If most people rank recent mystery novels in the same order, then the best will sell millions of copies, the second best might sell hundreds of thousands, and the third best might sell only thousands.

Even though all three novels might be very close in quality, a publisher will earn *10 times* more revenue selling the best novel compared to the second best, and 10 times more revenue selling the second best compared to the third best, and so on. Accordingly, a publisher will be willing to pay the same multiples in advances and royalties when bidding for contracts with mystery novelists of different rankings. Even if the top author is viewed as only *slightly* better than the next one down, as long as the vast majority of readers agree on the ranking, she can end up earning 10 times as much.

The same thing happens in markets for athletes, rock stars, movie stars, and news broadcasters.

> *In labor markets for talented professionals, in which there is mass-distribution of their product and substantial agreement about rankings, small differences in ability can lead to disproportionate differences in pay.*

The owners of the Texas Rangers and the Yankees were willing to pay Alex Rodriguez \$25 million or so each year because they believed that Rodriguez, as a superstar, would bring in *at least* that much additional revenue each year—from ticket sales, skybox rentals, TV and radio broadcasting fees, concession sales, parking fees, and more.

Beyond Superstars

The logic behind superstar pay applies beyond sports and entertainment markets. Suppose you had a net worth of \$100 million, and you were being sued for all of it. And suppose the *best* attorney you could hire had a 90 percent chance of winning your case. The *second best,* who was very close in ability, had an 85 percent chance of success. Ask yourself: How much more would you pay to hire the best rather than the second best? And if the best isn't available, what premium would you pay for the second best, if the third best had an 80 percent chance of success? With a little thought, you can apply the "economics of superstars" to many types of professions: physicians, political campaign strategists, asset managers, and more. In all of these cases, the stakes are very high, and small differences in perceived ability can lead to huge differences in the expected outcome.

---

[4] The seminal article on this theory is Sherwin Rosen, "The Economics of Superstars," *American Economic Review,* American Economic Association, Vol. 71, No. 5, 1981, pp. 845–58. A less-technical version is Sherwin Rosen, "The Economics of Superstars," *The American Scholar,* Vol. 52, No. 4, 1983. See also Robert H. Frank and Philip J. Cook, *The Winner Take All Society* (New York: The Free Press, 1995).

the percentage by which the *median* college graduate's wage exceeds the *median* high school graduate's wage. Even though economists expect the premium to remain high (at the medians) for many years, it will likely rise rapidly for some jobs as it falls rapidly for others. The reason: The new technologies that have been so highly complementary with college-educated labor in the past are now creating *substitutes* for that labor, at least in some jobs.

For example, consider tax accountants. In the 1980s and 1990s, tax software was a complementary input for high-skilled labor; it enabled accountants to create more accurate and helpful tax returns for individuals and small businesses, with faster turn-around time. But as the software improved and became faster and easier to use, taxpayers increasingly use it themselves, bypassing their accountants entirely. Tax software has become, to some degree, a substitutable input for individual and small-business tax accountants.

Or consider U.S. radiologists. At first, the Internet was a complementary input for these professionals, helping them consult with colleagues and hospitals on diagnoses, keep up with the field, and more. But as the Internet became faster and spread to other countries, it enabled hospitals to transmit X-rays for diagnosis to radiologists overseas, in countries like India. The result is a new substitutable input for U.S radiologists, namely, lower-paid but highly trained radiologists overseas.

As a rule of thumb, the high-skill jobs that will be most vulnerable to new substitutability inputs are jobs that involve routine work (which can increasingly be done by computers), or can be done by an equally educated (but lower-wage) worker overseas.

By contrast, jobs where the higher-education premium is likely to continue rising are those that require (1) considerable judgment and mental agility (defending a client in front of a jury, managing security for an airline); (2) close familiarity with American culture (designing a U.S. marketing campaign for a new product or political candidate); or (3) personal contact (as provided by a nurse, physical therapist or surgeon).

SUMMARY

Resources are traded in *factor markets* in which firms are demanders and households are suppliers. The *labor market* is a key factor market. A *perfectly competitive labor market* is one in which there are many buyers and sellers of standardized labor, with easy entry and exit of workers, and well-informed workers and firms. The demand for labor by a firm is a *derived demand*—derived from the demand for the product the firm produces.

In a competitive labor market, each firm faces a market-determined wage rate. The labor demand curve slopes downward because of the output effect (at higher wage rates, the firm produces less output) and the input-substitution effect (at higher wage rates, the firm substitutes other inputs for that type of labor). It shifts rightward when the demand for the product increases. A new or cheaper input will shift the demand curve rightward if the input is complementary with that labor and leftward if the input is substitutable for that labor. On the supply side, the *labor supply curve* slopes upward. Given the number qualified, more people will want to work in a labor market at higher wage rates. The labor supply curve shifts rightward when more people become qualified, when alternative labor markets become less attractive, or when tastes change in favor of that labor market.

The market labor supply and demand curves intersect to determine the market wage rate and employment in each labor market. Labor market equilibrium will change if either the labor demand or labor supply curve shifts. Wage differences can be explained by compensating wage differentials (for the nonwage characteristics of different jobs or for human capital costs), and because of differences in ability. Because of the "superstar" nature of many professions, small differences in ability can create extremely large wage differentials.

Barriers to entry created by occupational licensing, unions, or discrimination can create wage differences. The market works against discrimination that arises from employer prejudice, but not against that arising from customer or employee prejudice, nor against statistical discrimination.

One frequent proposal for reducing income inequality is an increase in the *minimum wage*. This is controversial because while the minimum wage benefits some low-income households, it harms other low-income households and benefits some high-income households. A higher minimum wage is believed to reduce employment among low-skilled workers, especially teenagers, and to reduce the wages of unskilled workers in industries not covered by the law. A more efficient redistributive policy is the *earned income tax credit* (EITC), which targets low-income working households.

PROBLEM SET

Answers to even-numbered Problems can be found on the text Web site through www.cengagebrain.com

1. In the nation of Barronia, the market for construction workers is perfectly competitive. Explain what would happen to the equilibrium wage rate and equilibrium employment of construction workers under each of the following circumstances:
   a. Young adults in Barronia begin to develop a taste for living in their own homes and apartments, instead of living with their parents until marriage.
   b. Construction firms begin to use newly developed robots that perform many tasks formerly done by construction workers.
   c. Because of a war in neighboring Erronia, Erronian construction workers flee across the border to Barronia.
   d. There is an increased demand for automobiles in Barronia, and Barronian construction workers have the skills necessary to produce automobiles.
   e. Tuition at trade schools that qualify Barronians for construction work become cheaper.

2. Suppose that dehydrated meat is an inferior good. Discuss the effect on the equilibrium wage rate and level of employment in the dehydrated meat industry of an increase in national income.

3. Suppose the supply of people who want to be "extras" in a film (people in the background of a film) is completely inelastic, because they will supply their labor to film production companies no matter what wage they are paid.
   a. Draw a diagram illustrating how the equilibrium wage and equilibrium employment level for extras is determined.
   b. On the same diagram, illustrate what will happen to the equilibrium wage and employment of extras if the demand in the product market (for films) increases.

4. Fifteen years ago, college professors frequently hired undergraduates as research assistants to gather basic information in the library. Today, most professors can get the information themselves using the Internet in less time than it would take to explain what is needed to a research assistant.
   a. In the labor market for undergraduate research assistants, has the Internet been a substitutable or complementary technological change?
   b. All else equal, what impact has the development of the Internet likely had on the wage and employment level of undergraduate research assistants?
   c. Many college professors find that *graduate* student research assistants are more productive than before because they can use the Internet. All else equal, has the Internet been a substitutable or complementary technological change for graduate student research assistants? What effect would this have on their equilibrium wage and employment level?

5. Suppose that in the market for U.S. meat packers, two things happen simultaneously: (1) Due to growth in less-developed countries, the demand for U.S. meat exports rises; and (2) Due to other job opportunities, fewer people find meat-packing an attractive job.
   a. Which curve or curves in the labor market for meat packers would be affected by these changes?
   b. If there were no other changes, could you predict the impact of these events on the equilibrium wage of meatpackers? On their equilibrium employment level? Explain.

6. The EITC is a subsidy given to workers for working. Suppose everyone in a particular unskilled labor market is receiving EITC payments of a given amount for each hour that they work.
   a. Draw a diagram showing the impact of the EITC on the labor market equilibrium. [Hint: The subsidy is paid directly to workers, not to firms.] On your graph, identify the wage rate and employment level both before and after EITC is introduced.

b. What happens to the wage rate that employers pay to their workers after the EITC? Explain briefly.

c. What happens to the wage rate the workers get (including the subsidy)? Explain briefly.

7. How would each of the following, *ceteris paribus*, affect the college wage premium over a long period of time?

a. Government scholarships are sharply curtailed.

b. Weird solar radiation renders all computers in the world inoperable.

c. Computers become even more complicated to operate.

8. Each of the following observations, *ceteris paribus*, implies something about a particular labor market. For each one, (1) identify the relevant labor market; (2) state whether you expect the wage rate in that market to be higher than otherwise, or lower than otherwise; and (3) identify which conceptual explanation for wage differences (among those discussed in the chapter) you are applying to reach your conclusion.

a. Elevator repairers have a higher accident rate than most other jobs.

b. People who work in New York City have to pay higher rent than other people.

c. People like to work in New York City because there is a lot to do there.

d. It takes rare diligence, motivation, and practice to become a concert pianist.

e. Los Angeles has passed legislation requiring that fortune tellers become certified by the city.

f. Office cleaning services don't like to risk hiring ex-convicts, because employers believe they are more likely to steal equipment than other employees.

9. [Appendix] The following gives employment and daily output information for Your Mama, a perfectly competitive manufacturer of computer motherboards.

Number of Workers	Total Output
10	80
11	88
12	94
13	97
14	99

A motherboard worker at Your Mama earns $80 a day, and motherboards sell for $27.50.

a. How many workers will be employed? How do you know?

b. Suppose the market wage for motherboard workers increases by $5 per day per worker, but the market price of motherboards remains unchanged. What will happen to employment at the firm? Why?

10. [Appendix] Add *MR* and *MC* columns to Table A.1 in the chapter and find the profit-maximizing output level using the *MR* and *MC* approach. When calculating *MR* and *MC*, don't forget to divide ΔTR and ΔTC by the change in output, which is *not* one unit in the table. Does the profit-maximizing output level differ from the one found in the appendix, using the $MRP = W$ approach? Explain briefly.

11. Many people think that immigration into the United States, because it causes competition for jobs, will lower the wage rates of U.S. workers. Yet, even though the United States admits hundreds of thousands of immigrants each year, the average U.S. wage has continued to grow. Can you explain why? Are there any groups of workers within the economy for whom the fear of lower wages is justified? Explain.

More Challenging

12. Some advocates of the minimum wage argue that any decrease in the employment of the unskilled will be slight. They assert that an increase in the minimum wage will actually increase the total amount paid to unskilled workers (i.e., wage × number of unskilled workers employed). Discuss what assumptions they are making about the wage elasticity of labor demand.

13. Suppose the demand for unskilled labor were completely *inelastic* with respect to the wage rate. Using graphs similar to those in Figure 14, but modified to reflect this new assumption, explain how a minimum wage above the equilibrium wage for covered unskilled workers would affect employment and the wage rate among:

a. Covered, unskilled workers

b. Uncovered, unskilled workers

c. Skilled workers

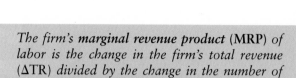

Using W to represent the daily wage rate, [...] the firm's guiding principle this way:

> *Hire another worker when* MRP > W [...] *when* MRP < W.

Let's apply this guideline to Spotless [...] When going from 0 to 1 worker, revenue [...] (*MRP* = $240) and cost rises by $120 (W [...] cause revenue rises more than cost (*MRP* [...] this first worker will add to the firm's pr[...] is true when the second, third, fourth, a[...] ers are hired. (Verify this on your own.) [...] from the fifth to the sixth worker, *MRP* [...] W = $120. Since *MRP* < W, the firm shou[...] sixth worker; it should stop at the fifth. V[...] the firm's profit-maximizing level of em[...] workers.

We can understand Spotless's emp[...] sion even better by graphing the margi[...] Table A.1, as we've done in Figure [...] marginal values are plotted *between* emp[...] since they tell us what happens as emplo[...]

FIGURE A.1   The Profit-Maximizing Em[...]

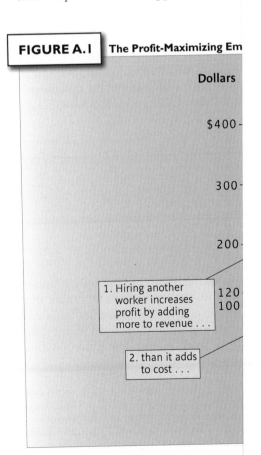

This appendix presents the formal mechanics behind the firm's employment decision, and shows how to derive a firm's labor demand curve from information on production and costs. We start with a general rule you learned in Chapter 8: the *marginal approach to profit*:

> *The marginal approach to profit states that a firm should take any action that adds more to its revenue that it adds to its cost.*

In the previous chapters, you've seen this rule applied to one kind of action: increasing production. Now, we'll apply it to a different type of action: increasing employment. Our rule translates to: Increase *employment* whenever it adds more to revenue than it adds to cost. Our first step is to see how an increase in employment affects a firm's revenue.

Employment and Revenue

In Table A.1, we return to an example we met earlier: Spotless Car Wash. The first two columns are based on information in Table 1 of Chapter 7, where we assumed that Spotless has one automated car-washing line. Column 1 shows different numbers of workers that Spotless can employ, and column 2 shows daily output (number of cars washed) for each level of employment.

We'll skip over column 3 for now, in order to calculate total revenue for each level of employment. In the table, we assume that Spotless sells its product in a competitive market, i.e., it's a *price taker*. It can wash all the cars it wants at the market price, which is $8. To get total revenue, we can just multiply the quantity of output (column 2) by the constant price (column 4). This gives us the total revenue in column 5.

The Marginal Revenue Product (*MRP*) of Labor

Column 6 introduces a new concept: the *marginal revenue product* of labor.

> *The firm's **marginal revenue product** (**MRP**) of labor is the change in the firm's total revenue (ΔTR) divided by the change in the number of workers employed (ΔL):*

$$MRP = \Delta TR / \Delta L$$

In words, the *MRP* of labor tells us how an additional worker will add to the firm's revenue. In the table, the *MRP* numbers are obtained by dividing the change in total revenue in column 5 by the change in employment in column 1. For example, when employment increases from 2 to 3 workers (an increase of 1 worker), its daily revenue rises from $720 to $1,040 (an increase of $320). So, for this change in employment,

$$MRP \text{ of Labor} = \Delta TR/\Delta L = \$320/1 = \$320$$

Another Way to Calculate *MRP*

We can also calculate (and think of) the *MRP* in another way. Column 3 shows the marginal product of labor (*MPL*)—a concept you also learned about in Chapter 7. The MPL tells us the additional *output* produced when one more worker is hired. For example, when the firm hires the third worker, output rises from 90 to 130, so the *MPL* for this change in employment is 40.

Now, each time the firm hires another worker, its output (car washes) rises by the marginal product of labor (*MPL*). Each unit of this additional output sells for $8. Therefore, each time another worker is hired, *revenue* must increase by *MPL* × $8.

More generally,

$$MRP \text{ of Labor} = MPL \times P$$

TABLE A.1

Data for Spotless Car Wash

	(1) Number of Workers
	0
	1
	2
	3
	4
	5
	6
	7

You can verify that each value for MRP in colu[mn]
to the MPL in column 3 times the price in col[umn]

Finally, notice how the MRP values c[hange as we]
travel down column 6. As employment inc[reases, MRP]
first rises (up to the hiring of the second w[orker]), then
falls (beginning with the hiring of the th[ird worker]).
This mirrors the behavior of the MP[L values in]
column 4. Recall, from Chapter 7, that at [low levels of]
employment and output, *increasing margi[nal returns to]
labor* (rising MPL) are likely. But eventuall[y, as employ-]
ment continues to rise, a firm will eventua[lly experience]
diminishing marginal returns to labor (fall[ing MPL). So]
whenever hiring another worker causes M[PL to rise or]
fall, it will cause MRP = MPL × P to rise [or fall as well.]
The rise and fall of MRP is based on the beh[avior of MPL.]

---

[12] $MRP = MPL \times P$ holds only when output is s[old in a perfectly]
competitive market, in which the firm faces a horizo[ntal demand curve]
for its product. If the firm faces a *downward-sloping* [demand curve for]
its product, as in monopoly or monopolistic comp[etition, there is a]
different relationship between MRP and MPL. Hirin[g another worker]
still increases output by the MPL, but now the firm m[ust lower its price]
in order to sell the additional output. In this cas[e, hiring another]
worker increases the firm's revenue by the additiona[l output produced]
(MPL) times the increase in revenue per unit increas[e in output (MR).]
Thus, a more general equation for MRP is MPL [× MR. When the]
product market is competitive, MR is just the mark[et price.]

This observation allows us to state a simple rule for the firm's employment decision:

> To *maximize profit*, the firm should hire the number of workers such that MRP = W—*that is, closest to the point where the* MRP *curve intersects the wage line.*

A Proviso

There is one proviso for the previous highlighted statement: Profits are maximized only if the *MRP* curve crosses the wage line *from above.* That is, we must be on the *downward-sloping* portion of the *MRP* curve. To prove this to yourself, draw an example in which the *MRP* curve crosses the wage line twice—once as it slopes upward and once as it slopes downward. In your drawing, you'll notice that the *MRP* will always be greater than the wage to the right of the crossing point, so it will always pay for the firm to *increase* employment beyond that point. Thus, that crossing point cannot be the profit-maximizing employment level. It is only the *downward-sloping* part of the *MRP* curve that matters for the firm's employment decision.

Two Approaches to Profit Maximization

Let's compare two different approaches that a firm can use to maximize its profit. In previous chapters, we used the *MR* = *MC* approach to find profit-maximizing *output*, which requires a certain amount of labor. In this appendix, we've used the *MRP* = *W* approach to find profit-maximizing *employment*, which will produce a certain level of output. Can these two approaches lead to different employment and output decisions at the firm? For example, for Spotless, we've discovered that *MRP* = *W* tells Spotless to employ five workers. But five workers (as you can see in Table 1) implies a total output of 184 car washes per day. Could the *MC* and *MR* approach guide Spotless to some *other* level of output, say, 196 car washes?

The answer is: No, because these two "different" approaches are actually the *same* approach viewed differently. To see why, remember that hiring another *worker* increases the firm's output and therefore changes both its revenue and its cost. For example, in Table A.1, increasing employment from four to five workers raises output by 24 units (from 160 to 184 units). This, in turn, increases revenue by $192 and cost by $120. Since hiring the fifth worker increases revenue more than it raises cost (i.e., *MRP* > *W*), then it must also be true

that increasing output by those *24 units* raises revenue by more than it raises cost (i.e., *MR* > *MC* for that increase in output).

This applies generally: Whenever *MRP* > *W* for a change in employment, *MR* > *MC* for the associated rise in output. Whenever *MRP* < *W* for a change in employment, *MR* < *MC* for the associated rise in output. And if *MRP* = *W* for a change in employment, then it must be that *MR* = *MC* for the associated change in output.[13]

The Firm's Labor Demand Curve

In Table 1, the firm took the wage rate of $120 per day as given. But what if the wage rate had been different, say, $90 per day? As you can verify by modifying the table, at this lower wage rate, the firm would have hired *six* workers instead of five. The optimal level of employment will always depend on the wage rate.

Figure A.2 shows what happens at the typical firm as the wage rate varies. For each wage rate, the optimal level of employment, where *MRP* = *W*, is found by traveling horizontally over to the *MRP* curve and then down to the horizontal axis. For example, with a wage rate of W_1, the firm will want to hire L_1 workers. If the wage drops to W_2, the optimal level of employment rises to L_2. As the wage rate drops, the firm moves along its *MRP* curve in deciding how many workers to employ. This is why we call the downward-sloping portion of the *MRP* curve the *firm's labor demand curve:*

> The downward-sloping portion of the MRP curve is the firm's labor demand curve, *telling us how much labor the firm will want to employ at each wage rate.*

From Firm to Market

The market labor demand curve is found by simply adding the labor demand curves for every firm that employs labor in that market. For example, at a daily wage of $120, Spotless's labor demand curve tells us it will employ 5 workers. Suppose a second firm

---

[13] To help you see the connection between these two approaches even more clearly, add two new columns for *MR* and *MC* in Table 1 and use them to find the profit-maximizing output level. But when calculating *MR* and *MC*, don't forget to divide ΔTR and ΔTC by the change in output as you move from row to row.

FIGURE A.2 The Firm's Labor Demand Curve

As the wage rate varies, the firm moves along its MRP curve in deciding how many workers to hire. As a result, the downward-sloping portion of the MRP curve is the firm's labor demand curve. It shows how many workers will be demanded at each wage rate.

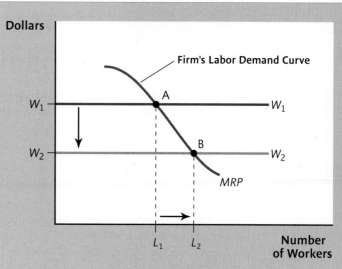

would hire 12 workers from the same labor market at that wage, and a third firm would hire 8, and so on. On the *market* labor demand curve, the quantity of labor demanded at a wage of $120 per day would be $5 + 12 + 8 + \cdots$ and so on (continuing to add the employment for all the firms in the market). As we've seen, at each of these firms, increasing the wage rate reduces employment. Therefore, in the labor market as a whole, increasing the wage rate reduces the quantity of labor demanded.

The market labor demand curve, like each firm's labor demand curve, slopes downward.

© ENIGMA/ALAMY

CHAPTER 13

Capital and Financial Markets

In 2011, the owners of Zipcar—a privately owned company that rents cars by the hour—wanted to expand their business. To do so, they would need millions of dollars to purchase cars for their fleet, expand service to more cities, hire new employees, increase advertising, and more. But Zipcar's owners had an important decision before they could do any of these things: How to obtain the funds?

There were several choices. They could delay the expansion until the firm became profitable, using the firm's own earnings to expand the business gradually. Or they could *borrow* the funds all at once from a bank or some other source. Or they could obtain the funds by bringing in new owners with money to invest, who would then be entitled to receive a share of all the firm's future profits. Zipcar went for the last option, choosing to sell ownership shares (called shares of *stock*) to the general public.

At that point, the spotlight shifted to another group of people: those *buying* shares in Zipcar. They had to decide whether the price Zipcar was asking—$18 for each share—was worth it. Zipcar had not earned a profit yet, and was not expected to for several years. But at some point in the future, investors thought the company had a good chance of becoming profitable. There was no guarantee, of course, nor could anyone be sure of just how much profit Zipcar might earn. But aside from these uncertainties, investors had another, more basic question to answer: How much should they pay *today* for money they might receive in the *future*?

In the end, investors decided that the dollars Zipcar wanted today for a share of the firm's future profits were worth it. They purchased more than 9.68 million shares at $18 each, providing Zipcar with about $175 million for immediate use. In this chapter, you'll see that the method they used to reach their conclusion—*assigning a value to future dollars*—can help us answer a variety of other questions.

This method is used by Staples when it decides whether to open or close a store. And by Pfizer when it decides how much of the firm's yearly income to put into research and development on new drugs. It can even be used by someone deciding whether or not—on purely financial grounds—attending college is likely to be a good investment. All of these decisions involve putting a value today on dollars to be received *in the future*.

In this chapter, we'll be discussing how such decisions are made. We'll first look at decisions about investing in physical capital, such as factory buildings or machinery. Then we'll turn our attention to the value of financial assets, specifically stocks and bonds. Finally, in the Using the Theory section, we'll turn to the decision to invest in human capital—specifically, your decision to attend college.

Physical Capital and the Firm's Investment Decision

The concept of *capital* was introduced in the first chapter of this book. There, you learned that capital is one of society's *resources*, along with land, labor, and entrepreneurship. You also learned that we can classify capital into two categories: *physical capital,* such as the plant and equipment owned by business firms, and *human capital,* the skills and training of the labor force. In this section, we'll focus on firms' decisions about physical capital.

How does a business firm decide how much physical capital to use? In the same way that it makes any other decision. The firm's goal is to maximize its profit—not just this year, but over many years into the future. What guidelines should a firm use?

That depends on how the firm *pays* for its capital. We'll look first at the decision to *rent* capital. Then, we'll move to the more complex decision to *purchase* capital.

A First, Simple Approach: Renting Capital

In this section we assume that a firm *rents* its capital at a constant price per unit of time (per hour, day, etc.), just as it "rents" its labor. We'll make our discussion more concrete with an example. Imagine you are the fleet manager at Quicksilver Delivery Service. Your firm delivers packages for small retailers in the Chicago metropolitan area. You are responsible for determining the number of trucks the firm should use.

Your first step is to remember the *marginal approach to profit*:

> *The marginal approach to profit states that a firm should take any action that adds more to its revenue than it adds to its cost.*

Here, the action is "rent another truck." Keep in mind that when we use this approach, revenue and cost are measured *per period,* such as revenue and cost per year. So, the marginal approach says that you should rent another truck if doing so will increase yearly revenue more than it increases yearly cost.

Table 1 lists the data that will help you make your decision. The first column tells us different numbers of trucks you could rent. The second tells us the additional revenue each truck would generate for your firm each year. Notice that the additional annual revenue decreases as you use more trucks. For example, renting the first truck increases your annual revenue by $52,000. The second truck adds a bit less—only $50,000. This pattern makes sense: With just one truck, you would use it on your busiest route (the one where you can deliver the most packages each day). If you rent a second truck, you'd use it on the next busiest route, and so on. So each additional truck you rent will generate less additional revenue than the truck before.

The third column tells us all of the annual *incidental* expenses of using a truck (costs other than renting the truck itself). These include the annual costs for a driver's wages, insurance, gasoline, and maintenance. We've assumed for simplicity that these truck-related expenses are $40,000 per year for each truck, no matter how many trucks are rented.

Ultimately, we want to compare the additional revenue from a truck with its additional cost. So what should we do with these incidental expenses? One option is to include them as a cost, along with the rent. Another option is to deduct these incidental expenses from revenue, and then compare what's left (net revenue) to the rent. Either option will lead us to the same conclusion about how many trucks to rent. But

TABLE 1					
Quicksilver Delivery's Truck Rental Decision	(1) Trucks	(2) Additional Annual Revenue	(3) Additional Annual *Incidental* Costs	(4) Additional Annual *Net* Revenue Column 2 – Column 3	(5) Additional Rental Cost
	First Truck	$52,000	$40,000	$12,000	$8,000
	Second Truck	$50,000	$40,000	$10,000	$8,000
	Third Truck	$47,500	$40,000	$ 7,500	$8,000
	Fourth Truck	$46,000	$40,000	$ 6,000	$8,000
	Fifth Truck	$44,000	$40,000	$ 4,000	$8,000

© CENGAGE LEARNING 2013

the latter approach—deducting these incidental expenses from revenue first—helps simplify things later on. So that's what we've done in Table 1.

Column 4 shows the result: the *net* revenue from each additional truck. For example, the second truck brings in annual revenue of $50,000, but after deducting expenses for the driver, gas, insurance, and so forth, the *net* additional revenue is $10,000. Notice that the *net* additional revenue in column 4, like the additional revenue, declines as you add more trucks.

Finally, in column 5, we come to the annual rent for each truck. We've assumed the annual rent is a constant $8,000 per truck, no matter how many trucks you rent.

Now we're ready to apply the marginal approach to profit, using the data in the table. You should *rent another truck* whenever its (net) additional revenue (column 4) is greater than the cost of renting the truck itself (column 5), because doing so will add to your profit.

Running down the table, we see that it makes sense to rent the first and second truck, because each one adds more in net revenue than it costs to rent. For example, the second truck adds $10,000 to net revenue each year, but costs only $8,000 to rent. But the third truck adds less to net revenue ($7,500) than to cost ($8,000). The same is true for the forth and fifth truck. Therefore, your profits are maximized by renting exactly two trucks.

> *When capital is rented, rather than purchased, the marginal approach to profit tells us the firm should rent another unit of capital whenever the additional (net) revenue per period is greater than the additional rental cost per period.*

The Limits of the Simple Approach

Our first simple approach—which assumed that firms rent their capital—has a serious limitation. Our assumption that capital can be *rented*—while it may work for *some* firms—does not work for the economy in general. That's because every unit of capital in use is owned by someone or some firm. Even if Quicksilver Delivery Service rents its trucks, it will be renting them from a truck rental firm that purchased them. For any unit of capital employed in the economy, some firm—somewhere along the line—must have made the decision to purchase it. So if we want to understand decisions about capital investment in the economy, we must ultimately account for the decisions of firms that *purchase* the capital before it is used. For that reason, from this point on, we'll focus on the firms that *purchase* their capital.

This changes the decision-making process, because capital equipment, once purchased, will last a long time. At Quicksilver, for example, suppose a truck will last for 10 years. Then you'd have to compare the cost of buying a truck—which you have to pay *now*—with the additional net revenue the truck would bring in over the next ten years.

"That's easy," you might think. "I'll just add up the revenue over those 10 years. The fourth truck, for example, brings in $6,000 per year, so in 10 years, it will bring in a total of $60,000. As long as the truck costs less than $60,000, it adds to my profit."

But if you reason this way, you are making a serious error: You're treating each year's revenue as equally valuable, regardless of *when* the revenue is earned. In reality, the value of a future payment depends on *when* that payment is received. To see why, we'll have to take a detour from Quicksilver Delivery and explore the issue of future payments more generally. We'll come back to Quicksilver and its trucks when we're done.

The Value of Future Dollars

To see why the value of a future payment depends on *when* that payment is received, just run through the following thought experiment. Imagine that you are given the choice between receiving $1,000 now and $1,000, with certainty, one year from now. Do you have to think hard before making up your mind? It's always better to have dollars earlier rather than later. But the *economic* reason is this: If you get the $1,000 now, you could put it in the bank and earn interest for a year, giving you *more* than $1,000 a year from now.

A truck, like most types of physical capital, will increase a firm's revenue for many years. As a result, the firm must calculate the present-dollar equivalent of future receipts.

> Because present dollars can earn interest, it is always preferable to receive a given sum of money earlier rather than later. Therefore, a dollar received later has less value than a dollar received now.

Knowing that a dollar received in the future is worth less than the same dollar received today is an important insight. But what, exactly, is the value to you right now of each dollar that you will receive *later*?

To answer that question, we use a concept called *present value*.

> The **present value** (PV) of a future payment is its equivalent value in today's dollars. Alternatively, it is the most anyone would pay today for the right to receive the future payment with certainty.

Present value The value, in today's dollars, of a sum of money to be received or paid at a specific date in the future with certainty.

To understand this concept better, let's work out a simple example: What is the present value of $1,000 to be received one year in the future? That is, what is the most you would pay *today* in order to receive $1,000 one year from today? The answer is clearly *not* $1,000. If you paid $1,000 today for a guaranteed $1,000 in one year, you would lose something: the interest you *could* have earned during the year. So it never makes sense to pay $1,000 now for $1,000 to be received one year from now.

But would you pay $800 for the guaranteed future payment? Or $900? That depends on how much interest you *could* earn by lending funds to someone else for a year. In fact, the most you'd pay is the amount that, if you lent it out for interest,

⚠ DANGEROUS CURVES

Percentages and decimals Be careful when working with interest rates: They can be expressed in either percentage form or decimal form. An interest rate of 5 percent (5%) can also be expressed in decimal form as 0.05.

In the expression $1 + r$, r is always in decimal form. For example, $1 + r$ is equal to 1.05 when the interest rate is 5 percent. Similarly, an interest rate of 0.5% (*one-half* of 1 percent) would translate to 0.005 in decimal form, and $1 + r$ would then equal 1.005.

would get you *exactly* $1,000 in one year. More concretely, suppose the interest rate you can earn if you lend out funds is 10 percent per year. Then the present value of $1,000 to be received one year from today is $909.09. Why? Because if you had $909.09 today, and loaned it out at 10 percent interest, then—one year from now—you'd have $909.09 × 1.10 = $1,000. As long as you can be sure you'll be repaid (an issue we'll discuss in more detail later), you shouldn't care whether you receive $909.09 today or $1,000 in the future.

But how did we *find* this present value of $909.09?

Calculating Present Value

To find the present value of $1,000 to be received one year in the future, we ask: What amount of money, loaned out today at a 10 percent annual interest rate, would give the lender $1,000 in one year? Let's call that amount of money "*X*." Then *X* has to satisfy the following equation: (*X*) (1.10) = $1,000. Solving this equation for *X*, we find that

$$X = \frac{\$1,000}{1.10} = \$909.09.$$

Now remember that "*X*" in this equation is the number of today's dollars that you could turn into $1,000 in one year. That is, "*X*" is just the present value we've been seeking. So let's use the symbol "*PV*" (for Present Value) in place of *X*. Then, when the annual interest rate is 10 percent, we can say:

$$PV \text{ of } \$1,000 \text{ in one year} = \frac{\$1,000}{1.10} = \$909.09.$$

In words, if you lent out $909.09 at 10 percent interest, you would have $1,000 one year from today. Therefore, $909.09 is the most you would be willing to give up today for $1,000 in one year. Or, more formally, *$909.09 is the present value of $1,000 received one year from now.*

We can generalize this result by noting that, if the interest rate had been something other than 0.10—we'll call it *r*—or the amount of money had been something other than $1,000—say, *Y* dollars—then the present value would satisfy the equation

$$PV \times (1 + r) = Y$$

or

$$PV = \frac{Y}{(1 + r)}.$$

What if the payment of $*Y* were to be received *two* years from now instead of one? Then we can use the same logic to find the present value. In that case, each dollar lent out now would become $(1 + r)$ dollars after one year. Then, when the dollar plus the earned interest was lent out again for a second year, it would become $(1 + r)(1 + r) = (1 + r)^2$ dollars at the end of the second year. Thus, the *PV* will satisfy

$$PV \times (1 + r)^2 = Y$$

and solving for *PV*, we obtain

$$PV = \frac{Y}{(1 + r)^2}.$$

Finally, for payments to be received one, two, or any number of years *n* in the future, we can state that

> *the present value of $Y to be received* n *years in the future is equal to*
> $$PV = \frac{Y}{(1 + r)^n}.$$

For example, with an interest rate of 10 percent, the present value of $1,000 to be received three years in the future would be

$$PV = \frac{\$1,000}{(1.10)^3} = \$751.31.$$

The process of making dollars of different dates comparable is called **discounting**. The value of *r* used in this process is often called the **discount rate**.[1]

Discounting The act of converting a future value into its present-day equivalent.

Discount rate The interest rate used in computing present values.

Determinants of Present Value

Table 2 shows the present value (rounded to the nearest penny) of a dollar to be received at different times in the future, at different interest rates. To see where the numbers come from, let's do an example. In the table, locate the entry for present value of $1 to be received 10 years from today when the interest rate is 10 percent. (The entry is $0.39.) Where did this number come from?

With an interest rate of 10 percent, our formula tells us that $PV = \$1/(1.10)^{10} = \$1/2.59 = \$0.39$. This tells us that, when the interest rate (discount rate) is 10 percent, anyone expecting to receive $1 ten years from today might just as well accept $0.39 now. After all, when loaned at 10 percent interest per year, 39 cents will get you $1 in ten years.

TABLE 2

Present Values of $1 Future Payments

No. of Years in Future	Value of $1 to Be Received at Various Numbers of Years in the Future, at Different Discount Rates		
	5 Percent	10 Percent	15 Percent
0	$1.00	$1.00	$1.00
1	$0.95	$0.91	$0.87
2	$0.91	$0.83	$0.76
3	$0.86	$0.75	$0.66
4	$0.82	$0.68	$0.57
5	$0.78	$0.62	$0.50
10	$0.61	$0.39	$0.25
20	$0.38	$0.15	$0.06

© CENGAGE LEARNING 2013

---

[1] In macroeconomics, the term *discount rate* has a completely different meaning: It's the interest rate that the Federal Reserve charges banks when it lends them reserves. There is no connection between the two different meanings of the term.

⚠ DANGEROUS CURVES

What about inflation? You may be wondering why we've ignored inflation (the general rise in prices) when calculating *PV*. After all, when there is inflation, there seem to be two types of costs from delaying receipt of money: (1) the sacrifice of the interest you *could* have earned if you had instead received the money today; and (2) the decrease in the purchasing power of each dollar you will get, due to inflation.

But it turns out that the first cost already includes the second. When you study macroeconomics, you'll learn that the ordinary interest rate (called the *nominal* interest rate in macro) that we've been using to determine *PV* is *higher* when people expect inflation, to compensate lenders for the decrease in each dollar's purchasing power. The higher interest rate makes our calculated *PV* lower. So our *PV already* includes any expected loss of purchasing power from inflation. The higher the expected inflation rate, the higher the ordinary interest rate will be, and the lower the *PV* of any given future payment.

© AXL/SHUTTERSTOCK.COM

Some patterns in the table are worth noting. One pattern is found by running down any of the *columns*. Notice that the present value entries get smaller: As the $1 payment is postponed further into the future, its present value declines.

This pattern is also seen in Figure 1, where the present value of $1 received in different future years is represented by the height of each bar. Panel (a) shows these present values when the interest rate is 5 percent, panel (b) for an interest rate of 10 percent, and panel (c) for 15%. Notice that in each panel, the more years the dollar payment is delayed, the shorter the bars.

The decline in present value when a payment is postponed follows a simple logic: The longer each dollar of payment is postponed, the more interest you forgo by the delay, so the less you would be willing to pay today for that future dollar.

> *All else equal, a payment received later has a lower present value than a payment received earlier.*

A second pattern is found in each *row* of Table 1. For a given future payment date, as the interest rate rises from 5 percent to 10 percent to 15 percent, the entries get smaller. In Figure 1, this causes the entire set of bars to become shorter as we move from panel (a) to panel (b), and from (b) to (c). This pattern make sense too: The higher the interest rate, the more interest you sacrifice by waiting to get your payment, so the less you'd pay for it now.

> *All else equal, the present value of a future payment is lower when the interest rate is higher.*

FIGURE 1 | **Present Values of $1 Future Payments: A Graphical Illustration**

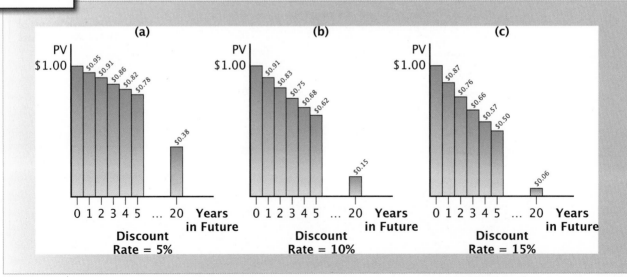

© CENGAGE LEARNING 2013

Finally, although this is not seen in the table, the present value of a future payment is greater when the future payment itself is greater. In fact, you can find the present value of any number of dollars by multiplying the entries in the table by that number of dollars. For example, the present value of $500 to be received 10 years in the future is 500 times the present value of $1 received at that time, or $500 \times \$0.39 = \$195$. However, because we've rounded the entries in the table to the nearest penny, the present values for larger dollar amounts will be approximations.

The Present Value of a Future *Stream* of Payments

The formula for present value calculations can also help us determine the value of a *stream* of future payments, with each individual payment to be received at a *different* time in the future. Consider the value, in today's dollars, of the following stream of future payments: $1,000 to be received one year from now, $900 to be received two years from now, and $600 to be received three years from now. To get the present value of this stream of payments, we first calculate the present value of each payment, and then we add those present values together:

$$PV = \frac{\$1,000}{(1 + r)} + \frac{\$900}{(1 + r)^2} + \frac{\$600}{(1 + r)^3}$$

With an interest rate of 10 percent, the *total* present value of the entire stream of payments is equal to:

$$PV = \frac{\$1,000}{(1.10)} + \frac{\$900}{(1.10)^2} + \frac{\$600}{(1.10)^3}$$
$$= \$909.09 + \$743.80 + \$450.79$$
$$= \$2,103.68$$

The logic of present value shows us why anyone who expects to receive a stream of future payments must discount each of those payments before adding them together. The next section provides an example of how firms use present value to make decisions about investing in new capital.

Purchasing Capital

Let's return to your problem at Quicksilver Delivery Service, where you've decided to purchase, rather than rent, your trucks. How many trucks should you buy? Table 3 shows the present value calculations you'd need to make, under the following conditions:

- The net additional revenue per year for each truck is as given in Table 1, a few pages earlier, and will occur with *certainty*.
- Each truck has an expected useful life of 10 years.
- You have the option to lend funds without risk at an annual interest rate of 10%. (So 10% is the appropriate discount rate for your present value calculations.)

For example, the first truck gives Quicksilver $12,000 per year in additional revenue for 10 years. Since we're assuming for simplicity that each year's revenue is received at the end of each year (see the Dangerous Curves feature above), the present value of the first year's revenue is $12,000/(1.1)$; the present value of the second year's revenue is $12,000/(1.1)^2$; and so on. When these present values are added together for all 10 years, we find that the first truck gives the firm $73,735 in net additional revenue in present value terms. The other entries are calculated similarly.

TABLE 3

The Present Value of Trucks at Quicksilver Delivery Service (with a Discount Rate of 10%)

Trucks	Additional Annual Net Revenue	Total Present Value of Additional Net Revenue over 10 years
First Truck	$12,000	$\dfrac{\$12,000}{(1.1)} + \dfrac{\$12,000}{(1.1)^2} + \cdots + \dfrac{\$12,000}{(1.1)^{10}} = \$73,735$
Second Truck	$10,000	$\dfrac{\$10,000}{(1.1)} + \dfrac{\$10,000}{(1.1)^2} + \cdots + \dfrac{\$10,000}{(1.1)^{10}} = \$61,446$
Third Truck	$ 7,500	$\dfrac{\$7,500}{(1.1)} + \dfrac{\$7,500}{(1.1)^2} + \cdots + \dfrac{\$7,500}{(1.1)^{10}} = \$46,084$
Fourth Truck	$ 6,000	$\dfrac{\$6,000}{(1.1)} + \dfrac{\$6,000}{(1.1)^2} + \cdots + \dfrac{\$6,000}{(1.1)^{10}} = \$36,867$
Fifth Truck	$ 4,000	$\dfrac{\$4,000}{(1.1)} + \dfrac{\$4,000}{(1.1)^2} + \cdots + \dfrac{\$4,000}{(1.1)^{10}} = \$24,578$

Now that we know the total present value that you gain from each truck, do we know how many trucks you should buy? Almost, but not quite. There is still the matter of how much each truck *costs*. But now that we've translated *all* the additional revenue from each truck into a single, present value number, we know the benefits of each truck measured in *today's dollars*. That measure can be compared to the truck's cost, which must *also* be *paid* in today's dollars. If trucks cost $45,000, the firm gains more benefits (in future revenue) than costs for the first three trucks. But the purchase of the fourth truck, whose benefit to the firm is only $36,867 in today's dollars, does not make sense, since the cost in today's dollars is $45,000. Quicksilver should buy only three trucks.

Our examples have focused on a special type of capital—delivery trucks. But the same logic works for any other type of physical capital—automated assembly lines, desktop computers, filing cabinets, locomotives, and construction cranes. In each of these cases, the first step in making a decision about a capital purchase is to put a value on the benefits of the capital. This value is the total present value of the future revenue generated by the capital.

This first step—putting a value on physical capital—is so important and so widely applicable that we can refer to it as a general principle:

Principle of asset valuation The idea that the value of an asset is equal to the total present value of all the future benefits it generates.

> The **principle of asset valuation** says that, when there is no uncertainty, the value of any asset is the sum of the present values of all the future benefits it will generate.

The principle of asset valuation tells us how to determine the marginal benefit from buying another unit of capital, such as another truck. Then, as we've done with Quicksilver, we compare this marginal benefit with the cost of the capital itself. As you've seen, the firm should then buy any unit of capital for which the marginal benefit (total present value of future revenue) is greater than the cost.

⚠ **DANGEROUS CURVES**

When are future payments received? Businesses typically earn revenue every day they are in operation. However, in calculating present discounted value, it would be cumbersome to discount each day's revenue by the appropriate discount factor. As a useful approximation, we can treat each year's revenue as if it is all received in one lump sum at the *end* of the year. This is the convention followed in this book for all future payments. Thus, when we say that a firm or individual receives a payment of $10,000 "in the first year," we mean "at the end of the first year." (Can you see how we've used this assumption in Table 3?)

An Important Proviso: Risk

In our discussion so far, we've been assuming that your future receipts at Quicksilver are known with certainty. But realistically, future receipts are risky. The demand for package deliveries might decrease, or a competitor might drain away some of your revenue, or the price of gasoline could spike. You can never be sure how much net revenue each truck will bring in to your firm.

Suppose that the net revenue entries in Table 1 are your best guess about the future. But there's also a small chance that each truck will bring in either $1,000 less or $1,000 more than your best guess. If you calculate the present value numbers for the *worst*-case scenario (in which each truck generates $1,000 less per year than in Table 1), the first two trucks would still have a present value greater than their cost. The third truck, however, would not.

Should you buy the third truck now? The worst case scenario isn't likely . . . but it's possible. On the other hand, the best case scenario—with every truck generating $1,000 more than your best guess each year—could happen as well. You now have a risky investment decision to make.

All else equal, most investors would prefer to face as little risk as possible. So the value of any future payment should be smaller when that payment is uncertain. Because we calculate present value assuming our "best guess" scenario is *certain* to occur, our present value calculations will *overestimate* the true value of future payments involving risk.

> *When there is uncertainty about future benefits, the principle of asset valuation is just our starting point. It tells us the* most *an asset would be worth. The greater the uncertainty or the greater one's aversion to risk, the more the value of a risky asset will fall short of its present value.*[2]

In this chapter, when there is uncertainty, we'll continue to calculate present values as if the "best guess" about the future is certain to occur. Therefore, risk will not affect present value itself. But risk will cause the true value of an asset to be *less* than its present value.

Going back to Quicksilver, under the "best guess" scenario, the third truck has a present value of $46,084—greater than its cost. But because of the risk, the third truck will be worth less than $46,084 to you—perhaps (if you dislike risk enough) less than $45,000. In that case, because of the uncertainty, you would not buy the third truck.

What Happens When Things Change: The Investment Curve

Investment is the term economists use to describe firms' purchases of new capital over some period of time. In the example above, if trucks cost $45,000 each, Quicksilver should buy three of them. If it bought all three trucks this year, its investment expenditures for the year would be $45,000 × 3 = $135,000.

But this conclusion about investment is based on the assumption that the interest rate, and Quicksilver's discount rate, is 10 percent. With a lower interest rate—say,

Investment Firms' purchases of new capital over some period of time.

---

[2] There are other ways to handle decision making under risk. For example, risk can be incorporated into the present value calculation itself, by using a higher discount rate (the interest rate for riskless lending plus a "risk premium"). In that case, uncertainty will reduce the present value itself. In this textbook, however, risk will not affect the way we calculate present value.

TABLE 4

Present Value Calculations for Various Interest Rates

Trucks	Additional Annual Revenue	Total Present Value with a Discount Rate of:		
		5%	10%	15%
First Truck	$12,000	$92,661	$73,735	$69,213
Second Truck	$10,000	$77,217	$61,446	$57,678
Third Truck	$ 7,500	$57,913	$46,084	$43,258
Fourth Truck	$ 6,000	$46,330	$36,867	$34,606
Fifth Truck	$ 4,000	$30,887	$24,578	$23,071

5 percent—each year's revenue would have a *higher* present value, so the total present value of each truck would be higher. Our conclusion about Quicksilver's investment spending might then change. Similarly, a rise in the interest rate—say, to 15 percent—would *lower* the present value of each year's revenue, and *decrease* the total present value for each truck.

Table 4 shows how our total present value calculations for each truck change as the interest rate changes. The numbers in the last three columns are each calculated just as were the numbers we calculated in Table 3. The only difference is that, instead of always assuming a discount rate of 10 percent, Table 4 shows the total present value for each truck under three different interest rates. Notice what happens as we move from left to right in the table for any particular truck: The interest rate rises, from 5 percent to 10 percent to 15 percent, and the value of the truck to the firm falls.

Now, if trucks cost $45,000 each, how much will Quicksilver invest (spend on new trucks) at any given interest rate? Let's see. If the interest rate is 5 percent, Quicksilver should buy four trucks, because each of the first four trucks has a total present value greater than $45,000 at that interest rate. The fifth truck, however, has a total present value of only $30,887, so the firm should not buy that one. Thus, if the interest rate is 5 percent, Quicksilver's investment spending will be $45,000 × 4 = $180,000.

If the interest rate rises to 10 percent, we are back to the conclusion we reached in Table 3, which assumed a 10 percent interest rate: Quicksilver should buy three trucks when the interest rate is 10 percent. (You can also verify this using the middle column of Table 3.) Quicksilver's total investment spending would *decrease* to $45,000 × 3 = $135,000. Finally, if the interest rate rises to 15 percent, Quicksilver should buy only two trucks, so its total investment spending is $45,000 × 2 = $90,000.

What is true for Quicksilver is true for every other truck-buying firm in the economy: The higher the interest rate, the fewer trucks delivery services and other truck-buying firms will want to purchase, and the smaller will be investment expenditures on trucks during the year.

Take a moment to think about why this happens. The trucks themselves are the same, and they are just as productive at any of the three interest rates. But each truck is less valuable to firms in *present-dollar* terms. That's because—with a higher interest rate—the future additional revenue from each truck is worth *less* in today's dollars. But the truck still costs the same in today's dollars, regardless of the interest rate. So with a high interest rate, firms will want to buy fewer trucks at any given price.

The same logic applies to other capital purchases. At high interest rates, U.S. firms end up buying less of all different kinds of capital—not just delivery trucks, but

FIGURE 2 | The Investment Curve

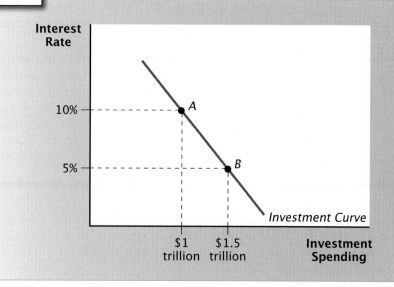

As the interest rate falls from 10 percent to 5 percent, each firm that buys a particular type of capital will buy more of it. As a result, the economy's total investment in physical capital rises from $1 trillion to $1.5 trillion. This is shown as the movement from point A to point B along the investment curve in the figure.

also other durable goods such as computers, machine tools, combines, and printing presses. It should be no surprise, then, that we come to the following conclusion:

> *As the interest rate rises, each business firm in the economy—using the principle of asset valuation—will place a lower value on additional capital, and decide to purchase less of it. Therefore, in the economy as a whole, a rise in the interest rate causes a decrease in investment expenditures.*

The Economy's Investment Curve

The relationship between the interest rate and investment expenditure is illustrated by the economy's investment curve, shown in Figure 2. The curve slopes downward, indicating that a drop in the interest rate causes investment spending to rise. When you study *macroeconomics,* you'll learn that the investment curve is important for the performance of the overall economy, for several reasons. But here's a hint as to one of them: When the interest rate falls, the increased investment in new capital means that the nation's *capital stock*—the total quantity of installed capital—will grow more rapidly than it otherwise would. With more capital, labor will be more productive, and our standard of living will be higher.

To recap:

> *Lower interest rates increase firms' investment in physical capital, causing the capital stock to be larger, and our overall standard of living to be higher.*

MARKETS FOR FINANCIAL ASSETS

You may be wondering what markets for financial assets, like stocks and bonds, have to do with the other subject of this chapter: markets for capital. After all, capital—like a machine or a factory—is something *real;* it enables a firm to produce real goods and services.

But in financial markets, the things being traded are just *pieces of paper,* which don't directly help anyone to produce anything. So what do these pieces of paper have to do with capital?

Actually, quite a bit. The pieces of paper being traded in financial markets are **financial assets**—promises to pay future income to their owners. Because capital lasts for many years, most firms get the funds to purchase their capital by issuing and selling these financial assets. For example, the firm might issue and sell shares of *stock* in the company, obligating it to pay those who hold the shares part of the firm's future profits. Or it might sell *bonds*, which are promises to pay back a sum of money in the future, along with interest payments. This leaves the firm with long-lasting capital, but also a long-lasting obligation to make future payments. So there is a close *economic* connection between a firm's decision to demand capital equipment and its decision to supply financial assets.

Primary and Secondary Asset Markets

When a newly issued financial asset is sold for the first time, we label this a **primary market** trade. But the buyer can then sell the asset to someone else, in which case we call it a **secondary market** trade. The difference between these two types of trades is illustrated in Figure 3.

Once a financial asset is issued and sold in the primary market, it can change hands many times in the secondary market. In fact, almost all of the trading that takes place in financial markets on any given day is secondary market trading. But it is only through primary market sales that firms actually obtain funds for investment projects. Secondary market trading is an exchange between private parties, and the original issuing firm or government agency is not involved.

Still, firms and government agencies follow secondary markets closely. Why? Because financial asset prices in the secondary and primary markets are closely related. In fact, at any given time, the prices of two otherwise identical assets in the primary market and secondary market should be identical.

Financial asset A promise to pay future income in some form, such as future profits or future interest payments.

Primary market The market in which newly issued financial assets are sold for the first time.

Secondary market The market in which previously issued financial assets are sold.

FIGURE 3   **Primary and Secondary Asset Markets**

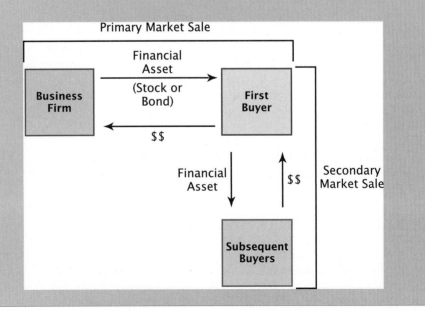

When a corporation creates a financial asset (such as a share of stock or a bond), it is sold to the public in the primary market. *This is how the corporation raises funds for investment. The financial asset can then be resold by its original purchaser to someone else in the* secondary market. *Secondary market transactions have no direct impact on the firm that originally issued the asset.*

Primary Market Sale

Financial Asset (Stock or Bond)

Business Firm

First Buyer

$ $

Financial Asset

$ $

Secondary Market Sale

Subsequent Buyers

For example, suppose that Microsoft wants to obtain funds by issuing new shares of stock in the primary market. In order to attract buyers, it will have to sell these *new* shares at the same price that *old* Microsoft shares are selling for in the secondary market. After all, every regular share of Microsoft stock provides the same benefits to its owner. So a buyer has no reason to prefer a new share to an old one, or vice versa.

> *Firms that issue financial assets in the primary market are affected by what happens in the secondary market. More specifically, if an asset's price rises in the secondary market, so will the price the firm can charge for similar, newly issued assets in the primary market.*

Now you can begin to see why firms care so much about secondary market trading. Each newly issued financial asset obligates the firm to make payments to its holder in the future. The higher the price at which the firm can sell the new financial asset, the more dollars it will get in exchange for the future obligations it is taking on. Or, viewed another way, the higher the selling price of a financial asset, the fewer assets the firm will have to issue to raise any given amount of money now.

Financial Assets and Present Value

We've discussed one connection between capital and financial markets. But here's another: A financial asset, just like capital equipment, gives its owner a stream of future benefits—in this case, dollar payments. Therefore, the value of a financial asset is calculated in the same way as the value of any other asset, such as a truck or a computer: We find the *total present value* of the future payments that the asset will generate. Thus, the method of valuation is another connection between markets for capital and markets for financial assets.

> *The principle of asset valuation applies to financial assets as well as physical assets. In each case, the value of the asset is the sum of the present values of the future benefits.*

In the rest of this chapter, we'll explore two types of financial assets: bonds and stocks.

BONDS

If a firm wants to buy a new fleet of trucks, build a new factory, or upgrade its computer system, it must decide how to finance that purchase. One way to do this is to sell **bonds**. A bond is simply a promise to pay a certain amount of money, called the *principal* or *face value*, at some future date. A bond's *maturity date* is the date on which the principal will be paid to the bond's owner. In addition to principal, some bonds also promise to make periodic payments, called *coupon payments*, before they mature.

A bond's **yield** (more formally, "yield to maturity") is the constant annual rate of return that the buyer would earn on his investment in the bond if it were held to maturity. For example, if you buy a bond that pays you $10,000 in two years for $8,900, your yield is 6%. How do we know? Because (as you can verify) if you took that same $8,900 and earned interest at a constant rate of 6% per year for two years, you'd end up with $10,000—the same as you'd get from the bond at maturity.

Bond A promise to pay back borrowed funds, issued by a corporation or government agency.

Yield The annual rate of return a bond earns for its owner.

How Much Is a Bond Worth?

To determine the value of a bond, let's start with a simple example: a bond that promises to pay $10,000 when it matures in exactly one year. The $10,000 is a future payment, and our method of calculating its value should not surprise you: It involves *present value*. Let's suppose (for now) that the bond will pay just what it promises, with certainty. That is, we'll assume no risk of *default* (failure to pay as promised).

Let's also suppose the interest rate at which you can lend funds elsewhere with just as much certainty is 10 percent. Then we can calculate (to the nearest dollar) the present value of the bond with our discounting formula as follows:

$$PV = \frac{\$Y}{(1 + r)} = \frac{\$10,000}{1.10} = \$9,091.$$

Because the present value of $10,000 to be received in one year is $9,091, that is the most you should pay for the bond. It is also the lowest price at which its current owner will sell the bond to you. We conclude that this bond will sell for $9,091, no more and no less.

The same principle applies to more complicated types of bonds, such as bonds that don't mature for many years, or bonds with coupon payments. For example, suppose a bond maturing in five years has a principal of $10,000, and also promises a coupon payment of $600 each year until maturity, with the first payment made one year from today. The total present value of this bond would be:

$$PV = \frac{\$600}{(1.10)} + \frac{\$600}{(1.10)^2} + \frac{\$600}{(1.10)^3} + \frac{\$600}{(1.10)^4} + \frac{\$600}{(1.10)^5} + \frac{\$10,000}{(1.10)^5} = \$8,484.$$

Once again, this total present value—$8,484—is what the bond is worth, and this is the price at which it will trade, as long as buyers and sellers use the same discount rate of 10 percent in their calculations.

⚠ DANGEROUS CURVES

Bond prices, bond yields, and opportunity cost You might think that the inverse relationship between bond prices and yields applies only to those *buying* bonds, and not those already holding them. After all, your yield is determined when you first buy a bond, and then it never changes, right?

Not right. If the price changes, the yield changes too, even for those who bought earlier at a different price. That's because the *opportunity cost* of continuing to own a bond is its *current* price, not the price you originally paid.

For example, suppose you initially pay $9,091 for a bond that gives you $10,000 in one year. The yield is initially $909/$9,091 or 10 percent. But now suppose, the day after you buy the bond, its price jumps to $9,500. If you continue to hold the bond, you give up ownership of $9,500 that you *could* have by selling it. In return, you will get $10,000 in one year. So your yield is now $500/$9,500 or 5.3 percent. This is the same yield that someone *buying* the bond for $9,500 would get. The point to remember is: When bond prices rise, the yield for *every* bondholder falls.

Bond Prices and Bond Yields

There is an important relationship between the price of a bond and the yield or rate of return that the bond earns for its owner. This is easiest to see with a simple case, such as the bond that pays $10,000 in one year in our earlier example. Suppose you bought this bond for $8,000. Then, at the end of the year, you would earn interest of $10,000 − $8,000 = $2,000 on an asset that cost you $8,000. Your yield would be $2,000/$8,000 = 0.25 or 25 percent.

But now suppose you paid $9,000 for that same bond. Then your interest earnings would be $10,000 − $9,000 = $1,000, and your yield would be $1,000/$9,000 = 0.111 or 11.1 percent.

As you can see, the yield a bond gives you depends on its price. For each price, there is a different yield. And the greater the price of a bond, the lower the yield on that bond. This applies not only to simple discount bonds, but also to more complicated bonds with coupon payments. And the reasoning is the same in both cases: A bond promises to pay fixed amounts of dollars at fixed dates in the future. The more you end up paying for those promised future payments, the lower your rate of return.

More generally:

> *There is an inverse relationship between bond prices and bond yields. The higher the price of any given bond, the lower the yield on that bond.*

Why Do Bond Yields Differ?

Thousands of different kinds of bonds are traded in financial markets every day. There are corporate bonds of various maturities, and bonds issued by local, state, and federal governments and government agencies, as well as bonds issued by foreign firms and governments. And each bond has its own unique yield. Why is this? Why don't all bonds give the same yield?

The answer is that bonds differ in important ways from one another. They have different maturity dates, are subject to different tax treatment, and differ in other ways. But one of the most important differences among bonds is their *default risk*.

A bond is a promise to pay in the future, and there is always a danger that the promise won't be kept, or won't be kept in full. This is called a *default* by the bond issuer. When a firm goes bankrupt, the holders of its bonds may receive none, or only some, of the payments they were promised.

For example, when General Motors declared bankruptcy in June 2009, it defaulted on bonds with a face value of $27 billion, declaring that there would be no further coupon or principal payments. In their place, bondholders were given shares of stock in a newly-formed successor corporation. But these shares were worth substantially less than the bonds they replaced.

Governments, too, sometimes default on their bonds. The risk that a government will default on its bonds is called *sovereign debt risk*. In 2010 and 2011, sovereign debt risk for several European countries' bonds dominated the news. There was a growing perception among investors that Portugal, Ireland, Italy, Spain, and Greece had borrowed so many euros in the past (by selling government bonds), and were projected to borrow so much more in the near future, that they might be unable or unwilling to honor their bonds in full.

All else equal, the greater the risk of default perceived by investors, the greater the yield on the bond. If a bond with a higher default risk had the same yield as an otherwise identical but safer bond, no one would hold the risky bond; everyone would prefer the safer one. The additional yield is the reward necessary to induce the bondholder to accept the higher risk of default.

When the default risk of a bond suddenly rises, people initially try to sell it, which makes the bond's price fall and it's yield rise until someone is willing to hold the bond at the higher yield. Or, to put it another way:

> *Bonds with default risk sell for less than the present value of their promised payments. All else equal, the greater the risk of default, the lower the bond's price, and the greater its yield.*

Figure 4 shows how rising sovereign debt risk in Europe affected long-term bond yields in 2010 and 2011. Notice how yields rose for three countries perceived to be getting riskier: Portugal, Greece, and Ireland. (Germany is included for comparison, because German bonds were considered free of default risk.)

| FIGURE 4 | 10-Year Government Bond Yields in Four Countries |

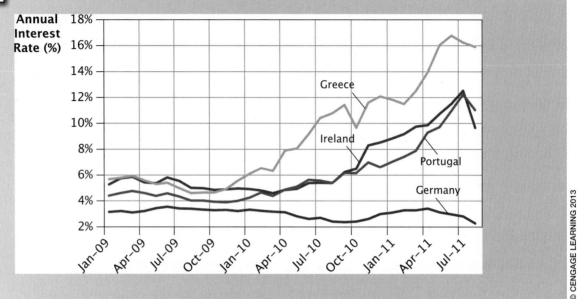

© CENGAGE LEARNING 2013

THE STOCK MARKET

Share of stock A share of ownership in a corporation.

A **share of stock,** like a bond, is a financial asset that promises its owner future payments. But the nature of the promise is different. When a corporation issues a bond, it is *borrowing* funds and promising to pay them back. But when a corporation issues a share of stock, it brings in new ownership of the firm itself. In fact, a share of stock is, by definition, a *share of ownership* in the corporation. Those who buy the shares provide the firm with funds, and, in return, they are entitled to a share of the firm's future profits.

Why Do People Hold Stock?

Why do so many individuals and fund managers choose to put their money into stocks? You already know part of the answer: When you own a share of stock, you own part of the corporation. Indeed, the fraction of the corporation that you own is equal to the fraction of the company's total shares that you own. For example, in August 2011, Starbucks Corporation had 746 million shares outstanding. If you owned 7,460 shares of Starbucks stock, then you owned 7,460/746,000,000 = .00001, or about one-thousandth of 1 percent of that firm. This means you are, in essence, entitled to a thousandth of a percent of the firm's after-tax profit.

In practice, however, most firms do not pay out *all* of their profit to shareholders. Instead, some of the profit is kept as *retained earnings,* for later use by the firm. The part of profit that is distributed to shareholders is called **dividends.** Of course, as a part owner of a firm, you are part owner of any retained earnings as well, even if you will not benefit from them until later.

Dividends Part of a firm's current profit that is distributed to shareholders.

Aside from dividends, a second—and usually more important—reason that people hold stocks is that they hope to enjoy **capital gains:** the return someone gets when they sell an asset at a higher price than they paid for it. For example, if you buy shares of Starbucks at $30 per share, and later sell them at $35 per share, your capital gain is $5 per share. This is in addition to any dividends the firm paid to you while you owned the stock.

Some stocks pay no dividends at all, because the management believes that stockholders are best served by reinvesting all profits within the firm so that *future* profits will be even higher. If the firm uses this money well, then future profits (and future dividends) can be even greater. And in the meantime, higher profits raise the price of the stock so that shareholders can get capital gains when they sell it.

Until 2010, Starbucks had never paid a dividend. But by plowing its profits back into the company, the firm was able to grow and become even more profitable. The company's shareholders had great faith that they would eventually get cash from the firm, and, in March 2010, it happened: Starbucks paid its first dividend.

Capital gain The return someone gets by selling a financial asset at a price higher than they paid for it.

Valuing a Share of Stock

Let's begin our attempt to value a share of stock with the simplest possible case. Imagine we know, with certainty, that a corporation's after-tax profit will be $10 million per year, every year. In that case, the value of a share should equal the present value of those future after-tax profits. (We use after-tax profits because this is what belongs to the firm's shareholders, whether they receive them as dividends or not. Any profits *not* received as dividends are plowed back into the firm on *behalf* of the shareholders.)

But the present value calculation, even in this simple case, is a little different than for a bond. A bond has a known maturity date, after which no further payments are made. A share of stock, by contrast, continues to entitle the owner to a share of the corporation's after-tax profit as long as the corporation exists. This is essentially forever, unless the firm is anticipated to go out of business.

Fortunately, there is a formula for calculating the present value in a case like this.

> *If a firm will earn a constant $Y in profit after taxes each year forever, then the total present value of these future profits is $Y/r, where r is the discount rate.*

Let's apply this formula to our example of $10 million in after-tax profit forever. If the discount rate—the interest rate you could earn on riskless lending—is 10 percent, the formula tells us that the *PV* of those future profits is $10 million/0.10 = $100 million.

What about the value of a single *share* of this firm's stock? If there are 1 million shares of stock outstanding for this firm, then each share should be worth one one-millionth of the firm's total value. So each share's price should be $100 million / 1 million = $100.

Now, our example was very simple in many respects, aside from assuming that there is no uncertainty. For one thing, profits at most firms do not remain constant year after year. There are other present value formulas for profit that is expected to *grow* at a constant rate, or grow for some period and then stabilize, and more. If you go further in your study of economics or finance, you will learn some of them. What's important here is that, regardless of which *PV* formula is called for,

> *if there were no uncertainty, the value of a share of stock would equal the total present value of its future after-tax profit, divided by the number of shares outstanding.*

Explaining Stock Prices

The prices of most stocks change every minute, and sometimes make large jumps in seconds. Why? The basic answer is: supply and demand. But the supply and demand curves require a careful interpretation (similar to housing markets in Chapter 4).

Figure 5 presents a supply and demand diagram for the shares of FedEx. The supply curve tells us the quantity of FedEx shares *in existence* at any moment in time. This is the number of shares that people are *actually* holding.

On any given day, the number of FedEx shares in existence is just the number that FedEx has issued and sold previously. Therefore, no matter what happens to the price today, the number of shares remains unchanged. Through August, 2011, FedEx had issued 317 million shares, so the supply curve is a vertical line at 317 million.

The quantity of FedEx shares that people want to *own* is given by the downward-sloping demand curve. As you can see, the lower the price of the stock, the more shares of FedEx people will want to hold. Why is this?

As discussed earlier, if FedEx's future profits per share were known by everyone with certainty, then everyone would place the same value on a share: the present value of those future profits. Everyone would want to own a share if they could buy it for any price equal to or less than that present value. This is a good starting point for valuing a share of stock.

The real world, of course, is more complicated. For one thing, people disagree about what FedEx's future profits are likely to be. If you think FedEx will be highly profitable in the future, you'll calculate a higher present value than someone who thinks FedEx's best days are behind it. Thus, even if everyone were certain about their own predictions, they would each calculate different present values for the shares, and each would have a different price at which they would be willing to own the stock.

FIGURE 5   **The Market for FedEx Shares**

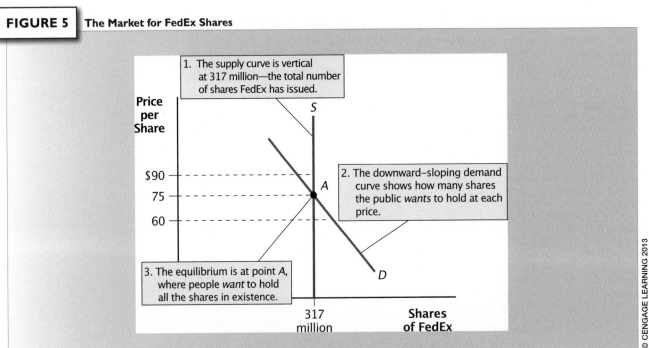

1. The supply curve is vertical at 317 million—the total number of shares FedEx has issued.

2. The downward–sloping demand curve shows how many shares the public *wants* to hold at each price.

3. The equilibrium is at point *A*, where people *want* to hold all the shares in existence.

Second, aside from different expectations of future profits, people may differ in their views about how *risky* those profits will be, and in their *attitudes* toward that risk. Because shares are risky, people will ordinarily hold them only if they can buy them for a price *less* than their basic present value. But for each person, the price that makes the stock attractive will be different.

Other factors, too, can influence the prices people are willing to pay, such as how many shares of FedEx they own already, what *other* assets they hold, how much wealth they have, and more. Clearly, the prices at which people want to own this stock will be different for different people. As the price of FedEx shares falls, and it becomes cheaper to potential investors, more of them will want to own it, and those who already own shares may want to own even more. This is what the downward sloping demand curve tells us.

In Figure 5, you can see that at any price other than $75 per share, the number of shares people *are* holding (on the supply curve) will differ from the number they *want* to hold (on the demand curve). For example, at a price of $60 per share, people would want to hold more shares than they are currently holding. Many would try to buy the stock, and the price would be bid up. At $90 per share, the opposite occurs: People find themselves holding more shares than they want to hold, and they will try to get rid of the excess by selling them. The sudden sales would cause the price to drop. Only at the equilibrium price of $75, where the supply and demand curves intersect, are people satisfied holding the number of shares they are *actually* holding.

As with bonds, stocks achieve their equilibrium prices almost instantly. Legions of stock traders—both individuals and professional fund managers—sit poised at their computers, ready to buy or sell a particular firm's shares the minute they feel they have an excess supply or a shortage of those shares. Thus, we can have confidence that the price of a share at any time is the equilibrium price.

What Happens When Things Change?

Why do stock prices *change* so often? Or, since stocks sell at their equilibrium prices at almost every instant, we can ask: Why do shares' *equilibrium* prices change so often?

Since a supply curve, like that in Figure 5, only shifts when the firm issues new shares (an infrequent occurrence), the day-to-day changes in equilibrium prices cannot be caused by shifts in the supply curve. So they must be caused by shifts in *demand* curve. Figure 6 shows how a rightward shift in the demand curve for shares of FedEx could cause the price to rise to $100 per share. Indeed, on rare occasions, the demand curve for a firm's shares has shifted so far rightward in a single day that the share price doubled or even tripled.

But what causes these sudden shifts in demand for a share of stock? Here are some important examples, each causing the demand curve to shift *rightward*:

Release of New Information. New information that suggests future profits will be higher than previously anticipated will increase the present value of a share. Remember that present value is our *starting point* for valuing a share. But if other factors (e.g., risk) remain unchanged, a greater present value will increase the number of shares people want to own at any price.

Drop in Interest Rates. With lower interest rates—including the interest rate for riskless lending—the discount rate used in present value calculations will be lower as well. This increases the present value of any given share and—all else equal—makes people want to own more of them at any price.

FIGURE 6 | **An Increase in Demand for Shares of FedEx**

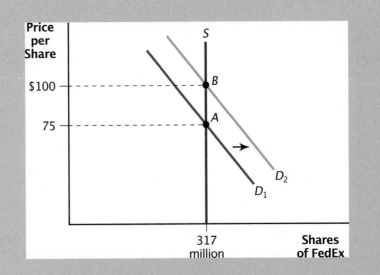

With 317 million FedEx shares available, and demand curve D_1, the equilibrium price is $75 per share. When demand for FedEx shares increases (to demand curve D_2), an excess demand is created at the original price: People want to hold more than the 317 million shares they are actually holding. Their efforts to buy more shares drive up the price, until a new equilibrium at $100 is reached. At this new, higher equilibrium price, the quantity of shares demanded is once again equal to the 317 million available.

© CENGAGE LEARNING 2013

Other Assets Less Attractive. All else equal, when other assets (bonds, real estate, commodities like gold and silver, or *other* firms' shares) become less attractive, people want to have more of their wealth in the shares we are analyzing, increasing demand.

Decrease in Risk. With less uncertainty surrounding future profits, the price that makes a share attractive to potential owners will rise closer to its present value. (Remember: we calculate present value assuming no uncertainty.) This implies that, at any given price, less uncertainty makes people want to own more shares.

Expectations of Any of the Above. If people expect any of the above changes to occur in the future, they will also expect the demand curve for shares to shift rightward, and the price of the stock to rise. The anticipation of capital gains in the future (when the price rises) makes people want to hold more shares at any given price *now.*

An Example: Stock Prices in 2008 and Early 2009

An example of a dramatic change in stock prices occurred in 2008 and early 2009. Recall from Chapter 4 that during this time, housing prices were collapsing, and the economy was in the midst of a severe recession. New economic data was released daily, suggesting that the ongoing recession was worsening, and that future corporate profits would plummet. Even worse was the risk of widespread corporate bankruptcies. When a firm goes bankrupt, stockholders are last in line to receive any value that might be left. When General Motors declared bankruptcy in 2009, for example, its stock became worthless.

These events shifted demand curves for most corporate shares leftward, and their equilibrium prices dropped. Figure 7 gives an idea of how dramatic the drop was. It shows the behavior of the Standard and Poor's 500 (S&P 500), which tracks the average price of 500 of the largest U.S. corporations. As you can see, stock prices

FIGURE 7 | **The S&P 500 Stock Market Index**

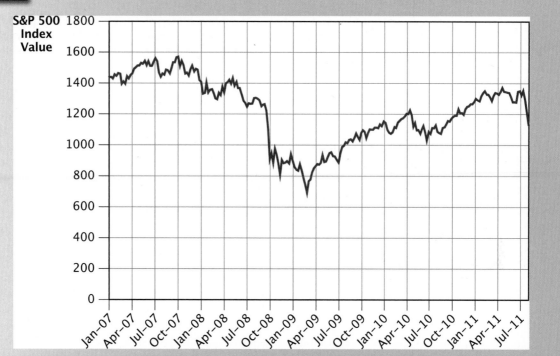

The S&P 500 Index is a popular stock market index that tracks share prices for 500 large corporations. In 2008 and early 2009, expected corporate profits fell and uncertainty rose, and share prices plummeted, hitting bottom only after they had fallen by more than 50%.

© CENGAGE LEARNING 2013

fell throughout 2008, especially in mid-September when the economic news was particularly bad. Stock prices continued dropping through early 2009, eventually falling to 50 percent of their previous high. During this period, the total value of the shares owned by U.S. households fell by about $8 trillion.

THE EFFICIENT MARKETS VIEW

Every day, financial news programs on cable stations like CNBC or Fox Business Network offer advice to millions of television viewers. The analysts interviewed on these shows tell us that they have done some careful research or that they have a secret formula, and that by following their advice, you'll earn more dividends, interest, and capital gains than you could hope to earn on your own. Of course, for the *really* good predictions, you'll have to pay a price and subscribe to their private newsletter or use them as your money manager.

Economists believe that analysts can often explain stock and bond price movements in the *past*. But they are extremely skeptical about anyone's ability to *predict* such price changes in advance. This is because economists tend to take the **efficient markets** view of markets in which assets are widely traded. According to this view, financial markets digest new information that might affect asset prices *efficiently*, that is, rapidly and thoroughly. To see what this view means, let's consider its implications for the stock market.

Efficient market A market that instantaneously incorporates all available information relevant to a stock's price.

The Meaning of an Efficient Stock Market

The efficient markets view implies that you cannot, on average, beat the market by doing research and finding and buying underpriced (or selling overpriced) stocks. You cannot do this because any research that *you* do will also be done by others and is therefore already incorporated into the stock's price. That means—if the goal is to outperform a broad stock market average like the Standard & Poor's 500—you are largely wasting your time.

For example, suppose that you spend a lot of time investigating the XYZ corporation, which is experimenting with a new, patented technology. If successful, it will generate enormous profits. Every day, you look at press clippings, search Web pages, and learn all about this new technology. You even do some complicated statistical work to estimate the potential profits the technology could earn for XYZ, Inc.

One day, XYZ, Inc., reports that a very preliminary experiment was promising. Only very savvy people like you could read the details and come to the proper conclusion: The chances that the new technology will work have just doubled. Instantly, you go to the Web and look up the stock's price . . . only to find that it has already jumped higher. Why? Because there were hundreds of others just like you—some of them professionals managing billions of dollars of other people's wealth—who did the same research you did. They all have recognized the likelihood of greater future profit, and have attached a greater present value to this corporation's stock. By the time you go to buy shares, the demand curve has already shifted rightward.

But wait. *Someone* had to get there first. Surely *that* person benefited from their research, right? Actually, no. Assuming that the news was a surprise, only those lucky enough to be *already* holding the stock at the time of the announcement will benefit. They will immediately adjust their asking price upward, so no one will be able to buy at the lower, preannouncement price.

The same is true of strategies to profit from *patterns* in stock trading, often called *technical analysis*. In the efficient markets view, this is a waste of time as well. Imagine a very simple pattern: Because of exuberance or fatigue or superstition, people like to buy stocks on Fridays, so on average, stock prices rise every Friday. Since everyone would anticipate this pattern, they would buy stocks on Thursday, hoping to profit from the Friday run-up. But this would cause stocks to rise on Thursday, not Friday, so people would buy on Wednesday, and so on. Soon, there would be no patterns at all; every day would be like any other day. Even though this is a very simple example, the logic applies to *any* pattern an analyst might uncover.

> *According to efficient markets theory, any information that helps one predict the future price of a specific stock or the market in general is instantly incorporated into stock prices. The only ones who benefit are those who are lucky enough to be holding the stock before the information became available.*[3]

The theory of efficient markets is one of the most exhaustively tested theories in all of economics. Thousands of studies have confirmed the efficiency of stock prices with respect to all sorts of information.

---

[3] One exception to this rule is *insiders*—those with connections to the firm and access to information *before* it becomes public. They can buy or sell stock early, before information is reflected in the price of the stock. Profiting from insider information is illegal. Those who do so, if they are caught, pay stiff fines and sometimes even go to jail. However, enforcement of insider trading laws is difficult, since it is often hard to detect.

Common Objections to Efficient Markets Theory

When students first learn about efficient markets theory, some objections often come to mind. Here is how economists often respond to them.

Efficient markets theory can't be true. Otherwise, why would financial institutions spend so much money doing research on particular stocks or on the market in general? The cynical response to this objection is that many financial institutions earn their income from commissions when their clients buy and sell stocks. Frequent research reports on stocks—"what's hot and what's not"—help these institutions convince their clients to trade more frequently.

A less cynical response draws on what you've learned about perfectly competitive markets in Chapter 8. Because there are no artificial barriers to doing stock market research and trading for profit, efficient markets theory assumes individuals and firms will continue to enter the market until the profit is reduced to zero.

But remember: It is *economic* profit that is reduced to zero through entry. In long-run equilibrium, stock researchers would earn just enough *accounting* profit to compensate for the implicit costs of their activities, such as forgone income. If it takes some special talent or ability to do this kind of research, then annual accounting profit would just cover the salary that people with these special talents or abilities could earn elsewhere. Thus, there is room to justify a positive salary for the thousands of professionals who analyze the market.

However, these professionals manage enormous amounts of other people's wealth. If they beat the market by only a tiny—almost imperceptible—fraction, they have covered their salary. For example, suppose a professional managing a portfolio of $3 billion in wealth can beat the market averages by 0.01 percent per year. That tiny edge would generate $300,000 in extra revenue for his or her firm—enough to justify up to that much in salary.

Now consider someone managing his or her own portfolio of, say, $100,000. Once entry by professionals has reduced the return to doing research down to 0.01 percent, this individual investor—doing his or her own full-time research, or using the research of others—increases his or her earnings by only $10 per year.

Efficient markets theory can't be true. I just saw a money manager interviewed on CNBC, and he beat the market by more than 5 percentage points, three years in a row! Efficient markets theory does not rule out luck. With thousands of professionally managed stock funds, we would expect some of them to be unusually lucky even if they operated by sheer guesswork. And we would expect some small number to do so many years in a row. An unusually good performance by a few—in a process involving many—does not prove any actual skill.

To prove this to yourself, imagine that 10,000 investment managers each picked their stocks by throwing darts at the stock page, and timed their buying and selling by flipping a coin every day. If we ignore trading commissions, this group would, on average, perform about as well as the stock market as a whole. But through luck alone, *some* would be very successful in any given year—beating the market averages significantly (say, by 5 percentage points or more).

Let's say that the first year, by chance alone, 10 percent of these managers significantly beat the market. That's 1,000 managers. The second year, 10 percent of this group—or 100 managers—would outperform the market again. And the third year, 10 percent of that group—or 10 managers—would do it again. These 10 managers—especially if interviewed on CNBC—would appear to have some special skill or talent

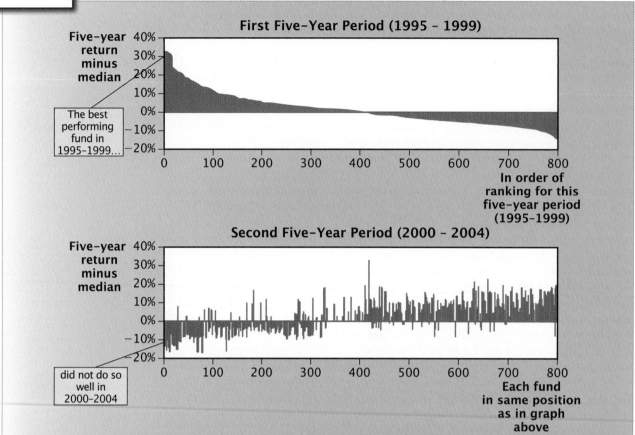

FIGURE 8 Lack of Persistence in Five-Year Performance of 800 Mutual Fund Managers

In the upper panel, the graph shows the percentage points by which the returns of each fund manager exceeded the returns of the median fund, during the five-year period 1995–1999. They are ordered from best performer to worst performer during those years. For example, the best performing fund earned a five-year return that was 32 percentage points greater than the median fund's return. In the lower panel, the funds are located in the same horizontal positions as in the upper panel. But now the graph shows by how much each fund beat the median during the subsequent five-year period (2000–2004). Comparing panels, the better performing funds in the first five-year period were not likely to be the better performing funds in the second five-year period.

Source: Index Funds Advisors, Inc., http://www.ifa.com/12steps/step5/step5page2.asp, accessed on June 17, 2009. Return is the number of percentage points by which each fund beat the median for each five-year period.

at picking stocks or timing buys and sells. But remember: In our thought experiment, they achieved their success by chance alone. The fourth year, each of them would be no more likely to beat the market than would any other randomly selected manager.[4]

This is not just academic theory—it is supported by the data. Figure 8 provides a startling example. It shows the performance of 800 professional stock funds during two

[4] A brief personal note: In December 2008, after one of us finished a lecture about efficient markets theory, a perplexed student came up after class. While he accepted the ideas in theory, he and his family had clearly found an exception: an investment manager who had greatly outperformed the market every year for more than a decade. The student asked if he could prove this by bringing a prospectus and some quarterly statements to office hours. Two days later, he e-mailed that he would not need to keep the appointment. The investment manager was Bernard Madoff, who had been arrested the night before for fraud—most notably, for creating fictitious investment returns. Madoff's clients lost an estimated $18 billion in total.

five-year periods. In the upper panel, the funds are ordered by their performance for the period 1995 to 1999, with the best performing on the left. The height of the graph shows the annual rate of return for a fund minus the annual return for the median fund. For example, from 1995 to 1999, the most successful (leftmost) fund earned about 32 percentage points more per year than did the median fund. The worst (rightmost) fund did about 12 percentage points worse per year than the median.

Now look at the lower panel, where each of the funds occupies the same position along the horizontal axis as it did in the upper panel. But the lower panel shows performance over the *next* five years, from 2000 to 2004. As you can see, there was no tendency for a top performing fund in the first period to be among the top in the next period. This is just what we'd expect if the performances in the first period were based on chance alone. (In fact, this data shows a tendency for top performers to drop to the bottom, and bottom performers to rise to the top. But that odd result may be due to chance as well.)

I've heard that economists no longer believe in efficient markets theory because of asset price bubbles. There has been some confusion about whether the efficient markets view still makes sense in light of economic research on asset price bubbles—episodes of exaggerated price spikes not connected to any fundamental change in underlying values. The confusion is partly based on different interpretations of the phrase "efficient markets."

The strongest interpretation—one that few economists hold to—is that markets always determine the "correct price" for an asset, one that accurately reflects the benefits and risks of owning it at the time. The mere fact that asset prices sometimes change rapidly—and that people gain and lose fortunes—does not by itself prove that the earlier prices were "incorrect." Prices are based on forecasts, and even a good forecast may not come true. If prices for particular stocks (or stocks in general) change rapidly, it could be because new information has changed the forecast.

Still, few economists today adhere to this "correct price" interpretation of efficient markets. Asset markets, including the stock market, *do* seem to experience occasional bubbles. There is a vigorous debate among economists about what causes them, and their implications for policy. Research in the field of *behavioral finance* suggests that various forms of herd behavior—some rational and some not—can cause bubbles to form, and exaggerate those that start for other reasons. In any case, it is widely agreed that, in the midst of a bubble, markets are not delivering the "correct" price.

But research continues to justify, and most economists still adhere, to the more *modest* interpretation of efficient markets theory we've been stressing: that markets for widely traded assets digest information rapidly, and that individual investors cannot systematically outperform the market averages.

That last statement might surprise you in light of our discussion of bubbles. After all, isn't it easy to spot asset bubbles? And don't they always burst? So can't you "beat the market" just by betting that prices will come down? The answers to these questions, in order, are: No, yes, and not necessarily. Let's explore this further.

Trying to Predict When Bubbles Will Burst

While an asset bubble may be obvious after the bubble has burst, it may *not* be so obvious while prices are rising. There is always the possibility that asset prices are soaring because of a change in long-term fundamentals rather than temporary herd behavior. For example, in the 1980s, many market analysts believed that the rapidly growing price differential between coastal and inland homes was a speculative "coastal home" bubble, which would soon burst. But the premium for coastal real estate remains as strong as ever. In retrospect, it appears to have been due to long-term market and institutional forces, rather than short-term herd behavior.

FIGURE 11   Housing Prices in Four Countries: The Full Graph

Seeing only the behavior of prices up to 2006 (see Figure 9), most observers would have guessed that because housing prices in the country with the purple line—Australia—had risen the most rapidly, Australian housing was the most likely bubble that would soon burst. In fact, Australia's home prices continued rising for several more years. By contrast, the U.S. (blue line) had the smallest price rise over the period shown. Yet U.S. housing prices started falling earlier, and fell further, than in the other countries shown.

Source: www.whocrashedtheeconomy.com

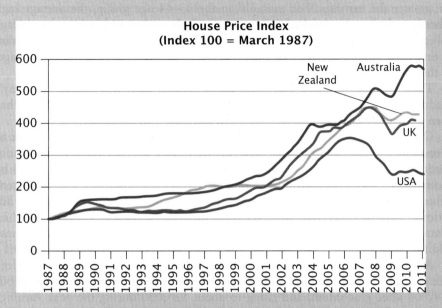

House Price Index
(Index 100 = March 1987)

© CENGAGE LEARNING 2013

public instead of private school tuition—finds the rate to a four-year degree to be even greater.[5]

Of course, these results make several simplifying assumptions. The experience of every graduate is different, and technological change may increase the risks for college graduates in certain careers (as discussed in Chapter 12). Still, if the past is any guide to the future, a college degree will remain an exceptionally good investment for most graduates.

[5] See, for example, Michael Greenstone and Adam Looney, "Where is the Best Place to Invest $102,000—In Stocks, Bonds, or a College Degree?" The Hamilton Project—Brookings Insitution, July 1, 2011. They find a rate of return of 15.2% for four-year degrees. For two-year associate's degrees, the rate of return is over 20%. (Although associate's degrees provide a smaller income gain, their cost is disproportionately lower than for a four-year degree.)

SUMMARY

A firm that rents its capital equipment can use the marginal approach to profit to decide how much to rent. The firm will increase its use of capital as long as the additional net revenue per period exceeds the rental cost of the capital. However, the decision to purchase, rather than rent, capital is more complex, requiring a comparison of future receipts with the current purchase price. Present value calculations help make these comparisons.

The *principle of asset valuation* tells us that—when there is complete certainty about future receipts—the value of any asset is the total *present value* of all the future income the asset will generate. With no risk, the firm should buy any unit of capital for which the total present value of all future years' net revenue is greater than the purchase price. This total present value will be smaller when interest rates are higher. Therefore, higher interest rates discourage investment in physical capital. When there is uncertainty, the value of physical capital will fall short of its present value by an amount that depends on the degree of risk and investor attitudes toward risk.

There are many types of financial assets, including bonds and corporate stock. Ignoring risk, the price of a *bond* will equal the total present value of its future payments. There is an inverse relationship between the price of a bond and its yield (rate of return). When there is risk of default, the price of a bond will be less than its present value, and its yield will be higher than under certainty.

The value of a share of corporate *stock*, in the absence of uncertainty, would equal the total present value of the future after-tax profits of the firm, divided by the number of shares outstanding. With uncertainty about future profit, the value of a share to any individual will be less than the presented value. The price of a share is determined by the intersection of a vertical supply curve and a downward-sloping demand curve.

Efficient markets theory suggests that the price of an asset, such as a share of stock, rapidly incorporates all available information that would enable someone to predict its future price. Therefore, research to help pick individual stocks or to detect trading patterns is not worth the typical investor's time or money. In an asset price bubble, stock prices can depart substantially from their underlying value, but this does not undermine the conclusions of efficient markets theory for individual investors.

PROBLEM SET

Answers to even-numbered Problems can be found on the text Web site through www.cengagebrain.com

1. You are considering buying a new laser printer to use in your part-time desktop publishing business. The printer will cost $380, and you are certain it will generate additional net revenue of $100 per year for each of the next five years. At the end of the fifth year, it will be worthless. Answer the following questions:
   a. What is the value of the printer if you could lend funds safely at an annual interest rate of 10 percent? Is the purchase of the printer justified?
   b. Would your answer to part (a) change if the interest rate were 8 percent? Is the purchase justified in that case? Explain.
   c. Would your answer to part (a) change if the printer cost $350? Is the purchase justified in that case?
   d. Would your answer to part (a) change if the printer could be sold for $500 at the end of the fifth year? Is the purchase justified in that case? Explain.

2. Your inventory manager has asked you to approve the purchase of a new inventory control software package. The software will cost $200,000 and will last for four years, after which it will become obsolete. If you do not approve this purchase, your company will have to hire two new inventory clerks, paying each $30,000 per year. Answer the following questions:
   a. Should you approve the purchase of the inventory control software if the relevant annual interest rate is 7 percent?
   b. Would your answer to part (a) change if the annual interest rate is 9 percent? Explain.
   c. Would your answer to part (a) change if the software cost $220,000? Explain.
   d. Would your answer to part (a) change if the software would not become obsolete until the last day of its sixth year?

3. Ice Age Ice is trying to decide how many $150,000 commercial ice makers to buy. Assume that each machine is expected to last for seven years. Complete the following table for an interest rate of 5 percent (and assuming no uncertainty). How many ice makers should Ice Age Ice purchase? How low would the price per machine have to fall before the firm would buy four ice makers?

Ice Machines	Additional Annual Revenue	Total Present Value of Additional Revenue over Seven Years
1	$26,000	
2	$25,000	
3	$16,000	
4	$12,000	
5	$ 6,000	

4. Your firm is considering purchasing some computers. Each computer costs $2,600, and each will add to your net revenue by known amounts. Because you plan to use the computers for different purposes, you have ranked those purposes in descending order of annual additional revenue as follows:

Computer	Net Additional Revenue per Year
1	$3,000
2	$2,000
3	$1,000
4	$ 500

   a. Assume that each computer has a useful life of three years, and no value thereafter. If the annual interest rate is 10 percent per year, how many computers should you purchase?
   b. If, before you purchased the computers, the interest rate dropped to 5 percent per year, how many computers would you purchase?

5. A drug manufacturer is considering how many of four new drugs to develop. Suppose it takes one year and $10 million to develop a new drug, with the entire cost being paid up front (immediately). The yearly profits from the new drugs will begin in the *second* year (with profits, as always, assumed to come at the end of the year) and are given in the table below:

Drug	Annual Profit
A	$7 million
B	$5.5 million
C	$5 million
D	$4 million

These profits, which are certain, accrue *only* while the drug is protected by a patent; once the patent runs out, profit is zero.

a. If the annual interest rate is 10 percent and patents are granted for just two years, which drugs should be developed?

b. If the annual interest rate is 10 percent and patents are granted for three years, which drugs should be developed?

c. Answer (a) and (b) again, this time assuming the discount rate is 5 percent.

d. Based on your answers above, what is the relationship between new drug development and (1) the discount rate; (2) the duration of patent protection?

e. Would the relationships in (d) still hold in the more realistic case where profits from new drugs are uncertain?

f. Is there any downside to a change in patent duration designed to speed the development of new drugs? Explain briefly.

6. Good news! Gold has just been discovered in your backyard. Mining engineers tell you that you can extract five ounces of gold per year forever. Gold is currently selling for $1,000 per ounce, and that price is not expected to change. If the discount rate is 5 percent per year, estimate the total value of your gold mine.

7. One year ago, you bought a two-year bond for $900. The bond has a face value of $1,000 and has one year left until maturity. It promises one additional interest payment of $50 at the maturity date. If the interest rate is 5 percent per year, what capital gain (or loss) would you get if you sell the bond today?

8. Suppose a risk-free bond has a face value of $100,000 with a maturity date three years from now. The bond also gives coupon payments of $5,000 at the end of each of the next three years. What will this bond sell for if the annual interest rate for risk-free lending in the economy is

a. 5 percent?

b. 10 percent?

9. Suppose a risk-free bond has a face value of $250,000 with a maturity date four years from now. The bond also gives coupon payments of $8,000 at the end of each of the next four years.

a. What will this bond sell for if the risk-free lending rate in the economy is 4 percent?

b. What will this bond sell for if the risk-free lending rate is 5 percent?

c. What is the relationship between the bond's price and the level of interest rates in the economy in this exercise?

10. Suppose that people are sure that a firm will earn annual profit of $10 per share forever. If the interest rate is 10 percent, how much will people pay for a share of this firm's stock? Suppose that people become uncertain about future profit. What would happen to the price they would be willing to pay? (Your answer will be descriptive only.)

11. In the market for Amazon.com stock, explain how each of the following events, *ceteris paribus*, would affect the demand curve for the stock and the stock's price.

a. The interest rate on U.S. government bonds, an asset considered safe from default, rises.

b. People *expect* the interest rate on U.S. government bonds to rise, but it hasn't yet risen.

c. Google announces that it will soon start competing with Amazon in the market for books, DVDs, and everything else that Amazon sells.

12. State whether each of the following, with no other change, would *increase* or *decrease* the economic attractiveness of going to college, and give a brief explanation for each.

a. A decrease in estimated working life.

b. An increase in the earnings of the average high school student.

c. Permanently higher interest rates in the economy.

13. In the Using the Theory section, we calculated the present value of the total cost of attending a private college, under the assumption that the costs remain the same for each of the four years. Recalculate the present value of these costs under the assumption that while implicit costs remain the same, tuition and other *explicit* costs rise by 8 percent per year, starting with the second year's tuition and expenses. (Continue to assume that all costs are paid at the end of each year.)

14. In the Using the Theory section, we calculated the present value of attending a private college, under the assumption that each year's costs are paid at the *end* of the year. Recalculate the present value of these costs under the assumption that all costs are paid at the *beginning* of each year.

15. In the Using the Theory section, we calculated the present value of the costs of attending a private college, with no financial aid.

    a. Using Table 1 in Chapter 1, what would have been the present value of the cost of college if we had done the analysis for a four-year public institution, with no financial aid? (Hint: Assume that future income does not depend on the type of college.)

    b. What is the percentage difference between the present value of costs at a private versus a public institution?

    c. Private college tuition is about four times higher than public college tuition. Explain briefly why the (present value) cost figures do not differ this widely.

More Challenging

16. In the chapter, you learned that when future income from an asset is uncertain, the asset's value will be less than the present value of its future payments. A different way to think about uncertainty is to calculate a *modified* present value, which uses a higher discount rate, equal to the *safe* lending interest rate *plus a risk premium*. In Problem 5, answer (a) through (d) again, assuming that (1) each interest rate provided in the problem is for riskless lending; and (2) the risk premium for developing new drugs is 20 percentage points.

17. Suppose that 1,000,000 people select which stocks to buy and hold for the year by throwing darts at the stock page. Suppose, too, that in any given year:
    • The average stock price rises by 7 percent.
    • In any given year, 50 percent of the dart throwers will have a return that is average or better.
    • In any given year and by luck alone, 20 percent of the dart throwers will "beat the average" by 5 percentage points or more.
    • In any given year and by luck alone, 10 percent of the dart throwers will beat the average by 10 percentage points or more.

    a. After five years, how many people will report that they've earned 7 percent (the market average) or more on their stocks in every one of the previous five years?

    b. After five years, how many people will report that they've earned 12 percent (5 percent above the average) or more on their stocks in every one of the previous five years?

    c. After five years, how many people will report that they've earned 17 percent or more on their stocks in every one of the previous five years?

© RUBBERBALL/NICOLE HILL/GETTY IMAGES

CHAPTER 14

Economic Efficiency and the Competitive Ideal

Throughout this book you've learned about the different types of markets in which products and resources are traded. Most of our discussion has been *descriptive:* For each type of market structure, we reached conclusions about price, quantity, firm profit, and how changes of various kinds affect the market equilibrium.

In this chapter, we will look at markets in a different way—*assessing* them in terms of their *economic efficiency.* As you'll soon see, there is more to the concept of efficiency than you might think.

We'll look first at the idea of economic efficiency itself: what it is and what it is not. Next, you'll learn how economists measure the gains from trading, and use this measure to gauge whether or not a market is efficient. You'll see why perfectly competitive markets are considered economically efficient, and why other market structures fall short of this ideal. We'll also explore how some government actions can *prevent* a market from achieving an efficient outcome.

Of course, the market—left on its own—is sometimes *not* efficient, and government action can be an appropriate remedy. We'll take up these situations, and government's role in fostering efficiency, in the next chapter.

THE MEANING OF ECONOMIC EFFICIENCY

What, exactly, do we mean by the word *efficiency?* We all use this word, or its opposite, in our everyday conversation: "I wish I could organize my time more efficiently," "He's such an inefficient worker," "Our office is organized very efficiently," and so on. In each of these cases, we use the word *inefficient* to mean "wasteful" and *efficient* to mean "the absence of waste."

In economics, too, efficiency means the absence of waste, although a very specific kind of waste: *the waste of an opportunity to make someone better off without harming anyone else.* More specifically,

> *economic efficiency is achieved when all activities that can make at least one person better off without making anybody else worse off are taking place.*

Notice that economic efficiency is a limited concept. Even though it is an important goal for a society, it is not the only goal. Most of us would list fairness as another important social goal. But an efficient economy is not necessarily a fair economy. For example, an economy could, in theory, be efficient even if 99 percent of its income went to a single person—a situation that almost everyone would regard as unfair.

Economists are concerned about both efficiency and fairness. But they generally spend more time and energy on efficiency. Why? Largely because it is so much easier for people to agree about efficiency. We all define fairness differently, depending on our different ethical and moral views. Issues of fairness must therefore be resolved politically.

But virtually all of us would agree that if we fail to take actions that would make some people in our society better off *without harming anyone*—that is, if we fail to achieve economic efficiency—we have wasted a valuable opportunity. Economics—by helping us understand the preconditions for economic efficiency and teaching us how we can bring about those preconditions—can make a major contribution to our material well-being.

Pareto Improvements

Imagine the following scenario: A boy and a girl are having lunch in elementary school. The boy frowns at a peanut butter and jelly sandwich, which, on this particular day, makes the girl's mouth water. She says, "Wanna trade?" The boy looks at her chicken sandwich, considers a moment, and says, "Okay."

This little scene, which is played out thousands of times every day in schools around the country, is an example of a trade that makes people better off without harming anyone. And as simple as it seems, such trading is at the core of the concept of economic efficiency. It is an example of a *Pareto* (pronounced puh-RAY-toe) *improvement,* named after the Italian economist, Vilfredo Pareto (1848–1923), who first systematically explored the issue of economic efficiency.

> A **Pareto improvement** *is any action that makes at least one person better off, and harms no one.*

Pareto improvement An action that makes at least one person better off, and harms no one.

In a market economy such as that in the United States, where trading is voluntary, literally hundreds of millions of Pareto improvements take place every day. Almost every purchase is an example of a Pareto improvement. If you pay $30 for a pair of jeans, then the jeans must be worth more to you than the $30 that you paid, or you wouldn't have bought them. Thus, you are better off after making the purchase. On the other side, the owner of the store must have valued your $30 more highly than he valued the jeans or he wouldn't have sold them to you. So he is better off, too. Your purchase of the jeans, like virtually every purchase made by every consumer every day, is an example of a Pareto improvement.

The notion of a Pareto improvement helps us arrive at a formal definition of economic efficiency:

> **Economic efficiency** *is a situation in which every possible Pareto improvement is being exploited.*

Economic efficiency A situation in which every possible Pareto improvement is being exploited.

This definition can be applied to any part of the economy, or to the economy as a whole. For example, if we want to know whether the U.S. market for airline travel is efficient, we would ask: Can we find any Pareto improvement that is *not* happening in this market? If the answer is yes, then the market is *in*efficient. If the answer is no, then all Pareto improvements *are* being exploited, so the market is efficient.

Similarly, we judge an economy to be efficient if it exploits all Pareto improvements that are possible.

Of course, no market or economy can exploit all Pareto improvements that might be possible. So the term is often applied loosely. An economy that encourages

Pareto improvements and largely exploits them is often labeled efficient. An economy in which Pareto improvements are difficult to achieve, with many important ones unexploited, is called inefficient.

Side Payments and Pareto Improvements

So far, the Pareto improvements we've considered are easily arranged transactions. Because both parties come out ahead, they have every incentive to find each other and trade.

But there are more complicated situations in which a Pareto improvement will come about only if one side makes a special kind of payment to the other, which we call a *side payment*. These are situations in which an action, without the side payment, would benefit one group and harm another.

Here's a simple example. The owner of an empty lot wants to build a movie theater on her property. Many people might gain from the theater: the owner of the lot, moviegoers, the theater's employees, and more. But the residents in the immediate vicinity might be harmed, because the theater will bring noise and traffic congestion.

Imagine that we can measure in dollars the gains and losses from building the theater for each person in the town. And when we sum them up, the total benefits to the gainers are valued at $100,000, while the total harm to the losers is valued at $70,000.

Building the theater—by itself—would *not* be a Pareto improvement, because even though some would benefit, others would be hurt. But suppose we can build the theater and also arrange for a *side payment*. Specifically, we collect $80,000 from those who benefit and pay it to those who are harmed. Those who benefit from the theater will still come out ahead: They initially gained $100,000 worth of benefits, so after paying $80,000, they are left with net benefits of $20,000. Those who initially opposed the theater come out ahead as well: They suffer harm worth $70,000, but the $80,000 payment gives them a net benefit of $10,000.

If you experiment around a bit, you'll see that *any* side payment between $70,000 and $100,000 would make building the theater a Pareto improvement.

More generally,

> *if any action creates greater total gains for some than total losses to others, then a side payment exists which, if transferred from the gainers to the losers, would make the action a Pareto improvement.*

Any side payment with a value between the total benefits to the gainers and the total losses to the losers will do the trick.

This has an important implication for economic efficiency. Suppose we find some transaction that could benefit some more than it harms others, and suppose *an appropriate side payment can be easily arranged*. Then *not* doing that transaction would be a waste of an opportunity to make people better off. Economic efficiency requires that we find, and exploit, opportunities that—with side payments—would be Pareto improvements.

But reread the italicized words in the paragraph above. The appropriate side payment—as you'll see in the next chapter—is *not* always easy to arrange. In many instances, arranging a side payment to ensure that everyone benefits has high costs. It may be that, after deducting these costs, too little would be left to adequately compensate the losers while still leaving the gainers better off.

When someone is harmed by an action and a side payment *cannot* be made—or for any reason is *not* made—then even though the action might create greater gain than harm, it might not be considered *fair*. Achieving the efficient outcome then becomes *one* consideration, but not the only one.

Productive Efficiency versus Economic Efficiency

In Chapter 2, you learned that an economy is considered *productively efficient* if it operates on its production possibility frontier (PPF). In such an economy, the only way we can produce more of any good is to produce less of some other good.

It is easy to prove that productive efficiency is a *necessary* condition for economic efficiency. Imagine that an economy is productively *in*efficient—operating inside its PPF. Then by moving to the frontier, the economy could produce more of one good without producing less of any other. Such a move could surely benefit some people—those who would receive the additional production—and need not harm anyone else. A productively inefficient economy—because it leaves an important Pareto improvement unexploited—is not economically efficient.

But productive efficiency does not guarantee economic efficiency. To see why, imagine a productively efficient economy—one operating on its PPF. But suppose the economy is producing very large quantities of goods that few people want (Garlic-flavored ice cream? Chocolate-covered shrimp?) and hardly any of the goods that most people *do* want. Then by changing the mix of goods produced and moving to a *different* productively efficient point on the PPF, we could make everyone better off. So economic efficiency also requires the quantity of each good produced matches our consumer preferences.

But that is not all. Suppose that we produce the right quantities of each good, but they end up going to the wrong households. (For example, suppose two-seater sports cars are provided to families with children, while single people get all the SUVs.) Exchanges among households would then be a Pareto improvement. But what if such trades are costly to make? Then we'd be wasting resources making trades that wouldn't have been necessary if the goods had been distributed properly in the first place. So economic efficiency requires that goods be allocated among consumers in a way that exploits all Pareto improvements, and doesn't waste resources by requiring unnecessary, after-the-fact trading.

> *Productive efficiency is a necessary but not sufficient condition for economic efficiency. To be economically efficient, an economy must produce a mix of goods and distribute them in a way that exploits all Pareto improvements.*

COMPETITIVE MARKETS AND ECONOMIC EFFICIENCY

In a market system, firms and consumers are largely free to produce and consume as they wish, without anyone orchestrating the process from above. In Chapter 2, you learned that market economies tend to be *productively* efficient. But can we expect such unsupervised trading to be *economically* efficient? That is, when markets are in equilibrium, will we be exploiting all possible Pareto improvements, so we are not wasting opportunities to make people better off?

In this section, you'll see that the answer is usually yes . . . *if* trading takes place in perfectly competitive markets. To explore this, we'll return to two familiar tools—the demand curve and the supply curve—but we'll be interpreting them in a new way.

Reinterpreting the Demand Curve

Figure 1 shows a market demand curve for guitar lessons. It also indicates the specific person who would be taking each lesson along the curve. For example, at a price of $25, only Flo—who values guitar lessons the most—takes a lesson, so weekly quantity demanded is one. If the price drops to $23, Joe will take one lesson, so quantity demanded is two. At $21, Flo will decide to take a second lesson each week, so quantity demanded rises to three. This is the standard way of thinking about a market demand curve: It tells us quantity demanded at each price.

But we can also view the curve in a different way: It tells us the maximum price someone would be willing to pay for each unit. Therefore, it tells us how much that unit is *worth* to the person who buys it. In Figure 1, for example, the maximum value of the first lesson to some consumer in the market is just a tiny bit greater than $25. How do we know this? Because Flo, who values this lesson more highly than anyone else, will not buy it at any price greater than $25. But if the price falls to $25, she will buy it. When she decides to buy it, she must be getting at least a tiny bit more in value than the $25 she is giving up. So the value of that first lesson must be just a tiny bit more than $25. Ignoring for the moment the phrase "tiny bit more," we can say that the first lesson in the market is worth $25 to some consumer (Flo), the second is worth $23 to some consumer (Joe), and the third is worth $21 (Flo again).

Of course, in Figure 1, we've simplified by assuming there are very few consumers in the market for guitar lessons. This makes the graph easier to read. But the point is the same whether there are five consumers in the market, or 500, or 50,000. In general,

the height of the market demand curve at any quantity shows us the value—to someone—of the last unit of the good consumed.

FIGURE 1 | **The Value of Another Guitar Lesson**

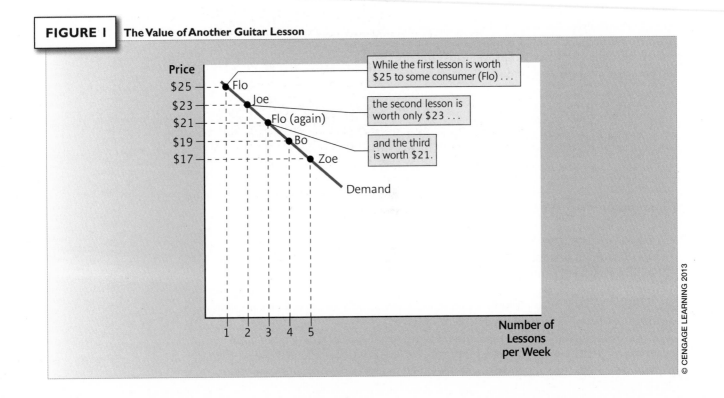

While the first lesson is worth $25 to some consumer (Flo) . . .

the second lesson is worth only $23 . . .

and the third is worth $21.

© CENGAGE LEARNING 2013

Reinterpreting the Supply Curve

Now let's look at the other side of the market: those who *supply* guitar lessons. Figure 2 shows us a supply curve for guitar lessons. The figure also indicates who would be supplying each lesson. For example, at a price of $13, Martin would offer one lesson each week. If the price rose to $15, Martin would offer two lessons per week, and at $17, another teacher—Gibson—would enter the market and offer a third. This is the standard way to view the supply curve: It tells us the quantity supplied at each price.

But we can also interpret the supply curve this way: It tells us the minimum price a seller must get in order to supply that lesson. For example, for the first lesson, the price would have to be at least $13. At any price less than that, no one will offer it. However, when the price reaches $13, one supplier (Martin) will decide to offer it. Similarly, $15 is the minimum price it would take to get some producer in this market (Martin again) to supply the second lesson, and $17 is what it would take for the third lesson to be supplied (Gibson this time).

Why does it take higher prices to get more lessons? Because offering lessons is *costly* to guitar teachers. Not only do they have to rent studio space, but they must also use their time, which comes at an opportunity cost. In order to get someone to supply a guitar lesson, the price must *at least* cover the additional costs of giving that lesson. We can expect this additional cost to rise as more lessons are given. (For example, the opportunity cost of a guitar teacher's time will rise as he gives more lessons and has less free time to do other things.)

The minimum price that would convince Martin, Gibson, or any other teacher to supply a lesson will be the amount that just barely compensates for

---

FIGURE 2   **The Cost of Another Guitar Lesson**

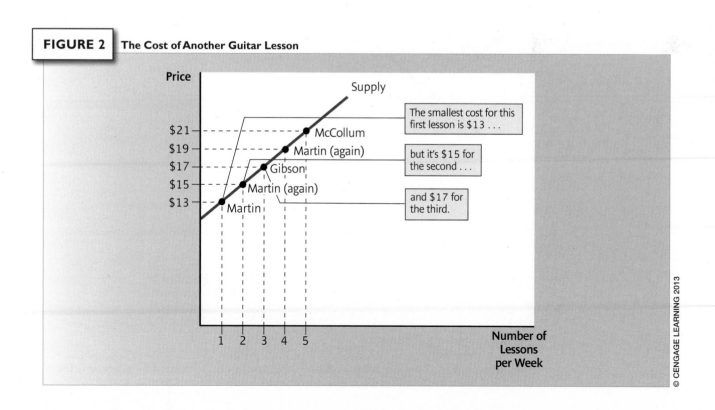

© CENGAGE LEARNING 2013

the additional cost of that lesson—and a tiny bit more. Ignoring the phrase "a tiny bit more," we can say that

the height of the market supply curve at any quantity shows us the additional cost—to some producer—of the last unit of the good supplied.[1]

The Efficient Quantity of a Good

Figure 3 combines the supply and demand curves for guitar lessons. Remember that the demand curve shows us the *value* of each lesson to some *consumer* and the supply curve shows us the additional *cost* of each lesson to some producer. We can then find the efficient quantity of weekly guitar lessons by using the following logical principle:

Whenever—at some quantity—the demand curve is higher than the supply curve, the value of one more unit to some consumer is greater than its additional cost to some producer.

This means that when the demand curve lies above the supply curve, we can always find a price for one more unit that makes both the consumer and the producer better off—a Pareto improvement.

Here's an example: Look at the *second* lesson in the figure. Tracing up vertically, we see that the demand curve (with a height of $23) lies above the supply

---

FIGURE 3 | **Efficiency in the Market for Guitar Lessons**

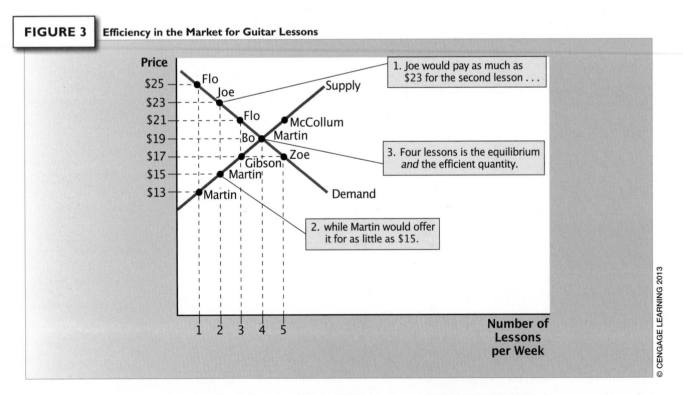

1. Joe would pay as much as $23 for the second lesson . . .

3. Four lessons is the equilibrium *and* the efficient quantity.

2. while Martin would offer it for as little as $15.

© CENGAGE LEARNING 2013

---

[1] If you've been reading the chapters in order, you'll recognize *additional cost* as *marginal cost*, first introduced in Chapter 7 and discussed in later chapters. That is, the height of the supply curve tells us the lowest marginal cost at which each unit could be supplied in the market.

curve (with a height of $15). That tells us that some consumer—Joe—values this lesson more than it would cost some teacher—Martin—to provide it. If Joe can *buy* the lesson at any price *less than $23,* he comes out ahead; if Martin can *sell* it for any price *greater than $15,* he comes out ahead. So, at any price *between $15 and $23,* both will come out ahead and no one is harmed: a Pareto improvement.

Continuing in this way, we find that the third lesson, and even the fourth, could be offered as Pareto improvements. (The fourth would be only a *slight* Pareto improvement, because its value is just a tiny bit greater than $19 and its cost a tiny bit less than $19.)

What about lessons for which the demand curve is *lower* than the supply curve—such as the fifth? Then there is *no* price at which both buyer and seller could come out ahead. To Zoe, the consumer who values the fifth weekly lesson the most, it's worth only $17. And for McCollum, the one who could provide it at the lowest additional cost, that cost would be $21. Producing this lesson could not be a Pareto improvement—no matter what the price—since the lowest cost of providing it is greater than its highest value to anyone in the market.

Let's recap: Whenever the demand curve lies *above* the supply curve, producing and selling another lesson (at a price between its value and its cost) is a Pareto improvement. Whenever the demand curve lies *below* the supply curve, producing another lesson can*not* be a Pareto improvement. This tells us that the efficient quantity of guitar lessons—the quantity at which all Pareto improvements are being exploited—is where the demand and supply curves intersect. At this quantity (4 lessons in the figure), the value of the last unit produced will be equal to (or possibly a tiny bit greater than) the cost of providing it.

If the market for guitar lessons is perfectly competitive, the equilibrium quantity will be the efficient quantity.

> *The efficient quantity of a good is the quantity at which the market demand curve and market supply curve intersect.*

How Perfect Competition Ensures the Efficient Quantity

As you learned in Chapter 3 (and again in Chapter 9), when markets behave as the model of perfect competition predicts, the price adjusts until the market quantity reaches its *equilibrium:* where the market demand curve and market supply curve intersect. In Figure 3, this occurs where four lessons are produced and consumed. But we've just seen that this quantity is also the *economically efficient* quantity—the one that exploits all possible Pareto improvements. This gives us a very important and powerful result:

> *A well-functioning, perfectly competitive market will automatically achieve the efficient quantity.*

Let's consider this statement carefully. It tells us that, if we leave producers and consumers alone to trade with each other as they wish, then in a perfectly competitive market, all units (and only those units) that are Pareto improving will be produced. The economy will not produce goods that no one wants (underwear made of steel wool?); will not overproduce the less-popular goods; and will not underproduce the goods that people want the most.

The Efficient Allocation of a Good

For the market to be economically efficient, we must not only produce the efficient quantity of a good, but also *distribute* it among consumers efficiently. This requires that units of the good be distributed to those who value them most. In Figure 3, the only efficient distribution of the four lessons would be for Flo to get two, and Joe and Bo to each get one.

To see why, suppose that the four guitar lessons were allocated by command, and Zoe (who values a lesson at $17) ended up getting one of the four lessons, while Joe (who values a lesson at $23) got none. Then we could easily imagine an exchange that would make both Joe and Zoe better off. For example, suppose Zoe gave up her lesson and allowed Joe to take it, and Joe paid Zoe $20. Joe would be better off (because he gets a lesson valued at $23 but pays only $20), and Zoe would be better off (she gives up a lesson worth only $17 but gets $20 instead). On the supply side, the guitar teacher—who would still be giving that same lesson—would be neither better nor worse off. Thus, changing the distribution of lessons as we've described would be a Pareto improvement, so the initial allocation was not economically efficient.

> A good is allocated efficiently when units are consumed by those who value them most.

How Perfect Competition Ensures the Efficient Allocation

A perfectly competitive market reaches equilibrium where the supply and demand curves intersect. At that point, the quantities supplied and demanded are equal, so anyone who chooses to buy the good will find it available. Those who value the good more than its market price will purchase it, and those who value it less than the price will not. So we can be sure that production of the good will end up going to those who value it the most, and no further trading among consumers can bring about additional gains. In our simple example in Figure 3, where the market equilibrium price of guitar lessons would be $19, only those who value lessons at $19 or more would get them (two for Flo, and one each for Joe and Martin).

> A well-functioning, perfectly competitive market will automatically achieve the efficient allocation of a good among consumers.

Evaluating the Efficiency of Perfect Competition

The notion that perfect competition—where many buyers and sellers each try to do the best for themselves—actually delivers efficient markets is one of the most important ideas in economics. In Chapter 2, you learned that the great economist Adam Smith coined the term *invisible hand* to describe the force that leads a market economy toward a desirable outcome. The Smith quote from that earlier chapter is worth repeating in this new context:

> [The individual] neither intends to promote the public interest, nor knows how much he is promoting it . . . he intends only his own gain, and he is in this, as in many other cases, led by an invisible hand to promote an end which was not part of his intention.[2]

[2] Adam Smith, *The Wealth of Nations* (Modern Library Classics edition, 2000), p. 423.

We can now recognize that the "end" promoted by the invisible hand is the economically efficient outcome. And now you've learned how the invisible hand achieves this end when markets are perfectly competitive.

The efficiency achieved by competitive markets is worthy of our admiration, even awe. But remember the caution earlier in this chapter: Efficiency is not our only economic goal; we also care about fairness. In discussions about efficiency, it is sometimes easy to forget this.

For example, several times in our discussion we've referred to the *value* of a good to some consumer. (We say that "Joe values a guitar lesson at $23," or that an efficient allocation distributes goods to those who "value them most.") In ordinary language, "value" has a psychological meaning, akin to how much you appreciate something or how happy it would make you. But in economics, *value* has a much narrower meaning: what a buyer is *willing and able to pay* for something. In Figure 3, the value of a guitar lesson to Joe is $23 and to Zoe is $17 because those are the amounts each is willing and able to pay.

Of course, what consumers are willing and able to pay depends on how much income or wealth they have at their disposal. Even if Zoe would *appreciate* the guitar lesson more than Joe, she may have more trouble affording it. When the market price is established at $19, Joe gets the lesson and Zoe doesn't. Similarly, you might appreciate a one-week vacation on your own private island more than, say, Bill Gates, the billionaire founder of Microsoft. But if the most you are willing and able to pay is $1,000, while Bill Gates is willing and able to pay $100,000, then in the purely economic sense that matters in the marketplace, Bill Gates values that vacation more than you.

For any *given* distribution of income and wealth among households, almost everyone would agree that Pareto improvements should be exploited, and that an efficient outcome is better than an inefficient outcome. But when we make this favorable judgment about efficiency, we put aside any concerns about whether income and wealth—or the *ability* to earn income and acquire wealth—are distributed fairly in the first place.

MEASURING MARKET GAINS

When markets are *not* perfectly competitive, or when they fail to function in other ways, they are *in*efficient. By comparing the actual benefits a market delivers with the benefits it *could* provide if it were operating efficiently, we can estimate what we lose from the inefficiency. In this section, you'll learn how economists measure the benefits traders receive in a market—and the potential benefits not realized.

Consumer Surplus

Let's start with the benefits enjoyed by consumers in a market. Consumers rarely have to pay what a unit of a good is actually worth to them. Regardless of how much they value the good, they can usually buy all they choose at the market price. For example, in panel (a) of Figure 4, the equilibrium price of guitar lessons is $19. So Flo is able to buy her first weekly lesson at $19, even though that lesson is *worth* $25 to her. By being able to purchase the lesson for less than its value to her, Flo gets a net benefit—called *consumer surplus*—on that lesson.

> A buyer's **consumer surplus** on a unit of a good is the difference between its value to the buyer and what the buyer actually pays for that unit.

Consumer surplus The difference between the value of a unit of a good to the buyer and what the buyer actually pays for it.

Pareto improvements are exploited. Therefore, efficiency means that we are exploiting all opportunities to increase total benefits. Or, to put it more succinctly:

> *A market is efficient when total benefits—the sum of consumer and producer surplus—are maximized in that market.*

Perfect Competition: The Total Benefits View

Total benefits The sum of consumer and producer surplus in a particular market.

Look again at Figure 6, which shows the perfectly competitive market for guitar lessons at the equilibrium price and quantity. When this market is in equilibrium, the **total benefits**—the sum of the blue- and red-shaded areas—are the maximum total benefits achievable in this market. How do we know this? Because any change in either the quantity or the price away from their equilibrium values will shrink the total benefits.

Let's first see what would happen if we arbitrarily moved the *quantity* of guitar lessons to some value other than 4,000. Suppose the market were forced to supply *more* than 4,000—say, 5,000. For lessons 4,001 to 5,000, the supply curve lies above the demand curve, so their cost to the seller would be greater than their value to the buyer. Providing these additional lessons cannot add to total benefits in the market. In fact, no matter what price is charged for them, each additional lesson would *reduce* total benefits. For example, if a lesson has a cost of $21 but a value of $17, then producing that lesson *reduces* total benefits by $4, regardless of the price charged. (Charging $21 or more puts the entire loss on the buyer; charging $17 or less puts the entire loss on the seller.) Therefore, as we increase quantity above 4,000, total benefits fall.

What about a quantity *less* than 4,000—say, 3,000? For lessons 3,001 to 4,000, the demand curve lies above the supply curve, so their value to the buyer would be greater than their cost to the seller. These potential gains are lost when quantity is reduced to 3,000. Therefore, as we decrease quantity below 4,000, we reduce total benefits.

Because increasing the quantity above or below 4,000 *reduces* total benefits, we know that at 4,000, total benefits are maximized. More generally,

> *in a well-functioning, perfectly competitive market, the equilibrium quantity maximizes total benefits. This is another illustration that the equilibrium under perfect competition is efficient.*

INEFFICIENCY AND DEADWEIGHT LOSS

Our example of the perfectly competitive market for guitar lessons can be regarded as a benchmark (and ideal) case. The market, left to itself, exploits every possible Pareto improvement involving buyers and sellers.

But markets don't always achieve this efficient outcome. In some cases, government intervention may be preventing efficiency. In other cases the nature of the market itself is responsible. In this section, we'll explore some examples of each of these cases of *in*efficiency.

A Price Ceiling

What happens in an otherwise efficient market if we impose a price ceiling below the equilibrium price?

If the quantity remained the same, the change in price would change the way benefits are allocated, but not their total. For example, consider a guitar lesson that is initially produced and sold for $19. If we force the price down to $17, and if that guitar lesson were *still* produced, the seller would enjoy $2 less in benefits, and the buyer would enjoy $2 more. By merely transferring benefits from one party to the other, we would not affect the total.

However, as you learned in Chapter 4, a price ceiling *does* change quantity. In a market economy we cannot force people to sell more than they want to. So a price ceiling that lowers the price will *reduce* the quantity sold.

Figure 7 shows the impact of a $15 price ceiling imposed on the market for guitar lessons. At that price, quantity supplied of 2,000 lessons per week is smaller than quantity demanded of 6,000. Since sellers are the short side of this market, and they can't be forced to offer more than 2,000 lessons, that will be the market quantity bought and sold.

The figure also shows how buyers' and sellers' market benefits are affected by the price ceiling, under two assumptions. First, we assume that no black market develops. Second, we assume that the smaller number of available lessons will be purchased by those who value them the most (and who would therefore get the greatest possible surplus from them). (In the problem set, you'll be asked to analyze price ceilings with different assumptions.) Producer surplus (shaded in red) is the area above the supply curve and below the new market price of $15, up to 2,000 units. Consumer surplus (in blue) is the area below the demand curve and above $15 also *up to 2,000 units.* Even though consumers would like to buy *more* than 2,000 units at a price of $15, we must stop at 2,000 when measuring their surplus: The lessons beyond 2,000 are no longer provided, so no consumer surplus is gained from them.

FIGURE 7   The Inefficiency of a Price Ceiling

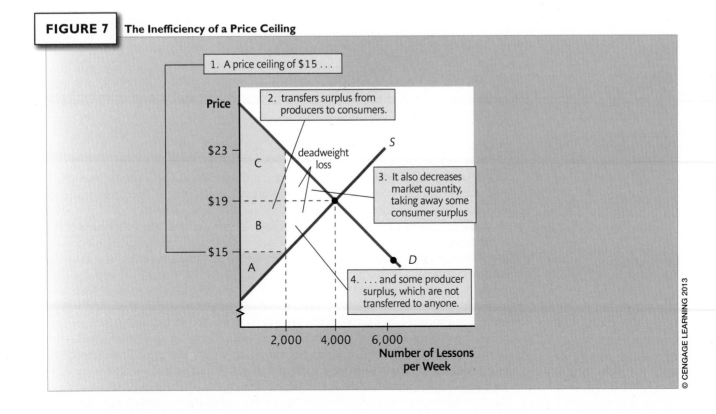

Comparing the market with the price ceiling (Figure 7) to the market *without* the price ceiling (Figure 6), it looks like the blue area measuring consumer surplus (marked B and C) has increased. (A price ceiling doesn't always increase consumer surplus, but it does in our example.) But the price ceiling *decreases* the red area (marked A) measuring producer surplus. (An effective price ceiling will *always* reduce producer surplus.)

What has happened to the *total* of producer and consumer surplus? If you compare total benefits in Figure 6 with total benefits in Figure 7, you'll see that the price ceiling causes total benefits to fall. Specifically, in Figure 7, total benefits have been reduced by the area of the unshaded triangle. This area represents benefits that *could* be achieved in the market but are *not* achieved, because the market quantity drops from its efficient level of 4,000 to the inefficient level of 2,000.

The unshaded triangle is an example of what economists call a *deadweight loss* (sometimes also called a *welfare loss* or *excess burden*).

Deadweight loss The dollar value of potential benefits not achieved due to inefficiency in a particular market.

> *The **deadweight loss** in a market is the loss of potential benefits (measured in dollars) due to a deviation from the efficient outcome.*

As you can see in the figure, a price ceiling causes a deadweight loss because it moves the market quantity away from its efficient level.

Calculating the Deadweight Loss

To make this more concrete, let's calculate the *dollar value* of the deadweight loss caused by the price ceiling—the area of the unshaded triangle. From basic geometry, we know that the area of any triangle is $\frac{1}{2} \times$ base $\times$ height. Imagine that our triangle has been tipped on its side, so that its *vertical* side is the *base*. This side goes from $15 to $23, so the base has a length of $23 − $15 = $8. The horizontal dashed line cutting through the middle of the triangle would be its *height*. This line goes from 2,000 to 4,000, so its length is 2,000. Applying the formula, we find that the loss = $\frac{1}{2} \times$ base $\times$ height = $\frac{1}{2} \times $8 \times 2,000 = $8,000.

In words, when this market is delivering only 2,000 lessons per week instead of the efficient 4,000, guitar teachers and students together lose $8,000 in potential benefits—per *week*. If measured yearly, the deadweight loss would be 52 weeks $\times$ $8,000 per week = $416,000 per year.

A Price Floor

What happens in an otherwise efficient market if we raise the price *above* its equilibrium value? That is, how does a price *floor* affect total benefits? The analysis is very similar to that for a price ceiling.

Figure 8 shows the impact of a price *floor* in our market, set at $21 per lesson. At that price, quantity demanded of 3,000 lessons per week is smaller than quantity supplied of 5,000. Now *buyers* are the short side of this market, so 3,000 will be the market quantity.

Let's assume that the 3,000 lessons supplied are provided by those sellers who would get the most surplus from them, i.e., those willing to supply them at the lowest prices. Producer surplus after the price floor is shaded in red and consumer surplus in blue. Notice that both surpluses are measured only up to 3,000 lessons—the quantity actually provided. Comparing the market with the price floor (Figure 8) to the market *without* the price floor (Figure 6), we find that the red area measuring producer surplus (marked F and G) has increased. (A price floor won't always increase producer surplus, but it does in our example.) But the price floor *decreases*

FIGURE 8   **The Inefficiency of a Price Floor**

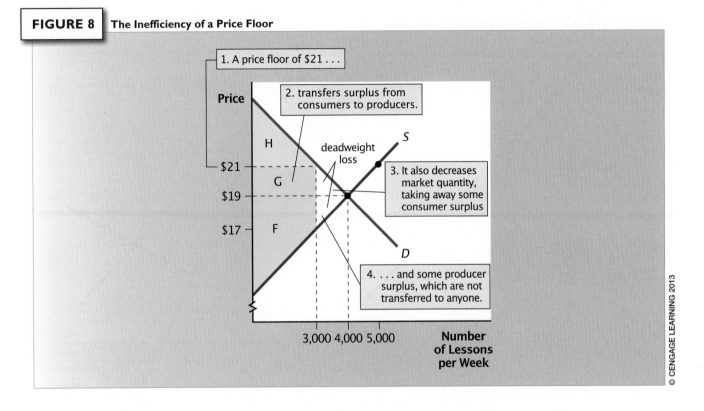

1. A price floor of $21 . . .

2. transfers surplus from consumers to producers.

3. It also decreases market quantity, taking away some consumer surplus

4. . . . and some producer surplus, which are not transferred to anyone.

Price

$21

$19

$17

H

G

F

deadweight loss

S

D

3,000 4,000 5,000

Number of Lessons per Week

© CENGAGE LEARNING 2013

the blue area (marked H) measuring consumer surplus. (An effective price floor will always reduce consumer surplus.)

What has happened to the *total* of producer and consumer surplus? If you compare total benefits in Figure 6 with total benefits in Figure 8, you'll see that the price floor causes total benefits to fall. In Figure 8, the *deadweight loss* from the floor is equal to the area of the unshaded triangle. (In the problem set, you'll be asked to calculate the dollar value of this deadweight loss.)

Market Power

A firm has *market power* when it can influence the price that it charges for its product. Monopolists, oligopolists, and monopolistic competitors all have some degree of market power because they *set* their price in order to maximize profit, rather than take the price as given.

In monopolistic competition, the presence of many competitors generally limits market power and helps keep prices low. But when a market has just one seller, or a few oligopolists who collude, the price can be significantly higher than in an otherwise similar competitive market. With a higher price, a lower quantity will be produced and sold—a quantity that is *less* than the efficient quantity.

To see how this works, look at Figure 9(a). The left panel shows a perfectly competitive market for wheat, in equilibrium at point *E*, with a market price of $3 per bushel and market output of 500,000 bushels per period.

Now imagine that a single company buys up all the farms in this market. We'll assume this new monopoly treats each of the old farms as an independent operation—with one exception: The monopoly owner will now set the price of wheat in the market so as to maximize its total profit.

FIGURE 9   The Deadweight Loss from Monopoly

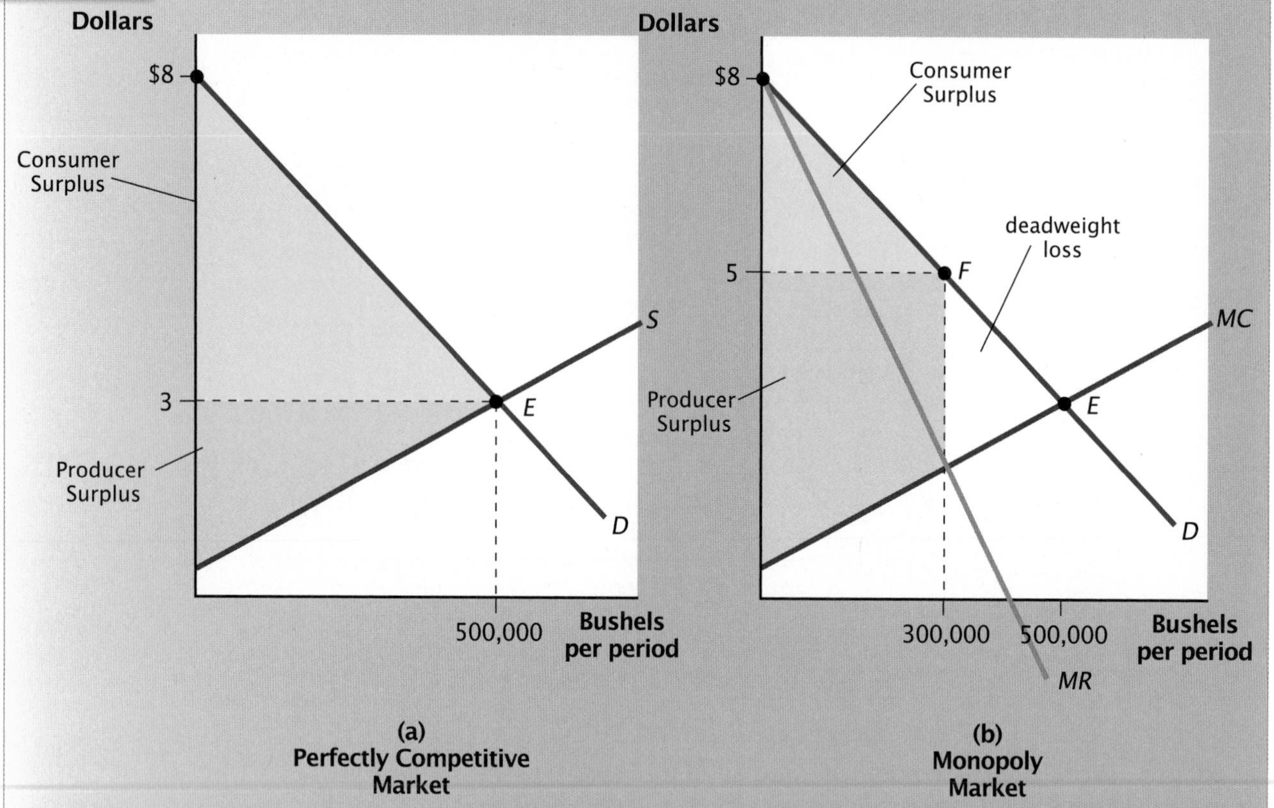

In panel (a), the market for wheat is perfectly competitive. Price is $3 per bushel, and output is 500,000 bushels per period. Total benefits are equal to the area of the two shaded triangles.

In panel (b), the market for wheat is monopolized. The competitive market supply curve becomes the monopoly's MC curve. The monopoly, at point F, supplies fewer bushels (300,000) at a higher price ($5). Potential benefits on bushels 300,001 to 500,000—for which the value to some buyer would be greater than the marginal cost—are not realized. The result is a deadweight loss equal to the area of the unshaded triangle.

© CENGAGE LEARNING 2013

Figure 9(b) shows the market from the perspective of the new monopoly. Each time the monopoly wants to sell an additional bushel of wheat, it will produce it on the individual farm that can do so at the lowest additional cost—that is, by the supplier who provided that bushel before, when the market was perfectly competitive. Thus, the monopoly's marginal cost curve in panel (b)—showing the additional cost of another bushel—is the same as the old market supply curve in panel (a).

The demand curves in the two panels are identical: *At any given price,* buyers in the market would choose to buy the same quantity of wheat before and after monopolization.

The monopoly maximizes profit by choosing the number of bushels at which marginal revenue and marginal cost are equal. However, the monopoly—unlike the competitive suppliers—must drop the price on *all* bushels in order to sell one more. That's why the monopoly's marginal revenue curve lies below the demand curve: Marginal revenue is less than the price of the last bushel.

In panel (b), you can see that the monopoly's profit-maximizing output level is 300,000 bushels, and it charges the highest price—$5—at which it can sell that quantity.

The Deadweight Loss from Monopoly

Now we'll calculate the deadweight loss—the extent to which total benefits fall short of their maximum—caused by the monopolization of this market. Our first step is to identify the new consumer surplus in panel (b). This is the blue-shaded area—below the demand curve and above the market price of $5.

Next, we identify the monopoly's producer surplus as the red-shaded area (above its new marginal cost curve and below the market price of $5). Why? Because producer surplus on each unit for the monopoly is the difference between the added cost of that unit (given by the *MC* curve) and what it actually gets for it ($5). When we sum up this surplus for all 300,000 units produced, the result is the red-shaded area.

What has happened to the *total* of producer and consumer surplus? Compare total benefits in the perfectly competitive market (the shaded areas in panel (a)) with total benefits under monopoly (the shaded areas of panel (b)). You'll see that the monopoly takeover has caused total benefits to fall. Specifically, total benefits have been reduced by the area of the *unshaded triangle*. This area is the *deadweight loss* from monopolization of the industry.

To understand the deadweight loss caused by monopolization, remember that 500,000 is the efficient quantity—the quantity supplied and demanded under perfect competition. But the monopoly provides only 300,000. Providing each bushel from number 300,001 to number 500,000 would be a Pareto improvement, but none of these is provided. Why not? Because *the monopoly charges a price that is greater than marginal cost.* Thus, buyers will choose *not* to buy some bushels even though their value exceeds the cost of providing them.

Note that if the monopoly could *price discriminate*—say, continuing to charge $5 on bushels 1 through 300,000, and then charge a lower price for additional bushels—it would produce more than 300,000 and move closer to the efficient quantity. (You may want to review price discrimination in Chapter 10 if you forgot why.) But as you've learned, not all firms can price discriminate. A *single-price* monopoly, like the one in panel (b), will be inefficient.

Our example generalizes to any firm facing a downward-sloping demand curve—that is, any firm with market power—that cannot price discriminate.

> *Monopoly and imperfectly competitive markets—in which firms charge a single price on all units that is greater than marginal cost—are generally inefficient. Price is too high, and output is too low, to maximize the total benefits in the market.*

In the next chapter, we'll explore some options for government policy in dealing with monopoly.

Taxes and Deadweight Losses

In Chapter 4, you learned that imposing a tax on a competitive market changes the equilibrium quantity. Based on what you've learned in *this* chapter, you won't be surprised that this change in quantity—in an otherwise efficient market—creates a deadweight loss.

Before we get to that result, let's briefly revisit how a tax affects a competitive market.

How a Tax Affects Price and Quantity: A Review

Figure 10 illustrates the impact of an excise on a competitive market for airline travel. The initial market equilibrium is at point *A*, with 22 million tickets sold per year at a price of $400 each. Then, the government imposes a $200 tax on the market, collected from sellers. We'll make that tax $200 per ticket.

As you learned in Chapter 4, it makes no difference to the market outcome whether this tax is imposed on buyers or sellers. In Figure 10, we've imposed the tax on sellers, causing the supply curve to shift upward by $200 to $S_{\text{After Tax}}$. The market equilibrium moves from point *A* to point *B*, with the new quantity equal to 12 million tickets per year. Buyers now pay $500 per ticket, and sellers receive $300 (after we deduct the $200 tax they must pay).

This part of the analysis should be familiar to you, based on what you learned about excise taxes in Chapter 4. But now, let's look at this tax from the point of view of economic efficiency.

How a Tax Affects Buyers, Sellers, and the Government

Before the tax was imposed in Figure 10, consumer surplus was equal to the area of the entire large triangle under the demand curve and above the price of $400. (Make sure you can identify this on the graph.) Producer surplus was equal to the area of the entire triangle above the supply curve and below the price of $400. Total benefits were equal to those two areas summed together.

But after the tax is imposed, both producer and consumer surplus shrink. Consumer surplus shrinks to the (blue shaded) area under the demand curve and above the price of $500 that consumers pay. Producer surplus shrinks to the (red shaded) area above the supply curve and below the price of $300 that sellers now receive.

FIGURE 10 | **Deadweight Loss from an Excise Tax**

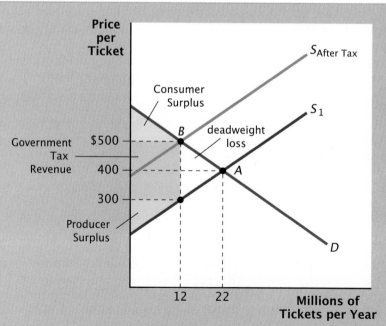

A $200 tax per airline ticket reduces consumer and producer surplus, while providing revenue to the government. But because the tax decreases the quantity bought and sold, total benefits decrease: The tax causes a deadweight loss.

© CENGAGE LEARNING 2013

The sum of these two shaded areas represents the total benefits to consumers and producers after the tax.

However, this sum is not *total* benefits, because there is one more benefit to consider: the government's revenue from the tax. After all, this revenue can be used to reduce other taxes (a benefit to other taxpayers) or to provide government services (a benefit to those who receive them).

In the figure, the government's revenue is equal to the area of the green-shaded rectangle. To see why, note that the tax per ticket is $200, the height of the green rectangle. It is collected on each of 12 million tickets per year, the base of the rectangle. When we multiply the tax per ticket times the number of tickets, we get $200 × 12 million = $2,400 million, which is the area of the green rectangle.

Measuring the Deadweight Loss from a Tax

If we now add together consumer surplus (blue), producer surplus (red), and the government's tax revenue (green), we get the total benefits after the tax is imposed on this market. Comparing this total to what benefits would be with *no* tax (all of the shaded areas together plus the unshaded triangle), we see that total benefits have been reduced by the area of the unshaded triangle—the deadweight loss from the tax.

As always, the deadweight loss occurs because quantity has changed. If the quantity had remained at the efficient level, the tax would have merely redistributed benefits from buyers and sellers to the government, with no change in the total. But the tax—by raising the price buyers pay and lowering the price sellers receive—results in fewer tickets being sold. The "missing tickets" (from 12,000,001 to 22,000,000) previously provided benefits to both buyers and sellers, but now they provide benefits to no one—not even the government.

The result we obtained for an excise tax applies to other types of taxes as well. In general,

> *a tax imposed on an otherwise efficient market creates a deadweight loss: The loss in benefits to buyers and sellers is greater than the gain in revenue to the government.*

For example, the payroll tax on wages creates a deadweight loss in *labor* markets. The loss in benefits to those who buy labor (firms) and sell it (households) is greater than the gain in revenue to the government, so total benefits decrease. (You'll be asked to analyze a labor market tax in the problem set.)

The personal income tax, which is a tax on wage income together with other sources of income, has a similar effect. And taxes on interest, dividends, and capital gains create deadweight losses in markets for capital.

How large are these deadweight losses from taxes? They can be substantial. Typical estimates of the deadweight loss from various taxes in the United States range from 20 to 60 cents on each dollar of revenue collected.[3] A deadweight loss of this size means that each dollar collected by the government reduces total consumer and producer surplus by between $1.20 and $1.60.

[3] Congressional Budget Office, *Budget Options*, February 2001, p. 381. More recently, Martin Feldstein analyzed the deadweight loss from an across-the-board 1 percent increase in everyone's marginal income tax rate (such as, those paying 10 percent in taxes on additional income would instead pay 10.1 percent, and so on). Feldstein found a deadweight loss of 76 cents for each dollar in government revenue collected. ("Effects of Taxes on Economic Behavior," *National Bureau of Economic Research Working Paper 13745*, January 2008.)

Does knowledge about deadweight losses help us? After all, doesn't the government need revenue? Doesn't it have to impose taxes? Indeed it does. But recognizing *why* a tax causes a deadweight loss can help us design more efficient tax policies.

Taxes, Deadweight Loss and Elasticity

A deadweight loss arises because the *quantity* of the good or resource being traded decreases below the efficient quantity. And, in turn, the quantity falls because the tax changes the *price* paid by buyers and received by sellers.

When demand or supply is very elastic (sensitive to price), even a small tax will result in a relatively large change in quantity, and deadweight losses will be relatively large. But the opposite applies as well: The more *inelastic* demand or supply, the smaller the deadweight loss.

Therefore,

> *all else equal, taxes create smaller deadweight losses when they are imposed on markets in which demand or supply is relatively inelastic.*

Figure 11 demonstrates this result. It shows the market for airline tickets, with the same supply curves as in Figure 10, and the same tax. But this time the demand curve is drawn to be less elastic over the price range we're considering. If you compare

---

FIGURE 11 **Deadweight Loss from a Tax When Demand Is More Inelastic**

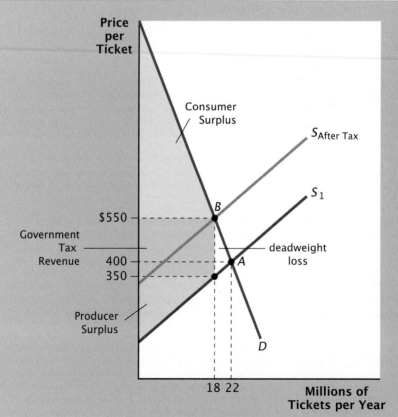

When demand and/or supply are more inelastic, a given tax causes a smaller change in quantity, so the deadweight loss from the tax will be smaller. In this figure, the same $200 tax is imposed on airline tickets as in Figure 10. But because the demand curve is more inelastic in this figure, the change in quantity and the deadweight loss are smaller.

© CENGAGE LEARNING 2013

the results in the two figures, you'll see that the same $200 tax causes a smaller drop in quantity in Figure 11, when demand is less elastic. With less elastic demand, consumers do not cut back their purchases as much when the tax is imposed. As a result, we know that (1) government revenue from the tax is greater in Figure 11, and (2) the deadweight loss (the loss of benefits on units no longer bought and sold) is smaller in Figure 11. Combining these two facts, we know that the deadweight loss *per dollar of government revenue* must be smaller in Figure 11 as well.

Our results suggest that to raise any given amount of revenue, deadweight losses will be smaller (and the economy more efficient) if we shift taxes toward those goods, services, and resources that are inelastically supplied or demanded. For example, the demand for food is more inelastic than the demand for airline travel. So, to be as efficient as possible, we would tax food more and air travel less.

However, once again, efficiency—while important—is not our only goal. In most modern market economies, there is agreement that a *fair* tax system should collect more revenue from those with the greatest *ability to pay*. Air travel is used disproportionately by households with high income or wealth. Taxing food more, and air travel less, would shift the tax burden away from the rich and toward the poor. This would not strike most people as a fair change in the tax code.

One more observation before we end our discussion. What if we had made supply (instead of demand) less inelastic when we drew Figure 11? If you experiment by drawing a new graph—this time making the *supply* curves steeper over the range of prices we're considering—you will see that when supply is less elastic, government revenue from the tax is greater, and the deadweight loss smaller. That is, inelastic supply has the same effects that we observed with inelastic demand.

In the extreme case, if supply or demand were *completely* inelastic, a tax would cause no change in quantity and no deadweight loss at all. We'll use this last insight to explore an interesting idea with a long history in the Using the Theory Section.

USING THE THEORY

A TAX ON LAND

In 1879, economist and social philosopher Henry George (1839–1897) wrote a very influential book called *Progress and Poverty*. In the book, he argued that people who work, and who save and invest their earnings, are entitled to their financial rewards; but pure gifts of nature—such as land—should be shared by everyone in society, rather than just the few who own them.

Henry George proposed that all other taxes should be abolished, and government should raise *all* of its revenue by taxing just one thing: land. The "single-tax" movement that was formed to advocate this idea was very popular for a time, and influenced many prominent intellectuals, including playwright George Bernard Shaw, and the creators of the board game Monopoly. Henry George ran for public office several times, including mayor of New York City, although he never won. His ideas, however, continue to have influence. And while George's single-tax proposal was based more on concerns for equity than efficiency, there is clearly an efficiency argument in favor of taxing land.

FIGURE 12 | A Tax on Land

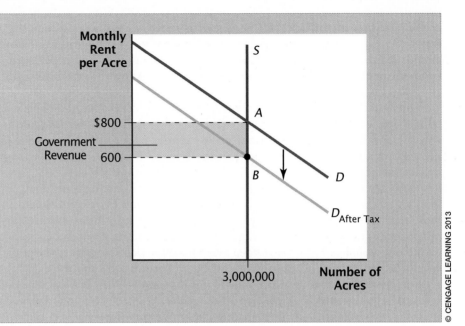

The market for land is initially in equilibrium at point A, with monthly rent equal to $800 per acre, and all 3 million acres rented. When a tax of $200 is imposed, the demand curve shifts downward to $D_{\text{After Tax}}$, and the new market equilibrium is at point B. Rent decreases from $800 to $600 (by the full amount of the tax), and the government's dollar revenue gain is equal to the dollar loss by landowners. Renters pay none of the tax. Since the equilibrium quantity of rented land remains unchanged, there is no deadweight loss.

Figure 12, which shows supply and demand curves in a local market for land, helps us understand why a land tax would have no deadweight loss. We assume for simplicity that all land in this market is rented. The demand curve tells us the quantity of land people would want to rent at each price (each monthly rent). The supply curve tells us the quantity of land that owners make available to renters.

Notice that the supply curve for land is vertical. The price may rise or fall, but the same quantity (3 million acres) will always be available. Why? In many cases, the total quantity of land available is fixed. If you are a landowner in one of these markets, it is always better to rent out your land, even at a very low price, rather than *not* rent it and earn nothing. So no matter how low the price, every acre of land owned by every landowner will still be available for rent. That is what we've assumed in the figure.

Initially, the market is in equilibrium at point *A*, with rent of $800 per acre per month. Then a tax of $200 per acre per month is imposed on land rentals. We'll first imagine that the tax is collected from the demand side of the market—those who rent land from landowners. The tax causes the demand curve to shift downward to $D_{\text{After Tax}}$. Why? To get renters to choose any given quantity, they must be charged $200 less than before, because now they also have to pay the tax.

The tax moves the market equilibrium from *A* to *B,* and rent drops by the full amount of the tax, from $800 to $600. This tells us that renters neither gain nor lose: Including the tax, they still pay $800 per acre and still rent 3 million acres. *Landowners*, however, receive only $600 per acre, so they lose $200 per acre. They end up paying the entire tax. The total loss for landowners is $200 × 3 million = $600 million per month, equal to the green-shaded area.

But notice that the landowners' loss is precisely equal to the government's gain in revenue, which is also $600 million (the same green-shaded area). The tax causes no deadweight loss at all; it has merely transferred dollars from landowners to the government.

What if the tax were imposed on *landowners* instead of renters? The result would be exactly the same. We can't shift the supply curve to illustrate that case, because a vertical curve can't be shifted upward or downward. But we *can* use logic to see what would happen. Suppose landowners *tried* to pass some or all of the tax on to renters by raising the rent they charge. As you can see in the figure, any rent greater than $800 creates an excess supply of land, so rent would fall back to $800. Because rent must remain at $800 per acre, but the $200 tax is collected from the owners, they are left getting $600 per acre. Once again, the entire burden of the tax falls on the owners.

A Land Tax Today?

Economists have long debated the idea of a land tax. Its efficiency is certainly attractive. And—in societies where landownership is primarily inherited by wealthy families—it is appealing on equity grounds as well. But in a modern market economy such as the United States, moving from current revenue sources toward a land tax would create some serious problems.

First, in order to avoid deadweight loss, the tax would have to be on the value of the *land only*—excluding the value of any improvements made to it. Such improvements include homes, factories, irrigation systems, private roads, and other infrastructure. If the value of such improvements is taxed, their quantity will fall in the long run, and we are back to the problem of deadweight losses on the improvements themselves. But once we limit ourselves to taxing the value of just land, minus the value of any improvements, the tax base shrinks significantly. It would be too small to substitute completely for other sources of revenue.

There are also equity considerations. In modern economies, land ownership is not inherited by feudal lords or limited to a certain social class. Rather, land is bought and sold easily and frequently, as an investment. A shift to a land tax would—by lowering rent—reduce the rate of return on land. This harm would occur *after* people had bought land at a price based on the current tax system. Those who had already bought land before the tax was imposed would be forced to either (1) suffer a lower-than-expected rate of return on their investment, or (2) suffer a capital loss if they try to sell their land. (Once rents fall, the price any new buyer would pay for land would drop as well.) Thus, current landowners—whether wealthy or not—would be harmed by this change in the rules.

In spite of these objections, the idea of shifting *some* of the tax burden toward gifts of nature like land, as well as toward other resources with a completely inelastic supply (such as radio spectrum or airline corridors), is alive and well.[4]

One final word about taxes and efficiency. If you've read this section carefully, you've seen that we've often used the phrase "otherwise efficient market" in discussing the deadweight loss from a tax. But in some cases, when a market is *not* otherwise efficient, imposing a tax can actually *make* it efficient. We'll explore these cases, as well as other situations in which government action can help to foster efficiency, in the next chapter.

---

[4] For a well-argued defense of such a shift, see Fred Foldvary, "Geo-Rent: A Plea to Public Economists," *Econ Journal Watch*, April 2005, pp. 106–132.

SUMMARY

A *Pareto improvement* is an action that makes at least one person better off and harms no one. A market or an economy is *economically efficient* when all Pareto improvements have been exploited. Economic efficiency requires more than just productive efficiency; it also requires that we exploit Pareto improvements in the mix of goods produced and their allocation among households. When well-functioning, perfectly competitive markets are left free to reach equilibrium, they are economically efficient.

Economic efficiency can also be viewed as the outcome that maximizes *total benefits* in a market. In a market without taxes, total benefits are the sum of *consumer surplus* (the dollar value to consumers minus what they actually pay) and *producer surplus* (the dollar value producers receive minus

the minimum payment necessary to get them to produce). In a competitive market, the equilibrium quantity, which is also the efficient quantity, maximizes total benefits.

When market quantity deviates from the efficient quantity, the result is a *deadweight loss:* the value of potential benefits not achieved due to inefficiency. A price *ceiling* or a price *floor* in an otherwise efficient market may or may not increase the surplus for one side of the market. But it changes the equilibrium quantity, and therefore decreases *total* benefits and creates a deadweight loss.

A deadweight loss also occurs when a competitive market is monopolized, or when a tax is imposed in an otherwise efficient market. The less elastic is demand or supply, the smaller is the deadweight loss from any given tax.

PROBLEM SET

Answers to even-numbered Problems can be found on the text Web site through www.cengagebrain.com

1. In Figure 3, suppose that, initially, McCollum is providing the fifth guitar lesson to Zoe for a price of $16. Who would gain and who would lose from this lesson and how much?

2. Figure 8 shows a price floor of $21 in the market for guitar lessons. Calculate the dollar value of the deadweight loss caused by the price floor, using the numbers on the graph.

3. The following table shows the quantities of bottled water demanded and supplied per week at different prices in a particular city:

Price	Quantity Demanded	Quantity Supplied
$1.10	8,000	0
$1.15	7,000	1,000
$1.20	6,000	2,000
$1.25	5,000	3,000
$1.30	4,000	4,000
$1.35	3,000	5,000
$1.40	2,000	6,000
$1.45	1,000	7,000
$1.50	0	8,000

a. Draw the supply and demand curves for this market, and identify the equilibrium price and quantity.
b. Identify on your graph areas for market consumer surplus and market producer surplus when the market is in equilibrium.
c. Using your graph, calculate the dollar value of market consumer surplus, market producer surplus, and the total net benefits in the market at equilibrium.

4. Suppose the government imposes a price *ceiling* of $1.20 in the market for bottled water in problem 3. Calculate the dollar value of each of the following:
a. Market consumer surplus
b. Market producer surplus
c. Total net benefits in the market
d. The deadweight loss from the price ceiling

5. Suppose the government imposes a price *floor* of $1.40 in the market for bottled water in problem 3. Calculate the dollar value of each of the following:
a. Market consumer surplus
b. Market producer surplus
c. Total benefits in the market
d. The deadweight loss from the price floor

6. Calculate the deadweight loss caused by the monopolization of the wheat industry in Figure 9. (Note: For marginal revenue at 300,000 bushels, use $2.)

7. Toward the end of the chapter, it was pointed out that a tax on labor income can cause a deadweight loss, just like an excise tax on a good.
a. Draw a diagram of a labor market in which the equilibrium wage is $20 per hour and total employment is 10,000 workers. On the graph, identify an area that represents total benefits to workers. (Hint: This area will be analogous to producer surplus in a goods market. Think about each point on the labor supply curve, and ask: What is the lowest wage at which this worker would supply labor, compared to the wage they are actually being paid?)

b. On the same graph, identify an area that represents total benefits to firms from hiring labor. [Hint: This area will be analogous to consumer surplus in a goods market. Think about each point on the labor demand curve, and ask: What is the highest wage the firm would pay to hire *this* particular worker, compared to the wage it is actually paying?]

c. Draw a second diagram showing the impact of a $10 per hour tax on labor income, collected from workers. On this diagram, identify areas that represent, after the tax, each of the following: (1) the total benefits to workers, (2) the total benefits to firms, (3) the government's tax revenue, and (4) the deadweight loss from the tax.

8. Suppose equilibrium price in a market is $5, and then a price ceiling of $3 is imposed. Assume (as in the chapter) that those who value the product the most are able to buy whatever quantity is available, and there is no black market.

a. If *supply* is completely price inelastic between $3 and $5, is there a deadweight loss? Briefly, why or why not?

b. If *demand* is completely price inelastic between $3 and $5, is there a deadweight loss? Briefly, why or why not?

9. Figure 10 shows the impact of a tax on airline tickets.

a. What is the annual deadweight loss of the tax in dollars? [Hint: Calculate the deadweight loss directly, viewing it as the area of a triangle turned on its side. Note that the area of a triangle is ½ × height × base.]

b. In the discussion of Figure 10 in the chapter, government revenue from the tax was calculated. Use this dollar figure, and your answer in (a) above, to calculate the deadweight loss *per dollar of government revenue*.

10. Figure 11 shows the deadweight loss from a tax on airline tickets when demand is less elastic than in Figure 10.

a. What is the annual deadweight loss from the tax in dollars? [See the hint in the previous problem.]

b. What is the annual government revenue from the tax in dollars?

c. Use your answers above to calculate the deadweight loss *per dollar of government revenue*.

More Challenging

11. In Figure 7, we assumed that the 2,000 lessons available would be purchased by those who value them most (i.e., those who would get the most surplus from them). But one problem with price ceilings is that available supplies are sometimes allocated haphazardly, so that some consumers who value the good less are able to buy it, while others who value it more are not. Redo the analysis of the price ceiling of $15 in Figure 7, this time under the (extreme) assumption that the 2,000 consumers who value lessons the *least* (but are willing to pay $15 or more) end up getting them. Specifically:

a. Identify the *new* area representing consumer surplus after the price ceiling.

b. Identify the *new* area representing the deadweight loss after the price ceiling.

c. Evaluate the following statement: "The unshaded triangles in the original Figure 7 show the *maximum* deadweight loss we would expect from a price ceiling in that market." True or false? Explain.

12. Figure 7 shows how a price ceiling affects consumer and producer surplus in the competitive market for guitar lessons. Suppose instead that Figure 7 (and all of the numbers in it) depicts the competitive market for tickets to rock concerts by local bands. Further, when the city imposes a $15 price ceiling, a black market develops in which ticket scalpers buy up all of the tickets available, and sell them all at the highest single price that the market will bear. Draw a graph and identify areas for each of the following after the price ceiling is imposed:

a. Consumer surplus

b. Producer surplus

c. Ticket scalpers' revenue.

d. Deadweight loss

13. Suppose the weekly quantity demanded (Q^D) for a good is given by the equation $Q^D = 10,000 - 80P$, and the weekly quantity supplied (Q^S) is given by $Q^S = 20P$, where P is the price per unit.

a. What is the equilibrium price and quantity?

b. When the market is in equilibrium, what are the values of consumer surplus, producer surplus, and total benefits? [Hint: Sketch a rough graph first.]

c. Find the value of the deadweight loss (dollars per week) if a price ceiling of $80 is imposed on this market.

d. Find the value of the deadweight loss (dollars per week) if a price floor of $110 is imposed on this market.

CHAPTER 15

Government's Role in Economic Efficiency

In nations around the world, virtually every disagreement about the economy ultimately leads to government. And some disagreements start there as well.

In the United States, for example, hardly a day goes by without a speech in Congress attacking or applauding the government's spending on defense, education, environmental programs, and more.

Underlying many of these speeches are sharp disagreements about the *role* that government should play in economic life. Should it help people send their children to private schools by giving them vouchers? Should it discourage the merger of two large airlines? Should local governments collect trash and run prisons, or should these services be contracted out to private firms? How far should the government go in regulating the activities of private businesses? Similar controversies exist in other developed market economies, such as the nations of the European Union or Japan.

But these disagreements tend to obscure a remarkable degree of *agreement* about the economy and the government's role in it. For example, in the United States and most other countries, the vast majority of goods and services you buy are provided by private firms. Almost everyone agrees that's how it should be. Hardly anyone proposes that the government should provide the economy's books, jeans, computers, entertainment, or soft drinks. At the same time, there is widespread agreement that certain goods and services should be provided by government alone, such as general police protection, the court system, and national defense. Much of this agreement is based on ideas about economic efficiency.

In the previous chapter, we looked at ways in which government intervention in an otherwise efficient market *reduced* total benefits and made those markets inefficient. In this chapter, by contrast, we'll be looking at how government can *increase* total benefits in a market, and create efficiency where it would not otherwise exist.

THE LEGAL AND REGULATORY INFRASTRUCTURE

The word *infrastructure* in this section's title suggests roads, bridges, airports, waterways, and the like. Indeed, this sort of *physical* infrastructure, often provided by government, is vital for a well-functioning market system.

But equally important is the government-provided *institutional* infrastructure: the legal and regulatory framework without which markets could function only primitively, if at all.

The Legal System

Laws are important for reasons that go far beyond economics. The law protects us from many kinds of physical and emotional harm, guarantees us freedom of speech and other vital civil liberties, and helps provide a sense of security and dignity in our lives.

But people often overlook the purely *economic* role of law—ways in which it supports markets and helps us achieve economic efficiency. Economically speaking, the law encourages people to channel their efforts into mutually beneficial, Pareto-improving exchanges by discouraging the chief alternative: trying to benefit *at the expense* of others. If there were no law, one way you could benefit is by breaking into your neighbor's house and stealing her television. You would gain, but your neighbor would lose. In fact, your neighbor's economic loss would be even greater than your economic gain, because your neighbor would lose her T.V. *and* have to take the time and trouble to replace it. *Criminal law*, however, reduces your expected gains from thievery by adding the possibility of arrest and penalties.

In addition to deterring harmful activity, the law also enables some types of Pareto improvements to take place that would be difficult or impossible without the law. For example, *contract law* enables parties to exchange promises involving future activities. It specifies what sorts of promises can be made, and establishes procedures for compensation if one party breaks the promise. Without well-enforced contract law, much productive activity would come to a halt, because people would be wary of fulfilling their side of a bargain first. You might not want to work for an employer or invest in a company, because you couldn't count on receiving your wages or a share of the company's profits in the future.

Table 1 summarizes several different types of law, along with a brief explanation of how each type helps to encourage economic efficiency.

Regulation

Regulation is fundamentally different from legal procedures. The legal system imposes fines or other penalties when a business violates the law. But regulation goes further. It directs businesses to take specific actions and prohibits other actions, often on a case-by-case basis. This can contribute to efficiency by protecting buyers, sellers, or third parties from some of the potential harm that market exchanges might otherwise cause.

For example, in the United States, the Food and Drug Administration (FDA) can prohibit a pharmaceutical company from selling a particular drug, or order that further research be done to prove its safety or effectiveness. The Environmental Protection Agency (EPA) has detailed control over what substances a business can release into the atmosphere or into the water. And the new Consumer Financial Protection Bureau, which began operations in 2011, requires financial companies to provide households with information about loans and investments in simple, specific formats. It can even prohibit certain financial products if they are deemed misleading or harmful to consumers.

Regulation is controversial. Tighter regulations can help protect the public from harm, but if they are too strict, they can stifle innovation. The FDA, for example, is criticized for delays in approving new drugs, and for moving too quickly when a drug it approved turns out to be harmful.

TABLE 1

Law and Economic Efficiency

Type of Law	Description	Efficiency Effect
Criminal Law	Prohibits actions that harm others, including theft, robbery, fraud, assault, and murder.	Shifts behavior away from harmful activities toward Pareto-improving activities.
Contract Law	Establishes rules for writing and enforcing contracts and penalties for failure to fulfill.	Enables Pareto improvements involving future promises, such as financial contracts or work performed by employees and independent contractors.
Property Law	Establishes rules for private ownership of land and other assets; ensures that rewards from assets accrue to the owners.	Enables owners to sell or rent property to those who can use it most profitably.
Tort Law	Allows those harmed by dangerous activities or products to sue for damages.	Facilitates Pareto improvements that require reasonable assumption of safety (e.g., "If I buy this car, I can expect the brakes will work properly, because the car company doesn't want to be sued.").
Anti-trust Law	Prevents business behavior that limits competition at the expense of consumers.	Limits market power, which generally means lower prices and production closer to economically efficient levels.

The Importance of Infrastructure

Americans take their institutional infrastructure almost completely for granted. The best way to appreciate the infrastructure of the United States is to visit a country that has a poor one. In many countries, the police are more likely to steal from citizens than to protect them from thievery. Many local economies, and a few national ones, are dominated by powerful mafias that extort protection money from businesses and threaten government officials when they try to enforce the law. The result is serious economic inefficiency that reduces living standards.

Figure 1 shows that when countries are divided into three groups, according to the quality of their institutional infrastructure, there is a strong relation between infrastructure and output per worker. The countries on the left—the ones with the lowest quality infrastructures—were able to produce only about $3,000 in output per worker per year in 1988. These are the nations where property rights were weak, contracts were not enforced, and the government was more often predator than protector of economic activity. In the middle of the figure are countries with medium-quality infrastructures, averaging about $5,500 in output per worker per year. On the right are the best-organized countries, averaging $17,000 in output per worker. Within this group, nations with the very best infrastructures—such as the United States, Sweden, and Japan—achieved output levels more than double that average.

More recent research has confirmed results like those in the figure. And a recent World Bank study[1] estimates that national legal and regulatory infrastructures

---

[1] *Where Is the Wealth of Nations? Measuring Capital for the 21st Century*, The World Bank (Washington, DC), 2006.

FIGURE 1   Government Infrastructure and Output per Worker

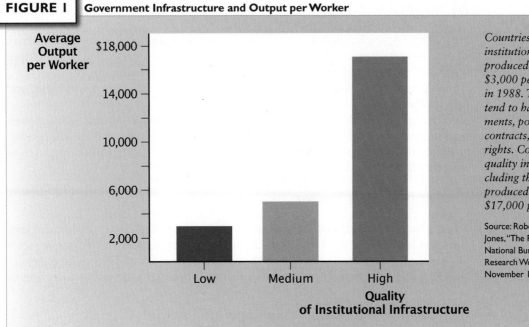

Average
Output
per Worker

$18,000
14,000
10,000
6,000
2,000

Low   Medium   High

**Quality
of Institutional Infrastructure**

Countries with low-quality institutional infrastructures produced an average of only $3,000 per worker per year in 1988. These countries tend to have corrupt governments, poor enforcement of contracts, and weak property rights. Countries with higher quality infrastructures, including the United States, produced an average of $17,000 per worker per year.

Source: Robert E. Hall and Charles I. Jones, "The Productivity of Nations," National Bureau of Economic Research Working Paper 5812, November 1997.

© CENGAGE LEARNING 2013

(measured using a "rule of law" index for each country) accounts for about 44% of the world's productive wealth—about the same percentage as the world's physical and human capital combined. The institutional infrastructure is an especially large percentage of total wealth in the most productive, highest-income countries.

Market Failures

So far, we've been discussing how the legal and regulatory infrastructure operates in the background, creating fertile ground for markets to operate and generate Pareto improvements. But this infrastructure also enables government to operate more aggressively in specific situations in which a market, left to itself, remains inefficient. These situations are called *market failures*.

> A **market failure** occurs when a market—even with the proper institutional support—is economically inefficient.

Market failure A market that operates inefficiently without government intervention.

In the remainder of this chapter, we'll focus on four general types of market failures to which economists have devoted a lot of attention. These are:

- monopoly markets
- externalities
- public goods
- information asymmetry

Although economists agree in theory on what causes each of these market failures, addressing them in the real world can create new problems. Dealing with market failures remains one of the most controversial aspects of microeconomic policy.

MONOPOLY

In Chapter 14, you learned that a monopoly market, or a market in which firms have significant market power, is inefficient. In such markets, price is too high, and output is too low, to maximize the total benefits achievable: a market failure.

Is there a proper role for government to make such markets more efficient, and thus cure a market failure?

That depends on the nature of the market and the reason for the monopoly power. In some cases, the government tries to *limit* market power by preventing the monopolization of markets. In others, the government accepts monopoly as unavoidable and tries to *cope* with it in various ways.

Limiting Market Power

When a market would function well under competitive conditions, government uses anti-trust law to limit market power. U.S. anti-trust law centers on two major pieces of legislation—the Sherman Act of 1890 and the Clayton Act of 1914—and their subsequent interpretation by the courts. Anti-trust law operates primarily in three areas.

Agreements among Competitors

U.S. antitrust law—expressed in Section 1 of the Sherman Act—prohibits "contracts, combinations or conspiracies" among competing firms that would harm consumers by raising prices. The most flagrant agreements by this law are those that directly fix prices. But the law also prohibits agreements that raise prices indirectly, such as when a group of firms agrees to divide up a market so each is served exclusively by one firm. For example, in the mid-1990s, the only two important sellers of review courses for the bar exam taken by prospective lawyers divided up their territory to avoid competition. The courts outlawed their agreement because it reduced competition.

Monopolization

Section 2 of the Sherman Act makes it illegal to monopolize or attempt to monopolize a market. As the law is now interpreted, it does not prohibit a firm from being or becoming a monopoly by, say, producing a better product. Rather, it prohibits *certain steps* to acquire or maintain monopoly status, such as spreading false information about a competitor's product or interfering with a competitor's operations in order to drive it from the market.

On rare occasions, the government has used the Sherman Act to break up a monopoly by splitting it up into smaller firms. Standard Oil was broken up in 1911 and AT&T in 1982. In 2000, Microsoft was ordered to split into two companies, but the decision was reversed on appeal and eventually settled out of court.

Mergers

In a merger, two firms combine to form one new firm. As you learned in Chapter 11, when a merger leads to a more concentrated oligopoly market, or even a monopoly, the result can be higher prices for consumers. Mergers of this type are often blocked by the U.S. government based on Section 7 of the Clayton Act. The Herfindahl-Hirschman Index (HHI) that you learned about in Chapter 11 plays a prominent role in the government's merger decisions. Many potential mergers are not even contemplated by firms because they know—based on the HHI—that the government will try to block it.

Coping with Market Power

In some cases, monopoly or significant market power is embraced by the government, because the market would not function well under conditions close to perfect competition. As you are about to see, coping with market power is fraught with problems, and requires the government to balance competing goals. Two important examples are monopolies due to patents or copyrights, and natural monopolies.

Patents and Copyrights

When a firm holds a patent on a scientific discovery, or a copyright on an artistic work, and there are no close substitutes, the firm operates as a monopoly. The government creates this monopoly in order to encourage new discoveries. As long as the copyright or patent lasts, the monopoly's price and its profit will be higher than under perfect competition. But during this time, the market provides a less-than-efficient quantity.

With patents and copyrights, the government tries to balance two conflicting interests: (1) providing incentives to make new discoveries, and (2) keeping prices low so that the efficient quantity will be provided. The shorter the duration of a patent or copyright, the sooner the efficient quantity will be produced, but the less incentive there will be for new discoveries and creations. For example, if we end the patent on a new drug after only a short time, the price would be lower and production more efficient *for that already-discovered drug*. But fewer new drugs would be developed in the future.

Another trade-off involves the types of discoveries that can get patent protection. Patents are increasingly granted for business practices, such as Amazon's "one-click" method of ordering online, or obvious and small technological improvements. Google's CEO estimates that the technology in a typical smartphone is subject to as many as 250,000 separate patent claims. Businesses have been formed for the sole purpose of buying up thousands of obscure patents and then suing firms that make products that infringe on them. Such lawsuits raise costs and disrupt production. While the proliferation of patents encourages new discoveries, it can also slow the development of new products *based* on those discoveries.

The Special Case of Natural Monopoly

In Chapter 10, you learned that a *natural monopoly* exists when, due to economies of scale, one firm can produce for the entire market at a lower cost per unit than could two or more firms. If the government steps aside, such a market will naturally evolve toward monopoly.

Figure 2 presents an example of a natural monopoly: a local cable company in a small city. The company has important *lumpy inputs*, including costly underground cable, a legal department to negotiate contracts with entertainment providers, and more. Spreading these costs over more subscribers creates economies of scale. In the figure, these economies of scale continue until the entire market is served: The *LRATC* curve slopes ever downward.

To serve an *additional* household, however, is *not* very costly to this cable company: just the installation appointment, some additional above-ground cable, and occasional customer service. Therefore, *marginal* cost is relatively low. In Figure 2, we assume for simplicity that marginal cost is a constant $30 per additional household per month, no matter how many households are served. Accordingly, the marginal cost curve is a horizontal line at $30.

| FIGURE 2 | Regulating a Natural Monopoly |

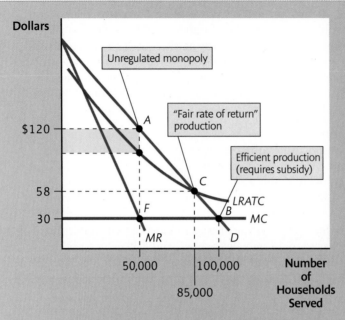

Left unregulated, the cable monopoly would serve 50,000 households, where MC = MR. *This is inefficient, because units 50,001 to 100,000 have value to some consumers greater than their marginal cost.*

By mandating a price of $30, government regulators could achieve the efficient outcome—100,000 households—at point B. But with price less than LRATC, the monopoly would suffer a loss, so it would have to be subsidized or go out of business.

The alternative, which is typically chosen, is to set price at $58—the lowest achievable average cost in this market, which includes a "fair rate of return." At this price, the monopoly serves 85,000 households—not quite efficient, but closer than without regulation.

If this market is left to itself, one cable firm would become the sole supplier. It would sign up the profit-maximizing number of households, where the *MR* and *MC* curves intersect: 50,000 households. The price, at point *A* on the demand curve, is $120 per month. Profit is the area of the shaded rectangle.

But point *A*—with an output of 50,000—is *inefficient*. The 50,001st through the 100,000th households still value cable service more than the additional cost of providing it to them, so total net benefits in the market would rise if they acquired service. But because the monopoly charges $120 for service, these households do not buy it. In fact, the efficient level of output is 100,000 households, at point *B*, where the *MC* curve crosses the demand curve. The monopoly—by failing to provide this quantity—is a market failure. What can the government do?

Using antitrust law to break this natural monopoly into several competing firms would not make sense. With several firms—each supplying to only a part of the market—each firm's cost per unit would be even higher than for the monopoly. Therefore, the price in a more competitive market could never be $30, so we would not get the efficient quantity of 100,000. In fact, competition, by raising cost per unit, might result in an even *higher* price and *lower* quantity than under monopoly.

But if breaking up a natural monopoly is not advisable, what *can* government do? One option is public *ownership* and *operation* of cable service, as is done with the post office, another natural monopoly. Public takeover of private business is rare, except when certain conditions are present (to be discussed later in this chapter).

That leaves one other option, and the one local governments actually choose for the cable industry: *regulation.*

Regulation of Natural Monopoly

At the beginning of this chapter, you learned that under regulation, a government agency digs deep into the operations of a business and takes some of the firm's decisions under its own control. In the case of a natural monopoly, regulators would tell the firm what price it can charge.

Marginal Cost Pricing

One option for regulators is **marginal cost pricing:** setting the price equal to the firm's marginal cost of production. In the figure, where marginal cost is constant at $30, the regulators would set price equal to $30. This will automatically bring the market to the efficient level of output: At a price of $30 for service, 100,000 households will sign up.

But there's a problem. If you look again at Figure 2, you'll notice that the *MC* curve lies everywhere *below* the *LRATC* curve. This must be the case for a natural monopoly, since economies of scale—the reason for the natural monopoly—means that average costs are decreasing, which can occur only when marginal cost is less than average cost. (See Chapter 7 on the marginal–average relationship if you've forgotten why. Here, both marginal cost and average cost refer to the long run.)

Now you can see the problem for regulators: If they set the efficient price of $30, then cost per unit (on the *LRATC* curve) will be greater than the price. The firm suffers a loss, and in the long run, it would go out of business. Therefore, with marginal cost pricing, the government must also *subsidize* the natural monopoly—to cover its losses with government funds. This is often controversial because it requires taxpayers in general, rather than just the monopoly's customers, to help pay for the product.

Marginal cost pricing Setting a monopoly's regulated price equal to its marginal cost of production at the efficient quantity.

Average Cost Pricing

Because of the problems with marginal cost pricing, regulators around the world more commonly choose an alternative, called **average cost pricing.** With this method, the price is set as low as possible—to serve as many customers as possible—while still covering the firm's cost per unit. Such a price is found where the *LRATC* curve crosses the demand curve ($58 in the figure).

Average cost pricing is sometimes called *fair rate of return* pricing. To see why, remember that average total cost incorporates *all* costs, including the opportunity cost of owners' funds. Thus, a fair rate of return to owners is already built into the *LRATC* curve. When the firm charges $58 per unit, it is covering *all* of its production costs—including a fair rate of return for owners. Moreover, $58 is the lowest price the natural monopoly could charge without suffering a loss. (Confirm for yourself that if it charged any less, it would operate at a point on the demand curve *below* the *LRATC* curve, creating a loss.)

More generally,

Average cost pricing Setting a monopoly's regulated price equal to long-run average cost where the *LRATC* curve crosses the market demand curve.

> with average cost pricing, regulators strive to set the price equal to cost per unit where the LRATC curve crosses the demand curve. The natural monopoly makes zero economic profit, which provides its owners with a fair rate of return and keeps the monopoly in business.

Average cost pricing does not quite make the market efficient. For example, in Figure 2, only 85,000 units are produced, instead of the efficient quantity of 100,000. But compared to no regulation at all, average cost pricing lowers the price to consumers and increases the quantity they buy, bringing us closer to the efficient level.

A bigger problem with average cost pricing is that it provides little or no incentive for the natural monopoly to control costs. The monopoly can grow larger and larger, buying more machinery, office buildings, and other forms of capital—confident that the regulators will always adjust the price upward to ensure a fair rate of return. This can lead to rising costs for customers, and a further movement away from the efficient output level.

EXTERNALITIES

If you live in a dormitory, you have no doubt had the unpleasant experience of trying to study while the stereo in the next room is blasting through your walls—and usually not your choice of music. This may not sound like an economic problem, but it is one. The problem is that your neighbor, in deciding to listen to loud music, is considering only the private costs (the sacrifice of his own time) and private benefits (the enjoyment of music) of his action. He is not considering the harm it causes to you. Indeed, the harm you suffer might be greater than the benefit he gets from blasting his music.

When a private action has side effects that affect other people in important ways, we have the problem of externalities:

Externality A by-product of consuming or producing a good that affects someone other than the buyer or seller.

> An **externality** is a by-product of consumption or production that affects someone other than the buyer or seller.

A *negative externality* is one that causes harm to others, while a *positive externality* creates benefits for others. As you'll see, both types of externalities can create economic inefficiency.

Suppose, for example, that because of a negative externality, some activity or transaction causes more harm than benefits. Then *total* benefits to society (including those harmed) are reduced. Because total benefits are not maximized, the situation is economically inefficient. However, under certain conditions, private parties can correct the inefficiency on their own, without the government's help.

The Private Solution

To see how the private market might solve a negative externality, let's consider a simple example. Every morning at 6 A.M., a noisy, heavy truck takes a shortcut off the main highway, drives along an isolated road past the single house there, and wakes up the resident. The truck driver benefits by using the road—it saves time. The resident is harmed by the loss of sleep. But the negative externality (the noise) harms the resident.

Suppose the harm to the resident is greater than the gain to the driver. Total benefits for "society" (the two people affected) would be greater if the truck driver avoided the short-cut. So, avoiding the shortcut is the efficient outcome.

In a case like this, if *either party* has clear legal rights over the activity, the outcome will be efficient: the truck driver will avoid the shortcut. To see why, let's first suppose that it's the *resident* who possesses the legal rights. (The shortcut is a private road, and the driver needs the resident's permission to use it.) Then the truck will avoid the shortcut, because the resident will certainly not grant permission.

But what if the shortcut is a public road, so the *truck driver* has the legal rights? Then the resident will find it worth his while to make a side payment to the driver to convince him to avoid the shortcut. The resident would be willing to pay any amount up to the harm he would suffer, which is more than the driver's benefit from using the shortcut. A mutually beneficial side-payment will be made, and the outcome will be efficient once again.

As you can see, regardless of who has the rights, the efficient outcome—the truck stays on the highway—will occur. No government intervention is required, other than the initial establishment of the legal rights.

What if the example were changed so that using the shortcut created more gains to the driver than harm to the resident? Then—as you'll see in an end-of-chapter question—the driver will take the shortcut, regardless of which party possesses the legal rights. Once again, the outcome will be the efficient one.

The Coase Theorem

Our example's conclusion—that the outcome will be efficient regardless of which party holds the rights—is an example of the *Coase theorem,* named after the Nobel-prize winning economist Ronald Coase:

> The **Coase theorem** states that—*when side payments can be negotiated and arranged without cost—the private market will solve the externality problem on its own, always arriving at the efficient outcome. The allocation of legal rights determines gains and losses among the parties, but does not affect the action taken.*

Coase theorem When a side payment can be arranged without cost, the market will solve an externality problem—and create the efficient outcome—on its own.

The Coase theorem points out that externalities do not always create market failures, and that private parties—with proper institutional backing—can sometimes work things out themselves. And although we've discussed only a negative externality here, the Coase theorem applies to positive externalities too, as you'll see in an end-of-chapter problem.

However, note that the Coase theorem requires that side payments can be arranged *without cost*—or, in practice, that the cost is so low relative to the gains or losses at stake that it doesn't matter. This requirement is most likely to be satisfied when: (1) legal rights are clearly established, and (2) the number of people involved is very small.

However, many real-world situations do not satisfy these conditions. Legal rights are often in dispute. If the rights are vaguely defined in our example, the truck driver and the resident might very well end up in court. Since courts are often more concerned about fairness or legal interpretation than efficiency, the outcome may not be the efficient one. (This is not necessarily bad; fairness, as we've stressed, is a concern as well as efficiency.)

But an even bigger problem in applying the Coase theorem is the second condition. In most real-world situations, a large number of people are involved. In our example, there could be *hundreds* of trucks traveling along the shortcut and hundreds of residents disturbed by the noise. Determining the gains and losses for each one, coming up with a mutually agreeable side payment, and getting everyone to contribute voluntarily would be very costly at best, and maybe impossible. As a result, we often turn to government to deal with externalities involving large numbers of people.

Government and Negative Externalities

To see how a negative externality can be economically inefficient, consider driving. When people drive their cars, they create local pollution, global greenhouse gas emissions, contribute to traffic congestion, and increase the probability of an accident. Because driving is so closely correlated with gasoline use, we can view these as negative externalities that arise in the market for gasoline. While estimates vary, research suggests that the costs imposed on third parties from driving in the United States can be reasonably valued at about $1 per gallon of gasoline consumed.[2] Additional accidents and road congestion are the two largest factors.

Figure 3 shows the market for gasoline in the United States, with hypothetical supply and demand curves. (Ignore the curve labeled *MSC* for now.) Before the government gets involved, the market reaches equilibrium at point *A*, where supply curve *S* and demand curve *D* intersect. But the equilibrium quantity, 400 million gallons per day, is *not* efficient. Why not? Recall (from Chapter 14) that the height of the supply curve at any output level tells us the cost to *producers* of providing gasoline. It does *not* reflect any of the costs to the general public from accidents, pollution, etc., because—without government involvement—producers do not *pay* these costs.

Let's suppose that each gallon of gasoline involves a negative externality of $1. If we add this to the marginal cost actually paid by gasoline producers, we get the

---

FIGURE 3   Inefficiency from a Negative Externality

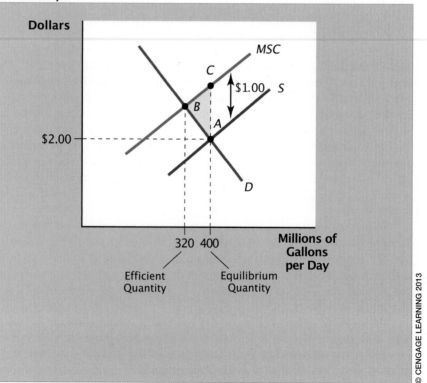

In the competitive market for gasoline, the market equilibrium is at point A with quantity at 400 million. But the supply curve includes only marginal costs to private suppliers, ignoring the negative externality of $1.00 per gallon. When the negative externality is added to other costs, the result is the marginal social cost curve (MSC). The efficient output level (320 million) is at point B. Without government intervention, the units from 320 million to 400 million are produced, even though their full cost (given by the MSC curve) is greater than their value (on the demand curve). The result is a deadweight loss equal to the area of the shaded triangle.

© CENGAGE LEARNING 2013

---

[2] See, for example, Ian W. H. Parry and Kenneth A. Small, "Does Britain or the United States Have the Right Gasoline Tax?" *American Economic Review*, Vol. 95, No. 4, September 2005.

marginal social cost (*MSC*) of another unit of gasoline. *MSC* includes *all* costs of producing another unit of gas: the resources used up and paid for by the industry, *and* the costs imposed on third parties. This is why the *MSC* curve in Figure 3 lies *above* the market supply curve.

Now let's find the efficient quantity of gasoline. Efficiency requires that the market provide only those units that are valued more highly by consumers than their cost. The *MSC* curve tells us the true, full cost of gasoline, when *all* costs are considered. For all units up to 320 million, the demand curve lies above the *MSC* curve, so those units are more highly valued than their costs. Total benefits in the market are increased by providing the first 320 million gallons.

But for all units *beyond* 320 million, the *MSC* curve lies above the demand curve. These units should *not* be produced, because they cost more—in the fullest sense—than their value to consumers. Each time a unit beyond 320 million is produced, total benefits—to producers, consumers, *and* society—shrink. Thus, the efficient quantity of gasoline—at which total benefits are maximized—is 320 million gallons per day. The area of the shaded triangle *ABC* is the *deadweight loss* for this market in equilibrium—the loss in benefits from producing too much output.

> *A market with a negative externality will produce more than the efficient quantity of the good, creating a deadweight loss.*

How can we deal with this inefficiency?

Regulation

Until recently, the most common method used in the United States for dealing with negative externalities—especially pollution—has been regulation. Federal, state, and local governments limit the amounts of certain pollutants released into the water and air by individual firms, and mandate pollution control devices on automobiles. If we wanted to take a purely regulatory approach to the gasoline market, we could limit the amount of gasoline each producer could produce, or that each consumer could use.

For example, if there are 100 million gasoline consumers, we could limit each one individually to 3.2 gallons of gas per day, achieving the efficient quantity of 320 million gallons. However, while this approach would give us the efficient total *quantity,* it would still leave significant inefficiency. That's because the total quantity would not be *allocated* efficiently among consumers.

Suppose Consumer A values gasoline very highly and would be willing to pay $10 for another gallon each day beyond the 3.2 gallons allowed. And suppose Consumer B values gasoline very little and would be willing to sell a gallon each day for $1. At any price between $1 and $10, a trade between consumers A and B would be a Pareto improvement. But the regulation—3.2 gallons per day for each consumer and no more—prevent this trade from occurring. We are leaving Pareto improvements unexploited.

A similar problem would occur if we used regulation to dictate gasoline *production* for each refining company. Suppose high-cost producers and low-cost producers are each told how much they are allowed to produce. Then they will not have to compete for business in the marketplace, so high-cost producers will end up producing gallons that could be produced more cheaply by low-cost producers. As a result, we would not be producing the given quantity of gasoline at the lowest possible cost.

Marginal social cost (MSC) The full cost of producing another unit of a good, including the marginal cost to the producer *and* any harm caused to third parties.

Ordinarily, in a competitive market, we don't need to worry about efficient allocation of goods among consumers and producers because the market does this automatically. In equilibrium, consumers can buy all the units that are worth more to them than the market price, and no consumers will buy any units that are worth less to them than the market price. Similarly, any firm that can produce units at a cost less than the market price will produce them, and any units that would cost more than the market price will not be produced. But with regulation, there is no such guarantee.

This inefficiency in allocating production and consumption among market participants is why economists often favor a different type of solution to negative externalities. With a *market-based approach,* we can achieve the efficient market quantity of a good (and therefore, the efficient market quantity of the externality), but with an important advantage: We can also ensure that we're exploiting all Pareto improvements in *allocating* that quantity among market participants.

Let's consider the two leading market-based approaches to negative externalities favored by economists.

Market-Based Approach #1: Taxes

One market-based approach is to impose a tax per unit equal to the negative externality created by each unit of the good. In the market for gasoline, for example, we've assumed that each gallon creates $1 of harm, so we could impose a tax on gasoline of $1 per gallon. As you learned in Chapter 4, it makes no difference whether we impose the tax on gasoline sellers or buyers—the effect on equilibrium quantity, and on the price for each side of the market, is the same in either case. But for negative externalities, imagining that the tax is imposed on sellers allows for a more straightforward discussion.

Figure 4 illustrates the impact of a $1 per gallon tax on gasoline sellers. As you've learned (Chapter 4), the tax shifts the supply curve upward by $1. If you

---

FIGURE 4   **A Tax on Producers to Correct a Negative Externality**

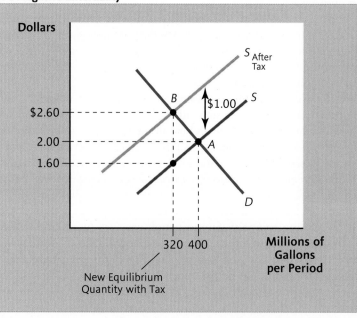

The negative externality is corrected with a tax on suppliers of $1—equal to the negative externality per unit. The supply curve shifts upward by the amount of the tax, moving the market equilibrium to the efficient point B. Only units valued at least as much as their full cost—the first 320 million units—are produced.

compare Figure 4 with Figure 3, you'll see that the tax shifts the supply curve until it is the same as the *MSC* curve. Once the tax is in place, the market reaches a new equilibrium at point *B*. The efficient quantity of gasoline (320 million gallons per day) is produced, resulting in the efficient amount of harm from the externality ($1 × 320 million = $320 million).

So far, the tax achieves just what regulation did. But notice one further result when we use the tax: Every gallon of gasoline valued by any consumer at more than $2.60 per gallon is purchased by that consumer. And no one ends up with gasoline that they value less than $2.60 (because no one would pay $2.60 in that case). So there are no further Pareto-improving trades among gasoline consumers. Moreover, every gallon of gasoline that can be produced and sold by any firm at less than $2.60 per gallon is being produced and sold. And no firm ends up selling any gallons that cost more than $2.60 to produce, because it would not be profitable to do so. So there is no reallocation of production among firms that could reduce costs for society.

> *A tax on each unit of a good equal to the external harm it causes can correct a negative externality, and bring the market to the efficient quantity of the good. Moreover, using a tax (rather than limits on individual firms and consumers) assures that the total market quantity of the good is allocated efficiently among consumers and producers.*

Notice that, in the new equilibrium after the tax, each consumer of gasoline is paying 60 cents more than initially, and each seller is receiving 40 cents less than initially for each unit. In this sense, both buyers and sellers share the burden of paying for the harm to society caused by each unit of gasoline sold. And society—represented by the government—receives the tax revenue, equal to $1 × 320 million = $320 million per day. This revenue can be used for environmental cleanup, reducing other taxes, or providing other government services valued by society. In effect, if used properly, the tax can serve as a kind of side payment from gasoline buyers and sellers to those (society in general) harmed by its use.

In our example so far, we've imposed a tax on a *good*—gasoline—whose use is associated with a negative externality. But a tax can also be imposed directly

DANGEROUS CURVES ⚠

Taxes, externalities, and deadweight losses In the previous chapter, our examples showed how taxes *create* a deadweight loss. In this chapter, you've seen an example in which taxes *eliminate* a deadweight loss. So which is it?

The answer is: A tax can do either, depending on the nature of the market in which the tax is imposed. In the previous chapter, we dealt with competitive markets that were *otherwise economically efficient.* Those markets were not characterized by any negative externalities. In such markets, a tax will *reduce* total benefits and create a deadweight loss. In this section, we're looking at competitive markets that are *not* otherwise efficient, because of a negative externality. In such markets, a tax of the right amount can *increase* total benefits and eliminate the deadweight loss.

© AXL/SHUTTERSTOCK.COM

on the harmful externality itself—say, on each unit of pollution emitted by each firm. A tax more narrowly focused on the harm itself creates additional incentives: to alter technology in order to reduce the harm from each unit. Gasoline producers, for example, would have an incentive to change the chemical composition of gasoline so it creates less pollution. Only those producers that can reduce pollution for less than the cost of paying the tax would have an incentive to do so. In this way, the tax ensures that any given amount of emissions reduction is achieved at the lowest possible cost.

> *A direct tax on the negative externality itself (like a tax on the associated good) can bring the market to the efficient quantity of the good. But taxing the externality has an added advantage: It encourages technological change that reduces the harm from each unit of the good produced or consumed.*

Many countries around the world have taxed a variety of negative externalities, including the pollution caused by discarded plastic bags and batteries, and atmospheric pollutants like nitrous oxide, and carbon dioxide emissions associated with global warming. However, another market-based approach has become increasingly popular, especially for atmospheric emissions associated with climate change.

Market-Based Approach # 2: Tradable Permits

Tradable permit A license that allows a company to release a unit of pollution into the environment over some period of time.

A **tradable permit** is a license that allows a company to release a unit of pollution into the environment over some period of time. Using tradable permits to limit emissions is often called *cap and trade*. By issuing a fixed number of permits, the government determines the total level of pollution that can be legally emitted each period (the "cap"). However, firms can sell their government-issued permits to other firms in an organized market.

Because the permits are tradable and sell for a price, a polluting firm faces an opportunity cost: For each unit of pollution that it creates, it must either buy a permit, or it must forgo the revenue it *could* earn by selling the permit to some other firm. Thus, the price of the permit becomes part of the marginal cost of producing the polluting good. With higher marginal cost, the market supply curve shifts upward, as in Figure 4, and the market equilibrium price of the polluting good rises as well. This can move the quantity of a polluting good toward its efficient level, similar to the effects of a tax.

And, also like a tax, tradable permits allow consumers and firms to respond to prices when determining how much of the negative externality to create individually. Overall efficiency is ensured by the limit on the total number of permits issued.

Let's take a closer look at how this works for producers.

A firm whose technology would make it very costly to reduce pollution generally *buys* permits in the market. By buying a permit at a price lower than its cost of reducing pollution by another unit, the high-cost firm comes out ahead. At the same time, a firm whose technology enables it to reduce pollution rather cheaply will *sell* permits. By giving up permits, the low-cost firm takes on the obligation to reduce its pollution further. But by selling the permit at a price greater than its pollution-control cost, the low-cost firm gains as well.

The trading of permits shifts the costs of any given level of environmental improvement toward those firms that can do so more cheaply. The general public, however, is not affected by the trade because total emissions remain unchanged. Therefore, for any given level of emissions, allowing firms to buy and sell licenses generates Pareto improvements.

> *A system of tradable permits for pollution, like a tax, can make the market quantity of polluting goods efficient. Moreover, unlike limits on individual consumers and producers, tradable permits assure that total production is allocated efficiently among producers.*

Tradable permits have been used since the early 1980s to reduce several types of pollution in the United States. Permits for adding lead to gasoline virtually eliminated leaded gasoline from the market within 5 years. A system of tradable permits begun in 1990 for sulfur dioxide (that causes acid rain) cut emissions in half within 5 years—well ahead of schedule and at much lower cost than anticipated.

Tradable Permits and Global Warming

In 1997, an international agreement known as the *Kyoto Protocol* was established, taking effect in 2005. The developed nations that were part of the protocol promised to use one of several methods—including tradable permits—to reduce their combined emissions to 5.2% below 1990 levels, by the year 2012. Today, almost all of the world's nations have agreed to the protocol.

In 2005, Europe introduced a tradable permit system for carbon dioxide emissions. Almost all of the countries in the European Union now participate in the system. The system had several problems in its initial phases (including the issuance of too many permits), but has since led to significant reductions in carbon emissions within those countries. Several other countries—including Australia and New Zealand—have begun phasing in tradable permits systems as part of their efforts to meet their protocol commitments. Worldwide, however, greenhouse gas emissions have continued to increase.

The United States has bounced back and forth on national efforts to limit carbon dioxide and other greenhouse gases. The United States signed the Kyoto Protocol in 1998 under President Clinton. But the Bush administration took the U.S. out of the treaty before it was ratified by Congress, based on skepticism about the science of climate change, the perceived high costs to the U.S. economy, and objection to the special exemptions granted to emerging economies such as China and India. In 2009, the Obama administration proposed a national cap and trade program for carbon emissions, similar in design to the European system. It passed the House but was never brought to a vote in the Senate. At present, the U.S. has only regional and state tradable permit systems to reduce greenhouse gases—some still in the planning stages. A nationwide cap and trade program remains an extremely contentious issue in U.S. politics.

Positive Externalities

Now we move away from negative externalities to examine positive ones. For a positive externality, the by-product of the good or service *benefits* other parties, rather than harms them. A home owner who plants flowers in the front yard creates enjoyment for everyone who walks by and helps to raise property values in the neighborhood. People who purchase hidden tracking devices for their cars that enable the police to arrest car thieves help to reduce the rate of auto theft. This benefits all car owners—not just those who bought the devices.

Why a Positive Externality Is a Market Failure

It may seem strange to think of activities that benefit other people as "failures," but remember that a market failure is an *inefficient* market—one that leaves Pareto improvements unexploited, and thus wastes the opportunity to make people better off. In the case of a positive externality, the market—left to itself—will produce *less* than the efficient quantity.

To see why, consider the market for a college education. In deciding whether to attend college, each of us takes into account only the costs to *us* (including tuition, and room and board) and the benefits to *us* (such as a higher-paying and more interesting job later on, or enjoyment of learning for its own sake). But when you become educated, you also create a number of benefits for other people. For example, you will be a more-informed voter and thereby help to steer the government in directions that benefit many people other than you. Or your education may make you more likely to make a scientific discovery or start a business that creates benefits for society in general. Thus, the market for college education involves a positive externality.

FIGURE 5 | **A Subsidy for Consumers to Correct a Positive Externality**

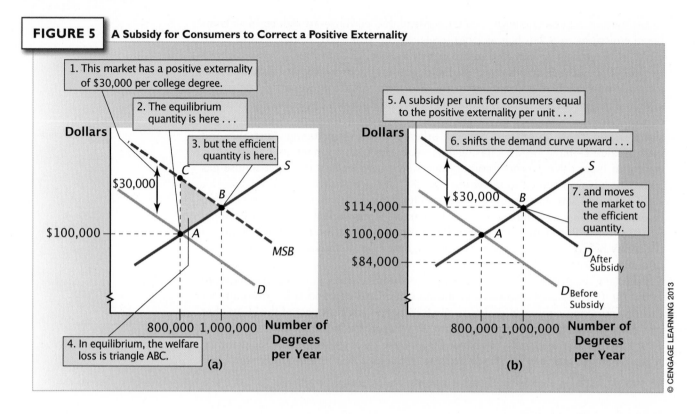

1. This market has a positive externality of $30,000 per college degree.

2. The equilibrium quantity is here . . .

3. but the efficient quantity is here.

4. In equilibrium, the welfare loss is triangle ABC.

(a)

5. A subsidy per unit for consumers equal to the positive externality per unit . . .

6. shifts the demand curve upward . . .

7. and moves the market to the efficient quantity.

(b)

© CENGAGE LEARNING 2013

Marginal social benefit (MSB) The full benefit provided by another unit of a good, including the benefit to the consumer *and* any benefits enjoyed by third parties.

Let's see why a competitive market in college education, with no government interference, would be inefficient. Figure 5(a) shows the market for bachelor's degrees. The horizontal axis measures the number of students acquiring bachelor's degrees each year, and the vertical axis measures the price the college charges for each degree.[3] The height of the supply curve S reflects the costs to a college or university to provide each degree and the height of the demand curve measures the value of each degree *to the student who gets it.* But the demand curve does not reflect any of the benefits that another college degree provides to the general public. Without government intervention, the market reaches equilibrium at point *A*, with 800,000 bachelor's degrees awarded each year, and a four-year price of $100,000.

But 800,000 is *not* the efficient number of degrees. We can see this by incorporating the positive externality into our diagram. Let's suppose that each degree gives the general public $30,000 in benefits. When we add this benefit to the benefit of the degree holders themselves, we get the **marginal social benefit** (*MSB*) of another degree. *MSB* includes *all* the benefits of acquiring another college degree—the benefits to the student *and* the benefits to society at large. This is why the *MSB* curve in Figure 5 lies above the market demand curve. The distance between the curves is $30,000, the value of the positive externality.

Once we draw the *MSB* curve in Figure 5(a), we discover that the efficient output level in this market is 1 million college degrees, where the *MSB* curve intersects the supply curve at point *B*. Why? Efficiency requires that the market provide any unit that has more value than it would cost to produce. The *MSB* curve tells us

[3] We could also measure price and quantity "per year of education" (as we did in Chapter 4) rather than "per degree" (as we do here). Either way, we come to the same conclusions.

what the value of each degree *really* is, when *all* benefits are considered. For all units up to 1 million, the *MSB* curve lies above the supply curve, so those units provide greater value than their costs. Total benefits in the market are increased by providing them. Because the market, left to itself, fails to produce any of the degrees between 800,000 and 1 million, we are wasting opportunities to increase total benefits in the market.

In fact, we can measure the benefits given up for any degree *not* provided as the distance between the *MSB* curve and the supply curve for that degree. For example, the 800,001st degree provides benefits of about $130,000 to both the student and society in general, but its cost is only $100,000, so we lose $30,000 in total benefits by not providing that degree. The total deadweight loss (welfare loss) from *all* the degrees not provided is the shaded triangle *ABC*.

> *A market with a positive externality associated with producing or consuming a good will produce less than the efficient quantity, creating a deadweight loss.*

How can we achieve the efficient quantity of 1 million college degrees each year?

Government Subsidies for Positive Externalities

When dealing with positive externalities, economists once again favor a market-based approach, which changes the price of the product but then allows individual consumers and producers to respond to those prices and make their own decisions. An effective market-based approach—and one used in the United States and many other countries for higher education—is a *subsidy*.

In Figure 5(b) we imagine that a subsidy of $30,000 per degree—the value of the positive externality—is paid to each student. (As you learned in Chapter 4, the impact on price and quantity for each side of the market is the same regardless of which side initially pays a tax or receives a subsidy.) The subsidy causes each student to add $30,000 to the value that he or she places on a degree, thereby shifting up the demand curve by that amount. The demand curve now rises to the level of the *MSB* curve, and the market equilibrium moves to 1 million degrees per year—the efficient number.

Notice how the subsidy causes buyers and sellers to take account of the positive externality in making their decisions. In the new equilibrium, the price of a degree rises—from $100,000 to $114,000 in the figure. This encourages colleges to increase enrollment. But students, after accounting for the subsidy, pay only $84,000 ($114,000 minus the $30,000 subsidy). This is why more of them choose to acquire degrees.

> *A subsidy on each unit of a good, equal to the external benefits it creates, can correct a positive externality and bring the market to an efficient output level.*

PUBLIC GOODS

So far, all of our examples of market failures have been goods that are left to the market to provide. The market failure arises because some government manipulation of the price is needed (via a tax, subsidy, or regulation) to induce firms to move the quantity closer to the efficient level.

But some types of goods, by their nature, are especially difficult for the market to provide, or to provide even close to efficiently. Such goods require a more *direct* form of involvement, in which the government itself provides the goods. These are called *public goods*. (A more formal definition follows a bit later.)

Private Goods

The best way to understand *public* goods is to consider their opposite: Private goods. These are goods that share two characteristics: rivalry and excludability.

Rivalry

Rivalry A situation in which one person's consumption of a unit of a good or service means that no one else can consume that unit.

A private good is characterized by **rivalry** in consumption—if one person consumes a unit someone else cannot consume that unit. If you rent an apartment, then someone else will *not* be able to rent that apartment. The same applies to most goods that you buy—food, computers, air travel, and so on. Rivalry also applies to privately provided services: the time you spend with your doctor, lawyer, or career counselor is time that someone else will *not* spend with that professional.

By allowing the market to provide rival goods at a *price,* we ensure that people take account of the opportunity costs to society of their decisions to use these goods. If they were provided free of charge, people would tend to use them even if their value were less than the value of the resources used to produce them. Moreover, offering a rival good free of charge would enable some people who don't value it very highly to grab up all available supplies, depriving others who might value the goods even more. Thus, leaving such goods to the market—where a price reflecting marginal cost is charged—tends to promote economic efficiency.

Excludability

Excludability The ability to exclude those who do not pay for a good from consuming it.

A second feature of a private good is **excludability**, the ability to exclude those who do not pay for a good from enjoying it. Excludability is what makes it *possible* for a private business to provide a good. After all, without excludability people would never pay, so any private firm that tried to provide the good would quickly go out of business.

Let's sum up the discussion so far: Excludability means that firms *can* provide a good. Rivalry means that a price *should* be charged for a good (something that private firms do automatically). If a good has both of these characteristics, it is called a *pure private good*.

Pure private good A good that is both rivalrous and excludable.

> A good *that is both rivalrous and excludable is a* **pure private good.** *In the absence of any significant market failure, private firms will provide these goods at close to efficient levels.*

But not all goods or services have these characteristics.

Pure Public Goods

Consider a small, urban park whose chief benefit is that people find it nice to look at when they walk by. To provide and maintain the park is costly. But its benefits are *nonexcludable*—there is no practical way to limit enjoyment just to those who pay.

In general, when goods are nonexcludable, private firms will not be able to provide them. Because everyone will be able to enjoy the benefits without paying, no one will pay. If asked to contribute to a voluntary fund to build or maintain the park, most people will reason, "I am one person among many—just a drop in the bucket. Whether I contribute or not will make no difference to the condition of the park, so I'll hope that others contribute and I can enjoy it without paying."

When most people think this way, the total contributions will be insufficient, and the nonexcludable good will not be provided at all. Economists call this the **free-rider problem**. It's as if everyone in a car pool thinks they can get a free ride to their destination, because others will pay for the gas. When everyone thinks this way, the tank remains empty.

Here, the free-rider problem prevents private firms from producing and selling a nonexcludable good. The only way to make the park excludable would be to construct a giant fence with a gate and charge admission. But then it's a different good—no longer a walk-by park, but rather a private club that you must go out of your way to enter and spend time in to get the benefit.

The walk-by park is also *nonrival*. One person's enjoyment while passing does not prevent or lessen the enjoyment of anyone else. Moreover, no more of society's resources are used up when another person views it. For this reason, even if a firm *could* figure out a way to charge for the park, charging would be inefficient. Each time an additional person sees the park, a Pareto improvement takes place: That person gains and no one loses. Thus, to be economically efficient, everyone who places *any value at all* on seeing the park should be able to see it. This can only happen if the price is *zero*.

Generalizing from this example: If a good is nonrival, a private firm will not provide the efficient quantity. The firm would have to charge a price, while efficiency requires a price of zero. And if the good is also nonexcludable, the private market is usually *unable* to provide it anyway. A good with both of these characteristics is called a *pure public good*.

> *A good that is both nonrival and nonexcludable is a* **pure public good**. *These goods are generally provided by government without charge, because the private market cannot supply them at all, or cannot supply them efficiently.*

TICKETS

LIFEGUARD
ON
DUTY

8 ST
VIEW
SUNSET
$10

© CENGAGE LEARNING

Free-rider problem When everyone tries to enjoy the benefits of a nonexcludable good without paying, so private firms cannot provide it.

Pure public good A good that is both nonrival and nonexcludable.

Figure 6 illustrates the classification of goods into pure private and pure public, and it provides some examples. (Ignore the other two categories for now.) Pure private goods are in the upper left corner. There is general agreement that private firms should provide such goods in the market and charge for them. While government may intervene in these markets, it does not generally provide the goods itself.

In the lower right corner are pure public goods. It is generally agreed that government should provide these goods without charge. A classic example is national defense. It would be virtually impossible to exclude those who did not pay from enjoying most of the benefits of national defense, as long as they remain in the country. And once a given quantity of national defense is provided, extending its benefits to an additional person requires no additional resources, nor does it lessen anyone else's defense.

Mixed Goods

Goods that appear in the other two corners of Figure 6 can be called *mixed goods* because they share features of both public and private goods. These goods are becoming increasingly important in our society.

FIGURE 6 | Pure Private, Pure Public, and Mixed Goods

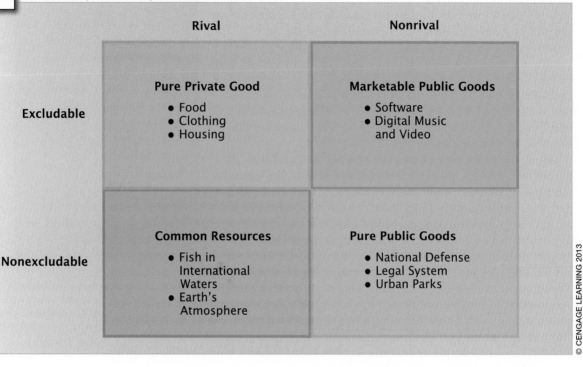

	Rival	Nonrival
Excludable	**Pure Private Good** • Food • Clothing • Housing	**Marketable Public Goods** • Software • Digital Music and Video
Nonexcludable	**Common Resources** • Fish in International Waters • Earth's Atmosphere	**Pure Public Goods** • National Defense • Legal System • Urban Parks

© CENGAGE LEARNING 2013

Marketable Public Goods

Marketable public good
An excludable and nonrival good. Generally provided by the market for a price, though efficiency would require a price of zero.

In the upper right corner are goods that are excludable, but nonrival. We'll call these **marketable public goods.** Because their benefits are excludable, the market generally can, and generally does, provide them at a price. But because they are nonrival, the quantity is less than efficient. Some people decide not to pay the price and don't consume, even though their consumption would not use up resources or lessen anyone else's enjoyment.

An example is digital music. Enforcement efforts have eliminated most unauthorized free downloading. As a result, digital music files are now largely excludable: private firms (such as Apple and Amazon) offer them for sale, and only those who pay can enjoy them. But firms could provide an *additional* music file—or allow customers to share files with anyone they wanted—without decreasing anyone else's enjoyment. The same is true of any other form of digital information or entertainment: software, movies, books, and more. All are provided privately at less than efficient quantities.

In some cases, if firms can rely on advertising for their revenue, we can get closer to the efficient quantity. Broadcast television and Google searches are examples of marketable public goods that are offered privately, at no charge, because they are supported entirely by advertising.

But in most cases, a price is charged, and we accept the resulting inefficiency. Most economists would not even describe a marketable public good as a market

⚠ DANGEROUS CURVES

Public *provision* versus public *production* Don't confuse public *provision* of a good with public *production.* The government must *provide* a pure public good in order to correct the market failure problem. But it can provide it by either producing the good itself (public production) or contracting production out to private firms (private production). Many local governments, for example, pay private firms to collect trash or run prisons. These services are privately produced, but they are purchased by government and *publicly provided* without charge to residents.

© AXL/SHUTTERSTOCK.COM

failure. It is true that, once such goods are created and we desire them, public provision at no charge would generate the efficient quantity. But having the government deeply involved in providing our music or software, and making decisions about which products to provide, would be unacceptable to most of us.

Common Resources

In the lower left corner of Figure 6 is another category of mixed good: nonexcludable, but rivalrous. Crowded city streets and some important natural resources fall into this category. They are often called **common resources** because they are available to everyone in common—no one can be excluded from consuming them. But their consumption lessens the benefits available for others.

Economists use the term *tragedy of the commons* to describe the problem caused by many of these goods. In a traditional English village, the commons was an area freely available to all families for grazing their animals. Grazing rights are a rivalrous good: If one cow eats the grass, another can't. But the commons had no method of exclusion, so it was overgrazed, causing harm to *all* families.

Common resource
A nonexcludable and rival good. Generally available free of charge, though efficiency would require a positive price.

> The **tragedy of the commons** occurs when rivalrous but nonexcludable goods are overused, to the detriment of all.

Tragedy of the commons The problem of overuse when a good is rivalrous but nonexcludable.

When common resources are used within a single country, that country's government can sometimes solve the market failure by passing laws or regulations to limit consumption. But when a nonexcludable resource is shared internationally, it is much harder to find a solution, and the tragedy of the commons often results.

An example is fishing in international waters, generally beyond 200 miles from national coastlines. No one owns these areas of the ocean, and no single government can tell people not to fish in them. And since no one charges for the fish removed, fishing boats use huge nets that catch just about every source of protein (most of which is ground up to be used as cattle feed). These methods are also changing the ocean's ecosystem, threatening species of ocean life further down the food chain. Although scientists have recommended specific limits on national governments since 1987, virtually every country—concerned about the welfare of its *own* fishing industry—has chosen to ignore the recommendations. Each government is a free rider in the international community, reasoning that its own fish catch is just a "drop in the bucket," and that whatever other governments do, it is better off allowing its *own* crews to continue depleting the fish.

Another example of a common resource is the earth's atmosphere. The planet is warming. To the extent that this trend is exacerbated by emissions of carbon dioxide and other greenhouse gases, the world has an interest in reducing this activity. But reducing emissions is costly. And slowing global warming would benefit everyone on the planet, whether they helped pay these costs or not. Therefore, each country—and even each person—can be a free rider, with the result that nothing is done. This was the logic behind the Kyoto Protocol and subsequent efforts to set up tradable permit systems.

© AXL/SHUTTERSTOCK.COM

DANGEROUS CURVES ⚠️

Categorizing market failures Don't be troubled if a particular market seems to fit more than one type of market failure. The categories are not mutually exclusive. For example, a walk-by park—which we've discussed in this section as a pure public good—could also be viewed as a good with an important positive externality. After all, if the park were provided by the private market, many people who did not produce it or pay to enjoy it would get external benefits. In general, when a positive externality becomes important enough, economists begin to think of the good as a pure public good.

Similarly, when a negative externality becomes large enough—such as with greenhouse gas emissions or other types of pollution—it can be useful to shift our thinking to the common resource model. We can regard the atmosphere as a common resource, because, although it is rival, the private market cannot establish excludability in using it.

ASYMMETRIC INFORMATION

In the previous chapter, we saw that a well-functioning competitive market provides the efficient quantity of a good. In this chapter, you've already learned some of the features behind the "well-functioning" condition. For example, the good must be a private good, characterized by excludability and rivalry. There should be no positive or negative externalities in production or consumption of the good. And remember that we've always been assuming a more or less *competitive* market (ideally, a *perfectly* competitive market).

When you learned about perfect competition in Chapter 9, one of the conditions was *easily obtained information*. In perfect competition, we assume that each party knows what it is getting and what it is giving up. We also assume that obtaining this information has no significant costs. But this is not always the case.

Suppose you buy a bottle of sugar pills for $50 because you believe they will help you shed pounds without diet or exercise. The seller is better off, but you are worse off. Moreover, this transaction likely *decreases* total benefits. You lost $50 and also suffered the humiliation of being fooled; the seller gained *less* than $50 because he has to deduct from his revenue the time and expense of making and marketing the pills.

Asymmetric information
A situation in which one party to a transaction has relevant information not known by the other party.

This transaction is an example of a problem known as **asymmetric information**—when one party to a transaction knows something about its value that the other party does not know. Asymmetric information can cause markets to fail in numerous ways, depending on the type of information involved.

Adverse Selection

One type of asymmetric information concerns the *quality* of a good. The classic example is the used-car market. The owner of a car knows much more about its quality than anyone else. From general knowledge, or consulting Web sites, or life experience, buyers may know the quality of the *average* used car of that model and with that mileage, but not the particular one being offered to them. The buyer's willingness to pay for any particular car will thus be based on the average quality of used cars of the same category.

In this sort of market, anyone who sells a "lemon"—an unusually poor car—stands to gain, because the car can be sold for more than its value. By contrast, anyone with a great used car would lose out in this market, because buyers will believe it to be of average quality. As a result, people with great used cars are reluctant to sell them to strangers in the market. But lemons are offered in large numbers.

Of course, once the market becomes awash in lemons, the average quality drops further, reducing used-car prices even more. Eventually, the market may offer nothing but lemons. The good-quality cars disappear: Used-car prices are so low that the good cars are kept by their owners or sold only to friends.

Adverse selection A situation in which asymmetric information about quality eliminates high-quality goods from a market.

In this example, asymmetric information about quality leads to the problem of **adverse selection**. The market acts as if it is "selecting" only the worst cars to offer for sale. Pareto improvements—in which people sell good used cars to strangers at mutually beneficial prices—remain unexploited.

Adverse selection occurs in many markets. In labor markets, employers are more likely to let go of their "lemons" and retain their highest-quality workers, so well-qualified but unemployed workers may have a harder time getting a job offer than someone who is currently working. In the private market for health insurance, those with the poorest health—who would get the best deal—are most likely to want to sign up for health insurance at any given price. This can drive up the cost of insurance until people of average or good health are priced out of the market.

Moral Hazard

Another information problem—especially for insurance markets—arises from lack of information about someone's *future behavior*. It is called **moral hazard**—the tendency for people to change their behavior and act less responsibly when they are protected from the harmful consequences of their behavior. For example, suppose you are away from home and realize you may have forgotten to lock your front door. Without theft insurance, you would think about the full value of what you'd lose if you were robbed. You might then go to considerable trouble to return home and check the lock. But if you have theft insurance you might only consider *part* of the cost—the part that *you* would pay. The rest of the cost—covered by your insurance company—would not matter to you. You would be less likely to return home to check the lock. In this way, theft insurance leads to fewer locked doors, a greater incidence of theft, and higher insurance costs for everyone.

Moral hazard is a problem, to some degree, for every kind of insurance in which the insured has some influence over the likelihood or amount of their future loss. Insuring people for floods or earthquakes not only makes them more likely to live in areas prone to those natural disasters but reduces their incentive to make their homes less vulnerable to damage. And though few people would choose to become ill just because they have health insurance, there is still a moral hazard problem: The more of my costs that are covered by the insurance company, the less I care whether my doctor charges excessive fees or uses inefficient and costly procedures as part of my health care. This causes insurance premiums to rise for everyone, driving many potential customers out of the market.

WHAT'S WRONG WITH THIS PICTURE?

Speeding Ticket Insurance
We pay ALL of your fines!
1-800-555-FAST

© CENGAGE LEARNING

Moral hazard When someone is protected from paying the full costs of their harmful actions and acts irresponsibly, making the harmful consequences more likely.

The Principal–Agent Problem

Finally, another potential market failure that arises from information asymmetry is the **principal–agent problem.** A principal is someone who hires someone else—an agent—to act in the principal's interest. The problem arises when the principal does not have full information about the agent's performance. This enables the agent to act in his *own* interest, at the expense of the principal.

A classic example is when you hire someone to fix your car. Unless you stand and watch (and also have expertise in car repair), you won't know whether the mechanic has done all he promised, and done it well. Some of your payment may just be a transfer of benefits from you to the mechanic, leaving you worse off. Knowing this, you may not want to take your car to a mechanic at all, and may do so only when the car stops running.

Principal–agent problems plague transactions involving individual contractors (roofers, plumbers, and so forth) and also many labor market relationships. In a corporation, managers are hired to be agents of the stockholders. But managers have their own goals that may conflict with those of the stockholders (higher-than-competitive salaries for themselves, larger-than-efficient offices, padded expense accounts, and more). Similarly, the managers act as principals when they hire hourly workers as agents. But hourly workers can find hidden ways of shirking that managers cannot monitor, such as spending time on Facebook or Twitter when the manager isn't looking.

Principal–agent problem When one party (the principal) hires another (the agent), who in turn can pursue goals that conflict with the principal's because of asymmetric information.

Market and Government Solutions

Information asymmetry—and the problems that arise from it—can reduce the total benefits in a market by preventing some transactions from taking place at all. In some cases, though, the information asymmetry can be addressed by the market itself. The problem of adverse selection in the used-car market, for example, can be partly corrected through *reputation*. A used-car dealer can hire mechanics to carefully screen the cars it buys and develop a reputation for selling only high-quality used cars. It could also signal to buyers that its cars are above-average quality by offering a warranty. The business could then charge a premium—which consumers would be willing to pay—to cover the additional costs of the mechanics and the warranty.

Or consider the problem of moral hazard. In some insurance markets, an insurance company could determine which consumers are most likely to exhibit costly behavior (for example, those who have made more theft insurance claims in the past). These people can be charged higher rates. In this way, those who behave more responsibly will not be priced out of the market.

The principal–agent problem can be partly addressed by offering agents incentives for good performance. One example is a *contingent contract,* which spells out rewards and penalties based on the agent's future behavior. (If I hire you to fix my roof, the contract requires you to fix it again if it leaks within the next six months.) Within business firms, the goals of employees and owners can be more closely aligned by long-term employment contracts, profit-sharing, and bonuses.

All of these market-based methods are often used by buyers and sellers to *reduce* the inefficiency caused by information asymmetry. But they cannot eliminate it. The market's corrective efforts always entail a cost—either to obtain the additional information or to deal with its absence. This additional cost is like a tax on the product. And, like a tax, it creates its own deadweight loss.

When the market failure is significant, and when government solutions have a lower cost than market solutions, the government's direct involvement can be justified on efficiency grounds.

An Example: The Market for Health Insurance

One of the major policy debates of recent years concerns the proper role for government in the market for health insurance. As discussed earlier, this market—when left to itself—is plagued by both moral hazard and adverse selection. But there are also special ethical and humanitarian concerns.

Private Solutions for Health Insurance

The private market can partially resolve some of the potential market failures. Consider, for example, one of the moral hazards: Once insured, patients need not be as careful about using costly medical expenses of dubious value because they are protected from paying the full costs themselves. Health insurance companies can—and to some degree, do—mitigate this problem by deciding which tests and procedures they will cover, and which they won't. In theory, if there were adequate competition among health insurance companies (perhaps assisted by anti-trust law), companies' coverage restrictions would strike the right balance between costs and benefits or lose customers to competitors who did.

The adverse selection problem, too, could be solved by the private market—*if* we were willing to accept the consequences. Recall that adverse selection arises because those who apply for insurance might know more about their health condition (and about likely future claims) than do the insurance companies. But if companies can obtain information about applicants' health at reasonable cost, they can charge more to someone with a preexisting condition, or offer coverage that excludes a prior condition, or refuse to insure the person at all if they believe they cannot do so profitably. This is analogous to someone trying to obtain information about a particular used car, to help them screen out lemons. Viewed from the narrow perspective of efficiency, it helps to solve the adverse selection problem: It prevents the applicant pool from becoming dominated by those with the most costly future health claims, so the companies can continue to offer health insurance at reasonable rates to those of average or better health.

But cars are not people. When car buyers have information, we don't object if an unlucky owner of a lemon cannot unload it. But many people *do* object when—because of information obtained by an insurance company—someone with an unlucky medical condition cannot get health insurance, or has to pay significantly more than others. In addition, some economists argue that the information costs are too high, and that insurance companies waste society's resources investigating applicants and rejecting claims that might be due to a prior medical condition.

Government Solutions for Health Insurance

In many countries in Europe and elsewhere, the government has chosen to solve the adverse selection problem by providing its own, universal health insurance to all citizens. The government then deals with the moral hazard problem by regulating the fees that doctors and hospitals can charge, and rationing health care among competing demands.

In the United States, government-funded health insurance has been more controversial, and until recently was provided only to veterans, the elderly, and the very poor. The rest of the population was either insured by private insurance companies (through their employer or on a policy purchased individually) or had no health insurance coverage at all.

In 2010, the United States followed Europe's example (at least in part) with the *Patient Protection and Affordable Care Act*, designed to expand health insurance coverage to virtually every citizen. The new law maintained existing government programs for veterans, the elderly, and the very poor, and worked with (rather than eliminated) existing private health insurance companies. But it set up a phased reform of the health insurance system. It also imposed tighter regulations on health insurance companies, including a prohibition on denying coverage to those with pre-existing conditions or dropping coverage when people became ill.

The reform solved the adverse selection problem by requiring *everyone* not covered by existing government programs—healthy or not—to purchase insurance or face a fine. Households with low incomes (but not low enough to be eligible for Medicaid) would get government assistance in paying.

The act also took a stab at the moral hazard problem. It set up an institute to determine and recommend (but not require) the most effective medical treatments and procedures. (Research has shown that in many areas of medicine, the most effective treatments are less costly than others in common use.) And it allowed the government wider authority to reduce Medicare reimbursements to hospitals whose patients—after being released—require further, expensive treatment by others.

As we've discussed, the health care reform act was highly controversial. It faced numerous court challenges in 2011, and it promised to be a major issue in the 2012 presidential election.

EFFICIENCY AND GOVERNMENT IN PERSPECTIVE

In this chapter, you've seen that an economy with *well-functioning, perfectly competitive markets* tends to be economically efficient. But notice the italicized words. As you've also learned in this chapter, markets need help from government (a legal and regulatory infrastructure) in order to function well. Moreover, efficiency can require direct government involvement to correct market failures.

These cases of government involvement are not without controversy. In fact, most of the controversies that pit Democrats against Republicans in the United States (or Conservatives against Labourites in Britain, or Social Democrats against Christian Democrats in Germany) relate to when, and to what extent, the government should be involved in the economy. Debates about public education, Social Security, international trade, health care, and immigration all center on questions of the proper role for government.

Why so much controversy?

Opposition to Government Intervention

Some of the opposition to government involvement is ideological. Government involvement works by placing restrictions on individual economic freedom. For example, regulations tell firms what they can and cannot do. Provision of public goods requires the government to collect taxes, even from those who don't benefit from or believe in a particular public good. If you don't pay your taxes, you face financial penalties at best, and possibly imprisonment at worst.

Many people believe that the opportunity cost in lost economic freedom outweighs the benefits of government interventions, even when the intervention *would* improve economic efficiency. Some opponents of the health care reform of 2010, for example, believed that requiring everyone to purchase health insurance or face a fine was an unjustified federal government encroachment upon individual economic freedom.

But in some cases, government intervention to correct a market failure is opposed on efficiency grounds alone. Why would government intervention be inefficient?

Government Failure

Even when a market failure could, *in theory*, be solved by government, we cannot be sure that government will do so effectively. And once government has the power to intervene, it could even make a market *less* efficient. That's because the public sector can be plagued by **government failure**—a situation in which government falls victim to the same types of problems that cause market failures in the private economy.

One source of government failure is the principal–agent problem. Government officials are the agents of the general public and are supposed to serve the public interest. But government officials may have their own incentives, such as expanding the size of their departmental budgets, covering up waste and mistakes to protect their jobs, or maximizing contributions to their campaign funds. Although there are checks and balances to monitor and limit this type of behavior, they are not always effective. Even in the most lawful democracies, lobbying by corporations, unions, and other interest-groups can lead politicians and government officials astray.

Those most skeptical of government intervention stress examples in which, arguably, government failure had led to substantial inefficiency. Those who view intervention more favorably stress examples where, arguably, the *lack* of government intervention has resulted in substantial inefficiency.

Deadweight Loss from Taxes

In order for government to have the funds it needs to support markets and do other things, it must raise revenue through taxes.

Some taxes actually help *eliminate* deadweight losses by correcting a market failure (such as a negative externality). But the government needs more tax revenue than it could get from these markets. In the absence of a market failure, a tax creates a deadweight loss of its own in the market that is taxed. In Chapter 14, you saw how an excise tax on a particular good (air travel) created such a deadweight loss. Taxes in other markets have a similar effect. Income and payroll taxes, for example, reduce total benefits for workers and employers by more than the amount the government collects in these taxes.

These deadweight losses from taxes are a cost of government activity, to be compared with its benefits. A particular government action (say, providing a new public good or adding a new regulatory agency) might provide benefits to society when the action is considered in isolation. But if the tax needed to fund the government activity creates deadweight loss greater than those benefits, then total benefits in the economy would shrink. Those who are pessimistic about the value or effectiveness of government actions conclude that, in many cases, the deadweight loss from the taxes exceeds the potential benefits. They tend to oppose expanding government's role in the economy on efficiency grounds.

Efficiency versus Equity

Fostering efficiency—the focus of this chapter—is just one of the government's roles in the economy. We also want our government to be concerned with equity or fairness. Much of the controversy surrounding government intervention in the economy arises from different definitions of what is fair or equitable.

Almost every government policy designed to improve efficiency also has consequences for equity. Taxing gasoline to correct an externality would hit the poor harder than the rich, while taxing airline travel would do the opposite. Eliminating price floors for agricultural goods might move the economy toward efficiency, but it would cause harm to many farmers and their families. Almost every change in the tax code designed to improve efficiency will raise a firestorm of protest because of the way it might affect equity. This limits the government's ability to focus on efficiency when dealing with market failures.

* * * *

The controversies we've discussed can be so heated and so varied that it is easy to forget how much agreement there is about the role of government. Anyone studying the role of government in the economies of the United States, Canada, Mexico, France, Germany, Britain, Japan, and the vast majority of other developed economies, is struck by one glaring fact: Most economic activity is carried out among private individuals. In all of these countries, there is widespread agreement that the most powerful forces that exploit Pareto improvements and drive the economy toward efficiency are the actions of individual producers and consumers. There is also widespread agreement that certain market failures *require* government correction. In the Using the Theory section, we look at one example: a market failure in the financial system caused by moral hazard.

To their surprise, they find that they are using a total of 1,000 gallons per month between them. Why? What concept discussed in this chapter is illustrated by this example?

6. Some have argued that the music industry is by nature inefficient because once a piece of music is produced, the firm that owns it has a monopoly and charges the monopoly price. Yet, the marginal cost of making the music available to one more member of the public (via the Internet) is zero. Draw a diagram, similar to Figure 2, to represent this situation. Identify on your diagram:
   a. The efficient level of production
   b. The level of production a government-regulated music industry would earn if it were permitted to charge just enough for a "fair rate of return"
   c. The level of production provided by the (currently unregulated) industry

7. In Figure 4, a negative externality was corrected with a $1 per gallon tax on gasoline producers. Draw a diagram to show that the total price paid by consumers, the total price received by firms, and the equilibrium quantity would have been exactly the same if the same tax had been imposed on gasoline consumers instead of producers.

8. In Figure 5(b), a positive externality was corrected with a $30,000 subsidy paid to students. Draw a diagram to show that the total price paid by students, the total price received by colleges, and the equilibrium quantity of degrees would have been exactly the same if the $30,000 subsidy per student had been given to colleges instead.

9. Each of the following is an example of (or would lead to) a particular type of market failure arising from information asymmetry. Identify the type of market failure and justify your answer briefly.
   a. A woman in the "dating market" complains, "All the good ones are taken."
   b. A college announces a new policy: Any senior with a GPA less than 2.0 will, upon graduation, have all grades of C− or lower retroactively raised to a grade of C.
   c. A restaurant in New York hires workers to pass out fliers to pedestrians all over the city, and pays them based on how many fliers are gone (and presumably distributed) when the workers return at the end of the day.

10. During the financial crisis of 2008, market failures occurred other than those discussed in the Using the Theory section. For each of the following, identify the market failure. (If asymmetric information, identify the specific type: moral hazard, principal–agent, or adverse selection.)

a. Troubled financial institutions tried to raise cash by quickly selling financial assets (such as bonds backed by mortgages) to other institutions. However, managers at the other institutions assumed the assets being offered were especially risky, and would pay very little for them. As a result, some troubled institutions stopped selling all but their most-risky assets.

b. Managers at financial institutions were given huge bonuses when they took risks that paid off. As a result, they took many risks that even their institutions' owners (stockholders) would not have approved of, knowing that the owners could not monitor their every move. In effect, they treated stockholders as "outsiders" rather than owners.

c. Some managers made risky investments that could cost their firms billions of dollars if the investments turned out badly. They knew, however, that they would not have to cover these losses; the worst that could happen to them was losing their jobs.

d. When making investments, managers at financial institutions often considered the costs and benefits to themselves and their stockholders, but they did not consider how their decisions might contribute to instability for the financial system as a whole.

More Challenging

11. The following table shows the quantities of car alarms demanded and supplied per year in a town:

Price	Quantity Demanded	Quantity Supplied
$ 75	800	0
$100	750	150
$125	700	300
$150	650	450
$175	600	600
$200	550	750
$225	500	900
$250	450	1,050

Without drawing a graph, determine the efficient quantity in this market under each of the following assumptions:

a. Each car alarm sold creates a negative externality (noise pollution) that causes $100 in harm to the public.

b. Each car alarm creates a *positive* externality (reduced law enforcement costs) that provides $100 in benefits to the public.

12. Suppose Douglas and Ziffel have properties that adjoin the farm of Mr. Haney. The current zoning law permits Haney to use the farm for any purpose. Haney has decided to raise pigs (the best use of the land). A pig farm will earn $50,000 per year, forever.

a. Assume the interest rate is 10 percent per year. What is Haney's pig farm worth? [Hint: Use a special formula from Chapter 13.]

b. Suppose the next best use of Haney's property is residential, where it could earn $20,000 per year. What is the minimum one-time payment Haney would accept to agree to restrict his land for residential use forever?

c. Suppose Douglas is willing to pay $200,000 for an end to pig farming on Haney's land, while Ziffel is willing to pay no more than $150,000. (For some reason, Ziffel does not mind pig farming as much as Douglas does.) If Douglas pays Haney $200,000, and Ziffel pays Haney $150,000, and Haney converts his land to residential use, is this a Pareto improvement? Who benefits, who loses, and by how much?

d. Suppose instead that Douglas pays $150,000 and Ziffel pays $150,000. Is this move a Pareto improvement? Who benefits, who loses, and by how much?

CHAPTER 16

Comparative Advantage and the Gains from International Trade

© LHB PHOTO/ALAMY

onsumers love bargains. And the rest of the world offers U.S. consumers bargains galore: cars from Japan, computer memory chips from Korea, shoes from China, tomatoes from Mexico, lumber from Canada, and sugar from the Caribbean. But Americans' purchases of foreign-made goods have always been a controversial subject. Should we let these bargain goods into the country? Consumers certainly benefit when we do so. But don't cheap foreign goods threaten the jobs of American workers and the profits of American producers? How do we balance the interests of specific workers and producers on the one hand with the interests of consumers in general? These questions are important not just in the United States, but in every country of the world.

Over the post–World War II period, there has been a worldwide movement toward a policy of *free trade*—the unhindered movement of goods and services across national boundaries. An example of this movement was the creation—in 1995—of a new international body: the World Trade Organization (WTO). The WTO's goal is to help resolve trade disputes among its members and to reduce obstacles to free trade around the world.

And to some extent it has succeeded: Import taxes, import limitations, and all kinds of crafty regulations designed to keep out imports are gradually falling away. In recent years, almost one-third of the world's production has been exported to other countries. One hundred fifty-three countries have joined the WTO, and 30 others are eager to join.

But even though many barriers have come down, others remain—and new ones have come up. In 2011, the United States was still refusing to eliminate its long-standing quota on sugar imports and took steps to limit imports of shrimp from China and steel from Korea. The European Union continued to restrict imports of U.S. beef while demanding that China and Canada open up their markets to its own high-tech equipment. Free trade agreements the U.S. had negotiated several years earlier with South Korea, Colombia and Panama continued to languish in Congress, which was reluctant to approve them. And a decades-long negotiation to reduce trade barriers around the world—sponsored by the WTO and known as the "Doha Round"—had gotten nowhere, with each new proposal eliciting strong objections from a variety of national governments.

Looking at the contradictory mix of trade policies that exist in the world, we are left to wonder: Is free international trade a good thing that makes us better off, or is it bad for us and something that should be kept in check? In this chapter, you'll learn to apply the tools of economics to issues surrounding international trade.

THE LOGIC OF FREE TRADE

Many of us like the idea of being self-reliant. A very few even prefer to live by themselves in a remote region of Alaska or the backcountry of Montana. But consider the defects of self-sufficiency: If you lived all by yourself, you would be poor. You could not *export* or sell to others any part of your own production, nor could you *import* or buy from others anything they have produced. You would be limited to consuming the goods and services that you produced. Undoubtedly, the food, clothing, and housing you would manage to produce by yourself would be small in quantity and poor in quality—nothing like the items you currently enjoy. And there would be many things you could not get at all—electricity, television, cars, airplane trips, or the antibiotics that could save your life.

The defects of self-sufficiency explain why most people do not choose it. Rather, people prefer to specialize and trade with each other. In Chapter 2, you learned that specialization and exchange enable us to enjoy greater production and higher living standards than would otherwise be possible.

This principle applies not just to individuals, but also to *groups* of individuals, such as those living within the boundaries that define cities, counties, states, or nations. That is, just as we all benefit when *individuals* specialize and exchange with each other, so, too, we can benefit when *groups* of individuals specialize in producing different goods and services, and exchange them with other *groups*.

Imagine what would happen if the residents of your state switched from a policy of open trading with other states to one of self-sufficiency, refusing to import anything from "foreign states" or to export anything to them. Such an arrangement would be preferable to individual self-sufficiency; at least there would be specialization and trade *within* the state. But the elimination of trading between states would surely result in many sacrifices. Lacking the necessary inputs for their production, for instance, your state might have to do without bananas, cotton, or tires. And the goods that *were* made in your state would likely be produced inefficiently. For example, while residents of Vermont *could* drill for oil, and Texans *could* produce maple syrup, they could do so only at great cost of resources.

Thus, it would make no sense to insist on the economic self-sufficiency of each of the 50 states. And the founders of the United States knew this. They placed prohibitions against tariffs, quotas, and other barriers to interstate commerce right in the U.S. Constitution. The people of Vermont and Texas are vastly better off under free trade among the states than they would be if each state were self-sufficient.

What is true for states is also true for entire nations. The members of the WTO have carried the argument to its ultimate conclusion: National specialization and exchange can expand world living standards through free *international* trade. Such trade involves the movement of goods and services across national boundaries. Goods and services produced domestically, but sold abroad, are called **exports**; those produced abroad, but consumed domestically, are called **imports**. The long-term goal of the WTO is to remove all barriers to exports and imports in order to encourage *among* nations the specialization and trade that have been so successful *within* nations.

Exports Goods and services produced domestically, but sold abroad.

Imports Goods and services produced abroad, but consumed domestically.

INTERNATIONAL COMPARATIVE ADVANTAGE

In Chapter 2, you were introduced to the notions of absolute and comparative advantage. Let's focus on these two concepts as they apply to trade between nations.

A country has an *absolute advantage* in a good when it can produce it using *fewer resources* than another country. Economists who first considered the benefits of international trade focused on absolute advantage. As the early economists saw it, the citizens of every nation could improve their economic welfare by specializing in the production of goods in which they had an absolute advantage and exporting them to other countries. In turn, they would import goods from countries that had an absolute advantage in those goods.

In 1817, however, the British economist David Ricardo disagreed. Absolute advantage, he argued, was not a necessary ingredient for mutually beneficial international trade. The key was *comparative advantage*:

> *A nation has a comparative advantage in producing a good if it can produce it at a lower opportunity cost than some other country.*

As you learned in Chapter 2, there is a key difference between absolute advantage and comparative advantage. While absolute advantage in a good is defined by the resources used to produce it, comparative advantage is based on the *opportunity cost* of producing it. The opportunity cost of producing something is the *other goods* that these resources *could* have produced instead.

Ricardo argued that a potential trading partner could be absolutely inferior in the production of every single good—requiring more resources per unit of each good than any other country—and still have a comparative advantage in some good. The comparative advantage would arise because the country was *less* inferior at producing some goods than others. Likewise, a country that had an absolute advantage in producing everything could—contrary to common opinion—still benefit from trade. It would have a comparative advantage only in some, but not all, goods.

To illustrate Ricardo's insight, let's go back to our example from Chapter 2, involving trade between the U.S. and China. We'll first review what you learned there, and then we'll carry our analysis and discussion further.

Determining a Nation's Comparative Advantage

In our example, the U.S. and China each produce two goods—soybeans and T-shirts—using just one resource: labor. Table 1 shows the number of labor hours required to produce one unit of each good, in each country. We assume that these labor requirements remain constant, no matter how much is produced.

Notice that the United States has an *absolute* advantage in producing both goods: It takes fewer hours to produce either a bushel of soybeans or a T-shirt in the U.S. than in China. But China has a *comparative advantage* in T-shirts. That is, the opportunity cost of producing T-shirts is lower in China than in the U.S. How do we know? For China to produce one more T-shirt, they must shift one hour of labor out of soybean production. Because each bushel of soybeans requires five hours in China, taking away

---

TABLE 1

Labor Requirements for Soybeans and T-Shirts

	Labor Required for:	
	1 Bushel of Soybeans	1 T-Shirt
United States	½ hour	¼ hour
China	5 hours	1 hour

© CENGAGE LEARNING 2013

one hour causes soybean production to fall by one-fifth of a bushel. So in China, the opportunity cost of one T-shirt is one-fifth of a bushel of soybeans.

In the United States, producing another T-shirt means shifting one-fourth of an hour from soybeans to T-shirts. This shift decreases soybean production by one-half of a bushel. Thus, in the U.S., the opportunity cost of one T-shirt is one-half of a bushel of soybeans. Because China has the lower opportunity cost (one-fifth of a bushel, rather than one-half of a bushel), China has the comparative advantage in T-shirts.

Similar reasoning (which you should do on your own) will show that the U.S. has a lower opportunity cost, and therefore a comparative advantage, in producing soybeans.

So far, this should all be familiar: It's the same analysis, done in the same way, as in Chapter 2. But now, as we continue with the example, we'll delve deeper. For each country, we'll compare production and consumption of each good before trade and after trade. And we'll see precisely how each country can gain by exporting its comparative advantage good.

How Specialization Increases World Production

Figure 1 shows production possibilities frontiers for the United States and China. In the left panel, we assume that the United States has 100 million hours of labor per year, which it must allocate between soybeans (on the horizontal axis) and T-shirts (on the vertical axis). To obtain the PPF for the U.S., we first suppose that all 100 million hours of labor were allocated to T-shirts. The U.S. could then produce 400 million of them per year (because each one requires $\frac{1}{4}$ hour of labor). Accordingly, the upper-most point on the PPF represents 400 million T-shirts and zero bushels of soybeans.

To get the rest of the points, remember that the opportunity cost of one more bushel of soybeans is 2 T-shirts. Therefore, each time we move rightward by one unit (one more bushel), we must move downward by 2 units (2 fewer T-shirts). Accordingly, the PPF for the U.S. will be a straight line, with a slope of +2. The PPF ends where the U.S. would be allocating all of its 100 million hours to soybeans, producing 200 million bushels.

Notice that this PPF is a straight line, unlike the curved PPFs in Chapter 2. A linear PPF follows from our assumption that hours per unit—and therefore opportunity costs—remain constant no matter how much of either good is produced. Essentially, to keep things simple, we are assuming *constant opportunity cost*, rather than increasing opportunity cost as in the PPFs drawn in Chapter 2. (We'll discuss the implications of this in a few pages.)

The right panel shows China's PPF, under the assumption that China has 500 million hours of labor per year. On your own, be sure you can see how the two end points of China's PPF are determined. Also, be sure you understand why the slope of China's PPF will be +5. (Hint: What is the opportunity cost of another bushel of soybeans in China?)

Before international trade occurs, we assume (arbitrarily) that both countries are operating in the middle of their respective PPFs. The United States is at point *A*, producing 100 million bushels of soybeans and 200 million T-shirts each year. This combination of goods is also U.S. *consumption* per year: Without trade, you can only consume what you produce. In the right panel, China is at point *A'*, producing and consuming 50 million bushels of soybeans and 250 million T-shirts.

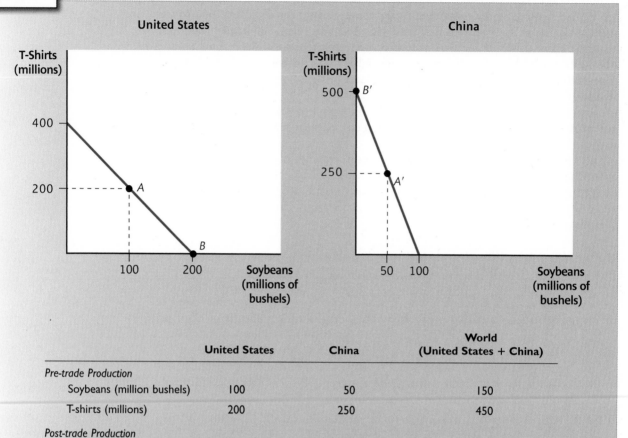

FIGURE 1 | **How Trade Changes Production**

	United States	China	World (United States + China)
Pre-trade Production			
Soybeans (million bushels)	100	50	150
T-shirts (millions)	200	250	450
Post-trade Production			
Soybeans (million bushels)	200	0	200
T-shirts (millions)	0	500	500

Before international trade opens up in soybeans and T-shirts, the United States is assumed to produce in the middle of its linear PPF at point A, representing 100 million bushels of soybeans and 200 million T-shirts. Similarly, China is assumed to produce at point A', representing 50 million bushels of soybeans and 250 million T-shirts.

After trade, each country will completely specialize in its comparative advantage good. The United States will shift all resources into soybeans (200 million bushels) at point B, and China will put all resources into T-shirts (500 million) at point B'. The result is greater world production of both goods. World soybean production rises from 150 million to 200 million bushels, and world T-shirt production rises from 450 million to 500 million.

© CENGAGE LEARNING 2013

Now look at the table that accompanies the figure. The first two rows tell us the production of each good in each country before trade opens up, and also world production of each good. As you can see, with the United States producing at point *A* along its PPF and China producing at point *A'*, the world (the United States and China combined) produces 150 million bushels of soybeans and 450 million T-shirts per year.

Let's now see what happens to world *production* when trade opens up. We'll have each country devote *all* of its resources to the good in which it has a comparative advantage. The United States, with a comparative advantage in soybeans, moves to point B on its PPF, producing 200 million bushels of soybeans and zero T-shirts. China moves to point B' on its PPF, producing 500 million T-shirts and zero soybeans. The new production levels for each country are entered in the last two rows of the table in Figure 1.

Finally, look at the last column of numbers in the table. For both goods, world production has increased. Soybean output is up from 150 million to 200 million bushels, and T-shirt production is up from 450 million to 500 million. This increase in world production has been accomplished without adding any resources to either country. The world's resources are simply being used more efficiently.

Although our example has just two countries and two goods, it illustrates a broader conclusion:

> *When countries specialize according to their comparative advantage, the world's resources are used more efficiently, enabling greater production of every good.*

How Each Nation Gains from International Trade

Now let's show that both countries can gain from trade. As you've seen, when the two countries specialize in their comparative advantage good, they produce more of that good but none of the other. For example, China produces more T-shirts but no soybeans. However, by trading some of its comparative advantage good for the other good, each country can *consume* more of both goods.

Table 2 illustrates this conclusion, under the assumption that the U.S. will trade 80 million bushels of soybeans for 240 million T-shirts from China. This is an arbitrary assumption, and we could change it and still come to the same conclusion. But let's see how international trade can benefit both countries in this case.

Because there is so much going on in this table, we'll go through it one step at a time, starting with the column of numbers for soybeans in the United States. The first entry for the U.S. shows how specialization changes U.S. *production* of soybeans, based on the movement along the PPF in Figure 1. When the U.S. moves from point A to point B in Figure 1, soybean production increases from 100 million to 200 million bushels. This is an increase of 100 million, hence the entry +100 in the first row. If there were no international trade, this would also be the change in U.S. consumption of soybeans.

TABLE 2

The Gains from Specialization and Trade

| | United States | | China | |
	Soybeans (million bushels)	T-Shirts (millions)	Soybeans (million bushels)	T-Shirts (millions)
Change in Production	+100	−200	−50	+250
Exports (−) or Imports (+)	−80	+240	+80	−240
Net Gain in Consumption	+20	+40	+30	+10

© CENGAGE LEARNING 2013

But because of international trade, the U.S. will *not* consume all the soybeans it produces. Instead, it will export some of them. Our assumption is that the U.S. exports 80 million bushels. These bushels have to be deducted from its production in order to determine how many bushels are left for the U.S. to consume. Hence, the entry −80 for U.S. exports of soybeans in the second row.

Finally, the third row subtracts exports from the change in production to get the change in *consumption* of soybeans. Since production increased by 100 million bushels, and 80 million of them were exported, U.S. consumption of soybeans rises by 100 − 80 = 20 million bushels.

Next, we move to the next column, U.S. T-shirts. When the U.S. moves from point *A* to point *B* in Figure 1, its T-shirt production decreases from 200 million to zero, represented by the entry −200. Without trade, this would mean that consumption of T-shirts decreases by 200 as well. However, remember our assumption: In exchange for its soybean exports, the U.S. gets 240 million T-shirts from China. These imports enter with a plus sign (+240). Combining the change in production (−200) with the T-shirts obtained as imports (+240), we are left with the change in U.S. *consumption* of T-shirts: +40. So U.S. consumption of T-shirts rises by 40 million.

Notice that the United States—by specializing in and exporting its comparative advantage good (soybeans)—ends up with more of *both* goods. One might think that if the U.S. ends up with more of both goods, then China must end up with less. But don't forget: world production of both goods has increased too. And in our example, China will end up with more of both goods as well.

The first row shows the consequences of China's move from point *A′* to point *B′* along its PPF in Figure 1. China's soybean production decreases from 50 million to zero (−50), while T-shirt production rises from 250 million to 500 million (+250). In the second row, we remember our assumption about trade: The U.S. exports 80 million bushels of soybeans to China. That means China must be *importing* 80 million bushels of soybeans (+80). Similarly, we assume the U.S. imports 240 million T-shirts from China, so that must be how many T-shirts China *exports* (−240). Summing up the numbers for China, we see that China's soybean consumption rises by 30 million (+30), while its T-shirt consumption rises by 10 million (+10).

Illustrating Gains from Trade Graphically

Figure 2 illustrates the change in consumption on a PPF diagram similar to Figure 1. Once again, we start with the PPFs for the United States and China. But now we compare consumption in each country before trade with consumption *after* trade. The United States began with 100 million bushels of soybeans and 200 million T-shirts (point *A*). After specialization and trade, it consumes 120 million bushels of soybeans and 240 million T-shirts (point *C*). Similarly, China began by consuming 50 million bushels of soybeans and 250 million T-shirts (point *A′*). After specialization and trade, it consumes 80 million bushels of soybeans and 260 million T-shirts (point *C′*).

Notice that points *C* and *C′* lie *beyond* each country's PPF. While the PPF still shows possibilities for *production* of the two goods, *consumption* is no longer limited to what is produced. Instead, with trade, a country can consume more of both goods than it would be capable of producing and consuming on its own.

Let's take a step back and consider what we've discovered. First, look back at Table 1. Based on the required labor hours, the U.S. has an *absolute advantage* in

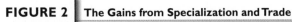

FIGURE 2 **The Gains from Specialization and Trade**

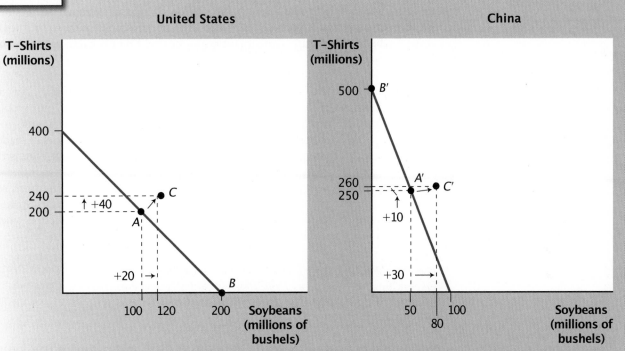

With international trade, the U.S. moves production from point A to point B, but consumes at point C—beyond its PPF. Soybean production increases from 100 million (at point A) to 200 million (at point B). After exporting 80 million bushels to China, the United States is left with 120 million (at point C), for a net gain of 20 million bushels. With terms of trade assumed to be 3 T-shirts for 1 bushel of soybeans, the United States trades its soybeans for 240 million T-shirts. United States T-shirt consumption rises from 200 million (point A) to 240 million (point C).

    In China, production moves from point A′ to point B′, but consumption is at point C′. T-shirt production rises from 250 million (at point A′) to 500 million (at point B′). After exporting 240 million T-shirts to the United States, China is left with 260 million (point C′), for a net gain of 10 million. China trades its T-shirts for 80 million bushels of soybeans from the United States, so China's soybean consumption rises from 50 million (at point A′) to 80 million (at point C′).

both goods: It can produce both soybeans and T-shirts using fewer hours of labor than can China. But we've determined that the U.S. has a *comparative advantage* in only *one* of these goods—soybeans—and China has a comparative advantage in the other—T-shirts. This is because the *opportunity costs* of each good differ in the two countries. Then, in Figure 1, we saw how world production of both goods increases when each country shifts its resources toward its comparative advantage good. Finally, in the last row of Table 2 and in Figure 2, we saw that *international trade* can enable *each* country to end up with more of *both* goods.

Although we've illustrated this result for just two countries and two goods, it also holds more generally:

> *Through international trade based on comparative advantage, all nations can achieve greater total consumption of goods and services, and therefore higher living standards, than is possible without trade.*

The Terms of Trade

Terms of trade The ratio at which a country can trade domestically produced products for foreign-produced products.

In our ongoing example, China exports 240 million T-shirts in exchange for 80 million bushels of soybeans. This exchange ratio (240 million to 80 million, or 3 to 1) is known as the **terms of trade**—the quantity of one good that is exchanged for one unit of the other.

The terms of trade determine how the gains from international trade are *distributed* among countries. Our particular choice of 3 to 1 apportioned the gains as shown in the last row of Table 2. But with different terms of trade, the gains would have been apportioned differently. In the problems at the end of this chapter, you will be asked to recalculate the gains for each country with different terms of trade. You'll see that with different terms of trade, both countries still gain, but the distribution of the gains between countries changes.

But notice that the terms of trade were not even *used* in our example until we arrived at Table 2. The gains from trade for the *world as a whole* were demonstrated in Figure 1, and they were based entirely on the increase in world production when countries specialize according to comparative advantage.

> *For the world as a whole, the gains from international trade are due to increased production as nations specialize according to comparative advantage.* How *those world gains are distributed among specific countries depends on the terms of trade.*

We won't consider here precisely *how* the terms of trade are determined (it's a matter of supply and demand). But we *will* establish the limits within which the terms of trade must fall.

Look again at Table 1. China would never give up *more* than 5 T-shirts to import 1 bushel of soybeans. Why not? Because it could always get a bushel for 5 T-shirts *domestically*, simply by shifting resources into soybean production.

Similarly, the United States would never export a bushel of soybeans for *fewer* than 2 T-shirts because it could get 2 T-shirts for a bushel domestically (again, by shifting resources). Therefore, when these two nations trade, we know the terms of trade will lie *somewhere between* 5 T-shirts for 1 bushel and 2 T-shirts for 1 bushel. Outside of that range, one of the two countries would refuse to trade. Note that in our example, we assume terms of trade of 3 T-shirts for 1 bushel—well within the acceptable range.

Countries can gain when they shift production toward their comparative advantage goods (such as soybeans in the United States), and trade them for other goods from other countries (such as textiles in China).

© GLOWIMAGES/GETTY IMAGES

Some Provisos about Specialization

Our simple example seems to suggest that countries should specialize *completely,* producing *only* the goods in which they have a comparative advantage. That is, it seems that China should get out of soybean production *entirely,* and the United States should get out of T-shirt production *entirely.*

The real world, however, is more complicated than our simplified example might suggest. Despite divergent opportunity costs, sometimes it does *not* make sense for two countries to trade with each other, or it might make sense to trade, but *not* completely specialize. Following are some real-world considerations that can lead to reduced trade or incomplete specialization.

Costs of Trading

If there are high transportation costs or high costs of making deals across national boundaries, trade may be reduced and even become prohibitively expensive. High transportation costs are especially important for perishable goods, such as ice cream, which must be shipped frozen, and most personal services, such as haircuts, eye exams, and restaurant meals. These goods are less subject to trade according to comparative advantage. (Imagine the travel cost for a U.S. resident to see an optometrist in China, where eye exams are less expensive.)

The costs of making deals are generally higher for international trade than for trade within domestic borders. For one thing, different laws must be dealt with and different business and marketing customs must be mastered. In addition, international trade involves the exchange of one country's currency for another. This can introduce additional costs and risks that don't exist for domestic trade, because exchange rates can change before a contract is settled with payment. High transportation costs and high costs of making deals help explain why nations continue to produce some goods in which they do not have a comparative advantage and why there is less than complete specialization in the world.

Sizes of Countries

Our earlier example featured two large economies capable of fully satisfying each other's demands. But sometimes a very large country, such as the United States, trades with a very small one, such as the Pacific island nation of Tonga. If the smaller country specialized completely, its output would be insufficient to fully meet the demand of the larger one. While the smaller country would specialize *completely,* the larger country would not. Instead, the larger country would continue to produce both goods. This helps to explain why the United States continues to produce bananas, even though we do so at a much higher opportunity cost than many small Latin American nations.

Increasing Opportunity Cost

In our example, we have assumed that the labor hours required to produce another unit of each good remains constant as production changes. Therefore, opportunity costs remain constant as well. For example, the opportunity cost of a bushel of soybeans remains at 2 T-shirts for the United States, regardless of how many bushels it produces.

But more typically, the opportunity cost of a good rises as more of it is produced. (Why? You may want to review the law of increasing opportunity cost in Chapter 2.) In that case, each step on the road to specialization would change the opportunity cost. A point might be reached—before complete specialization—in which opportunity costs became *equal* in the two countries, and there would be no further mutual gains from trading. (Remember: Opportunity costs must *differ* between the two countries in order for trade to be mutually beneficial.) In the end, while trading will occur, there will not be complete specialization. Instead, each country will produce both goods, just as China and the United States each produce T-shirts *and* soybeans in the real world.

Government Barriers to Trade

Governments can enact barriers to trading. In some cases, these barriers increase trading costs; in other cases, they make trade impossible. Since this is such an important topic, we'll consider government-imposed barriers to trade in a separate section, later in the chapter.

THE SOURCES OF COMPARATIVE ADVANTAGE

We've just seen how nations can benefit from specialization and trade when they have comparative advantages. But what determines comparative advantage in the first place?

Resource Abundance and Comparative Advantage

In many cases, comparative advantage arises from the *resources* a country has at its disposal.

> *A country that has relatively large amounts of a particular resource will tend to have a comparative advantage in goods that make heavy use of that resource.*

Remember that resources include not just land and natural resources, such as coal or oil, but also labor, human and physical capital, and entrepreneurship. A country that is relatively abundant in *any* of these resources will tend to have a comparative advantage in those goods that use relatively large quantities of that resource.

Comparative Advantage Based on Natural Resources and Climate

The most obvious cases of comparative advantage arise from gifts of nature, such as a specific natural resource like oil or coal, or a climate especially suited to a particular product.

The top part of Table 3 contains some examples. Saudi Arabia has a comparative advantage in the production of oil because it has oil fields with billions of barrels of oil that can be extracted at low cost. The United States comparative advantage in crops such as wheat and soybeans is partly explained by its abundant farmland. Canada is a major exporter of timber because its climate and geography make its land more suitable for growing trees than other crops. Canada is a good example of comparative advantage without absolute advantage: It grows a lot of timber, not because it can do so using fewer resources than other countries, but because its land is even more poorly suited to growing other things.

But now look at the bottom half of Table 3. It shows examples of international specialization that arise from some cause *other* than natural resources. Japan has a strong comparative advantage in making automobiles. Yet none of the *natural* resources needed to make cars are available in Japan; the iron ore, coal, and oil needed to produce cars are all imported.

What explains the cases of comparative advantage in the bottom half of Table 3?

Comparative Advantage from Other Resources

Some of the examples in the lower half of Table 3 arise from resources *other* than natural resources or climate. The United States is rich in both physical capital and human capital. As a result, the United States tends to have a comparative advantage in goods and services that make heavy use of computers, tractors, and satellite technology, as well as goods that require highly skilled labor. This, in part, explains the U.S. comparative advantage in the design and production of aircraft, a good that makes heavy use of physical capital (such as computer-based design systems) and human capital (highly trained engineers).

The United States is also relatively abundant in entrepreneurship. This helps explain why many of the Internet-related innovations in recent years (Google's

Country	Specialization Resulting from Natural Resources or Climate
Saudi Arabia	Oil
Canada	Timber
United States	Grain
Spain	Olive oil
Mexico	Tomatoes
Jamaica	Aluminum ore
Italy	Wine
Israel	Citrus fruit
Niger	Uranium
China	Rare-earth minerals

Country	Specialization Not Based on Natural Resources or Climate
Japan	Cars, consumer electronics
United States	Software, movies, aircraft, higher education
Switzerland	Watches
Korea	Cars, ships, consumer electronics
China	Textiles, shoes, consumer electronics
Great Britain	Financial services
Pakistan	Textiles

search engine, Facebook, YouTube, Twitter) and first-generation high-tech products (Apple's iPhone, Tivo's Digital Video Recorder) were developed in the United States. Creating these inventions and bringing them to market not only requires the human capital of scientists and managers, but it also requires entrepreneurs who perceive market opportunities and are willing to take risks to exploit them.

In less-developed countries, by contrast, capital and skilled labor are relatively scarce, but less-skilled labor is plentiful. Accordingly, these countries tend to have a comparative advantage in products that make heavy use of less-skilled labor, such as textiles and light manufacturing. Note, however, that as a country develops—and acquires more physical and human capital—its pattern of comparative advantage can change. Japan, Korea, and Singapore, after a few decades of very rapid development, acquired a comparative advantage in several goods that, at one time, were specialties of the United States and Europe—including automobiles, steel, and sophisticated consumer electronics. China is now moving rapidly up this development ladder.

Beyond Resources

Another aspect of the bottom half of Table 3 is harder to explain: Why do specific countries develop a *particular* specialty? For example, you may take the worldwide dominance of American movies for granted. But if you try to explain it based on the availability of resources like physical capital or highly skilled labor, or cultural traditions that encouraged artists, writers, or actors, then why not Britain or France? At the time the film industry developed in the United States, these two countries had similar endowments of physical and human capital, and much older and stronger theatrical traditions than the United States. Yet their film industries—in spite of massive government subsidies—are a very distant second and third compared to that of the United States.

The exports in the bottom half of Table 3 are certainly *consistent* with the physical and human capital each nation has at its disposal, but explaining why each *specific* case of comparative advantage arose in the first place is not easy.

We can, however, explain why a country *retains* its comparative advantage once it gets started. Japan and Korea today enjoy a comparative advantage in cars and consumer electronics in large part because they have accumulated a capital stock— both physical capital and human capital—well suited to producing those goods. The physical capital includes the many manufacturing plants and design facilities that these countries have built over the years. The human capital includes the accumulated knowledge and skills of their managers, scientists, product designers, and factory workers.

The existing physical and human capital in Japan and Korea sustain their comparative advantage just as natural resources sustain comparative advantage in other countries. More likely than not, Japan and Korea will continue to have a comparative advantage in cars and electronics, just as the United States will continue to have a comparative advantage in making movies.

> *Countries often develop strong comparative advantages in the goods they have produced in the past, regardless of why they began producing those goods in the first place.*

WHY SOME PEOPLE OBJECT TO FREE TRADE

Given the clear benefits that nations can derive by specializing and trading, why would anyone ever *object* to free international trade? Why do the same governments that join the WTO turn around and create roadblocks to unhindered trade? The answer is not too difficult to find: Despite the benefit to the nation as a whole, some groups within the country, especially in the short run, are likely to lose from free trade, even while others gain a great deal more. Unfortunately, instead of finding ways to compensate the losers—to make them better off as well—we often allow them to block free trade policies. The simple model of supply and demand helps illustrate this story.

Figure 3 shows the market for shrimp in the United States. Both the supply and demand curve in the figure represent the *domestic* market only. That is, the supply curve tells us the quantity supplied at each price by U.S. producers; the demand curve tells us quantity demanded at each price by U.S. consumers. With no international trade in shrimp, the U.S. market would achieve equilibrium at point *A*, at a price of $7 per pound. This relatively high price reflects the relatively high opportunity cost of producing shrimp in the United States. Both production and consumption would be 400 million pounds per year.

The United States does not have a comparative advantage in shrimp. Other countries that *do* have a comparative advantage (such as Vietnam, Thailand, and

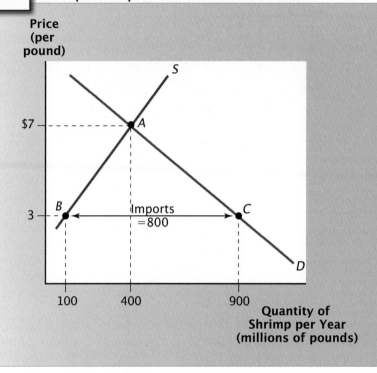

FIGURE 3   **The Impact of Imports on Consumers and Producers**

With no international trade, equilibrium in the U.S. market for shrimp is at point A, where domestic quantity supplied equals domestic quantity demanded. Price is $7 per pound, and 400 million pounds are consumed each year.

When U.S. consumers can import shrimp at the lower world price of $3 per pound, quantity supplied falls to 100 million pounds, while quantity demanded rises to 900 million. The difference—800 million pounds—is imports from the world market.

Consumers of shrimp gain from trade—they enjoy a greater quantity at a lower price. But producers lose— they sell less at a lower price.

Brazil) would like to sell it to us. Moreover, because their opportunity cost of producing shrimp is less than in the United States, their price tends to be lower as well. Let's suppose that the *world price* of shrimp—the price at which other countries offer to sell it to Americans—is $3 per pound. To keep our example simple, we'll also assume this price remains constant, no matter how much shrimp Americans buy from the rest of the world. (In effect, we're assuming that under international trade, the United States would be a relatively small buyer in a much larger world market.)

Now let's open up free trade in shrimp. Because Americans can buy unlimited quantities of imported shrimp at $3, domestic producers will have to lower their price to $3 as well in order to sell any. So the price of *all* shrimp in the U.S. market falls to $3 per pound—the same as the world price.

As the price drops, two things happen. On the one hand, we move along the demand curve from point *A* to point *C*: U.S. consumers buy more shrimp (900 million pounds) because it is cheaper. On the other hand, we move along the supply curve from point *A* to point *B*: U.S. producers decrease their quantity supplied (to 100 million pounds). The difference between domestic supply of 100 million and domestic demand of 900 million is the amount of shrimp the United States imports each year: 800 million pounds.

You've already learned (in the last section) that international trade according to comparative advantage makes each country as a whole better off: It increases total world production and enables consumers to enjoy greater quantities of goods and services. But not *everyone* is better off. It is easy to figure out who will be happy and who will be unhappy in the United States. American consumers are delighted: They are buying more shrimp at a lower price. American shrimp producers are miserable: They are selling less shrimp at a lower price.

> *International trade makes each country, as a whole, better off. But not everyone gains, because cheap imports from abroad—while beneficial to domestic consumers—are harmful to domestic producers.*

The Anti-Trade Bias

Imagine that a bill comes before Congress to prohibit or restrict the sale of cheap shrimp from abroad, so that its U.S. price can rise above $3. Domestic producers would favor the bill. Domestic consumers would oppose it. But not with equally loud voices. After all, the harm to consumers from this restriction of trade would be spread widely among *all* U.S. consumers. The loss to any individual would be very small. For example, if the total loss to U.S. consumers were $200 million per year, the total harm to any single consumer would be less than a dollar. As a result, no individual consumer of shrimp has a strong incentive to lobby Congress, or to join a dues-paying organization that would act on behalf of shrimp consumers to oppose this anti-trade bill.

By contrast, the benefits from this restriction of trade would be highly concentrated on a much smaller group of people: those who work in or own firms in the domestic shrimp industry. They have a powerful incentive to lobby against free trade in shrimp. Not surprisingly, when it comes to trade policy, the voices raised *against imports* are loud and clear, while those *for imports* are often nonexistent. Since a country has the power to restrict imports from other countries, the lobbying can—and often does—lead to a restriction on free trade. The United States, for example, continues to restrict imports of shrimp from low-cost producers, largely due to powerful lobbying by the U.S. shrimp industry.

> *For any particular good or service, the costs from expanded trade are highly concentrated among relatively few parties, while the benefits are widely dispersed among many. As a result, those harmed by international trade generally have more incentive to mobilize and lobby than those who benefit.*

A similar process works against U.S. *exports* to other countries. In this case, the *foreign* producers who would have to compete with U.S. goods will complain loudest, while foreign consumers who stand to gain will be mostly silent. The U.S. exporters—who are not constituents of these foreign governments—will have little influence in the debate. Thus, just as there is a policy bias against U.S. imports in the United States, there is a policy bias against U.S. exports in other countries.

Pro-Trade Forces

As we've seen, those harmed by international trade in a good often have a stronger incentive to mobilize than those who benefit. As a result, new agreements to reduce trade barriers are often blocked, and new barriers are often created. There are, however, some forces that work *against* the anti-trade bias and in favor of expanded international trade.

The World Trade Organization

One important antidote to the anti-trade bias is the World Trade Organization. By setting standards for acceptable and unacceptable trade restrictions and making rulings in specific cases, the WTO has some power to influence nations' trade policies. But its influence is limited, because the WTO has no enforcement power. For example, the WTO has ruled several times against European trade barriers against U.S. beef, with little effect. Still, a negative WTO ruling puts public relations pressure on a country and allows a nation harmed by restrictions on its exports to retaliate, in good conscience, with its own trade barriers.

All or Nothing Trade Agreements

In a bilateral or multilateral trade agreement, two or more countries agree to trade freely in many goods—or even all goods—simultaneously. These agreements are sometimes negotiated by government officials and then presented to legislatures as "all-or-nothing" deals: The agreement must be approved or rejected as a whole, without any amendments that make exceptions for specific industries.

"All-or-nothing" agreements can bring in another constituent to lobby for free trade: *exporters* in both countries. Ordinarily, exporters have no ability to influence the debate because their ability to export is decided in the *importing* country, where they have little influence. But in an all-or-nothing free trade deal, they can lobby their *own* country to allow imports as a way of enabling them to sell their exports. In this way, a balance of forces is created. Domestic producers threatened by imports will lobby against trade agreements in each country. But potential exporters will lobby just as strongly *for* the agreement.

In the United States, the president can present a trade deal to Congress as "all-or-nothing" only if Congress has voted to give the president *Trade Promotion Authority* (sometimes called "fast track authority"). Before this authority expired in 2007, it helped the U.S. reach several multi-lateral trade agreements.

An example was the *North American Free Trade Agreement (NAFTA)* between the United States, Canada, and Mexico, which went into effect in 1994, and has eliminated barriers on most products produced by the three nations. Another example was the Dominican Republic-Central American Free Trade Agreement, which was presented in the U.S. and six other partner-countries as an "all-or-nothing" deal, and took effect in 2007. In both of these cases, the producers who would have to compete with imports lobbied against the agreement. But the producers who were also exporters lobbied for it, and they prevailed. The biggest gainers—consumers in each country—were hardly involved in the debate, for reasons we've discussed.

Industries as Importers

When we hear the word *imports,* we might think only about consumer goods: French wine, Japanese cars, Colombian coffee. But many imported goods and services are *inputs* used by domestic industries. If imported inputs are an important part of firms' costs, they have an incentive to lobby for free trade in the good. For U.S. retailers and importers, clothing from Vietnam and Pakistan and electronics from China and Korea are inputs, to which the U.S. firms add value by making them available on store shelves. Large retail chains, such as Walmart, Best Buy and Macy's, have lobbied in support of free-trade agreements in recent years.

HOW FREE TRADE IS RESTRICTED

So far in this chapter, you've learned that specialization and trade according to comparative advantage can dramatically improve the well-being of entire nations. This is why governments generally favor free trade. Yet international trade can, in the short run, hurt particular groups of people. These groups often lobby their government to restrict free trade.

When governments decide to accommodate the opponents of free trade, they are apt to use one of two devices to restrict trade: tariffs or quotas.

Tariffs

Tariff A tax on imports.

A **tariff** is a tax on imported goods. It can be a fixed dollar amount per physical unit, or it can be a percentage of the good's value. In either case, the effect in the tariff-imposing country is similar.

Figure 4 illustrates the effect of a U.S. tariff of $2 per pound on imported shrimp. Before the tariff is imposed, the price of shrimp under free trade is the world price: $3 per pound. The U.S. imports 800 million pounds per year (the distance *BC*).

FIGURE 4 | **The Effects of a Tariff**

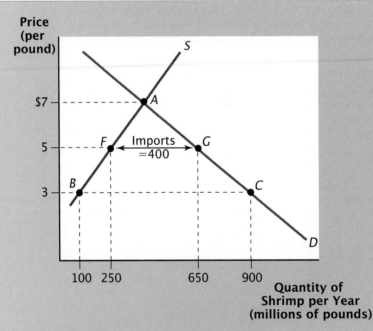

With free trade in shrimp, the price in the United States is the same as the world price: $3 per pound. U.S. imports are equal to the distance from B to C, 800 million pounds per year.

A tariff of $2 per pound raises the price of imported shrimp to $5 per pound, and the price of domestically produced shrimp rises to the same level. Domestic quantity supplied increases from 100 million to 250 million (the move from B to F), while domestic quantity demanded falls from 900 million to 650 million (the move from C to G). The result is lower imports of 400 million pounds.

Domestic suppliers gain from the tariff: They sell more shrimp at a higher price. But domestic consumers lose: They pay a higher price and consume less.

When the tariff is imposed, U.S. importers must still pay the same $3 per pound to their foreign suppliers. But now they must also pay $2 per pound to the U.S. government. Thus, the price of imported shrimp will rise from $3 to $5 per pound to cover the additional cost of the tariff.[1]

The higher price for imported shrimp allows U.S. producers to charge $5 for their domestic shrimp as well. As the price of shrimp rises, domestic quantity supplied increases (a movement along the supply curve from point B to point F). At the same time, domestic quantity demanded *decreases* (a movement along the demand curve from point C to point G). The final result is a reduction in imports, from 800 million before the tariff to 400 million after the tariff.

As you can see, U.S. consumers are worse off: They pay more for shrimp and enjoy less of it. But U.S. producers are better off: They sell more shrimp at a higher price.

But we also know this: Since the volume of trade has decreased, the gains from trade according to comparative advantage have been reduced as well. The United States, as a whole, is worse off as a result of the tariff.

> *A tariff reduces the volume of trade and raises the domestic price of an imported good. In the country that imposes the tariff, producers of the good gain, but consumers lose. The country as a whole loses, because tariffs decrease the volume of trade and therefore decrease the gains from trade.*

Quotas

A **quota** is a government decree that limits the imports of a good to a specified maximum physical quantity, such as 400 million pounds of shrimp per year. Because the goal is to restrict imports, a quota is set below the level of imports that would occur under free trade. Its general effects are very similar to the effects of a tariff.

Quota A limit on the physical quantity of imports.

Figure 4, which we used to illustrate tariffs, can also be used to analyze the impact of a quota. In the figure, we start with our free trade price of $3. Consumers are buying 900 million pounds, and domestic producers are selling 100 million pounds per year. The difference of 800 million pounds is satisfied by imports.

Now suppose the United States imposes a quota of 400 million pounds (equal to the distance FG in the figure). At $3 per pound, the gap between the domestic supply curve and the domestic demand curve would still be 900 million pounds, which is more than the 400 million pounds of foreign shrimp allowed into the country. There is an excess demand for shrimp, which drives up the price. The price will keep rising until the gap between the supply and demand curves shrinks to the quantity allowed under the quota. As you can see in the figure, only when the price rises to $5 would the gap shrink to 400 million pounds. Thus, a quota of 400 million gives us exactly the same result as did a tariff of $2: In both cases, the price rises to $5, and yearly imports shrink to 400 million pounds.

> *A quota has effects similar to a tariff: It reduces imports and raises the domestic price, thereby helping domestic producers of the good but reducing the gains from trade to the country as a whole.*

---

[1] If the United States is a large buyer in the world market for shrimp, the reduction in imports caused by the tariff would cause the world price to fall. This would change the quantitative results in our example. However, the price in the United States would still rise above $3, and all of our conclusions about the impact of tariffs would still hold.

Quotas versus Tariffs

The previous discussion seems to suggest that tariffs and quotas are pretty much the same. But even though the price and level of imports may end up being the same, there is one important difference between these two trade-restricting policies. A tariff, after all, is a *tax* on imported goods. Therefore, when a government imposes a tariff, it collects some revenue every time a good is imported. Even though the country loses from a tariff, it loses a bit less (compared to a quota) because at least it collects some revenue from the tariff. This revenue can be used to fund government programs or reduce other taxes, to the benefit of the country as a whole. When a government imposes a quota, however, it typically gains no revenue at all.

> *Both quotas and tariffs reduce the gains from trade. But a tariff has one saving grace that a quota lacks: increased tax revenue.*

Economists, who generally oppose measures such as quotas and tariffs to restrict trade, argue that, if one of these devices must be used, tariffs are the better choice. While both policies reduce the gains that countries can enjoy from specializing and trading with each other, the tariff provides some compensation in the form of additional government revenue.

PROTECTIONISM

This chapter has outlined the *gains* that arise from international trade, but it has also outlined some of the *pain* trade can cause to different groups within a country. While the country as a whole benefits, those who own or work in firms that have to compete with cheap imports will be harmed. The groups who suffer from trade with other nations have developed a number of arguments against free trade. Together, these arguments form a position known as **protectionism**—the belief that a nation's industries should be *protected* from free trade with other nations.

Protectionism The belief that a nation's industries should be protected from foreign competition.

Protectionist Myths

Some protectionist arguments are rather sophisticated and require careful consideration. We'll consider some of these a bit later. But anti-trade groups have also promulgated a number of myths to support their protectionist beliefs. Let's consider some of these myths.

Myth #1: The Threat to Living Standards

"IF A HIGH-WAGE COUNTRY TRADES WITH A LOW-WAGE COUNTRY, THE HIGH-WAGE COUNTRY'S WORKERS WILL HAVE TO ACCEPT EQUALLY LOW WAGE RATES AND EQUALLY LOW LIVING STANDARDS IN ORDER TO COMPETE WITH THE LOW-WAGE COUNTRY."

It's true that some countries have much higher wages than others. Table 4 shows average hourly wages for manufacturing workers (including benefits such as paid vacations and health insurance) in several countries. It's tempting to conclude

TABLE 4

**Hourly Wages
(Including Benefits)
in Manufacturing: 2009**

Country	Hourly Wage
Germany	$36.14
United States	**$25.63**
Japan	$24.95
Spain	$20.46
Singapore	$15.06
Korea	$14.20
Brazil	$ 5.63
Mexico	$ 3.93
China	$ 1.50
India	$ 1.25

Source: Bureau of Labor Statistics, "International Comparisons of Hourly Compensation Costs in Manufacturing, 2009," Table 3 (Total Direct Pay), Released March 2011. Entries for China and India extrapolated from 2008 estimates.

that lower-wage countries will always be able to charge lower prices for their goods, putting American workers out of jobs unless they, too, agree to work for low wages.

But there are several problems with this conclusion. First, it ignores differences in *productivity*, or output per hour. American workers tend to be more educated and work with more sophisticated machinery than their counterparts, so U.S. productivity is relatively high. For example, the table shows us that the manufacturing wage rate is almost twice as high in the U.S. as it is in Korea. But the average American factory worker produces more than twice as much output per hour as his or her Korean counterpart. So wages *per unit produced* are actually lower in the United States than in Korea.

Second, even in countries where—after accounting for productivity differences—the low-wage country has a cost advantage, the high-wage country will still have a *comparative advantage* in some goods, and can benefit by trading. Let's take an extreme case. Suppose that productivity were the same in the United States and China, so that China—with far lower wages—could produce everything more cheaply than the United States could. Both countries would still gain if China specialized in products in which its cost advantage was relatively large and if the United States specialized in goods in which China's cost advantage was relatively small. That is, the United States would still have a comparative advantage in some things, and there would be mutual gains from trade.

Finally, viewing trade as a threat to our living standard ignores a key fact: The foundation of a country's living standard is its general level of productivity. The more goods and services a country's workers can produce each hour, the more the average person can consume. A country's productivity depends on its social infrastructure, the skills and education of its labor force, and its physical capital. These features of an economy are not weakened by international trade. What trade does, as we've seen, is allow a country to consume even *more* goods and services than its own productivity, without trade, would allow it to consume. Trade with another country can only *raise* its average standard of living.

Myth #2: The Threat to Jobs

"INTERNATIONAL TRADE DECREASES THE TOTAL NUMBER OF JOBS IN A COUNTRY."

It is true that a sudden opening up of trade temporarily disrupts markets. There can even be a temporary drop in employment as jobs are lost in some sectors before they are created in other sectors. But neither logic nor observation supports the view that international trade causes any long-lasting drop in total employment.

This myth about losses in total employment comes from looking at only one side of the international trade coin: imports. It is true that international trade destroys jobs in those industries that now have to compete with cheaper imports from abroad. But trade also creates *new* jobs in the export sector. When trade is balanced—exports and imports are equal—there is no reason to expect the jobs lost in the import-competing sector to exceed the jobs gained in the export sector.

What about when trade is unbalanced, as when a country runs a *trade deficit* (the value of imports exceeds the value of exports)? Even in this case, there is no reason for total employment to decrease. The United States has run a trade deficit every year for decades: We spend more dollars buying imports from other countries than they return to us by buying our products. As a result, producers in these other countries start to pile up dollar balances.

But foreigners don't just hold onto these dollar balances, which pay no interest or other return. Instead, they invest these dollars in U.S. financial markets, purchasing stocks and bonds and making bank deposits. The funds are then lent out to U.S. firms and households who, in turn, spend them—on new capital equipment, new housing construction, or other things. In this way, while some jobs are lost when Americans spend their dollars on imports rather than U.S. goods, other jobs are created when the dollars flow back into the U.S. through the financial markets. A trade deficit can cause other problems for a country (as you will learn when you study macroeconomics), but it does not cause a permanent reduction in total employment.

Myth #3: Trade as the Main Cause of Rising Inequality

"THE DECLINING RELATIVE WAGES OF AMERICA'S UNSKILLED WORKERS ARE DUE MOSTLY TO THE EXPANSION OF TRADE BETWEEN THE UNITED STATES AND OTHER COUNTRIES."

True enough, unskilled workers have lost ground over the past few decades. College graduates have enjoyed growing purchasing power from their earnings, while those with only a high school education or less have lost purchasing power. Rising trade with low-wage countries is often blamed as the main (or even the *only*) cause for this adverse trend.

But before we jump to conclusions, let's take a closer look. Recall (from Chapter 12) that the college wage premium can be explained by supply and demand. For college graduates, demand has been increasing rapidly due to *skill-biased technological change*, while supply has not kept pace. For high school graduates, the same technological change has *slowed* the growth of demand. Most research concludes that technological change, along with slowing growth in the supply of college graduates, is the main cause of the widening gap between the wages of college and high school graduates.

Still, international trade contributes to this gap. All else equal, U.S. imports of goods that would otherwise be produced by low-wage labor shrink the demand for low-wage labor in the United States. And U.S. exports of goods produced by high-wage labor raise the demand for such labor in the United States.

Does rising income inequality justify trade barriers like quotas and tariffs? Only if it also justifies barriers to technological progress. After all, both technological progress and international trade have remarkably similar effects. They both raise living standards and benefit the country as a whole. And they both disproportionately benefit high-wage workers while causing harm to many low-wage workers. If concern for low-wage workers is grounds for opposing international trade, then logical consistency suggests it is grounds for opposing technological progress too.

Most economists believe that neither technological change nor international trade should be opposed. Rather, we should take advantage of the higher average living standards they enable, and use other policies to address the problems of low-wage workers more directly. The other policies include the earned income tax credit (discussed in Chapter 12), the removal of artificial barriers to attending college, government assistance for college tuition, job retraining programs, and more.

Sophisticated Arguments for Protection

Most of the protectionist arguments discussed in the media are based on the three myths we've just discussed. But some arguments for protecting domestic industries are based on a more sophisticated understanding of how markets work. For example, some economists favor a **strategic trade policy** that protects certain industries that benefit society as a whole, but that may not thrive in an environment of free trade.

Strategic trade policy is most effective in situations where a market is dominated by a few large firms. With few firms, the forces of competition—which ordinarily reduce profits in an industry to very low levels—will not operate. Therefore, each firm in the industry may earn high profits. These profits benefit not only the owners of the firm but also the nation more generally, since the government will be able to capture some of the profit with the corporate profits tax. When a government helps an industry compete internationally, it increases the likelihood that high profits—and the resulting general benefits—will be shifted from a foreign country to its own country. Thus, interfering with free trade—through quotas, tariffs, or even a direct subsidy to domestic firms—might actually benefit the country.

Another justification for strategic trade policy is the **infant industry argument**. This argument begins with a simple observation: In order to enjoy the full benefits of trade, markets must allocate resources toward those goods in which a nation has a comparative advantage. This requires well-organized markets for resources such as labor and land, and also well-organized *financial markets,* where firms obtain funds for new investment. But in some countries—especially less-developed countries—financial markets do not work very well. Poor legal systems or incomplete information about firms and products may prevent a new industry from obtaining financing, even though the country would have a comparative advantage in that industry once it was formed. In this case, protecting the infant industry from foreign competition may be warranted until the industry can stand on its own feet.

Infant industry argument The argument that a new industry in which a country has a comparative advantage might need protection from foreign competition in order to flourish.

Strategic trade policy and support for infant industries are controversial. Opponents of these ideas stress three problems:

1. Once the principle of government assistance to an industry is accepted, special-interest groups of all kinds will lobby to get the assistance, whether it benefits the general public or not.
2. When one country provides assistance to an industry by keeping out foreign goods, other nations may respond in kind. If they respond with tariffs and quotas of their own, the result is a shrinking volume of world trade and falling living standards.
3. Strategic trade policy assumes that the government has the information to determine which industries, infant or otherwise, are truly strategic and which are not.

Still, the arguments related to strategic trade policy suggest that government protection or assistance *may* be warranted in some circumstances, even if putting this support into practice proves difficult. Moreover, the arguments help to remind us of the conditions under which free trade is most beneficial to a nation:

Production is most likely to reflect the principle of comparative advantage when firms can obtain funds for investment projects and when they can freely enter industries that are profitable. Thus, free trade, without government intervention, works best when markets are working well.

Protectionism in the United States

Americans can enjoy the benefits of importing many of the products listed several pages ago in Table 3: olive oil from Spain, watches from Switzerland, tomatoes from Mexico, and cars from Japan. But on the other side of the ledger, U.S. consumers have suffered, and U.S. producers have gained, from some persistent barriers

TABLE 5

Some Examples of U.S. Protectionism

Protected Industry	Annual Cost to Consumers	Number of Jobs Saved	Annual Cost per Job Saved
Apparel and Textiles	$33,629 million	168,786	$ 199,241
Maritime Services	$ 2,522 million	4,411	$ 571,668
Sugar	$ 1,868 million	2,261	$ 826,104
Dairy Products	$ 1,630 million	2,378	$ 685,323
Softwood Lumber	$ 632 million	605	$1,044,271
Women's Nonathletic Footwear	$ 518 million	3,702	$ 139,800
Glassware	$ 366 million	1,477	$ 247,889
Luggage	$ 290 million	226	$1,285,078
Peanuts	$ 74 million	397	$ 187,223

Source: *The Fruits of Free Trade*, Federal Reserve Bank of Dallas, Annual Report, 2002, Exhibit 11.

to trade. Table 5 lists some examples of American protectionism—through tariffs, quotas, or similar policies—that have continued for years.

As you can see, protectionism is costly. Quotas and tariffs on apparel and textiles, the most costly U.S. trade barrier, force American consumers to pay $33.6 billion more for clothes each year. And while protection saves an estimated 168,786 workers in this industry from having to make the painful adjustment of finding other work, it does so at an *annual* cost of $199,241 per worker. Both workers and consumers could be made better off if textile workers were paid some amount up to $199,241 and asked *not* to work, while allowing consumers to buy inexpensive textiles from abroad.

In some cases, the cost per job saved is staggering. The table shows that trade barriers preventing Americans from buying inexpensive luggage save just a couple of hundred jobs, at a yearly cost of more than $1 million each. Trade barriers on sugar are almost as bad: While 2,261 jobs are saved, the annual cost per job is $826,104.

In addition to the dozens of industries in the United States permanently protected from foreign competition, dozens more each year are granted temporary protection when the U.S. government finds a foreign producer or industry guilty of *dumping*—selling their products in the United States at "unfairly" low prices that harm a U.S. industry. Most economists believe that these low prices are most often the result of comparative advantage, and that the United States as a whole would gain from importing the good. Vietnam, for example, has a clear comparative advantage in producing shrimp. But in 2005, based on a complaint by the Southern Shrimp Alliance, the U.S. government imposed tariffs of up to 26 percent on Vietnamese shrimp.

In the Using the Theory section that follows, we take a closer look at one of the longest-running examples of protectionism in the United States.

USING THE THEORY

© RICHARD LORD/PHOTOEDIT

THE U.S. SUGAR QUOTA

The United States has protected U.S. sugar producers from foreign competition since the 1930s. Since the 1980s, the U.S. sugar program has included price guarantees for domestic producers, tariffs, and import quotas set individually on sugar from 40 different countries. The quotas, in particular, restrict the supply of sugar to the U.S. market, and keep U.S. sugar prices higher than in the rest of the world, as shown in Figure 5. From 2000 to 2010, the world price of sugar averaged about 15 cents a pound, while Americans paid an average of 30 cents a pound.

The *primary* effects of the sugar quota are on domestic sugar producers and sugar consumers. As you've learned, an import quota raises the domestic price of sugar (the quota's purpose). Sugar producers benefit. But sugar consumers are hurt even more.

FIGURE 5 | Sugar Prices in the U.S. and the Rest of the World

Source: U.S. Department of Agriculture Economic Research Service, Sugar and Sweeteners (http://www.ers.usda.gov/Briefing/Sugar/data.htm#yearbook), Tables 2 and 5.

© CENGAGE LEARNING 2013

And the harm is substantial. In 2010 alone, the artificially high price of sugar in the U.S. cost American consumers an extra $4.5 billion. But spread widely over the U.S. population, this amounts to less than $15 per person per year. This probably explains why you haven't bothered to lobby for free trade in sugar.

But the costs of the sugar quota go beyond ordinary consumers. Industrial sugar users—such as the ice cream industry—are affected by the higher price too, not all of which can be passed on to consumers. So they try to avoid the quota's harm in other ways. One way is to waste resources buying sugar abroad disguised as other products. In the late 1990s and early 2000s, U.S. firms bought about 125,000 tons of sugar each year mixed with molasses, which was not restricted by the sugar quota. The sugar was then separated from the molasses. Even with these additional (and wasteful) processing costs, it was still a better deal to buy the disguised sugar abroad than to buy it through regular channels in the United States.

And sometimes a firm decides it's just not worth it anymore. In the past decade, several candy and baked-goods manufacturers have simply given up trying to pay the high cost of sugar in the United States, and moved their production facilities to other countries that don't have quotas, and where sugar can be purchased at the lower, world price.

Taxpayers, too, pay a cost for the sugar quota because as part of its price support program, the U.S. government must occasionally buy and store excess sugar from producers. The government must also hire special agents to detect and prevent sugar from entering the country illegally.

A final cost of the sugar quota is one that we have not yet considered in our discussion of international trade. In Figure 4, when a U.S. tariff or quota caused imports to shrink, we assumed that the world price of the good remained unchanged. But when a country is a very large buyer in the world market, a reduction in its purchases can cause the world price to drop. Essentially, the quota—by keeping sugar out—causes greater quantities of sugar to be dumped onto the world market, depressing its price. This hurts the poorest countries in the world that rely on sugar as an important source of export revenue. The sugar quota's harm to these countries has been estimated at about $1.5 billion per year.

Why do we bear all of these costs? Because of lobbying by groups who enjoy highly concentrated benefits. There are about 13,000 sugar farms in the United States. When the $4.5 billion in additional spending by U.S. consumers is spread among this small number of farms, the additional revenue averages out to more than $350,000 per farm per year. Those benefits are sizable enough to mobilize sugar producers each time their protection is threatened.

And mobilize they do. In 2004, the United States negotiated a free trade agreement with Australia that eliminated barriers on almost every good or service . . . except sugar. In 2005, the United States approved DR-CAFTA—a free trade agreement with five Central American countries and the Dominican Republic. Once again, sugar was an exception: Additional sugar imports from all six countries combined were restricted to less than 2 percent of the U.S. market.

Even the NAFTA agreement between the U.S., Mexico, and Canada put sugar in a special category: Restrictions on sugar from Mexico remained in place until 2008. When that year arrived, so did Mexican sugar. But the U.S. Congress came to the rescue with a new farm bill that promised even higher prices for U.S. sugar producers, mostly by shrinking the quotas on imports from other countries.

There is another group that receives concentrated benefits from the sugar quota: producers of high-fructose corn syrup, the closest substitute for sugar. Because of the sugar quota, high-fructose corn syrup can be sold at a substantially higher price.

Not surprisingly, the largest producer of high-fructose corn syrup in the U.S. market—the Archer Daniels Midland (ADM) company—has funded organizations that lobby Congress and try to sway public opinion in the United States. Occasionally, you may see a full-page newspaper advertisement paid for by one of these groups, arguing that sugar in the United States is cheap. And it is . . . until you find out what other countries are paying.

SUMMARY

A country has a *comparative advantage* in a good when it can produce it at a lower opportunity cost than another country. When countries specialize in the production of their comparative advantage goods, world production rises. Both countries benefit as consumption rises in each country. The distribution of the benefits between countries depends on the *terms of trade*—the rate at which the imported goods are traded for the exported goods.

Despite the benefits to each nation as a whole, those who supply goods that must compete with cheaper imports are harmed. Because the gains from expanding trade are spread widely while the harm is concentrated among a smaller number of people, the latter have an incentive to lobby against free trade. Those harmed often encourage government to block or reduce trade through the use of *tariffs* (taxes on imported goods) and *quotas* (limits on the volume of imports). Both tariffs and quotas decrease the gains from trade by raising domestic prices and reducing domestic consumption of the good. But tariffs at least provide additional government revenue, while quotas generally do not.

A variety of arguments have been proposed in support of protectionism. Some are clearly invalid and fail to recognize the principle that both sides gain when countries trade according to their comparative advantage. More sophisticated arguments for restricting trade may have merit in certain circumstances. *Strategic trade policy*—the notion that governments should assist certain strategic industries—can be justified in certain situations. These include markets dominated by a few large firms, and *infant industries* that need protection in countries without well-functioning financial markets.

PROBLEM SET

Answers to even-numbered Problems can be found on the text Web site through www.cengagebrain.com

1. Suppose that the costs of production of winter hats and wheat in two countries are as follows:

	United States	Russia
Per winter hat	$10	5,000 rubles
Per bushel of wheat	$ 1	2,500 rubles

   a. What is the opportunity cost of producing one more winter hat in the United States? In Russia?
   b. What is the opportunity cost of producing one more bushel of wheat in the United States? In Russia?
   c. Which country has a comparative advantage in winter hats? In wheat?

2. Suppose that the Marshall Islands does not trade with the outside world. It has a competitive domestic market for TV sets. The market supply and demand curves are reflected in this table:

Price ($/TV)	Quantity Demanded	Quantity Supplied
500	0	500
400	100	400
300	200	300
200	300	200
100	400	100
0	500	0

   a. Plot the supply and demand curves and determine the domestic equilibrium price and quantity.
   b. Suddenly, the islanders discover the virtues of free exchange and begin trading with the outside world. The Marshall Islands is a very small country, and so its trading has no effect on the price established in the world market. It can import as many TVs as it wishes at the world price of $100 per TV. In this situation, how many TVs will be purchased in the Marshall Islands? How many will be produced there? How many will be imported?
   c. After protests from domestic producers, the government decides to impose a tariff of $100 per imported TV. Now how many TVs will be purchased in the Marshall Islands? How many will be produced there? How many will be imported?
   d. What is the government's revenue from the tariff described in part (c)?
   e. Compare the effect of the tariff described in part (c) with a quota that limits imports to 100 TVs per year.

3. The following table provides hypothetical data about the supply and demand for beef in the European Union. The prices are in euros, and quantities are millions of pounds of beef per month. (You may wish to draw the supply and demand curves to help you visualize what is happening.)

Price	Quantity Supplied	Quantity Demanded
0	0	160
2	20	140
4	40	120
6	60	100
8	80	80
10	100	60
12	120	40

   a. In the absence of international trade, what is the equilibrium price and quantity of beef?
   b. If trade opens up, and the world price of beef is (and remains) 2 euros per pound of beef, how much beef will EU producers supply? How much beef will EU consumers demand? How much beef will be imported?
   c. Within the EU, who gains and who loses when trade opens up?

4. Using the data on supply and demand in problem 3, suppose the EU imposed a tariff of 2 euros on each pound of beef.
   a. How much beef would EU producers supply?
   b. How much beef would EU consumers demand?
   c. How much beef would the EU import?
   d. How much total revenue would EU government authorities collect from the tariff?

5. Using the data on supply and demand in problem 3, suppose the EU imposed a quota on imports of beef equal to 40 million pounds of beef per month.
   a. What would be the price of beef in the EU?
   b. How much beef would EU producers supply?
   c. How much beef would EU consumers demand?

6. Refer to Table 2 in the chapter. Suppose the terms of trade are *two and a half* T-shirts for each bushel of soybeans (instead of three for one as in the chapter). As in the chapter, assume the United States increases soybean production by 100 million bushels and exports 80 million of them to China, and that China decreases its own soybean production by 50 million bushels. Some of the remaining numbers in the table will have to change to be consistent with these new specifications. Then, answer each of the following questions.
   a. Does China still gain from trade? Explain briefly.
   b. Does the United States still gain from trade? Explain briefly.
   c. Compare the effects of trade for China under the new and old terms of trade. In which case does China fare better? Explain briefly.
   d. Compare the effects of trade for the United States under the new and old terms of trade. In which case does the United States fare better? Explain briefly.

7. Refer to Table 2 in the chapter. Suppose the terms of trade are *four* T-shirts for each bushel of soybeans (instead of three for one as in the chapter). Assume the United States increases soybean production by 100 million bushels and exports 60 million to China. China increases its T-shirt production by 250 million. Some of the remaining numbers in the table will have to change, to be consistent with these new specifications. Then, answer each of the following questions.
   a. Does China still gain from trade? Explain briefly.
   b. Does the United States still gain from trade? Explain briefly.
   c. Compare the effects of trade for China under the new and old terms of trade. In which case does China fare better? Explain briefly.
   d. Compare the effects of trade for the United States under the new and old terms of trade. In which case does the United States fare better? Explain briefly.

8. Redraw the PPFs for the United States and China from Figure 2 in the chapter. Assume that the initial production and consumption points (*A* and *A'*) and the new production points (*B* and *B'*) are the same as in that figure. Plot the new consumption points (*C* and *C'*) that correspond to your results from the previous problem (7).

9. The following table shows the hypothetical labor requirements per ton of wool and per hand-knotted rug, for New Zealand and for India.

Labor Requirements per Unit

	New Zealand	India
Per ton of wool	10 hours	40 hours
Per hand-knotted rug	60 hours	80 hours

   a. Which country has an absolute advantage in each product?
   b. Calculate the opportunity cost in each country for each of the two products. Which country has a comparative advantage in each product?
   c. If India produces one more rug and exports it to New Zealand, what is the lowest price (measured in tons of wool) that it would accept? What is the highest price that New Zealand would pay? Within what range will the equilibrium terms of trade lie?

10. Using the data from problem 9, suppose that New Zealand has 300 million hours of labor per period, while India has 800 million hours.
   a. Draw PPFs for both countries for the two goods (put quantity of wool on the vertical axis).
   b. Suppose that, before trade, each country uses half of its labor to produce wool and half to produce rugs. Locate each country's production point on its PPF (label it *A* for New Zealand, and *A'* for India).
   c. After trade opens up and each country completely specializes in its comparative advantage good, locate each country's production point on its PPF (label it *B* for New Zealand, and *B'* for India).

More Challenging

11. This problem uses the data from problem 9, and the graphs you drew in problem 10. Suppose that the terms of trade end up at 4 tons of wool for 1 hand-knotted rug. Suppose, too, that New Zealand decides to export 12 million tons of wool to India.
   a. How many rugs will New Zealand import from India?
   b. What will be New Zealand's consumption of each good after trade?
   c. What will be India's consumption of each good after trade?
   d. On the PPFs you drew for problem 10, plot each country's consumption point after trade. Label it *C* for New Zealand, and *C'* for India.

12. In Figures 3 and 4, we assumed that the world price of a good was fixed, and not affected by the quantity of imports a country chooses. But if a country is large relative to the world market, its imports can influence the world price.

Suppose the market for good X involves only two large countries (A and B), with supply and demand schedules as shown below:

Country A			Country B		
Price per Unit of Good X (measured in dollars)	Quantity Demanded of Good X	Quantity Supplied of Good X	Price per Unit of Good X (measured in dollars)	Quantity Demanded of Good X	Quantity Supplied of Good X
$10	1	25	$10	5	11
9	2	22	9	6	10
8	3	19	8	7	9
7	4	16	7	8	8
6	5	13	6	9	7
5	6	10	5	10	6
4	7	7	4	11	5
3	8	4	3	12	4

a. Plot the supply and demand curves for each country.
b. Before international trade, what is the equilibrium price and quantity in each country? For the remaining questions, assume that the two countries can trade in good X.
c. Which country will export good X?
d. What will be the equilibrium world price? [Hint: This will be the price at which the quantity of exports from one country equals the quantity of imports to the other.]
e. What will happen to production and consumption in Country A?
f. What will happen to production and consumption in Country B?
g. What quantity will be exported (and also imported) in equilibrium?
h. On your graph, label the new levels of production and consumption in each country, as well as distances representing exports and imports.

A

Absolute advantage The ability to produce a good or service, using fewer resources than other producers use.

Accounting profit Total revenue minus accounting costs.

Adverse selection A situation in which asymmetric information about quality eliminates high-quality goods from a market.

Aggregation The process of combining distinct things into a single whole.

Alternate goods Other goods that firms in a market could produce instead of the good in question.

Alternate market A market other than the one being analyzed in which the same good could be sold.

Asymmetric information A situation in which one party to a transaction has relevant information not known by the other party.

Average cost pricing Setting a monopoly's regulated price equal to long-run average cost where the *LRATC* curve crosses the market demand curve.

Average fixed cost Total fixed cost divided by the quantity of output produced.

Average total cost Total cost divided by the quantity of output produced.

Average variable cost Total variable cost divided by the quantity of output produced.

B

Behavioral economics A subfield of economics focusing on decision-making patterns that deviate from those predicted by traditional consumer theory.

Black market A market in which goods are sold illegally at a price above the legal ceiling.

Bond A promise to pay back borrowed funds, issued by a corporation or government agency.

Budget constraint The different combinations of goods a consumer can afford with a limited budget, at given prices.

Budget line The graphical representation of a budget constraint, showing the maximum affordable quantity of one good for given amounts of another good.

Business firm An organization, owned and operated by private individuals, that specializes in production.

C

Capital A long-lasting tool that is used to produce other goods.

Capital gain The gain to the owner of an asset when it is sold for a price higher than its original purchase price.

Capital loss The loss to the owner of an asset when it is sold for a price lower than its original purchase price.

Capital stock The total amount of capital in a nation that is productively useful at a particular point in time.

Cartel A group of firms that selects a common price that maximizes their combined profits.

Ceteris paribus Latin for "all else remaining the same."

Change in demand A shift of a demand curve in response to a change in some variable other than price.

Change in quantity demanded A movement along a demand curve in response to a change in price.

Change in quantity supplied A movement along a supply curve in response to a change in price.

Change in supply A shift of a supply curve in response to a change in some variable other than price.

Circular flow A simple model that shows how goods, resources, and dollar payments flow between households and firms.

Coase theorem When a side payment can be arranged without cost, the market will solve an externality problem—and create the efficient outcome—on its own.

Command or centrally planned economy An economic system in which resources are allocated according to explicit instructions from a central authority.

Common resource A nonexcludable and rival good. Generally available free of charge, though efficiency would require a positive price.

Comparative advantage The ability to produce a good or service at a lower opportunity cost than other producers.

Compensating wage differential A difference in wages that makes two jobs equally attractive to a worker.

Complement A good that is used together with some other good.

Complementary input An input that is used *by* a particular type of labor, making it more productive.

Concentration ratio The percentage of total output or sales by a given number of the largest firms in the market.

Constant cost industry An industry in which the long-run supply curve is horizontal because each firm's cost curves are unaffected by changes in industry output.

Constant returns to scale Long-run average total cost is unchanged as output increases.

Consumer surplus The difference between the value of a unit of a good to the buyer and what the buyer actually pays for it.

Copyright A grant of exclusive rights to sell a literary, musical, or artistic work.

Critical assumption Any assumption that affects the conclusions of a model in an important way.

Cross-price elasticity of demand The percentage change in the quantity demanded of one good caused by a 1 percent change in the price of another good.

D

Deadweight loss The dollar value of potential benefits not achieved due to inefficiency in a particular market.

Decreasing cost industry An industry in which the long-run supply curve slopes downward because each firm's *LRATC* curve shifts downward as industry output increases.

Demand curve A graph of a demand schedule; a curve showing the quantity of a good or service demanded at various prices, with all other variables held constant.

Demand curve facing the firm A curve that indicates, for different prices, the quantity of output that customers will purchase from a particular firm.

Demand curve for housing A curve showing, at each price, the total number of homes that everyone in the market would like to own, given the constraints that they face.

Demand schedule A list showing the quantities of a good that consumers would choose to purchase at different prices, with all other variables held constant.

Derived demand The demand for a resource that arises from, and varies with, the demand for the product it helps to produce.

Diminishing marginal returns to labor The marginal product of labor decreases as more labor is hired.

Discount rate The interest rate used in computing present values.

Discounting The act of converting a future value into its present-day equivalent.

Discrimination When a group of people have different opportunities because of personal characteristics that have nothing to do with their abilities.

Diseconomies of scale Long-run average total cost increases as output increases.

Dividends Part of a firm's current profit that is distributed to shareholders.

Dominant strategy A strategy that is best for a player no matter what strategy the other player chooses.

Duopoly An oligopoly market with only two sellers.

E

Economic efficiency A situation in which every possible Pareto improvement is being exploited.

Economic profit Total revenue minus all costs of production, explicit and implicit.

Economics The study of choice under conditions of scarcity.

Economies of scale Long-run average total cost decreases as output increases.

Efficient market A market that instantaneously incorporates all available information relevant to a stock's price.

Elastic demand A price elasticity of demand greater than 1.

Entrepreneurship The ability and willingness to combine the other resources—labor, capital, and land—into a productive enterprise.

Equilibrium price The market price that, once achieved, remains constant until either the demand curve or supply curve shifts.

Equilibrium quantity The market quantity bought and sold per period that, once achieved, remains constant until either the demand curve or supply curve shifts.

Excess demand At a given price, the amount by which quantity demanded exceeds quantity supplied.

Excess supply At a given price, the amount by which quantity supplied exceeds quantity demanded.

Exchange The act of trading with others to obtain what we desire.

Excise tax A tax on a specific good or service.

Excludability The ability to exclude those who do not pay for a good from consuming it.

Exit A permanent cessation of production when a firm leaves an industry.

Explicit collusion Cooperation involving direct communication between competing firms about setting prices.

Explicit cost The dollars sacrificed—and actually paid out—for a choice.

Exports Goods and services produced domestically, but sold abroad.

Externality A by-product of consuming or producing a good that affects someone other than the buyer or seller.

F

Factor markets Markets in which resources—labor, capital, land and natural resources, and entrepreneurship—are sold to firms.

Financial asset A promise to pay future income in some form, such as future profits or future interest payments.

Firm's supply curve A curve that shows the quantity of output a competitive firm will produce at different prices.

Fixed costs Costs of fixed inputs, which remain constant as output changes.

Fixed input An input whose quantity must remain constant over some time period.

Flow variable A variable representing a process that takes place over some time period.

Free-rider problem When everyone tries to enjoy the benefits of a nonexcludable good without paying, so private firms cannot provide it.

G

Game theory An approach to modeling the strategic interaction of oligopolists in terms of moves and counter-moves.

Government franchise A government-granted right to be the sole seller of a product or service.

H

Herfindahl-Hirschman Index (HHI) A measure of market concentration obtained by summing the squares of each firm's market share.

Human capital The skills and training of the labor force.

I

Imperfect competition A market structure in which there is more than one firm but one or more of the requirements of perfect competition is violated.

Implicit cost The value of something sacrificed when no direct payment is made.

Imports Goods and services produced abroad, but consumed domestically.

Income The amount that a person or firm earns over a particular period.

Income effect As the price of a good decreases, the consumer's purchasing power increases, causing a change in quantity demanded for the good.

Income elasticity of demand The percentage change in quantity demanded caused by a 1 percent change in income.

Increasing cost industry An industry in which the long-run supply curve slopes upward because each firm's *LRATC* curve shifts upward as industry output increases.

Increasing marginal returns to labor The marginal product of labor increases as more labor is hired.

Inelastic demand A price elasticity of demand between 0 and 1.

Infant industry argument The argument that a new industry in which a country has a comparative advantage might need protection from foreign competition in order to flourish.

Inferior good A good that people demand less of as their income rises.

Input Anything (including a resource) used to produce a good or service.

Input-substitution effect A change in the wage rate alters the price of labor relative to the costs of other inputs, and therefore changes the quantity of labor demanded.

Investment Firms' purchases of new capital over some period of time.

L

Labor The time human beings spend producing goods and services.

Labor demand curve Curve indicating the total number of workers all firms in a labor market want to employ at each wage rate.

Labor supply curve A curve indicating the number of people who want jobs in a labor market at each wage rate.

Land The physical space on which production takes place, as well as the natural resources that come with it.

Law of demand As the price of a good increases, the quantity demanded decreases.

Law of diminishing (marginal) returns As more and more of any input is added to a fixed amount of other inputs, its marginal product will eventually decline.

Law of diminishing marginal utility As consumption of a good or service increases, marginal utility decreases.

Law of supply As the price of a good increases, the quantity supplied increases.

Least-Cost Rule A firm produces any given output level using the lowest cost combination of inputs available.

Long run A time horizon long enough for a firm to vary all of its inputs.

Long-run average total cost The cost per unit of producing each quantity of output in the long run, when all inputs are variable.

Long-run elasticity An elasticity measured a year or more after a price change.

Long-run supply curve A curve indicating price and quantity combinations in an industry after all long-run adjustments have taken place.

Long-run total cost The cost of producing each quantity of output when all inputs are variable and the least-cost input mix is chosen.

Loss The difference between total cost (*TC*) and total revenue (*TR*), when *TC* > *TR*.

Lumpy input An input whose quantity cannot be increased gradually as output increases, but must instead be adjusted in large jumps.

M

Macroeconomics The study of the behavior of the overall economy.

Marginal approach to profit A firm maximizes its profit by taking any action that adds more to its revenue than to its cost.

Marginal cost The increase in total cost from producing one more unit of output.

Marginal cost pricing Setting a monopoly's regulated price equal to its marginal cost of production at the efficient quantity.

Marginal product of labor The additional output produced when one more worker is hired.

Marginal revenue The change in total revenue from producing one more unit of output.

Marginal social benefit (*MSB*) The full benefit provided by another unit of a good, including the benefit to the consumer *and* any benefits enjoyed by third parties.

Marginal social cost (*MSC*) The full cost of producing another unit of a good, including the marginal cost to the producer *and* any harm caused to third parties.

Marginal utility The change in total utility an individual obtains from consuming an additional unit of a good or service.

Market A group of buyers and sellers with the potential to trade with each other.

Market consumer surplus The total consumer surplus enjoyed by all consumers in a market.

Market economy An economic system in which resources are allocated through individual decision making.

Market failure A market that operates inefficiently without government intervention.

Market power The ability of a seller to raise price without losing all demand for the product being sold.

Market producer surplus The total producer surplus gained by all sellers in a market.

Market signals Price changes that cause changes in production to match changes in consumer demand.

Market structure The characteristics of a market that influence how trading takes place.

Market supply curve A curve indicating the quantity of output that all sellers in a market will produce at different prices in the short run.

Marketable public good An excludable and nonrival good. Generally provided by the market for a price, though efficiency would require a price of zero.

Microeconomics The study of the behavior of individual households, firms, and governments; the choices they make; and their interaction in specific markets.

Minimum efficient scale The lowest output level at which the firm's *LRATC* curve hits bottom.

Mixed economy A market economy in which the government also plays an important role in allocating resources.

Model An abstract representation of reality.

Monopolistic competition A market structure in which there are many firms selling products that are differentiated, and in which there is easy entry and exit.

Monopoly The only seller in a market, or a market with just one seller.

Moral hazard When someone is protected from paying the full costs of their harmful actions and acts irresponsibly, making the harmful consequences more likely.

Mortgage A loan given to a home-buyer for part of the purchase price of the home.

N

Natural monopoly A monopoly that arises when, due to economies of scale, a single firm can produce for the entire market at lower cost per unit than could two or more firms.

Natural oligopoly A market that tends naturally toward oligopoly because the minimum efficient scale of the typical firm is a large fraction of the market.

Network externalities Additional benefits enjoyed by all users of a good or service because others use it as well.

Nonprice competition Any action a firm takes to shift its demand curve rightward.

Nonwage job characteristic Any aspect of a job—other than the wage—that matters to a potential or current employee.

Normal good A good that people demand more of as their income rises.

Normal profit Another name for zero economic profit.

Normative economics The practice of recommending policies to solve economic problems.

O

Oligopoly A market dominated by a small number of strategically interacting firms.

Opportunity cost What is given up when taking an action or making a choice.

Output effect A change in the wage rate alters the profit-maximizing output level, and therefore changes the quantity of labor demanded.

P

Pareto improvement An action that makes at least one person better off, and harms no one.

Patent A temporary grant of monopoly rights over a new product or scientific discovery.

Payoff matrix A table showing the payoffs to each of two players for each pair of strategies they choose.

Perfect competition A market structure in which there are many buyers and sellers, the product is standardized, sellers can easily enter or exit the market, and buyers and sellers are well-informed.

Perfect price discrimination Charging each customer the most he or she would be willing to pay for each unit purchased.

Perfectly (infinitely) elastic demand A price elasticity of demand approaching infinity.

Perfectly competitive labor market A market with many well-informed buyers and sellers of standardized labor, with no barriers to entry and exit.

Perfectly competitive market (informal definition) A market in which no buyer or seller has the power to influence the price.

Perfectly inelastic demand A price elasticity of demand equal to 0.

Physical capital The part of the capital stock consisting of physical goods, such as machinery, equipment, and factories.

Plant The collection of fixed inputs at a firm's disposal.

Positive economics The study of how the economy works.

Present value The value, in today's dollars, of a sum of money to be received or paid at a specific date in the future with certainty.

Price The amount of money that must be paid to a seller to obtain a good or service.

Price ceiling A government-imposed maximum price in a market.

Price discrimination Charging different prices to different customers for reasons other than differences in cost.

Price elasticity of demand The sensitivity of quantity demanded to price; the percentage change in quantity demanded caused by a 1 percent change in price.

Price elasticity of supply The percentage change in quantity supplied caused by a 1 percent change in price.

Price floor A government-imposed minimum price in a market.

Price leadership A form of tacit collusion in which one firm sets a price that other firms copy.

Price setter A firm (with market power) that selects its price, rather than accepting the market price as a given.

Price taker A firm that treats the price of its product as given and beyond its control.

Primary market The market in which newly issued financial assets are sold for the first time.

Principal–agent problem When one party (the principal) hires another (the agent), who in turn can pursue goals that conflict with the principal's because of asymmetric information.

Principle of asset valuation The idea that the value of an asset is equal to the total present value of all the future benefits it generates.

Producer surplus The difference between what the seller actually gets for a unit of a good and the cost of providing it.

Product markets Markets in which firms sell goods and services to households.

Production possibilities frontier (PPF) A curve showing all combinations of two goods that can be produced with the resources and technology currently available.

Productively inefficient A situation in which more of at least one good can be produced without sacrificing the production of any other good.

Profit Total revenue minus total cost.

Protectionism The belief that a nation's industries should be protected from foreign competition.

Pure private good A good that is both rivalrous and excludable.

Pure public good A good that is both nonrival and nonexcludable.

Q

Quantity demanded The quantity of a good that all buyers in a market would choose to buy during a period of time, given their constraints.

Quantity supplied The specific amount of a good that all sellers in a market would choose to sell over some time period, given their constraints.

Quota A limit on the physical quantity of imports.

R

Rational preferences Preferences that satisfy two conditions: (1) Any two alternatives can be compared, and one is preferred or else the two are valued equally, and (2) the comparisons are logically consistent or transitive.

Relative price The price of one good relative to the price of another.

Rent controls Government-imposed maximum rents on apartments and homes.

Rent-seeking activity Any costly action a firm undertakes to establish or maintain its monopoly status.

Repeated play A situation in which strategically interdependent sellers compete over many time periods.

Resource markets Markets in which households that own resources sell them to firms.

Resources The labor, capital, land (including natural resources), and entrepreneurship that are used to produce goods and services.

Rivalry A situation in which one person's consumption of a unit of a good or service means that no one else can consume that unit.

S

Scarcity A situation in which the amount of something available is insufficient to satisfy the desire for it.

Secondary market The market in which previously issued financial assets are sold.

Share of stock A share of ownership in a corporation.

Short run A time horizon during which at least one of the firm's inputs cannot be varied.

Short side of the market The smaller of quantity supplied and quantity demanded at a particular price.

Short-run elasticity An elasticity measured just a short time after a price change.

Shortage An excess demand not eliminated by a rise in price, so that quantity demanded continues to exceed quantity supplied.

Shutdown price The price at which a firm is indifferent between producing and shutting down.

Shutdown rule In the short run, the firm should continue to produce if total revenue exceeds total variable costs; otherwise, it should shut down.

Simplifying assumption Any assumption that makes a model simpler without affecting any of its important conclusions.

Single-price monopoly A monopoly firm that is limited to charging the same price for each unit of output sold.

Specialization A method of production in which each person concentrates on a limited number of activities.

Stock variable A variable representing a quantity at a moment in time.

Subsidy A government payment to buyers or sellers on each unit purchased or sold.

Substitutable input An input that can be used *instead of* a particular type of labor.

Substitute A good that can be used in place of some other good and that fulfills more or less the same purpose.

Substitution effect As the price of a good falls, the consumer substitutes that good in place of other goods whose prices have not changed.

Sunk cost A cost that has been paid or must be paid, regardless of any future action being considered.

Supply curve A graph of a supply schedule, showing the quantity of a good or service supplied at various prices, with all other variables held constant.

Supply curve for housing A vertical line showing the total number of homes in a market that are available for ownership.

Supply schedule A list showing the quantities of a good or service that firms would choose to produce and sell at different prices, with all other variables held constant.

Surplus An excess supply not eliminated by a fall in price, so that quantity supplied continues to exceed quantity demanded.

T

Tacit collusion Any form of oligopolistic cooperation that does not involve an explicit agreement.

Tariff A tax on imports.

Tax incidence The division of a tax payment between buyers and sellers, determined by comparing the new (after tax) and old (pretax) market equilibriums.

Technology The methods available for combining inputs to produce a good or service.

Terms of trade The ratio at which a country can trade domestically produced products for foreign-produced products.

Tit-for-tat A game-theoretic strategy of doing to another player this period what he has done to you in the previous period.

Total benefits The sum of consumer and producer surplus in a particular market.

Total cost The costs of all inputs—fixed and variable—used to produce a given output level in the short run.

Total fixed cost The cost of all inputs that are fixed in the short run.

Total product The maximum quantity of output that can be produced from a given combination of inputs.

Total revenue The total inflow of receipts from selling a given amount of output.

Total variable cost The cost of all variable inputs used in producing a particular level of output.

Tradable permit A license that allows a company to release a unit of pollution into the environment over some period of time.

Traditional economy An economy in which resources are allocated according to long-lived practices from the past.

Tragedy of the commons The problem of overuse when a good is rivalrous but nonexcludable.

U

Unit elastic demand A price elasticity of demand equal to 1.

Utility A quantitative measure of pleasure or satisfaction obtained from consuming goods and services.

V

Variable costs Costs of variable inputs, which change with output.

Variable input An input whose usage can change over some time period.

W

Wealth The total value of everything a person or firm owns, at a point in time, minus the total amount owed.

Y

Yield The annual rate of return a bond earns for its owner.